THEATRE
THE LIVELY ART

EIGHTH EDITION

Edwin Wilson
Professor Emeritus
Graduate School and University Center
The City University of New York

Alvin Goldfarb
President Emeritus
Western Illinois University

McGraw Hill

Boston   Burr Ridge, IL   Dubuque, IA   Madison, WI   New York   San Francisco   St. Louis
Bangkok   Bogota   Caracas   Kuala Lumpur   Lisbon   London   Madrid   Mexico City
Milan   Montreal   New Delhi   Santiago   Seoul   Singapore   Sydney   Taipei   Toronto

Published by McGraw-Hill, an imprint of The McGraw-Hill Companies, Inc., 1221 Avenue of the Americas, New York, NY 10020. Copyright © 2012, 2010, 2008, 2005, 2002, 1999, 1996, 1991 by Edwin Wilson and Alvin Goldfarb. All rights reserved. Printed in the United States of America. No part of this publication may be reproduced or distributed in any form or by any means, or stored in a database or retrieval system, without the prior written consent of The McGraw-Hill Companies, Inc., including, but not limited to, in any network or other electronic storage or transmission, or broadcast for distance learning.

This book is printed on acid-free paper.

To our wives,
Catherine Wilson and Elaine Goldfarb.

2 3 4 5 6 7 8 9 0 DOW/DOW 1 0 9 8 7 6 5 4 3 2

ISBN: 978-0-07-351420-8
MHID: 0-07-351420-9

Sponsoring Editor: *Betty Chen*
Marketing Manager: *Stacy Ruel*
Developmental Editor: *Arthur Pomponio*
Production Editor: *Jasmin Tokatlian*
Manuscript Editor: *Deborah Kopka*
Design Manager: *Cassandra Chu*
Text Designer: *Cassandra Chu*
Cover Designer: *Heidi Baughman*
Photo Research: *Natalia Peschiera, Inge King*
Buyer: *Tandra Jorgensen*
Media Project Manager: *Jennifer Barrick*
Composition: *10.5/13 Adobe Garamond Pro Regular by Thompson Type*
Printing: *45# New Era Matte Plus, Quad/Graphics*

Vice President Editorial: *Michael Ryan*
Publisher: *Chris Freitag*
Editorial Director: *William R. Glass*
Director of Development: *Rhona Robbin*

On the cover: The cast of Roundabout Theatre Company's *Anything Goes,* starring Sutton Foster and Joel Grey, directed and choreographed by Kathleen Marshall with music and lyrics by Cole Porter; original book by P. G. Wodehouse, Guy Bolton, Howard Lindsay and Russel Crouse, new book by Timothy Crouse and John Weidman; set design by Derek McLane; costume design by Martin Pakledinaz; lighting design by Peter Kaczorowski; sound design by Brian Ronan; hair and wig design by Paul Huntley.
Photo by Joan Marcus

Credits: The credits section for this book begins on page C-1 and is considered an extension of the copyright page.

Library of Congress Cataloging-in-Publication Data
Wilson, Edwin.
    Theatre : the lively art / Edwin Wilson, Alvin Goldfarb.—8th ed.
        p. cm.
    Includes bibliographical references and index.
    ISBN-13: 978-0-07-351420-8 (alk. paper)
    ISBN-10: 0-07-351420-9 (alk. paper)
  1. Theater. 2. Theater—History. I. Goldfarb, Alvin. II. Title.
    PN2037.W57 2012
    792—dc23
        2011040640

The Internet addresses listed in the text were accurate at the time of publication. The inclusion of a website does not indicate an endorsement by the authors or McGraw-Hill, and McGraw-Hill does not guarantee the accuracy of the information presented at these sites.

Edwin Wilson, as a teacher, author, critic, and director, has worked in many aspects of theatre. Educated at Vanderbilt University, the University of Edinburgh, and Yale University, he received a master of fine arts degree, as well as the first doctor of fine arts degree awarded by the Yale Drama School. He has taught at Yale, Hofstra, Vanderbilt, Hunter College, and the CUNY Graduate Center. At Hunter he served as chair of the Department of Theatre and Film and head of the graduate theatre program. At CUNY he was the Executive Director of the Martin E. Segal Theatre Center.

He was the theatre critic for *The Wall Street Journal* for 22 years and edited and wrote the introduction for *Shaw on Shakespeare.* He is the author of *The Theatre Experience* and a coauthor, with Alvin Goldfarb, of *Living Theatre,* as well as coeditor of *The Anthology of Living Theatre,* all published by McGraw-Hill. He served as president of the New York Drama Critics' Circle, as well as a member of the selection committees of the Pulitzer Prize in drama and the Tony awards. He is currently on the board of the Susan Smith Blackburn Prize and the John Golden Fund, and for many years was on the board of the Theatre Development Fund, of which he served as president.

At the beginning of his career, Wilson was assistant to the producer for the film *Lord of the Flies* directed by Peter Brook and the Broadway play *Big Fish, Little Fish* directed by John Gielgud. He served as resident director for a season at the Barter Theatre in Virginia and was the executive producer of the film *The Nashville Sound.*

Alvin Goldfarb is President Emeritus of Western Illinois University, where he will continue to teach theatre. Dr. Goldfarb also served as Provost, Dean of Fine Arts, and Chair of the Department of Theatre at Illinois State University. He holds a Ph.D. in theatre history from the City University of New York and a master's degree from Hunter College.

He is the coauthor of *Living Theatre* as well as *The Anthology of Living Theatre* with Edwin Wilson. Dr. Goldfarb is also the coeditor, with Rebecca Rovit, of *Theatrical Performance during the Holocaust: Texts, Documents, Memoirs,* which was a finalist for the National Jewish Book Award. He has published numerous articles and reviews in scholarly journals and anthologies.

Dr. Goldfarb served as a member of the Illinois Arts Council and president of the Illinois Alliance for Arts Education. He has received service awards from the latter organization as well as from the American College Theatre Festival. Dr. Goldfarb also received an Alumni Achievement Award from the CUNY Graduate Center's Alumni Association, and another Alumni Award from Hunter College, CUNY.

CONTENTS IN BRIEF

Part 1
Theatre in Today's World   3
1. THEATRE: THE ART FORM   5
2. THE AUDIENCE—SPECTATORS AND PARTICIPANTS   23

Part 2
Creating Theatre: The Playwright   45
3. CREATING THE DRAMATIC SCRIPT   47
4. THEATRICAL GENRES   75

Part 3
Creating Theatre: The Production   95
5. ACTING FOR THE STAGE   97
6. THE DIRECTOR AND THE PRODUCER   119
7. THEATRE SPACES   137
8. THE DESIGNERS: SCENERY AND COSTUMES   157
9. THE DESIGNERS: LIGHTING AND SOUND   189

Part 4
Global Theatres: Past and Present   207
10. EARLY THEATRES: GREEK, ROMAN, AND MEDIEVAL   209
11. EARLY THEATRE: ASIAN   239
12. RENAISSANCE THEATRES   265
13. THEATRES FROM THE RESTORATION THROUGH ROMANTICISM   299
14. THE MODERN THEATRE EMERGES   327
15. TODAY'S DIVERSE GLOBAL THEATRE   365

INDEX   401

CONTENTS

PART 1
THEATRE IN TODAY'S WORLD 3

CHAPTER 1 THEATRE: THE ART FORM 5

THE UNIQUE QUALITY OF THEATRE 6

A Historical Reason to Attend Theatre 8

Theater and the Human Condition 9

THEATRE AS AN ART FORM 9

What Is Art? 9

The Art of Theatre 12

GLOBALIZATION AND TODAY'S THEATRE 15

DIVERSITY AND MULTICULTURALISM 18

Diversity in Contemporary Theatre 18

SUMMARY 20

THINKING ABOUT THEATRE 20

KEY TERMS 21

THEATRE ON THE WEB 21

CHAPTER 2 THE AUDIENCE—SPECTATORS AND PARTICIPANTS 23

HOW THEATER PERMEATES OUR LIVES 24

THEATRE AND TELEVISION 25

THEATRE AND FILM 26

THEATRE AND ROCK AND ROLL 27

THEATRICALITY IN AMUSEMENT PARKS, MUSEUMS, LAS VEGAS, AND SPORTING EVENTS 29

THEATER AND DIGITAL MEDIA 31

Differences between Theatre-Related Activities and Theatre Itself 32

THE ROLE OF THE AUDIENCE 33

How the Audience Participates 35

Diversity of Audiences 36

WIDER PERSPECTIVE: *Attending the Theater* 39

THE CRITIC AND THE REVIEWER 39

Preparing for Criticism 40

Criteria for Criticism 40

Decline of the Critics' and Reviewers' Influence   41

The Audience Member's Independent Judgment   42

SUMMARY   42

THINKING ABOUT THEATRE   43

KEY TERMS   43

THEATRE ON THE WEB   43

PART 2
CREATING THEATRE: THE PLAYWRIGHT   45

CHAPTER 3   CREATING THE DRAMATIC SCRIPT   47

THE PLAYWRIGHT CREATES THE SCRIPT   48

THE PLAYWRITING PROCESS   48

SUBJECT   49

FOCUS   49

DRAMATIC PURPOSE   50

WIDER PERSPECTIVE: *The Playwright's Role*   51

STRUCTURE IN DRAMA   52

Essentials of Dramatic Structure   52

MAKING CONNECTIONS: *Writers*   53

GLOBAL CROSS CURRENTS: *The Asian Influence on the Playwrights Brecht and Wilder*   56

Sequence in Dramatic Structure   57

Two Basic Forms of Structure: Climactic and Episodic   59

Other Forms of Dramatic Structure   64

CREATING DRAMATIC CHARACTERS   66

Types of Dramatic Characters   66

Juxtaposition of Characters   71

SUMMARY   71

THINKING ABOUT THEATRE   72

KEY TERMS   72

THEATRE ON THE WEB   73

CHAPTER 4   THEATRICAL GENRES   75

DRAMATIC GENRES   76

TRAGEDY   76

Traditional Tragedy   77

WIDER PERSPECTIVE: *Conditions for Tragedy: Theatre and Society*   78

Modern Tragedy   80

COMEDY   80

Characteristics of Comedy   81

Forms of Comedy   83

HEROIC DRAMA   86

MELODRAMA 87

DOMESTIC DRAMA 88

TRAGICOMEDY 89

Shakespearean Tragicomedy   90

Modern Tragicomedy   91

SUMMARY   92

THINKING ABOUT THEATRE   92

KEY TERMS   93

THEATRE ON THE WEB   93

PART 3

CREATING THEATRE: THE PRODUCTION   95

CHAPTER 5   ACTING FOR THE STAGE   97

THREE CHALLENGES OF ACTING   98

Making Characters Believable   98

MAKING CONNECTIONS: *Acting*   104

WIDER PERSPECTIVE: *A Historical Perspective: Demands of Classical Acting*   106

Physical Acting: Voice and Body   106

Synthesis and Integration   113

GLOBAL CROSS CURRENTS: *Puppetry around the World*   114

JUDGING PERFORMANCES   116

SUMMARY   116

THINKING ABOUT THEATRE   117

KEY TERMS   117

THEATRE ON THE WEB   117

CHAPTER 6   THE DIRECTOR AND THE PRODUCER   119

THE DIRECTOR   120

Evolution of the Director   120

The Director at Work   121

GLOBAL CROSS CURRENTS: *Peter Brook: International Director*   124

The Director's Collaborators   127

WIDER PERSPECTIVE: *The Auteur Director and the Postmodern Director* 128

THE PRODUCER OR MANAGER   130

Producers in Commercial Theatre   130

Noncommercial Theatres   131

SUMMARY   134

THINKING ABOUT THEATRE   134

KEY TERMS   135

THEATRE ON THE WEB   135

CHAPTER 7 THEATRE SPACES 137

PROSCENIUM OR PICTURE-FRAME STAGE: HISTORY AND CHARACTERISTICS 138

THRUST STAGE: HISTORY AND CHARACTERISTICS 141

ARENA STAGE: HISTORY AND CHARACTERISTICS 146

CREATED OR FOUND SPACES 149

MULTIFOCUS ENVIRONMENTS 150

ALL-PURPOSE AND EXPERIMENTAL SPACES 150

> **MAKING CONNECTIONS:** *Popular Performance Spaces* 151

SUMMARY 154

THINKING ABOUT THEATRE 154

KEY TERMS 155

THEATRE ON THE WEB 155

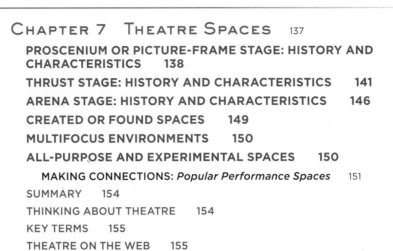

CHAPTER 8 THE DESIGNERS: SCENERY AND COSTUMES 157

SCENE DESIGN 158

THE SCENE DESIGNER'S OBJECTIVES 158

> Elements of Scene Design 162
>
> **GLOBAL CROSS CURRENTS:** *The Magic of the Designer Josef Svoboda* 165
>
> The Process of Scene Design: Steps in the Design Process 168
>
> The Scene Designer's Collaborators and the Production Process169
>
> Designing a Total Environment 171

COSTUME DESIGN 172

> The Costume Designer 172
>
> The Costume Designer's Objectives 173
>
> **PHOTO ESSAY:** *The Costume Designer at Work* 174
>
> Elements of Costume Design 179
>
> The Costume Designer's Collaborators 181
>
> Related Elements of Costume Design 181

SUMMARY 186

THINKING ABOUT THEATRE 186

KEY TERMS 187

THEATRE ON THE WEB 187

CHAPTER 9 THE DESIGNERS: LIGHTING AND SOUND 189

STAGE LIGHTING 190

> Lighting in Theatre History 190
>
> Objectives of Lighting Design 191
>
> Elements of Stage Lighting 193
>
> The Lighting Designer's Resources 195
>
> The Lighting Designer's Collaborators 198

SOUND IN THE THEATRE   199
Sound Reproduction: Advantages and Disadvantages   199
The Sound Designer   201
Understanding Sound Reproduction and Sound Reinforcement 201
Sound Technology   202
SPECIAL EFFECTS IN LIGHTING AND SOUND   203
SUMMARY   204
THINKING ABOUT THEATRE   204
KEY TERMS   205
THEATRE ON THE WEB   205

PART 4
GLOBAL THEATRES: PAST AND PRESENT   207

CHAPTER 10   EARLY THEATRES: GREEK, ROMAN, AND MEDIEVAL   209

ORIGINS OF THEATRE   210
GREECE   211
Background: The Golden Age of Greece   211
Theatre and Culture: Greek Theatre Emerges   211
Greek Tragedy   213
TIMELINE: *Greece*   215
Greek Comedy   216
Theatre Production in Greece   217
LIVING HISTORY: Antigone   218
Dramatic Criticism in Greece: Aristotle   219
Later Greek Theater   220
ROME   220
Background: Rome and Its Civilization   220
TIMELINE: *Rome*   221
Theatre and Culture in Rome   222
Popular Entertainment in Rome   222
Roman Comedy: Platus and Terence   223
LIVING HISTORY: The Menaechmi   224
Roman Tragedy: Seneca   225
Dramatic Criticism in Rome: Horace   225
Theater Production in Rome   225
MAKING CONNECTIONS: *Greek and Roman*   226
Decline of Roman Theatre   228
THE MIDDLE AGES   228
Background: Medieval Europe   228
Theatre and Culture in the Middle Ages   229
Medieval Drama: Mystery and Morality Plays   229

TIMELINE: *Middle Ages*   230

Medieval Theatre Production   232

LIVING HISTORY: *Noah's Ark*   233

SUMMARY   235

THINKING ABOUT THEATRE   236

KEY TERMS   236

THEATRE ON THE WEB   237

CHAPTER 11   EARLY THEATRE: ASIAN   239

THE THEATRES OF ASIA   240

Background   240

TIMELINE: *Asia*   241

INDIAN THEATRE   242

Sakskrit Drama   242

Later Indian Drama   245

CHINESE THEATRE   245

Early Theatre in China   246

Theatre in the Yuan Dynasty   247

Theater in the Ming Dynasty   248

JAPANESE THEATRE   250

Early Theatre in Japan   250

Nō   250

LIVING HISTORY: *Sotoba Komachi*   252

Banraku   254

Kabuki   256

SOUTHEAST ASIA: SHADOW PLAYS   260

SUMMARY   262

THINKING ABOUT THEATRE   262

KEY TERMS   263

THEATRE ON THE WEB   263

CHAPTER 12   RENAISSANCE THEATRES   265

ITALY   266

Background: The Renaissance Era   266

Italian Theatre: Commedia dell'Arte   266

TIMELINE: *Italian Renaissance*   267

Italian Dramatic Rules: The Neoclassical Ideals   269

LIVING HISTORY: *Commedia dell'Arte*   270

Theatre Production in Italy   271

ENGLAND   274

Background: Elizabethan England   274

TIMELINE: *English Renaissance*   275

Elizabethan Drama   276

LIVING HISTORY: Hamlet   278

Elizabethan Theatre Production   279

    MAKING CONNECTIONS: *The Popular Arts of Shakespeare's Time*   282

Theatre after Elizabeth's Reign   283

SPAIN   284

Background: The Spanish Golden Age   284

Spanish Drama   285

    TIMELINE: *Spanish Golden Age*   286

    LIVING HISTORY: The King, the Greatest Alcalde287

Theatre Production in Spain   288

FRANCE   290

Background: France in the Seventeenth Century   290

French Drama: The Neoclassical Era   290

    TIMELINE: *Neoclassical France*   292

    THEATRE PRODUCTION IN FRANCE   293

    LIVING HISTORY: Tartuffe   294

SUMMARY   296

THINKING ABOUT THEATRE   296

KEY TERMS   297

THEATRE ON THE WEB   297

CHAPTER 13 THEATRES FROM THE RESTORATION THROUGH ROMANTICISM   299

THE ENGLISH RESTORATION   300

Background: England in the Seventeenth Century   300

Restoration Drama: Comedies of Manners   300

    TIMELINE: *English Restoration*   301

Theatre Production in the Restoration   303

    LIVING HISTORY: The Country Wife   304

THE EIGHTEENTH CENTURY   306

Background: A More Complex World   306

Eighteenth-Century Drama: New Dramatic Forms   307

    TIMELINE: *Eighteenth Century*   309

Theatre Production in the Eighteenth Century   310

    LIVING HISTORY: The Marriage of Figaro   313

THE NINETEENTH CENTURY   314

Background: A Time of Social Change   314

    MAKING CONNECTIONS: *Nineteenth-Century Popular Theatrical Arts*   315

    TIMELINE: *Nineteenth Century, 1800 to 1875*   316

Theatre in Nineteenth-Century Life   317

Nineteenth-Century Dramatic Forms   318

Theatre Production in the Nineteenth Century   320

SUMMARY   324

THINKING ABOUT THEATRE   325

KEY TERMS   325

THEATRE ON THE WEB   325

Chapter 14 The Modern Theatre Emerges 327

REALISM AND THE MODERN ERA 328

Background: The Modern Era 328

TIMELINE: *1875 to 1915* 329

Theatrical Realism 330

Realistic Playwrights 331

Naturalism 332

Producers of Realism: Independent Theatres 333

LIVING HISTORY: The Sea Gull 335

DEPARTURES FROM REALISM 339

Antirealist Playwrights: Ibsen, Strindberg and Wedekind 340

Symbolism 340

Antirealist Designers: Appia and Craig 341

Russian Theatricalism: Meyerhold 342

Expressionism 343

Futurism and Surrealism 343

The Theatre of Cruelty and Epic Theatre 343

Unique Voices 345

Impact of Totalitarianism on Theatre 345

TIMELINE: *1915 to 1945* 346

Experimentation and Departures from Realism Continue 347

LIVING HISTORY: Waiting for Godot 349

ECLECTICS 350

POPULAR THEATRE 351

American Musical Theatre 352

GLOBAL THEATRE IN THE TWENTIETH CENTURY 356

TIMELINE: *1945 to 1975* 357

Some Background on Asian Theatre 358

Global Exchanges 359

GLOBAL CROSS CURRENTS: *Two Important International Directors* 360

SUMMARY 362

THINKING ABOUT THEATRE 362

KEY TERMS 362

THEATRE ON THE WEB 363

Chapter 15 Today's Diverse Global Theatre 365

THE DAWNING OF A NEW CENTURY 366

TIMELINE: *1975 to Present* 367

TODAY'S THEATRE: GLOBAL, DIVERSE, AND ECLECTIC 368

Performance Art 368

Postmodernism 370

DIVERSE THEATRES IN THE UNITED STATES 372

American Alternative Theatre 372

African American Theatre   374

Latino-Latina Theatre   377

Asian American Theatre   378

Native American Theatre   380

Feminist Theatre and Gender Diversity   381

Gay and Lesbian Theatre   382

GLOBAL THEATRE   384

A Continuing Global Trend: Documentary Drama   384

English and Irish Theatre   385

Canada and Australia   387

Asia, Africa, and Latin America   388

GLOBAL CROSS CURRENTS: *Tadashi Suzuki: Japanese Internationalist*   390

GLOBAL CROSS CURRENTS: *Augusto Boal: The Theatre of the Oppressed*   396

TODAY AND TOMORROW: A LOOK AHEAD   396

SUMMARY   398

THINKING ABOUT THEATRE   398

KEY TERMS   399

THEATRE ON THE WEB   399

T heatre is not only an art form; it is one of the performing arts. As a result, its quality is elusive because it exists only at the moment when a performance occurs. To study it in a book or classroom is to be one step removed from that immediate experience. This fact is uppermost in the minds of those who teach theatre in a classroom setting. At the same time, it is also known that an introductory theatre course can immeasurably enhance an audience's comprehension of theatre.

Understanding all of the theatre's elements and its history helps enrich the audience member's experience and appreciation of this performing art. (Sara Krulwich/The New York Times/Redux)

The experience of seeing theatre can be many times more meaningful if audience members understand a number of things: the component parts of theatre, the various creative artists and technicians who make it happen, the tradition and historical background from which theatre springs, and the genre or movement of which a particular play is a part. It is our hope that *Theatre: The Lively Art* will provide the background to make this possible and that it will encourage and inspire students to become life-long audience members, if not actual theatre artists.

Theatre: The Lively Art introduces readers to the exciting world of theatre in all its dimensions, behind the scenes as well as in the finished performance. Shown here is director Tina Landau rehearsing with performers.
(© T. Charles Erickson)

ABOUT THE EIGHTH EDITION

In its eighth edition, *Theatre: The Lively Art* remains a comprehensive introductory text that incorporates a number of elements in one volume:

- An introduction to the audience's experience of theatre
- An investigation of the elements of theatre: the audience; the text; theatre artists, including actors and directors; theatrical space; and scenic, costume, lighting, and sound design
- A study of the important developments in the history of theatre

Several qualities set *Theatre: The Lively Art* apart from other introductory texts. A particularly important element is our emphasis on the audience. All students reading the book are potential theatre-goers, not just during their college years but throughout their lives. We have therefore attempted to make *Theatre: The Lively Art* an ideal one-volume text to prepare students as future audience members. It will give them a grasp of how theatre functions, of how it should be viewed and judged, and of the tradition behind any performance they may attend.

In addition to serving as an ideal text for nonmajors, *Theatre: The Lively Art* will also prepare students who wish to continue studies in theatre, as majors, minors, or students from other disciplines who take advanced courses.

ORGANIZATION

We ordered the chapters in a logical and helpful way to make studying as intuitive as possible. However, as in previous editions, *Theatre: The Lively Art* can be studied in any order the instructor prefers.

We listened to instructors who asked us to improve the overall organization by streamlining some material for easier classroom use. In response, we combined

Chapters 2 and 3 from the seventh edition to form a single chapter in this edition—Chapter 2: The Audience: Spectators and Participants. Also, we combined Chapters 15, 16, and 17 from the seventh edition into two chapters—Chapter 14: The Modern Theatre Emerges and Chapter 15: Today's Diverse Global Theatre. Our goal here was to clarify the coverage of the modern and global theaters, with greater emphasis on providing students with key trends since 1875.

In addition to the changes noted above, the eighth edition fine-tunes Part 1, Theatre in Today's World. As in previous editions, this part opens the book by discussing the unique nature of theatre as an art form and by highlighting the multicultural nature of theatre that today's students will experience. In addition, throughout this edition, we focus on the global nature of theatre to give students the groundwork for understanding the wide diversity of theatre today. Other topics in Part 1 are theatre in everyday life and the theatre audience. This part provides a foundation for studying the elements of theatre in Parts 2 and 3.

In Part 2, Creating Theatre: The Playwright, we introduce students to the person or group creating a script, in particular the dramatic structure and dramatic characters. We then continue with dramatic genres and investigate point of view in a text as expressed in tragedy, comedy, tragicomedy, and other genres.

The photographs in *Theatre: The Lively Art* bring to life the vividness of all elements of theatre: acting, directing, script, and visual elements. (Kira Horvath © University of Colorado/ Colorado Shakespeare Festival)

In Part 3, Creating Theatre: The Production, we discuss the people and elements that make theatre possible: the actors, the director, the producer, and the designers who together bring the theatre to stunning life. Important too are the theatre spaces where a production occurs. Design and production techniques (in particular lighting, costume, and makeup) have been updated to include the latest advances in technology.

In Part 4, Global Theatres: Past and Present, we offer a survey of theatre history, beginning with Greek theatre and continuing to the present. Chapters 14 and 15 are devoted to theatre of the past one hundred or so years. The forces that began just more than a century ago—in realism and departures from realism, in acting techniques, in the emergence of the director, and in scene and lighting design—define theatre as it exists today.

TEXT FEATURES

Based on feedback from instructors and students, the eighth edition of *Theatre: The Lively Art* offers both time-tested and newly revised text features that help students deepen their understanding and appreciation of the theatrical experience.

URLs to Online Plays. At appropriate places in the text, students are directed to websites that provide complete plays for them to read and consider in context with what they are learning.

Thinking About Theatre Questions. A set of critical thinking questions has been added at the end of each chapter as part of an expanded pedagogical program. These questions not only help students to think critically about what they have read in the chapter, but also help them to connect what they've read to their own experiences. The Thinking About Theatre questions can be used as homework assignments or to inspire classroom discussion.

Global Cross Currents. These boxes, occurring throughout the text, highlight specific examples of global influence on theatre. Artists discussed include Peter Brook, Josef Svoboda, Julie Taymor, Bertolt Brecht, and Thornton Wilder. *NEW!* Boxes on legendary theatre artists Augusto Boal, Ariane Mnouchkine, and Tadashi Suzuki.

GLOBAL CROSS CURRENTS

THE MAGIC OF THE DESIGNER JOSEF SVOBODA

The Czech scene designer Josef Svoboda (1920–2002) developed a number of significant techniques in stage design, which have since been adopted and utilized by designers in many countries around the world. Svoboda's work centered on his understanding of the *kinetic stage* and *scenography*. The term *kinetic stage* refers to his belief that the set should not function independently of the actors, but rather should develop and adapt as a performance progresses. *Scenography* was what he called his art, conveying the sense that he created a whole physical space, not just designs on paper intended for the back of the stage. His experiments with these ideas led to many significant concepts in modern stage design, most notably the *laterna magika*, *polyekran*, and *diapolyekran*.

Polyekran literally means multiscreen and was the practice, devised by Svoboda, of using multiple screens at multiple angles and heights. Although real people and objects were projected, the aim was to convince the spectators not that they were looking at the real object, but rather that they were looking at a projection, or a collage of projections. A later development of this technique was *diapolyekran*, which employed whole walls of small, square screens making up a composite image. The wall of screens could be used to present one unified image, cubist images, or a collage.

Laterna magika, the best-known of his innovations, used screens in conjunction with actors; the actors were part of the film, and the film was part of the action. The projections used in this form were not simply for decoration, or for communicating images independent of the action; rather, the projections and action functioned together, creating a new manner of performance.

These developments were introduced to the global community in 1958 at the Brussels World Fair, where they instantly commanded attention from the wider theatrical community. Svoboda had been the chief designer at the National

Josef Svoboda. (© Franco Origlia/Sygma/Corbis)

Theatre in Prague at the time of the World Fair, and a showcase of the work of the theatre was displayed to the global audience, winning him three medals. What was seen as ingenious in 1958 was quickly adopted and adapted by numerous practitioners in many countries, and the effect of these means of design can still be witnessed in contemporary theatre, in performance art, and on Broadway, as well as at rock concerts and sporting events. This incorporation of screens and projections into onstage action has infiltrated the world of the theatre to the extent that it has become one of the conventional tools of theatre worldwide.

Prepared by Naomi Stubbs, CUNY Graduate Center.

WIDER PERSPECTIVE

ATTENDING THE THEATRE: AUDIENCE RESPONSIBILITY

Western theatre, particularly since the nineteenth century, has developed certain rules of behavior for audience members—expectations about what audiences do and don't do. However, it should be kept in mind that any given theatre event might have some unique expectations about the audience's behavior.

At a traditional theatre performance, the audience is expected to remain silent for the most part, and not interrupt the performers. Audience members should not talk to each other as if they were at home watching television; they should not send or receive text messages, use cell phones, hum or sing along with music, unwrap candy or other food, eat loudly, search through a purse or backpack; they should also shut off wristwatch alarms and beepers. Remember that the actors can hear the audience: noises and distracting behavior will have an impact on their concentration and performance. Noise and distractions also affect the experience of other spectators.

Students may be concerned about note-taking since they often will need to make notes in order to remember key elements of the production. An unobtrusive way of taking notes is to jot down only brief phrases or terms that will jog your memory later. Then, you can embellish your

notes during the intermission or intermissions, or after the end of the performance.

Of course, traditional audiences are not always absolutely quiet: audiences at comedies laugh, for instance. Audiences at musicals applaud after a song (in fact, they're expected to). On the other hand, audiences at serious plays generally do not applaud until the end of the performance—and even then, an audience may be so stunned or so deeply moved that there will be a moment of silence before the applause begins.

As noted above, not all of these traditional expectations may apply at every theatre event. Dinner theatres are one example since the audience may be eating during the presentation. (We might also note that audiences eat during the performance in many traditional Asian theatres, and they may speak back to the stage.) Audiences at some productions are expected to interact with the performers: in some comic presentations, for instance, actors may enter the audience space or actually speak to individual audience members; and in some nontraditional productions, audience members may even be expected to participate in the performance.

Wider Perspectives. These new boxes are found in the chapters discussing the audience, the playwright, the actor, and the director. Each box focuses on a unique issue in the contemporary theatre and can be used to engage students in discussion and debate.

MAKING CONNECTIONS

GREEK AND ROMAN POPULAR ARTS

Although we focus on the great dramas and comedies created during the Greek and Roman eras, we should not forget that there was a strong tradition of popular entertainment during these time periods. The types of popular arts that flourished during these eras were to have a great influence on popular culture through our own times.

During the classical and Hellenistic Greek eras, we know that there were traveling mimes who performed throughout the Greek world. Historians believe that mime may have developed in the fifth and fourth centuries B.C.E., but there is a great deal of debate over how to define the form. Greek mime is often described as dealing with domestic and sexual situations in a popular and highly bawdy manner, though it may have first been a form that parodied mythological figures and stories.

Mimes sometimes performed by themselves, but by the Hellenistic era they were usually organized into troupes. Mime was never introduced into the festivals and was seen as a lower form of theatrical art. Women eventually were performers in mime troupes, and frequently the actors in

economically, mime troupes traveled extensively. For that reason, it is often argued that Greek mime performers influenced the development of Roman theatre and popular entertainments.

Roman theatre had great competition in the popular arts that were available to the Roman public. Mime troupes continued to perform in Roman times. The Romans also developed a form referred to as *pantomime*, in which a single male dancer interpreted classical literature, sometimes accompanied by a chorus that chanted and by musicians.

But the Romans also organized even greater spectacles. As we have noted, they created huge circuses, stadiums, and amphitheatres for popular arts. Some of the circuses, for example, had tracks for chariot races. Stadiums held animal battles, battles between gladiators, and fights between humans

GLADIATOR BATTLES
Shown here is a Roman mosaic depicting a gladiator battling a leopard. Such battles between human combatants and animals were extremely popular, particularly during the Roman empire. (© Alinari Archives/Corbis)

In modern times, we can see many similarities to the popular arts of Greece and Rome. Stand-up comedians and small troupes of improvisatory comics entertain us regularly in events that are very re...
Sports...
house...
footba...
events...
pregan...

Making Connections. The Making Connections boxes explore the close relationship between theatre and other forms of popular entertainment through the ages, from the mimes and jugglers of ancient Rome to the circuses and vaudeville of the nineteenth century to the rock concerts and theme parks of today.

LIVING HISTORY

COMMEDIA DELL'ARTE

1500s, ROME The time is the late 1500s; the place is a town square in Rome. Set up in the square is a wooden platform stage with a backdrop at the rear. This backdrop, or curtain, not only forms the scenic background of the action on the platform but also provides a hidden space in which the performers can adjust their costumes and from which they can make their entrances and exits.

A crowd is beginning to gather, and people are trying to get the best position to see the performance that is about to begin. In front of the stage, people are already standing several rows deep; at the sides the audience members push closer, but they won't be facing the stage directly. As the spectators look around, they can see that the audience represents a cross section of Roman citizens.

There is great anticipation in the air ... rmers are members of ... nown theatre compa- ... troupe called I Gelosi, ... and Isabella Andreini. ... s of the company have ... dia dell'arte, a form of ... omedy that has be- ... opular type of theatre ... different from many ... eatre. There is no ... l sense. There is an ... ion—the characters ... ne, what happens, ... velops—but the ... ritten out. The lines

the characters speak are not provided. The performers, therefore, improvise their speeches—that is, they make the dialogue up as they go along. This, plus the fact that the movements also are improvised, adds a great air of immediacy to the production. It is most challenging to the performers, and this makes the presentation all the more exciting for those now assembled to watch.

Soon the performance is under way, and the fun begins. The story is partly about an actress who is pursued by every man—unmarried or married—in town, and partly about the adulterous intrigues of her pursuers' wives. There are insults, cases of mistaken identity, and plans gone wrong, and people's misbehavior is exposed.

The characters are stock figures: an old Venetian merchant, a foolish pedant, a cowardly braggart soldier, comic servants, and young lovers. All the characters except the lovers wear masks, most of which are half masks covering the upper part of the face. Each character wears a costume that makes him or her easily recognizable: the pedant, for instance, wears academic robes; the captain wears a uniform; the young lovers are fashionably dressed. One source of great pleasure in watching the performance is seeing the pompous, self-important characters get their comeuppance during the course of the action.

The servants are a special delight. They are known as *zanni* and are usually of two types. The first, called Buffetto

and various other names, is a clever, domineering intriguer who motivates the plot through various schemes. The other, even better known, is Arlecchino, or Harlequin. He wears a patchwork outfit of many colors, is given to pratfalls, and is often the victim of knockdown physical humor. Frequently, the servants outwit their masters and help the young lovers get together.

One plot twist operates around the notion that older characters attempt to thwart the desires of the young lovers, and it is only at the conclusion that the lovers achieve their objective.

The spectators crowded around the platform, knowing that the performers are improvising, are amazed at how quick on their feet the performers are and how readily they respond to the dialogue thrown at them.

The interaction of the performers is very physical. In one scene, a master beats a servant with a stick, which is hinged with a flap to make an exaggerated sound when it hits the servant's backside. In another scene, a soldier challenges a lover to a duel and becomes hopelessly entangled with his own sword; at times his sword sticks out from between his legs, taking on a sexual connotation. The more entangled he becomes, the louder the audience laughs.

At the end of the play, as they make their way home, audience members talk among themselves, sometimes laughing out loud as they recall highlights of the performance.

Living History. We present in these boxes narratives of actual events in theatre history, taking the readers back in time so they have a sense of being in the audience at a performance of, say, *Antigone* in Athens in 441 B.C.E., or at the premier of *Hamlet* at the Globe Theatre in London around 1600.

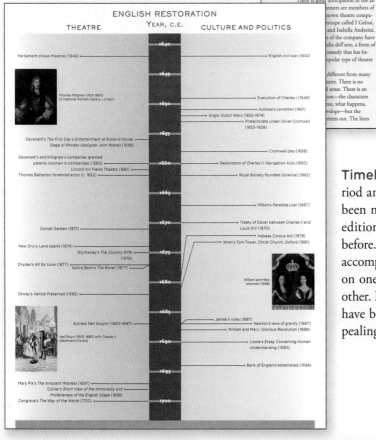

ENGLISH RESTORATION

THEATRE	YEAR, C.E.	CULTURE AND POLITICS
Parliament closes theatres (1642)	1640	English civil war (1642)
Thomas Killigrew (1612–1683) (© National Portrait Gallery, London)	1645	
	1650	Execution of Charles I (1649)
		Hobbes's *Leviathan* (1651)
		Anglo-Dutch Wars (1652–1674)
		Protectorate under Oliver Cromwell (1653–1658)
Davenant's *The First Day's Entertainment at Rutland House*; *Siege of Rhodes* (designer John Webb) (1656)	1655	
Davenant's and Killigrew's companies granted patents (women in companies) (1660)		Cromwell dies (1658)
Lincoln Inn Fields Theatre (1661)	1660	Restoration of Charles II; Navigation Acts (1660)
Thomas Betterton foremost actor (c. 1662)		Royal Society founded (science) (1662)
	1665	
		Milton's *Paradise Lost* (1667)
Dorset Garden (1671)	1670	Treaty of Dover between Charles II and Louis XIV (1670)
New Drury Lane opens (1674)		Habeas Corpus Act (1679)
Wycherley's *The Country Wife* (1675)	1675	Wren's Tom Tower, Christ Church, Oxford (1681)
Dryden's *All for Love* (1677)		
Aphra Behn's *The Rover* (1677)		*William and Mary crowned (1688)*
Otway's *Venice Preserved* (1682)	1680	
	1685	James II rules (1687)
Actress Nell Gwynn (1650–1687)		Newton's laws of gravity (1687)
Nell Gwyn (1650–1687) with Charles II (Bettmann/Corbis)		William and Mary; Glorious Revolution (1688)
	1690	Locke's *Essay Concerning Human Understanding* (1690)
	1695	Bank of England established (1694)
Mary Pix's *The Innocent Mistress* (1697)		
Collier's *Short View of the Immorality and Profaneness of the English Stage* (1698)		
Congreve's *The Way of the World* (1700)	1700	

Timelines. Timelines are included for each period and country addressed. These timelines have been markedly improved from those in previous editions, with entries much easier to read than before. Each timeline shows landmark events and accomplishments in the social and political arenas on one side and significant theatre events on the other. In addition, photos of key people and events have been added to make the timelines more appealing and informative.

Writing Style. A sense of immediacy and personalization has been a goal in our writing style. We have attempted to write *Theatre: The Lively Art* in the most readable language possible. The book contains a wealth of information presented in a manner that makes it vivid and alive.

Production Photos. Altogether there are 243 photographs in the eighth edition of which 151 are new color photos. As always, the vast majority of the photos in the book are not only in full color but are generously sized to help students see and appreciate the dynamic and dramatic world of the theatre. The new photos include images from such recent productions as *The Plough and the Stars, The Emperor Jones, A View from the Bridge, True West, The Book of Mormon, War Horse,* and many more. Also, a number of global theatre productions have been included in this edition, such as Ninagawa's Kabuki *Twelfth Night,* An African-themed *The Tempest* by the Royal Shakespeare Company, and Soyinka's *Death and the King's Horseman.* The illustrations we've chosen—both photographs and line drawings—explain and enhance the material in the text.

Illustrations in *Theatre: The Lively Art* are not only dynamic but timely and up-to-date. Shown here is a scene from the musical, *The Book of Mormon.* (Sara Krulwich/The New York Times/ Redux)

Photo Essays. Students are placed in the audiences of important productions in these pictorial essays to bring to life key elements discussed in each Part. These essays provide context for theatre-viewing experiences, while highlighting outstanding performances and designs.

WHAT'S NEW IN THE CHAPTERS?

In addition to the major changes outlined above, we have included significant new material throughout the text, including the following:

Chapter 1: Theatre: The Art Form

- New accent on the art form itself and a revised introduction to the discipline

Chapter 2: The Audience—Spectators and Participants

- New box on Attending the Theatre: Audience Responsibility
- New material on how social networking technology affects the traditional role of the theatre critic

Chapter 3: Creating the Dramatic Script

- New coverage of the concepts of dénouement and the theatrical foil
- Introduction of the concept of dramatic structure

Chapter 6: The Director and the Producer

- New box on the postmodern director
- New box on modern versus postmodern theatre

Chapter 10: Early Theatres: Greek, Roman, and Medieval

- Enhanced coverage of the role of music in Greek and Medieval theatre

Chapter 11: Early Theatre: Asian

- Introduction of Wayang and Joruri puppet theatre.

Chapter 15: Today's Diverse Global Theatre

- New Global Cross Currents box on Augusto Boal
- New coverage of non-text-based theatre

TEACHING AND LEARNING RESOURCES

SUPPORT FOR INSTRUCTORS

This text offers a wealth of supplemental materials to aid both students and instructors. The Online Learning Center at **www.mhhe.com/livelyart8e** is an Internet-based resource for students and faculty members. Instructor's resources are password protected and offer the following:

- **Instructor's Manual,** including an outline and overview for each chapter, a list of significant names and terms found in the chapter, questions for student essays or discussions, and suggestions for demonstrations and exercises to use in class.
- **Test Bank,** including multiple choice, true-false, and matching questions.
- **Lecture PowerPoint** slides from the text.

STUDENT RESOURCES

The Online Learning Center at **www.mhhe.com/livelyart8e** is a robust tool for students providing a wide range of material to enhance learning and to simplify studying. Resources are keyed directly to this edition and include the following:

- **The Theatregoer's Guide** is an excellent introduction to the art of attending and critiquing a play. This guide will assist students in everything from making theatre reservations and knowing when to applaud to evaluating a performance and doing research on the Internet.
- A **bibliography** to accompany the text.
- **Student Quizzes** that allow students to check their understanding of the course material. The quizzes can be e-mailed directly to instructors.
- **Essay Quizzes** that can be e-mailed directly to instructors.
- **Play Synopses.**

Anthology of Plays

Anthology of Living Theater (978-0-07-351413-0) offers 18 plays for use with *Theatre: The Lively Art.*

Electronic Textbook

This text is available as an eTextbook at **www.CourseSmart.com.** At CourseSmart students can take advantage of significant savings off the cost of a print textbook, reduce their impact on the environment, and gain access to powerful Web tools for student learning. You can view CourseSmart eTextbooks online or download them to a computer. CourseSmart eTextbooks allow students to do full text searches, add highlighting and notes, and share notes with classmates. Visit www.CourseSmart .com to learn more and try a sample chapter.

Create

Craft your teaching resources to match the way you teach. With McGraw-Hill Create, **www.mcgrawhillcreate.com,** you can easily rearrange chapters, combine material from other content sources, and quickly upload content you have written like your course syllabus or teaching notes. Find the content you need in Create by searching through thousands of leading McGraw-Hill textbooks. Arrange your book to fit your teaching style. Create even allows you to personalize your book's appearance by selecting the cover and adding your name, school, and course information. Order a Create book and you'll receive a complimentary print review copy in three to five business days or a complimentary electronic review copy (eComp) via e-mail in about one hour. Go to www.mcgrawhillcreate.com today and register. Experience how McGraw-Hill Create empowers you to teach your students your way.

ACKNOWLEDGMENTS

In the preparation of this book there is a long list of colleagues whose assistance in providing important insights and material has been invaluable. These include the following: Professor J. Thomas Rimer—Asian Theatre; Professor James V. Hatch—African American Theatre; Professor Sam Leiter—Asian Theatre; Professor Ann Haugo—Native American Theatre. We are grateful to Professor Jeff Entwistle for his important contribution to the chapters on design—scenic, costume, lighting, and sound—and we also thank Professor Laura Pulio for her helpful suggestions on acting. Our thanks, too, to Stephen Harrick of Western Illinois University for his assistance. For others whose names we have failed to include, we apologize.

At McGraw-Hill, we wish to express appreciation to the following people: Betty Chen, associate sponsoring editor; Art Pomponio, developmental editor; Rhona Robbin, director of development; Stacey Ruel, marketing manager; Chris Freitag, publisher; Jasmin Tokatlian, production editor; Cassandra Chu, designer; and Tandra Jorgensen, buyer.

Through the years, many instructors have given us helpful comments and suggestions. For their assistance in developing the eighth edition of *Theatre: The Lively Art,* we wish to thank the following people:

Philip Atlakson, *Boise State University*

Brian Desmond, *Pacific Lutheran University*

Mary Field, *Mid-South Community College*

Monique Holt, *Gallaudet University*

Mary A. Ketchum, *Texas Christian University*

Dawn Larsen, *Francis Marion University*

Cathy O'Dell, *West Virginia University*

Joyce Pauley, *Moberly Area Community College*

Reginald G. Peters, *Angelina College*

James R. Rambo, *McLennan College*

Anita Tecce, *Chesapeake College*

David Underwood, *University of North Carolina at Pembroke*

One person who we must single out for special thanks is Inge King. Unquestionably the finest photo researcher on theatre in the United States, Inge has worked with us tirelessly and brilliantly on every one of our books: this is the twenty-seventh volume for which she has assisted in selecting and securing the photographs. Her contribution to the appeal and success of our books is incalculable.

THEATRE
THE LIVELY ART

PART 1

THEATRE: DIVERSE, GLOBAL, MULTICULTURAL

Today's theatre encompasses several worlds; it cuts across many art forms, many cultural phenomena, many nations, and many individual preferences and identities. An excellent example of diversity and multiculturalism in theatre is the African-themed Shakespeare's *The Tempest* directed by Janice Honeyman at the Royal Shakespeare Company in collaboration with the Baxter Theatre Centre of Cape Town, South Africa. Illka Louw, as the production designer, was responsible for creating the spectacular puppets in this scene from the wedding masque.

(© Donald Cooper/Photo*STAGE*)

THEATRE IN TODAY'S WORLD

1 THEATRE: THE ART FORM

2 THE AUDIENCE—SPECTATORS AND PARTICIPANTS

THEATRE: THE ART FORM

1

THE UNIQUE QUALITY OF THEATRE

A HISTORICAL REASON TO ATTEND THEATRE

THEATRE AND THE HUMAN CONDITION

THEATRE AS AN ART FORM

WHAT IS ART?

THE ART OF THEATRE

GLOBALIZATION AND TODAY'S THEATRE

DIVERSITY AND MULTICULTURALISM

DIVERSITY IN CONTEMPORARY THEATRE

SUMMARY

THINKING ABOUT THEATRE

KEY TERMS

THEATRE ON THE WEB

◄ **THEATRE AND THE IMAGINATION** The art of theatre involves many components. One crucial component is the audience's imagination. In the play *War Horse,* the audience is asked to imagine that a life-size puppet made of slats and operated by three men is a live horse. Thanks to the artistry of those involved, that magical transformation occurs for the audience in every performance of *War Horse.* The play, adapted by Nick Stafford from a novel by Michael Morpurgo, was originally a National Theatre production in association with Handspring Puppet Company, and also played at Lincoln Center Theater in New York. The London production was directed by Marianne Elliott and Tom Morris. In this scene we see David Emmings (the head puppeteer), Joey (the horse), and Bettrys Jones (Emilie) ecstatically astride the horse. (© Donald Cooper/Photo*STAGE*)

P rior to the twentieth century, for more than 2,000 years in the West and 1,500 years in Asia, the only way audiences could see theatre of any kind was to attend a live performance. Spectators had to leave their homes and go to a space where a theatrical production was being presented, where they would join others to watch the event. If people wanted to see a tragedy, with kings and queens, heroes and villains, or a comedy making fun of human foibles, they would have to become participants along with their fellow audience members.

Then, after all these centuries, at the beginning of the twentieth century, everything began to change. In rapid succession a series of technological innovations offered alternative ways to hear and observe drama. First, there was radio, and then silent film, and after that, movies with sound. Black-and-white film gave way to movies in color; not much later, film was joined by television, first in black and white and later in color. Film and television now also use 3D technology as well as computerization to create amazingly realistic effects. Today, the computer and a series of hand-held electronic devices, including smartphones and tablets, allow viewers to watch films and television shows anywhere.

With all of these inventions, arriving in quick succession, dramatic presentations became much more accessible and much less expensive. With film, for example, audiences could go to the movies and see a Shakespeare play or a knock-about farce for a fraction of the cost of a theatre ticket. They could also attend anywhere and at any time. In the case of television, the same offerings were available absolutely free and constantly available.

From the beginning, with radio and silent film, there were predictions that such inventions would mark the death knell of live theatre. With sound film and television, especially when color came in, dire predictions were even more pronounced. After all, it was argued, talking pictures eliminated silent film just as later, color television obliterated black-and-white TV. It seemed logical that drama on film and television, and now on computers and other digital devices, might well eradicate live theatre.

Contrary to predictions, however, theatre has not only survived but has thrived. In his play *Antony and Cleopatra,* Shakespeare has a character describe Cleopatra's "infinite variety." Today the words can apply equally well to the vitality and diversity of theatre in the United States and elsewhere. Audiences in every major city across the country, from Boston and Baltimore to San Francisco and Seattle, can see elaborate, spectacular musical productions such as *Wicked* and *The Lion King.* In smaller, intimate theatres, in each of the 50 states, audiences can view both new works and revivals of every description: serious dramas on thought-provoking subjects, experimental works, as well as a host of new plays by new playwrights and multicultural works by Hispanic, African American, and Asian playwrights from other nations. College and university theatre departments offer a range of plays from the most significant classics to the newest avant-garde works, in addition to everything in between. In every respect, from the types of theatre spaces available—large or small, indoors or outdoors—to the kinds of drama, from Greek and Asian classics straight through to modern American musicals, audiences today can find a cornucopia of theatrical experiences.

THE UNIQUE QUALITY OF THEATRE

In the face of such formidable competition from all forms of electronic media, why do people continue to go to the theatre? There are a number of reasons, but the most important single reason can be found in the title of this book. We call theatre the *lively art* not only because it is exciting, suspenseful, and amusing, but also because it is alive in a way that makes it different from every other form of dramatic presentation. It is the live quality of theatre that makes it so durable and so indispensible.

The special nature of theatre becomes more apparent when we contrast the experience of seeing a drama in a theatre with seeing a drama on film or television. In many ways the dramas presented are alike. Both offer a story told in dramatic form—an enactment of scenes by performers who speak and act as if they are the people they represent—and film and television can give us many of the same feelings and experiences that we have when watching a theatre performance. One can learn a great deal about theatre from watching a play on film or television, and the accessibility of film and television means that they have a crucial role in our overall exposure to the depiction of dramatic events and dramatic characters.

Nevertheless, there is a fundamental difference, and we become aware of that difference when we contrast theatre with movies. This contrast does not have to do with technical matters, such as the way films can show outdoor shots made from helicopters, cut instantaneously from one scene to another, or create interplanetary wars or cataclysmic events by using computer-generated special effects. The most significant difference between films and theatre is the *relationship between the performer and the audience.* The experience of being in the presence of the performer is more important to theatre than anything else. No matter how closely a film follows the story of a play, no matter how involved we are with the people on the screen, we are always in the presence of an *image,* never a person.

We all know the difference between an image of someone and the flesh-and-blood reality. How often we rehearse a speech we plan to make to someone we love or fear. We run through the scene in our mind, picturing ourselves talking to the other person—declaring our love, asking for help, asking for a raise. But when we meet face-to-face, it is not the same. We freeze and find ourselves unable to speak; or perhaps our words gush forth incoherently. Seldom does the encounter take place as we planned.

Like films, television seems very close to theatre; sometimes it seems even closer than film. Television programs sometimes begin with words such as "This program comes to you live from Burbank, California." But the word *live* must be qualified. Before television, *live* in the entertainment world meant "in person": not only was the event taking place at that moment; it was taking place in the physical *presence* of the spectators. Usually, the term *live television* still means that an event is taking place at this moment, but "live" television does *not* take place in the presence of the viewer. In fact, it is generally far removed from the television audience, possibly half a world away. In television, like film, we see an image—in the case of TV, on a screen—and we are free to look or not to look, or even to leave the room.

The fascination of being in the presence of a person is difficult to explain but not difficult to verify, as the popularity of rock stars attests. No matter how often fans have seen a favorite star in the movies or heard a rock singer on iPod, CD, television, or a computer screen, they will go to any lengths to see her or him in person. In the same way, at one time or another, each of us has braved bad weather and shoving crowds to see celebrities at a parade or a political rally. The same pull of personal contact draws us to the theatre.

At the heart of the theatre experience, therefore, is the performer-audience relationship—the immediate, personal exchange whose chemistry and magic give

TAKING PART IN THEATRE HISTORY

When we attend a theatre performance, each one of us is participating in theatre history: seeing either a new play or a revival of an older one. A good example is the audience shown here at a production of Shakespeare's *The Comedy of Errors,* directed by Stephanie Shine, with Jake Hart as Angelo, at the Mary Rippon outdoor theatre, home of the Colorado Shakespeare Festival at Boulder. These spectators are part of a Shakespearean tradition that dates back to England 400 years ago. Farther back, attendance at outdoor theatre events began in Greece in the fifth century B.C.E. (Casey A. Cass, © Regents of the Univeristy of Colorado)

theatre its special quality. During a stage performance the actresses and actors can hear laughter, can sense silence, and can feel tension in the audience. In short, the audience can affect, and in subtle ways change, the performance.

At the same time, members of the audience watch the performers closely, consciously or unconsciously asking themselves questions: Are the performers talented? Have they learned their parts well? Are they convincing in their roles? Will they do something surprising? Will they make a mistake? At each moment, in every stage performance, the audience is looking for answers to questions like these. The performers are alive—and so is the very air itself—with the electricity of expectation. It is for this reason that we speak of theatre as the lively art. It is for this reason, as well as a number of others, that we study theatre as an art form.

A HISTORICAL REASON TO ATTEND THEATRE

There is a second reason to attend and study theatre: namely, its history. Theatre is the foundation of all drama: in films, on television, on computer screens, in theme parks, and in fact in every medium. The ancient Greeks, 2,500 years ago, established the categories of tragedy and comedy that are still used today. They also developed dramatic structure, acting, and theatre architecture. Roman domestic comedies are the prototype of every situation comedy we see in the movies or on television.

In other words, though we may not be aware of it, each time we see a performance we are taking part in theatre history. Wherever theatre takes place, its foundation, its roots are always found in theatre. When audiences watch a performance of a Shakespearean play in an outdoor theatre—for example, at the Shakespeare festival in Ashland, Oregon, or at the Old Globe in San Diego, California—they are not only watching a play by a dramatist who lived 400 years ago but are also sharing in an environment, a configuration of audience and stage space that goes back much farther to the ancient Greeks.

When an audience is in a theatre with a picture-frame stage, seeing a drama by the French playwright Molière, the spectators are not only partaking of a theatrical tradition that traces its roots to seventeenth-century France. They are also partaking of a tradition that goes back to Italian commedia dell'arte, which came to prominence a century earlier. And the theatre space goes back to the proscenium stage, which originated during the Italian Renaissance in the early seventeenth century.

Similarly, at a college production of Bertolt Brecht's *The Good Person of Setzuan*, the audience members are not only seeing a play by one of the most innovative playwrights of the twentieth century; they are seeing a play that was strongly influenced by techniques of ancient Asian theatre.

THEATRE AND THE HUMAN CONDITION

There is a third reason to attend and study theatre. Throughout its history theatre has had a two-fold appeal. One attraction is the sheer excitement or amusement of a theatre event. The other is the unique ability of theatre to incorporate in dramatic material profound, provocative, timeless observations about the human condition. Ideas, moral dilemmas, probing insights—these have long found vivid expression in exceptional plays and exceptional performances. Moreover, in theatre these performances are live, not reproduced on a film or television screen.

In Greek and Shakespearean tragedy, and in the works of modern playwrights like Henrik Ibsen, Anton Chekhov, Eugene O'Neill, Tennessee Williams, Arthur Miller, Lorraine Hansberry, and August Wilson, we encounter questions and issues that strike at the very heart of human existence. In the comedies of the French playwright Molière, we see personal foibles exposed as they have rarely been before or since.

Finally, theatre also differs in significant ways from the live performances of entertainers such as rock stars. Rock musicians make no pretense of offering the same kind of experience as a production by a theatre company. A drama or a piece of performance art has a structure—a beginning, middle, and end—a purpose, a cast of characters, a unique completeness that a concert by a rock artist would never aspire to.

In other words, theatre is an art form with its own characteristics: its own quality, coherence, and integrity.

THEATRE AS AN ART FORM

To understand theatre as an art form, it is useful to look first at art in general.

WHAT IS ART?

As has often been observed, art is a mirror or reflection of life: an extension or a projection of how we live, think, and feel. Art reveals to us what people treasure and admire, and what they fear most deeply. Art is not only something we find desirable and enjoyable; it seems to be an absolute necessity for human survival.

There are feelings, emotions, and ideas that cannot be expressed in any way other than through art. The beauty of a face or a haunting landscape may be impossible to convey in words, but it can be revealed in a painting; a complex personality can be captured in a novel or a play in a way that reveals the person's innermost soul; joy or anguish can often be communicated most directly and completely through music, poetry, or drama. Without these modes of expression—that is, without art—human beings would be as impoverished and as helpless as they would be if they tried to live without language.

Characteristics of Art Art can be divided into three categories: *literary, visual,* and *performing.* The literary arts include novels, short stories, and poetry. The visual arts include painting, sculpture, architecture, and photography. The **performing arts** are theatre, dance, opera, and music. (Film, another art form, partakes of both the visual and the performing arts.)

Performing arts Theatre, dance, opera, and music. Film also partakes of the performing arts.

THE PERMANENCE OF THE VISUAL ARTS
If they are preserved, painting and sculpture—unlike performing arts such as theatre, dance, and music—are permanent and unchanging. An example is this sculpture of the Nike of Samothrace, goddess of victory, on display at the Louvre Museum in Paris, France. The torso enfolded in flowing robes and the outstretched wings appear much as they did when the sculpture was first created on the island of Samothrace in Greece around 200 B.C.E., about 2,200 years ago.
(© Erich Lessing/Art Resource, NY)

One characteristic of all art—visual, literary, or performing—is that it is selective. As the three categories suggest, different art forms focus on certain elements and eliminate others. The visual arts, for example, deal solely with sight and touch – what we can see and feel—and they exclude sound. When we visit an art gallery, there is a hush in the air because the concentration is purely on what the eye observes. Moreover, in the visual arts, a composition is frozen and constant. We value the visual arts partly because they capture subjects—faces, landscapes, a series of colors or shapes—and hold them fast in a painting or a sculpture. We can look at a statue of a Roman soldier from 2,000 years ago, or a Madonna and Child painted 500 years ago, and see exactly the same artifact that its first viewers observed.

Music, to take another example, concentrates on sound. Although we may watch a violinist playing with a symphony orchestra or observe a soprano singing at a recital, the essence of music is sound. We prove this whenever we close our eyes at a concert, and whenever we listen to recorded music. In both cases, the emphasis is totally on sound. By concentrating on sound, we block out distractions and give our full attention to the music itself. This kind of selectivity is one quality that makes any art form effective.

Another characteristic of art is its relationship to time or space; thus a second way to differentiate the arts is in temporal and spatial terms. The visual arts exist in space, which is their primary mode of existence. They occupy a canvas, for instance, or—in the case of architecture—a building. By contrast, music moves through time. It does not occupy space; musicians performing a symphony exist in space, of course, but the music they perform does not. The music is an unfolding series of sounds, and the duration of the notes and the pauses between notes create a rhythm that is an essential part of music. This, in turn, becomes a time continuum as we move from one note to the next.

THE PERFORMING ARTS
Like theatre, opera, and music, dance shares a number of characteristics with these other performing arts. For example, all these arts move through time, they require interpreters as well as creators, and they must be seen live by an audience. In this photo we see the Kremlin Ballet performing *Swan Lake* in Skopje, Macedonia. (Chris Pizzello/AP Images)

Unlike painting and sculpture on the one hand or music on the other, theatre, dance, and opera occupy both time and space. Let's now consider the special characteristics of the performing arts.

Characteristics of the Performing Arts   The performing arts, of which music, theatre, and dance are a part, have several characteristics in common. One is the movement through time described above. Another is that they require interpreters as well as creators. A playwright writes a play, but actors and actresses perform it; a composer writes a piece of music that singers and instrumentalists will perform; a choreographer develops a ballet that dancers will interpret.

Another quality shared by the performing arts is that they require an audience. A performance can be recorded on film or tape, but the event itself must be "live," that is, it must occur in one place at one time with both performers and audience present. If a theatre performance is recorded on film or tape without the presence of an audience, it becomes a movie or a television show rather than a theatre experience. To put this distinction another way, when an audience watches a film in a movie theatre, there are no performers onstage; there are only images on a screen. Hence there is no interaction

PERFORMANCE: THE HEART OF THEATRE

At the center of a theatrical event and a theatrical experience is a performance by actors and actresses, viewed by an audience. This personal interaction, between spectator and performer, separates theatre from film and television as well as from the other arts. The scene shown here is from *The Glass Menagerie* by Tennessee Williams, with Judith Ivey as Amanda Wingfield and Keira Keeley as her daughter Laura in a production directed by Gordon Edelstein at the Long Wharf Theatre. (© T. Charles Erickson)

between performers and audience. Such interaction is absolutely essential to the performing arts. In Chapter 2, we will talk more about the special nature of "live" performance and the crucial role of the audience.

In addition to the general qualities we have been discussing, each art form has unique qualities and principles that set it apart from other art forms and help us to understand it better. When we know how shapes and designs relate to overall composition, for instance, and how colors contrast with and complement one another, we are in a better position to judge and understand painting. In the same way, we can appreciate theatre much more if we understand how it is created and what elements it consists of. We'll now consider theatre as an art form, and the creation and elements of theatre will be the focus of Part 2 of this book.

THE ART OF THEATRE

Elements of Theatre   When we begin to examine theatre as an art form, we discover that there are certain elements common to all theatre. These elements are present whenever a theatre event takes place; without them, an event ceases to be theatre and becomes a different art form and a different experience.

Audience   As we have suggested, a necessary element for theatre is the audience. In fact, the essence of theatre is the interaction between performer and audience. A theatre, dance, or musical event is not complete—one could almost say it does not occur—unless there are people to see and hear it. When we read a play in book form, or listen to recorded music, what we experience is similar to looking at a painting or reading a poem: it is a private event, not a public one, and the live performance is recreated and imagined rather than experienced firsthand.

Later, we will explain this in more detail, but now we can note simply that in the performing arts a performance occurs when the event takes place, not before and not after. All the performing arts, including theatre, are like an electrical connection: the connection is not made until positive and negative wires touch and complete the circuit. Performers are half of that connection, and audiences are the other half.

Performers   Another absolutely essential element for theatre are the performers: people onstage presenting characters in dramatic action.

Acting is at the heart of all theatre. One person stands in front of other people and begins to portray a character—to speak and move in ways that convey an image of the character. At this point the magic of theatre has begun: the transformation through which an audience accepts, for a time, that a performer is actually someone else. The character portrayed can be a historical figure, an imaginary figure, or even a self-presentation; still, everyone accepts the notion that it is the character, not the actor or actress, who is speaking.

Acting is a demanding profession. In addition to native talent—the poise and authority needed to appear onstage before others, and the innate ability to create a character convincingly—acting requires considerable craft and skill. Performers must learn to use both voice and body with flexibility and control; they must be able, for example, to make themselves heard in a large theatre even when speaking in a whisper. (This takes extensive physical and vocal training, which we will discuss in more detail in Chapter 5.) Performers must also be able to create believability, or the emotional truth of the characters they portray; that is, the audience must be convinced that the actor or actress is thinking and feeling what the character would think and feel. (This, too, is a difficult task requiring a special kind of training—which we will also discuss in Chapter 5.)

Script or Text   Another element essential to theatre is the *script* or *text* that is performed. It could also be called the *blueprint* for a production. The playwright transforms the raw material—the incident, the biographical event, the myth—into a drama, a sequence of events that features characters talking and interacting with one another. Making this transformation is not easy. It requires intimate knowledge of stage practices, of how to breathe life into characters, of how to build action so that it will hold the interest of the audience and arouse anticipation for what is coming next. In other words, the playwright must create characters and develop a dramatic structure. The term *text* is used to discuss any type of theatrical activity presented onstage: for example, all forms of pop entertainment, as well as performances created by performers or directors. Frequently, the term *text* is all-inclusive, and it is sometimes used in place of *script*. A specific example of a nonliterary theatrical text would be an improvisitory presentation created by actors on a street, in a remodeled school, or in a theatre.

Along with structure, a text must have a focus and a point of view. Who and what is the text about? Are we supposed to regard the characters and the events as sad or funny? The person or persons who create the text have the power as well as the responsibility to direct our attention toward certain characters and away from others. We will discover more about how these tasks are accomplished when we look at the nature of a dramatic text in Chapters 3 and 4.

Director   An additional key element of a theatre production is the work of the *director:* the person who rehearses the performers and coordinates the work of the designers and others to make certain that the production is cohesive as well as exciting. As we will see in Chapter 6, the separate role of the director became prominent for the first time in modern theatre, but many of the functions of the director have always been present.

Theatre Space   Another necessary element of theatre is the *space* in which performers and audiences come together. It is essential to have a stage, or some equivalent area, where actors and actresses can perform. It is also essential to have a place for audience members to sit or stand. We will discover that there have been several basic

Script Also, *text.* Story, incident, or event put into theatrical form.

Director The person who rehearses and coordinates performers to ensure that they interpret the text appropriately.

Theatre space The place where performers and audiences come together.

A PRIMARY COMPONENT OF THEATRE: THE DESIGN ELEMENTS
Key aspects of a theatrical production are the design elements: scenery, costumes, lights, and sound. Shown here is a scene from *She Stoops to Conquer* by Oliver Goldsmith, directed by Nicholas Martin at the McCarter Theatre. This eighteenth-century play, known as a "laughing comedy," requires elaborate sets and costumes. Sets: David Korins; lighting: Ben Stanton; costumes: Gabriel Berry. (© T. Charles Erickson)

configurations of stage spaces and audience seating. Whatever the configuration, however, a stage and a space for the audience must be a part of it. Also, there must be a place for the actors and actresses to change costumes, as well as a way for them to enter and exit from the stage.

Design Elements   Closely related to the physical stage is another important element: the design aspects of a production. Design includes visual aspects—costumes, lighting, and some form of scenic background—and a nonvisual aspect, sound.

A play can be produced on a bare stage with minimal lighting, and with the performers wearing everyday street clothes. Even in these conditions, however, some attention must be paid to visual elements; there must, for instance, be sufficient illumination for us to see the performers, and clothes worn onstage will take on a special meaning even if they are quite ordinary.

Usually, visual elements are prominent in theatre productions. Costumes, especially, have been a hallmark of theatre from the beginning; and scenery has sometimes become more prominent than the performers. In certain arrangements, visual aspects come to the forefront; in others—such as the arena stage, where the audience surrounds the action—elaborate scenery is impractical or even impossible.

The visual aspects of theatre are particularly interesting to trace through history because their place in theatre production has shifted markedly from time to time. For example, stage lighting changed dramatically when the electric lightbulb came into use at the end of the nineteenth century.

As we noted above, a design element that is not visual is sound. This, too, is a modern element that has come into its own with modern technology. Of course, there were always sound effects, such as thunder and wind created by offstage machines; and there was frequently music, especially during certain periods, when every intermission was accompanied by orchestral performances. In modern times, though, with electronic inventions, there are far more elaborate sound effects; and frequently there are also microphones, sometimes in the general stage area and sometimes actually worn by the performers.

To sum up, the following are the major elements of theatre:

Audience

Performers

Script, with its structure, characters, and point of view

Director

Theatre space

Design aspects: scenery, costume, lighting, and sound

Theatre as a Collaborative Art   It should be clear from what we have said that theatre is a collaborative art. For a theatre event to take place, its various elements must be brought together and coordinated.

The director must stage the play written by the playwright and must share with the playwright an understanding of structure, theme, and style. At the same time, the director must work closely with performers in rehearsing the play, and with the designers of scenery, lights, costumes, and sound, to bring the production to fruition. During performances many elements must be coordinated: the work of actors and actresses along with technical aspects—scene changes, lighting shifts, and sound cues. The people working on these elements are joined, in turn, by a number of collaborators: stage manager, stage carpenters, makeup experts, those who make costumes, and computer lighting experts. In an ensemble piece, where the play is actually composed by a group of actors working with a director, collaboration is more important than ever.

Another essential component in this collaborative enterprise is the business and administrative side of a production or theatre organization. This includes producers and managers, and their staffs—the people who organize and administer press and public relations, advertising, scheduling, fund-raising, and all the details of keeping the theatre running smoothly, including ticket sales, ticket taking, and ushering.

Ultimately, the many elements integrated in a production—text, direction, design, and acting, assisted by the technical side and the business side—must be presented to an audience. At that point occurs the final collaboration in any theatre enterprise: the performance itself before spectators.

GLOBALIZATION AND TODAY'S THEATRE

Theatrical performances occur all over the world. There are unique theatrical arts found in many cultures, as well as performances that reflect the fusion of differing world theatre traditions. For this reason, one of the most important trends in our theatre today is globalization: the various ways in which different nations and cultures

Global Having to do with any activity—political, economic, artistic, cultural—in which nations and people around the world relate and interact.

influence one another's theatrical traditions. **Global** connections were relatively rare prior to the 1800s, but today we live in a world where such cross-cultural relationships are extremely easy, owing to modern transportation and communication.

In approaching global theatre, three points should be kept in mind. The first is that in many cultures, theatre has a long, illustrious history. Unlike American theatre, which has a relatively short history, theatre in both Europe and Asia goes back more than 2,000 years. In Europe, preceding contemporary theatre, there is a long tradition beginning with Greek theatre and moving through Roman, medieval, Renaissance, eighteenth-century, and nineteenth-century theatre and into modern theatre. In Asia, theatre in India began more than 2,000 years ago and Chinese theatre a few centuries after that; Japanese theatre was established by 800 C.E.

In other parts of the world—for instance, in Africa, in pre-Columbian Latin America, and in the Native American culture of North America—there is rich tradition of rituals and ceremonies that have recognizable elements of theatre: costumes; song and dance; and impersonation of people, animals, and divinities. These presentations form a rich tradition of theatre-like reenactments. When we look at European, Asian, and other theatres, therefore, we are looking at a tradition preceding the theatre that exists in those parts of the world today.

A second point to be borne in mind is that beginning around 1900, Asian and other non-European theatres were influenced by developments of modern theatre in the West: the realism introduced by Ibsen, Strindberg, and Chekhov, and a number of departures from realism such as expressionism. Thus in a country like Japan, you had the traditional theatre of nō and kabuki alongside modern theatre.

The third point—and in many ways the most significant point for modern audiences—is the development of global exchanges in communication, in ideas, in commerce, and in the arts. Thomas Friedman, in his acclaimed book *The World Is Flat,* analyzes how globalization has affected business and industry in contemporary society. One can no longer tell whether a product is made by a company of a specific country since most major corporations are multinational. The automobile industry clearly reflects the trend toward industrial globalization, as does the personal computer industry. A car created today by a Japanese, Korean, or German manufacturer may be assembled in the United States. A PC may be assembled in the United States, but the 24-hour help desk may be located in India.

The same is true in today's theatre. Many diverse groups influence one another to create the contemporary theatrical landscape. Theatre artists cross national boundaries to stage their works with artists of other countries. Popular works tour the world and cross-pollinate other theatrical ventures. International theatre festivals bring artists of various nationalities to interact with those in the host community.

An indication of the global nature of today's theatre can be seen in the offerings each summer at the International Theatre Festival at Lincoln Center in New York City. Productions from all parts of the world are presented side by side. In recent years the countries represented have included Japan, Indonesia, China, Singapore, Switzerland, Germany, Ireland, Argentina, Chile, Spain, Mexico, Italy, and France.

Experimental artists appropriate the styles and techniques of traditional theatres from around the world. Artists mix and match all sorts of styles, historical antecedents, materials, and techniques. For example, in 2009 a 10-day festival in India presented

TODAY'S GLOBAL THEATRE
Today's theatre features an impressive amount of exchange and interchange among different countries and different cultures. Twenty-first century theatre is truly global, far more so than theatre of earlier years. An excellent example is the work of the acclaimed Japanese director Yukio Ninagawa. The scene shown here is from his Kabuki adaptation of Shakespeare's *Twelfth Night* staged in London. (© Geraint Lewis)

Asian and Arab adaptations of the well-known plays by the late nineteenth-century playwright Henrik Ibsen.

What these examples suggest is that we can no longer easily classify theatre productions and artists by specific national designations. Ease of travel, electronic communication, and the commerce of theatre have all led to a blurring of national theatres. Instead, like the global economy, theatre is a global activity.

What these trends also suggest is that we can categorize globalization into three general patterns: interaction, adaptation, and collaboration.

Theatres across the world have been transformed through cultural interactions. For example, western theatre borrowed the concept of the revolving stage from traditional Japanese theatre after interactions between Asia and Europe in the nineteenth century. Today, many Asian theatres, as a result of their interactions with European and American theatre artists in the late nineteenth century and the twentieth century, present realistic dramas and musicals. A theatre company in one nation may invite a company from another country to present one of its works.

In addition, there have been cross-cultural adaptations of storylines as well as performance and production techniques. We will see many examples later, when we discuss the theatre of the past 100 years. The twentieth-century director and playwright Bertolt Brecht used Asian techniques in his plays; the French theorist Antonin Artaud argued that contemporary acting should follow the traditions of Balinese theatre.

And, as noted, there are frequent collaborations across international boundaries. Individual artists work with artists from different nations. Multinational casts and production teams are more common than ever before.

As we shall see in our discussions of theatrical elements, theatre artists, and theatre history, globalization is omnipresent in our contemporary theatre.

DIVERSITY AND MULTICULTURALISM

Multiethnic/multicultural
Referring to any nation, community, or group in which people of various ethnic or cultural origins or beliefs coexist and interact.

Two words that also characterize today's theatre are *diversity* and ***multiculturalism:*** diversity because the types of theatre available to audiences are so wide ranging and because the audiences themselves are so diverse; and multiculturalism because contemporary theatre embraces such a wide variety of social groups and concerns. When we explore contemporary theatre history in Chapters 14 and 15, it will become even clearer how diverse and multicultural the theatrical landscape remains in the twenty-first century.

DIVERSITY IN CONTEMPORARY THEATRE

The diversity of contemporary theatre is striking. There are artists who reflect the multicultural landscape of our global society and focus on significant concerns and issues of many historically underrepresented groups.

Clearly, there is an impressive variety of theatrical events in contemporary theatre. Audiences today can see revivals of the best theatre from the past: Greek, Elizabethan, French, and Spanish. They can see theatre from Asia, Africa, and Latin America; new plays; and avant-garde and experimental works. There are productions in translation of the best new plays from many countries. American audiences, for example, can see multiethnic or multicultural theatre—African American, Asian American, Hispanic, Native American. They can also see political theatre, and theatre reflecting the viewpoints of a number of minorities and special groups such as feminist theatre and gay and lesbian theatre. What's more, these productions can be seen in a wide variety of theatre environments.

One hallmark of contemporary theatre is that all these strands exist simultaneously. As all this suggests, our contemporary theatre is complex. If theatre mirrors the society in which it is produced, it is not surprising that ours is fragmented, reflecting the complexity of today's life.

However, we do need to emphasize one point when discussing the diverse points of view in the contemporary theatre. Although many theatre artists do want to write from a specific ethnic or gender point of view, there are others who happen to be members of an ethnic group, or who espouse feminism or a political outlook, but who do not want to be identified solely, or even primarily, on that basis—or on the basis of their gender. For instance, there are playwrights who happen to be Latin American or African American but want to be known simply as playwrights, without any ethnic

MULTIETHNIC, MULTICULTURAL THEATRE
In the past half century, theatre from many cultures and many ethnic groups has found its way into the mainstream of theatre offerings on view. One strong example is Hispanic theatre, which itself has a number of branches. A case in point is a joint production by the Goodman Theatre and Teatro Vista in presenting *El Nogalar* by the Mexican American dramatist Tanya Saracho. The play, a scene from which is shown here, is a moving, yet comical, story about the choice between adapting to today's changing world or being left behind. (Photo: Eric Y. Exit)

identification. In the same way, there are people who are gay or lesbian, or who are strong feminists, but who want to be known chiefly, or even exclusively, as dramatists, not as gay dramatists, lesbian dramatists, or feminist dramatists.

It is also true that theatre companies, producers, or playwrights identified with an ethnic or gender group may well include in their presentations characters belonging to those groups, and wish to see them treated with understanding and insight, but who include them as part of a larger picture. We will explore our diverse and multiethnic contemporary theatre in Chapters 14 and 15.

We will understand the collaborative process, the individual elements, and the diversity of theatre when we examine these elements in the chapters to come. But before we turn to those elements and how theatre is created, we need to discuss more specifically how theatre is the foundation for many other contemporary popular entertainments and dramatic arts. We need to discover how theatrical traditions affect film, television, digital media, and even rock and roll and sporting events.

SUMMARY

The theatre experience has been created many thousands of times over the centuries and continues to be created every day throughout the world. A great variety of theatre experiences can be found in the United States today.

To have a full and rewarding appreciation of theatre, it is important to understand that theatre is an art form, and that theatre has a long and fascinating history.

Art forms can be categorized as literary, visual, and performing; theatre is one of the performing arts. All art is selective, and selectivity is one way of distinguishing one art form from another. Art forms may also be distinguished in terms of time and space: the visual arts exist primarily in space; music exists in time rather than space; and theatre (along with dance and opera) exists in both time and space.

Important characteristics of the performing arts include the need for interpreters and the need for an audience.

Understanding theatre involves understanding its history, its elements, and how it is created.

The major elements of theatre are audience, performers, text, director, theatre space, and design. Because these elements must be coordinated, theatre is a collaborative art. Today's theatre is also global and reflects the diversity of our contemporary society.

THINKING ABOUT THEATRE

▶ Take an example with which you are familiar from three different art forms: (1) visual (a painting or a piece of sculpture); (2) literary (a poem, a novel, or a biography); (3) the performing arts (theatre, a ballet, a musical concert). Describe your experience of encountering each of the three: what you felt, what you thought, what you focused on. Explain how the experience of responding to each one differed from that of seeing or hearing the other two.

▶ In the past half-century, theatre has become increasingly global and much more ethnically diverse. Have you seen a theatre production of a foreign play (Chinese, Japanese, African) or a play that depicts an ethnic group different from your own (African American, Hispanic, Asian American)? If so, did you identify with the situation and the characters in the play? Explain how identifying with people and events from another culture might be possible.

KEY TERMS

Director The person who rehearses and coordinates performers to ensure that they interpret the text appropriately.

Global Having to do with any activity—political, economic, artistic, cultural—in which nations and people around the world relate and interact.

Multiethnic/multicultural Referring to any nation, community, or group in which people of various ethnic or cultural origins or beliefs coexist and interact.

Performing arts Theatre, dance, opera, and music. Film also partakes of the performing arts.

Script Also, *text.* Story, incident, or event put into theatrical form.

Theatre space The place where performers and audiences come together.

THEATRE ON THE WEB

For more research and to learn more about the topics in this chapter, please visit the Online Learning Center at **www.mhhe.com/livelyart8e.**

The Audience— Spectators and Participants

How Theatre Permeates Our Lives

Theatre and Television

Theatre and Film

Theatre and Rock and Roll

Theatricality in Amusement Parks, Museums, Las Vegas, and Sporting Events

Theatre and Digital Media

DIFFERENCES BETWEEN THEATRE-RELATED ACTIVITIES AND THEATRE ITSELF

The Role of the Audience

HOW THE AUDIENCE PARTICIPATES

DIVERSITY OF AUDIENCES

Wider Perspective: Attending the Theatre

The Critic and the Reviewer

PREPARING FOR CRITICISM

CRITERIA FOR CRITICISM

DECLINE OF CRITICS' AND REVIEWERS' INFLUENCE

THE AUDIENCE MEMBER'S INDEPENDENT JUDGMENT

SUMMARY

THINKING ABOUT THEATRE

KEY TERMS

THEATRE ON THE WEB

◀ **THE AUDIENCE** The audience and the performers are the two basic elements of theatre: for theatre to occur, both are required. The presence of the audience observing live performers sets theatre apart from other forms of entertainment such as film, television, or scenes viewed on computer screens. In the scene here, we see a special kind of interaction between performers and spectators in the Broadway musical *Spider-Man: Turn Off the Dark,* where Spider-Man and the Green Goblin fight in the air above the heads of the audience. The musical features not only the kind of performance audiences are accustomed to on stage itself, but many flying sequences above and around the audience. (Sara Krulwich/The New York Times/Redux)

n this chapter, we will explore two areas. First, we will look at a number of activities in the world of entertainment that bear a close affinity with theatrical presentations or are strongly influenced by them. These cover a broad range of spectacles and public attractions as we will see. Second, we will examine the crucial, indispensable role of the audience in theatrical productions. The relationship of the audience to the actors in a drama casts these audience members in a different role from that of spectators at other entertainment events, as we will discover.

HOW THEATRE PERMEATES OUR LIVES

Most of us would be surprised at the extent to which theatre permeates and informs every aspect of our lives. Think of how often we use theatre as a metaphor to describe an activity in daily life. We say that someone is melodramatic or highly theatrical or acts like a prima donna. When we don't believe children, we say that they are play-acting. We refer to the battleground on which a war is fought as its theatre. Clearly, theatre is an activity that we use to describe how we live.

In addition, as we will note in Chapter 5, acting is part of our everyday lives. We describe the role-playing we do in our professional and personal spheres as if we were performers on the stage of life. Children and adults imitate behaviors that they admire in the same way that actors and actresses mimic behavior. As we go through our college careers, we play many roles, such as student, friend, romantic partner, organization member, and student government leader. As adults we also play a number of roles: doctor, lawyer, engineer, nurse, mother, teacher, wife, political figure.

Theatre is incorporated in our lives in other ways. Taken in its broadest sense, it is everywhere around us. A wedding is theatre; a funeral is theatre. A Thanksgiving

THEATRICAL ELEMENTS IN RITUALS AND CEREMONIES
Weddings, funerals, other religious ceremonies as well as family and society rituals have strong elements of theatre in them. Costumes, a set script, various roles to be played: all of these are similar to counterparts in theatre. Shown here is a wedding ceremony with the bride and groom in appropriate attire, and a presiding official. Often the one officiating is a priest, minister, or rabbi. (Blend Images/Punchstock)

Day parade, a Mardi Gras parade, a trial in a courtroom—all these have decided theatrical elements: costumes or uniforms, a ritualistic structure, performers and spectators. The same is true of such activities as a presidential nominating convention, a Senate hearing, or a White House press conference. Even seemingly spontaneous, unrehearsed events, such as a high-speed automobile chase or a gunman holding hostages in a suburban home, have become a form of theatre by the time they are seen on television. The person holding the television camera has framed the "shots" showing the event; and for the evening news, the people who edit and report a segment on a family tragedy have taken great care to present the story as a brief drama, with an attention-grabbing opening followed by a suspenseful or shocking revelation and then a closing quotation, perhaps from a relative or neighbor. We even encounter drama in seemingly real-life reports on television: not only the evening news but documentaries and so-called "reality" shows.

These are instances of theatre in "real life." In the case of theatre in relationship to film and television, the similarity is even closer.

THEATRE AND TELEVISION

The structure, the dynamics, the subject matter of both television and film can be traced directly to antecedents in theatre. The characters of film and television—the heroes, the villains, the victims, the comic figures—all come straight from predecessors in theatre. The way stories are structured—the early scenes, the succession of crises, the withholding and revealing of information—were there first, hundreds of years ago, in the theatre.

On television, we can see a wide range of dramatic offerings that have a clear counterpart in theatrical prototypes. Daytime soap operas present a variety of domestic crises in family and other relationships. These dramas use many theatrical devices to ensure our continued viewing. A suspenseful moment concludes each segment; heightened music and emotions capture our attention. Recognizable character types—young lovers, difficult parents, doctors, lawyers, and criminals—inhabit the world of the soap operas, such as the long-running *General Hospital.*

Nighttime hospital and police shows, as well as earlier popular westerns, present the thrills and suspense of traditional melodrama. The stereotypical characters, including the heroes and villains; the focus on the spectacular and the grotesque; and the neat and happy resolutions are all related, as we shall see, to nineteenth-century melodrama. The popularity of the television series *CSI* and *Law & Order* is related to their use of traditional characteristics of the suspenseful melodramas of earlier eras.

Situation comedies depict young as well as middle-age characters in farcical and humorous encounters. These comic television shows have, throughout the history of the medium, focused on domestic situations, language filled with sexual double meaning, physical humor, and recognizable situations. Classic situation comedies, such as *I Love Lucy, The Cosby Show, The Dick Van Dyke Show, The Mary Tyler Moore Show, Seinfeld, Will & Grace, Friends, Two and a Half Men,* and *Modern Family* all reflect comic traditions, techniques, characters, and structures developed earlier in theatre.

Popular television variety shows throughout the medium's history have all been influenced by earlier popular theatrical forms that we will discuss later, such as minstrelsy, burlesque, and vaudeville. The long-running format of *Saturday Night Live,* which combines take-offs of serious films or literature, satire of political figures, exaggerated fictional characters, and popular musical acts, is a close replica of vaudeville, a popular theatre form of the early twentieth century.

On television, even news documentaries are framed in dramatic terms: a car crash in which a prom queen dies; a spy caught because of an e-mail message; a high government official or corporate officer accused of sexual harassment. Extremely popular reality shows are also staged like theatrical events. Many of the shows focus on highly dramatic situations and turn the real-life individuals into theatrical characters. And we all know that the reality shows are theatrically manipulated to create a sense of dramatic tension, ongoing suspense, and heightened conflict among the participants.

THEATRE AND FILM

Even more clearly, film has been greatly influenced by theatre. Movies provide dramatic material of many kinds: science fiction; romantic and domestic comedies; action-packed stories of intrigue; historical epics; and even film versions of classical plays, such as Shakespeare's *Hamlet, Othello,* and *Romeo and Juliet.* And we should note that there is a combination of film and video when we watch movies at home on a DVD or Blu-ray player.

Various types and categories of theatrical offerings have been appropriated by film. Recent successful film musicals, such as *Dreamgirls* and *Nine,* are movie versions of hugely successful stage musicals. Stage musicals, such as *Hairspray* and *Mary Poppins,* have also been made from films. As mentioned earlier, classical and contemporary plays are frequently adapted into movies.

In addition, most film genres borrow from past theatrical traditions. For example, popular cinematic melodramas, such as the *Harry Potter* and *Batman* films, reflect the characteristics of the theatrical genre and earlier theatrical innovations. We shall see that the intense interest in creating awe-inspiring special effects was as prevalent in nineteenth-century theatre as it is in twenty-first-century film.

Just as we are intrigued by the lives of film stars, earlier theatrical audiences were often obsessed with theatrical stars. There are many earlier theatrical parallels to the great personalities who dominate film today. Stars such as Will Smith, Brad Pitt, Angelina Jolie, Jamie Foxx, and Sandra Bullock continue the tradition of the theatrical idols of earlier eras.

In addition, since the inception of commercial film, there has been a great deal of crossover by theatre and film artists. As we shall see, many film stars began their careers in theatre. For that matter, Hollywood frequently raided the New York theatre for actors, directors, and writers during the 1930s, 1940s, and 1950s. Many current film and television stars began their careers in theatre and return to it on occasion; one example is Denzel Washington, who won a Tony Award for a Broadway revival of *Fences* in 2010. And many playwrights, such as Harold Pinter, Sam Shepard, and David Mamet, write for film. (Shepard is also a successful film actor.) Tony Kushner and Neil LaBute are also successful theatre and screenplay authors.

In recent years, many movie and television stars, whose entire careers have been in these media, have performed onstage as an artistic challenge. For example, in New York in 2008, Katie Holmes appeared in a revival of Arthur Miller's *All My Sons,* and

Daniel Radcliffe, from the *Harry Potter* movies, starred in revivals of Peter Shaffer's *Equus* and the musical *How to Succeed in Business Without Really Trying* (2011). What attracted audiences were the production's stars.

And just as film stars are admired for their wealth and status, while at the same time their personal lives are viewed suspiciously—for example, consider the furor over the romantic intrigue involving Jennifer Aniston, Brad Pitt, and Angelina Jolie—so, too, were theatrical stars from the earliest times on. This obsession with the lives of stars is reflected today in the popularity of such tabloids and magazines as *Star, National Enquirer,* and *People;* and in just the same way, there were earlier theatrical publications that reported about the lives of stage personalities.

THEATRE AND ROCK AND ROLL

When we turn from electronic media to live performance, we see that theatre has pervaded and influenced a popular music form with which we are all familiar: rock and roll. Throughout its history, rock has appropriated theatrical elements. The singer and dancer Lady Gaga is a perfect example. Her outrageous, extravagant outfits and over-the-top visual effects are directly derived from theatrical antecedents, as are her lighting and special effects. The purpose, of course, is to draw attention to the performer. "One of my greatest art works," she has said, "is the art of fame." Her recent "Monster Ball" tour was a highly stylized theatrical event. For that matter, a January 22, 2010, article in the *New York Times* describing her Radio City Music Hall performance was entitled, "For Lady Gaga, Every Concert Is a Drama."

Like Lady Gaga, numerous rock stars have created theatrical characters for their performances. Beginning with Little Richard and Elvis Presley in the 1950s, and continuing with the Beatles in the 1960s, through punk rock, glam rock, rap, hip-hop, and other forms, musical performers have used costumes, props, and makeup to create

THEATRICALITY IN THE POPULAR ARTS
Good examples of the crossover of theatrical elements between the popular arts and traditional theatre are the elaborate, outsize presentations by individual performers and popular rock groups, which use extravagant costumes, spectacular lighting, sound, and full-scale scenic effects. Shown here is the star Lady Gaga performing in a dress made of bubbles. (Yana Paskova/The New York Times/Redux)

theatrical characterizations. The actual performers were often less recognizable than their stage personae.

The connection between rock performance and theatre is also illustrated by the many rock stars who have acted, including Elvis Presley, the Beatles, Madonna, Mark Wahlberg, Ice T, Tupac Shakur, Eminem, Jack Black, Beyoncé, André Benjamin from OutKast, Ludacris, LL Cool J, Queen Latifah, Alicia Keyes, and 50 Cent, to name just a few. Sean ("Puff Daddy") Combs appeared in a 2004 Broadway production of *A Raisin in the Sun.* The hip-hop and rap star Mos Def has also been a successful actor; he performed on television as a teenager and starred on Broadway in the 2002 Pulitzer Prize–winning play *Top Dog/Underdog* and in the 2010 production of *A Free Man of Color,* as well as films such as *The Italian Job* (2003), *16 Blocks* (2006), and *Cadillac Records* (2008).

The popularity of music videos on MTV and VH1 also reflects the integration of theatrical elements into rock and roll. These videos turn many songs into visual, dramatic narratives. Current rock concerts are also highly theatrical events, using live performers, lights, sound, and properties in ways that are like multimedia presentations. For example, the popular group U2 used all these elements in a concert tour, "Elevation," performing in front of a heart-shaped set, with a "runway" stage that allowed the lead singer to be almost completely surrounded by the audience. The pop stars Justin Timberlake, Christina Aguilera, and the aforementioned Lady Gaga have also staged their concerts like theatre performances, with spectacular lighting effects and dance routines. Even classic rock groups, such as the Rolling Stones, have added highly visual theatrical elements to their touring shows to appeal to more contemporary fans.

For that matter, recent acoustic tours by some well-known rock stars are a reaction against these intensely theatricalized concerts and reflect a desire to return the focus to the live performer. We shall see that some contemporary theatrical theorists and experimental artists also argue for diminishing spectacular scenery and using fewer special effects, to reestablish the primacy of live performance.

In the past few years, there has also been a new phenomenon in musical theatre: the use of rock as the score for musicals. The most popular example of such musicals is *Mamma Mia!* (1999), which used the songs of a group from the 1980s, ABBA. Other examples include *All Shook Up* (2005), which used Elvis Presley's hits; *Jersey Boys* (2004), which traced the career of a pop group of the 1960s, the Four Seasons; *Rock of Ages* (2006), which used 1980s rock music, and *American Idiot* (2009), based on Green Day's concept album. In Savannah, Georgia, the musical revue *Jukebox*

A POPULAR MUSICAL FORM: THE "JUKEBOX MUSICAL"
American musicals are based on all kinds of sources: novels, straight plays, and films, as well as biographies and history. A popular source in recent years have been popular songs: songs written by one person or group, and songs made popular by a single singer or a group. *Mamma Mia!*—featuring the songs of ABBA—is a good example. A more recent example is *Jersey Boys,* seen here, a musical based on songs made popular by Frankie Valli and the Four Seasons. The performers, from the left, are: J. Robert Spencer as Nick Massi; Christian Hoff as Tommy DeVito; John Lloyd Young as Frankie Valli; and Daniel Reichard as Bob Gaudio. (Sara Krulwich/The New York Times/Redux)

Journey ran for more than 1,000 performances at the Savannah Theatre, which is on a site where there has been a playhouse since 1818.

Some rock composers have also composed scores for musicals, including Elton John for *Aida* (1998) and *Billy Elliott* (2005), and Bono and Edge of U2 for *Spider-man: Turn Off the Dark* (2011). We will discuss the influence of rock and roll on the American musical more fully later when we survey the history of this popular theatrical form.

THEATRICALITY IN AMUSEMENT PARKS, MUSEUMS, LAS VEGAS, AND SPORTING EVENTS

Rock illustrates that we have come to expect theatrical elements as part of our popular entertainments and that theatre is around us in many unexpected venues. Amusement parks like Disney World, Sea World, and Universal Studios incorporate theatrical material; most, for example, present staged productions based on films, which attract huge audiences. The rides at these amusement parks also incorporate theatricality by placing the participant in a theatrical environment and a dramatic situation. Rides such as *ET, Raiders of the Lost Ark,* and *Twilight Zone: Tower of Terror,* allow the rider

to be an actor in a dramatic plotline often based on films, in a space that functions as a kind of stage setting.

We can also see theatre around us in many other everyday activities. Many restaurants, such as the Rainforest Cafes, have theatricalized environments. Shopping centers and specialty stores, such as Niketown and American Girl, contain spaces for performances that highlight specific holiday seasons or product lines.

Museums have recently adopted some of these theatrical techniques to attract visitors. For example, the new Abraham Lincoln Presidential Library and Museum in Springfield, Illinois, includes stage presentations about this famous president as well as about how historians and archivists work. The museum also contains many exhibits that function like stage settings, including a reproduction of the log cabin in which Lincoln originally lived.[1]

In cities such as Orlando, Florida, dinner theatres present theatrical entertainments based on Roman gladiators, medieval knights, and gangsters of the 1930s. *Medieval Nights* is an extremely popular dinner theatre entertainment in Orlando, New Jersey, and Chicago.

Las Vegas is a highly theatricalized environment. Its hotels—such as New York, New York; the Bellagio; Luxor; and Mandelay Bay—are constructed like huge theatrical sets. Lavish stage shows use all the elements of theatre to entertain audiences. Possibly the most spectacular is *KA,* a $165 million production of Cirque du Soleil, staged at the MGM Grand by the avant-garde Canadian director Robert LePage. In addition,

---

[1]We would like to thank Chris Jones, chief theatre critic of the *Chicago Tribune,* who presented some of these concepts in a talk at Western Illinois University on April 17, 2006.

LAVISH SPECTACLES

A first cousin to dramatic productions, and a staple of popular entertainment, are elaborate stage spectacles presented in such places as Las Vegas and theme parks. An organization that has made a specialty of such presentations is Cirque du Soleil whose extravagant presentations are part circus, part acrobatic display, and part musical theatre. Shown here is a colorful, complex trapeze routine in *Zarkana,* a recent Cirque presentation at Radio City Music Hall in New York City. (Sara Krulich/The New York Times/Redux)

many performance artists and Broadway productions have set up resident companies in Las Vegas, including *Blue Man Group, Jersey Boys,* and *Mamma Mia!* These theatre productions are even modified to meet the time limitations of the traditional Las Vegas stage show.

Contemporary sporting events also integrate significant theatrical elements. Sports arenas, as we will note later, function much like theatre spaces. The introduction of sports teams before the start of competitions is often highly staged, with spectacular sound, lighting, and visual effects. Halftime shows, particularly at championship games such as the Super Bowl, are often huge stage spectacles with musicians, dancers, and special effects.

THEATRE AND DIGITAL MEDIA

At the start of the twenty-first century, digital media are omnipresent, ranging from the computer to the Xbox to the iPad. One result is the immense popularity of the interactive computer, the Internet, and video games, all of which are clearly influenced by theatre. Whether they are games we play on our computer or on a PlayStation, an Xbox, or a Wii, these digital entertainments usually present a theatrical plotline in

which we engage. Many of these storylines are based on popular melodramatic premises taken from films, comic books, and other entertainments. Some are based on historic events, such as actual wars and battles; others are fictional tales. Their goal is to make us feel as if we are actors within the universe of the game. The desire to create realistic special effects graphics continues a tradition that began with nineteenth-century stage melodrama, continued into film and television, and now is an engaging element of these digital games.

There are also interactive theatrical role-playing websites on the Internet. These websites all allow the participant to feel as if she or he is an actor in a theatricalized fantasy world. Even websites that are supposedly realistic chat rooms allow us to play roles as if we are actors in a performance for an unseen audience. Although there is an abundance of dramatic materials available in movie houses, on television, on Blu-ray or DVD, in amusement parks, at sporting events, in video games, and on the Internet, theatre itself is also a highly diverse and eclectic art form that attracts a wide spectrum of audience members and artists.

DIFFERENCES BETWEEN THEATRE-RELATED ACTIVITIES AND THEATRE ITSELF

We have been looking at a number of activities in daily life that have recognizable theatrical elements. None of them, however, is the same as theatre itself. These other, theatre-related events fall into two categories, each of which separates those activities from pure theatre, which can be defined as the presentation by live actors of a dramatic work in the presence of an audience.

The first group—movies, television, films shown on computers or hand-held devices—depict dramatic fare just as theatre does: dramas of all kinds from Shakespeare to musicals and contemporary comedies. But there is this important difference: though there is a spectator, a viewer, who is observing the drama, the object seen is not a group of flesh-and-blood actors. Rather, it is an image on a screen. And the series of images that constitute the film or TV show is finished, complete. It is frozen and cannot change. Put another way: those watching it can have no effect on it whatsoever.

The other category of events—rock performances, amusement parks, theme restaurants, half-time shows at football games—unlike film, are live; they are happening at the same time that they are being observed. But the content, what is being seen, makes no pretense of being a dramatic production. It is a concert, a spectacle, an environment, but not a play or musical.

All of this suggests that the unique quality of theatre, in addition to what happens behind the scenes and what happens on stage, is that it requires a live audience: a group of people observing, responding to, and deeply involved in what is unfolding in their presence. It is to this phenomenon that we now turn as we focus on the role of the audience in a theatrical event.

THE ROLE OF THE AUDIENCE

If you asked someone to list the essential components of a theatre experience, the chances are the person might say the actors, the script, and the stage; he or she might also mention the scenery and costumes. If you pressed for further elements, however, the list still might not include a crucial ingredient—the audience.

This is understandable—particularly today, when film and television are so pervasive. In these two media, which are so much like theatre in many ways, the "product," as it is sometimes called, stands alone as a finished production. When you watch a film at home on a DVD, it has been completed and is in its absolutely final form. The same is true of a film in a movie theatre; when released it might be shown in 1,000 theatres simultaneously across the United States, and it will be exactly the same in each location, night after night. The audience watches but plays no part in what appears on the screen.

Theatre is different. Even when the story and the characters presented in the two are identical—in a film and stage presentation of Shakespeare's *Romeo and Juliet,* for instance—there is the crucial and important difference, namely, that each theatre performance is unique and occurs in the presence of an *audience.* The ramifications of the audience are far-reaching. To begin with, the performers have no opportunity to play a scene over or to correct mistakes. Most people are aware that in creating a film most scenes are filmed a number of times. These repetitions are called "takes," and there may be four, five, or even twenty takes before the director feels that a scene is "right." Moreover, once scenes are filmed, the director decides in the editing room where each scene begins and ends and how scenes are joined together.

In theatre, there is no repeating and no editing. The performers onstage move through a production from beginning to end, and if there is a mishap—if an actor forgets a line, or an unexpected noise occurs offstage—the performers must recover and carry on. The result of all this is that each theatre event is live, immediate, and unique.

The dynamics and the excitement of being in the presence of a living person are as old as time and have not changed despite the many technological advances of recent years. People still wait for hours or stand in the rain to see a rock star or a hip-hop

performer in person, although the same performer is readily available on a CD, video, or DVD. The same is true of film personalities and charismatic political figures—people eagerly throng to see someone "in person." At the inauguration of President Barack Obama in 2009, an estimated 2 million people stood for many hours in freezing weather on the Washington Mall and along the parade route in order to be in the physical presence of the new president. This same chemistry is possible at every stage performance when the actors and actresses and the members of the audience are in the same place at the same time.

There is another aspect in which the audience plays a significant part: the effect the audience has on performers. The drama critic Walter Kerr (1913–1996) explained the special relationship between audience and performers at a theatre event:

> It doesn't just mean that we are in the personal presence of performers. It means that they are in our presence, conscious of us, speaking to us, working for and with us until a circuit that is not mechanical becomes established between us, a circuit that is fluid, unpredictable, ever-changing in its impulses, crackling, intimate. Our presence, the way we respond, flows back to the performer and alters what he does, to some degree and sometimes astonishingly so, every single night. We are contenders, making the play and the evening and the emotion together. We are playmates, building a structure.[2]

In other words, the audience has an enormous effect on actors and actresses. They are buoyed up by a responsive audience and discouraged by an unresponsive one. Sometimes, if an audience is not reacting, they might try harder than ever to make contact. This is the case not only with comedy, where laughter is a clear gauge of the audience's response, but also with serious drama. Performers know whether or not spectators are caught up in the action. When audience members are involved in a serious play, they

---

[2]Walter Kerr, "We Call It 'Live' Theater, but Is It?" *The New York Times,* January 2, 1972. Copyright 1972 by The New York Times Company. Reprinted by permission.

become very quiet; you can sense their fierce concentration. When an audience is not engaged, there may be noticeable coughing or rustling of programs. Reacting to this, actors and actresses will change their performances in subtle but very real ways.

HOW THE AUDIENCE PARTICIPATES

At the heart of the theatre experience, then, is the performer-audience relationship: the immediate, personal exchange; the chemistry and magic that give theatre its special quality. We might ask how the audience becomes involved in a theatre event, aside from sending the performers such obvious signals as laughter, silence, and palpable tension. The answer lies in the power of the imagination.

Audience members do not participate physically in a theatre performance, the way they would if they were riding a bicycle, working at a computer, or singing in a chorus. Rather, they participate *vicariously,* through the mind and the heart. The astonishing thing is how powerful these aspects of the human psyche are. Through our imagination, we come to believe in the reality of what we see onstage and to identify with the characters. We feel deep sympathy for those we sense are being treated unjustly, and we suffer with them; we feel hatred for those we consider mean or despicable; we laugh at those we consider foolish.

The events onstage become so real that we often forget who we are and where we are and enter the imaginary world we see before us. We can be transported to a foreign country, to another century, to an imaginary place—or to the kitchen of people who might be our own neighbors. Some situations in theatre are so vivid and so engrossing that we cry real tears, even though a part of us knows that the events onstage are not actually happening and that the people are only actors and actresses. This experience comes about because of a phenomenon that the English poet and critic Samuel Taylor Coleridge (1772–1834) called *willing suspension of disbelief.* In other words, we want so much to believe in the reality of what is happening onstage that we willingly put aside all literal and practical considerations in order to enter into the world of the drama.

Another factor that allows us to enter into an imaginative world—even though we are aware that it is separate from everyday reality—is referred to as ***aesthetic distance.*** Aesthetic distance is a requirement of virtually all involvement with the arts. It means that the viewer, spectator, or audience member must be in some sense separated from the performance or object—and must be aware that it is a work of art—in order to experience its aesthetic qualities. Paradoxically, once the proper distance is established, the observer can enter into the experience fully and completely.

Aesthetic distance Physical or psychological separation or detachment of audience from dramatic action, usually considered necessary for artistic illusion.

Throughout theatre history, the power of the audience's mental and emotional participation has manifested itself in both positive and negative ways. Negatively, it has taken the form of censorship—which indicates that those in authority fear the effect theatre can have on audiences. The Greeks of ancient Athens considered certain subjects unfit for drama and banned them. In fourth-century Rome, in the early days of Christianity, the church had a great deal to do with stopping theatrical activity. In 1642, the Puritans closed the theatres in England. In modern times, there have been many examples of censorship, especially in places like China and various totalitarian countries, where only drama that has been approved of by the political authorities can be presented.

Positively, the power of audience participation can be seen in many ways. To take just one example, many political groups and other groups use theatre as a means

PHYSICAL THEATRE HELPS SHAPE THE EXPERIENCE
The size, shape, and configuration of a theatre affect the audience's experience. The theatre may be small and intimate; it may be indoors or outdoors; it might be large and expansive: all these factors will have an impact on the experience of attending the performance, even though we usually think that the only important aspect is what occurs onstage. Here the informal outdoors setting for a production of *Greenshow* at the Utah Shakespearean Festival establishes a mood and atmosphere that is far different from what would be experienced at a formal, indoor theatre, especially if it had elegant furnishings and a traditional appearance. (© Utah Shakespearean Festival. Photo by Karl Hugh.)

of educating people or furthering a cause. In recent times, we have seen theatre representing various groups: feminist theatre, gay theatre, and radical political theatre, for instance. The people who present such productions feel that the imaginative and symbolic power of theatre will affect their audiences.

In sum, the ability of the audience to enter into the world presented onstage is one reason why it is always a key factor in any theatre event.

DIVERSITY OF AUDIENCES

Makeup of Audiences: Past and Present   As we trace the history of theatre, one thing we will note is that the makeup of audiences has varied from time to time and from place to place. In ancient Greece, for example, a large percentage of an entire city, such as Athens or Epidaurus, would attend the theatre. The same was true of medieval theatre in western Europe and England. However, when we come to Restoration theatre in England during the late seventeenth century, we find that the audience was often rarefied, consisting primarily of the upper classes. This affected the kind of writing and acting seen onstage; as a result, Restoration plays still remain less accessible to the general population. In Europe in the nineteenth century, theatre once again came to be a form of art popular with a wide range of people. In various Asian countries, as well, theatre in some eras was only for an elite audience or for the upper classes; but at other times it included audiences from the general population.

THE CRUCIAL ROLE OF THE AUDIENCE

In any theatre event, the audience plays an essential part. A performance is a two-way street, with impulses passing back and forth between members of the audience and the actors and actresses onstage. An electrical circuit is established to which each contributes, making the experience a joint, communal one. Shown here is the audience attending a production at the restored Shakespeare's Globe Theatre in London. (© Andrea Pistolesi/The Image Bank/Getty)

In today's theatre there is great diversity in both the size and the makeup of those who are present at a theatre event. As to size, in a small, intimate theatre, there may be no more than 100 or 200 people attending. On the other hand, at a large city auditorium, there may be 2,000 or 3,000 people, or even more, watching a large-scale musical. This factor will make a difference, both to audience members and to performers. In an intimate space there is more awareness, on the part of everyone, of the interaction between actors and spectators. In a large amphitheatre, a different, less personal relationship exists. In a theatre somewhere in between—a house that seats 800 or 900 people—the relationship will be a mixture of the two. (We will consider the actor-audience relationship in the context of theatre spaces in more detail in Chapter 7.)

Aside from the question of size, today there is often a wide variety in the makeup of theatre audiences. Some audiences are homogeneous: the audience members come mostly from similar backgrounds and experiences. A good example would be a college or university theatre production in which the audience consists primarily of students, faculty members, and their friends. Another example would be a performance presented to a group of senior citizens in a retirement village. Other audiences are heterogeneous, such as the spectators at free performances of Shakespeare in an outdoor amphitheatre in a city park. Here you would find people of many ethnic and social backgrounds and of all ages. A third audience mix would be found at a Broadway theatre or in a similar theatre in any large city. The members of the audience would be mostly middle-class and upper-class but might include children, students, or foreign visitors. Even among traditional audience groups such as these, however, the chemistry of the audience will change from night to night for no apparent reason. At a comedy, for instance, on some nights the audience will laugh at everything; on other nights, audience members may enjoy the show just as much, but they will barely chuckle and seem never to indulge in a hearty laugh.

Where We See Theatre   In addition to diversity in the makeup of audiences and in their reactions, there are various places where theatre can be seen. One place is a Broadway theatre or its counterpart in other parts of the country. This is usually a large, formal theatre, frequently with a picture-frame stage. Another category is resident professional theatre. Such a theatre is generally smaller than a Broadway-type space and is a not-for-profit operation. Resident professional theatres are found in cities throughout the United States and Canada. A third category consists of small theatres—usually under 250 seats—as well as theatres created from other spaces such as lofts, warehouses, and former churches. Still another group of theatres can be found on the campuses of colleges and universities. Intended for the productions of theatre and drama departments, they range from small to somewhat larger theatres, and from formal arrangements to experimental spaces. Along with those listed above are stages reserved for children's theatre or theatre for youth, focusing on productions for and about young people.

Audiences Today: Multicultural and Diverse   Along with the variety of spaces and audiences described above, there is a further factor that has affected the makeup of contemporary audiences. Increasingly, people in the United States and throughout the world are becoming aware of the multiracial and multicultural aspects of our society. In the late nineteenth century and the early twentieth century, the United States was known as a "melting pot," a term implying that the aim of many foreign-born people who came here was to become assimilated and integrated into the prevailing white, male, European culture. (Women during this era had to fight for very basic rights, such as voting.) In recent decades, however, many people in our society have come to believe that such a homogeneous culture has many biases; as a result, they urge us to recognize, maintain, and celebrate our differences. This trend toward diversity has been reflected in theatre; many organizations have emerged that present productions by and for groups with special interests. They represent a number of political, ethnic, gender, sexual-orientation, and racial entities, discussed in detail in Chapters 14 and 15, including African American, Asian American, Latino and Latina, Native American, feminist, and gay and lesbian.

In brief, the role of the audience is crucial to a theatre event because of the importance of the performer-audience relationship. The audience completes a sort of electrical circuit that provides the immediacy and excitement of the live theatre performance. In addition, the makeup of the audience is a key factor, and one that audience members themselves should be aware of. When you are attending a performance, the following are questions for you, as an individual audience member, to consider. Is the audience a homogeneous group—similar in background and attitude—or a diverse one? Do you, as a member of the audience, relate to other audience members or not? Is the event being presented primarily by and for a particular group—cultural, social, gender, or political? If so, are you a member of the group or outside it? During the performance, is the audience involved in the production or not? If it is a serious event, is the audience concentrating and empathizing? If the event is comic, is the audience caught up in the amusement and laughter?

Western theatre, particularly since the nineteenth century, has developed certain rules of behavior for audience members—expectations about what audiences do and don't do. However, it should be kept in mind that any given theatre event might have some unique expectations about the audience's behavior.

At a traditional theatre performance, the audience is expected to remain silent for the most part, and not interrupt the performers. Audience members should not talk to each other as if they were at home watching television; they should not send or receive text messages, use cell phones, hum or sing along with music, unwrap candy or other food, eat loudly, search through a purse or backpack; they should also shut off wristwatch alarms and beepers. Remember that the actors can hear the audience: noises and distracting behavior will have an impact on their concentration and performance. Noise and distractions also affect the experience of other spectators.

Students may be concerned about note-taking since they often will need to make notes in order to remember key elements of the production. An unobtrusive way of taking notes is to jot down only brief phrases or terms that will jog your memory later. Then, you can embellish your notes during the intermission or intermissions, or after the end of the performance.

Of course, traditional audiences are not always absolutely quiet: audiences at comedies laugh, for instance. Audiences at musicals applaud after a song (in fact, they're expected to). On the other hand, audiences at serious plays generally do not applaud until the end of the performance— and even then, an audience may be so stunned or so deeply moved that there will be a moment of silence before the applause begins.

As noted above, not all of these traditional expectations may apply at every theatre event. Dinner theatres are one example since the audience may be eating during the presentation. (We might also note that audiences eat during the performance in many traditional Asian theatres, and they may speak back to the stage.) Audiences at some productions are expected to interact with the performers: in some comic presentations, for instance, actors may enter the audience space or actually speak to individual audience members; and in some nontraditional productions, audience members may even be expected to participate in the performance.

THE CRITIC AND THE REVIEWER

A person who can be considered a special type of audience member, an audience of one, is the *critic* or the *reviewer*. A simple definition of a critic or reviewer is someone who observes theatre and then analyzes and comments on it. In a sense this person stands between the theatre event and the audience, serving in ideal circumstances as a knowledgeable and sensitive audience member. At the same time, most theatergoers are amateur critics. When a person says about a performance, "It started off great, but it fizzled," or "The star was terrific, just like someone in real life," or "The woman was OK, but the man overacted," he or she is making a critical judgment. The difference between a critic and an ordinary spectator is that the critic presumably is better informed about the event and has developed a set of standards by which to judge it.

Critics, as distinct from reviewers, generally publish their analyses in magazines and scholarly journals. At times they go beyond articles and essays to write books about playwrights, plays, or theatrical movements. Critics also attempt to put a playwright or a group of plays into the larger context of theatre history and into the broad framework of the arts and society.

Ideally, a critic should have a thorough grounding in the history of theatre, in the elements that make up theatre, and in the nature of acting and production. He or she should be able to analyze a script for structure and meaning, should understand various styles of acting, and should be aware of the visual aesthetics of theatre. The critic should then use this knowledge to discuss—both for audiences and for the theatre community—just what is right and wrong about a production. The critic's readers or viewers have a right to expect informed judgments and helpful background information.

The reason audiences can learn from critics is not only that critics impart information and judgments, but also, as suggested above, that the critic shares with audience members the spectator's point of view. Unlike those who create theatre—writers, performers, designers—critics sit out front and watch a performance just as other members of the audience do.

A *reviewer* usually works for a newspaper, magazine, television station, or Internet site and reports on what has occurred at a theatre event. He or she will explain briefly what the theatre event is about, describing its plot and stating whether it is a musical, a comedy, or a serious play. The reviewer will generally add an opinion on whether or not the event was done well and is worth seeing. In most instances, a reviewer in a newspaper, on a television news program, or on the Internet is restricted by time or space. Reviewers may have taken college courses in theatre and the other arts, and may have had practical experience in the theatre, but frequently they come to reviewing from other positions in television, print journalism, or blogging. Once they are assigned to theatre, however, conscientious reviewers should make it their job to become as knowledgeable as possible. This type of review is important to the general audience, which turns to reviewers for information about arts events and guidance in deciding whether or not to attend, especially when an event is expensive.

PREPARING FOR CRITICISM

How do critics and reviewers prepare for their work? We said above that, ideally, a critic should have a complete and thorough knowledge of all aspects of theatre. A reviewer's knowledge is not expected to be as extensive as that of a critic, but it should be as comprehensive as possible.

In the case of a revival of a well-known play, reviewers or critics have individual preferences with regard to whether or not to read the play before seeing a performance. Because acting and directorial interpretation are crucial in a theatre experience, some prefer to see a performance without specific preparation. Others, especially when they are seeing a classic such as a Shakespearean play, prefer to refresh their memory by reading the play beforehand.

CRITERIA FOR CRITICISM

It has been suggested that there are three questions the critic/reviewer should ask in assessing a theatre event (incidentally, these are also questions audience members can ask):

1. What is the playwright or production attempting to do?
2. How well has it been done?
3. Is it worth doing?

In looking at these three questions, it must be remembered that in theatre both the play and the production are under consideration. The critic/reviewer, therefore, must make it clear whether he or she is assessing a script, a production, or both.

Question 1: What Is Being Attempted?

In answering the first question, the critic/reviewer must explain exactly what is being attempted, both by the playwright and by the director. Sometimes this is clear—in a comedy or farce, for example—but sometimes it is not.

A playwright, for instance, may be attempting to use satire to criticize excessive behavior, but this might not be obvious from what the audience sees onstage. Perhaps a playwright is parodying the work of another writer—that is, deliberately imitating and making fun of the other writer. If the audience understands this, it will make the play clearer.

Regarding the work of the director, the critic again must determine what is being attempted. Is the director trying to present a play exactly as the playwright intended, or is he or she trying something different? An *auteur director* (discussed in Chapter 6) usually attempts to present his or her own version of a dramatic work, not necessarily that of the playwright. The critic should make this clear to the reader to help audiences understand what is happening onstage.

Auteur director A director who believes that his or her role is to be the author of a production. An auteur director's point of view dominates that of the playwright, and the director may make textual changes and modifications.

Question 2: How Well Has the Attempt Succeeded?

In answering the second question, the critic/reviewer makes a personal evaluation. How well has the playwright realized his or her goals, and how well have the performers and the director brought the play to life? Generally a reviewer or critic makes personal evaluations in arriving at a conclusion and does not take into account the reactions of the audience. At times, however, the critic/reviewer might comment on the response of the audience, especially if audience members reacted favorably to a play that the reviewer did not regard as well written or well acted.

Question 3: Was the Attempt Worth Making?

In answering the third question, the critic/reviewer evaluates the overall undertaking. Is this kind of play or production valid? Does it fulfill a legitimate purpose? Is it meaningful or significant? Is the play or production itself a worthwhile undertaking?

Theatre encompasses a broad range of activities, from low farce to high tragedy, and so value is not merely a question of depth or profundity but often a question of comparing the goal with the achievement. If the purpose of a play is clearly understood to be entertainment, for example, then the question becomes how well this intention is carried out in the production. On the other hand, a play can be pretentious, claiming to have depth when it actually does not, and a critic should point that out.

DECLINE OF THE CRITICS' AND REVIEWERS' INFLUENCE

At one time, critics and reviewers exerted much more influence on the opinions of audiences and on the fate of a theatre production. Newspaper and television reviewers were particularly powerful. For example, in the twentieth century, a positive review in the *New York Times* could lead to a Broadway show having an extended run, while a negative one could result in the show closing.

Today, there are many more factors that influence audiences' attendance. There are blogs that comment on shows and almost function like online reviews. Productions are discussed on Internet social media, such as Facebook; celebrities and everyday audience members send Twitter messages about shows they enjoyed. Media stars are cast in productions to attract new audiences and become the reason many attend even when the reviews are negative. Large-scale advertising campaigns target specific categories of audience members to assure a successful run.

THE AUDIENCE MEMBER'S INDEPENDENT JUDGMENT

It is important to remember, with regard to evaluative criticism, that reactions to theatre—as to all art—are highly subjective. In theatre, unlike geometry or physics, there is no right or wrong answer. Nor are there absolutes in theatre, like the mathematical fact that $8 \times 9 = 72$. Sincere, intelligent people often disagree on whether or not a play is profound, moving, or skillfully written. There are principles of dramatic structure, as we will discover in Chapter 3, and there are aesthetic criteria that we can apply to scenery and costumes. However, the ultimate test is whether or not one is affected by a performance, and whether one thinks a play is exceptional or merely routine—and this is up to the individual spectator.

At the same time, there is no doubt that the critic/reviewer as well as the online blogger can be helpful in answering such questions. These observers can provide valuable information and incisive opinions that help us arrive at our own independent judgment. Perhaps one way to view the critic/reviewer or the blogger is to say that while we should not slavishly follow their ideas, we should at the same time learn from them everything we can.

In Chapter 3, we turn to the way a script is created—the script being the blueprint for a theatre production.

SUMMARY

We can see the impact of theatre all around us today. Theatre exists in many aspects of our everyday lives and has influenced many of our popular entertainments.

Theatre permeates our everyday lives as we and those with whom we interact play roles. We play such roles at work, at home, and with those we know and love.

Theatre has greatly influenced television and film. We can see the impact of theatre in the content of television shows and movies.

Our interest in media stars' performances and lives parallels the way audiences throughout the history of theatre have engaged with actors and actresses.

Rock and roll performances emphasize stage spectacle, lighting, and sound effects.

We can also see theatrical influences in our visits to amusement parks and museums. When we visit dinner theatres throughout the country, and when we visit Las Vegas, we recognize the pervasiveness of theatrical element.

The presence of an audience is an essential element in a live theatre performance. Just as no two performances of the same production are ever exactly alike, no two audiences are identical. Each audience is composed of a different mix of people, with varied ages, educational backgrounds, and occupations. Among the diverse groups toward which productions are aimed and whose members constitute specific audience groups are African Americans, Asian Americans, Latinos and Latinas, Native Americans, feminists, gays and lesbians, and other political and experimental groups. Also, the particular response of each audience affects the acting of the performers.

A special member of the audience is the critic or reviewer, who is assumed to be a knowledgeable observer of the theatre event. A reviewer is usually a reporter for a newspaper, magazine, or television station. After viewing a theatre event, the reviewer describes it and gives his or her own opinion as to whether it was well done and is worth seeing.

A critic, usually writing for a magazine or scholarly journal, describes and analyzes a theatre event in greater detail than the reviewer does. The critic should have a solid education in theatre history, dramatic literature, and theatrical production so that he or she can offer readers an informed judgment along with useful background information.

Theatre criticism may be either descriptive, explaining what actually happens onstage; or prescriptive, offering advice and prescribing what should take place.

THINKING ABOUT THEATRE

▶ During a performance you may observe a puppet or group of puppets who appear as real as people we deal with every day. (If you have not seen puppets on stage, you have surely seen them on film or TV.) At the same time, you may see on a bare stage two or three props (a tree, for example, or a throne) and assume you are in a forest or a royal palace. Why do you think during a performance we are able to let our imaginations take over—with a bare stage becoming a forest, or a puppet becoming a person? Is this something we also do in everyday life?

▶ While watching a performance you may dissolve into laughter or cry real tears. The whole time, on some level, you know what you are observing is not "real." Does this difference matter? In some sense is the experience real? Is it imaginary? Is it a bit of both? What is the relationship between a theatre experience such as this and an experience in daily life?

▶ Imagine two friends viewing the same theatre production. One friend is captivated, feeling that what she saw was genuine and moving, an experience that affected her deeply. The other friend was not moved and felt that the performance was artificial and inauthentic. Why do you think the same performance can elicit two such different reactions?

KEY TERMS

Aesthetic distance Physical or psychological separation or detachment of audience from dramatic action, usually considered necessary for artistic illusion.

Auteur director A director who believes that his or her role is to be the author of a production. An auteur director's point of view dominates that of the playwright, and the director may make textual changes and modifications.

 THEATRE ON THE WEB

For more research and to learn more about the topics in this chapter, please visit the Online Learning Center at **www.mhhe.com/livelyart8e.**

PART 2

CREATING THEATRE THE PLAYWRIGHT

3 CREATING THE DRAMATIC SCRIPT

4 THEATRICAL GENRES

THE SCRIPT: THE BLUEPRINT FOR A PRODUCTION

Every theatre event begins with an idea, an outline, a concept that is the basis for the production that emerges. This "blueprint" might be the work of a performance group, a performance artist, or a director. Traditionally, however, the concept or blueprint has been created by the playwright in his or her text. One of the most masterful playwrights of all times is William Shakespeare. Shown here is a scene from Shakespeare's *Twelfth Night,* directed by Gregory Doran at the Royal Shakespeare Company, featuring Nancy Carroll as Viola (left) and Jo Stone-Fewings as Orsino. (© Robbie Jack/Corbis)

CREATING THE DRAMATIC SCRIPT

3

THE PLAYWRIGHT CREATES THE SCRIPT

THE PLAYWRITING PROCESS

SUBJECT

FOCUS

DRAMATIC PURPOSE

WIDER PERSPECTIVE:
The Playwright's Role

STRUCTURE IN DRAMA

MAKING CONNECTIONS:
Writers

ESSENTIALS OF DRAMATIC STRUCTURE

GLOBAL CROSSCURRENTS:
The Asian Influence on the Playwrights Brecht and Wilder

SEQUENCE IN DRAMATIC STRUCTURE

TWO BASIC FORMS OF STRUCTURE: CLIMACTIC AND EPISODIC

OTHER FORMS OF DRAMATIC STRUCTURE

CREATING DRAMATIC CHARACTERS

TYPES OF DRAMATIC CHARACTERS

JUXTAPOSITION OF CHARACTERS

SUMMARY

THINKING ABOUT THEATRE

KEY TERMS

THEATRE ON THE WEB

◄ **THE PLAYWRIGHT CREATES THE SCRIPT**   Shown here is Luis Valdez (center), the author of *Zoot Suit,* flanked by Edward James Olmos who played El Pachuco and his brother Daniel Valdez, who wrote the music and also appears in the play. Valdez, writing about racial violence in Los Angeles in 1943, developed the dramatic script with all of its confrontations as well as its twists and turns, and also created each of the dramatic characters. The photo here was taken in front of the Winter Garden Theatre, April 1979. (© Stephanie Maze/Corbis)

THE PLAYWRIGHT CREATES THE SCRIPT

A theatre production is a collaboration, not only between the audience and the performers but among a whole range of people who make it happen: actors, directors, designers, the playwright. All of these are essential, but like any enterprise, a theatre production must begin somewhere, and in most cases that starting point is the script, also referred to as the *text*. The script provides the plan for a production in somewhat the same way that an architect's blueprint provides guidelines for constructing a building. In fact, the script can be looked on as a concept or blueprint. For nearly 2,500 years the script or text was understood to be the domain of the playwright, also referred to as the dramatist. He or she chose the story to be told; selected the dramatic episodes, including the order in which they were to unfold; and wrote the dialogue for the characters to speak.

THE PLAYWRITING PROCESS

The playwright has a number of questions to answer and many choices to make, involving at least six aspects of a drama. Before we discuss these in detail, however, a word about the writing process is in order. In choosing a subject, developing a structure, or creating characters, the playwright will often work intuitively, sometimes even subconsciously. When the playwright's imagination, for instance, is captured by a certain episode or attracted to certain characters, he or she begins to create a drama. Usually a play evolves rather than being put together in a mechanical fashion.

In past eras, the type of structure used and the characters chosen by a playwright were in some measure the traditionally accepted practices of a given period and society. Playwrights in ancient Greece, for example, based both their plots and their characters on well-known myths. In modern times, however, playwrights often begin without a clear plan and only later discover the type of structure and the nature of the characters they have chosen to create.

Below are the six aspects of a script the playwright must address and make choices about.

1. Selecting the specific subject of the play
2. Determining focus
3. Establishing purpose
4. Developing dramatic structure
5. Creating dramatic characters
6. Establishing point of view

In this chapter, we will examine the first five of these aspects. In Chapter 5, we will look at point of view. Consciously or unconsciously, when a playwright creates a script he or she adopts a point of view toward the story and the material. This viewpoint determines whether the play is a tragedy or comedy, a farce or a melodrama, a didactic teaching tool or intended merely for entertainment. We will extensively examine these and other categories of drama in the next chapter.

Subject

The subject matter of drama is always human beings. In theatre, unlike certain other art forms—music, for instance, or abstract painting—people are invariably at the center. At the same time, a play cannot simply be about "human beings" or "people" in general, or even about "people's concerns," and the first task of the person creating a dramatic text is therefore to decide what aspect of human existence to write about.

Will the drama be based on history—for example, an episode or incident from the Civil War, from World War II, or from the war in Iraq? Or will it be based on biography—on the life of Abraham Lincoln, Eleanor Roosevelt, or Martin Luther King Jr.? Another possibility is the dramatization of someone's personal life: confronting some problem of growing up, or facing a personal crisis as an adult. A different possibility would be an imaginary story resembling everyday life or based on a fantasy or nightmare.

Focus

Along with selecting a subject to be dramatized, the playwright or dramatist must decide whom and what to focus on. For example, the same playwright can emphasize a particular character trait in one play and a very different trait in another play. This is what the Norwegian playwright Henrik Ibsen often did. In his *Brand,* the leading character is a stark, uncompromising religious man who will sacrifice everything—family, friends, love—for his principles. On the other hand, in Ibsen's *Peer Gynt,* the central character is just the opposite: a man with no principles who is always compromising, always running away.

In determining focus, a playwright may need to decide how to interpret the characters and events of an existing story; in doing this, the playwright may even change the order of events. A good example is the way three tragic dramatists of ancient Greece dealt with the myth of Electra. This myth concerns Electra's revenge on her mother, Clytemnestra, who has murdered Electra's father, Agamemnon, and then married a lover, Aegisthus. In wreaking revenge on Clytemnestra, Electra enlists the help of her brother, Orestes, who has just returned from exile. In *The Libation Bearers* (458 B.C.E.) by Aeschylus, and also in *Electra* (c. 412 B.C.E.) by Euripides, Electra and Orestes first murder Clytemnestra's lover, Aegisthus, and then murder Clytemnestra herself—their mother. This puts emphasis on the horror and aberration of killing one's own mother. But Sophocles saw the story differently. He wanted to emphasize that Electra and Orestes are acting honorably and obeying an order from the gods. He therefore needed to play down the murder of the mother, and so in his version of *Electra* (c. 410 B.C.E.) he reversed the order of the murders: Clytemnestra is killed first, and then the action builds to the righteous murder of Aegisthus.

By means of focus, then, the playwright lets us know whom the play is about—the main character or characters—and how we are to view the characters: whether we are to look at them favorably or unfavorably. See the URLs noted throughout the book to read the plays under discussion in the text.

EMPHASIS AND POINT OF VIEW
Henrik Ibsen makes it clear that his play *Peer Gynt* is about the title character, who is in virtually every scene. The play itself—which is clearly serious but has numerous comic and tragicomic episodes—ranges over many years and many locations. The character of Peer is always compromising, always running away, and Ibsen shows the consequences of that. In this scene are Mark Rylance (as Peer, wearing the crown), Jim Lichtscheidl, Jonas Goslow, Tyson Forbes, and Richard Ooms. *Peer Gynt,* translated and adapted by Robert Bly from the original by Henrik Ibsen; directed by Tim Carroll; set and costume design by Laura Hopkins; lighting design by Stan Pressner. (© Michal Daniel/Guthrie Theater, Minneapolis)

> **READ** Compare the *Libation Bearers,* Euripides's *Electra,* and Sophocles's *Electra* by reading them online at:
>
> http://records.viu.ca/~johnstoi/aeschylus/libationbearers.htm; http://classics.mit .edu/Euripides/electra_eur.html; http://classics.mit.edu/Sophocles/electra.html.

DRAMATIC PURPOSE

Another challenge in creating a script or text is to determine the purpose of a play. A purpose may be casual or unconscious, or conscious and deliberate, but every theatre event is intended to serve some purpose.

Throughout theatre history, plays have been written to serve different purposes: to entertain, to impart information, to probe the human condition, to provide an escape. Various types of contemporary theatre are frequently presented for a specific purpose: these include feminist theatre, Latino or Latina theatre, and African American theatre. In theatre of this kind, those who create the event are addressing the concerns of a particular constituency.

There is a long tradition of theatre as a source of entertainment—similar to modern situation comedies on television and comic films that offer us pleasure and an

Some contemporary commentators have questioned what they refer to as the "centrality" of the playwright and the play. These critics point out that there have been companies whose performers or directors, sometimes with the assistance of audiences, improvise presentations: they create a presentation while actually performing it. There have also been times when texts were developed by performers or by a director who assembled material from various sources. Some theorists argue, therefore, that an "authorless" theatre exists: theatre in which performers create their own works, sometimes using a traditional text only as a jumping-off point.

Theorists who question the centrality of the text also argue that the playwright's importance has been overstated—that a play is simply a suggestion or starting point and that the artists who create a stage presentation are its true "authors." In addition, they hold that each audience member may create his or her own "reading" of a production; in this sense, the spectator is the "author," and any discussion of a play's theme or meaning is inappropriate. It should be pointed out that this argument seems largely a question of semantics. If a theatre piece is created by a group of performers or by a director, then these people are in effect operating as playwrights. The playwright's function has not been eliminated; it is simply being carried out by someone else.

As for the matter of the "centrality" of the playwright, this argument, too, does not eliminate the necessity of what we are calling the blueprint that every theatre event requires. Whether the blueprint is a text, a script, an idea, a scenario, an improvisation, or anything similar, it is an indispensable element in the process of creating a theatre production. The work of the playwright or other "authors" need not be "central" or predominant to be essential and irreplaceable. Also, the fact remains that throughout the history of both western and eastern theatre, the significant role of the playwright has been widely accepted. Whether it is a dramatist like Sophocles, Shakespeare, or Ibsen in the West, or Chikamatsu—an eighteenth-century Japanese dramatist—in the East, both their own contemporaries and later generations have seen their dramatic texts as foundations on which productions are based.

escape from the cares of everyday life. The comedies of the Roman playwrights Plautus and Terence, written 2,000 years ago, were designed for this sort of entertainment. In the United States, for many years Broadway provided comedies that were written purely for fun.

There have been times when plays were intended primarily to teach. In the medieval period, prior to the late fifteenth century, very few people could read or write. In order to teach people about the Bible, the church encouraged plays that presented religious stories and precepts. Today, political dramatists often write plays specifically to put forward their own opinions and ideas.

At times, the purpose of drama has been to raise philosophical questions or to probe timeless themes, such as why the innocent suffer or why there is so much hatred and violence in the world.

Sometimes a play is intended simply to thrill or frighten us. A horror story or a melodrama is not supposed to make us think or meditate; it is intended to draw us into the action so that we will experience the same fears and apprehensions as the characters.

At times a play serves more than one purpose. Satirical comedies may be intended not only to make us laugh, but also to take stabs at hypocrites or charlatans. The works of the French playwright Molière are frequently of this kind: comical, but also revealing human folly. His *Tartuffe,* for instance—about a man who moves into a household falsely posing as a pious cleric—is an indictment of hypocrisy but is also amusing.

Sometimes a playwright may begin working without an exact purpose—the purpose may emerge only as the script goes through several revisions. Before a play goes into production, however, the playwright should know where it is headed. Once the purpose is clear, the director, performers, and designers join the playwright in working to achieve it.

After subject, focus, and purpose have been decided, two crucial steps in developing a play are creating dramatic structure and creating dramatic characters.

STRUCTURE IN DRAMA

Though it may not be readily apparent, every work of art has some type of structure. When does the action of a play begin? How are the scenes put together? How does the action unfold? What is the high point of the action? Questions like these are related to dramatic structure, but we should note that structure is significant in all art.

In a sense, the structure of a play is analogous to that of a building. In designing a building, an architect plans a skeleton or substructure that will provide inner strength; the architect determines the depth of the foundation, the weight of the support beams, and the stress on the side walls. Similarly, a playwright develops a dramatic structure. The playwright introduces various stresses and strains in the form of conflicts; sets boundaries and outer limits, such as how many characters participate, how long the action lasts, and where it takes place; and calculates dynamics—when tension increases and slackens. Some feminist critics argue that the playwright's gender might also influence structure and that feminist dramas are less linear and less traditional in building dramatic tension.

Buildings vary enormously in size and shape: they can be as diverse as a skyscraper, a cathedral, and a cottage. Engineering requirements vary according to the needs of individual structures: a gymnasium roof must span a vast open area, and this calls for a construction different from that of a sixty-story skyscraper. Plays, too, vary; they can be tightly or loosely constructed, for instance. The important point is that each play, like each piece of architecture, should have its own internal laws and its own framework, which give it shape, strength, and meaning. Without structure, a building will collapse, and a play will fall apart.

Naturally, structure is manifested differently in theatre and architecture. A play is not a building; it unfolds through time, developing like a living organism. As we experience this development, we become aware of a play's structure because we sense its underlying pattern and rhythm. The repeated impulses of two characters in conflict, the quickening pace and mounting tension of a heated argument—these elements insinuate themselves into our subconscious like a drumbeat. Moment by moment we see what is happening onstage; but below the surface we sense the structure, the framework of the dramatic action.

ESSENTIALS OF DRAMATIC STRUCTURE

There are several essentials of dramatic structure. First, the story on which a drama is based must be turned into a plot. Second, the plot involves action. Third, the plot includes conflict. Fourth, there are strongly opposed forces. Fifth, a reasonable balance is struck between the opposed forces.

WRITERS

How do we compare writing for the stage and writing for films or television? Obviously, many writers engage in both, moving from theatre to films or television and back again. Some writers, however, seem to have a natural affinity for one field or the other. There are playwrights who have never attempted to write screenplays and never want to. By the same token, there are people who write for films or television who have never been interested in writing plays or musicals for the stage.

David Mamet is a good example of a writer who frequently moves back and forth between theatre and film. Others who write primarily for theatre at times write films as well; they include Neil Simon, John Guare, and Marcia Norman. Many playwrights write almost exclusively for theatre; they include Edward Albee, Paula Vogel, Terence McNally, A. R. Gurney, Tina Howe, and Lanford Wilson. Among younger writers who have moved back and forth between theatre and film or television are Gina Gionfriddo, Rolin Jones, and Adam Rapp.

Whatever path a writer takes, he or she must meet the requirements we discuss in this chapter: decide on the subject, develop a plot, create the characters, compose the dialogue, and undertake all other necessary steps in creating a completed script. In undertaking these tasks, the writer for film or television must follow a path similar to that of the playwright for the stage, but there are important differences. The requirements of film, for instance, are not the same as those for the stage. Many scenes in film are action scenes: shots from a helicopter, shots of car crashes, shots of a villain stalking his prey. Such scenes may be described by the writer, but their realization is mostly in the hands of the director and cinematographer. They contain almost no dialogue. As a rule, whatever the storyline, there is far less dialogue in a film than in a play.

Because of the nature of theatre, as opposed to film or television, the role of the writer is different in other ways. The Dramatists Guild contract, under which most dramas are produced, states unequivocally that no dialogue in a production may be deleted or changed without the permission of the author. By contrast, in films and television two things happen. First, there are often a number of writers on a script. There may be two, three, or more. This means that no one writer has the authority to maintain his or her vision over the material. Second, the writer is unable to prevent changes in the script

The playwright David Mamet. (© Kevin Winter/Getty Images)

made by directors, producers, performers, or other writers. Thus in films and television, as compared with theatre, the writer has less control over what happens to his or her words.

Another crossover area for dramatic writers would be opera and musical theatre, in which the playwright would provide the libretto and perhaps the lyrics as well. When working on an opera or musical piece, the dramatist must collaborate with a composer as well as with a director and others.

Plot Our first essential of dramatic structure, *plot,* is the arrangement of events or the selection and order of scenes in a play. The term *plot* can mean a secret scheme or plan. The word is also used to describe the sequence of scenes or events in a novel, but we are speaking here specifically of plot in drama.

A dramatic plot is usually based on a story. Stories are as old as the human race, and today stories form much of the substance of our daily conversation, of newspapers and television, of novels and films. Every medium presents a story in a different form. In theatre, the story must be presented by living actors and actresses on a stage in a

Plot As distinct from story, the patterned arrangement in a drama of events and characters, with incidents selected and arranged for maximum dramatic impact. Also, in Elizabethan theatres, an outline of the play that was posted backstage for the actors.

ACTION: AN ESSENTIAL OF DRAMATIC STRUCTURE
Among the elements required to create a dramatic script is action: the confrontation, the conflicts, the overcoming of obstacles that constitute the events of the drama. In Arthur Miller's *All My Sons* there are numerous conflicts and complications: A son versus his father, the wife versus her husband, the son's fiance confronting his parents. Shown here from the left are Patrick Wilson, Katie Holmes, and Christian Camargo in a production directed by Simon McBurney on Broadway. (© Joan Marcus)

limited period of time, and this requires selectivity. Thus the plot of a play differs from a story. A *story* is a full account of an event or series of events, usually in chronological order; a *plot* is a selection and arrangement of scenes from a story for presentation onstage. The plot is what actually happens onstage, not what is talked about.

For example, the story of Abraham Lincoln begins with his birth in a log cabin and continues to the day he is shot at Ford's Theatre in Washington. In developing a plot for a play about Lincoln, however, the playwright must make choices. Will the play include scenes in Springfield, Illinois, where Lincoln served as a lawyer and held his famous debates with Stephen A. Douglas? Or will the entire play take place in Washington after Lincoln has become president? Will there be scenes with Lincoln's wife, Mary Todd; or will all the scenes involve government and military officials? Decisions like these must be made even when a play is based on a fictional story: the plot must be more restricted and structured than the story itself.

Action   A second essential of dramatic structure is ***action.*** If we were to construct a "grammar of theatre," the subject would always be human beings—dramatic characters who represent human concerns. In linguistic grammar, every subject needs a verb; similarly, in the grammar of theatre, dramatic characters need a verb—some form of action that defines them. The word *drama* actually derives from a Greek root, the verb *dran,* meaning "to do" or "to act." At its heart, theatre involves action.

Action According to the Greek philosopher Aristotle, a sequence of events linked by cause and effect, with a beginning, middle, and end. Said by Aristotle to be the best way to unify a play. More generally, the central, unifying conflict and movement through a drama.

STRONGLY OPPOSED
FORCES

In developing a dramatic structure, a playwright sets powerful
forces and characters against
one another to provide conflict
and dramatic confrontations.
A good example is the opposition between Othello (Eamonn
Walker) and Iago (Tim McIn-
nerny) in Shakespeare's play
Othello. The production shown
here was directed by Wilson
Milam at Shakespeare's Globe
in London. (© Geraint Lewis)

Conflict A third essential of dramatic structure is **conflict,** the collision or opposition of persons or forces in a drama that gives rise to dramatic action. We can perhaps
best understand dramatic conflict in terms of everyday experience. People often define
themselves by the way they respond to challenges, such as marriage, a job, sudden
good fortune, or a serious illness. If they cannot face up to a challenge, that tells us one
thing; if they meet it with dignity, even though defeated, that tells us another; if they
triumph, that tells us something else. We come to know our family, our friends, and
our enemies by being with them over a period of time. We see how they respond to us
and to other people, and how they meet crises in their own lives and in ours.

In life, this process can take years—in fact, it continues to unfold for as long as
we know a person—but in theatre we have only a few hours. The playwright, therefore, must devise means by which characters will face challenges and be tested in a
short time. The American playwright Arthur Miller called one of his plays *The Crucible*
(1953). Literally, a crucible is a vessel in which metal is tested by being exposed to
extreme heat. Figuratively, a crucible has come to stand for any severe test of human
worth and endurance—a trial by fire. Every play provides a crucible of a sort: a test
devised by the playwright to show how the characters behave under stress. Such a test,
and the characters' reaction to it, is one way that the meaning of a play is brought out.

Strongly Opposed Forces A fourth essential of dramatic structure, closely related to conflict, is *strongly opposed forces.* By this we mean that the people in conflict in
a play are fiercely determined to achieve their goals; moreover, they are powerful adver-
saries for one another. The conflicting characters have clear, strong goals or objectives;
that is, they have goals they want desperately to achieve, and they will go to any length
to achieve them. For example, Macbeth, in the play by Shakespeare, wants to become
king; Jean, the servant in August Strindberg's *Miss Julie,* wants to achieve independence;

Conflict Tension between
two or more characters that
leads to crisis or a climax;
a fundamental struggle or
imbalance—involving ideologies, actions, personalities,
etc.—underlying a play.

THE ASIAN INFLUENCE ON THE PLAYWRIGHTS BRECHT AND WILDER

In this chapter we are discussing the work of the playwright. We see in this area, as well as others, the global aspect of theatre today. Two mid-twentieth-century dramatists from the West who were strongly influenced by Asian theatre were the German playwright Bertolt Brecht (1889–1956) and American playwright Thornton Wilder (1897–1975).

Brecht, for example, drew from Asian legends and used techniques borrowed from Chinese, Japanese, and Indian theatre. Chinese theatre and literature were to prove particularly important with his *Good Woman of Setzuan* (1938–1949) which was set in China, and *The Caucasian Chalk Circle* (1944–1945), based on the Chinese play, *The Story of the Chalk Circle.*

Both Brecht and Wilder had seen Beijing opera and adopted certain features of this dramatic style into their own work. Beijing opera (also called *jingju* and Peking opera) blends song, dance, martial arts, theatre, acrobatics, and dance and uses much symbolism. Beijing opera takes place on an almost bare stage (often with just a table and a few chairs onstage throughout); it uses simple props brought on by stage attendants, and symbolic movements by the actors. For example, an actor walking in a circle around the stage indicates a long journey; a banner with a fish design indicates water, while rolled up on a tray, the same banner would represent a fish.

Brecht used such symbolic props and actions to achieve his alienation or distancing effect, which prevented the audience from identifying emotionally with the drama. In 1935, Brecht saw a performance by the Beijing opera star Mei Lanfang (1894–1961) in Moscow, and the following year wrote his essay "Alienation Effects in Chinese Acting," which noted aspects of Beijing opera conducive to the distancing effect he desired.

Similarly, Wilder had been exposed to Chinese theatre first at an early age, when his father's work took him to Hong Kong and Shanghai; and then as an adult, when he saw Mei Lanfang perform in New York in 1930. Aspects of Beijing opera that Wilder adopted can best be seen in his Pulitzer Prize–winning *Our Town* (1938). In this play, Wilder uses an almost bare stage with just two tables and six chairs positioned by the stage manager (who also acts as a narrator), and other locales are suggested by very simple alterations; in the

Brecht's *The Good Woman of Setzuan,* original Berliner Ensemble production. (Percy Paukschta)

third act, for example, the cemetery is suggested by just ten or twelve people sitting in chairs.

Both playwrights illustrate the increasing prevalence of Asian influences in twentieth-century playwriting.

Prepared by Naomi Stubbs, CUNY Graduate Center.

Blanche DuBois, in Tennessee Williams's *A Streetcar Named Desire,* wants to find a haven in the home of her sister. In fighting for their goals, two or more characters find themselves in opposition; and the strength of both sides must be formidable.

A perfect example of two characters bound to clash is found in *A Streetcar Named Desire.* Blanche DuBois is a faded southern belle trying desperately to hold onto her gentility; the crude, aggressive Stanley Kowalski is the chief threat to her stability and her survival. On his side, Stanley, who is insecure about his lack of education and refinement, is provoked almost to the breaking point by Blanche and her superior airs.

One device dramatists often use to establish friction or tension between forces is restricting the characters to members of a single family. Relatives have built-in rivalries and affinities: parents versus children, sisters versus brothers. As members of the same family, moreover, they have no avenue of escape.

Mythology, on which so much drama is based, abounds with familial relationships. Shakespeare also frequently set members of one family against each other: Hamlet opposes his mother; King Lear is opposed by his daughters. In modern drama, virtually every writer of note has dealt with close family situations. The American dramatist Eugene O'Neill wrote what many consider his finest play, *Long Day's Journey into Night,* about the four members of his own family.

In plays not directly involving families, the characters are usually still in close proximity. They are fighting for the same turf, the same throne, the same woman or man.

Balance of Forces   A fifth essential of dramatic structure is some sort of *balance* between the opposed forces: that is, the people or forces in conflict must be evenly matched. In almost every case, one side eventually wins, but before this final outcome the opposing forces must be roughly equal in strength and determination.

In most sporting events, there are rules ensuring that the contest will be as equal as possible without coming to a draw, and this notion is equally important in theatre. In sports, fans want their team to win, but they would prefer a close, exciting contest to a one-sided runaway. The struggle, as much as the outcome, is a source of pleasure; and so rules are set up, with handicaps or other devices for equalizing forces. In basketball or football, when one team scores, the other team gets the ball so that it will have a chance to even the score. In theatre, too, a hard-fought and relatively equal contest is usually set up between opposing forces: the vulnerable, artistic Blanche, for example, faces the brutish Stanley.

SEQUENCE IN DRAMATIC STRUCTURE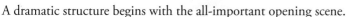

A dramatic structure begins with the all-important opening scene.

Opening Scene   The first scene of a drama starts the action and sets the tone and style for everything that follows. It tells us whether we are going to see a serious or a comic play, and whether the play will deal with affairs of everyday life or with fantasy. The opening scene also sets the action in motion, giving the characters a shove and hurtling them toward their destination.

Providing the characters with a problem or establishing an imbalance of forces compels the characters to respond. Generally, the problem or imbalance has occurred

OBSTACLES AND COMPLICATIONS

In developing a dramatic plot, the playwright often incorporates obstacles and complications that impede the movement of the main characters as they attempt to reach their goals. Complications and obstacles also add interest, suspense, and intricacy to the dramatic action. A good example of a play with many obstacles and complications is Shakespeare's *Hamlet*. The scene here is the "play within a play" in which Hamlet traps the king for having killed his father. Production by the Colorado Shakespeare Festival. (Kira Horvath © University of Colorado/Colorado Shakespeare Festival)

just before the play begins, or it arises immediately after the play opens. In *King Oedipus,* for example, a plague has struck the city just before the opening of the play. In *Hamlet,* "something is rotten in the state of Denmark," and early in the play the ghost of Hamlet's father appears to tell Hamlet that he must seek revenge. At the beginning of *Romeo and Juliet,* the Capulets and the Montagues are at one another's throats in a street fight.

As these examples suggest, in the opening scene the characters are thrust into a situation that provides the starting point for the play.

Obstacle That which delays or prevents the achieving of a goal by a character. An obstacle creates complication and conflict.

Complication Introduction, in a play, of a new force that creates a new balance of power and entails a delay in reaching the climax.

Obstacles and Complications   Having confronted the initial challenge of the play, the characters then move through a series of steps alternating between achievement and defeat, between hope and despair. The moment they accomplish one goal, something cuts across the play; a new hurdle or challenge is thrown up that they must overcome. These hurdles blocking a character's path—or outside forces that are introduced at an inopportune moment—are known as *obstacles* and *complications.*

Shakespeare's *Hamlet* provides numerous examples of obstacles and complications. Hamlet, suspecting that his uncle, Claudius, has killed his father, seeks revenge; but Claudius, as king, controls the army and other instruments of power. Thus the authority of the throne is one obstacle standing in Hamlet's way.

When Hamlet stages the "play within a play," Claudius's reaction confirms his guilt, and Hamlet's path to revenge seems clear. But on first trying to kill Claudius, Hamlet discovers him at prayer. A complication has been introduced: if Claudius dies while praying, he may go to heaven rather than to hell, and so Hamlet does not kill him.

Later, Hamlet is in his mother's bedroom when he hears a noise behind a curtain. Surely Claudius is lurking there, and Hamlet can kill him instantly. But when Hamlet thrusts his sword through the curtain, he finds that he has killed Polonius, who is the father of Ophelia, the young woman Hamlet is supposed to marry. This is another complication: the murder of Polonius gives Claudius a pretext for sending Hamlet to England with Rosencrantz and Guildenstern, who carry a letter instructing the king of England to put Hamlet to death.

Hamlet gets out of this trap and returns to Denmark. Now, at last, it seems that he can carry out his revenge. But he discovers that Ophelia has killed herself while he was away; and her brother, Laertes, is seeking revenge on Hamlet. This is still another complication: Hamlet is prevented from killing Claudius because he must also deal with Laertes. In the end, Hamlet does carry out his mission—but only after many interruptions.

READ *Hamlet*

http://www.Shakespeare-literature.com/Hamlet/1.html

Crises and Climaxes   As a result of conflicts, obstacles, and complications, dramatic characters become involved in a series of *crises.* Some crises are less complicated than those in *Hamlet,* some even more complicated. A play builds from one crisis to another; when the first crisis is resolved, the action leads to a second crisis, and so on. The final and most significant crisis is referred to as the *climax.* Sometimes there is a minor climax earlier in a play and a major climax near the conclusion. In the final climax, the issues of the play are resolved—either happily or tragically, depending on the genre.

Often, after the final climax of a drama, there will be a dénouement, a French word meaning the untying of the knot or the winding down of the plot.

TWO BASIC FORMS OF STRUCTURE: CLIMACTIC AND EPISODIC

Over the long history of western theatre, playwrights have usually adopted one or the other of two basic dramatic structures: *climactic,* or *intensive,* **structure;** and *episodic,* or *extensive,* **structure.** In certain periods, playwrights have combined the two. There are other forms of structure, which we will discuss, but let us consider climactic and episodic structure first.

Climactic Plot Construction   A dramatic form first used in Greece in the fifth century B.C.E. reemerged, somewhat altered, in France in the seventeenth century; in the late nineteenth century and the twentieth century, this same form was adopted in Norway, Sweden, France, and (somewhat later) the United States. This we call *climactic* or *intensive.* We use these terms because in this kind of dramatic construction, all aspects of a play—duration, locale, action, and number of characters—are severely

Crisis Point within a play when the action reaches an important confrontation or takes a critical turn. In the tradition of the well-made play, a drama includes a series of crises that lead to the final crisis, known as the climax.

Climax Often defined as the high point in the action or the final and most significant crisis in the action.

Climactic structure Also referred to as *intensive structure.* Dramatic structure in which there are few scenes, a short time passes, there are few locales, and the action begins chronologically close to the climax.

Episodic structure Also referred to as *extensive structure.* Dramatic structure in which there are many scenes, taking place over a considerable period of time in a number of locations. Many episodic plays also use such devices as subplots.

restricted; this results in a contained, or intense, structure, in which little time passes until the climax occurs.

A good example of climactic structure is found in *Miss Julie* by the Swedish playwright August Strindberg. The play takes place in one space, the kitchen of a home; it focuses on two people, a young woman and a male servant; and it occurs over a brief period, one and a half hours. Also, it has a single action: the young woman and the servant, from different social levels, are drawn compulsively into a fatal sexual encounter.

Climactic plots have several distinctive characteristics, which we'll consider one by one.

The Plot Begins Late in the Story

The first hallmark of climactic drama is that the plot begins quite late in the story, at a point where the story has reached a climax. It focuses on a moment when everything comes to a head, lives fall apart, fate closes in, and there is a final showdown between characters. Because the plot deals with a culmination of events, climactic form is sometimes called *crisis drama,* or *drama of catastrophe.*

King Oedipus by Sophocles offers a good example. When Oedipus is born, it is predicted that he will kill his father and marry his mother; and so his parents, the king and queen of Thebes, order that he be left in the wilderness to die. He is saved, however, and taken to another country where he is raised by another king and queen as their own son. As he grows up, he hears the prophecy about himself; and, assuming that his adoptive parents are his real ones, he leaves home. He goes to Thebes, where he does kill his natural father and marry his mother, not knowing who they are. He becomes king of Thebes; and when a plague strikes the kingdom, he sets out to find the person who has murdered the former king—not knowing that he himself is the murderer. All this happens *before* the play begins. The drama itself focuses on the single day when the full story emerges.

Exposition Imparting of information necessary for an understanding of the story but not covered by the action onstage; events or knowledge from the past, or occurring outside the play, which must be introduced for the audience to understand the characters or plot.

Whether it is *King Oedipus,* Ibsen's *A Doll's House,* or Tennessee Williams's *Cat on a Hot Tin Roof,* any play in climactic form concentrates on the final hours of a long sequence of events. Because so much has happened before the play begins, details about the past must be provided during the course of the play. In drama, the term for this information is ***exposition.***

The effect of beginning the action near the climax of events is to give a play a very sharp focus and a strong sense of immediacy. In climactic form, everything is concentrated on the showdown, the payoff, the final confrontation.

READ *King Oedipus* and Ibsen's *A Doll's House*

http://classics.mit.edu/Sophocles/oedipus.html and
http://www.gutenberg.org/ebooks/2542

Scenes, Locales, and Characters Are Restricted

Climactic structure is restricted not only in time but also in other ways. For example, it has a limited number of long scenes or acts, or perhaps only one act. Critics in the Renaissance said that a play must have five acts. For much of the nineteenth and twentieth centuries, three acts were standard. Today, the norm is two acts, though the long one-act play, performed without intermission, is also common.

CLIMACTIC STRUCTURE

In climactic structure, everything is restricted: the action occurs in a brief time, in limited locations, and with very few characters involved. Climactic structure was first developed in Western theatre by the Greek dramatists of the fifth century B.C.E. in Athens. In his play *No Exit,* Jean-Paul Sartre offers an excellent example of limited space. He presents three characters involved in an impossible love triangle confined to one room, from which, as the title suggests, there is no escape. Karen MacDonald as Estelle, Will Lebow as Garcin, and Paula Plum as Inez are shown in this scene from a production directed by Jerry Mouawad at the A.R.T. in Boston. (© T. Charles Erickson)

Limited scenes in a play usually entail a restricted locale. All the action in *King Oedipus* takes place in front of the royal palace. *No Exit,* a climactic play by the French writer Jean-Paul Sartre, confines its three characters to one room from which, as the title suggests, there is no escape. Writers like Ibsen and Strindberg also frequently confined their plays to one room, and contemporary plays provide numerous instances of this device.

Climactic dramatic structure also has a limited number of characters. Greek drama generally has four or five principal characters. *King Oedipus* has four: Oedipus, Jocasta, Creon, and Teiresias. French neoclassical drama and many modern plays have the same number of principal characters: four or five.

Construction Is Tight   Construction is tight in a climactic play: events are arranged in an orderly, compact way, with no loose ends. It is like a chain linked by cause and effect. As in a detective story, A leads to B, B to C, which causes D, leading in turn to E, and so on. This chain of events is unbreakable: once the action begins, there is no stopping it.

The French playwright Jean Anouilh (1910–1987), in his *Antigone* (1943), compares tragedy to the workings of a machine.

EPISODIC STRUCTURE: MANY CHARACTERS, PLACES, AND EVENTS
A good example of the typically wide-ranging episodic structure is *Julius Caesar* by William Shakespeare, during which the action shifts to many different sites in Rome, some public, some private. Shown here are Dan Kremer in the title role, with Kryztov Lindquist as the Soothsayer and the cast of the Shakespeare Theatre Company in its production, directed by David Muse. (© Carol Rosegg)

The spring is wound up tight. It will uncoil itself. That is what is so convenient in tragedy. The least little turn of the wrist will do the job. . . . The rest is automatic. You don't need to lift a finger. The machine is in perfect order; it has been oiled ever since time began and it runs without friction.[1]

Deus ex machina (DEH-oos eks MAH-kih-nah) Literally, "god from a machine," a resolution device in classic Greek drama; hence, intervention of supernatural forces—usually at the last moment—to save the action from its logical conclusion. In modern drama, an arbitrary and coincidental solution.

This applies to every play in climactic form. The aim is always to make events so inevitable that there is no escape—at least, not until the very last moment, when a **deus ex machina** may intervene to untangle the knot. *Deus ex machina* is Latin for "god from a machine" and comes from ancient Greece and Rome, when a mechanical contraption on the roof of the stage house was used to bring the gods onstage to resolve the action at the end of a play. The term *deus ex machina* has come to stand for any plot contrivance used to resolve a play at the end.

Episodic Plot Construction When we turn from climactic structure to episodic structure, we find a very clear contrast in almost every respect.

Episodic structure emerged during the Renaissance in England—Shakespeare's plays offer a prime example—and in Spain, in the plays of Lope de Vega and his contemporaries. Later, episodic form was adopted by the German playwrights Goethe and Schiller during the romantic period, in the late eighteenth century and the early

---

[1]Jean Anouilh, *Antigone*, Lewis Galantière (trans. and adaptor), Random House, New York, 1946, p. 36. Copyright 1946 by Random House.

nineteenth century. It was also used in the late nineteenth century by the Norwegian playwright Henrik Ibsen and in the twentieth century by the German playwright Bertolt Brecht. The following are the characteristics of episodic structure.

People, Places, and Events Proliferate

A typical episodic play covers an extended period of time, sometimes many years, and ranges over a number of locations. In one play, we can go anywhere: to a small antechamber, a large banquet hall, the open countryside, a mountaintop.

Short scenes alternate with longer scenes. The large number of characters and scenes in three plays will serve to indicate the expansive nature of episodic drama: Shakespeare's *Antony and Cleopatra* has thirty-four characters and more than forty scenes; his *Julius Caesar* has thirty-four characters and eighteen scenes; *The Sheep Well* by his Spanish contemporary Lope de Vega has twenty-six characters and seventeen scenes.

There May Be a Parallel Plot or a Subplot

One technique of episodic drama is the *parallel plot,* or **subplot.** In Shakespeare's *King Lear,* for example, Lear has three daughters, two evil and one good. The two evil daughters have convinced their father that they are good and that their sister is wicked. In the subplot—a counterpart of the main plot—the Earl of Gloucester has two sons, one loyal and one disloyal; and the disloyal one has deceived his father into thinking that he is the loyal one. Both old men have misjudged their children's true worth, and in the end each is punished for his mistake: Lear is bereft of his kingdom and his sanity; Gloucester loses his eyes. The Gloucester plot parallels and reinforces the Lear plot.

Subplot Secondary plot that reinforces or runs parallel to the major plot in an episodic play.

Contrast and Juxtaposition Are Used

Another technique of episodic drama is juxtaposition or contrast. Rather than moving in linear fashion, the action alternates between different kinds of elements.

For one thing, as we have noted, short scenes alternate with longer scenes. *King Lear* begins with a short scene between Kent and Gloucester, goes next to a long scene in which Lear divides his kingdom, then returns to a brief scene in which Edmund declares his intention to deceive his father.

Also, public scenes alternate with private scenes. Shakespeare's *Romeo and Juliet* opens with a public scene: a street fight between the Capulet family and the Montague family. This is followed by three private scenes. Then comes a public street scene, followed by a public scene at a masked ball.

In addition, comic scenes often alternate with serious scenes. In *Macbeth,* just after Macbeth has murdered King Duncan, there is a knock on the door of the castle. This is one of the most serious moments in the play, but the man who goes to open the door is a comic character, a drunken porter, whose speech is a humorous interlude in the grim business of the drama. In *Hamlet,* a gravedigger and his assistant are preparing a grave for Ophelia when Hamlet comes onto the scene. The gravediggers are joking about death; but for Hamlet, who soon learns that the grave is Ophelia's, it is a somber moment.

READ *Macbeth* and *Romeo and Juliet*

http://www.Shakespeare-literature.com/Macbeth/index.html and
http://www.Shakespeare-literature.com/Romeo_and_Juliet/index.html

The Overall Effect Is Cumulative   Unlike climactic drama, in which each action follows logically from what precedes it, episodic drama creates an impression of events piling up: a tidal wave of circumstances and emotions sweeping over the characters. Rarely is a character's fate determined by a single letter, a single incident, or a single piece of new knowledge. Time and again, Hamlet has proof that Claudius has killed his father; but it is a whole onrush of events—not a single piece of hard evidence—that eventually leads him to kill Claudius.

Combinations of Climactic and Episodic Construction   There is no rule requiring a play to be exclusively episodic or exclusively climactic; these forms are not watertight compartments. It is true that during certain periods one form or the other has been predominant. And it is not easy to mix the two because each has its own laws and its own inner logic. In various periods, however, they have been successfully integrated.

For example, climactic and episodic construction are combined in the comedies of late-seventeenth-century England—the Restoration period. In the late nineteenth century, the Russian dramatist Anton Chekhov combined elements of both forms, and in the twentieth century the two forms were frequently integrated.

OTHER FORMS OF DRAMATIC STRUCTURE

During the twentieth century and into the twenty-first, new types of dramatic structure appeared. In some cases, such as ritual structure, the form amounted to adaptation of an ancient structure for modern use. We will now look briefly at these variations in dramatic structure, returning to many of them in Part 4, when we study the historical periods in which they first appeared.

Ritual as Structure   Just as acting is a part of everyday life so is ritual. Basically, *ritual* is a repetition or reenactment of some proceeding or transaction that has acquired special meaning. It may be a simple ritual like singing the national anthem before a ball game or a deeply religious ritual like the Catholic mass. We all develop ritualistic patterns of behavior in our personal lives, such as following the same routine

Ritual Specifically ordered ceremonial event, often religious.

COMPARING CLIMACTIC AND EPISODIC FORMS OF STRUCTURE

Climactic	Episodic
1. Plot begins late in the story, toward the very end or climax.	**1.** Plot begins relatively early in the story and moves through a series of episodes.
2. Covers a short space of time, perhaps a few hours or at most a few days.	**2.** Covers a longer period of time: weeks, months, and sometimes many years.
3. Contains a few solid, extended scenes, such as three acts with each act comprising one long scene.	**3.** Has many short, fragmented scenes; sometimes alternates short and long scenes.
4. Occurs in a restricted locale, such as one room or one house.	**4.** May range over an entire city or even several countries.
5. Number of characters is severely limited—usually no more than six or eight.	**5.** Has a profusion of characters, sometimes several dozen.
6. Plot is linear and moves in a single line with few subplots or counterplots.	**6.** Is frequently marked by several threads of action, such as two parallel plots, or scenes of comic relief in a serious play.
7. Line of action proceeds in a cause-and-effect chain. The characters and events are closely linked in a sequence of logical, almost inevitable development.	**7.** Scenes are juxtaposed to one another. An event may result from several causes, or from no apparent cause, but arises in a network or web of circumstances.

The table above outlines the chief characteristics of climactic and episodic forms and illustrates the differences between them. It is clear that the climactic and episodic forms differ from each other in their fundamental approaches. One emphasizes constriction and compression on all fronts; the other takes a far broader view and aims at a cumulative effect, piling up people, places, and events.

when we get up in the morning or taking a day off on Sunday. As we shall see, some historians have theorized that theatre grew out of rituals and ritualistic enactments of ancient peoples.

Patterns as Structure   Related to ritual are *patterns* of events. In Samuel Beckett's *Waiting for Godot,* the characters have no personal history, and the play does not build to a climax in the ordinary way. But if Beckett has abandoned many techniques of traditional structure, he has replaced them with something else—a repeated sequence of events containing its own order and logic.

Cyclical Structure   A number of feminist commentators have argued that women playwrights often write in a cyclical form, one that does not build to a climax but rather stresses what Professor Sue-Ellen Case calls "contiguity," which is "fragmentary rather than whole" and "interrupted rather than complete." Traditional plot is replaced by an open-ended, serial structure.

Serial Structure   Another kind of structure is a *series* of acts or episodes—individual theatre events—offered as a single presentation. In this case, individual segments are strung together like charms on a bracelet or beads on a necklace. Sometimes a central theme or common thread holds the various parts together; sometimes there is little or no connection between the parts.

One example of serial structure is the musical revue, which has a series of short scenes, songs, and dance numbers. An evening of one-act plays is another example.

Avant-Garde and Experimental Structures

In the second half of the twentieth century, several groups in Europe and the United States experimented with ritual as a dramatic form. These groups included the Polish Laboratory Theatre, the Living Theatre, the Performance Group, and the Wooster Group. One purpose of their experiments was to return to the ritualistic, religious roots of theatre.

From their experiments, these groups developed several significant departures from traditional theatre practice. Among them were (1) interest in *ritual* and *ceremony;* (2) emphasis on *nonverbal theatre,* that is, theatre stressing gestures, body movements, and wordless sounds rather than logical or intelligible language; (3) reliance on *improvisation,* or scenarios developed by performers and directors; (4) stress on the physical *environment* of theatre, including a restructuring of the spatial relationship between performers and audience; and (5) stress on each audience member's developing his or her own interpretation of the work being presented.

Segments and Tableaux as Structure

Robert Wilson and Richard Foreman, who will be discussed in Chapter 15, organize their avant-garde productions into units analogous to the frames of film and television, or to the still-life tableaux of painting or the moving tableaux of dance. Frequently, directors like Foreman and Wilson will use rapid movements—as in silent films—or slow motion. At times, several actions will occur simultaneously. All of these, however, relate both to an image and to a tableaux or frame.

CREATING DRAMATIC CHARACTERS

Dialogue Conversation between characters in a play.

Along with creating dramatic structure, the playwright must create the characters who will carry out the action. In drama, as opposed to a novel or a short story, everything must be transformed into conversation between characters—called ***dialogue***—or into action. Literature can rely on passages describing what the characters are thinking and how they react to each other; in theatre, everything must be enacted by the characters.

Though they often seem like real people, dramatic characters are actually created in the imagination of a playwright. By carefully emphasizing certain features of a character's personality and eliminating others, the dramatist can show us in two hours the entire history of a person whom we might need a lifetime to know in the real world. In *A Streetcar Named Desire,* for example, we come to know Blanche DuBois, in all her emotional complexity, better than we know people we see every day. As we become intimately acquainted with Blanche, the dramatist reveals to us not only her biography but her mind and soul.

In deciding what to emphasize about a character and how to present the character, a playwright has wide latitude. A stage character can be drawn with a few quick strokes, as a caricaturist sketches a political figure; can be given the surface detail and reality of a photograph; or can be fleshed out with the more interpretive, fully rounded quality of an oil portrait.

TYPES OF DRAMATIC CHARACTERS

Extraordinary Characters

Heroes and heroines of most important dramatic works before the modern period are *extraordinary* in some way—that is, "larger than life." Historically, major characters have been kings, queens, generals, members of the nobility, or other figures clearly marked as holding a special place in society.

EXTRAORDINARY CHARACTERS
The heroes and heroines of drama of the past—classical tragedies and historical plays—were usually kings, queens, members of the nobility, and military leaders: in other words, figures who by their very positions were exceptional. They may have been evil characters or noble ones, but they stood above the crowd, both because of their positions in society and because of their characteristics. A good example is the title character in Shakespeare's *King Lear,* played here by David Calder (center) with Paul Copley (as Kent) and Jodie McNee (as Cordelia) at Shakespeare's Globe Theatre in London. (© Photoshot/Getty Images)

In addition, extraordinary characters generally represent some extreme of human behavior—men and women at their worst or best. Lady Macbeth is not only a noblewoman; she is one of the most ambitious women ever depicted. In virtually every instance, extraordinary characters are men and women at the breaking point, at the outer limits of human capability and endurance.

For example, the young Greek heroine Antigone and the medieval religious figure Joan of Arc are the epitome of the independent, courageous female, willing to stand up to male authority with strength and dignity. Two heroes from ancient Greece, Prometheus and Oedipus, are men willing to face the worst the gods can throw at them and accept the consequences. Among those qualifying as human beings at their worst is the Greek heroine Medea, who murders her own children.

Comic characters can also be extremes. For instance, the chief character in *Volpone,* by Shakespeare's contemporary, the English comic dramatist Ben Jonson, is an avaricious miser who gets people to present him with expensive gifts because they mistakenly think he will remember them in his will.

In much of modern realistic theatre, the main characters are distinguished not by being extraordinary or larger than life, but by being "representative" of a group or type. In the play *A Doll's House* by Henrik Ibsen, Nora and her husband, Torvald, are such characters. The two are played here by Janet McTeer and Owen Teale in a production on Broadway. (© Joan Marcus)

Beginning in the eighteenth century, ordinary people took over more and more from royalty and the nobility as the heroes and heroines of drama—a reflection of what was occurring in real life as monarchies became less powerful and democracy took hold. Nevertheless, the leading figures of drama continued to be exceptional men and women at their best and worst. The heroine of August Strindberg's *Miss Julie* is a neurotic, obsessive woman at the end of her rope. In *Mother Courage* by Bertolt Brecht, we see a woman who will sacrifice almost anything to survive; she even loses a son by haggling over the price of his release from detention. *The Emperor Jones,* by Eugene O'Neill, shows the downfall of a powerful black man who has made himself the ruler of a Caribbean island.

READ *Antigone* and *Miss Julie*

http://classics.mit.edu/Sophocles/antigone.html and
http://openlibrary.org/Books/OL7038162M/Miss_Julie_and_other_plays

Representative or Quintessential Characters   Though many characters of modern drama are extraordinary, a new type of main character has emerged—one who is three-dimensional and highly individual but at the same time ordinary. He or she stands apart not by being exceptional but by being typical of a large, important sector of the population. Rather than being "worst," "best," or some other extreme, such characters are notable because they embody the characteristics of an entire group. We can call these characters ***representative*** or *quintessential.*

A good example of a representative character is Nora Helmer, the heroine of Henrik Ibsen's *A Doll's House.* Though Nora secretly forged a signature to get money that saved the life of her husband when he was very ill, he regards her as spoiled and flighty.

Representative characters
Characters in a play who embody characteristics that represent an entire group.

All her life, in fact—first by her father and now by her husband—she has been treated as a doll or a plaything, never as a mature, responsible woman. In the last act of the play, Nora rebels: she makes a declaration of independence to her husband, slams the door on him, and walks out. It has been said that Nora's slamming of the door marked the beginning not only of modern drama but of the emancipation of modern women. Nora's demand that she be treated as an equal has made her typical of all housewives who refuse to be regarded as pets. *A Doll's House* was written in 1879, but today—well over a century later—Nora still symbolizes the often inferior position of women.

Another example of a representative character is Willy Loman, in Arthur Miller's *Death of a Salesman.* Willy stands for all salesmen, traveling on "a smile and a shoeshine." He has accepted a false dream: the idea that he can be successful and rich by putting up a good front and being "well liked."

Nora Helmer and Willy Loman are both examples of characters who stand apart from the crowd, not by standing above it but by embodying the attributes of a certain type of ordinary person.

Stock Characters

Many characters in drama are not "complete," not "three-dimensional." Rather, they symbolize and throw into bold relief a particular type of person to the exclusion of virtually everything else. They are called **stock characters,** and although they can be found in almost all kinds of drama, they appear particularly in comedy and melodrama.

Among the most famous examples of stock characters are those in ***commedia dell'arte,*** a form of comic improvisational theatre that flourished in Italy from the late sixteenth century to the eighteenth century. In commedia dell'arte, there were no scripts; there was only an outline of the action, and the performers supplied the words. There was a set group of stereotypical characters, each one invariably wearing the same costume and displaying the same personality traits. The bragging soldier, called Capitano, always boasted of his courage in a series of fictitious military victories. Pantalone, an elderly merchant, spoke in clichés and chased young women; and a pompous character, Dottore, spouted Latin phrases to impress others with his learning. Among the servant characters, Harlequin was the most popular; both cunning and stupid, he was at the heart of every plot complication.

The familiar figures in situation comedies on television are good examples of stock characters in our own day. The conceited high school boy, the prejudiced father, the harried mother, the dumb blond waitress, the efficient career person, the tough private detective—we can see such stereotypical characters every day on television. We recognize their familiar traits, and their attitudes and actions are always predictable.

Characters with a Dominant Trait

Closely related to stock characters are characters with a **dominant trait,** or *humor.* One aspect of such a character dominates, making for an unbalanced, often comic, personality. Ben Jonson titled two of his plays *Every Man in His Humour* (1616) and *Every Man Out of His Humour* (1616); and he usually named his characters for their single trait or humor. In his play *The Alchemist* (1610), the characters have names like Subtle, Face, Dapper, Surly, Wholesome, and Dame Pliant.

Playwrights of the English Restoration also gave characters names that described their personalities. In *The Way of the World,* by William Congreve, one character is

Stock character Character who has one outstanding trait of human behavior to the exclusion of virtually all other attributes. These characters often seem like stereotypes and are most often used in comedy and melodrama.

Commedia dell'arte (koh-MAY-dee-ah dehl-AHR-teh) Form of comic theatre, originating in sixteenth-century Italy, in which dialogue was improvised around a loose scenario calling for a set of stock characters.

Dominant trait Found in certain theatrical characters: one paramount trait or tendency that overshadows all others and appears to control the conduct of the character. Examples could include greed, jealousy, anger, and self-importance.

A DOMINANT TRAIT

A favorite character of many comic writers through the ages has been one with a clear, strong trait that overrides all others: jealousy, avarice, miserliness, pomposity, and so forth. A good example is Mrs. Malaprop in *The Rivals* by Richard Brinsley Sheridan. Mrs. Malaprop invariably uses long words in the wrong way, making her an immensely comic figure. Here, she is played by Mary Louise Wilson in a production at the Huntington Theatre. (© T. Charles Erickson)

called Fainall, meaning "feign all"—that is, he constantly pretends. Other characters are Petulant, Sir Wilful Witwoud, Waitwell, and Lady Wishfort, the last being a contraction of "wish for it." Molière frequently emphasized the dominant trait of the main character in his titles: *The Miser*, *The Misanthrope*, *The Would-Be Gentleman*, *The Imaginary Invalid*.

Minor characters In a drama, those characters who have small, secondary, or supporting roles. These could include soldiers and servants.

Minor Characters Characters who play a small part in the overall action are called *minor characters*. Usually, they appear briefly and serve chiefly to further the story or to serve as a foil to more important characters.

Narrator or Chorus Generally, a *narrator* speaks directly to the audience, frequently commenting on the action. The narrator may or may not have a dramatic persona in the same sense as the other characters. In Tennessee Williams's *The Glass Menagerie*, the narrator is also a character in the play; in Thornton Wilder's *Our Town*, the narrator becomes several characters during the course of the action. Greek drama used a *chorus* that commented, in song and dance, on the action of the main plot and reacted to it.

Chorus In ancient Greek drama, a group of performers who sang and danced, sometimes participating in the action but usually simply commenting on it. In modern times, performers in a musical play who sing and dance as a group.

Nonhuman Characters In many primitive cultures, performers portrayed birds and animals, and this practice has continued to the present. Aristophanes, the Greek comic playwright, used a chorus to play the title parts in his plays *The Birds* (414 B.C.E.) and *The Frogs* (405 B.C.E.). In the modern era, the absurdist playwright Eugène Ionesco has people turn into animals in *Rhinoceros* (1959). The contemporary American playwright Edward Albee has performers play lizards in *Seascape* (1974).

While authors may create nonhuman characters, however, we should note that their focus is always on drawing parallels with the human experience.

JUXTAPOSITION OF CHARACTERS

In creating characters, a playwright can use them in combinations that will bring out certain qualities.

One such combination consists of a ***protagonist*** and an ***antagonist.*** These terms come from Greek theatre. A *protagonist* is the leading character in a play, the chief or outstanding figure in the action. An *antagonist* is the character who opposes the protagonist. In Shakespeare's *Othello,* for example, the protagonist is Othello and the antagonist is Iago, his chief opponent. Through the interaction and conflict between protagonist and antagonist, the individual qualities of both characters emerge.

Another way to contrast characters is to set them side by side rather than in opposition. Frequently, a dramatist will introduce secondary characters to serve as *foils* or *counterparts* to the main characters. A foil is a person who stands in contrast to another. In *Hedda Gabler,* by Henrik Ibsen, the main character, Hedda, is destructive and willful, bent on having her own way. Mrs. Elvsted, another character in the play, is Hedda's opposite in almost every regard.

Protagonist Principal character in a play, the one whom the drama is about.

Antagonist Opponent of the protagonist in a drama.

In this chapter, we have examined the work of the person or persons creating a dramatic text. We have looked at the development of subject, focus, and purpose and the creation of dramatic structure and dramatic characters. In Chapter 4 we turn to another aspect of the script: point of view as it manifests itself in theatrical genres.

SUMMARY

The person or persons creating a dramatic text have a number of tasks and responsibilities: to develop the subject, focus, and purpose of the text. Beyond that, those creating a text must develop a dramatic structure and dramatic characters.

Like an architect planning a building, those who create a text must develop a structure for a play. Essentials of dramatic structure include plot, conflict, strongly opposed forces, and a reasonable balance between those forces. Working with these essentials, the playwright creates the structure. An opening scene starts the action and sets the tone and style. Then the characters, motivated by objectives or goals, encounter a series of obstacles and complications. The result is a succession of crises leading to the most important crisis, the climax.

In the past, playwrights generally used either climactic or episodic structure. In climactic form, all aspects of a play—such as action, duration, and number of characters and locales—are restricted; in episodic form, these aspects are all expanded. At certain times in theatre history, climactic and episodic form have been combined.

A playwright or the equivalent must also create characters, using dialogue and action. Playwrights of the past usually presented extraordinary, "larger than life" characters. A modern dramatist is less likely to present elevated characters such as kings and queens, but present-day playwrights still often give us exceptional characters—people at their best or their worst. Today's playwrights might also choose to present ordinary but representative characters, typical of a large portion of the population. A playwright may also use stock characters, easily recognizable stereotypes.

The playwright or whoever creates a text juxtaposes characters to highlight their individual traits—for example, opposing the main character or protagonist with an antagonist or a contrasting character.

THINKING ABOUT THEATRE

▶ Look at the cast of characters in a Shakespearean play you have seen or read. (See the URLs in this chapter for *Hamlet, Macbeth,* and *Romeo and Juliet.*) Place each character in a category: major character, minor character, or a character in between, that is, a character with a clear personality but not a large role. Which characters are in opposition to one another? Which characters in the play predominate in the struggle? Is there a reversal of their fortunes?

▶ During the last performance you attended (or the last play you read), did the action take place in one locale (one room, for instance) or instead, in three or four locations? Did the action move frequently, returning at times to a former location? What effect did these elements of place or location have on the experience of the play?

▶ While watching a modern play or drama involving a small group of characters locked in a struggle for dominance or control, how does the action usually play out? (For example, read *A Doll's House* at the URL in this chapter.) Is first one person in the ascendency and then another? What do shifts of power and control have to do with revealing the personalities of the characters? What do these changes have to do with the meaning of the play?

(NOTE: *Hamlet* and *A Doll's House* are also available in *Anthology of Living Theatre,* Third Edition, by Edwin Wilson and Alvin Goldfarb.)

KEY TERMS

Action According to the Greek philosopher Aristotle, a sequence of events linked by cause and effect, with a beginning, middle, and end. Said by Aristotle to be the best way to unify a play. More generally, the central, unifying conflict and movement through a drama.

Antagonist Opponent of the protagonist in a drama.

Chorus In ancient Greek drama, a group of performers who sang and danced, sometimes participating in the action but usually simply commenting on it. In modern times, performers in a musical play who sing and dance as a group.

Climactic structure Also referred to as *intensive structure.* Dramatic structure in which there are few scenes, a short time passes, there are few locales, and the action begins chronologically close to the climax.

Climax Often defined as the high point in the action or the final and most significant crisis in the action.

Commedia dell'arte (koh-MAY-dee-ah dehl-AHR-teh) Form of comic theatre, originating in sixteenth-century Italy, in which dialogue was improvised around a loose scenario calling for a set of stock characters.

Complication Introduction, in a play, of a new force that creates a new balance of power and entails a delay in reaching the climax.

Conflict Tension between two or more characters that leads to crisis or a climax; a fundamental struggle or imbalance—involving ideologies, actions, personalities, etc.—underlying a play.

Crisis Point within a play when the action reaches an important confrontation or takes a critical turn. In the tradition of the well-made play, a drama includes a series of crises that lead to the final crisis, known as the climax.

Deus ex machina (DEH-oos eks MAH-kih-nah) Literally, "god from a machine," a resolution device in classic Greek drama; hence, intervention of supernatural forces—usually at the last moment—to save the action from its logical conclusion. In modern drama, an arbitrary and coincidental solution.

Dialogue Conversation between characters in a play.

Dominant trait Found in certain theatrical characters: one paramount trait or tendency that overshadows all others and appears to control the conduct of the character. Examples could include greed, jealousy, anger, and self-importance.

Dramatic structure The way a play is put together: the sequences of scenes, the rise and fall in the action, the conflicts and crises, the resolution.

Episodic structure Also referred to as *extensive structure*. Dramatic structure in which there are many scenes, taking place over a considerable period of time in a number of locations. Many episodic plays also use such devices as subplots.

Exposition Imparting of information necessary for an understanding of the story but not covered by the action onstage; events or knowledge from the past, or occurring outside the play, which must be introduced for the audience to understand the characters or plot.

Minor characters In a drama, those characters who have small, secondary, or supporting roles. These could include soldiers and servants.

Obstacle That which delays or prevents the achieving of a goal by a character. An obstacle creates complication and conflict.

Plot As distinct from story, the patterned arrangement in a drama of events and characters, with incidents selected and arranged for maximum dramatic impact. Also, in Elizabethan theatres, an outline of the play that was posted backstage for the actors.

Protagonist Principal character in a play, the one whom the drama is about.

Representative characters Characters in a play who embody characteristics that represent an entire group.

Ritual Specifically ordered ceremonial event, often religious.

Stock character Character who has one outstanding trait of human behavior to the exclusion of virtually all other attributes. These characters often seem like stereotypes and are most often used in comedy and melodrama.

Subplot Secondary plot that reinforces or runs parallel to the major plot in an episodic play.

THEATRE ON THE WEB

For more research and to learn more about the topics in this chapter, please visit the Online Learning Center at **www.mhhe.com/livelyart8e.**

THEATRICAL GENRES

DRAMATIC GENRES

TRAGEDY

WIDER PERSPECTIVE:
Conditions for Tragedy:
Theatre and Society

TRADITIONAL TRAGEDY

MODERN TRAGEDY

COMEDY

CHARACTERISTICS OF COMEDY

FORMS OF COMEDY

HEROIC DRAMA

MELODRAMA

DOMESTIC DRAMA

TRAGICOMEDY

SHAKESPEAREAN TRAGICOMEDY

MODERN TRAGICOMEDY

SUMMARY
THINKING ABOUT THEATRE
KEY TERMS
THEATRE ON THE WEB

◀ **GENRES**   Drama is often put into categories: tragedy, comedy, tragicomedy, melodrama, and so forth. Sometimes these categories overlap, but ever since the ancient Greeks separated tragedy and comedy and provided a different mask for each, the practice of dividing drama into various types or genres has proved helpful to practitioners and audiences alike. And, of course, there are categories other than tragedy and comedy, such as tragicomedy, domestic drama, and heroic drama. Seen here are Jeffrey Bean and Todd Waite in a scene from *The Underpants*, a hilarious social satire, a form of comedy, by Steve Martin, directed by Scott Schwartz at the Alley Theatre in Houston, Texas. (© T Charles Erickson)

I n Greece in the fifth century B.C.E., where Western theatre began, the actors wore masks covering their faces when they performed. The Greeks took the idea of the mask to create symbols of the two kinds of plays presented at their dramatic festivals—the mask of tragedy and the mask of comedy—symbols that are still used today. Similarly, in Japan in the fourteenth century C.E., a theatre called nō had become established as the serious form of drama. Alongside nō, however, was a comical, farcical type of drama called Kyogen.

In other words, wherever theatre has appeared, there has been a tendency to divide it into categories or types, often referred to by the French term *genre* (JAHN-ruh). In addition to tragedy and comedy, additional genres have developed: farce, melodrama, tragicomedy, and a number of others.

This tendency to divide dramatic works into categories is not confined to theatre. We find it widespread, not only in the arts, but in many aspects of life. Not only those who create theatre adopt different points of view toward events and toward life in general; all of us do. Depending on our perspective, we can see the same subject as funny or sad, take it seriously or laugh at it, make it an object of pity or of ridicule. Just why we look at events from different points of view is difficult to say, but there is no question that we do. The English author Horace Walpole (1717–1797) wrote: "This world is a comedy to those that think, a tragedy to those that feel."

In theatre, this question of viewpoint—looking at people or events from a particular perspective—becomes crucial. Viewpoint is not taken for granted, as it is in everyday life; rather, it is a conscious act on the part of whoever creates the text. To take an example, in most cases death is considered a somber matter; but in his play *Arsenic and Old Lace* (1941), the dramatist Joseph Kesselring (1902–1967) makes it clear that in his play we are to regard death as comic. Kesselring presents two elderly women who kill no fewer than 12 old men by serving them arsenic in glasses of wine. But because the dramatist removes from the play any feeling that the deaths are to be taken seriously, he engenders in the audience the notion that it is all in fun.

DRAMATIC GENRES

Before examining genre, we should note that often a play does not fit neatly into a single category. Those who create a text do not write categories or types of plays; they write individual, unique works—and preoccupation with genre may distract us from the individuality of a play or a production. Still, if we keep these reservations in mind, we will find that it is helpful to understand the traditional genres into which Western dramatic literature has fallen.

TRAGEDY

Tragedy is serious drama involving important personages caught in calamitous circumstances; it evokes in the audience fear and apprehension for the characters who are suffering, and admiration for the courage they display. Many people consider tragedy the loftiest and most profound form of theatre—in fact, one of the most meaningful forms of expression in any of the arts. Why is this so? For one thing, tragedy probes very basic questions about human existence. Why are people sometimes extremely

Genre Category or type of play.

THE MASKS OF TRAGEDY AND COMEDY
The notion of dividing theatre into various categories began with Greeks who separated tragedy from comedy and created a mask for each. (© Ingram Publishing/Alamy)

Tragedy Dramatic form involving serious actions of universal significance and with important moral and philosophical implications, usually with an unhappy ending.

THE TRAGIC HERO
In classic or traditional tragedy, the hero or heroine is caught in circumstances from which there is no escape and which lead inevitably to a fateful end. A good example is the title character in Shakespeare's *Othello.* The production shown here was directed by Wilson Milam at Shakespeare's Globe, featuring Eamonn Walker as Othello, Zoe Tapper as Desdemona. (© Johan Persson/ ArenaPAL)

cruel? Why is the world so unjust? Why are men and women called on to endure suffering? What are the limits of human suffering and endurance? In the midst of cruelty and despair, what are the possibilities of human achievement? To what heights of courage, strength, generosity, and integrity can human beings rise?

Tragedy assumes that the universe is indifferent to human concerns, and often cruel or malevolent. Sometimes the innocent suffer while the evil prosper. Some human beings are capable of despicable deeds; others confront and overcome adversity, attaining a nobility that places them, in the words of the psalmist in the Bible, "a little lower than the angels."

TRADITIONAL TRAGEDY

Tragedy can be divided into two basic kinds: traditional and modern. Let's begin by looking at traditional tragedy. We have noted that Greece in the fifth century B.C.E. and certain European countries in the Renaissance were conducive to tragedy. What characteristics do the traditional tragedies of these periods have in common?

Tragic Heroes and Heroines   Generally, the hero or heroine of a traditional tragedy is an extraordinary person: a king, a queen, a general, a member of the nobility—in other words, a person of stature. Because these heroes and heroines are important, they stand not only as individuals but as symbols of an entire culture or society. Also, the central figure of a traditional tragedy is caught in a set of tragic circumstances. In traditional tragedy, the universe seems to trap the hero or heroine in a fateful web.

Tragic Fate   The tragic situation becomes irreversible and irretrievable: there is no turning back, no way out. Tragic heroes and heroines suffer a cumulative series of reversals. The figures of traditional tragedy find themselves in situations from which

When we study theatre history, we recognize that theatre, like any art form, does not occur in a vacuum. It is created by artists who live in a given culture at a given time. These artists are shaped by their culture, even though they may question it or rebel against it.

For example, in Western civilization, the eighteenth century was known as the Age of Enlightenment and the nineteenth century as the Century of Progress. Over the course of these two centuries, there were political revolutions in France and America, the Industrial Revolution, and many scientific advances. As a result, the eighteenth and nineteenth centuries were optimistic periods, when it was felt that our worst problems—poverty, disease, injustice—could be solved. This point of view is hardly conducive to tragedy.

By contrast, other periods of Western civilization were characterized by a point of view receptive to tragedy. The outlook of these societies created what might be called the *conditions* or *climate* for tragedy. In general, there seem to be two such conditions—which at first appear mutually contradictory but are actually two sides of the same coin. One side of this tragic coin is the idea that human beings are capable of extraordinary accomplishments; the other is the idea that the world is potentially cruel and unjust. Both conditions are evidently necessary; for example, the eighteenth and nineteenth centuries in Europe reflected the concept of humanity as capable of vast accomplishments but not the concept of the world as cruel and unjust.

Two periods in which both ideas were prominent, and which did prove conducive to tragedy, were the Golden Age of Greece in the fifth century B.C.E. and the Renaissance (the fourteenth through seventeenth centuries) in Europe. In both eras, human beings were exalted above all else; the gods and nature were given much less prominence. In the fifth century B.C.E., Greece was truly enjoying its Golden Age, in commerce, politics, science,

and art: Pythagoras had recently formulated his theories of mathematics; Socrates was holding his philosophical discourses; and the Parthenon was being built atop the Acropolis in Athens. Nothing seemed impossible in the way of architecture, mathematics, trade, or philosophy. The same was true in Europe and England during the Renaissance. Columbus had reached the new world in 1492; the possibilities for trade and exploration appeared infinite; science and the arts were on the threshold of a new day.

In both periods, celebration of the individual was apparent in all the arts, including drama. The Greek dramatist Sophocles exclaimed:

> Numberless are the wonders of the world.
> but none
> More wonderful than man.

And in the Renaissance, Shakespeare has Hamlet say:

> What a piece of work is man! How noble in
>   reason! How infinite in faculty!
> In form, in moving, how express and admirable!
>   In action how like an angel!
> In apprehension how like a god!

The credo of both ages was expressed by Protagoras, a Greek philosopher of the fifth century B.C.E.:

> Man is the measure of all things.

But both periods also reflect the other side of the tragic coin. Along with exalted humanism, there was a simultaneous awareness of what life can do to men and women: an unflinching admission that life can be, and in fact frequently is, cruel, unjust, and even meaningless. Shakespeare, writing in 1606, put it this way in *King Lear:*

> As flies to wanton boys, are we to the gods;
> They kill us for their sport.

In *Macbeth,* he expressed it in these words:

there is no honorable avenue of escape; they must go forward to meet their tragic fate. Once the Greek heroine Antigone faces down her uncle King Creon, she is doomed.

Acceptance of Responsibility   A tragic hero or heroine accepts responsibility for his or her actions and also shows a willingness to suffer and an immense capacity for suffering. In many traditional tragedies, the hero or heroine recognizes the flaw or fault of character that leads to the tragic downfall.

A CLIMATE FOR TRAGEDY
Two historical periods particularly suited for the creation of dramatic tragedies were ancient Greece and the Renaissance. Shown here in a production of a play from the Greek period is the British actress Vanessa Redgrave, portraying the title character in Euripides' *Hecuba* at the Brooklyn Academy of Music. (© Richard Termine)

Out, out brief candle!
Life's but a walking shadow, a poor player
That struts and frets his hour upon the stage
And then is heard no more; it is a tale
Told by an idiot, full of sound and fury,
Signifying nothing.

The Greek Golden Age and the Renaissance, then, encompassed both attitudes toward existence: the greatness of human beings on the one hand, and the cruelty of life on the other. These two sides of the tragic coin are indispensable conditions for the creation of tragedy.

We must note, however, that—important as it is—the outlook of a society serves only as a background in creating theatre. The foreground is the highly personal point of view of the individual artist. This is proved by the fact that playwrights within the same era vary greatly. At the same time that Euripides was writing tragedies in ancient Greece, Aristophanes was writing satirical farces. In France in the seventeenth century, Molière was writing comedies while Jean Racine was writing tragedies. In the modern period particularly, drama expresses a multiplicity of individual viewpoints.

Tragic Verse The language of traditional tragedy is *verse*. Because it deals with lofty and profound ideas, tragedy soars to the heights and descends to the depths of human experience; and many people feel that such thoughts and emotions can be best expressed in poetry.

The Effect of Tragedy When the elements of traditional tragedy are combined, they appear to produce two contradictory reactions simultaneously. One reaction

MODERN TRAGEDY

A number of works by serious playwrights of the past 145 years can be classified as contemporary or modern tragedies. Though they do not contain certain elements of traditional tragedy—such as poetry or characters from the nobility—they deal with similar themes in a profound way. A good example is *Miss Julie* by Strindberg, in which a neurotic young woman from a well-to-do family is locked in a struggle of love and hate with a servant, Jean. In the production shown here, by the Two River Theatre Company, Heather Lea Anderson plays Julie and Ed Onipede Blunt portrays the servant Jean. (© T. Charles Erickson)

is pessimistic: the heroes or heroines are "damned if they do and damned if they don't," and the world is a cruel, uncompromising place. And yet, in even the bleakest tragedy, there is affirmation. One source of this positive reaction is the drama itself. Traditional tragic playwrights, although telling us that the world is in chaos, at the same time strike a note of affirmation by the very act of creating such carefully shaped and brilliant works of art. Another positive source is the ultimate dignity of the tragic figure in accepting his or her fate.

When we come to the theatres of fifth-century Greece (in Chapter 10), the English Renaissance (in Chapter 12), and neoclassical France (also in Chapter 12), we will look at specific examples of traditional tragedy and their unique characteristics.

MODERN TRAGEDY

Tragedies of the modern period—that is, beginning in the late nineteenth century—do not have queens or kings as central figures, and they are written in prose rather than poetry. Though the characters are not as exalted and the language is not as formal, modern dramatists probe the same depths and ask the same questions as their predecessors: Why do men and women suffer? Why is there violence and injustice in the world? And perhaps most fundamental of all: What is the meaning of life? When we turn to theatre of the late nineteenth century and the twentieth century, we will examine specific examples of plays that have been called "modern tragedies."

COMEDY

Comedy In general, a play that is light in tone, is concerned with issues that are not serious, has a happy ending, and is designed to amuse.

Comedy is humorous drama whose characters, actions, and events are intended to provoke amusement and laughter. People who create comedy are not necessarily frivolous or unconcerned with important matters; they may be extremely serious in their own way. Consider three comic dramatists from different periods—Aristophanes in classical Greece, Molière in seventeenth-century France, and George Bernard Shaw in modern Britain. All three cared passionately about human affairs and human problems. But they—and others like them—took a comic view of life; they saw the world differently from someone whose outlook is somber; they made their points with a smile, an arched eyebrow, a deep laugh. As they observed human follies and excesses, they developed a keen sense of the ridiculous, showing us things that make us laugh.

Laughter is one of the most elusive of human reactions; no one—from philosophers to psychoanalysts—has provided a fully satisfactory explanation of why we laugh. Most people do agree, however, that laughter is quintessentially human. Other creatures express pain and sorrow—emotions we associate with tragedy—but apparently only human beings laugh.

It should also be noted that there are many kinds of laughter, ranging all the way from mild amusement at a witty saying or a humorous situation to a belly laugh at wild physical comedy, to cruel derisive laughter at someone who is different. (An example of derisive laughter would be a group of children mocking a newcomer to their school or neighborhood who seems "different"—perhaps a child with a physical disability or a speech impediment.) Theatre, which reflects society, includes a similar range of comedy, from light comedies to outrageous farces.

CHARACTERISTICS OF COMEDY

If we cannot fully explain comedy, we can at least understand some of the principles that make it possible.

Suspension of Natural Laws   One feature of most comedy is a temporary suspension of the natural laws of probability and logic. Actions in a comic play do not have the same consequences as actions in real life.

In comedy, when a haughty man walking down a street steps on a child's skateboard and goes sprawling on the sidewalk, we do not fear for his safety or wonder if he has been hurt. In comedy, the focus is on the man being tripped up and getting his comeuppance. We have in some sense suspended our belief in injury. In burlesque, a comic character can be hit on the backside with a fierce thwack, and we laugh, because we know that only his or her pride is hurt. In fact, at one point in stage history a special stick, made of two flat wooden slats fastened closely together, was developed to make the sound of hitting even more fearsome: when this stick hit someone, the two slats would slap together, making the whack much louder. The device was known as a *slapstick,* and its name came to describe all kinds of raucous, knockabout comedy.

Prime examples of the suspension of natural laws in comedy are silent movies and film cartoons. In animated cartoons, characters are hurled through the air like missiles, shot full of holes, and flattened on the sidewalk after falling from buildings; but they always get up, with little more than a shake of the head. The audience has no thought of real injury, of cuts or bruises because the real-life chain of cause and effect does not apply.

Under such conditions, murder itself can be viewed as comic. The American playwright Arthur Kopit (1937–   ) titled one of his plays *Oh, Dad, Poor Dad, Mama's Hung You in the Closet and I'm Feeling So Sad* (1960). In Kopit's play, as in *Arsenic and Old Lace,* the serious aspects of murder have been eliminated. We do not dwell on the fact that people are being killed, and we have none of the feelings we would usually have for victims; as a result, we are free to enjoy the irony and incongruity of the situation.

Slapstick Type of comedy or comic business that relies on ridiculous physical activity—often violent in nature—for its humor.

SUSPENSION OF NATURAL LAWS IN COMEDY
Frequently in various kinds of comedy, particularly in farce, our natural reaction to events is reordered to achieve the comic effect, and the audience goes along with this. An excellent example is the play *Arsenic and Old Lace* by Joseph Kesselring, in which two elderly women, who appear to be helpless and harmless, actually murder a number of old men by giving them elderberry wine laced with poison. Because we have accepted the comic premise of the play, we do not condemn their acts but rather become amused. Shown here in a London production of the play are Marcia Warren, Stephen Tompkinson, Thelma Barlow, and Brian Poyser. (© Geraint Lewis)

Contrast between Individuals and the Social Order Comedy develops when two elements—a basic assumption about society and the events of the play—cut against each other like the blades of a pair of scissors. In most instances, comic writers accept the notion of a clear social and moral order in their society; it is not the social order that is at fault but the defiance of that order by individuals. Human excess, fraud, hypocrisy, and folly are laughed at against a background of normality and moderation. This view is in contrast to the view of many tragedies, which assume that society itself is upside down, or that, in Hamlet's words, "the time is out of joint."

In Molière's comedy *Tartuffe*, for example, the chief character is a charlatan and hypocrite who pretends to be pious and holy, going so far as to wear clerical garb. He lives in the house of Orgon, a foolish man who trusts him implicitly. The truth is that Tartuffe is trying to acquire Orgon's wife as well as his money; but Orgon, blind to Tartuffe's real nature, is completely taken in by him. The audience and Orgon's family are aware of what is going on; they can see how ludicrous these two characters are, and in the end both Tartuffe's hypocrisy and Orgon's gullibility are exposed. But it is the individual—not religion or marriage—that is ridiculed. What Molière criticizes is the *abuse* of religion and marriage.

Many modern comedies reverse the scissors blades; their basic assumption is that the world is not orderly but absurd or ridiculous. Against this background, ordinary people are set at odds with the world around them, and the comedy results from thrusting normal people into an abnormal world. This condition—a normal person in an upside-down world—is found especially in tragicomedy and theatre of the absurd, both of which will be discussed later in this chapter.

READ *Tartuffe*
http://www.gutenberg.org/ebooks/2027

The Comic Premise Suspension of natural laws (together with the scissors effect of setting a ridiculous person in a normal world or a normal person in a ridiculous world) makes possible the development of a comic premise. A ***comic premise*** is an idea or concept that turns the accepted notion of things upside down. This idea becomes the basis of a play: it provides thematic and structural unity and serves as a springboard for comic dialogue, comic characters, and comic situations.

Comic premise Idea or concept in a comedy that turns the accepted notion of things upside down.

The Greek satiric dramatist Aristophanes was a master at developing a comic premise. In *The Clouds* (423 B.C.E.), Aristophanes pictures the philosopher Socrates as a man who can think only when perched in a basket suspended in midair. In *The Birds,* two ordinary men persuade a chorus of birds to build a city between heaven and earth. The birds comply, calling the place Cloudcuckoo Land, and the two men sprout wings to join them. In *Lysistrata,* Aristophanes has the women of Greece go on a sex strike; they will not make love to their husbands until the husbands stop fighting a prolonged war and sign a peace treaty with their opponents.

The comic premise—along with the suspension of natural laws—leads to exaggeration and incongruity in several areas of comedy: verbal humor, characterization, and comic situations. These will be explored in detail when we discuss individual comedies in Part 4.

READ *The Birds* and *Lysistrata*
http://classics.mit.edu/Aristophanes/birds.html and
http://www.gutenberg.org/ebooks/7700

FORMS OF COMEDY

Depending on the dramatist's intent and comic techniques, comedy takes various forms, including farce, burlesque, satire, domestic comedy, comedy of manners, and comedy of ideas.

Farce *Farce* thrives on all forms of exaggeration—broad physical humor, plot complications, stereotyped characters. It has no intellectual pretensions but aims simply at entertainment and laughter. One hallmark of farce is excessive plot complications, and

Farce Dramatic genre usually regarded as a subclass of comedy, with emphasis on plot complications and with few or no intellectual pretensions.

THE FUN OF FARCE
In farce everything is in fun, and events do not have the serious consequences they do in real life. Exaggeration—in language, in characters, in plot developments—is one of the main ingredients of farce. Shown here is a scene from a modern farce, *Noises Off*, by Michael Frayn, directed by Malcolm Morrison for the Hartford Stage Company. The actors are Michael Bakkensen and Liv Rooth. *Noises Off* is a backstage farce. Onstage a play is being presented called *Nothing On*, and the play details the mishaps occurring offstage during rehearsals and performances. (© T. Charles Erickson)

its humor usually results from ridiculous situations as well as pratfalls and horseplay. It relies less on verbal wit than the more intellectual forms of comedy do, though puns are used frequently in farce.

In modern times, the Marx brothers' films of the 1930s are examples of farce, as are many of the films starring Jim Carrey (1962–), Vince Vaughn (1970–), Steve Carell (1962–), and Adam Sandler (1966–). Mistaken identity, chase scenes, mock violence, rapid movement, and accelerating pace—as in a slapstick scene in a hotel room or a restaurant—are typical of farce. In bedroom farce, marriage and sex

are objects of fun; in other types of farce, medicine, law, and business can serve as the butt of jokes.

Burlesque   *Burlesque* also relies on knockabout physical humor, gross exaggerations, and occasional vulgarity. Historically, burlesque was a form of parody, a ludicrous imitation of other forms of drama or of individual plays. *Dance Flick* (2009), *MacGuber* (2010), and *Vampires Suck* (2010) are contemporary examples. In the United States, the term *burlesque* came to describe a type of variety show featuring low comedy skits and attractive women.

Burlesque Formerly parody; later a serious form of satire.

Satire   *Satire* uses wit—especially sophisticated language—irony, and exaggeration to expose or attack evil and foolishness. Satire can attack one specific figure, or it can be more inclusive, as in Molière's *Tartuffe,* which ridicules religious hypocrisy generally.

Satire Dramatic form using techniques of comedy—such as wit, irony, and exaggeration—to attack and expose folly and vice.

Domestic Comedy   *Domestic comedy* usually deals with family situations and is found most frequently today in television situation comedies—sitcoms—that feature members of a family or neighborhood friends caught up in a series of complicated but amusing situations. Television shows like *Everybody Loves Raymond, Will & Grace, Two and a Half Men,* and *Desperate Housewives* are good examples.

Comedy of Manners   Concerned with pointing up the foibles and peculiarities of the upper class, *comedy of manners* uses verbal wit to depict the charm of its characters and expose their social pretensions. Rather than relying on horseplay, it stresses witty phrases and clever barbs. In England, a line of comedies of manners runs from William Wycherley, William Congreve, and Oliver Goldsmith in the seventeenth and

Comedy of manners Form of comic drama that became popular in seventeenth-century France and the English Restoration, emphasizing a cultivated or sophisticated atmosphere and witty dialogue.

HEROIC DRAMA
Though having many of the characteristics of tragedy, heroic drama usually differs in having a happy ending, or an ending in which the dead hero or heroine is exalted in some way. A drama by George Bernard Shaw in this category is *Saint Joan*. The title character dies at the end but is seen as triumphant. Shown here in the title role is Anne-Marie Duff in a production at the National Theatre, London. (© Kevin Cummins)

eighteenth centuries to Oscar Wilde (1854–1900) in the nineteenth century and Noël Coward (1899–1973) in the twentieth.

Comedy of Ideas   Many plays of the British writer George Bernard Shaw could be put under a special heading: *comedy of ideas.* In plays like *Arms and the Man* (1894), Shaw used comic techniques to debate intellectual propositions such as the nature of war, cowardice, and romance.

Clearly, comedy comes in many forms, from the most basic type, designed only to provide a laugh, to the more intellectual type, designed to make us think while we are being entertained. In between are many combinations of these two types. Underlying them all, though, is an emphasis on humor.

HEROIC DRAMA

Heroic drama Serious but basically optimistic drama, written in verse or elevated prose, with noble or heroic characters in extreme situations or unusual adventures.

We have begun with the two fundamental genres: tragedy and comedy. However, other genres have also been important in theatre history, including heroic drama, melodrama, domestic drama, and tragicomedy.

The term ***heroic drama*** refers to serious drama that has heroic or noble characters and certain other traits of classic tragedy—such as dialogue in verse, elevated language, or extreme situations—but differs from tragedy in important respects. One way is in having a happy ending; another is in assuming a basically optimistic worldview, even when the ending is sad.

If heroic drama has a happy ending, the chief characters go through many trials and tribulations but finally emerge victorious. We agonize with the hero or heroine, but we are aware all the time that the play will end well. Several Greek plays that are ordinarily classified as tragedies are actually closer to what we are calling heroic drama. In the late seventeenth century in England, a form of drama called heroic drama or *heroic tragedy* was precisely the type of which we are speaking—a serious play with a happy ending for the hero or heroine. Although many Asian dramas—from India, China, and Japan—resist the usual classifications and involve much dance and music, they often bear a close resemblance to heroic drama. Frequently, for example, a hero goes through a series of dangerous adventures, emerging victorious at the end. The vast majority of Asian dramas end happily.

A second form of heroic drama involves the death of the hero or heroine, but neither the events along the way nor the conclusion can be thought of as tragic. *Cyrano de Bergerac,* written in 1897 by Edmond Rostand, is a good example. The title character, Cyrano, dies at the end, but only after his love for Roxanne, hidden for fifteen years, has been revealed. He dies a happy man, declaring his opposition to oppression and secure in the knowledge that he did not love in vain. *Saint Joan* (1923), by George Bernard Shaw, is another example: Joan is burned at the stake, but her death is actually a form of triumph; moreover, Shaw provides an epilogue in which Joan reappears after her death.

In the history of theatre, heroic drama occupies a large and important niche, cutting across Asian and Western civilization, and across periods from the Greek Golden Age to the present.

MELODRAMA

The term **melodrama** means "song drama" or "music drama." Though it originally comes from the Greek, it usually refers to a theatrical form made popular by the French at the end of the eighteenth century and the beginning of the nineteenth. "Music" here refers to the background music that accompanied these plays, similar to the music played along with silent films and to background music in sound films.

In early melodrama, a premium was put on surface effects, especially those creating suspense, fear, nostalgia, and other strong emotions in the audience. The heroes and heroines of melodrama were clearly delineated and stood in sharp contrast to the villains; the audience sympathized with the good characters and despised the bad ones. Melodrama had easily recognizable stock characters: the threatened young woman, the sidekick (a comic foil to the hero), and the calculating villain. The highly moral tone of traditional melodrama meant that the conflict between good and evil was clearly and firmly established, and virtue was always victorious. In order to keep the audience's interest, melodrama—both past and present—has a suspenseful plot, with a climax at the end of each act. Today, melodramas on television, such as adventure stories, detective stories, and cop shows, have a climax—a car crash, a sudden confrontation, a discovery of important evidence—just before each commercial break.

Melodrama Dramatic form made popular in the nineteenth century that emphasized action and spectacular effects and also used music; it had stock characters and clearly defined villains and heroes.

DOMESTIC DRAMA
Domestic or bourgeois drama concerns itself with family problems: parents and children, husbands and wives, growing up, growing old. Usually set in a family or domestic situation involving recognizable people, it has been a mainstay of modern drama. Shown here is a scene from *The Member of the Wedding* by Carson McCullers, about an awkward young girl growing up, and the maid who helps her. The production here, at the Westport Country Playhouse, featured Liz Morton (Frankie Addams), LaTanya Richardson Jackson (Bernice Sadie Brown), and Jack Metzger (John Henry West). (© Michal Daniel)

Most types of nineteenth-century melodrama have modern equivalents. Domestic melodrama has a counterpart in television soap opera. Frontier melodrama has become the western. Crime melodrama is now the popular mystery or detective show. Nautical melodrama, which dealt with sailors and pirates, was the forerunner of the swashbuckler or underwater film. Equestrian melodrama, which featured horses performing spectacular tricks, was the ancestor of various television and film melodramas starring animals.

DOMESTIC DRAMA

In the eighteenth and nineteenth centuries, there was a marked rise in the importance of ordinary men and women. With the Industrial Revolution and the expansion of trade, the merchant class came very much to the forefront and began to replace kings, queens, and the nobility—dukes and duchesses, earls and countesses—as both social and political leaders. With the emergence of this new class of ordinary citizens, there was a call for drama dealing not with royal families but with people from everyday life. As a result, drama began to change.

In England in 1731, George Lillo (1691–1739) wrote *The London Merchant,* about a merchant's apprentice who is led astray by a prostitute and betrays his good-hearted employer. This play, like others that came after it, overstated the case for simple working-class virtues; but it dealt with recognizable people from the daily life of Britain, and audiences welcomed it.

From these beginnings, ***domestic*** or ***bourgeois drama*** developed throughout the balance of the eighteenth century and the whole of the nineteenth, until it achieved a place of prominence in the works of Ibsen, Strindberg, and later writers such as Arthur Miller, Tennessee Williams, Lorraine Hansberry, and August Wilson. Problems of society, struggles within a family, dashed hopes, and renewed determination are characteristic of domestic drama. *Domestic* means "related to the household or the family," and most of the plays in this category deal with people from everyday life—usually the members of a family—in their own homes.

In the last 150 years, domestic drama has replaced both classical tragedy, as written by the Greeks and the Elizabethans, and heroic drama as the predominant type of serious drama. Domestic drama that is serious but has a happy ending has replaced heroic drama; and domestic drama with an unhappy ending that is sufficiently penetrating or profound has become a modern form of tragedy.

Domestic or bourgeois drama Drama dealing with problems—particularly family problems—of middle- and lower-class characters. There are serious and comic domestic dramas.

TRAGICOMEDY

Drama has often combined serious and comic material in the same play, and at times in the past there have been dramas classified as tragicomedies. It was in the twentieth century, however, that the genre of tragicomedy came to the forefront. What exactly is ***tragicomedy?***

Traditionally, comedy has been set in opposition to tragedy or serious drama: serious drama is sad, comedy is funny; serious drama makes people cry, comedy makes them laugh; serious drama arouses anger, comedy brings a smile. The two, however, are not always as clearly separated as this polarity suggests. For instance, a great deal of serious drama has comic elements. Shakespeare included comic characters in several of his serious plays: the drunken porter in *Macbeth,* the gravedigger in *Hamlet,* and Falstaff in *Henry IV, Part 1* are examples. One of the best-known of all medieval plays, *The Second Shepherds' Play,* concerns the visit of the shepherds to the manger of the newborn Christ child. While they are spending the night in a field, Mak, a comic character, steals a sheep and takes it to his house; he and his wife put it into a crib, pretending that it is their baby (a parody of Christ in the manger). When the shepherds discover what Mak has done, they toss him in a blanket, and after this horseplay the serious part of the story resumes.

Such alternation of serious and comic elements is a practice of long standing, but *tragicomedy* does not refer to plays that simply shift from serious to comic and back again. In tragicomedy, the point of view is itself mixed; the overall or prevailing attitude is a *synthesis,* or fusion, of the serious and the comic. One eye looks through a

Tragicomedy During the Renaissance, a play having tragic themes and noble characters but a happy ending; today, a play in which serious and comic elements are integrated.

MODERN TRAGICOMEDY

A form of drama that came very much to the forefront during the twentieth century is tragicomedy in which serious and humorous elements are intermingled and fused. This genre reflects the confusing and complex nature of today's world. A good example of tragicomedy—and one of the first in modern drama—is *The Cherry Orchard* by Anton Chekhov. The production shown here was directed by Curt Columbus at Trinity Repertory Company. (© T. Charles Erickson)

comic lens and the other through a serious lens; and the two points of view are so intermingled as to become one—like a food that tastes sweet and sour at the same time.

SHAKESPEAREAN TRAGICOMEDY

In addition to his basically serious plays and his basically comic plays, Shakespeare wrote others, such as *Measure for Measure* (1604) and *All's Well That Ends Well* (1602), which seem to be a combination of tragedy and comedy. Because they do not fit neatly into one category or the other, these plays have been dubbed *problem plays.* The "problem," however, arises largely because of a difficulty in accepting the tragicomic point of view, for these plays have many attributes of a fusion of tragic and comic. In *Measure for Measure,* for instance, Angelo—a puritanical, austere man—condemns young Claudio to death for having made his fiancée pregnant. When Claudio's sister, Isabella, comes to plead for her brother, Angelo is overcome by passion and tries to make

Isabella his mistress. Angelo's sentencing of Claudio is serious, but the bitter irony that arises when Angelo himself is guilty of even worse "sins of the flesh" is comic. The result is a situation that is simultaneously tragic and comic.

MODERN TRAGICOMEDY

In the modern period—during the last 100 years or so—tragicomedy has become a predominant form. A statement made by the Danish philosopher Søren Kierkegaard (1813–1855) as early as 1842 can serve to set the tone for the tragicomic attitude: "Existence itself, the act of existence, is a striving and is both pathetic and comic in the same degree."

The plays of Anton Chekhov, written at the end of the nineteenth century, reflect this spirit. Chekhov called two of his major plays comedies; but Stanislavski, who directed them, called them tragedies—a confusion arising from Chekhov's mixture of the serious and the comic. One illustration of Chekhov's approach is found in a scene at the end of the third act of his play *Uncle Vanya,* first produced in 1899. Vanya and his niece, Sonya, have worked and sacrificed for years to keep an estate going in order to support her father, a professor. At the worst possible moment, just when Vanya and Sonya have both been rebuffed by people they love, the professor announces that he wants to sell the estate, leaving Vanya and Sonya with nothing. A few moments later Vanya comes in to shoot the professor. He waves his gun in the air like a madman and shoots twice, but he misses both times and then collapses on the floor. In this scene, Vanya and Sonya are condemned to a lifetime of drudgery and despair—a grim fate—but Vanya's behavior with the gun (it is doubtful that he honestly means to kill the professor) is wildly comic.

After World War II, a new type of drama emerged called **theatre of the absurd,** and many absurdist plays can be considered tragicomedy. They probe deeply into human problems and cast a dark eye on the world; yet they are also imbued with a comic spirit—among other traditional manifestations of humor, they include juggling, acrobatics, clowning, and verbal nonsense. Three important absurdist playwrights are Eugène Ionesco, Samuel Beckett, and Harold Pinter. (Beckett's play *Waiting for Godot* will be discussed in detail in Chapter 15.) Pinter called his plays *comedies of menace,* suggesting their juxtaposition of the serious and the comic. His characters are often pursued and persecuted by unknown people and forces, but the action also has a comic component.

Theatre of the absurd Plays expressing the dramatist's sense of the absurdity and futility of existence.

READ *Uncle Vanya*

http://www.ibiblio.org/eldritch/ac/vanya.htm

In tragicomedy, a smile is frequently cynical, a chuckle may be tinged with a threat, and a laugh is sometimes bitter. In the past, the attitude that produced such combinations was the exception rather than the rule, but in our day it seems far more prevalent—and relevant. As a result, tragicomedy has taken its place as a major genre alongside more traditional approaches.

In this chapter we have examined the point of view—tragic, comic, tragicomic—that informs the theatre experience. In Part 3 we turn to theatre production.

Summary

An essential element of theatre is a dramatic text or script created by a playwright, or by someone else functioning as a playwright.

An important aspect of a dramatic text is the point of view, which determines *genre*—a French term for "type" or "category." The two oldest and best-known theatrical genres are tragedy and comedy.

Particular societies as well as individual playwrights are often predisposed to a tragic point of view. For example, two historical periods conducive to tragedy were the fifth century B.C.E. in Greece and the period from the late sixteenth century to the early seventeenth century in the European Renaissance.

Comedy may take a variety of forms, including farce, burlesque, satire, domestic comedy, comedy of manners, and comedy of ideas.

Although tragedy and comedy are the two fundamental genres, there are other important genres, including heroic drama, melodrama, domestic or bourgeois drama, and tragicomedy.

Thinking about Theatre

▶ Which kind of play do you prefer: a classic tragedy, a serious contemporary drama, a knockabout farce, a comedy, a musical? Can you explain why you prefer one type over the others? Perhaps you enjoy several types of theatre.

▶ Do you favor a play with a strong storyline, a tight plot, and unexpected twists and turns, or do you prefer a looser play that reflects the randomness of everyday life? What do you think attracts you to the characteristics you prefer?

▶ A play by Henrik Ibsen, Anton Chekhov, Tennessee Williams, Lorraine Hansberry, or August Wilson might be set in a time period of 50 or 100 years ago. What do you think it is about these dramas that allows an audience member in the twenty-first century to identify strongly with the characters and the situations in the play? (Read, for example, *A Doll's House* or *Uncle Vanya* at the URLs provided.)

(NOTE: Plays by Henrik Ibsen, Anton Chekhov, Tennessee Williams, and August Wilson are also available in *Anthology of Living Theatre,* Third Edition, by Edwin Wilson and Alvin Goldfarb.)

KEY TERMS

Burlesque Formerly parody; later a serious form of satire.

Comedy In general, a play that is light in tone, is concerned with issues that are not serious, has a happy ending, and is designed to amuse.

Comedy of manners Form of comic drama that became popular in seventeenth-century France and the English Restoration, emphasizing a cultivated or sophisticated atmosphere and witty dialogue.

Comic premise Idea or concept in a comedy that turns the accepted notion of things upside down.

Domestic or bourgeois drama Drama dealing with problems—particularly family problems—of middle- and lower-class characters. There are serious and comic domestic dramas.

Farce Dramatic genre usually regarded as a subclass of comedy, with emphasis on plot complications and with few or no intellectual pretensions.

Genre Category or type of play.

Heroic drama Serious but basically optimistic drama, written in verse or elevated prose, with noble or heroic characters in extreme situations or unusual adventures.

Melodrama Dramatic form made popular in the nineteenth century that emphasized action and spectacular effects and also used music; it had stock characters and clearly defined villains and heroes.

Satire Dramatic form using techniques of comedy—such as wit, irony, and exaggeration—to attack and expose folly and vice.

Slapstick Type of comedy or comic business that relies on ridiculous physical activity—often violent in nature—for its humor.

Theatre of the absurd Plays expressing the dramatist's sense of the absurdity and futility of existence.

Tragedy Dramatic form involving serious actions of universal significance and with important moral and philosophical implications, usually with an unhappy ending.

Tragicomedy During the Renaissance, a play having tragic themes and noble characters but a happy ending; today, a play in which serious and comic elements are integrated.

 THEATRE ON THE WEB

For more research and to learn more about the topics in this chapter, please visit the Online Learning Center at **www.mhhe.com/livelyart8e**.

PART 3

CREATING THEATRE THE PRODUCTION

5 ACTING FOR THE STAGE
6 THE DIRECTOR AND THE PRODUCER
7 THEATRE SPACES
8 THE DESIGNERS: SCENERY AND COSTUMES
9 THE DESIGNERS: LIGHTING AND SOUND

THE THEATRE PRODUCTION

A theatre production is most often created when a director takes a text—either a new play or one from the past—and works with actors and designers to develop a stage piece. The production shown here, *John Gabriel Borkman* by Henrik Ibsen, directed by James Macdonald at Dublin's Abbey Theatre, was also staged at BAM in New York. The actors are Cathy Belton, Joan Sheehy, Fiona Shaw, and Lindsay Duncan; the set was designed by Tom Pye, lighting by Jean Kalman, costumes by Jan Bergin, and sound by Ian Dickinson. The director decides what the "tone" will be (comic or serious), how characters will interact, their positions and movements on stage, and many other aspects that will make up the final look and "feel" of the production. (© Ros Kavanagh)

ACTING FOR THE STAGE

THREE CHALLENGES OF ACTING

MAKING CHARACTERS BELIEVABLE

MAKING CONNECTIONS: Acting

WIDER PERSPECTIVE: A Historical Perspective:
The Demands of Classical Acting

PHYSICAL ACTING: VOICE AND BODY

GLOBAL CROSSCURRENTS: Puppetry around the World

SYNTHESIS AND INTEGRATION

JUDGING PERFORMANCES

SUMMARY
THINKING ABOUT THEATRE
KEY TERMS
THEATRE ON THE WEB

◀ **STAGE ACTING** Acting is a demanding profession, requiring extensive training in vocal work, physical movement, character development, and many other skills. Along with the craft are certain indefinable qualities, such as being able to connect with the audience and project the personality and complexity of the character being portrayed. Seen here is Mark Rylance as Valere, an outrageous character, in the London production of *La Bete,* a play by David Hirson, set in seventeenth-century France, directed by Matthew Warchus. (© Geraint Lewis)

Two indispensable elements in a theatrical event are the audience and the performers. Having looked at the audience in Chapter 2, we turn in this chapter to the other part of the actor-audience relationship—the performers. Acting is almost as old as the human race. From the earliest days of civilization, people have mimicked other people and have told stories, imitating the voices and gestures of the characters in those stories. There have also been rituals and ceremonies in which the celebrants wore costumes and performed assigned roles—one example is a priest in a church service.

Today, in schools, on street corners, and at parties we often see people performing or imitating others in some way. When telling a story, a person often adopts the voices and attitudes of the characters; some people seem to be particularly adept at doing this and are referred to as "natural" actors or actresses. The desire to imitate others, or to take on the personality of an imaginary character, seems irresistible; and the pleasure we take in watching others do this is universal. In this process of enactment and impersonation is the origin of stage acting. A closely connected type of "acting" in daily life is role-playing. The current term *role model* refers to a person whose life, or "role," serves as a model or guide for others to emulate or imitate.

In theatre, this practice of imitation becomes conscious and deliberate. *Acting* can be defined as assuming a role onstage; to put it another way, acting is impersonating a character in a dramatic presentation before an audience. Actors and actresses develop their craft and then carefully rehearse a play in order to bring the text to life. In the process, they speak words and perform actions that give flesh and blood to the characters on the page.

THREE CHALLENGES OF ACTING

Throughout theatre history it can be said that three main challenges have faced an actor or actress:

1. To make characters believable
2. Physical acting—the use of the voice and body
3. Synthesis and integration: combining inner and outer skills

To understand the first two aspects of acting, we will examine them separately. We begin with making characters believable and then turn to the craft of acting—specific physical and vocal techniques required in performance.

MAKING CHARACTERS BELIEVABLE

Along with developing the craft of acting, a performer's second major task is credibility. If the audience is to believe in the characters that appear onstage, performers must be convincing.

The Development of Realistic Acting From the mid-seventeenth century on, serious attempts were made to define the craft or technique of credible, natural acting. Such an approach became more important than ever at the end of the nineteenth century, when drama began to depict characters and situations close to everyday life. Three playwrights—Henrik Ibsen of Norway, August Strindberg of Sweden, and Anton

PORTRAYING A BELIEVABLE CHARACTER
Since the advent of realistic theatre, at the end of the nineteenth century, a primary challenge for performers is making the characters they portray convincing and credible. Many techniques and exercises have been developed for this, but it also calls for total sincerity on the part of the performer. Shown here are Robin McLeavy as Stella Kowalski and Cate Blanchett as Blanche Dubois, one securely married, the other in desperate straights, in the Sydney Theatre Company's *A Streetcar Named Desire* by Tennessee Williams, directed by Liv Ullmann, at BAM. (© Richard Termine)

Chekhov of Russia—perfected a type of drama that came to be known as *realism.* This drama was called realistic because it closely resembled what people could identify with and verify from their own experience. In performing plays by these dramatists, not only the spirit of the individual dramatic characters but also the details of their behavior had to conform to what people saw of life around them.

Realism Broadly, an attempt to present onstage people and events corresponding to those in everyday life.

The Stanislavski System: A Technique for Realistic Acting   Before the realistic drama of the late 1800s, individual actresses and actors, through their own talent and genius, had achieved believability onstage, but no one had developed a system whereby it could be taught to others and passed on to future generations. The person who eventually did this most successfully was the Russian actor and director Konstantin Stanislavski.

A cofounder of the Moscow Art Theater in Russia and the director of Anton Chekhov's most important plays, Stanislavski was also an actor. By closely observing the work of great performers of his day, and by drawing on his own acting experience, Stanislavski identified and described what these gifted performers did naturally and intuitively. From his observations he compiled and then codified a series of principles and techniques.

We might assume that believable acting is simply a matter of being natural; but Stanislavski discovered first of all that acting realistically onstage is extremely artificial and difficult. He wrote:

> All of our acts, even the simplest, which are so familiar to us in everyday life, become strained when we appear behind the footlights before a public of a thousand people. That is why it is necessary to correct ourselves and learn again how to walk, sit, or lie down. It is essential to reeducate ourselves to look and see, on the stage, to listen and to hear.[1]

To achieve this "reeducation," Stanislavski said, "the actor must first of all believe in everything that takes place onstage, and most of all, he must believe what he himself is doing. And one can only believe in the truth." To give substance to his ideas, Stanislavski developed a series of exercises and techniques for the performer, among them the following.

Relaxation. When he observed the great actors and actresses of his day, Stanislavski noticed how fluid and lifelike their movements were. They seemed to be in a state of complete freedom and relaxation, letting the behavior of the character come through effortlessly. He concluded that unwanted tension has to be eliminated and that the performer must at all times attain a state of physical and vocal relaxation.

Concentration and observation. Stanislavski also discovered that gifted performers always appeared fully concentrated on some object, person, or event while onstage. Stanislavski referred to the extent or range of concentration as a *circle of attention.* This circle of attention can be compared to a circle of light on a darkened stage. The performer should begin with the idea that it is a small, tight circle including only himself or herself and perhaps one other person or one piece of furniture. When the performer has established a strong circle of attention, he or she can enlarge the circle outward to include the entire stage area. In this way performers will stop worrying about the audience and lose their self-consciousness.

Importance of specifics. One of Stanislavski's techniques was an emphasis on concrete details. A performer should never try to act in general, he said, and should never try to convey a feeling such as fear or love in some vague, amorphous way. In life, Stanislavski said, we express emotions in terms of specifics: an anxious woman twists a handkerchief, an angry boy throws a rock at a trash can, a nervous businessman jangles his keys. Performers must find similar concrete activities. Stanislavski points out how Shakespeare has Lady Macbeth in her sleepwalking scene—at the height of her guilt and emotional upheaval—try to rub blood off her hands.

The performer must also conceive of the situation in which a character exists—what Stanislavski referred to as the *given circumstances*—in terms of specifics. In what kind of space does an event take place: formal, informal, public, domestic? How does it feel? What is the temperature? The lighting? What has gone on just before? What is expected in the moments ahead? Again, these questions must be answered in concrete terms.

Inner truth. An innovative aspect of Stanislavski's work has to do with inner truth, which deals with the internal or subjective world of characters—that is, their thoughts and emotions. The early phases of Stanislavski's research took place while he was also

---

[1]Constantin Stanislavski, *An Actor Prepares,* Theater Arts, New York, 1948, p. 73.

THE IMPORTANCE OF SPECIFICS
One of the techniques for acting emphasized by Stanislavski is concentrating on specific actions and details. An example, in a performance of Shakespeare's *Macbeth*, is having Lady Macbeth attempt to rub the blood off her hands. Seen here are Kate Fleetwood and Patrick Stewart as Lady Macbeth and Macbeth, in a production of the play at the Brooklyn Academy of Music. (Ruth Fremson/The New York Times/Redux)

directing the major dramas of Anton Chekhov. Plays like *The Sea Gull* and *The Cherry Orchard* have less to do with external action or what the characters say than with what the characters are feeling and thinking but often do not verbalize. It becomes apparent that Stanislavski's approach would be very beneficial in realizing the inner life of such characters.

Stanislavski had several ideas about how to achieve a sense of inner truth, one being the ***magic if.*** *If* is a word that can transform our thoughts; through it we can imagine ourselves in virtually any situation. "*If* I suddenly became wealthy . . ." "*If* I were vacationing on a Caribbean island . . ." "*If* I had great talent . . ." "*If* that person who insulted me comes near me again . . ." The word *if* becomes a powerful lever for the mind; it can lift us out of ourselves and give us a sense of absolute certainty about imaginary circumstances.

Action onstage: What? Why? How? Another important principle of Stanislavski's system is that all action onstage must have a purpose. This means that the performer's attention must always be focused on a series of physical actions (also called *psychophysical actions*), linked together by the circumstances of the play. Stanislavski determined these actions by asking three essential questions: What? Why? How? An action is performed,

Magic if Stanislavski's acting exercise that requires the performer to ask, "How would I react if I were in this character's position?"

ENSEMBLE PLAYING
Experienced performers are aware of the importance of playing together: listening carefully to one another, sensing each other's actions and moods, and responding alertly. Ensemble playing is especially important in plays where interaction between characters is crucial. In the scene here, we see a number of characters from Chekhov's *The Cherry Orchard* in a production directed by Bonnie J. Monte at The Shakespeare Theatre of New Jersey. (© Gerry Goodstein)

such as opening a letter (the *what*). The letter is opened because someone has said that it contains extremely damaging information about the character (the *why*). The letter is opened anxiously, fearfully (the *how*), because of the calamitous effect it might have on the character.

Through line of a role. According to Stanislavski, in order to develop continuity in a part, the actor or actress should find the *superobjective* of a character. What is it, above all else, that the character wants during the course of the play? What is the character's driving force? If a goal can be established toward which the character strives, it will give the performer an overall objective. From this objective can be developed a *through line* that can be grasped, as a skier on a ski lift grabs a towline and is carried to the top. Another term for through line is *spine*.

To help develop the through line, Stanislavski urged performers to divide scenes into units (sometimes called *beats*). In each unit there is an objective, and the intermediate objectives running through a play lead ultimately to the overall objective.

Ensemble playing. Except in one-person shows, performers do not act alone; they interact with other people. Stanislavski was aware that many performers tend to "stop acting," or lose their concentration, when they are not the main characters in a scene or when someone else is talking. This tendency destroys the through line and causes the performer to move into and out of a role. That, in turn, weakens ***ensemble playing***—the playing together of all the performers.

Ensemble playing Acting that stresses the total artistic unity of a group performance rather than individual performances.

Stanislavski and Psychophysical Action

Stanislavski began to develop his technique in the early twentieth century, and at first he emphasized the inner aspects of training: for example, various ways of getting in touch with the performer's unconscious. Beginning around 1917, however, he began to look more and more at purposeful action, or what he called *psychophysical action.* A student at one of his lectures that year took note of the change: "Whereas action previously had been taught as the expression of a previously-established 'emotional state,' it is now action itself which predominates and is the key to the psychological."[2] Rather than seeing emotions as leading to action, Stanislavski came to believe that it was the other way around: purposeful action undertaken to fulfill a character's goals was the most direct route to the emotions.

Modern Approaches to Realistic Acting

In the second half of the twentieth century, there were three broad approaches to actors' training in the United States. Two of these derived from the methods of Stanislavski.

In the 1930s and 1940s a number of performers and directors in the United States became greatly interested in the ideas of Stanislavski. One of these, Lee Strasberg, a founder of the Actors Studio in New York City, focused on the inner aspects of Stanislavskian theory. Strasberg emphasized a technique called ***emotional recall,*** a tool intended to help performers achieve a sense of emotional truth onstage. By recalling sensory impressions of an experience in the past (such as what a room looked like, and the temperature and any prevalent odors in the room), emotions associated with that experience are aroused and can be used as the basis of feelings called for in a role in a play.

Emotional recall Stanislavski's exercise that helps the performer present realistic emotions. The performer feels a character's emotion by thinking of an event in his or her own life that led to a similar emotion.

Though the teachings of Strasberg and his followers were successful with certain performers, other acting teachers, such as Stella Adler (1902–1992), Sanford Meisner (1905–1997), and Uta Hagen (1919–2004), felt that Strasberg emphasized the inner aspects of acting to the exclusion of everything else. Following the lead of Stanislavski in his later approach with psychophysical action, they balanced the emphasis on inner resources with the inclusion of given circumstances and purposeful action.

Three examples of current approaches to training actors are represented by Uta Hagen, Robert Cohen (1938–), and Robert Benedetti (1939–). Hagen, in her book *Respect for Acting,* places a large emphasis on emotional recall and memory in general. She provides a number of exercises that enable the students to pull from past experiences in their own lives as a means of reaching the emotions required within the context of any given role. Hagen's idea is not to allow the student to become overwhelmed by past emotion, but to use it as a springboard into the action of the play.

In *Acting One* Cohen encourages students to use text as an instrument of action. In an exercise that he calls the "Content-less Scene," he has students memorize the same text. He then asks them to perform the scene but changes the given circumstances of

---

[2]Jean Beneditti, *Stanislavski,* Routledge, New York, 1988, p. 217.

MAKING CONNECTIONS

ACTING

Many performers have been successful in theatre as well as film and television. They include such well-known actresses and actors as Meryl Streep, Al Pacino, Glenn Close, Kevin Spacey, Sarah Jessica Parker, Matthew Broderick, and Calista Flockhart. An excellent example of an actress who has distinguished herself on the stage as well as in films and television is Phylicia Rashād. The recipient of numerous awards, Rashād has had many outstanding roles on television, perhaps the best-known being her running part as the wife of Bill Cosby's character Cliff Huxtable in *The Cosby Show.* Onstage, she has starred in *A Raisin in the Sun, Gem of the Ocean,* and *Cat on a Hot Tin Roof.*

Another good example of a stage performer who has also had a remarkable film and television career is Meryl Streep. Streep was trained at the Yale School of Drama and came to the attention of New York theatre audiences for her work at Joseph Papp's off-Broadway Public Theatre. Her film work includes memorable roles in *The Deer Hunter* (1978), *Kramer vs. Kramer* (1979), *Sophie's Choice* (1982), *Out of Africa* (1985), *Music of the Heart* (1999), *The Hours* (2002), *Adaptation* (2002), *The Devil Wears Prada* (2006), and *Mama Mia!* Streep has received 13 Oscar nominations for her film work

and in 1978 won an Emmy award for her performance in the television mini-series *Holocaust.* Her memorable stage performances include leading roles in *The Cherry Orchard, The Taming of the Shrew, The Seagull,* and *Mother Courage and Her Children.* In 2003, she appeared in the critically acclaimed HBO television adaptation of *Angels in America,* directed by Mike Nichols, who has also worked in theatre, film, and television.

The British actress Judi Dench has worked extensively in three mediums: stage, film, and television. As a stage performer she has been seen frequently in Shakespearean and other classic works in London, as well as in a number of contemporary plays, and she is the winner of seven Laurence Olivier Awards for her stage work. She won an Oscar for her role as Queen Elizabeth I in the film *Shakespeare in Love* and, among other things, has played the part of M in six James Bond films. In television, she starred with Geoffrey Palmer in the long-running television series *As Time Goes By.* These accomplishments, by the way, represent only a fraction of her total body of work in all three fields.

What are the similarities and differences between performing on a stage in front of an audience and acting before

Judi Dench as Mistress Quickly in a musical version of Shakespeare's *The Merry Wives of Windsor,* directed and adapted by Gregory Doran for a London Production. (© Geraint Lewis)

a camera for film or television? Among the similarities are the fact that in both fields the performer must create a character, usually someone unlike himself or herself. The performer in both cases must memorize lines, perfect

the scene each time. The outcome is the obvious realization that the words are not nearly as important as the meaning behind them. And, clearly, without solid given circumstances, actors are simply saying lines instead of using those lines to further the action of the play.

Finally, Benedetti in *The Actor at Work* focuses on the actor's body and how performers can use it to help shape character. Using a variety of movement exercises, Benedetti encourages students to explore elements of rhythm, time, weight, intensity,

Judi Dench as "M" in Ian Fleming's *Casino Royale*. (© MGM/Columbia Pictures Photographer: Jay Maidment/Photofest)

How a scene is edited can also influence how the audience perceives the performance. The film director Alfred Hitchcock (1899–1980) claimed that he, not his actors, created their performances.

In contrast to this, the performer onstage must go straight through the play from start to finish with no interruptions, except possibly an intermission. Stage actors must also develop the ability to project their voices throughout the theatre. The stage performers in a realistic play must be able, for example, to convince the audience that they are speaking quietly but yet project so that even those seated in the back row of the auditorium can hear. Also, the stage actor must be able to create a physical performance that can be seen by all the audience members; this requires that even the slightest gesture must be somewhat heightened.

In addition, performers onstage are playing before an audience, so that, in a sense, they are being tested every moment. Moreover, the audience throughout a performance is sending signals to the actors, some silent and some in the form of laughter or exclamations. The presence of the audience, therefore, is a constant challenge and reinforcement.

movements, develop the personality of the character, and interact with other performers. The research and preparation for these tasks are quite similar for stage, film, and television.

But there are significant differences. In movies and television, short scenes are filmed, often not in the sequence in which they will ultimately appear. Several scenes, for instance, might take place in a town square; one will come at the beginning, one at the end, and two in between. These scenes would all be filmed at one time. In this case, the mood and circumstances at the beginning and end would be different, but the performer would have to move from one to the other with little transition or preparation.

Also, in film or television, a scene may be shot over and over until the director is satisfied with the results. For that matter, the film director exerts great control over the film performance. How the director frames the actor or chooses the shot (for example, a close-up or long shot), determines how the audience views the performer.

and space through improvisational work. These exercises allow the students to start with the "outside" (physical) aspects of a character's definition. Once the physical form is found, they can then use it to define the character's inner life (emotion).

The important thing for students of acting is to explore different methods of and approaches to acting, such as those outlined above, and to decide which techniques and types of training—or which combination of these—work best for them. Ultimately each individual actor must develop his or her own methodology.

Before the twentieth century, the challenges facing performers were dictated by the very specific demands of the type of theatre in which performers appeared. Both classic Greek theatre and traditional Asian theatre stressed formal movement and stylized gestures similar to classical ballet. The chorus in Greek drama both sang and danced its odes, and Asian theatre has always had a significant component of singing and dancing. In addition, Greek performers wore masks and Asian performers often wore richly textured makeup.

In Western theatre, from the time of the Renaissance through the nineteenth century, actions onstage were not intended to replicate the movements or gestures of everyday life. For example, performers would often speak not to the character they were addressing but directly to the audience.

In England during the eighteenth and nineteenth centuries, acting alternated between exaggerated and more natural styles. Throughout this period, every generation or so an actor or actress would emerge who was praised for performing in a less grandiose, more down-to-earth way. But exaggerated or not, performance before the twentieth century was more formal and stylized than the acting we are accustomed to onstage, and especially in films and on television.

No one would expect an actress or actor today to perform a classical play in the manner in which it was originally presented; such a performance would seem ludicrous. Besides, we do not know exactly how classical acting looked or sounded. At the same time, it should be clear that any performer today who is appearing in a play from the past must develop a special set of skills and be able to respond successfully to a number of challenges.

As an example, let us consider an actor undertaking the role of Hamlet. He must convince the audience that he is experiencing numerous and often contradictory emotions: that he is aware of lies and treachery taking place around him; that he is saddened by the recent death of his father and the hasty marriage of his mother to his uncle; that he believes his uncle has murdered his father; that he wants to murder his uncle but cannot bring himself to do so; that he berates himself for not being more decisive; that he loves Ophelia but is repelled by the web of circumstances in which he is caught and of which she is an unwitting part.

For an actor, one aspect of conveying these emotions lies in developing the inner feelings that Hamlet has from moment to moment. How does it feel to have such conflicting emotions about your mother or about your duty? An actor playing Hamlet must answer such questions; he must understand in his own innermost depths what Hamlet's emotions are like and then communicate them to the audience.

At the same time, the actor must have a sense of the physical and vocal qualities that a man like Hamlet would have. How would Hamlet walk? How would he handle a sword? How would he greet a friend like Horatio? What movements and gestures would he use? How would he speak? What vocal range and speech patterns would he use?

Along with these personal characteristics, moreover, the actor playing Hamlet must be able to speak Shakespeare's lines distinctly and intelligently. This is particularly true of Hamlet's soliloquies—the speeches he delivers while alone onstage. Because much of the language of Shakespeare's plays is poetry, and because there are many extended phrases that must be spoken without interruption, the speeches call for tremendous breath control. To achieve beauty of sound, the performer must, in addition, have a resonant voice; and to achieve clarity, he must have an accurate understanding of the words.

In portraying Hamlet, an actor must also have athletic ability and control of his body. If the stage setting has ramps and platforms, he must be able to navigate them with ease; and since he must engage in a sword fight with

PHYSICAL ACTING: VOICE AND BODY

We have been looking at training that helps actors make stage characters truthful and believable. We turn now to another aspect of actor training: the instruments of the performer, specifically the voice and the body.

Physical elements have always been important in the art of acting. Traditional theatre makes strong demands on the performer's body. In Shakespeare, for instance,

Laertes in a scene near the end of the play, he must have mastered many of the techniques of fencing.

Similarly, an actress playing Ophelia must have a wide range of accomplishments. She must be able to portray the interior emotions of the character convincingly, speak clearly and intelligently, move with poise and authority, and interact with the other performers. In addition, the role calls for the actress to sing and to play a scene in which she must convince us that Ophelia has lost her sanity, although of course the actress herself is perfectly sane.

Along with the attributes we have been discussing, acting in the classics calls for special training in voice. In Western theatre before the modern period, from the fifth century B.C.E. in Greece to the middle of the nineteenth century, vocal demands on actors and actresses were even greater than they are today. The language of plays was most often poetry; and poetry—with its demanding rhythms, sustained phrases, and exacting meters—required intensive training in order for the performer to speak the lines intelligently and distinctly. There were problems of projection, too. A Greek amphitheatre was an acoustical marvel, but it seated as many as 15,000 spectators in the open air, and throwing the voice to every part of the theatre was no small task.

In Elizabethan England, Christopher Marlowe, a contemporary of Shakespeare, wrote superb blank verse that made severe demands on performers' vocal abilities. One example is found in Marlowe's *Doctor Faustus.* Here is a speech by Faustus to Helen of Troy, who has been called back from the dead to be with him:

> O' thou art fairer than the evening's air
> Clad in the beauty of a thousand stars;
> Brighter art thou than flaming Jupiter
> When he appear'd to hapless Semele;
> More lovely than the monarch of the sky
> In wanton Arethusa's azured arms;
> And none but thou shalt be my paramour!

John Douglas Thompson in the title role in Shakespeare's *Richard III*, directed by Jonathan Croy at Shakespeare & Company in Lenox, Massachusetts. (© Kevin Sprague/Studio Two)

These seven lines of verse are a single sentence and, spoken properly, will be delivered as one overall unit, with the meaning carried from one line to the next. How many of us could manage that? A fine classical actor can speak the entire passage as a whole, giving it the necessary resonance and inflection as well. Beyond that, he can stand onstage for two or three hours delivering such lines.

performers must frequently run up and down steps or ramps, confront other characters in sword fights, and enact prolonged death scenes. Anyone who has seen an impressive sword fight onstage senses how difficult it must be. A duel, in which the combatants strike quickly at one another—clashing swords continually without hitting each other—resembles a ballet in its precision and grace, and it entails a great deal of physical exertion. Adept physical movement is also required in modern realistic acting. For

example, an activity in a modern play analogous to a sword fight would be a headlong fall down a flight of stairs or two people engaged in a knife fight, like the one in Arthur Miller's *A View from the Bridge.*

As to the importance of voice training, because of microphones and sound amplifications, today we have increasingly lost our appreciation of the power of the human voice. But in the past, public speakers from Cicero to Abraham Lincoln stirred men and women with their oratory; and throughout its history, the stage has provided a natural platform for stirring speeches. Beginning with the Greeks and continuing through the Elizabethans, the French and Spanish theatres of the seventeenth century, and other European theatres at the close of the nineteenth century, playwrights wrote magnificent lines that performers, having honed their vocal skills to a fine point, delivered with zest. Any performer today who intends to act in a revival of a traditional play must learn to speak and project stage verse, which requires much the same kind of vocal power and breath control as opera.

In order to develop projection and balance it with credibility, a performer must train and rehearse extensively. For example, an actor or actress might use breathing exercises, controlling the breath from the diaphragm rather than the throat so that vocal reproduction will have power and can be sustained. Many of these exercises are similar to those used by singers. Also, head, neck, and shoulder exercises can be used to relax the muscles in those areas, thus freeing the throat for ease of projection. In the chart on p. 111, we see a group of elementary vocal and body exercises. It must be stressed that these are basic exercises that represent only the earliest beginnings of a true regimen of exercises for the voice and body.

The Actor's Instrument: Voice and Body Throughout the twentieth century, at the same time that many acting teachers were focusing on the inner life of the actor, another group of teachers and theoreticians were turning to a different aspect, they physical side of performing. This includes the freeing and development of the voice and body and combining these with improvisation to create maximum flexibility, relaxation, and imagination in the actor's instrument—his or her voice and body.

There were a number of key figures who contributed to this movement. For example, in the second and third decades of the twentieth century, the Russian director Vsevolod Meyerhold (1874–1942) developed a program called *biomechanics* that emphasized physical exercises and full control of the body, in the manner of circus performers such as acrobats and trapeze artists. In France in the 1920s, Jacques Copeau (1878–1949) incorporated such disciplines as mime, masks, Italian commedia dell'arte, and Asian acting into his system of training. Beginning in mid-century and continuing for the next fifty years, a Frenchman, Jacques Lecoq (1921–1999), ran an influential school in Paris dedicated to explaining and exploring the physical side of performance. In addition to emphasizing the elements on which Copeau concentrated, Lecoq also incorporated a clown figure in his work.

Along with European influences, there has also been a strong global presence in the new approaches to actor training. A good example is Asian theatre. Stylization and symbolism characterize the acting of the classical theatres of India, China, and Japan. To achieve the absolute control, the concentration, and the mastery of the body and nerves necessary to carry out the stylized movements, performers in the various classical Asian theatres train for years under the supervision of master teachers. Every movement of these performers is prescribed and carefully controlled, combining elements of formal ballet, pantomime, and sign language. Each gesture tells a story and means something quite specific—contributing to a true symbolism of physical movement.

VOICE PROJECTION

Among the skills that actors and actresses must develop is using the voice to project it to the far reaches of an auditorium, to modulate it, to articulate poetry properly, and in some cases to master accents. Shown here is actor Jude Law playing the title character in *Doctor Faustus* at the Young Vic Theatre in London. Marlowe's play makes both physical and vocal demands on the performer, with extended, intricate poetry that must be spoken clearly and forcefully. (© Donald Cooper/*Photostage*, England)

One Asian discipline, not from theatre but from martial arts, which modern acting teachers have found helpful is tai chi chuan, commonly called *tai chi*. Unlike some martial arts, tai chi is not aggressive: it is a graceful, gentle exercise regimen performed widely by men, women, and children in China. It has spread to other countries, where it is sometimes practiced in conjunction with meditation or body awareness. The movements of tai chi are stylized and often seem to be carried out in slow motion. Among other things, tai chi requires concentration and control, both valuable qualities for a performer.

The Japanese director, Tadashi Suzuki (1939–   ), developed a training technique, again taken from ancient Japanese practices, emphasizing the connection between the feet and the ground underneath. Consciousness of this connection is accomplished by exercises involving "stomping."

An approach to training that originated in the United States and has gained acceptance and wider use in our contemporary theatre is known as *viewpoints theory*. Based

on ideas from the avant-garde choreographer Merce Cunningham (1919–2009) and the experimental director Jerzy Grotowski (1933–1999), it combines elements of dance and stage movement with concepts of time and space. Viewpoints theory initially had six components: space, time, shape, movement, story, and emotion. The director Anne Bogart (1951–   ), one of its chief proponents, feels that it provides a new vocabulary for certain elements that have always been significant in performance and directing: spatial relationships onstage, movement, and the notion of time, among others.

In the United States in the twenty-first century the emphasis on physical movement—training in the use of the voice and the body—has become more pronounced and widespread than ever. In the words of author David Bridel in an article in *American Theatre* magazine:

> Body awareness and alignment, mask work, clowning and circus skills, physical characterization, spatial relationships, ensemble work, improvisation, games, mime . . . so many forms of movement training exist today, and so many specialists work in these related fields, that the opportunity to connect the craft of acting with the movement of the body has never been richer.

Today, no one approach, no one master, no one technique appears to have become universally recognized as the single authority in the field. Rather, teachers, coaches, and directors draw on a wide variety of sources, including those mentioned above as well as others, to develop their individual approaches to training the voice and body. The field also goes by various names: body movement, physical theatre, and a term favored by many, physical acting.

Centering   As a way of integrating and unifying various approaches to body and voice training, many acting teachers emphasize a process called *centering*. This is a way of pulling everything together and allowing the performer to eliminate any blocks that impede either the body or the voice. Centering involves locating the place—roughly in the middle of the torso—where all the lines of force in the body come together. When performers are able to "center" themselves, they achieve a balance, a freedom, and a flexibility they could rarely find otherwise.

All this should make it clear that to master the many techniques required to play a variety of roles and to be at ease onstage—moving and speaking with authority, pur-

WARM-UP EXERCISES FOR BODY AND VOICE

To give an indication of the types of exercises performers must undertake during their years of training—and during their careers as professionals—it is interesting to look at some samples of warm-up exercises. The exercises here are designed to relax the body and the voice.

The following are typical warm-up exercises for body movement:

1. Lie on your back; beginning with the feet, tense and relax each part of the body—knees, thighs, abdomen, chest, neck—moving up to the face. Note the difference in the relaxation of various muscles and of the body generally after the exercise is completed.

2. Stand with feet parallel, approximately as far apart as the width of the shoulders. Lift one foot off the ground and loosen all the joints in the foot, ankle, and knee. Repeat with the other foot off the ground. Put the feet down and move to the hip, spine, arms, neck, etc., loosening all joints.

3. Stand with feet parallel. Allow all tension to drain out of the body through the feet. In the process, bend the knees, straighten the pelvis, and release the lower back.

4. Begin walking in a circle; walk on the outside of the feet, then on the inside, then on the toes, and then on the heels. Notice what this does to the rest of the body. Try changing other parts of the body in a similar fashion and observe the effect on feelings and reactions.

5. Imagine the body filled with either helium or lead. Notice the effect of each of these sensations, both while standing in place and while walking. Do the same with one body part at a time—each arm, each leg, the head, etc.

The following *vocal exercises* free the throat and vocal cords:

1. Standing, begin a lazy, unhurried stretch. Reach with your arms to the ceiling, meanwhile lengthening and widening the whole of your back. Yawn as you take in a deep breath and hum on an exhalation. Release your torso so that it rests down toward your legs. Yawn on another deep breath and hum on an exhalation. On an inhalation, roll up the spine until you are standing with your arms at your sides. Look at something on the ceiling and then at something on the floor; then let your head return to a balance point, so that the neck and shoulder muscles are relaxed.

2. Put your hands on your ribs, take a deep breath, and hum a short tune. Repeat several times. Hum an *m* or *n* up and down the scale. Drop your arms; lift the shoulders an inch and drop them, releasing all tension.

3. Take a deep breath and with the palm of your hand push gently down on your stomach as you exhale. Do this several times. Exhale on sighs and then on vowels.

4. Standing, yawn with your throat and mouth open and be aware of vibrations in the front of your mouth, just behind your front teeth, as you vocalize on the vowels *ee, ei,* and *o.* Take these up and down the scales. Sing a simple song and then say it, and see if you have just as much vibration in your mouth when you are speaking as when you are singing.

5. Using a light, quick tempo, shift to a tongue twister (such as *Peter Piper picked a peck of pickled peppers*). Feel a lively touch of the tongue on the gum ridge on the *t*'s and *d*'s, and a bounce of the back of the tongue on the *k*'s and *g*'s. Feel the bouncing action on the lips on the *p*'s and *b*'s.

Source: Provided by Professor John Sipes of the Oregon Shakespeare Festival and Professor Barbara F. Acker of Arizona State University.

pose, and conviction—performers must undergo arduous training and be genuinely dedicated to their profession.

Training for Special Forms of Theatre   Certain types of theatre and theatre events require special discipline or training. For example, musical theatre obviously requires talent in singing and dancing. Coordination is also important in musical theatre: the members of a chorus must frequently sing and dance in unison.

Pantomime is another demanding category of performance: without words or props, a performer must indicate everything by physical suggestion, convincingly lifting an imaginary box or walking against an imaginary wind.

TRAINING FOR MUSICAL THEATRE
Musical theatre makes its own demands, just as classical or avant-garde theatre does. Musical performers often must be able to sing and dance, as well as to enact convincing characters. A prime example is the exuberant dancing in *Memphis*, the Broadway musical. (© Joan Marcus)

Various forms of modern avant-garde and experimental theatre also require special techniques. A good example is Samuel Beckett's *Happy Days,* in which an actress is buried onstage in a mound of earth up to her waist in the first act, and up to her neck in the second. She must carry on her performance through the entire play while virtually immobile. In some types of avant-garde theatre, the performers become acrobats, make human pyramids, or are used like pieces of furniture. In the theatres of Robert Wilson, Mabou Mines, and similar groups, the elements of story, character, and text are minimized or even eliminated. The stress, rather than being on a narrative or on exploring recognizable characters, is on the visual and ritualistic aspects of theatre, like a series of tableaux or a moving collage. Stage movement in this approach to theatre is often closely related to dance; thus the performers must have the same discipline, training, and control as dancers. In Wilson's work, performers are frequently called on either to move constantly or to remain perfectly still. In *A Letter to Queen Victoria,* two performers turn continuously in circles like dervishes for long periods of time—perhaps thirty or forty minutes. In other works by Wilson, performers must remain frozen like statues.

THE ART OF ACTING
Acting is a difficult artistic endeavor, requiring not only arduous training in vocal and movement techniques but also the ability to create believable characters. In addition, it is necessary to rehearse with fellow actors so that action is coordinated, and all performers work together. Shown here are the actor and playwright John Kani as Caliban and his son Atandwa Kani as Ariel in Shakespeare's *The Tempest,* directed by Janice Honeyman, in a production by the Baxter Theatre Centre of South Africa in association with The Royal Shakespeare Company, Stratford-Upon-Avon. (© Geraint Lewis)

In concluding this section, it should be noted that many of the figures covered in the above analysis of actor training, both those who focus on interior development and motivation and those who focus on physical acting, will be discussed again in the chapters on theatre history.

SYNTHESIS AND INTEGRATION

The demands made on performers by experimental and avant-garde theatres are only the most recent example of the rigorous, intensive training that acting generally requires. The goal of all this training—both internal and external—is to create for the performer an instrument that is flexible, resourceful, and disciplined. Above all, the actor must bring together the inner approach to acting, the work on truthfulness and believability, with the physical aspects discussed above. He or she must combine inner and outer into one indivisible whole. What is important to remember is that whatever the starting point, the end result must be a synthesis of these two aspects. The inner emotions and feelings and the outer physical and vocal characteristics become one.

PUPPETRY AROUND THE WORLD

Puppetry in its various forms (puppets, marionettes, shadow puppets) has a long and honorable history. Remarkably, it emerged independently in widely separated parts of the world: in Indonesia, in Japan, in sections of Europe, and among Native Americans in the far northwest of what is now the United States.

Stick puppets in a Wayeng Golek play presented at a puppet workshop in Java, Indonesia. (© Michael Freeman/Corbis)

Only then will the character be forcefully and convincingly portrayed. This process is termed *integration.*

When a performer is approaching a role in a play, the first task is to read and analyze the script. The actress or actor must discover the superobjective of the character she or he is playing and put together not only the spine of the role but the many smaller moments, each with its own objective and given circumstances.

The next challenge is to begin specific work on the role. In taking this step, some performers begin with the *outer* aspects of the character—with a walk, a posture, or a peculiar vocal delivery. They get a sense of how the character looks in terms of makeup and other characteristics, such as a mustache or hairstyle. They consider the clothes the character wears and any idiosyncrasies of speech or movement, such as a limp or a swagger. Only then will they move on to the inner aspects of the character: how the character feels; how the character reacts to people and events; what disturbs the character's emotional equilibrium; what fears, hopes, and dreams the character has.

In whatever form, the puppet figure is the image, reflection, and embodiment of a theatrical character and, therefore, a replacement for the actor. Puppets can run the gamut of emotions. They can be evil, demonic figures; they can be eerie, otherworldly creatures; they can be wildly comic, as in Punch and Judy shows when they biff one another across the head and knock one another down; they can be intensely human, as in the suffering characters in Japanese bunraku. In short, when puppets are onstage, audiences usually experience these silent, nonhuman characters as real people.

It should be noted as well that while puppet or marionette characters are often either comic or tragic figures, they are also frequently employed as advocates for a political point of view. The Bread and Puppet Theatre of San Francisco, founded by Peter Schuman (1934–   ), features larger-than-life, exaggerated figures made of papier-mâché. This theatre began with protests about the Vietnam War but has continued, often with the figures processing down city streets, in protests against all wars, including the Iraq War.

Puppet characters are created and manipulated in various ways. In Indonesia and other parts of southeast Asia, two kinds of puppets were developed. One kind is rod puppets, so called because the movements of these puppets are controlled by rods attached to the head and limbs and operated by one or more persons, from either above or below. (Though they are most often associated with southeast Asia, rod puppets, nearly life-size, were developed as well on the island of Sicily

in the Mediterranean.) The other type of puppet popular in southeast Asia—in Java and Bali as well as Indonesia—is the shadow puppet. In this case, silhouette figures, often made of leather, are highlighted on a screen that is lit from behind.

Marionettes are puppets controlled by strings attached to the head, arms, and legs, and operated from above. A unique type of puppet is the bunraku puppet from Japan, which will be discussed in more detail in Chapter 11. Originating in the late seventeenth century, it was firmly established by the eighteenth century and has continued to this day. In the early eighteenth century, one of the most famous playwrights of all time, Chikamatsu Monzaemon, wrote masterful plays for bunraku theatre. In the case of bunraku figures, which today are roughly two-thirds life-size, one man operates the feet, another operates the left hand, and a third controls the face, head, and right hand.

Probably the puppet figures most familiar to Western audiences are hand puppets, operated by a person who has one or two hands inside the puppet itself. Among the immediately recognizable hand puppets are the Muppets, featuring such popular and enduring characters as Kermit the Frog and Miss Piggy. Another example of hand puppets onstage appeared in the successful Broadway production *Avenue Q.* Remarkable recent examples of puppetry were the horses and other animals created for the play *War Horse.*

Puppetry remains, and will continue to remain, a vital art form in its own right, and an important adjunct to live theatre.

Other performers, by contrast, begin with the *internal* aspects: with the feelings and emotions of the character. These performers delve deeply into the psyche of the character to try to understand and duplicate what the character feels inside. Only after doing this will they go on to develop the outer characteristics. Still other performers work on both aspects—inner and outer—simultaneously.

Finally, we must realize that although a competent, well-trained performer may become a successful actress or actor, another ingredient is required in order to electrify an audience as truly memorable stage artists do. This results from intangibles—qualities that cannot be taught in acting schools—that distinguish an acceptable, accomplished actor or actress from one who ignites the stage. *Presence, charisma, personality, star quality:* these are among the terms used to describe a performer who communicates directly and kinetically with the audience. Whatever term one uses, the electricity and excitement of theatre are enhanced immeasurably by performers who possess this indefinable attribute.

JUDGING PERFORMANCES

As observers, we study the techniques and problems of acting so that we will be able to understand and judge the performances we see. If a performer in unconvincing in a part, we know that he or she has not mastered a technique for truthful acting. We recognize that a performer who moves awkwardly or cannot be heard clearly has not been properly trained in body movement or vocal projection. We learn to notice how well performers play together: whether they listen to one another and respond appropriately. We also observe how well performers establish and maintain contact with the audience.

Before leaving the subject of the performer, we should note that actors and actresses have always held a fascination for audiences. In some cases this is because they portray larger-than-life characters; it can also result from the exceptional talent they bring to their performances. Also, of course, some performers have personal charisma or appeal. Theatre audiences have often responded to stars onstage in the same way that people tend to respond to a rock star or a film star. There is something in these personalities that audiences find immensely attractive or intriguing. Moreover, the personal lives of actors are often of great interest to the public, and some people find it difficult to separate a stage character from the offstage woman or man.

In Chapter 6, we turn to the individual responsible for coordinating the elements and creating a vision for the production: the director.

SUMMARY

All human beings engage in certain forms of acting; imitation and role-playing are excellent examples of acting in everyday life. Acting onstage, however, differs from acting in everyday life. Historically, stage performances have required exceptional physical and vocal skills: moving with agility and grace to engage in such things as sword fights and death scenes; dealing with poetic devices (meter, imagery, alliteration, etc.); and projecting the voice to the farthest reaches of the theatre space.

From the end of the nineteenth century to the present day, many plays have been written in a very realistic, lifelike style. The characters in these plays resemble ordinary people in their dialogue, behavior, etc. Presenting them requires that performers make the characters they portray believable and convincing.

A Russian director, Konstantin Stanislavski, developed a system or method of acting to enable performers to believe in the "truth" of what they say and do, and to project this to the audience.

Modern approaches to realistic acting by such teachers as Lee Strasberg, Stella Adler, Sanford Meisner, and Uta Hagen have built on and departed from aspects of Stanislavski's theories. Two other approaches are those of Robert Cohen and Robert Benedetti.

Global influences on actors' training include the work of the Russian director Vsevolod Meyerhold and the French director Jacques Copeau, as well as the Polish director Jerzy Grotowski.

Exercises and tasks have been developed to train performers. These include numerous physical and vocal exercises and techniques taken from other disciplines such as tai chi and the circus. Centering is often emphasized as part of body and voice training. Avant-garde theatre and other types of theatre make additional demands on the performer with regard to voice and body training.

Audience members should familiarize themselves with the problems and techniques of acting in order to judge performances properly.

Thinking about Theatre

▶ What is the most convincing performance you've seen where you felt the actor on stage was really the person being portrayed? What was it about the performance that made it believable? In contrast, what was the least convincing and effective performance you have seen? Explain why this was so.

▶ In Shakespearean and other classic plays, the actors often speak in verse. In what way are the various vocal techniques described in this chapter important to actors in preparing to play a role in this kind of play and in the performance itself?

▶ Identify a scene in a play in which two, three, or four actors are locked in conflict. What can individual actors do to hold the attention of the audience and make their actions and feelings convincing? How do you think these actors can best prepare for conflict scenes?

▶ Read either *Miss Julie* or *A Doll's House* at the URLs provided in Chapter 3. What kinds of background information would the actors in these plays need to know? What are the physical attributes actors would need to create for some of the key characters? Choose one scene and one character and discuss what is motivating the character. How might you employ some of Stanislavski's concepts in order to bring the character to life?

(NOTE: *A Doll's House* is also available in *Anthology of Living Theatre,* Third Edition, by Edwin Wilson and Alvin Goldfarb.)

Key Terms

Emotional recall Stanislavski's exercise that helps the performer present realistic emotions. The performer feels a character's emotion by thinking of an event in his or her own life that led to a similar emotion.

Ensemble playing Acting that stresses the total artistic unity of a group performance rather than individual performances.

Magic if Stanislavski's acting exercise that requires the performer to ask, "How would I react if I were in this character's position?"

Realism Broadly, an attempt to present onstage people and events corresponding to those in everyday life.

Theatre on the Web

For more research and to learn more about the topics in this chapter, please visit the Online Learning Center at **www.mhhe.com/livelyart8e.**

THE DIRECTOR
AND THE PRODUCER

6

THE DIRECTOR

EVOLUTION OF THE DIRECTOR

THE DIRECTOR AT WORK

Global Crosscurrents:
Peter Brook: International Director

THE DIRECTOR'S COLLABORATORS

Wider Perspective:
The Auteur Director and the
Postmodern Director

THE PRODUCER OR MANAGER

PRODUCERS IN COMMERCIAL THEATRE

NONCOMMERCIAL THEATRES

SUMMARY
THINKING ABOUT THEATRE
KEY TERMS
THEATRE ON THE WEB

◀ **THE DIRECTOR**   The director coordinates the activities of performers and designers in bringing the playwright's script to life. The director confers with the dramatist, studies the script, chooses and rehearses the actors, and guides the work of the designers. Shown here is director and choreographer Bill T. Jones during a rehearsal for the musical *Fela!*, guiding Sahr Ngaujah, who plays the title role. (© Richard Termine)

119

THE DIRECTOR

In preparing a production, the person most closely associated with the performers is the director, who not only guides them but coordinates the entire artistic side of the production. More than any other person, the director is responsible for the overall style, pace, and visual appearance of a production. The entire process requires organizational skills as well as aesthetic sensibility—qualities the director must have in abundance. In modern theatre the director is indispensable, but this role was not always so comprehensive.

EVOLUTION OF THE DIRECTOR

It is sometimes argued that the theatre director did not exist before 1874, when George II, duke of Saxe-Meiningen, determined to make the productions of his court theatre in Germany as effective as possible. He supervised every element, paid great attention to details, and strove for historical accuracy in order to create an integrated whole. It is true that beginning with Saxe-Meiningen, the director emerged as a full-fledged, indispensable member of the theatrical team, taking a place alongside the playwright, the performers, and the designers. Though the title may have been new, however, the function of the director has always been present in one way or another.

We know, for example, that the Greek playwright Aeschylus directed his own plays and that the chorus in a Greek play rehearsed under the supervision of a leader for many weeks before a performance. At various times in theatre history, the leading performer or playwright of a company served as a director, though without the name. Molière, for instance, not only was the playwright and the chief actor of his company but functioned as its director also. We know from Molière's short play *The Impromptu of Versailles* that he had definite ideas about how actors and actresses should perform; no doubt the same advice he offered in that play was frequently given to his performers in rehearsal. When Hamlet gives instructions and advice to the players who are about to perform the "play within the play," we could say that he is functioning as a director of this visiting theatrical troupe. In fact, in England after the time of Shakespeare, from the seventeenth century through the nineteenth, there was a long line of actor-managers who gave strong leadership to their theatre companies and performed many of the functions of the director, although they still were not called by that name.

The actual term ***director*** came into common usage at the end of the nineteenth century. It is perhaps significant that the emergence of the director as a separate creative functionary coincides with important social changes that began to take place during the nineteenth century. First, with Karl Marx, Charles Darwin, and Sigmund Freud there came a shift in established social, religious, and political concepts. Second, there was a marked increase in communication. Industrialization also impacted the theatre; an increased focus on complex technical elements and the hiring of additional theatrical professionals required a strong coordinator. With the advent of the telegraph, the telephone, photography, motion pictures, and eventually television and the Internet, various cultures that had remained remote from or even unknown to one another suddenly became linked. The effect of these two changes was to alter the monolithic, ordered view of the world that individual societies had maintained. There is a close relationship between theatre and society: when a society has an ordered, unified view of the world, its drama reflects this; and when a society views the world as a changing, heterogeneous, global culture, its drama will reflect that outlook.

Director In American usage, the person responsible for the overall unity of a production and for coordinating the work of contributing artists. The American director is the equivalent of the British producer and the French *metteur-en-scène*.

PART 3 Creating Theatre: The Production

Before the changes of the late nineteenth century and the early twentieth century, consistency of style in theatre was easier to achieve. Within a given society, writers, performers, and audiences stood on common ground. For example, the comedies of the English playwrights William Wycherley and William Congreve, written at the end of the seventeenth century, were aimed at an elite, upper-class audience that relished gossip, acid remarks, and well-turned phrases. The society's code of behavior was well understood by performers and audiences alike. Questions of style in a production hardly arose because a common approach to style was already present in the very fabric of society. The way a man took a pinch of snuff, or a nobleman flirted with a maid, or a lady flung open her fan was so clearly delineated in daily behavior that performers had only to refine and perfect these actions for the stage.

In such a society, the task of the manager or leader of a theatrical company was not really to impose a style on a production but simply to prevent the performers from overacting, to see that they spoke their lines properly, and to ensure that the cast worked together as a unit. Today, however, because style, unity, and a cohesive view of society are so elusive, the director's task is more important. The director must draw disparate elements together to create a unified whole.

Today's directors get their training in a variety of ways. Many of them begin as actors and actresses and find that they have a talent for working with other people and for coordinating the work of designers as well as performers. Others train in the many academic institutions that have specific programs for directors. These institutions include large universities that offer theatre as part of a liberal arts program, as well as conservatories and other specialized schools.

THE DIRECTOR AT WORK

In this chapter we focus on the traditional director and how he or she undertakes to guide a production. A traditional director begins with a close examination of the text. This is true whether the play is from the past—a work by Shakespeare or Molière, for instance—or is a new work that has not been produced before.

The director must first of all understand dramatic purpose and dramatic structure (covered in Chapters 3 and 4). What is the playwright's intention: to entertain, to educate, or to arouse strong feelings in the audience? What is the playwright's point of view toward the characters and events of the play: does he or she see them as tragic or comic? How has the playwright developed the action in the play: in other words, how is the play constructed? Such considerations are crucial because the director is the one person who must have an overall grasp of the text in order to guide the performers in making it come alive. If an actor or actress has a question about a character or about the meaning of a scene, the director must be able to provide an answer.

In preparing a production, one of the director's first steps is to discover the *spine* of the play. The American director and critic Harold Clurman says in his book *On Directing* that a director's first task is to find in the text the general action that "motivates the play." The director must determine the "fundamental drama or conflict" of which "the script's plot and people are the instruments."[1] Clurman calls this fundamental action or conflict the "spine"; it could also be called the *main action* of the play.

As they seek an approach to a text—a way to translate it from page to stage—directors sometimes develop a *directorial concept.* The directorial concept is an overall image

Spine In the Stanislavski method, a character's dominant desire or motivation; usually thought of as an action and expressed as a verb.

---

[1]Harold Clurman, *On Directing,* Macmillan, New York, 1992, p. 27.

THE DIRECTOR AT WORK

The modern director works closely with the playwright on a new script or develops an understanding and interpretation of a well-known script, casts and rehearses the play, and works closely with the designers and others to bring the play to fruition. Shown at the top is Joe Dowling, in the center, directing actors in *A Midsummer Night's Dream* at the Guthrie Theater in Minneapolis. Below, Tina Landau (right) is directing Shakespeare's *Antony and Cleopatra,* featuring Kate Mulgrew and John Douglas Thompson at the Hartford Stage Company. (© T. Charles Erickson)

THE DIRECTORIAL CONCEPT
At times, directors create an overall image or metaphor for interpreting a play. This serves both to illuminate the text and to give the production unity and cohesion. Frequently the director develops an approach that throws new light on the text, reminds us of past approaches to a play, or develops a radical new interpretation. For a production called *Dollhouse,* based on Ibsen's *A Doll's House,* Mabou Mines director Lee Breuer decided to have all the men in the production played by little people to make a point about the relationship of men to women in the play. The production was directed by Lee Breuer and Maude Mitchell with Maude Mitchell as Nora and Mark Povinelli as Torvald, shown here in a performance at the Edinburgh International Festival. (© Geraint Lewis)

or metaphor of a play. For example, a director might develop a concept of Shakespeare's *Macbeth* in terms of "blind ambition." In their insatiable desire for power, both Macbeth and Lady Macbeth are blind to the immorality, the dangers, and the consequences of their actions. Following this notion, the concept of blindness—of what people can and cannot see—would permeate the play.

At the same time that the director becomes thoroughly familiar with all aspects of the text, he or she begins casting the play. The term *casting* comes from sculpture— from casting a mold. In theatre, it refers to finding an actor or actress for each role. In the past—in Shakespeare's day, for example—a company of performers worked together regularly, and it was understood who would play the hero, who the clown, who the young female lead, and so forth. In modern times, when very few theatres have a repertory company of regular performers, directors hold *auditions* at which actors and actresses try out for various roles. Sometimes performers will be interviewed, and sometimes they will be asked to read scenes from the play being produced or from another play. Sometimes, too, a director is already familiar with the work of a performer, having seen or worked with the person before. From a combination of

Casting Assigning roles to performers in a production; this is usually done by the director.

Auditions Tryouts held for performers who want to be considered for roles in a production.

PETER BROOK: INTERNATIONAL DIRECTOR

English director Peter Brook (1925–) presented some of the most memorable productions of the late twentieth century, a number of which drew extensively from the theatrical traditions and source materials of many countries. His major productions include Peter Weiss's *Marat/Sade* (1964), Shakespeare's *Midsummer Night's Dream* (1970), and his ad-

Peter Brook in Paris, 1987. (© Julio Donoso/Corbis Sygma)

aptation of the Indian epic, *The Mahabharata* (1985). His best-known writings include *The Empty Space* (1968), *The Shifting Point* (1987), and *The Open Door* (1993).

As a means of escaping commercial theatre and allowing himself to address the universality of the theatrical experience, Brook founded the International Center for Theatre Research in Paris in 1970. This company was formed of actors from a variety of countries including Algeria, Japan, England, France, America, Spain, and Portugal, with directors from Armenia, England, and Romania and a designer from Switzerland. There was much sharing of ideas and techniques with the Japanese actor teaching daily classes in nō, for example. Brook's vision was for the actors to learn from each other and to approach a kind of universal theatrical language. A production entitled *Orghast* (1971) first allowed the company to present its experimentation with language. The text was written by Ted Hughes in an invented language influenced heavily by Latin and Ancient Greek, and was performed in Iran.

In 1989, Brook's continued interest in identifying a universality of language in theatre was manifest in his production of *The Mahabharata*. The source text for this play was the Indian epic of the same name which is more than 90,000 verses long. It concerns wars between the Pandavas and the Kauravas, and addresses a great number of philosophical questions. Brook's production of this epic text originally took place at the Avignon Festival in France and took a full nine hours to perform. The source text was Indian, the director English, the theatre company French, the composer Japanese, and the actors from all over the globe. This production, which toured widely, clearly drew from a large number of different cultures.

Although Brook has been criticized for exploiting some of his source material (such as *The Mahabharata*, which he greatly simplified), his work has shown a creative and continued interest in drawing from many different theatrical traditions. Unlike many other directors who have "borrowed" certain aspects of other theatrical traditions, Brook has sought to use them to identify a common language or universality understood by them all.

Prepared by Naomi Stubbs, CUNY Graduate Center.

auditions and previous knowledge, the director casts the play, deciding which actor or actress will play each of the parts. At times a casting director is employed to assist in this process.

While the director is preparing the script and choosing the performers, he or she is also working closely with the scene, costume, lighting, and sound designers to develop the visual and aural aspects of the production. This is the point at which questions of style and genre become important. The director and the designers must work closely together to be certain that the acting style will be reinforced by the visual elements, and vice versa. Performers who will be speaking high-flown language, as in an Elizabethan play, would seem out of place in a setting that looked like a suburban backyard. In the same way, if a play is set in a modern living room, one would not want the performers to act as if they were the chorus in a Greek tragedy. The director also makes certain that the physical appearance of the production is itself consistent and unified.

A few weeks before the play is to be performed for the public, the director begins rehearsals. This is the period when he or she works most intensively with the performers. The director explains the text—not only the meaning of the play but the style in which it will be presented—and then begins to work with the actors and actresses. At first they may read through the text while simply sitting around a table; next they "get the play on its feet," beginning to sketch in the details of the setting and the characters' interaction.

Initially, the performers work with the text still in their hands. Gradually, they memorize their lines and flesh out their characters. Each performer begins to discover emotional depths in his or her character and becomes aware of the dynamics of scenes where the character confronts others. In the beginning, individual scenes are prepared separately; later, a whole act is put together. After that, the entire play is rehearsed so that the performers get a sense of its overall shape.

GUIDING THE PERFORMERS' MOVEMENTS
In a musical, the person who directs the dancers is the choreographer. But there is also other movement, for entrances and exits, for crosses on stage, for interaction of characters, which is the responsibility of the director. Shown here is Mark Lamos, directing actors in a scene from *Edgardo Mine* by Alfred Uhry at the Guthrie Theater. (© T. Charles Erickson)

In preparing the action onstage, the director keeps in mind what the production will look like to the audience. In a sense, the director is the eye of the audience—a person who sits out front and sees the performance before the public does. To ensure a smooth, clear flow of stage action, the director develops the blocking with the performers. ***Blocking*** means the arrangement and movements of performers relative to each other as well as to furniture and to the places where they enter and leave the stage. If two performers are playing a scene together, they must both be seen clearly by the audience, and they must be in positions that allow them to play the scene to maximum effect. The director also coordinates stage business. In contrast to blocking, which has to do with movements and physical arrangements onstage, *business* is the term for activities of performers such as opening an umbrella, writing a letter at a desk, arranging pillows on a sofa, and the like.

Blocking Pattern and arrangement of performers' movements onstage with respect to each other and to the stage space, usually set by the director.

In all this, the director is aware of the ***stage picture*** or *visual composition,* that is, how the entire scene onstage will appear to the audience. Is the placement of performers balanced? Is it aesthetically pleasing? One goal of the director is to make the visual images onstage striking and effective. Also, the director underscores the meaning of specific scenes through visual composition. The spatial relationships of performers convey information about characters. For example, important characters are frequently placed on a level above other characters—on a platform, say, or a flight of stairs.

Another spatial device is to place an important character alone in one area of the stage while grouping other characters in another area; this draws the spectator's eye to the character standing alone. In addition, if two characters are opposed to each other, they should be placed in positions of physical confrontation on the stage. Visual composition is more crucial in plays with large casts, such as Shakespearean productions, than in plays with only two or three characters.

The director gives shape and structure to a play in two dimensions: in *space,* as was just described, and in *time.* Since a production occurs through time, it is important for the director to see that the *movement,* the ***pace,*** and the *rhythm* of the play are appropriate. If the play moves too quickly, if we miss words and do not understand what is going on, it is the director's fault. The director must determine whether there is too little or too much time between speeches or whether a performer moves too slowly or too quickly across the stage. The director must attempt to control the pace and rhythm within a scene—the dynamics and the manner in which the actors and actresses move from moment to moment—and the rhythm between scenes.

Pace Rate at which a performance is played; also, to play a scene or an entire event to determine its proper speed.

The director must see to it that the movement from moment to moment and scene to scene has enough thrust and drive to maintain our interest. Nothing interrupts the flow, the rhythm, the focus of a production more than action that is sporadic or too slow. However, variety is also important. If a play moves ahead at only one pace, the audience will become fatigued simply by the monotony of that pace.

Before rehearsals, the director has met with the scene, costume, lighting, and sound designers to develop the approach to the play in each of these areas. While rehearsals with the performers are proceeding, other activities that will eventually be under the director's control are also going forward: the people building the scenery and costumes and the technicians preparing the lights and sound are doing their work.

Technical rehearsal Rehearsal at which all the design and technical elements are brought together.

Run-through Rehearsal in which the cast goes through the entire text of the play in the order that it will be performed.

Dress rehearsal Rehearsal in which a play is performed as it will be for the public, including all the scenery, costumes, and technical effects.

Just before the play is to be shown to the public, these elements are brought together, under the supervision of the director, in a ***technical rehearsal.*** At this point, production elements are integrated in a ***run-through:*** the performers wear their costumes to get accustomed to them, and the lighting and sound "cues" are set with the performers onstage. Scene changes are rehearsed and coordinated. Following this comes the ***dress rehearsal,*** when the play is performed as it will be for the public. This is when last-minute problems are discovered and dealt with.

Then the play is performed for the first time before audiences. These first performances, often called *previews,* are dress rehearsals for an invited audience. We have seen in Chapter 2 how vital the audience is to a production. In previews, the audience's reaction first becomes part of the production process. The response from the audience lets the director and performers know whether a comedy is as funny as they thought, or whether a serious play holds people's attention. The audience lets everyone know which scenes are successful and which are not so that adjustments can be made if there are problems.

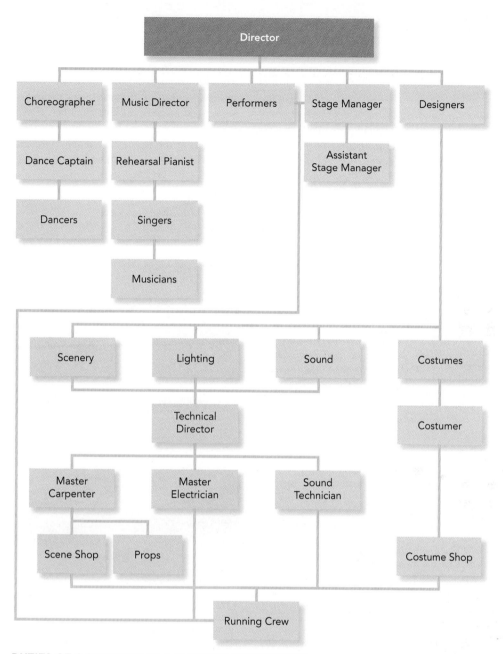

DUTIES OF A DIRECTOR IN A THEATRE PRODUCTION
Once a director has decided on a script (and worked with the playwright, if it is a new play), he or she must organize the entire artistic side of the production. This chart indicates the many people the director must work with and the many elements that must be coordinated.

THE DIRECTOR'S COLLABORATORS

In addition to working closely with performers, the director, the designers, and the playwright, the director has other collaborators who are essential to a production. In musical theatre, these others would include the composer, lyricist, choreographer, and music director. In a nonmusical play, various technicians and artists may be indispensable to

THE AUTEUR DIRECTOR AND THE POSTMODERN DIRECTOR

The traditional director treats the script as the source of the words and actions in a production. In addition to this type of director, however, there are two other types of stage directors who approach a production differently: the auteur director and the postmodern director. There are a number of similarities between these two, but we will look at them one at a time, beginning with the auteur director.

THE AUTEUR DIRECTOR

Auteur is a French word meaning "author." Just after World War II, French critics began using the term ***auteur director*** to describe certain

Auteur director A director who believes that his or her role is to be the author of a production. An auteur director's point of view dominates that of the playwright, and the director may make textual changes and modifications.

film directors, who, they said, were really the authors of the films they made. In these films the point of view and the implementation of that point of view came almost entirely from the director, not from a writer. The term

has since been applied to a type of stage director as well. We are not speaking here of directors who alter the time or place in which the action occurs but retain the original script—the playwright's words, the sequence of scenes, and so forth. We are speaking rather of directors who make more drastic alterations or transformations in the material, taking responsibility for shaping *every* element in the production, including the script.

Interestingly, one of the first and most important auteur directors began his work with Stanislavsky and then went out on his own. He was the Russian director Vsevolod Meyerhold (1874–1940), and he developed a type of theatre in which he controlled all the elements. The script was only one of many aspects that Meyerhold used for his own purposes. He would rewrite or eliminate text in order to present his own vision of the material. Performers, too, were subject to his overall ideas. Often they were called on to perform like circus acrobats or robots. The finished product was frequently exciting and almost always innovative, but it reflected Meyerhold's point of view, strongly imposed on all the elements, not the viewpoint of a writer or anyone else.

Following in Meyerhold's footsteps, many avant-garde directors, such as Jerzi Grotowski (1933–1999), Richard Foreman, and Robert Wilson, can also be classified as auteur directors in the sense that they demanded that a text

serve their purposes, not the other way around. In some cases, such as many of Wilson's pieces, the text is only fragmentary and is one of the least important elements. In the former Soviet Union and Eastern Europe before the political changes of the early 1990s, certain directors, who had not been allowed to deal with material that questioned the

TWO AUTEUR DIRECTORS
Robert Wilson is one of the foremost auteur directors in today's theatre. Such directors create their own theatre pieces, providing the vision and the interpretation. They serve not only as directors but as authors, taking elements from many sources and melding them into their own version of what we see onstage. The script or scenario is under their control, as are all the elements of the production. Shown in the photo above are (left to right) Rachel Eberhart, Benoît Maréchal, Ariel Garcia Valdès, and Isabelle Huppert in Robert Wilson's adaptation of *Quartett* by Heiner Müller. (© Richard Termine) The avant-garde director Anne Bogart decided to present Sophocles's *Antigone* in a stark modern style at the Dance Theatre Workshop/SITI Company. Shown here are Makela Spielman, in the title role, with Leon Ingulsrud. (Nicole Bengiveno/The New York Times/Redux)

government hierarchy, drastically reworked established texts in order to make a political comment. These directors, too, imposed their own vision, rather than that of the playwright, on the material.

Another recent auteur director is Ivo van Hove, a Flemish director who enjoys reinventing the classics. In his *A Streetcar Named Desire,* Blanche Dubois performs a good part of the play naked in a bathtub; and his version of *The Misanthrope* by Molière, which he transfers to the present day, features cell phones, laptops, BlackBerrys, and digital cameras. Two additional highly regarded contemporary American auteur directors are Julie Taymor (b. 1952) and Mary Zimmerman (b. 1960).

THE POSTMODERN DIRECTOR

There is a great deal of overlap between the auteur director and the postmodern director. What is postmodernism? Probably the best way to answer the question is historically. The modern period in drama began in the late nineteenth century with plays like those of Ibsen and Strindberg that broke long-held taboos. The subject matter of their plays included explicit sexual content, social diseases, the subjugation of women, and the hypocrisy of religious figures. The twentieth century, therefore, was the period of modern drama.

At mid-century, however, there were people in theatre who felt that as advanced as theatre had become, it remained bound by the strictures of the text. In their minds this state of affairs did not properly reflect the chaos, the confusion, and the alienation of the world around us. Two groups especially advanced these ideas: the theoreticians who propounded the doctrine of postmodernism; and a series of stage directors who embodied postmodernism in their work with a radical, rebellious, freeform approach to theatre production.

What are the hallmarks of postmodern production? One, which began with Meyerhold and continued with Grotowski in his "poor theatre," was a taking apart of the text, often called *deconstruction,* in which portions of a text may be altered, deleted, taken out of context, or reassembled.

A second hallmark is the abandonment of a narrative or linear structure in a theatre piece. For example, Robert Wilson (b. 1941) and

Richard Foreman (b. 1937) in his Ontological Hysteric Theatre both replace traditional structure with the use of segments, tableaux, and other nonsequential devices.

A third hallmark is unfamiliar, cross-gender, multicultural casting. Lee Breuer (b. 1937) in a Mabou Mines production of *King Lear* recast the title role as a female ranch owner in the southern United States who has difficulty leaving her inheritance to her three "good ole boy" sons. *The Emperor Jones* is a play by Eugene O'Neill (1888–1953) about the ruler of a Caribbean island who is gradually stripped of his powers. When the Wooster Group produced this play, an actress, Kate Valk, played the ruler, appearing in blackface. Sometimes the alteration of a script in this way results in a lawsuit. When the director Joanne Akalaitis (b. 1937) of Mabou Mines attempted to present an ethnically altered version of Samuel Beckett's *EndGame* in a New York subway, she was legally prevented from doing so by the Beckett estate.

A fourth hallmark of postmodern productions is the integration of dance, film, video, and computer material into the production.

In addition to those discussed above, other postmodern directors who deserve to be mentioned are Anne Bogart (b. 1951) and her SITI organization and Elizabeth LeCompte (b. 1944) with the Wooster Group.

DYNAMICS OF DRAMA

MODERN VERSUS POSTMODERN PRODUCTION AESTHETICS

Modern	Postmodern
Organic unity	Interdisciplinary
Single view	No single view can predominate
Single viewer approach	Multiperspective, multifocus
Shared values of audience	Multicultural
Metaphorical or representational	Presentational
Linear	Nonlinear, simultaneous
Closeness	Distance
Time is singularly staged	Multiple time frames are presented simultaneously
Space is unified	Space is fragmented and can be simultaneously conceived

(Prepared by Tom Mikotowicz)

the director. For example, a fencing or fight consultant may be needed for a classic play, such as a play by Shakespeare. If a play calls for regional accents—as in a play by Tennessee Williams set in the south—a vocal coach would be helpful.

Stage manager Person who coordinates all the rehearsals for the director and runs the actual show during its performances.

Another important member of the production team is the ***stage manager,*** the person who coordinates all the rehearsals and the actual running of a performance. The stage manager calls rehearsals; lets the performers know their rehearsal schedule; makes all important announcements concerning technical rehearsals and other events involving performers; coordinates all the elements of light, sound, and scene changes during the technical rehearsals and previews; and is in charge of all the same elements, as well as the entrances and exits of performers, during each performance. Clearly, the stage manager is an essential member of any production team: he or she has the immense responsibility of preplanning, of organizing rehearsals, of coordinating all elements, and of seeing to it that performances come off satisfactorily.

Dramaturg Literary manager or dramatic adviser of a theatre company.

In Europe, there is a long-standing practice of having a ***dramaturg*** or ***literary manager*** collaborate with the director. In the United States in recent years, many regional professional groups and nonprofit theatres have engaged full-time dramaturgs. In a number of the directorial decisions outlined above, a dramaturg or literary manager can be extremely helpful. Among the duties frequently undertaken by the dramaturg are discovering and reading new plays, working with playwrights to develop new scripts, identifying overlooked plays from the past, preparing information on the history of classical works, researching past productions and criticism, and writing program articles. The dramaturg can also aid the director in making decisions regarding style, approach, and concept.

THE PRODUCER OR MANAGER

Producer In American usage, the person responsible for the business side of a production, including raising the necessary money. (In British usage, a producer is the equivalent of an American director.)

Audiences frequently confuse directors with producers, perhaps because both the director and the producer function behind the scenes. Actually, the ***producer,*** or *manager,* is the director's counterpart in the business and management side of a theatre production. Here, too, coordination of elements is crucial, and the producer or manager is the person chiefly responsible. As the term itself suggests, the producer is a key figure in a production.

PRODUCERS IN COMMERCIAL THEATRE

In commercial theatre, a producer has many responsibilities. In general, the producer oversees the entire business side of a production, including publicity. His or her duties include the following:

1. Raising money to finance the production
2. Securing rights to the script
3. Dealing with the agents for the playwright, director, and performers
4. Hiring the director, performers, designers, and stage crews
5. Dealing with theatrical unions
6. Renting the theatre space
7. Supervising the work of those running the theatre: in the box office, auditorium, and business office

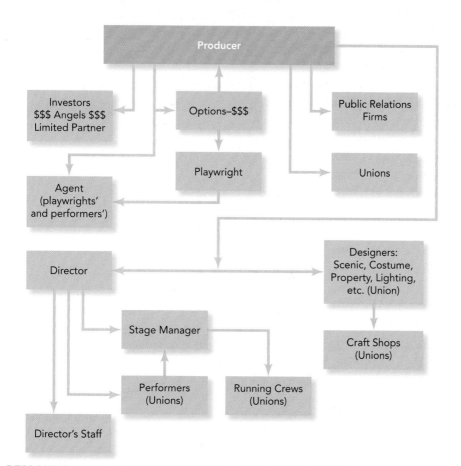

RESPONSIBILITIES OF THE COMMERCIAL THEATRE PRODUCER
When a commercial theatre production is mounted, the person responsible for organizing the full range of nonartistic activities is the producer. This chart, which shows the producer at the top, indicates the people the producer must deal with and the numerous elements he or she must coordinate.

8. Supervising the advertising
9. Overseeing the budget and the week-to-week financial management of the production

If a production is to succeed, the producer must have the artistic sensibility to choose the right text and hire the right director. Aside from raising capital and having the final say in hiring and firing, the producer oversees all financial and business operations in a production.

NONCOMMERCIAL THEATRES

Administrative Organization of a Nonprofit Theatre Most nonprofit theatres—including those in smaller urban centers as well as large noncommercial theatres in major cities like New York, Chicago, and Los Angeles—are organized with a board of directors, an artistic director, and an executive or managing director.

The board is responsible for selecting both the artistic and the managing directors. The board is also responsible for overseeing the financial affairs of the theatre, for

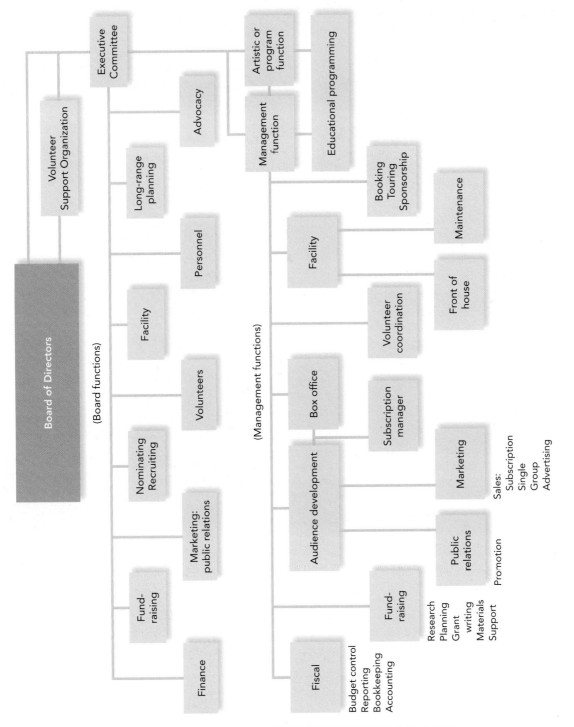

ORGANIZATIONAL STRUCTURE OF A NONPROFIT THEATRE COMPANY

A nonprofit theatre is a complex institution with many facets. This chart shows the various activities that must be organized for the successful management of such a theatre.

fund-raising, for long-range planning, and the like. To carry out some of these tasks, the board frequently delegates authority to an executive committee.

The ***artistic director*** is responsible for all creative and artistic activities. He or she selects the plays that will constitute the season and chooses directors, designers, and other creative personnel. Frequently the artistic director also directs one or more plays during the season.

Artistic director Person responsible for all creative and artistic activities for resident and repertory companies.

Responsibilities of the Noncommercial Managing Director The managing director in a noncommercial theatre is, in many respects, the counterpart of a producer and manager in commercial theatre. In both a commercial production and the running of a nonprofit theatre organization, the tasks of the person in charge of administration are many and complex.

The managing director is responsible for the maintenance of the theatre building, as well as for the budget, making certain that the production stays within established limits. The budget includes salaries for the director, designers, performers, and stage crews, and expenditures for scenery, costumes, and music. Again, an artistic element enters the picture; some artistic decisions—such as whether a costume needs to be replaced or scenery needs to be altered—affect costs. The managing director must work very closely with the director and the designers in balancing artistic and financial needs.

The managing director is also responsible for publicity. The audience would never get to the theatre if it did not know when and where a play was being presented. A host of other tasks come under the supervision of the managing director: tickets must be ordered, the box office must be maintained, and plans must be made ahead of time for how tickets are to be sold. The securing of ushers, the printing of programs, and the maintenance of the auditorium—usually called the ***front of the house***—are also the responsibility of the managing director.

Front of the house All of the nonproduction elements of the theatre space that relate to the audience's experience, including the auditorium, lobby, and box office.

Once again, plans must be made well in advance. In many theatre organizations, an entire season—the plays that will be produced, the personnel who will be in charge, and the supplies that will be required—is planned a year ahead of time. Coordination and cooperation are as important in this area as they are for the production onstage. (For the organization of a nonprofit theatre company, see the chart on the facing page.)

In Chapter 7 we will turn our attention to the places where audiences interact with performers and where directors stage their productions, as we examine the variety of theatre spaces available to contemporary audiences.

SUMMARY

The special function of the director emerged during modern times, when the great diversity of styles in modern theatre and the international nature of theatre required someone to provide an overall vision for a production and to coordinate all the elements. The director begins by analyzing the text, whether it is a classic or a new play. The director discovers the meaning and the intention of the playwright in order to translate these into stage terms. To do this organically and effectively, the director frequently develops a concept, an overall image or point of view, that will guide and inform the work of everyone connected with the production. An auteur director usually substitutes his or her own vision for that of the playwright, choosing texts to be used and rearranging time periods and other elements.

The director works with the actors and actresses, supervising rehearsals and guiding their performances. The director has many other duties as well. He or she casts the play, selecting an actor or actress for each role. Also, the director works closely with scene, costume, lighting, and sound designers, coordinating the visual elements of the production. The overall artistic quality of the production—its style, pace, and visual appearance—is also the responsibility of the director.

The director may have many collaborators, such as a choreographer, a stage manager, and a dramaturg. Behind the scenes, the producer or manager works to coordinate the business and management elements.

THINKING ABOUT THEATRE

▶ Imagine that while watching a production one performer is over-acting badly, to the point that he or she is quite unbelievable. Another performer is listless and has no energy. In each case, to what extent do you think this is the director's fault? To what extent is it each performer's failure? Is it, perhaps, a combination of the two?

▶ If you get bored or impatient when watching a performance, what do you think the director could have done in preparing the production to prevent this from happening?

▶ Is it fair to say, as some critics do, that when everything "clicks" in a production, that is, when the acting, the scenery and lighting, and the pace of the action all seem to be beautifully coordinated, that the director's hand is "invisible"? Why or why not?

▶ Read *Uncle Vanya* at the URL provided in Chapter 4. Do you think the play has a "spine"? If so, what is it? What would be your "directorial concept" if you were directing a production of the play?

KEY TERMS

Artistic director Person responsible for all creative and artistic activities for resident and repertory companies.

Auditions Tryouts held for performers who want to be considered for roles in a production.

Auteur director A director who believes that his or her role is to be the author of a production. An auteur director's point of view dominates that of the playwright, and the director may make textual changes and modifications.

Blocking Pattern and arrangement of performers' movements onstage with respect to each other and to the stage space, usually set by the director.

Casting Assigning roles to performers in a production; this is usually done by the director.

Director In American usage, the person responsible for the overall unity of a production and for coordinating the work of contributing artists. The American director is the equivalent of the British producer and the French *metteur-en-scène*.

Dramaturg Literary manager or dramatic adviser of a theatre company.

Dress rehearsal Rehearsal in which a play is performed as it will be for the public, including all the scenery, costumes, and technical effects.

Front of the house All of the nonproduction elements of the theatre space that relate to the audience's experience, including the auditorium, lobby, and box office.

Pace Rate at which a performance is played; also, to play a scene or an entire event to determine its proper speed.

Producer In American usage, the person responsible for the business side of a production, including raising the necessary money. (In British usage, a producer is the equivalent of an American director.)

Run-through Rehearsal in which the cast goes through the entire text of the play in the order that it will be performed.

Spine In the Stanislavski method, a character's dominant desire or motivation; usually thought of as an action and expressed as a verb.

Stage manager Person who coordinates all the rehearsals for the director and runs the actual show during its performances.

Stage picture Visual composition: how an entire scene onstage will appear to the audience.

Technical rehearsal Rehearsal at which all the design and technical elements are brought together.

 THEATRE ON THE WEB

For more research and to learn more about the topics in this chapter, please visit the Online Learning Center at **www.mhhe.com/livelyart8e**.

THEATRE
SPACES

7

PROSCENIUM OR PICTURE-FRAME STAGE:
HISTORY AND CHARACTERISTICS

THRUST STAGE:
HISTORY AND CHARACTERISTICS

ARENA STAGE:
HISTORY AND CHARACTERISTICS

CREATED OR FOUND SPACES

MAKING CONNECTIONS: Popular Performance Spaces

MULTIFOCUS ENVIRONMENTS

ALL-PURPOSE AND EXPERIMENTAL SPACES

SUMMARY
THINKING ABOUT THEATRE
KEY TERMS
THEATRE ON THE WEB

◀ **SPACES FOR THEATRE** Western theatre began in ancient Greece, where, to present their plays, the Greeks created amphitheatres by placing seats on a hillside surrounding a circle and a stage space at the base of the hill. Through the years, performance spaces have been developed in many sizes and shapes: large and small, indoors and outdoors, and with important variations in the physical relationship of the stage to the spectators. The Romans built entire stone buildings modeled after Greek theatres. The ancient theatre seen here is Leptis Magna, a Roman theatre in Libya dating from 1–2 C.E. (© Roger Wood/Corbis)

A theatre event occurs in a place where the audience and performers come together. Since theatre is a live experience, the physical environment where it occurs becomes an essential ingredient.

In addition to a stage—the area where the actors and actresses perform—and an adjoining space where the spectators sit or stand, a theatre space also includes a place adjacent to the stage where performers can change costumes and from which they can make entrances and exits. For the audience, provision is made for a lobby and other public spaces.

A theatre space can be indoors or outdoors, permanent or temporary, large or small. However, it is interesting to note that throughout theatre history four fundamental stage arrangements have been predominant. Each has its own advantages and disadvantages, each is suited to certain types of plays and certain types of productions, and each provides the audience with a somewhat different experience.

The four basic arrangements are: (1) the proscenium, or picture-frame, stage; (2) the thrust stage with three-quarters seating; (3) the arena, or circle, stage; and (4) created and found stage spaces. We will learn their features and characteristics as we look at each more closely, beginning with the proscenium stage. (There are also spaces that combine characteristics of these four types.)

PROSCENIUM OR PICTURE-FRAME STAGE: HISTORY AND CHARACTERISTICS

For many people, the most familiar type of stage is the **proscenium** (pro-SEEN-ee-um), or *picture-frame*, stage. In this arrangement, the audience faces in one direction, as in a movie theatre, and the action onstage is seen through a frame of some kind.

The term *proscenium* comes from the *proscenium arch,* the frame that separates the stage from the auditorium and forms an outline for the stage. This frame was first introduced in Italy during the Renaissance in the early seventeenth century. Although in the past it was an actual arch, today it is usually a rectangle. Before the 1950s, there was usually a curtain just behind the proscenium opening; when the curtain rose, it revealed the "picture." Another term for this type of stage is **fourth wall,** from the idea of the proscenium opening as an invisible or transparent wall through which the audience looks at the other three walls of a room.

The auditorium itself is slanted downward from the back of the auditorium to the stage. (In theatre usage, the slant of an auditorium or stage floor is called a **rake.**) The stage itself is raised several feet above the auditorium floor, to increase visibility.

The main floor where the audience sits is called the **orchestra.** (This is the modern usage of the term *orchestra;* in ancient Greek theatre, the orchestra was the circular acting area at the base of a hillside amphitheatre.) There is usually a balcony (sometimes there are two balconies), protruding

PROSCENIUM THEATRE
The audience faces in one direction, toward an enclosed stage encased by a picture-frame opening. Scene changes and performers' entrances and exits are made behind the proscenium opening, out of sight of the audience.

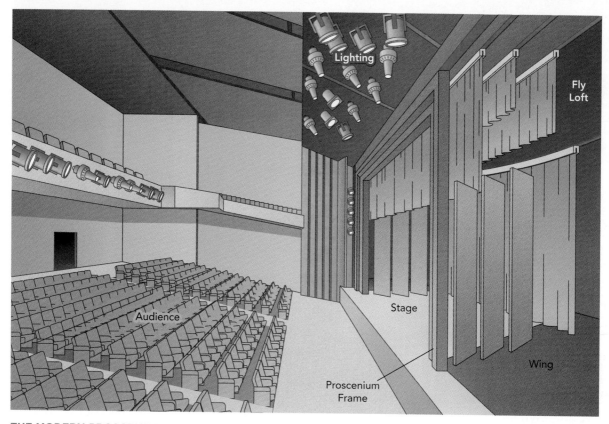

THE MODERN PROSCENIUM-STAGE THEATRE
In this cutaway drawing, we see the audience seating at the left, all facing in the one direction toward the stage. Behind the orchestra pit in the center is the apron on the stage, and then the proscenium frame, behind which are the flats and other scenic elements. Overhead, scenery can be raised into the fly loft above the stage area.

about halfway over the main floor, to provide additional seating. In certain theatres, as well as in similar concert halls and opera houses, there are horseshoe-shaped tiers or boxes ringing the auditorium for several floors above the orchestra.

Beginning in the late seventeenth century, the proscenium theatre was adopted in virtually every European country. The popularity of this type of stage spread throughout the United States in the nineteenth century and the early twentieth.

The stage area of all these proscenium theatres was usually deep, allowing for elaborate scenery and scene shifts; and there was a tall ***fly loft*** above the stage to hold scenery. The loft had to be more than twice as high as the proscenium opening so that scenery could be concealed when it was raised, or *flown,* above the stage. Scenery was usually hung by ropes or cables on a series of parallel pipes, one behind the other, running from side to side across the stage. With this arrangement, many pieces of scenery could be raised and lowered. Ingenious mechanisms for raising and lowering scenery were developed during the Italian Renaissance, when the proscenium stage was being refined.

Throughout the seventeenth and eighteenth centuries, there were times when everyone—audiences, scene designers, and technicians—seemed so carried away with spectacle that it was emphasized above everything else, sometimes even above the text

Fly loft Space above the stage where scenery may be lifted out of sight by means of ropes and pulleys.

THE PROSCENIUM STAGE

The traditional proscenium theatre resembles a movie theatre with respect to audience seating: all the seats face in one direction, toward the stage. The frame of the stage is like a picture frame, and behind the frame are the elements of the visual production, such as scenery, painted drops, pieces that move across the stage, platforms, steps, and perhaps the interior of a room or several rooms. It is particularly effective for elaborate scenic effects. The theatre shown here, the Bolton Theatre at the Cleveland Play House, which seats 548 people, is an excellent example of a proscenium theatre. Founded in 1915, the Cleveland Play House is the oldest regional theatre in America; its Bolton Theatre was redesigned by the architect Philip Johnson and renovated in 1983. (Photo by Paul Tepley, Courtesy of The Cleveland Play House)

and the acting. In Paris, for example, there was a theatre called the *Salle des Machines*—"Hall of Machines"—its name indicating that visual effects were its chief attraction. At times there was nothing onstage but visual display: cloud machines brought angels or deities from up high; rocks opened to reveal wood nymphs; a banquet hall was changed to a forest; smoke, fire, twinkling lights, and every imaginable effect appeared as if by magic. Later, such heavy concentration on spectacle went out of favor for many years; but fascination with this type of theatre returned in the latter part of the twentieth century and in the early twenty-first century, in musicals such as *The Phantom of the Opera, Hairspray, Wicked, The Lion King, Mary Poppins,* and *Billy Elliot.* The proscenium stage is ideal for such spectacles because the machinery and the workings of the scene changes can be concealed behind the proscenium opening.

In addition to providing an opportunity for spectacle, the proscenium stage offers other advantages. Realistic settings—a living room, an office, a kitchen—are particularly effective in a proscenium theatre. The illusion of a genuine, complete room can be created more easily with a proscenium stage than with any other kind. Also, the

THE PROSCENIUM: IDEAL FOR SPECTACLE
One advantage of a proscenium theatre is that it allows elaborate scenery and effects to be created behind the proscenium opening. Machinery for changing scenery can be hidden, and impressive visual pictures can appear as if by magic. Here is a scene from the Broadway musical *Wicked,* which features the kinds of elaborate set changes and scenic effects associated with large-scale musical productions. (© Joan Marcus)

strong central focus provided by the frame rivets the attention of the audience. There are times, too, when the audience wants the detachment—the distancing—that a proscenium provides.

There are disadvantages as well, however. As we have seen, the proscenium stage creates a temptation to get carried away with visual pyrotechnics. In addition, a proscenium stage tends to be remote and formal. Some spectators prefer the intimacy and informality—the experience of being close to the action—found in the thrust and arena theatres.

THRUST STAGE: HISTORY AND CHARACTERISTICS

In one form or another, the ***thrust stage*** has been the most widely used of all theatre spaces. In the basic thrust arrangement, the audience sits on three sides, or in a semicircle, enclosing a stage that projects into the center. At the back of the playing area is some form of stage house providing for the performers' entrances and exits, and for scene changes. The thrust stage offers a sense of intimacy, giving the "wraparound"

Thrust stage Theatre space in which the audience sits on three sides of the stage.

audience a feeling of surrounding the action. At the same time, the rear wall of the thrust stage—the facade of the stage house—provides a focused background for the action in the playing area.

The thrust stage was developed by the Greeks for their tragedies and comedies. Before they had formal theatres, the Greeks had areas for religious ceremonies and tribal rituals. It is believed that these areas sometimes took the form of a circle in a field, with an altar at the center. In forming their theatres, the Greeks modified this arrangement by placing the circle, which they called the *orchestra,* at the base of a curving hillside. The slope of the hill formed a natural amphitheatre for the spectators, and the level circle at the foot formed the stage. At the back of the circle, facing the hillside, there was a stage house that had formal doors for the performers' entrances and exits. It also created a background for the action, and provided a place for changing costumes. The stage house and the audience seating in Greek theatres began as wooden structures in the fifth century B.C.E., but during the next two centuries they came to be made of stone. The largest Greek theatres seated 15,000 or more spectators. This design was duplicated all over Greece, particularly in the years following the conquests of Alexander the Great during the early fourth century B.C.E. Remnants of these theatres remain today throughout that part of the world, in such places as Epidaurus, Priene, Ephesus, Delphi, and Corinth.

The Romans adapted the Greek form, making it a complete structure and developing a theatre that was not strictly a thrust but a forerunner of the proscenium. Instead of using the natural amphitheatre of a hillside, they created a freestanding stone structure in which the stage house was joined to the seating area and the orchestra was

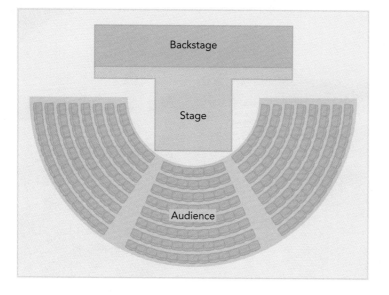

THRUST STAGE WITH THREE-QUARTERS SEATING
The stage is surrounded on three sides by the audience. Sometimes seating is a semi-circle. Entrances and exits are made from the sides and backstage. Spectators surround the action, but scene changes and other stage effects are still possible.

a semicircle. In front of the stage house, which was decorated with arches and statues, they erected a long platform stage where most of the action occurred.

In the medieval period, formal theatre, which had disappeared for several hundred years, was revived. Short religious plays in Latin began to be presented in churches and cathedrals in England and parts of continental Europe. Around 1300 C.E., religious plays written in the common language were presented outdoors. One popular space for these outdoor performances was another form of the thrust, known as a *platform stage.* A simple platform was set on wooden supports called *trestles* (hence, this arrangement is sometimes also called a *trestle stage*), with a curtain at the back that the performers used for entrances and costume changes. The area underneath the stage was closed off and provided a space from which devils and other characters could appear, sometimes in a cloud of smoke. In some places the platform was mounted on wheels (a *wagon stage*) and moved from place to place through a town. The audience stood on three sides of the platform, making it an improvised thrust stage. This type of performance space was widely used between the thirteenth and fifteenth centuries in England and various parts of continental Europe. (We will discuss more fully debates surrounding pageant wagon staging in Chapter 11.)

In the sixteenth century, just before Shakespeare began writing for the theatre, a particular type of thrust stage took shape in England. A platform stage was set up at one end of the open inner courtyard of an inn. Such a courtyard was surrounded on four sides by the interior walls of the inn, three or four stories high. The rooms facing the courtyard served as boxes for some of the spectators; on the ground level, other spectators stood on three sides of the stage. The fourth side of the courtyard, behind the platform, served as the stage house. Interestingly, an almost identical theatre took shape in Spain at the same time. Spanish inns were called *corrales,* and this name was given to the courtyard theatres that developed there.

Formal English theatres of Shakespeare's day, such as the Globe and the Fortune, were similar to the inn theatres: some of the spectators stood in an open area around a

Platform stage Elevated stage with no proscenium.

Wagon stage Low platform mounted on wheels by means of which an entire stage is moved place to place.

Corral Theatre of the Spanish Golden Age, usually located in the courtyard of a series of adjoining buildings.

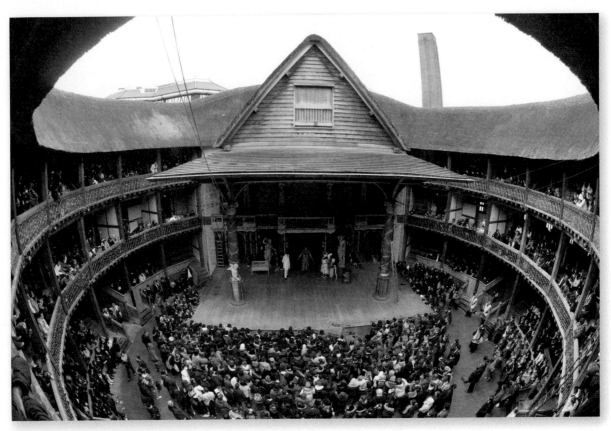

THE RESTORED GLOBE THEATRE
On the South Bank of the Thames River in London, a theatre has been constructed quite near the site of the original Globe, built in 1599. It was for this theatre that Shakespeare and several of his contemporaries wrote their most masterful dramas. The reconstruction has attempted to duplicate the original dimensions, use the same materials, and in general create for audiences an experience similar to the one for audiences in Shakespeare's time. Shown here is the audience attending a production at the reconstructed Globe. (Shakespeare's Globe Image Library)

platform stage while others sat in three levels of closed galleries at the back and sides. A roof covered part of the stage; at the back, some form of raised area served for balcony scenes, such as the one in *Romeo and Juliet.* On each side at the rear were doors used for entrances and exits. (In the spring of 1997, a reproduction of the Globe Theatre was opened on the South Bank of the Thames River in London, only a short distance from the site of the original Globe. Built to the same dimensions as the original and using authentic materials, it recreates the feeling of the thrust theatre used in Shakespeare's day.)

English theatres like the Globe and the Fortune were a fascinating combination of diverse elements: they were both indoors and outdoors, and some spectators stood while others sat; also, the audience was made up of almost all levels of society. The physical environment must have been stimulating since performers standing at the front of the thrust stage were in the center of a hemisphere of spectators—on three sides around them as well as above and below. Although such a theatre held 2,000 spectators or more, no one in the audience was more than sixty feet or so from the stage, and most people were much closer. Being in the midst of so many people, enclosed on all sides, but with the open sky above, must have instilled a feeling of great

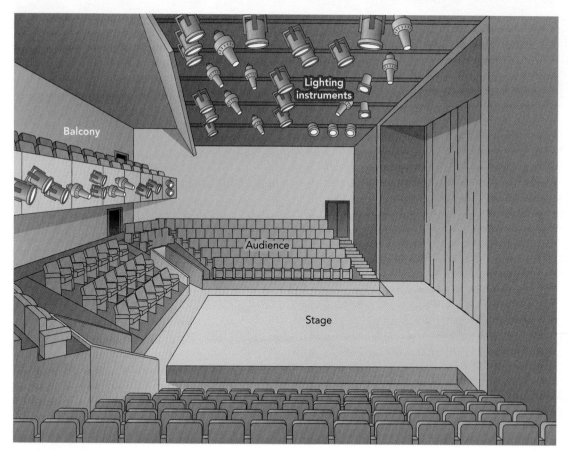

THE STAGE AND SEATING AREA OF A THRUST-STAGE THEATRE
This cutaway drawing of a thrust stage shows how the playing area juts into the audience, which surrounds the stage on three sides. This configuration affords intimacy, but at the back (shown here at the right) is an area that furnishes a natural backdrop for the action.

communion among the spectators and the performers. (A drawing of a typical Elizabethan theatre can be found in Chapter 13.)

However, we should note that there were several smaller indoor theatres built during Shakepeare's time. Shortly after Shakespeare's day, in the latter part of the seventeenth century, two things occurred, not only in England and Spain but throughout Europe: theatre moved completely indoors, and the stage began a slow but steady retreat behind a frame—the proscenium opening—which enclosed the stage action. For the next two centuries the thrust theatre was in eclipse, and it was not to reappear until around 1900, when a few theatres in England began using a version of the thrust stage to produce Shakespeare.

The return of the thrust stage in Great Britain and the United States during the past 100 years has resulted from a growing realization that certain plays—not only works of Shakespeare but those of his fellow Elizabethans and the playwrights of the Spanish Golden Age—can be done best on a stage similar to the one for which they were written. In the United States and Canada, the thrust stage was not revived until after World War II; since then, however, a number of fine thrust-stage theatres have been built, including the Tyrone Guthrie in Minneapolis; the Shakespeare Theatre in

THE JAPANESE NŌ STAGE
An ancient Asian form of the thrust stage is the nō stage in Japan. As shown here, it is a platform stage with the audience sitting on one side and in front. Originally it was an outdoor theatre with a covered stage. In modern times, the entire theatre is enclosed, as if the outdoor space had been moved indoors, but the theatre itself remains the same. Shown here is a production of the nō play *Ataka,* at the National Nō Theatre, Tokyo. (© Toshiro Morita/HAGA/The Image Works)

Stratford, Ontario; the Mark Taper Forum in Los Angeles; and the Long Wharf in New Haven.

The basic stage of traditional Chinese and Japanese drama (including nō theatre in Japan) is a form of thrust stage: a raised, open platform, frequently covered by a roof, with the audience sitting on two or three sides around the stage. Entrances and exits are made from doors or ramps at the rear of the stage.

The obvious advantages of the thrust stage—the intimacy of the three-quarters seating, the close audience-performer relationship, and the fact that so many of the world's great dramatic works were written for it—give it a significant place in theatre.

ARENA STAGE:
HISTORY AND CHARACTERISTICS

Arena stage Stage entirely surrounded by the audience; also known as theatre-in-the-round.

The **arena stage,** also called *circle theatre* or *theatre-in-the-round,* has a playing space in the center of a square or circle, with seats for spectators surrounding it. This arrangement is similar to that in sports arenas that feature boxing or basketball. The stage may

ARENA STAGE
With an arena stage, also referred to as a circle stage or theatre-in-the-round, the audience surrounds the stage area on all sides. In addition to aisles for audience members to enter, there are passages that the performers use to enter and leave the stage. One effect of the arena stage is to create a close rapport between actors and audience. Seen here is the newly renovated Fitchander Stage at the Arena Stage in Washington, D.C. (Photo by Nic Lehoux courtesy of Bing Thom Architects)

be raised a few feet off the main floor, with seats rising from the floor level; or it may be on the floor itself, with seats raised on levels around it. When the seating is close to the stage, there is usually some kind of demarcation indicating the boundaries of the playing area.

One advantage of the arena theatre is that it offers the most intimacy, particularly in comparison with the picture-frame stage. With the performers in the center, even in a large theatre, the audience can be closer to the action because seating is on all four sides instead of only one side. If the same number of people attend a performance in an arena theatre and a picture-frame theatre, at least half of those in the arena theatre will be nearer the stage. Moreover, in an arena theatre there is no frame or barrier to separate the performers from the audience.

An arena arrangement also allows for the unconscious communion that is created when people form a circle. The configuration of a circle seems to come naturally to human beings: we embrace with encircling arms, form circles to play children's games, and make human enclosures around fires and altars. An unusual event will automatically draw people into a circle to watch; during a street fight, for instance, notice how the onlookers form a circle to take a close look without getting so near that they would

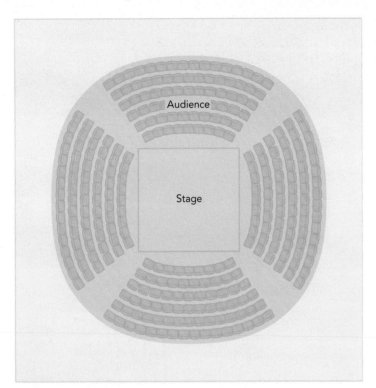

PLAN OF AN ARENA STAGE
The audience sits on four sides or in a circle surrounding the stage. Entrances and exits are made through the aisles or through tunnels underneath the aisles. A feeling of intimacy is achieved because the audience is close to the action and encloses it.

become involved. In view of this universal instinct to form circles, it is not surprising that virtually all of the earliest forms of theatre were "in the round."

There is also a practical, economic advantage to the arena stage: any large room can be converted into this arrangement. You simply designate a playing space, arrange rows of seats around the sides, and hang lights on pipes above, and you have a theatre. Elaborate scenery is unnecessary; in fact, it is impossible because it would block the view of large parts of the audience. A few pieces of furniture, with perhaps a lamp or sign hung from the ceiling, are all you need to indicate where a scene takes place. Many low-budget groups have found that they can build a workable and even attractive theatre-in-the-round when a picture-frame theatre would be out of the question.

These two factors—intimacy and economy—no doubt explain why the arena theatre is one of the oldest stage spaces. As we have mentioned, ceremonies in ancient Greece were held in a circular space, which was the forerunner of the Greek thrust stage. From as far back as we have records,

THE STAGE AND SEATING IN AN ARENA THEATRE
The arena theatre attempts to capture the intimacy and immediacy of primitive theatre. It uses the barest essentials of stage scenery but the full resources of contemporary stage lighting.

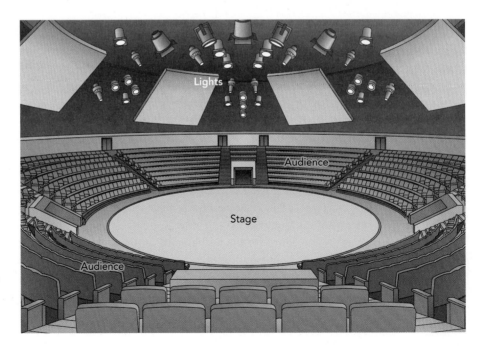

we know that religious observances and tribal rituals in all parts of the world have been held in some form of circle theatre. One example is the war dance of the Apache; another is the festival plays of Tibet, which portray the struggle of Buddhism to supplant an earlier religion. In the medieval period, several of the religious plays in England and France were performed in arena-type spaces. In the modern period in the United States, there was a proliferation of arena stages after World War II.

In spite of its long history and its recent resurgence, however, the arena stage has often been eclipsed by other forms. One reason is that its design, while allowing for intimacy, also dictates a certain austerity: elaborate scenery, for example, is impossible because it would block the view of many spectators. Also, performers must make all their entrances and exits along aisles that run through the audience, and so they can sometimes be seen before and after they are supposed to appear onstage.

These problems may explain why some of the circle theatres that opened in the United States thirty or forty years ago have since closed. A number survive, however, and continue to do well, one of the best-known being the Arena Stage in Washington, D.C. In addition, throughout the country there are a number of tent theatres in arena form, where concerts and revivals of musicals are given.

Before we leave the three major types of theatre arrangements—proscenium, thrust, and arena—we should point out that with each of them, there is customarily space just outside the main seating and stage areas where the audience assembles and tickets are sold and taken. Also, backstage or offstage, there must be dressing rooms for performers and facilities for the stage manager, the stage crews, and anyone else concerned with mounting and running a show. (***Running*** is the term used to describe the unfolding of a performance, including changes in lighting and scenery. When actors, actresses, and stage crew move through a performance, they are said to be *running* the show.)

Run Operation of a show; also, the length of time a production is performed.

CREATED OR FOUND SPACES

A fourth type of stage is called ***created space*** or ***found space.*** This term means that a theatre is set up in a space not ordinarily used for performance. All early theatres probably began in some type of created or found space. Tribal ceremonies, for example, were performed in outdoor spaces such as a circle with an altar at the center. In the Middle Ages, theatre performances were originally held in churches or cathedrals. When these performances became longer and more secular in nature, they were presented outside; but even then, there were no permanent theatres—only temporary stages erected in the "found" space of town squares.

In recent years, there has been renewed interest in the concept of theatre performed in unusual places: street corners, public parks, and the like. This is meant partly to bring theatre closer to people, and partly to put theatre into a new and different context so that people will think about its purpose and impact. Nontheatre spaces are often of special interest to experimental, avant-garde, or political theatre practitioners. In the 1960s, the Polish director Jerzy Grotowski made novel use of space an important part of his productions, rearranging an open area in different configurations for different plays. In his production of a play about Doctor Faustus, for example, Faustus gives a banquet; for this, Grotowski filled the open theatre space with two long tables at which audience members sat, as if they were guests at a dinner party, while the actors

Created space or **found space** Space not originally intended for theatre use which is converted for productions. Avant-garde artists often produce in found spaces.

and actresses performed on the tabletops. For another play, which took place in a mental hospital, the action was set inside a simulated hospital ward, with the performers on beds and the spectators moving around the beds.

One manifestation of found or created space has been *street theatre,* which takes place—as the name suggests—in the streets. One purpose of street theatre is to bring performances to neighborhoods, especially in inner cities, where people do not normally attend traditional theatre. Street theatre can also serve a political purpose: it is sometimes used to make a moral or political point by people who feel that being in the streets will bring their message home to audiences more forcefully.

By now, every conceivable type of space has been used for theatre: lofts, warehouses, fire stations, basements, churches, breweries, gymnasiums, jails, parks, subway stations. Of course, such sites present problems for any kind of long-range theatre. They are, obviously, impermanent, and matters such as how to handle tickets raise difficult questions. Also, there is usually only a minimum of scenery, and the accommodations for spectators can be less than ideal. Nevertheless, created and found spaces have been important at various times in theatre history and take their place as one of the four major theatre arrangements or environments.

MULTIFOCUS ENVIRONMENTS

Multifocus theatre Theatre in which something is going on simultaneously in several playing areas.

An approach that sometimes accompanies unusual theatre arrangements is *multifocus theatre.* Put simply, this means that there is more than one playing area (such as the four corners of a room), and that something is going on simultaneously in several areas. Multifocus theatre is somewhat like a three-ring circus, where we see an activity in each ring and must either concentrate on one ring or divide our attention.

There are several theories behind the idea of multifocus theatre. One theory is that a multifocus event is more like everyday life; if you stand on a street corner, for instance, there is activity all around you—in the four directions of the streets and in the buildings above—not just in one spot. You select which area you will observe, or perhaps you watch several areas at once. The argument is that you should have the same choice in theatre.

In a multifocus production, no single space or activity is supposed to be more important than any other. Each spectator either takes in and synthesizes several impressions at once or selects one impression as most arresting and concentrates on that. There is no such thing as the "best seat in the house"; all seats are equally good because the activity in all parts of the theatre is equally important. Sometimes multifocus theatre is joined with *multimedia theatre*—a presentation using some combination of acting, film, dance, music, slides, video, and light shows.

Multimedia theatre Use of electronic media—such as slides, film, and videotape—in live theatrical presentations.

ALL-PURPOSE AND EXPERIMENTAL SPACES

Black box A theatre space that is open, flexible, and adaptable, usually without fixed seating or a permanent stage area. It is economical and particularly well suited to experimental work.

Because of the interest in a variety of spaces in modern theatre productions, and to meet the requirements of different kinds of productions, a number of theatre complexes—including many college theatre departments—have built spaces that can be adapted to an almost infinite range of configurations. These spaces are sometimes referred to as *black boxes.* Seats, lights, platforms, levels—every aspect is flexible and movable. In this kind of space, designers can create a proscenium, a thrust, an arena, or some

POPULAR PERFORMANCE SPACES

Many spaces used for live popular entertainments are reminiscent of theatre environments. Arenas used for sports, circuses, and rock concerts are configured much like the theatrical spaces discussed in this chapter. Madison Square Garden in New York, Soldier Field in Chicago, and the Rose Bowl in Pasadena, California, are all large spaces that primarily house sporting events but are also used for rock concerts and other popular spectacles.

Madison Square Garden, for example, has housed the Ringling Brothers and Barnum and Bailey Circus, an extravagant staging of *The Wizard of Oz,* Frank Sinatra, Barbra Streisand, Bruce Springsteen, the Grammys, and the VH1 Awards, to name just a few events. This means that an arena like the Garden is often equipped with the most innovative technology for lighting, stage, and sound effects.

Spectacular performance spaces for magicians, circuses, and concerts are also found in all of the extravagant hotels in Las Vegas. There is live entertainment presented in spaces at fairgrounds and amusement parks as well.

These spaces for popular performance are most often configured in the round, with spectators surrounding the events. (Some are configured three-quarter-round.) The reason is to maximize the number of audience members as well as to create an electrifying, interactive environment. With these configurations, the spectators are also able to watch and possibly influence each other's reactions.

Such popular performance spaces are usually extremely large, much larger than environments created exclusively for theatre. For example, the Rose Bowl accommodates 92,542 for football games. Even a comparatively small

collegiate athletics facility, Western Hall on the campus of Western Illinois University, can accommodate approximately 5,100 spectators.

The relationship between spaces for popular entertainment and theatrical environments is complex. In later chapters, we will see that often in theatre history, spaces were used for popular arts and for theatrical performances. Modern theatre artists have experimented with staging dramatic performances within spaces created for circuses and concerts.

For that matter, the performance qualities of sports, the circus, and rock concerts underscore their shared heritage with the theatrical arts. It is not surprising, then, that their spaces for performance are also similar.

A SPORTS SPECTACLE
An event such as a game in a sports arena has a number of similarities to a theatrical event: a focus of attention like a stage; an audience surrounding it; a common bond between spectators and athletes, where the athletes resemble performers in theatre. The arena shown here is the Cowboys Stadium in Arlington, Texas, which hosted the 2011 Super Bowl. (© Tom Pennington/ Getty Images)

SITE-SPECIFIC THEATRE: CREATED AND FOUND SPACE

Shown here are two examples of site-specific theatre. In the first, a production loosely based on *Macbeth,* entitled *Sleep No More* by the British group Punchdrunk, was presented in three abandoned warehouses in New York City through which the audience was led to see various segments, some of which involved movement, some of which were like tableaus. In the scene here, the Macbeth character (Nicholas Bruder) is seen in a bathtub, with the Lady Macbeth character (Sophie Bortolussi) outside the tub. (Sara Krulwich/The New York Times/Redux) The second example shows the Polish theatre company Biuro Podrozy in a street theatre version of Shakespeare's *Macbeth* using its trademark stilts near the Royal Mile at the Edinburgh Festival Fringe in Edinburgh, Scotland. (© Jeff Mitchell/Getty Images)

combination of these. Moreover, the designers can also create corner stages, island stages, and multifocus arrangements with playing areas in several parts of the studio or another flexible space.

Open studios and similar adaptable, experimental spaces are especially important for avant-garde theatre troupes, college theatre organizations, and groups engaged in workshop productions of new works, whether by individual playwrights, performance artists, or collectives.

In conclusion, we should note that simply assigning a theatre to a category does not adequately describe the environment; we must also take into account a number of other variables in theatre architecture. Two theatres may be of the same type but still be quite different in location, size, ornateness, and atmosphere; for instance, one may be indoors and the other outdoors.

We should also note that questions of appropriateness and aesthetic distance arise. By *appropriateness,* we mean the relationship of a stage space to a play or production. With regard to environment, ***aesthetic distance*** denotes the appropriate amount of spatial separation between performers and audience. For example, the theatre space for a large-scale spectacular musical should be different from that for a small-scale intimate drama.

In discussing theatre spaces, another thing to remember is that the modern period is unique in having so many forms available simultaneously. Audiences in the United States today can enjoy theatre in a multitude of settings. Not only do we have examples of all four major types of theatre spaces; there is great variety within each of those types. There are thrust stages outdoors, such as the Shakespeare Festival theatre in New York's Central Park and other similar outdoor theatres; and there are small indoor thrust stages in cities all across the country, as well as larger ones such as the Guthrie Theatre in Minneapolis and the Mark Taper Forum in Los Angeles. The same variety is seen in arena and proscenium theatres.

In Chapters 8 and 9 we will turn to aspects of theatre closely associated with theatre space: the visual elements—scenery, costumes, and lighting—that become a part of the space, and the sound that fills it.

THE MULTIPURPOSE OR "BLACK BOX" THEATRE
A popular type of modern theatre is the multipurpose space, sometimes called a "black box." It consists of an open space with perhaps a pipe grid on the ceiling from which lighting and sound instruments can be suspended. A stage platform can be positioned at any place in the space, and movable chairs for spectators can be placed around the playing area. The diagrams suggest some of the possibilities of stage arrangements in a multipurpose theatre.

Aesthetic distance Physical or psychological separation or detachment of audience from dramatic action, usually considered necessary for artistic illusion.

Summary

An indispensable element of all theatrical productions is the physical space in which the performance occurs. A theatre space must include a place for the spectators to sit or stand. Theatre spaces may be indoors or outdoors, and of any size or shape, but four basic arrangements have prevailed throughout theatre history.

Probably the best-known arrangement is the proscenium-arch or picture-frame stage. First introduced in Europe during the Italian Renaissance, it grew in popularity throughout Europe and the United States, and it is still frequently used. The action takes place behind the proscenium arch, which can also be used to conceal elaborate machinery for creating realistic or spectacular scenic effects.

In the earliest Western theatres, the most popular arrangement was the thrust stage with three-quarters seating, developed by the ancient Greeks and adapted by the Romans. Variations of the thrust stage were also used in English courtyard theatres and Spanish corrales, and for traditional Chinese and Japanese drama.

Another basic arrangement of theatre space is the arena stage, or theatre-in-the-round. Arena staging brings more of the audience closer to the stage than is possible with a proscenium or thrust arrangement; thus one of the advantages of the arena stage is a sense of intimacy between audience and performers.

The fourth type of theatre arrangement is created or found space: performances that take place not in a permanent theatre but in a park, a church, a garage, or some other place that does not usually serve as a theatre.

All four types of theatre spaces are used in the United States today, as are many variations, including the multifocus space and the flexible experimental theatre.

Thinking about Theatre

▶ As discussed in this chapter, there are four major types of stage spaces: proscenium, thrust, arena, and found space. What do you think are the advantages and disadvantages of each? On which type of stage space would you prefer to watch a performance?

▶ Using information from this chapter, explain which type of stage space you feel is best suited to each of the following productions: a large-scale musical, an intimate personal drama, a Shakespearean drama, and a play of political protest.

▶ The size of theatre spaces can range from more than 3,000 spectators to fewer than 100. What do you consider an ideal-sized theatre for particular types of theatre: a musical, a Shakespeare play, a modern family drama? Suggest the ideal number of audience seats for each, and the shape and size of the ideal stage space for each type of production.

KEY TERMS

Aesthetic distance Physical or psychological separation or detachment of audience from dramatic action, usually considered necessary for artistic illusion.

Arena stage Stage entirely surrounded by the audience; also known as theatre-in-the-round.

Black box A theatre space that is open, flexible, and adaptable, usually without fixed seating or a permanent stage area. It is economical and particularly well suited to experimental work.

Corral Theatre of the Spanish Golden Age, usually located in the courtyard of a series of adjoining buildings.

Created space or **found space** Space not originally intended for theatre use which is converted for productions. Avant-garde artists often produce in found spaces.

Fly loft Space above the stage where scenery may be lifted out of sight by means of ropes and pulleys.

Fourth-wall convention Pretense that in a proscenium-arch theatre the audience is looking into a room through an invisible fourth wall.

Multifocus theatre Theatre in which something is going on simultaneously in several playing areas.

Multimedia theatre Use of electronic media—such as slides, film, and videotape—in live theatrical presentations.

Orchestra Ground-floor seating in an auditorium; also, a circular playing space in ancient Greek theatres.

Platform stage Elevated stage with no proscenium.

Proscenium Arch or frame surrounding the stage opening in a box or picture stage.

Rake An upward slope of the stage floor away from the audience; also, to position scenery on a slant or at an angle other than parallel or perpendicular to the curtain line.

Run Operation of a show; also, the length of time a production is performed.

Thrust stage Theatre space in which the audience sits on three sides of the stage.

Wagon stage Low platform mounted on wheels or casters by means of which scenery is moved on- and offstage.

THEATRE ON THE WEB

For more research and to learn more about the topics in this chapter, please visit the Online Learning Center at **www.mhhe.com/livelyart8e.**

THE DESIGNERS: SCENERY AND COSTUMES

SCENE DESIGN

THE SCENE DESIGNER'S OBJECTIVES

ELEMENTS OF SCENE DESIGN

Global Crosscurrents:
The Magic of the Designer
Josef Svoboda

THE PROCESS OF SCENE DESIGN: STEPS IN THE DESIGN PROCESS

THE SCENE DESIGNER'S COLLABORATORS AND THE PRODUCTION PROCESS

DESIGNING A TOTAL ENVIRONMENT

COSTUME DESIGN

THE COSTUME DESIGNER

THE COSTUME DESIGNER'S OBJECTIVES

Photo Essay:
The Costume Designer at Work

ELEMENTS OF COSTUME DESIGN

THE COSTUME DESIGNER'S COLLABORATORS

RELATED ELEMENTS OF COSTUME DESIGN

SUMMARY
THINKING ABOUT THEATRE
KEY TERMS
THEATRE ON THE WEB

◀ **SCENERY AND COSTUME DESIGNERS** Designers—especially scene and costume designers—determine the look of a production. These visual elements tell us whether a production is realistic or nonrealistic and whether it is modern or historical; they also add color and visual excitement. Seen here are Joseph Marcell, Jeffrey Wright, and Mos Def in *A Free Man of Color,* a play by John Guare set in early nineteenth-century New Orleans, about a wealthy African American who was free until the United States purchased Louisiana from the French, when he was no longer free. Directed by George C. Wolfe at Lincoln Center Theater; set: David Rockwell; costumes: Ann Hould-Ward; lighting: Jules Fisher and Peggy Eisenhauer; wigs: Paul Huntley. (© T. Charles Erickson)

As spectators sit in a theatre, watching what unfolds before them, they naturally focus most keenly on the performers. But audiences also notice the visual images created by scenery, costumes, and lighting—and they may also hear music underscoring the action, and sound effects such as rain, thunder, or traffic. These visual and aural elements, which add a significant ingredient to the total mixture of theatre, are created and organized by designers.

The *scene designer* is responsible for the stage set, which can run the gamut from a bare stage furnished only with stools or orange crates to the most elaborate large-scale production. No matter how simple, however, every set has a design. Even the absence of scenery constitutes a stage set and can benefit from the ideas of a scene designer. The *costume designer* is responsible for selecting, and in many cases creating, the outfits and accessories worn by performers.

Designers must deal with practical as well as aesthetic considerations. A scene designer must know in which direction a door should open onstage, how high each riser should be on a flight of stairs, what materials work best in building scenery, and what kinds of paint to use for painting it. A costume designer must know how much material it takes to make a certain kind of dress and how to "build" clothes so that performers can wear them with confidence and have freedom of movement.

In this chapter, we will deal with scene and costume design. Chapter 9 will take up lighting and sound design.

SCENE DESIGN

THE SCENE DESIGNER'S OBJECTIVES

In preparing scenery for a stage production, a scene designer has the following objectives:

1. Help set the tone and style of the production
2. Establish the locale and period in which the play takes place
3. Develop a design concept consistent with the director's concept
4. Provide a central image or metaphor, where appropriate
5. Ensure that scenery is coordinated with other production elements
6. Solve practical design problems

Establishing Tone and Style   A stage setting can help establish the mood, style, and meaning of a play. In the arts, *style* refers to the *manner* in which a work is done: how scenery looks, how a playwright uses language or exaggerates dramatic elements, how performers portray characters. (A realistic acting style, for example, resembles the way people behave in everyday life; in contrast, the lofty quality of traditional tragedy calls for formal, larger-than-life movements and gestures.)

A slapstick farce might call for a design style involving comic, exaggerated scenery, like a cartoon; and perhaps for outrageous colors, such as bright reds and oranges. Such scenery would match the acting, which would also be exaggerated, with lots of physical comedy—people tripping over carpets, opening the wrong doors, and so forth. A satire would call for a comment in the design, like the twist in the lines of a caricature in a political cartoon. A serious play would call for less exaggerated or less comic scenery.

SCENE DESIGN SETS THE STAGE
In Federico García Lorca's play *The House of Bernarda Alba,* a widow who has grown to hate and distrust men keeps her daughters confined as virtual prisoners in their own home, preventing them from going out. In this production, directed by Elizabeth Huddle at the Madison Repertory Theatre, we see four of the daughters, with the mother in the center. Left to right, the performers are Jamie England, Monica Lyons, Elisabeth Adwin, Margaret Ingraham, and Diane Robinson. For this production, scene designer Frank Schneeberger created in the set a hemmed-in, confining space appropriate for the play. Costumes by Mary Waldhart. (Zane Williams/Madison Repertory Theatre)

As an illustration of what is called for in scene design, let us consider two plays by the Spanish playwright Federico García Lorca. His *Blood Wedding* is the story of a young bride-to-be who runs away with a former lover on the day she is to be married. The two flee to a forest. In the forest, allegorical figures of the Moon and a Beggar Woman, who represents Death, seem to echo the fierce emotional struggle taking place within the characters, who are torn between duty to their families and passion for each other. For this part of the play, the scenery and costumes must have the same sense of mystery, of the unreal, which rules the characters. The forest should not have real trees but should represent the thicket of emotions in which the man and woman are entangled; the costumes of the Moon and the Beggar Woman should not be realistic but should suggest the forces that endanger the lovers.

Another play by García Lorca, *The House of Bernarda Alba,* is a contrast in style: it has no fantasy or symbolic characters. This play concerns a woman and her five daughters. The mother has grown to hate and distrust men, and so she locks up her house, like a closed convent, preventing her daughters from going out. From a design

REALISM AND NONREALISM IN SCENIC DESIGN

Scene design helps indicate whether a production is realistic or a departure from realism. Shown here are good examples of the two approaches. The scene at top is from *American Buffalo,* directed by Amy Morton for Steppenwolf and McCarter Theatres; the scenic designer was Kevin Depinet; lighting was by Pat Collins; costumes by Nan Cibula-Jenkins. Pictured are Patrick Andrews as Bobby, Kurt Ehrmann as Don. (© T. Charles Erickson) In contrast we see an example of nonrealistic scenery designed by Robert Wilson for his rock opera, POEtry, about Edgar Allan Poe. There is no attempt to portray reality; rather, there is a surrealistic presentation of images and ideas. (© Hermann and Clärchen Baus)

point of view, it is important to convey the closed-in, cloistered feeling of the house in which the daughters are held as virtual prisoners. The walls of the house and its furniture should all have solid reality, creating an atmosphere that will convey a sense of entrapment.

Scene design is especially important in indicating to the audience whether a play is realistic or departs from realism. ***Realism*** in theatre means that everything connected with a production conforms to our observation of the world around us. This includes the way characters speak and behave, the clothes they wear, the events that occur in the play, and the physical environment. Characters presented in a living room or a bar, for example, will look and act as we expect people in those settings to look and act.

Realism Broadly, an attempt to present onstage people and events corresponding to those in everyday life.

On the other hand, *nonrealism* or *departures from realism* means all types of theatre that depart from observable reality. A musical in which characters sing and dance is nonrealistic because people do not ordinarily go around singing and dancing in public places. A play like Shakespeare's *Macbeth* is unrealistic because it has witches and ghosts—two types of creatures not encountered in everyday existence. Also, the language of the play is poetry, and there are soliloquies in which characters speak thoughts out loud—again, these are elements that depart from the reality we see in our daily lives. Nonrealistic elements are, of course, highly theatrical and can increase our pleasure and excitement. Moreover, they often indicate a deeper reality than we see on the surface. Thus *departures from realism* does not imply that something is not genuine or not true; it simply means that something is a departure from what we see in the world around us.

The terms, then, are simply ways of categorizing aspects of theatre; and they are particularly important in scene design, because scenery can quickly signal to an audience which type of theatre we are viewing.

Establishing Locale and Period   Whether realistic or not, a stage set should tell the audience where and when the play takes place. Is the locale a saloon? A bedroom? A courtroom? A palace? A forest? The set should also indicate the time period. A kitchen with old-fashioned utensils and no electric appliances sets the play in the past. An early radio and an icebox might tell us that the period is the 1920s. A spaceship or the landscape of a faraway planet would suggest that the play is set in the future.

In addition to indicating time and place, the setting can also tell us what kinds of characters a play is about. For example, the characters may be neat and formal or lazy and sloppy. They may be kings and queens or members of an ordinary suburban family. The scenery should suggest these things immediately.

Developing a Design Concept   In order to convey information, the scene designer frequently develops a *design concept.* Such a concept should be arrived at in consultation with the director and should complement the directorial concept (discussed in Chapter 6). The design concept is a unifying idea carried out visually. For García Lorca's *The House of Bernarda Alba,* for example, such a concept would be a claustrophobic setting that sets the tone for the entire play.

A strong design concept is particularly important when the time and place of a play have been shifted. Modern stage designs for Shakespeare's *A Midsummer Night's Dream* illustrate this point. In most productions, this play is performed in a palace and a forest, as suggested by the text. But the director Peter Brook wanted to give the play a modern, clean, spare look so that the audience would see its contemporary implications. Accordingly, the scene designer, Sally Jacobs (1932–   ), fashioned a single set consisting of three bare white walls, rather like the walls of a gymnasium. This single set was used as the background for all the scenes in the play, giving visual unity to the production and also creating a modern, somewhat abstract atmosphere. As part of the action, trapezes were lowered onto the stage at various times, and in some scenes the performers actually played their parts suspended in midair.

Providing a Central Image or Metaphor   The design concept is closely related to the idea of a *central image* or *metaphor.* Stage design not only must be consistent

A CENTRAL DESIGN IMAGE

For a production of John Steinbeck's *The Grapes of Wrath*, the scene designer, Marion Williams, selected an old jalopy as a central design image. The design conveys the futility of a deserted land, the Dust Bowl in the 1930s. In later scenes, trapdoors open to reveal a stream, and then a horrendous rainfall showers down, showing the extremes of weather faced by these wanderers. Through it all, however, an overstuffed jalopy is pushed around the stage by some of the actors, remaining a constant visual image and giving a sense of the characters' movements from place to place. The play was adapted by Frank Galati and directed by Joe Discher at the Shakespeare Theatre of New Jersey, with costumes by Maggie Dick. (© Gerry Goodstein)

with the play; it should have its own integrity. The elements of the design—lines, shapes, and colors—should add up to a complete visual universe for the play. Often, therefore, the designer tries to develop a central image or metaphor.

In a production of Stephen Sondheim's *Sweeney Todd,* the designer, John Doyle, who was also the director, created a vast wooden cabinet in the center of the back wall. The subtitle of this musical is *The Demon Barber of Fleet Street;* and the cabinet, about twenty feet tall, had shelves for razors and all the tools of the barber trade as well as other bric-a-brac. A black coffin, which served other functions as well as its original purpose, stood at center stage throughout. But it was the menacing presence of the towering cabinet that dominated the scene and served as a central design image for the entire production.

Coordinating Scenery with the Whole   Because scenic elements have such strong symbolic value and are so important to the overall effect of a production, the designer needs to provide scenery consistent with the playwright's intent and the director's concept. If the text and acting are highly stylized, the setting should be stylized too. If the text and acting are realistic, the setting should also be realistic, rather than, say, a fantastic or overpowering spectacle. As with other elements, the setting should contribute to the overall effect of a production.

Solving Practical Design Problems   Finally, the scene designer must deal with practical problems of design. Many of these involve physical elements of stage design, to which we'll now turn.

ELEMENTS OF SCENE DESIGN

Five Elements of Scene Design   As the scene designer proceeds, he or she makes use of the following elements:

1. *Line,* the outline or silhouette of elements onstage; for example, predominantly curved lines versus sharply angular lines.

2. *Mass,* the overall bulk or weight of scenic elements; for example, a series of high, heavy platforms or fortress walls versus a bare stage or a stage with only a single tree on it.

3. *Composition,* the balance and arrangement of elements; the way elements are arranged: for example, mostly to one side of the stage, in a vertical or horizontal configuration, or equally distributed onstage.

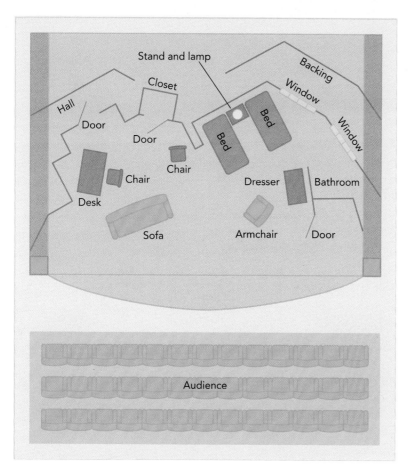

Stand and lamp
Closet
Hall
Door
Door
Desk
Chair
Chair
Sofa
Backing
Window
Window
Bed
Bed
Dresser
Bathroom
Armchair
Door

Audience

GROUND PLAN
To aid the director, performers, and stage technicians, the
designer draws a ground plan
of the stage, showing the exact
locations of furniture, walls,
windows, doors, and other
scenic elements.

4. *Texture,* the "feel" projected by surfaces and fabrics; for example, the slickness of chrome or glass versus the roughness of brick or burlap.

5. *Color,* the shadings and contrasts of color combinations.

The designer will use these elements to affect audiences, in conjunction with the action and other aspects of the production.

Physical Layout: The Playing Area   A playing area must, obviously, fit into a certain stage space and accommodate the performers. A designer cannot plan a gigantic stage setting for a theatre where the proscenium opening is only twenty feet wide and the stage is no more than fifteen feet deep. By the same token, to design a small room in the midst of a forty-foot stage opening might be ludicrous.

The designer must also take into account the physical layout of the stage space. If a performer must leave by a door on the right side of the stage and return a few moments later by a door on the left, the designer must obviously provide space for crossing behind the scenery. If performers need to change costumes quickly offstage, the scene designer must make certain that there is room offstage for changing. If there is to be a sword fight, the actors must have space in which to make their turns, to advance and retreat.

Any type of physical movement requires a certain amount of space, and the scene designer must allow for this in his or her ground plan. A ***ground plan*** is a floor plan

Ground plan Floor plan or layout of stage design that outlines the various levels on the stage and indicates the placement of scenery, furniture, doors, windows, and other necessary scenic elements.

STAGE AREA

Various parts of the stage are given specific designations. Near the audience is *down-stage;* away from the audience is *upstage. Right* and *left* are from the performers' point of view, not the audience's. Everything out of sight of the audience is *offstage.* Using this scheme, everyone working in the theatre can carefully pin-point stage areas.

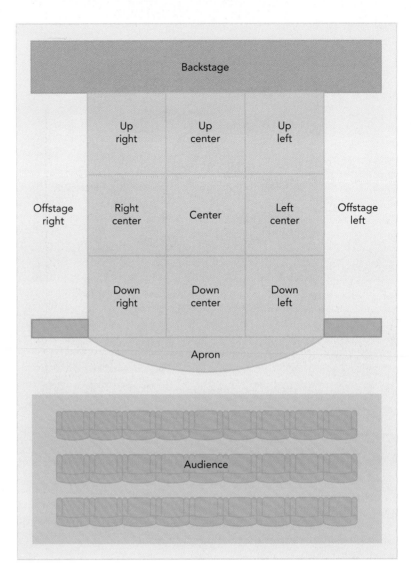

Right stage Right side of the stage from the point of view of a performer facing the audience.

Left stage Left side of the stage from the point of view of a performer facing the audience.

outlining the various levels on the stage and indicating the placement of all scenery, furniture, doors, windows, and so on. The designer, working in conjunction with the director, is chiefly responsible for ensuring a practical ground plan.

How doors open and close, where a sofa is placed, at what angle steps will lead to a second floor—all these are important. Performers must be able to execute stairs easily and to sit in such a way that the audience can readily see them, and they must have enough space to interact with each other naturally and convincingly. If a performer opens a door onstage and is immediately blocked from the view of the audience, this is obviously an error on the part of the scene designer.

To designate areas of the stage, scene designers, directors, performers, and technicians use terminology peculiar to theatre. *Stage right* and *stage left* mean the right side and the left side of the stage, respectively, as seen from the position of a performer facing the audience. (In other words, when spectators in the auditorium look at the stage, the area to their left is known as ***right stage*** and the area to their right as ***left stage.***)

THE MAGIC OF THE DESIGNER JOSEF SVOBODA

The Czech scene designer Josef Svoboda (1920–2002) developed a number of significant techniques in stage design, which have since been adopted and utilized by designers in many countries around the world. Svoboda's work centered on his understanding of the *kinetic stage* and *scenography*. The term *kinetic stage* refers to his belief that the set should not function independently of the actors, but rather should develop and adapt as a performance progresses. *Scenography* was what he called his art, conveying the sense that he created a whole physical space, not just designs on paper intended for the back of the stage. His experiments with these ideas led to many significant concepts in modern stage design, most notably the *laterna magika, polyekran,* and *diapolyekran.*

Polyekran literally means multiscreen and was the practice, devised by Svoboda, of using multiple screens at multiple angles and heights. Although real people and objects were projected, the aim was to convince the spectators not that they were looking at the real object, but rather that they were looking at a projection, or a collage of projections. A later development of this technique was *diapolyekran,* which employed whole walls of small, square screens making up a composite image. The wall of screens could be used to present one unified image, cubist images, or a collage.

Laterna magika, the best-known of his innovations, used screens in conjunction with actors; the actors were part of the film, and the film was part of the action. The projections used in this form were not simply for decoration, or for communicating images independent of the action; rather, the projections and action functioned together, creating a new manner of performance.

These developments were introduced to the global community in 1958 at the Brussels World Fair, where they instantly commanded attention from the wider theatrical community. Svoboda had been the chief designer at the National

Josef Svoboda. (© Franco Origlia/Sygma/Corbis)

Theatre in Prague at the time of the World Fair, and a showcase of the work of the theatre was displayed to the global audience, winning him three medals. What was seen as ingenious in 1958 was quickly adopted and adapted by numerous practitioners in many countries, and the effect of these means of design can still be witnessed in contemporary theatre, in performance art, and on Broadway, as well as at rock concerts and sporting events. This incorporation of screens and projections into onstage action has infiltrated the world of the theatre to the extent that it has become one of the conventional tools of theatre worldwide.

Prepared by Naomi Stubbs, CUNY Graduate Center.

The stage area nearest the audience is known as **downstage;** the area farthest away from the audience is **upstage.** The designations *downstage* and *upstage* come from the eighteenth and nineteenth centuries, when the stage was raked—that is, it sloped downward from back to front. As a result of this downward slope, the performer farthest away from the audience was higher, or "up," and could be seen better. Also, performers downstage from—below—an upstage performer would be forced to turn their backs on the audience when addressing him or her. This is the origin of the expression *to upstage someone.* Today the term is used whenever one performer grabs the spotlight from

Downstage Front of the stage toward the audience.

Upstage At or toward the back of the stage, away from the front edge of the stage.

everyone else or calls attention to himself or herself by any means whatever. At first, however, it meant simply that one performer was in a better position than the others because he or she was standing farther back on the raked stage and hence was higher.

Materials and Devices of Scene Design

In creating a stage set, a designer begins with the stage floor. At times, trapdoors are set into the floor; through them, performers can enter or leave the stage. For some productions, tracks or slots are set into the stage floor, and set pieces or wagons are brought onstage in these tracks. A *wagon* is a low platform set on wheels. Wagon stages are brought onstage electronically or by stagehands hidden behind them. This type of scene change is frequently used in musical theatre. Another device used along the stage floor is a *treadmill,* which can carry performers, furniture, or props from one side of the stage to the other. Sometimes the stage floor includes a *turntable*—a circle, set into the floor, which is rotated mechanically or electronically to bring one set into view as another disappears.

Formerly, equipment such as turntables, wagons, and treadmills would be moved mechanically or by hand. In recent years, however, these operations have been computerized. Complicated scene changes can be controlled by computer so that they take place efficiently and simultaneously. Computers can also control the turning and shifting of scenic elements. In addition, safety features are built into the new computerized equipment. When performers are on a moving treadmill, for example, light beams or pressure-sensitive plates can detect a malfunction and shut the system down before anyone is hurt.

Instead of coming from the sides, scenery can be dropped from the *fly loft; to fly* is the term used when scenery is raised into the area above the stage, out of sight of the audience.

From floor level, ramps and platforms can be built to any height desired. To create walls or divisions of other kinds, for many years the most commonly used element was the *flat,* so named because it is a single flat unit, consisting of canvas stretched on a wood frame. The side of the flat facing the audience was painted to look like a solid wall, and flats used connected together were made to look like a complete room.

Wagon Low platform mounted on wheels or casters by means of which scenery is moved on- and offstage.

Fly loft Space above the stage where scenery may be lifted out of sight by means of ropes and pulleys.

Flat Single piece of flat, rectangular scenery, used with other similar units to create a set.

SCENIC PROJECTIONS
Effective scenic sup-
plements to traditional
scenery are video and
screen projections—
either still images or
moving images. Visual
effects can be super-
imposed or used in the
background of stage
action. Shown here is a
scene from *War Horse*,
which takes place
during the First World
War, presented at
Lincoln Center Theater.
The sets, costumes,
and drawings were
done by Rae Smith,
with animation and
projection design by
59 Productions. (Sara
Krulwich/The New York
Times/Redux)

Today scene designers and shop technicians have turned more and more to the *hard flat*, sometimes called a *movie* or *Hollywood* flat; it consists of a thin, solid material, called *lauan*, mounted on a wooden or hollow metal frame. A hard flat can be painted, and three-dimensional plastic moldings can be attached to it, creating cornices, chair rails, and other interesting features. Other vertical units are *cutouts*—small pieces made like flats or cut out of plywood. These too can be painted.

A special type of scenery is the **scrim**—a gauze or cloth screen. A scrim can be painted like a regular flat; however, the wide mesh of the cloth allows light to pass through. When light shines on a scrim from the front—that is, from the audience's point of view—it is reflected off the painted surface, and the scrim appears to be a solid surface. When light comes from behind, the scrim becomes transparent and the audience can see performers and scenery behind it. Scrims are particularly effective in scenes where ghosts appear or when eerie effects are desired. Scrims are also useful in memory plays or plays with flashbacks: the audience sees the scene in the present in front of the scrim; then, as the lights in front fade and the lights behind come up, a scene with a cloudy, translucent quality appears through the gauzelike scrim, indicating a scene taking place in someone's memory or in the past.

Scrim Thin, open-weave fabric which is nearly transparent when lit from behind and opaque when lit from the front.

Another scenic device is *screen projection.* A picture or drawing is projected on a screen either from in front—as in an ordinary movie theatre—or from behind. The advantage of projection from behind is that the performers will not be in the beam of light, and thus there will be no shadows or silhouettes. Obviously, projections offer many advantages: pictures can change with the rapidity of cinema, and vast scenes can be presented onstage in a way that would otherwise require tremendously elaborate scene painting. Two recent productions that used projections extensively and successfully were a Broadway revival of the musical *Sunday in the Park with George* and a Goodman Theatre production in Chicago of *The Ballad of Emmett Till.* Till was a young African American from Chicago who was brutally murdered in Mississippi when he was visiting there. His murder sparked a reaction that became an important part of the civil rights movement.

In recent years, many avant-garde artists have also incorporated video screens and video projections into production design, frequently to draw stark parallels or contrasts between the live performance and something captured on video.

Special Effects Scrims and projections bring us to a consideration of *special effects.* These are effects of scenery, lighting, sound, and props that seem unusual or even miraculous. (The term **prop** comes from the word *property;* it refers to any object that will be used onstage but is not a permanent part of the scenery or costumes. Props are such things as lamps, mirrors, computers, walking sticks, umbrellas, and fans.) Special effects include fog, ghosts, knives or swords that appear to stab victims, walls and windows that fall apart, and so on. Today, films and television—because of their technical capabilities—have very realistic special effects, like burning buildings and exploding cars. Also, computers can create the world of dinosaurs or storms at sea. Special effects onstage, however, are almost as old as theatre itself. From the Greeks on, theatre has tried to create the illusion of the miraculous or extraordinary.

A modern version occurs in *The Phantom of the Opera,* when a huge chandelier falls from the top of the auditorium onto the stage. In Chapter 9, we will see that there are also many special effects using lighting and sound.

SPECIAL EFFECTS

All manner of stage displays, from the eerie to the comic, come under the heading of special effects. An ancient tradition in theatre, these effects can include fog, ghosts, and swords that appear to run through victims. In the play *Thirty Nine Steps,* fog is called for at one point when we see the main characters, Pamela (Ferrin) and Hannay (Edwards), running for their lives, hoping to escape up a ladder from an area covered with fog. The play, which had its American premiere with the Huntington Theatre Company, is based on the Alfred Hitchcock film of the same name. (© T. Charles Erickson)

THE PROCESS OF SCENE DESIGN: STEPS IN THE DESIGN PROCESS

In meeting the objectives described above, how does the scene designer proceed? Although every designer has his or her own method, usually the same general pattern is followed.

The designer reads the script and develops ideas about scene designs and a design concept. He or she may even make a few rough sketches to illustrate thoughts about the designs. Meanwhile, the director also has ideas about the scenery. These ideas may vary considerably, depending on the director: they may be vague, or they may be an exact picture of what the scenery should look like.

Director and designer meet for a preliminary conference to exchange ideas about the design. During these discussions, they will develop and discuss questions of style, a visual concept for the production, the needs of the performers, and so on.

Next, the designer develops preliminary sketches, called *thumbnail sketches,* and rough plans to provide a basis for further discussions about the scenic elements.

As the designer proceeds, he or she attempts to fill out the visual concept with sketches, drawings, models, and the like. Sometimes the designer will bring the director sketches showing several possible ideas, each emphasizing different elements to achieve different results.

When the director and the designer have decided on an idea and a rough design, the designer will make a more complete sketch, usually in color, called a *rendering*. If the director approves of the rendering, the designer will make a small-scale three-dimensional *model* that the director can use to help stage the show. There are two types of models. One shows only the location of the platform and walls, with perhaps some light detail drawn in; it is usually all white. The other is a complete, finished model: everything is duplicated as fully as possible, including color and perhaps moldings and texture.

Today, more and more designers are using computers and computer graphics to develop not only ground plans but also three-dimensional models of what a set will look like. Computerized design, known technically as **computer-assisted design (CAD),** is very flexible: the designer can make instantaneous changes in what appears on the screen and can easily indicate to the director and others alternative plans and features of a stage set. Not only ground plans but also the three-dimensional look of a set can be instantaneously rearranged to let both director and designer see what various configurations would look like. In this way, the scene can be shown in three dimensions; it can also be looked at from various perspectives: from the right or left, from above, from the front.

Computer-assisted design (CAD) The use of computers to create design components such as ground plans, elevations, and three-dimensional views.

THE SCENE DESIGNER'S COLLABORATORS AND THE PRODUCTION PROCESS

As with every element of theatre, there is a collaborative aspect to scene design: in addition to the director there are a number of other important people with whom the scene designer works. In fact, any scene design would be little more than a creative idea without the input of the following collaborators: technical directors, property designers, scenic charge artists, stage managers, design assistants, and skilled technicians working in every one of these areas, often with expanded new technologies. These scenic collaborators are essential at every level of production, from university theatre to regional professional theatre to Broadway.

A few definitions: the **technical director** is responsible for solving overall technical problems; he or she is in charge of scheduling, constructing and painting scenery, and in general making certain that all designs are executed as conceived by the scene designer. The **property designer** creates and executes all props; this work may include building special pieces of furniture, finding or devising magical equipment, and selecting items such as lamps and other accessories. **Scenic charge artists** are responsible for seeing that sets are built and painted according to the specifications of the scene designer. In the case of painting the set, the person in charge is referred to as the **paint charge artist.** As noted earlier in this chapter, projection design is becoming a more common feature of the scenic environment, also requiring additional skilled technicians to bring the world of the play to life.

Realizing the design typically begins with drafting (predominantly with CAD these days) all production ground plans, also known as floor plans, which are detailed layouts of each scenic location drafted within the context of a specific theatre space. Drawings that show all exact scenic details from the point of view of the audience

Technical director Person who oversees all technical aspects of a theatre production, especially the building, painting, and installation of scenery and related elements.

Property designer The person who creates and executes all properties (props).

Scenic charge artist The person responsible for seeing that the sets are built and painted according to the specifications of the designer.

Paint charge artist The person responsible for seeing that all painting of scenery is carried out in accordance with the specifications of the designer.

are known as *designer/front elevations.* The drafting of the designer/front elevations is completed either by the scene designer or by various design assistants. These drawings are then used to construct accurate scenic models or perspective renderings that are useful visual tools for anyone involved in the production. Once they have been given final approval by the director, the floor plans are delivered to the stage manager, who will tape on the floor of the rehearsal spaces an accurate, full-scale version of all platforms, ramps, staircases, and entrances and exits to be used by the director and the actors in rehearsal. The technical director uses the floor plans to determine where all the construction elements will go, as well as to determine backstage escapes for actors. The technical director then completes construction drawings for all those floor plan elements. The technical director also converts the complete set of designer/front elevations into a complete set of rear elevations or working drawings for construction purposes. Without this critical engineering and drafting step, the scenery could never be built accurately or safely. The technical director and scenic designer work together in much the same way an engineer will work with an architect in completing the blueprints to plan construction of a building.

It is interesting to note that the realm of scene design on Broadway is one of the last areas to begin the switch over to CAD drafting and design. Many of the designers who have been working for years on Broadway were already well along in their professional careers when CAD became common. Therefore they required their assistants to "draft by hand" as they themselves had done in the past. The use of CAD is now happening more rapidly as younger trained associate and assistant designers are bringing advanced CAD skills with them to Broadway design studios and demonstrating the flexibility of CAD and the opportunity to make changes very quickly.

The visual world of many production designs is so complex that a property designer typically works as an essential collaborator with the scenic designer. The property area is also broken down into areas: (1) functional props used by actors, and (2) set dressing, which fills out the visual stage reality. Once the scene designer has approved all of the property designer's research, solutions, and drawings, those are also forwarded to the technical director to be worked into the construction schedule. It is also frequently the property designer who completes the mechanical special effects used in theatrical production. Owing to developments in computer and electronic technology, special effect solutions are frequently crafted by projection designers or electricians as well. Although not many productions utilize the level of scenic projection noted previously, projection technology solutions are finding their way into many production designs for special visual effects requiring the presence of yet another essential scenic collaborator.

The scene designer and his or her assistants also complete a full series of paint elevations that are delivered to the scenic charge artist who works with a group of scenic artists in completing the painting of the actual scenery. Paint charge and scenic artists require both talent and technique: for instance, to create the feeling of rare old wood in a library, or of bricks, or of a glossy, elegant surface in an expensive living room. In commercial theatre, construction drawings and paint elevations are sent to scenic houses separate from the theatre that specialize in both construction and painting. In regional theatres and university settings there are typically support spaces and support staff for scenic, property, painting, and costume construction on-site. In these settings the entire production team is typically present at all times, allowing for convenient tracking of the construction and painting process. In Broadway and other professional producing theatres without technical support spaces and staff, it is necessary for the

DESIGNING AN ENVIRONMENT
In addition to creating a specific space, such as a kitchen or a bedroom, the designer often creates an "environment," meaning the entire physical landscape in which a production takes place. A good example is the bi-level set for *The Diary of Anne Frank,* with the attic on the upper level, designed by Jo Winiarski. The production was directed by James Edmondson at the Utah Shakespearean Festival. (Photo by Karl Hugh. Copyright Utah Shakespeare Festival 2010)

designer or the assistant designers (or both) to visit the scenic houses and paint studios to check on progress and to assure consistency with the original design intent.

When the time comes for technical rehearsals, dress rehearsals, and the actual performances after the official opening, a production requires backstage leadership by the stage management team. The members of this team call all the cues for lights, sound, projections, scenic shifts, and actors' entrances. An entire crew of stagehands will work together to coordinate every change, no matter how small, in the visual world of the play. These changes may involve a fly crew for flown scenery, a shift crew for either automated or manual shifting of entire settings, and a property crew for any preparation or movement of furniture and properties onstage or off. Meanwhile a crew of dressers, whose work will be covered in more detail later in the chapter, will work backstage with the actors, helping prepare them for the next scene. Once a production moves beyond opening night, it is controlled by the stage manager, who is also responsible for maintaining the director's artistic intent as well as maintaining consistency in cue placement and the visual world of the play.

DESIGNING A TOTAL ENVIRONMENT

Sometimes, in addition to all these duties, a designer goes further, designing not only scenery and special effects but the entire theatre space. For example, a designer might decide to rearrange the position of the stage and the audience seating area around it. Seats might be removed to make way for additional stage space; or, in a flexible area without fixed seating, the stage might be put in one corner rather than in a central position.

COSTUME DESIGN

Of all the visual elements in theatre, costumes are the most personal because they are worn by the performers. Visually, performer and costume are perceived as one; they merge into a single image onstage. At the same time, costumes have a value of their own, adding color, shape, texture, and symbolism to the overall effect. Closely related to costumes are makeup, hairstyles, and masks.

Outside the theatre, most people think of costumes in terms of a holiday parade, a masquerade ball, an occasion like Halloween or Mardi Gras, or a historical pageant. Costumes, however, also play a significant role in daily life. People wear clothes not only for comfort but to convey information about themselves. If we look around us, we are actually surrounded by costumes: the formal, subdued uniform of a police officer; the sparkling outfits of a marching band at a football game; sports gear, such as hockey and baseball uniforms; caps and gowns at a graduation; a priest's cassock; brightly colored bathing suits at a swimming pool.

Clothes have always suggested a number of things about the wearer:

- Position and status
- Gender
- Occupation
- Flamboyance or modesty
- Independence or regimentation
- Occasion—work or leisure, a routine event or a special event

As soon as we see what people are wearing, we receive a great many messages and impressions about them; we instantaneously relate those messages to our own experiences and preconceptions; and we form judgments, including value judgments. Even if we have never before laid eyes on people, we feel we know a great deal about them when we first see the clothing they wear.

In theatre, clothing also sends us signals; but, as with other elements of theatre, there are significant differences between theatrical costumes and costumes in everyday life. Although stage costumes, like ordinary clothes, communicate information about gender, status, and occupation, this information is magnified onstage because it is in the spotlight. Also, of course, stage costumes must meet other requirements not normally imposed on everyday clothing.

THE COSTUME DESIGNER

Costume designer The person responsible for the appearance of each performer onstage.

The person responsible for creating costumes for performers is the ***costume designer.*** Like a scene designer, a costume designer must develop visual ideas with the director and communicate those ideas through drawings. Drawings by a costume designer are frequently accompanied by swatches of material of the kind to be used in actual costumes. It is the costume designer's responsibility to determine how costumes will actually look on performers in front of an audience. Obviously, all this requires both training and talent.

The costume designer should begin with a thorough knowledge of the play—its subject matter, period, style, and point of view—and with an intimate understanding of the characters. The costume designer must also be aware of the physical demands of the text—what is called for in terms of sitting, moving, dancing, fighting, and so on. Finally, the designer must be acquainted with the physical characteristics of the performers themselves in order to create costumes accommodating their individual physiques and patterns of movement.

Additionally, the costume designer must decide whether the costumes are to be *pulled* or *built*. **Pulling** costumes means renting them from a costume warehouse or choosing them from an inventory owned by a theatre company. **Building** costumes means creating them in a costume shop under the supervision of the designer. Built costumes must be sewn, fitted, and completed with accessories and ornamentation. Sometimes, a designer will pull some costumes for a production but build the more unusual ones.

Pull To choose a costume from an inventory owned by a theatre company.

Build To create a costume from scratch in a costume shop.

THE COSTUME DESIGNER'S OBJECTIVES

Stage costumes should meet six requirements:

1. Help establish the tone and style of a production
2. Indicate the historical period of a play and the locale in which it is set
3. Indicate the nature of individual characters or groups in a play: their stations in life, their occupations, their personalities
4. Show relationships among characters: separate major characters from minor ones, contrast one group with another
5. Meet the needs of individual performers: make it possible for an actor or actress to move freely in a costume; allow a performer to dance or engage in a sword fight, for instance; when necessary, allow performers to change quickly from one costume to another
6. Be consistent with the production as a whole, especially with other visual elements

Let us look at these objectives one at a time.

Setting Tone and Style   Along with scenery and lighting, costumes should inform the audience about the style of a play. For a production taking place in outer space, for instance, the costumes would be futuristic. For a Restoration comedy set in the late 1600s, the costumes would be elegant, with lace at the men's collars and cuffs, and elaborate gowns for the women. For a tragedy, the clothes would be somber and dignified; seeing them, the audience would know immediately that the play itself was somber and its tone serious.

Indicating Time and Place   Costumes indicate the period and location of a play: whether it is historical or modern, set in a foreign country or the United States, and so on. A play might take place in ancient Egypt, for instance; in seventeenth-century Spain; or in modern Africa. In some productions, the director and designers want to indicate timelessness, in which case the costumes should not suggest any one period.

Sometimes, as we have already seen, a costume designer and a director decide to shift the period of a play. Such a shift may come as a shock to the audience, and it is up to the costume designer to help the audience adjust to it. For example, if *Hamlet* is to be performed in modern dress, the costume designer in certain scenes might have Hamlet wear a tuxedo and Gertrude an evening gown.

(© Carol Rosegg)

Costume designer Jane Greenwood, who has designed costumes for more than 100 Broadway shows, several dozen regional theatre productions, and numerous films, is seen here in her studio. Shown also are her sketch for Hermione's red costume in a production of Shaw's *Heartbreak House* and Swoosie Kurtz wearing the red costume on stage. Greenwood makes sketches of what the costumes will look like, chooses the colors and fabrics, fits the costumes to the performer, and oversees the construction of the costume.

(© Joan Marcus)

(Courtesy of Jane Greenwood)

One of the most active costume designers of recent times is William Ivey Long. Like many costume designers, he often sketches the costumes of the characters in the play, indicating the style of the clothes, the fabrics, the colors, and the silhouette. Long developed a collage board for all the characters in the "grand finale" of the musical *Hairspray,* not only sketching the costumes themselves but—below the sketches—adding swatches of fabric indicating colors and other qualities of the fabrics. Shown here are several of the costumes taken from the full cast of the finale, giving an indication of how the final costumes were developed.

At the right we see William Ivey Long with his costume sketches for *The Lost Colony,* the nation's longest running historical drama, presented annually on Roanoke Island, on the outer banks of North Carolina.

(The Virginian-Pilot, Chris Curry/AP Images)

COSTUMES INDICATE TIME AND PLACE
Designers determine the look of a production, especially in scenery and costumes. They emphasize whether a production is realistic or nonrealistic, whether it is modern or historical, and whether the characters are upper-class or ordinary people. Designers add color and visual excitement. Seen here are Ben Daniels and Laura Linney in aristocratic period costumes (late eighteenth century) designed by Katrina Lindsay for the Broadway production of *Les Liaisons Dangereuses*. (Sara Krulwich/The New York Times/Redux)

Indicating Characterization   Just as everyday clothes often do, costumes tell us whether their wearers are aristocrats or ordinary people, blue-collar workers or professionals. In the theatre, such signals must be clear and unmistakable. For example, a person in a long white coat could be a doctor, a laboratory technician, or a hairdresser. A stage costume must indicate the exact occupation, and so it may be necessary to add accessories, such as a stethoscope for a doctor.

Costumes also tell us about characters' personalities: a flamboyant person will be dressed in flashy colors; a shy, retiring person will wear subdued clothes.

Costumes can also be used to create symbolic or nonhuman characters. Many plays call for special costumes, denoting abstract ideas or giving shape to fantastic creatures. Here the costume designer must develop an outfit that has the appropriate imaginative and symbolic qualities. A good example would be the Moon and Beggar Woman in *Blood Wedding*.

COSTUMES INDICATE SOCIAL RELATIONSHIPS
Along with their many other properties, costumes can signal the relationships and contrasts among characters in a production. The lead character may be dressed more vividly than those surrounding her or him; opposing forces such as the two families in *Romeo and Juliet* may be dressed in different colors. Not only can costumes indicate the time period when a drama takes place, and the locale where it occurs—Europe, Asia, Africa, America—but they can and should indicate occupations and relative social positions. Who, for example, is a laborer or tradesman and who is a professional businessperson? Who is a housewife and who is a career woman? In this scene from August Wilson's *Radio Golf* at the Goodman Theatre, we see John Earl Jelks as Sterling Johnson and Hassan El-Amin as Harmond Wilks in costumes designed by Susan Hilferty. The man on the right is a successful businessman; the man on the left is a laborer. (Peter Wynn Thompson)

Indicating Relationships among Characters Characters can be set apart by the way they are costumed. Major characters, for example, will be dressed differently from minor characters. Frequently, a costume designer will point up the major characters by dressing them in distinctive colors, in sharp contrast to the colors worn by other characters. Consider, for instance, Shaw's *Saint Joan,* a play about Joan of Arc. Obviously, Joan should stand out from the soldiers surrounding her. Therefore, her costume might be bright blue while theirs are steel-gray. In another play of Shaw's, *Caesar and Cleopatra,* Cleopatra should stand out from her servants and soldiers.

Costumes also underline important differences between groups. In *Romeo and Juliet,* the Montagues wear costumes of one color; the Capulets wear another color. In a modern counterpart of *Romeo and Juliet,* the musical *West Side Story,* the two street gangs are dressed in contrasting colors: the Jets might wear various shades of pink, purple, and lavender; the Sharks might wear green, yellow, and chartreuse.

STYLE, FABRIC, AND CUT IN COSTUMES
With costumes, the type of fabric used, the line and shape of the outfit, the ornateness of the trim and finishing, all of these tell us a great deal about the characters in a play. The costumes here, designed by Michael Krass, speak of elegance, style, and fantasy in the all-white palette. The actors are Ellen McLaughlin as Titania and Jay Goede as Oberon in Shakespeare's *A Midsummer Night's Dream* at the McCarter Theatre, Princeton, directed by Tina Landau. (© T. Charles Erickson)

Meeting Performers' Needs Virtually every aspect of theatre has practical as well as aesthetic requirements, and costume design is no exception. No matter how attractive or how symbolic a costume may be, it must work for the performer. A long flowing gown may look beautiful; but if it is too long and the actress wearing it trips every time she walks down a flight of steps, the designer has overlooked an important practical consideration. If an actor is called on to engage in hand-to-hand combat or fight a duel, his costume must stand up to this wear and tear; and his arms and legs must be free to move, not constrained by the costume. If performers are to dance, they must be able to turn and leap freely.

Ensuring Consistency with the Whole Finally, costumes must be consistent with the entire production, especially with the other visual elements. A realistic production set in the home of everyday people calls for down-to-earth costumes. A highly stylized production requires costumes designed with flair and imagination.

COSTUMES: COLOR AND STYLE
Color and style are two elements costumes add to the visual aspect of a theatre production. An example is a production of *Much Ado About Nothing* by William Shakespeare, directed by Scott Schwartz at the Alley Theatre, Houston. Costume design: Fabio Toblini; set design: Walt Spangler; lighting design: Michael Gilliam. The palette and the lively, bright colors underscore the fact that this is a comedy. (© T. Charles Erickson)

ELEMENTS OF COSTUME DESIGN

Resources of the Costume Designer   Among the resources a costume designer works with are:

Line, shape, and silhouette

Color

Fabric

Accessories

Line   Of prime importance is the cut or line of a costume. Do the lines of the outfit flow, or are they sharp and jagged? Does the clothing follow the lines of the body, or is there some element of exaggeration, such as shoulder pads in a man's jacket or a bustle at the back of a woman's dress?

Color   A second important resource for costume designers is color. Earlier, we saw that major characters can be dressed in a color that contrasts with the colors worn by minor characters, and that the characters in one family can be dressed in a different color from those in a rival family. Color also suggests mood: bright, warm colors for a happy mood; dark, somber colors for a more serious mood.

ORNAMENTATION IN COSTUME

Those who create costumes, wigs, and hairstyles often use a wide variety of objects and accessories: feathers, fabrics, jewelry, and the like. A vivid example is found in the elaborate costume, wig, and hairpiece for the actress Patricia O'Connell (seen here with Remak Ramsay) in a production of *She Stoops to Conquer* at the Irish Repertory Theatre, with costumes by Linda Fisher. (© Carol Rosegg)

Fabric   Fabric is a third resource of the costume designer. In one sense, fabric is the medium of the costume designer, for it is in fabric that silhouette and color are displayed. Texture and bulk of a fabric are also important. Does a fabric have a smoothness or sheen that reflects light? Or is it rough, so that it absorbs light? How does it drape on the wearer? Does it fall lightly to the floor, outlining the body, or does it hide the body? Does it wrinkle naturally, or is it smooth? Beyond its inherent qualities, fabric has symbolic values. Burlap or other rough-textured cloth, for example, suggests peasants or earthy people. Silks and satins, on the other hand, suggest elegance, refinement, and perhaps even royalty.

In terms of fabric, a number of improvements have been made in recent years, just as they have in other fields of design. William Ivey Long (1947–   ) is an award-winning designer who designs for Broadway, off-Broadway, and the long-running outdoor drama *The Lost Colony* in North Carolina. In an interview, Long explained the improvements in fabric: "We're actually using more accurate fabrics. When I was growing up, polyester was what was available, and blends. Flax is now available—wool, silk, cotton, linen, flax. We are able to use more plastics (to support the costumes), and we have better products for maintaining the costumes that are fabric-, people- and environment-friendly."

Accessories Ornamentation and accessories are another resource for costume designers. Fringe, lace, ruffles, feathers, belts, and beads can add to the attractiveness and individuality of a costume. Walking sticks, parasols, purses, and other items that are carried or worn can give distinction and definition. Using the combined resources of line, color, fabric, and accessories, the costume designer arrives at individual outfits that tell us a great deal about the characters who wear them and convey important visual signals about the style and meaning of the play as a whole.

THE COSTUME DESIGNER'S COLLABORATORS

Once again, it is important to recognize that a number of collaborators aid in the process of costume design. The *costume shop supervisor* is the lead costume technician, and there are many other very specific job responsibilities in a typical costume shop. Often young professionals beginning a career will scour sources to find actual fabrics that best match the designer's renderings and notes. Once found, the fabric comes back to the shop, and after the muslin mock-ups are made, it will go to a cutter-draper. A costume designer's *first hand* (see below) will often build the initial costume and complete the fitting with the designer and the actor.

It is important to note that the stage manager is typically responsible for scheduling all actors' fittings to work out times that coordinate with rehearsals and company calls and also work efficiently with the designer's shop schedule. Once the fitting has been completed, the costume will proceed to the costume designer's first hand, or a lead stitcher, who completes the detailed sewing and adds all costume closures. It is not always desirable that costumes look like crisp, new, clean clothes; and once construction is completed the costumes are frequently turned over to design assistants or costume crafts specialists for purposes of *distressing*. Try to imagine a *Pirates of the Caribbean* movie with all the pirates wearing clothes that look brand new.

Once costumes are completed and ready for dress rehearsals and performances, they become the responsibility of the *wardrobe supervisor,* who coordinates the wardrobe crew for a production. All decisions related to costume organization and preparation in the theatre are made by the wardrobe supervisor. The wardrobe crew's responsibilities begin with backstage preparation before every performance until the laundry is completed following every performance. During rehearsal and performance, depending on the complexity of the production, there are numerous dressers from the wardrobe crew assigned to various actors. Some dressers will work solely with a single lead actor in the show, whereas others will work with various members of the production ensemble.

RELATED ELEMENTS OF COSTUME DESIGN

Three elements that are closely related to costumes are makeup, hairstyle, and masks.

Makeup A part of costume is makeup—the application of cosmetics (paints, powders, and rouges) to the face and body. With regard to age and the special facial features associated with ethnic origins, an important function of makeup is to help the performer personify and embody a character.

Anything beyond the most simple theatrical makeup demands an accomplished makeup designer to plan specifically what changes will take place. This design process

MAKEUP

Makeup is frequently applied so that facial features will not be washed out by bright theatre lights, or to change the look of a performer. In traditional Asian theatre, makeup has always been a key element in the performer's appearance. Often it is applied quite heavily and becomes almost like a mask, with colors, lines, and designs. Shown here is an actor in Cantonese opera applying stage makeup. (© Bob Krist/ Corbis)

will typically start with photographs or drawings of the actors with design overlay drawings indicating details of makeup. In a modern small theatre, performers playing realistic parts will often go without makeup of any consequence; in that case, the actors handle their own makeup. However, historical figures are frequently incorporated into realistic plays, and such figures may demand extensive use of extremely realistic prosthetic makeup. A recent example was William Gibson's one-woman play *Golda's Balcony,* with Tovah Feldshuh as the former Israeli Prime Minister, Golda Meir. One makeup artist from Long Island, New York, made nine prosthetic noses, cast in foam latex, each week for more than a year while the show ran on Broadway. The same show then toured nationally for eight more months with Valerie Harper requiring a different set of noses each week to fit her face perfectly.

Makeup has a long and important history in theatre, and sometimes it is a necessity—one good example being makeup to highlight facial features that would not otherwise be visible in a large theatre. Even in a smaller theatre, bright lights tend to wash out cheekbones, eyebrows, and other facial features.

Makeup is often essential because the age of a character differs from that of the performer. Suppose that a 19-year-old performer is playing a 60-year-old character. Through the use of makeup—a little gray in the hair or simulated wrinkles on the face—the appropriate age can be suggested. Another situation calling for makeup to indicate age is a play in which the characters grow older during the course of the action. Makeup is also a necessity for fantastic or other nonrealistic creatures. Douglas Turner Ward (1930–), a black playwright, wrote *Day of Absence* to be performed by black actors in whiteface. The implications of this effect are many, not the least being the reversal of the old minstrel performances in which white actors wore blackface. Ward was not the first to put black actors in whiteface; Genet had part of the cast of his play *The Blacks* wear white masks. A popular musical on Broadway, Steven Schwartz's *Wicked,* portrays a green witch named Elpheba, better known as the Wicked Witch of the West. Perhaps even more amazing in *Wicked* is the makeup used on the numerous flying monkeys in the production.

Asian theatre frequently relies on heavy makeup. For instance, Japanese kabuki, a highly stylized theatre, uses completely nonrealistic makeup. The main characters must apply a base of white covering the entire face, over which bold patterns of red, blue, black, and brown are painted. The colors and patterns are symbolic of the character. In Chinese theatre, too, the colors of makeup are symbolic: all white suggests treachery, black means fierce integrity, red means loyalty, green indicates demons, yellow stands for hidden cunning, and so forth.

WIGS AND HAIRSTYLES
Hairstyle indicates social status and other facts about a character; it provides information about when and where a play is taking place. Beyond that, hairstyles and wigs can make a comment. Shown here, in period costumes, are two characters wearing elaborate wigs in a hairstyle that exaggerates the normal and has an immediate comic effect all on its own: Mara Davi (Mrs. Whitehead) and Joey Slotnick (Captain Jeffrey T. Spaulding/Groucho) in *Animal Crackers*, written by George S. Kaufman and Morrie Ryskind, directed by Henry Wishcamper at the Goodman Theatre; costumes designed by Jenny Mannis. (Photo by Eric Y. Exit)

When makeup is used, the human face becomes almost like a canvas for a painting. The features of the face may be heightened or exaggerated; or symbolic aspects of the face may be emphasized. In either case, makeup serves as an additional tool for the performer in creating an image of the character.

Hairstyles and Wigs   Another important component of costume design includes hairstyles and wigs. When costume designers create their renderings they include characters' hairstyles as a part of the design, which will later require a hair and wig specialist as a part of the crew. In certain periods men have worn wigs: the time of the American Revolution is one example. In England, judges wear wigs to this day.

For women, hairstyles can denote period and social class. In the middle of the nineteenth century, for example, women often wore ringlets like Scarlett O'Hara's in the film *Gone with the Wind*. A few decades later, in the late 1800s, women wore their hair piled on top of the head in a pompadour; this was referred to as the "Gibson girl" look. In the 1920s, women wore their hair marcelled in waves, sometimes slicked down close to the head. In the modern period, women wear their hair in more natural styles; but again there is tremendous variety. The musical *Hairspray* featured young women in the bouffant hairdos of the 1960s. For men, too, hairstyles are significant and sometimes symbolic. A military brush cut, an Elvis Presley–style pompadour, and a ponytail each point to a certain lifestyle.

Audiences would actually be surprised to know how often wigs are used in theatrical productions. They may not even recognize an actor or actress outside the theatre because such a complete visual transformation can be accomplished with the use of wigs made from real hair. Hair and wig specialists are typically assigned to every production. The hair designers will fashion the wigs in the shop before dress rehearsals. A hair and wig specialist is also required backstage to care for the wigs throughout the performance process to keep the hair looking exactly as the designer envisioned it and to maintain the actors' comfort. One of the most amazing uses of a wig in recent memory on Broadway was the extraordinary design by Paul Huntley for *Jekyll and Hyde the Musical:* the actor could manipulate the character's wig instantaneously, allowing him to shift back and forth between Jekyll and Hyde within the same song.

Masks Masks seem to be as old as theatre, having been used in ancient Greek theatre and in the drama developed by primitive tribes. In one sense, the mask is an extension of the performer—a face on top of a face. There are several ways to look at masks. They remind us, first of all, that we are in a theatre, that the action going on before our eyes is not real in a literal sense but is a symbolic or an artistic presentation. For another thing, masks allow a face to be frozen in one expression: a look of horror, perhaps, which we see throughout a production. Masks can also make a face larger than life, and they can create stereotypes, similar to stock characters (see Chapter 3) in which one particular feature—for example, cunning or haughtiness—is emphasized to the exclusion of everything else.

Often today, audiences will see half-masks, like those used in commedia dell'arte, as they allow for stylized character expressions but also give the actor more freedom to speak clearly and effectively. Characters' mask designs are also incorporated into the costume renderings and are typically built by a makeup or crafts specialist in the costume shop. Neutral masks are also frequently used in actors' training to prompt them to use more dynamic physical movement without the benefit of facial expression to express character.

Masks offer other symbolic possibilities. In his play *The Great God Brown,* Eugene O'Neill calls for the performers at certain times to hold masks in front of their faces. When the masks are in place, the characters present a facade to the public, withholding their true selves. When the masks are down, the characters reveal their inner feelings.

Millinery, Accessories, and Crafts A number of the seven objectives of costume design noted earlier in this chapter are actually achieved through the design and

MASKS

Masks have a long tradition in both Eastern and Western theatre, where they began in classic Greek theatre. In Renaissance Italy, commedia dell'arte employed masks: shown here are Tommaso Minniti as Dr. Lombardi, Stefano Guizzi as Brighella, and Giorgio Bongiovanni as Pantalone in *Arlecchino: Servant of Two Masters* by Carlo Goldoni in a production by the Piccolo Teatro di Milano; costumes, Ezio Frigerio. (© Diego Ciminaghi/Piccolo Teatro di Milano–Teatro d'Europa)

use of accessories added to the base costume pieces. Accessories include items like hats, walking sticks, jewelry, purses, parasols, and royal staffs. All of these items instantly refer to various historical periods and also make visual statements about character and locale. Virtually every major costume shop will have a technician who specializes in millinery and crafts. Each of these pieces must be carefully designed and constructed to connect visually to the costumes and to other areas of design. It is hard to imagine a production of Shakespeare's *A Midsummer Night's Dream* without some kind of delightful donkey's headpiece or mask made specifically for the character Bottom. Theatre design and execution in all areas rely heavily on extensive details to make the visual world of the play compelling for audiences.

In Chapter 9 we turn to two other important contributors to the visual and aural elements of theatre productions: the light and sound designers.

SUMMARY

Two important visual elements of theatre are scenery and costumes. These elements are used both to convey information and for aesthetic effect. Scene and costume designers create and organize these visual aspects of theatre production.

The scene designer's goals are to help set the tone and style of the production, establish locale and period, develop a design concept, coordinate scenery with other production elements, and solve any practical design problems. Basic elements used by the scene designer are line, mass and composition, texture, and color.

The costume designer also helps establish tone, style, historical period, and locale. In addition, the costume designer helps indicate the personality and social status of individual characters and shows relationships between characters. Costumes—like settings—must be designed so that performers can use them safely and easily. Related to costume are hairstyles, masks, millinery, accessories, and crafts, which must also be appropriate and functional.

Scene and costume designers work closely with people who construct sets, props, and costumes and see that they function properly during productions.

THINKING ABOUT THEATRE

▶ What production that you have attended had the most elaborate scenery, lighting, costumes, and special effects? What effect did these visual elements have on you? Were you captivated by the visual elements, or did you think that they were overdone? Explain your answer.

▶ What production that you have seen had the least amount of scenery and visual effects? Did you miss seeing extensive design elements, or did you enjoy using your imagination to create the visual environment inside your head?

▶ What kinds of "costumes" do you encounter in everyday life? (Identify three.) What do the costumes convey about the people wearing them?

▶ Think back to the last play you attended (or alternately, select a photograph of a production from the text). How did the costume designer use color, fabric, and other elements to set up visual coordination and contrast among the figures on stage? Did the designer establish a visual color palette? If so, do you recall what it was?

▶ Read one of the plays at a URL provided in Chapters 3 and 4. Do you believe that the scenery and costumes must come from the time period in which the play was written? Why or why not?

KEY TERMS

Build To create a costume from scratch in a costume shop.

Computer-assisted design (CAD) The use of computers to create design components such as ground plans, elevations, and three-dimensional views.

Costume designer The person responsible for the appearance of each performer onstage.

Downstage Front of the stage toward the audience.

Flat Single piece of flat, rectangular scenery, used with other similar units to create a set.

Fly loft Space above the stage where scenery may be lifted out of sight by means of ropes and pulleys.

Ground plan Floor plan or layout of stage design that outlines the various levels on the stage and indicates the placement of scenery, furniture, doors, windows, and other necessary scenic elements.

Left stage Left side of the stage from the point of view of a performer facing the audience.

Paint charge artist The person responsible for seeing that all painting of scenery is carried out in accordance with the specifications of the designer.

Property designer The person who creates and executes all properties (props).

Props Properties; objects that are used by performers onstage or are necessary to complete a set.

Pull To choose a costume from an inventory owned by a theatre company.

Realism Broadly, an attempt to present onstage people and events corresponding to those in everyday life.

Right stage Right side of the stage from the point of view of a performer facing the audience.

Scenic charge artist The person responsible for seeing that the sets are built and painted according to the specifications of the designer.

Scrim Thin, open-weave fabric which is nearly transparent when lit from behind and opaque when lit from the front.

Technical director Person who oversees all technical aspects of a theatre production, especially the building, painting, and installation of scenery and related elements.

Upstage At or toward the back of the stage, away from the front edge of the stage.

Wagon Low platform mounted on wheels or casters by means of which scenery is moved on- and offstage.

THEATRE ON THE WEB

For more research and to learn more about the topics in this chapter, please visit the Online Learning Center at **www.mhhe.com/livelyart8e**.

THE DESIGNERS: LIGHTING AND SOUND

9

STAGE LIGHTING

LIGHTING IN THEATRE HISTORY

OBJECTIVES OF LIGHTING DESIGN

ELEMENTS OF STAGE LIGHTING

THE LIGHTING DESIGNER'S RESOURCES

THE LIGHTING DESIGNER'S COLLABORATORS

SOUND IN THE THEATRE

SOUND REPRODUCTION: ADVANTAGES AND DISADVANTAGES

THE SOUND DESIGNER

UNDERSTANDING SOUND REPRODUCTION AND SOUND REINFORCEMENT

SOUND TECHNOLOGY

SPECIAL EFFECTS IN LIGHTING AND SOUND

SUMMARY
THINKING ABOUT THEATRE
KEY TERMS
THEATRE ON THE WEB

◀ **THE MAGIC OF STAGE LIGHTING** Lighting can define a stage area, create mood, indicate changes of scene, and contribute many other effects to a theatre production. In the scene here, lighting creates a dramatic backdrop for the action and also highlights the star, Kellee Knighten, in a production of the musical *The Civil War,* directed by Jeff Calhoun for Ford's Theatre. Scenic design: Tobin Ost; costumes: Wade Laboissoniere; lighting: Michael Gilliam; video design: Aaron Rhyne. (© T. Charles Erickson)

STAGE LIGHTING

In Chapter 8, we explored the work of scene and costume designers. In this chapter, we turn to two other important aspects of theatrical design: lighting and sound. We begin with lighting, which must be coordinated closely with scene design. We'll consider how lighting has been used in earlier periods of theatre history, what its aesthetic functions and qualities are, and how a lighting designer works. Next, we discuss sound design and its use. Finally, we'll look at special effects in lighting and sound design.

LIGHTING IN THEATRE HISTORY

For the first 2,000 years of its recorded history, theatre took place mostly outdoors during the day, one important reason being the need for illumination—the sun, after all, is an excellent source of light.

Since artificial lighting was unavailable, playwrights used the imagination to suggest nighttime, or shifts in lighting. Performers would bring on torches—or a candle, as Lady Macbeth does—to indicate night. Playwrights also used language in place of lighting. When Shakespeare has Lorenzo say, in *The Merchant of Venice* (1596–1597), "How sweet the moonlight sleeps upon this bank," this is not just a pretty line of poetry but also serves to remind us that it is nighttime. The same is true of the eloquent passage in which Romeo tells Juliet that he must leave because dawn is breaking:

> Look, love, what envious streaks
> Do lace the severing clouds in yonder East:
> Night's candles are burnt out, and jocund day
> Stands tiptoe on the misty mountain tops.

Around 1600, theatre began to move indoors. Candles and oil lamps were used for illumination until 1803, when a theatre in London installed gaslights. With gas, lighting became more manageable, allowing some control of intensity and color, but it remained crude, primitive, and limited in its effectiveness. In addition, gas and other lighting systems of the time involved open flames and thus posed a constant threat of fire. During this period, there were several tragic and costly fires in theatres, in both Europe and the United States.

In 1879, Thomas Edison invented the incandescent lamp—the electric lightbulb—and the era of technological theatre lighting began. Not only are incandescent lamps safe, but their intensity can be controlled by means of rheostats and other devices. Brightness can be increased or decreased, so that the same lighting instrument can produce the full light of noon or the dim light of dusk. Also, the color of the light can be controlled by putting a colored film over the source, or by other means.

Beyond the power and versatility of electric light, there have been numerous other advances in controls and equipment over the past fifty years. Lighting instruments have been constantly refined to become more powerful, as well as more subtle, and to throw a more concentrated, more sharply defined beam. Moreover, miniaturization and computerization have been incorporated into lighting more successfully than into any other element of theatre. After all, costumes must still be sewn individually, and scenes on flats or backdrops must still be painted by hand. Lighting, however, is controlled by electricity and therefore offers a perfect opportunity to take advantage of innovations in electronics and technology. First came resistance systems, then thyratron vacuum tubes, and after that a series of technologies with names such as *magnetic amplifiers* and *silicon-controlled rectifiers.*

Applied to lighting, these innovations allowed for increasingly complex and sophisticated controls. For a large college theatre production, 200 to 300 lighting instruments may be hung around and above the stage; for a large Broadway musical, there may be 800 or more, depending on the type of show and the technology being used. Each of these instruments can be connected to a central computer board, and light settings—the level, direction, and color of the lighting instruments—can be stored in the computer. By pushing a single button, an operator can bring about a shift in literally dozens of instruments in a split second. The resulting flexibility and control are a remarkable tool for achieving stage effects.

OBJECTIVES OF LIGHTING DESIGN

The following are the functions and objectives of stage lighting:

1. Provide visibility
2. Help establish time and place
3. Help create mood
4. Reinforce the style of the production
5. Provide focus onstage and create visual compositions
6. Establish rhythm of visual movement

Providing Visibility   The chief practical function of lighting is, of course, illumination or visibility. First and foremost, we must be able to see the performers' faces and actions. Occasionally, lighting designers, carried away with the atmospheric possibilities of light, will make a scene so dark that we can hardly see what is happening. Mood is important, of course, but seeing the performers is obviously more important. At times, a script does call for the lights to dim; in a suspense play, for instance, the lights in a haunted house might go out. But these are exceptions. Ordinarily, if you cannot see the performers, the lighting designer has not carried out his or her first assignment.

Establishing Time and Place   The color, shade, and intensity of lighting can suggest time of day, giving us the pale light of dawn, the bright light of midday, the vivid colors of sunset, or the muted light of evening. Lighting can also indicate the season of the year because the sun strikes objects at very different angles in winter and summer. Lighting can also suggest place—indoor or outdoor light, for instance.

Creating Mood   Light, together with scenery and costumes, can help create a certain mood. Rarely, however, can lighting alone create mood. For example, if a stage is filled with blue light, it might be inviting, romantic moonlight, but it could also be a cold, dark, evil setting. When action, scenery, and words are combined with light, they tell us exactly what the mood is. In general, a happy, carefree play calls for bright, warm colors, such as yellows, oranges, and pinks. A more somber piece will lean toward blues, blue-greens, and muted tones.

Lighting can create a mood;
it can spotlight and highlight
important characters; it can
focus action; it can be visually striking. All these qualities
are present in this scene from
*Mother Courage and Her Chil-
dren* by Bertolt Brecht, translated by Tony Kushner, staged
at the Public Theater in New
York City under the direction
of George C. Wolfe. Sets by
Riccardo Hernández; costumes
by Marina Draghici; lighting
by Paul Gallo; sound by Acme
Sound Partners (© Michal Daniel)
A second example of striking
stage lighting is the expressionist lighting in *The Adding
Machine* in which Amy Warren plays Daisy, Mr. Zero's
assistant. Lighting design by
Keith Parham; sets by Takeshi
Kata; and costumes by Kristine
Knanishu. (Sara Krulwich/The New
York Times/Redux)

Reinforcing Style With regard to style, lighting can indicate whether a play is realistic or nonrealistic. In a realistic play, the lighting will simulate the effect of ordinary
sources, such as table lamps and sunlight. In a nonrealistic production, the designer
can be more imaginative: shafts of light can cut through the dark, sculpturing performers onstage; a glowing red light can envelop a scene of damnation; a ghostly green light
can cast a spell over a nightmare scene.

Providing Focus and Composition   In photography, the focus has to do with adjusting the lens of a camera so that the picture recorded on the film is sharp and clear. In theatre lighting, *focus* means that beams of light are aimed at, or "focused on," a particular area. Focus in theatre lighting directs our attention to one part of the stage—generally the part where the important action is occurring—and away from other areas.

Focus Aiming light on a particular area of the stage.

Furthermore, lights should illuminate the playing area, not the scenery. If more light is on the scenery than on the performers, the audience's attention will be drawn to the scenery and away from the actors and actresses. Therefore, the first objective of focus is to aim the light at the right place. A good example of the use of focus occurs when there is a split stage, with half the action on one side and half on the other side. The lights can direct our attention from side to side as they are dimmed in one area and come up in another.

Composition is the way lighted areas are arranged onstage in relationship to one another—which areas are dimmed, which are brightly lit, and what the overall stage effect is with regard to light. By means of focus, light can create a series of visual compositions onstage. The effects can vary from turning the stage into one large area to creating small, isolated areas.

Composition How lighted areas are arranged onstage relative to each other.

Establishing Rhythm   Since changes in light occur over a time continuum, they establish a rhythm running through a production. Abrupt, staccato changes with stark blackouts will convey one rhythm; languid, slow fades and gradual cross-fades will convey another.

Lighting changes are timed in coordination with scene changes. The importance of this coordination is recognized by directors and designers, who take great care to "choreograph" shifts in light and scenery, like the movements of dancers.

ELEMENTS OF STAGE LIGHTING

A *lighting designer* knows which elements or qualities of light will achieve the objectives we have just been discussing. Let's consider these qualities.

Intensity   First of all, light has brightness, or *intensity.* Intensity is controlled by an electronic device called a *dimmer,* which can make a scene brighter or darker. Dimmers allow a scene at night to take place in very little light and a daylight scene to take place in bright light.

Dimmer Device for changing lighting intensity smoothly and at varying rates.

Color   Another quality, a very powerful aspect of light, is *color.* Theatre lights can be changed very easily to any one of several hundred colors simply by putting colored material in slots at the front of the lighting instruments or by other means. The traditional material used to alter color is usually called *gel*—short for *gelatin,* the cellophane of which it was originally made. Today, however, these color mediums are generally made of plastic mylars and acetates. With modern technology, color can even be changed electronically without gels (the special equipment for this is described below in the section on the lighting designer's resources).

Color is mixed so that the strong tones of one shade will not dominate, creating an unnatural appearance. Warm lights (amber, straw, gold) are mixed with cool (blue,

COLOR IN LIGHTING

One key quality of stage lighting is color. By the use of gels and other electronic means, an almost infinite variety of colors can be created and combined. Note the reds at the top and the blues in the bottom photo. By using different colored lights, an entirely different mood and feeling is conveyed with the same set. The scenes are from *A Funny Thing Happened on the Way to the Forum* by Burt Shevelove and Larry Gelbart, music and lyrics by Stephen Sondheim, directed by Mark Waldrop at Papermill Playhouse; Ray Klausen: sets; Matthew Hemesath: costumes; F. Mitchell Dana: lighting. (© T. Charles Erickson)

blue-green, lavender) to produce depth, texture, and naturalness. One exception to the usual mixing of angles and colors of light, however, would be a scene calling for special effects: for example, we would expect stark shadows and strange colors—such as an eerie blue—in a suspenseful scene in a graveyard.

Direction   A third quality of light is direction, that is, the way lights are placed on or near the stage so that illumination comes from a particular angle. In earlier days, footlights—a row of lights across the front of the stage floor—were popular. However, because the light source was below the performers, footlights had the disadvantage of casting ghostly shadows on their faces. Footlights also created a barrier between performers and audience. With the development of more powerful, versatile lights, footlights have been eliminated.

Today, most lighting hits the stage from above, coming from instruments in front of the stage and at the sides. The vertical angle of the light beams is frequently close to forty-five degrees, to approximate the average angle of sunlight. The lights converge from different sides to avoid the harsh shadows that result when light hits only one side of a performer's face.

Once performers are properly illuminated by lights from the front and sides and from above, other lighting is added—***downlighting*** from directly overhead and ***backlighting*** from behind—to give further dimension and depths to figures onstage.

Downlighting Lighting that comes from directly overhead.

Backlighting Lighting that comes from behind.

Form   The *form* or *shape* of light is a fourth quality. It can be a single shaft of light, like a nightclub spotlight, a single beam of moonlight through trees, or general lighting. Light can also create a pattern, such as dappled sunlight through the leaves of trees in a forest. The edges of the light can be sharp and clearly defined, or soft and diffused. To accomplish either kind of definition, light can be shaped by special shutters that close in at the edges and give it an outline as it hits the stage area.

Movement   A fifth quality of light is movement. With various types of dimmers, light can shift its focus from location to location and can also change from color to color. In addition, light can move to suggest changing time of day, sunsets, and so on, providing more information for the audience.

For an example of how these qualities function, consider the lighting for a production of *Hamlet*. To emphasize the somber, tragic quality of this play, with its murders and graveyard scene, the lighting would be generally cool rather than warm. In addition to lighting from the front of the stage, there might be lighting angled down from above and backlighting to give a sculptured, occasionally unreal quality to the characters. In terms of movement, the lights would change each time there was a shift in locale. This would create a rhythm of movement through the play and would also serve to focus the audience's attention on particular areas of the stage.

THE LIGHTING DESIGNER'S RESOURCES

Among the resources of the lighting designer are various kinds of lighting instruments and other kinds of technical and electronic equipment.

Types of Stage Lights   Most stage lights have three main elements: a lamp that is the source of the light, a reflector, and a lens through which the beams pass. The two basic categories of lighting fixtures are conventional lighting instruments and automated or moving light fixtures. Conventional lights are fixed instruments with a single focus and design purpose; intelligent moving light fixtures are able to alter focus, change color, project multiple patterns, rotate the patterns at varying speeds, change the size of the beam, and give a sharp or diffused focus. Different types of stage lights include the following: ellipsoidal reflector spotlights, Fresnel spotlights, strip/cyc/flood/border lights, PARs, and follow spots.

Ellipsoidal Reflector Spotlight   Also known as the Variable Beam Profile Spot, this is the most widely used conventional fixture. It creates a bright, hard-edged spot. However, the edges can be softened with focus adjustment or with a diffusion filter, and lenses of different focal lengths allow this instrument to be useful from almost any position in the theatre.

Known as the "workhorse" of contemporary lighting practice, it has four independent shutters to shape the light and it also has a special ***gobo*** slot for pattern projection. At the front end of virtually all conventional lighting fixtures there is a slot for color filters. A ***follow spot*** is another typically hard-edged spotlight controlled by an operator that is designed to follow the audience's favorite leading performer across the stage. This type of follow spot has been in use since about 1856. Originally, the light was created by igniting the mineral lime in front of a reflector in the back end of a long metal tube. The chemical reaction created a bright but slightly green light, which led to a common expression for getting attention as "being in the limelight."

Soft-Edged Spotlights   The most popular soft-edged spotlight is the ***Fresnel*** (fruh-NEL). It is a high-wattage spot, and the Fresnel lens helps dissipate the heat, but it can create only a soft-edged beam of light that can be focused down to a small spot or flooded to cover a larger stage area. The lens is named for Auguste Fresnel, who designed, for lighthouses, the first lenses that would not crack with intense heating and cooling. The concentric rings he cut into the lens allowed the lens to function properly while preventing the buildup of heat from cracking the lens after the light was turned off. Many lighting designers use this instrument for toplighting and backlighting and to cover a large stage area with a wash of color. The Fresnel is generally used in positions near the stage—behind the proscenium opening, or mounted close to the action on an arena or thrust stage.

Another common soft-edged lighting instrument is the parabolic aluminized reflector (PAR), which emits an oval beam that comes in four different sizes (newer PARs produce a circular beam). PARs are extremely lightweight, and they are also the

Gobo   Template in a theatre lighting instrument that determines the shape and arrangement of the beam or pool of light thrown by the instrument. For example, a pattern created by a gobo or template could result in stripes, leaves on trees, the outline of a windowpane, or the like.

Follow spot   Large, powerful spotlight with a sharp focus and narrow beam that is used to follow principal performers as they move about the stage.

Fresnel   Type of spotlight used over relatively short distances with a soft beam edge that allows the light to blend easily with light from other sources; also, the type of lenses used in such spotlights.

VARIABLE BEAM PROFILE SPOT
(Courtesy of Selecon)

SELECON 1200 FRESNEL
(Courtesy of Selecon)

least expensive stage lighting instrument made; for these reasons they are used extensively on the road to provide a great deal of concert lighting. *Barn doors,* with flaps that can cut off an edge of the beam; and *changers/scrollers,* which increase the options from one color to fifteen colors on a single instrument, are common accessories used on both PARs and Fresnels.

Floodlights, Strip Lights, and Border Lights   These lights bathe a section of the stage or scenery in a smooth, diffused wash of light. ***Floodlights*** are used, singly or in groups, to provide general illumination for the stage or scenery. The light from floods can be blended in acting areas, or used to "tone" settings and costumes. They are most often used to illuminate cycloramas at the rear of the stage, or ground rows along the floor of the stage.

Floodlight Lighting instrument used for large or general area lighting.

Automated or Moving Light   The moving light is the newest and most versatile instrument of the group, although there are still only a few moving lights with an independent shutter function that can be focused in a theatre like an ellipsoidal spotlight. ***Automated light fixtures*** (sometimes called *movers*) are able to alter focus, change color using dichroic color mixing, project multiple patterns, rotate the patterns at varying speeds, change the size of the beam, and give a sharp or diffused focus. Most moving lights actually move the yoke and the instrument itself, increasing the onstage "noise"—which is bothersome in quiet dramas or even in opera. Some automated instruments keep the light stationary and simply move a small mirror to reflect the light in different ways. These types of moving lights are extremely cumbersome and take up too much room overhead, so they may be gradually phased out. Automated fixtures are particularly useful in elaborate musical productions and are widely used in rock concerts.

Automated lights (moving lights) Generic term for a new type of lighting instrument that can tilt, pan, rotate, change colors, and change focus—all electronically by computerized remote control.

Lighting Controls   Technologically, lighting is easily the most highly developed aspect of theatre; we have already considered some of the advances in this area. Lighting

SELECON ACCLAIM FLOOD
(Courtesy of Selecon)

VARI*LITE VL6 SPOT LUMINAIRE
(Courtesy of Vari*Lite)

instruments can be hung all over the theatre and aimed at every part of the stage; and these many instruments can be controlled by one person sitting at a console. The development of intelligent lighting fixtures and other digital accessories has also prompted a great deal of change in the design of lighting control systems. Ideally, in a theatre it is best to have a newly designed console that combines the typical theatrical programming for conventional light cues with full moving light capability and ease of operation. In recent years such lighting boards have been developed. Currently there are ideal control systems for movers with the ability to control more traditional lighting cues, though not in the traditional fashion; and there are traditional theatrical lighting boards that can control movers, though the programming for those moving lights is cumbersome and time-consuming. Lighting control systems are extremely expensive, so the eventual change to another system for most theatre operations will happen only gradually.

Lighting changes—or **cues,** as they are called—are arranged ahead of time. Sometimes, in a complicated production (a musical, say, or a Shakespearean play), there will be from 100 to several hundred light cues. A cue can range from a ***blackout*** (in which all the lights are shut off at once), to a ***fade*** (the lights dim slowly, changing the scene from brighter to darker), to a *cross-fade* (one set of lights comes down while another comes up) or a split cross-fade (the lights that are coming up are on a different fade count from the lights that are coming down). Thanks to computerized control, the split cross-fade is the most common. Although light board programming is complicated and somewhat time-consuming, the actual running of a show has become a fairly simple task because of well-designed computer control systems. The most critical aspect of the lighting design is the ability of the stage manager to fully understand the pacing and design aesthetics in calling the lighting and sound cues. Even the process of calling cues has been simplified in some ways by technology. In lighting for dance or for large-scale musicals, it is critical to merge the lighting and sound cues. Through the use of new digital sound technology a computer-controlled sound program can interface with a computer light board and both light and sound cues can be run simultaneously with one tap of the keyboard space bar.

For instance, Strindberg's *A Dream Play* has innumerable scene changes—like a dream, as the title implies—in which one scene fades into another before our eyes. At one point in the play, a young woman, called the Daughter, sits at an organ in a church. In Strindberg's words, "The stage darkens as the Daughter rises and approaches the Lawyer. By means of lighting the organ is transformed into a wall of a grotto. The sea seeps in between basal pillars with a harmony of waves and wind." At the light cue for this change, a button is pushed, and all the lights creating the majesty of the church fade as the lights creating the grotto come up. In many ways stage lighting technology has finally started to catch up with, and serve, the creative ideas that artists like Strindberg and the pioneer scene designer Adolph Appia had at the start of the twentieth century.

THE LIGHTING DESIGNER'S COLLABORATORS

As in every aspect of theatre, in lighting too there is collaboration. A number of people work with the lighting designer. These include assistant designers and people who help create the ***light plot;*** and a master electrician responsible for the preparation, hanging, and focusing of the lights and all accessories (often, if not always, electricians must climb on catwalks and ladders to remote areas above, behind, and in front of

Cue Any prearranged signal, such as the last words in a speech, a piece of business, or any action or lighting change, that indicates to a performer or stage manager that it is time to proceed to the next line of action.

Blackout Total darkening of the stage.

Fade Slow dimming of lights, changing from brighter to darker, or vice versa.

Light plot Detailed outline or diagram showing where each lighting instrument is placed in relationship to the stage.

PART 3 Creating Theatre: The Production

the stage). One of the newer jobs is that of the moving light programmer. Until the advent of moving lights, programming light cues had always fallen to either the lighting designer or the lead associate designer; more recently, however, the complexity of programming has grown exponentially with automated fixtures and other digital accessories, thus requiring another technical specialty. Large-scale music productions, for example, are often so complex that even calling all the cues is impossible for one person to do. For that reason, all follow-spot cues (usually three or four follow spots in a design) are typically called by the lead spot operator. In the concert industry, this gets even more complex, as there are usually a minimum of eight follow spots and often as many as sixteen or more on a major tour, in addition to almost unimaginably complex moving light packages.

Sound in the Theatre

Scenery, costumes, and lighting can be described as visual elements of theatre. Another design element, sound, is aural. In recent years, it has become increasingly important in theatre, with its own artistry, technology, and designers. In fact, beginning in 2008, sound design was added as a category to Broadway's Tony Awards.

SOUND REPRODUCTION: ADVANTAGES AND DISADVANTAGES

Amplification   In the past few decades, not only has sound reproduction become more prominent in the theatre; it has sometimes proved to be controversial as well. At rock concerts, intense amplification has come to be expected, and personal recordings have made listeners expect more pronounced sound reproduction in the theatre. As a result, large musicals, whether presented in Broadway houses or in spacious performing arts centers across the country, are now heavily amplified.

The controversy centers on this amplification. Should it be used for singing? If so, how loud should it be? Should speech also be amplified? Critics charge that often amplification is overdone, with the sound too loud and also too mechanical and artificial. It may be difficult for young people in the early twenty-first century to imagine, but the great American musicals of the 1940s and 1950s—by composers like Rodgers and Hammerstein, Cole Porter, Jerome Kern, and Irving Berlin—were all produced without any sound amplification whatsoever.

Today, electronic amplification is a way of life in theatre. Nevertheless, the controversy continues and has been extended to opera. In the fall of 1999, for example, there was considerable debate when the New York City Opera announced that it was installing a voice "enhancement" system. Frankly, given the trends in our contemporary society, sound reinforcement has often become necessary because of the failing hearing of several generations of our citizens. Continual improvement in technology now gives amplified sound a more natural quality.

Sound Effects   Aside from the argument about the volume or pervasiveness of amplification systems, it should be noted that sound has always been an important, and necessary, component of theatre production. One aspect of this is sound effects. In earlier years—for several centuries, in fact—various devices were developed to create such sounds. The sound of wind, for example, can be produced by a wooden drum

THE SIGNIFICANCE OF SOUND
There are times when sound takes over in a production. Of course, in most musical productions, all the voices, as well as the instruments of the orchestra, are enhanced by sound equipment. But in many productions there are certain moments when sound is crucial. An example is the scene shown here from a production of *Summer And Smoke* by Tennessee Williams, directed by Michael Wilson at the Hartford Stage Company. One of the characters fires a gun at another character. All action stops; the shot becomes the defining event. In this production the sound design was by John Gromada. (© T. Charles Erickson)

made from slats; the drum is usually two or three feet in diameter and covered with a muslin cloth. When the drum is turned, by means of a handle, it makes a noise like howling wind. For the sound of a door slamming, a miniature door or even a full-size door in a frame can be placed just offstage and opened and shut. Two hinged pieces of wood slammed shut can also simulate the sound of a closing door. This effect sounds like a gunshot as well, or a gunshot sound can be created by firing a gun loaded with blank cartridges. (In some states, blank guns are illegal, and live ammunition should never be used onstage.) Thunder can be simulated by hanging a large, thick metal sheet backstage and gently shaking it.

Today, of course, sound effects are far more sophisticated. The developments in computer programs to support sound design and playback are extensive. There are many programs available on the Internet that can be downloaded free, so it is not difficult to use such simple sound programs. Most often the free programs have more advanced, more complex capabilities that are available for purchase. You can record and play back a myriad of sound cues; but if you want to interface those sound cues through a lighting control board or a projection system, then you must use some form of *MIDI* interface. MIDI was originally developed to connect musical instruments to synthesizers; however, since it converts the music to digital information, it can actually communicate with many digital control systems, allowing for extremely sophisticated solutions to the needs of sound, lighting, and projection design in the theatre.

THE SOUND DESIGNER

The person responsible for arranging and orchestrating all the aural aspects of a production is the sound designer. Like his or her counterparts in visual design, the sound designer begins by reading the script, noting all the places where sound might be needed. For a large-scale musical, the designer also decides on the number and type of microphones to be used, the placement of speakers throughout the theatre, and all other aspects of sound reproduction.

After reading the script, the sound designer consults with the director to determine the exact nature of the sound requirements, including sound effects and amplification. The designer then sets about preparing the full range of components that constitute sound for a production. Encompassing anything from preshow and intermission music to any and all microphones to special prerecorded sound effects to preshow announcements about cell phones to live voice-overs, sound is an essential component of every production in the theatre.

UNDERSTANDING SOUND REPRODUCTION AND SOUND REINFORCEMENT

One way to classify sound design is either as ***sound reproduction*** or as ***sound reinforcement.*** Reproduction is the use of motivated or environmental sounds. ***Motivated sounds*** would be, for instance, the noise of a car crunching on gravel, a car motor turning off, and a door slamming—a sequence that would announce the arrival in a car of a character at a house where a scene is taking place. ***Environmental sounds*** are noises of everyday life that help create verisimilitude in a production: street traffic in a city, crickets in the country, loud rock music coming from a stereo in a college dormitory. Such sounds are usually heard as background.

In recent years, sound effects have been recorded on compact discs or now digitally downloaded to computers. Virtually every sound imaginable—from birds singing to dogs barking to jet planes flying—is available on CDs or digitally on computers, not only for expensive professional productions but also for college, university, and community theatres.

Reinforcement is the amplification of sounds produced by a performer or a musical instrument. With the growth of electronics in music, more and more instruments have been amplified. At any rock concert, you can see wires coming out of the basses and guitars. In an orchestra pit in a theatre, the quieter acoustic instruments such as the guitar are miked to achieve a balance of sound with the louder instruments. In today's Broadway theatres it is not unusual to have some members of the orchestra in a separate room in another part of the building with a television monitor showing the conductor. In most cases, the audience would never know this was the case. The total sound can overwhelm a singer, especially one who has not been trained—as opera singers are—to project the voice into the farther reaches of a theatre. As a result, we have body mikes on the performers.

At first, a body mike was a small microphone attached in some way to the performer's clothing. A wire ran from the mike to a small radio transmitter concealed on the performer; from the transmitter, the sound was sent to an offstage listening device that fed it into a central sound-control system. In today's large musical productions, the microphone worn by a performer is frequently a small instrument, hardly larger

Sound reproduction The use of motivated or environmental sounds.

Sound reinforcement Amplification of sounds in the theatre.

Motivated sounds Sounds called for in the script that usually come from recognizable sources.

Environmental sounds Noises from everyday life that provide background sound in a production.

than a piece of wire, worn over one ear alongside the temple or placed elsewhere near the performer's head. Head microphones are used so that they will be as close as possible to the performer's mouth and at a constant distance away from it. How many people realize while watching a musical that tap dancers are frequently wearing wireless microphones at their feet, inside their dance tights?

SOUND TECHNOLOGY

Microphones and Loudspeakers   In preparing the sound for a production, the designers and engineers not only must assemble all the necessary sounds but also must be certain that the appropriate microphones are used correctly and must place the speakers effectively onstage and in the auditorium.

Several types of microphones are used. A *shotgun mike* is highly directional and is aimed from a distance at a specific area. A *general mike* picks up sounds in the general area toward which it is aimed. A *body mike,* as described above, is a wireless microphone attached to a performer's body or clothing. Microphones not worn by performers are placed in various locations. One position is alongside the downstage edge of the stage. Another position is hanging in the air near the lights. Any type of microphone must be hooked up to an amplifier that increases the electronic energy of the sound and sends it through the speakers.

The placement of loudspeakers is both an art and a science. It is necessary to determine the correct speakers for the size and shape of the theatre, and to position them so that they carry sound clearly and evenly into the auditorium—to the upper reaches of the balcony, to the side seats, and to areas underneath the balcony as well as the first few rows in the orchestra. Also, live sound from the performers must reach the sides and back of the theatre at the same time that it reaches the spectators in front. One problem in this regard is that sound travels much more slowly than light. The speed of sound is only 1,100 feet per second—which means that for a spectator seated at the back of a large theatre, sound from a speaker at the rear of the auditorium will be heard before the human voice from the stage. Developments in digital electronics have led to devices that process, sample, and synthesize sound for various effects; and one useful device addresses this problem, delaying the electronic sound so that it arrives through a loudspeaker at the same time as the much slower live sound.

Sound Recordings   The process of assembling sound recordings is similar for professional and nonprofessional productions. First, a list is made of all nonmusical sound effects required. This list is usually developed by the sound designer in consultation with the director, and possibly with a composer: for a show with a great deal of sound or music, there may be both a sound designer and a music composer. Once the list is drawn up, a master recording is made and the sounds are arranged in their order of appearance in the script. This process is called *editing.* When the production moves into the theatre, there is a technical rehearsal without performers during which each sound cue is listened to and the volume is set. When rehearsals with the performers start in the theatre, more changes will be made. Depending on the action and the timing of scenes, some cues will be too loud and others too soft; some will have to be made shorter and others made longer.

During an actual performance of a production using sound reinforcement, an operator must sit at a complex sound console *mixing* sound—that is, blending all elements from the many microphones and from the master sound recording—so that there is a smooth, seamless blend of sound. Also, the operator must make certain not only that all sound is in balance, but also that sound does not intrude on the performance or call attention to itself, away from the stage and the performers.

New Technologies in Sound   As with lighting, in recent years we have seen frequent advances and breakthroughs in sound equipment and technology. The new body microphones and a device that delays the delivery of electronic sound have already been mentioned. There are other developments as well.

Analog reel-to-reel tape decks, which were standard years ago, gave way to digital technology such as digital audiotape (DAT), recordable compact discs, minidiscs, and direct playback from a computer's hard drive. Sound is now recorded and edited at digital audio workstations, based on personal computers. Such stations allow easier editing of sound, more complex effects, and higher-quality sound. Digital playback systems allow very easy and precise cueing of shows as well as greatly improved sound quality.

SPECIAL EFFECTS IN LIGHTING AND SOUND

As in scene design, some effects of lighting and sound can seem unusual or even miraculous.

There are several special lighting effects that can be used to create interesting visual pictures. One simple effect is to position a source of light near the stage floor and shine the light on the performers from below. This creates shadows under the eyes and chin and gives performers a ghostly or horrifying quality. Another common special effect is ultraviolet light, a very dark blue light that causes phosphorus to glow; when the stage is very dark, or completely dark, costumes or scenery that have been painted with a special phosphorus paint will "light up."

An effect of slow motion or of silent movies—where the performers seem to be moving in jerks—is created by a *strobe light,* a very powerful, bright gas-discharge light that flashes at rapid intervals. As we saw earlier, technological advances in lighting have made it possible to create even more spectacular effects.

There are also a number of special sound effects. Sometimes speakers are placed completely around the audience so that the sound can move from side to side. Echoes can be created by a machine that causes reverberations in sound waves. Expanding audio technology also allows for more complex sound effects. Computerized noises and electronic music can be used to create special sounds for various situations, and compact discs give instantaneous access to any element of the sound design. Also, with computerized synthesizers, a few musicians can replace a large orchestra.

Lighting and sound, like scenery and costumes, are means to an end: they implement the artistic and aesthetic aspects of a production. The colors, shapes, and lines of lighting effects and the qualities of sound interact with other elements of theatre and contribute to the overall experience.

In Part Three we have looked at the production of the theatre experience—at acting and directing as well as at both the aesthetic and the technical sides of various aspects of design: scenic, costume, lighting, and sound. In Part Four we move to a survey of theatrical activity through history.

Summary

Lighting—historically the last of the visual elements of theatre to be fully developed—is today the most technically sophisticated of all. Once the incandescent electric lamp was introduced, it was possible to achieve almost total control of the color, intensity, and timing of lights. Lighting controls have also benefited from computerization; extensive light shifts can now be hooked up to computer boards and controlled by an operator at a console.

Lighting design is intended to provide illumination onstage, to establish time and place, to help set the mood and style of a production, to focus the action, and to establish a rhythm of visual movement. Lighting should be consistent with all other elements. The lighting designer uses a variety of lighting instruments and controls to achieve effects and works closely with a group of collaborators to place lighting instruments in the theatre and to see that lighting changes are carried out effectively during a performance.

Another design element in theatre is sound. In today's theatre, sound is reproduced and reinforced by various means, many of them technologically advanced. For example, sound effects can be created by primitive mechanical means—such as pieces of wood slapped together to simulate a closing door—or by sophisticated computer and digital technology. These techniques are continually improving and affect the way sound is created, reproduced, and conveyed throughout a theatre auditorium.

Special effects in lighting and sound include ultraviolet light, strobe lights, echo effects, and computerized synthesizers.

Thinking about Theatre

▶ During the last play you attended, what did you notice about the lighting? Were there lighting instruments throughout the theater aimed at the stage? When the performance began, where did the beams of light appear to come from?

▶ What colors were created on the stage by lighting? Did you think the colors were appropriate for the production? How did the color of the lights affect your overall experience?

▶ Were you able to spot the sound speakers? Where were they located? During the performance, did you notice if microphones were attached to the actors? Do you think there were microphones elsewhere on stage? Can you speculate as to where they were?

▶ Read *Uncle Vanya* (Chapter 4), *Miss Julie* (Chapter 3), or *A Doll's House* (Chapter 3) at the URL provided. Choose a scene in which the lighting could be used to help set mood. Choose a scene in which lighting established the time of day. Choose a scene in which realistic sound effects are needed. Choose a scene in which sound might be used to enhance mood.

(NOTE: Plays by Henrik Ibsen, August Strindberg, and Anton Chekhov are also available in *Anthology of Living Theatre,* Third Edition, by Edwin Wilson and Alvin Goldfarb.)

KEY TERMS

Automated lights (moving lights) Generic term for a new type of lighting instrument that can tilt, pan, rotate, change colors, and change focus—all electronically by computerized remote control.

Backlighting Lighting that comes from behind.

Blackout Total darkening of the stage.

Composition How lighted areas are arranged onstage relative to each other.

Cue Any prearranged signal, such as the last words in a speech, a piece of business, or any action or lighting change, that indicates to a performer or stage manager that it is time to proceed to the next line of action.

Dimmer Device for changing lighting intensity smoothly and at varying rates.

Downlighting Lighting that comes from directly overhead.

Environmental sounds Noises from everyday life that provide background sound in a production.

Fade Slow dimming of lights, changing from brighter to darker, or vice versa.

Focus Aiming light on a particular area of the stage.

Floodlight Lighting instrument used for large or general area lighting.

Follow spot Large, powerful spotlight with a sharp focus and narrow beam that is used to follow principal performers as they move about the stage.

Fresnel Type of spotlight used over relatively short distances with a soft beam edge that allows the light to blend easily with light from other sources; also, the type of lenses used in such spotlights.

Gobo Template in a theatre lighting instrument that determines the shape and arrangement of the beam or pool of light thrown by the instrument. For example, a pattern created by a gobo or template could result in stripes, leaves on trees, the outline of a windowpane, or the like.

Light plot Detailed outline or diagram showing where each lighting instrument is placed in relationship to the stage.

Motivated sounds Sounds called for in the script that usually come from recognizable sources.

Sound reinforcement Amplification of sounds in the theatre.

Sound reproduction The use of motivated or environmental sounds.

 THEATRE ON THE WEB

For more research and to learn more about the topics in this chapter, please visit the Online Learning Center at **www.mhhe.com/livelyart8e.**

GLOBAL THEATRES
PAST AND PRESENT

PART 4

10 EARLY THEATRES: GREEK, ROMAN, AND MEDIEVAL

11 EARLY THEATRE: ASIAN

12 RENAISSANCE THEATRES

13 THEATRES FROM THE RESTORATION THROUGH ROMANTICISM

14 THE MODERN THEATRE EMERGES

15 TODAY'S DIVERSE GLOBAL THEATRE

GLOBAL THEATRES

In Part 4 we explore global theatres of the past and of today. The two are inextricably linked: contemporary theatre around the world builds on theatre from the past in both the Western and Asian traditions. This is a scene from *The Cherry Orchard* by Anton Chekhov, directed by Nicholas Martin in a new translation by Richard Nelson, staged at the Huntington Theatre. Chekhov is a writer whose work has resonated not only in the West but throughout the world for more than a century. (© T. Charles Erickson)

EARLY THEATRES: GREEK, ROMAN, AND MEDIEVAL

10

ORIGINS OF THEATRE

GREECE

BACKGROUND: THE GOLDEN AGE OF GREECE

THEATRE AND CULTURE: GREEK THEATRE EMERGES

GREEK TRAGEDY

TIMELINE: Greece

GREEK COMEDY

THEATRE PRODUCTION IN GREECE

LIVING HISTORY: *Antigone*

DRAMATIC CRITICISM IN GREECE: ARISTOTLE

LATER GREEK THEATRE

ROME

BACKGROUND: ROME AND ITS CIVILIZATION

TIMELINE: Rome

THEATRE AND CULTURE IN ROME

POPULAR ENTERTAINMENT IN ROME

ROMAN COMEDY: PLAUTUS AND TERENCE

LIVING HISTORY: *The Menaechmi*

ROMAN TRAGEDY: SENECA

DRAMATIC CRITICISM IN ROME: HORACE

THEATRE PRODUCTION IN ROME

MAKING CONNECTIONS: Greek and Roman Popular Arts

DECLINE OF ROMAN THEATRE

THE MIDDLE AGES

BACKGROUND: MEDIEVAL EUROPE

THEATRE AND CULTURE IN THE MIDDLE AGES

MEDIEVAL DRAMA: MYSTERY AND MORALITY PLAYS

TIMELINE: Middle Ages

MEDIEVAL THEATRE PRODUCTION

LIVING HISTORY: *Noah's Ark*

SUMMARY
THINKING ABOUT THEATRE
KEY TERMS
THEATRE ON THE WEB

◀ **THE BEGINNING OF WESTERN THEATRE**   Western theatre began with Greek and Roman theatre and, after a hiatus of many centuries, continued with medieval theatre. The early Greek theatre is well known for its tragedies by Aeschylus, Sophocles, and Euripides, but its comedies by Aristophanes were also significant. Shown here is a scene from Aristophenes's *The Birds,* as presented by the National Theatre, London. Franky Mwangi (right) portrays Sparrow and Josette Bushell-Mingo is Hoopoe. (© Pete Jones/ArenaPAL/Topham/The Image Works)

ORIGINS OF THEATRE
Most ritual ceremonies—whether in Africa, for instance, or among Native Americans, or in southeast Asia—have a strong theatrical component. This includes masks, costumes, repeated phrases, music, and dancing. Here, in Mali, West Africa, teetering on stilts high above a crowd of villagers, masked Dogon dancers in a traditional ceremony imitate a long-legged waterbird. (© Charles & Josette Lenars/Corbis)

The ancient civilizations of Greece and Rome have had a profound impact on Western civilization. Their innovations in the arts, architecture, culture, science, philosophy, law, engineering, and government shaped much of later thought and practice in the Western world. The theatres of Greece and Rome laid the foundations of many traditions of today's Western theatre. The theatre of the Middle Ages was the bridge between these eras and the Renaissance. Before turning to these three remarkable eras, however, we should first briefly discuss some of the possible origins of theatre.

ORIGINS OF THEATRE

No one knows exactly how theatre began, or where or when it originated. We do know, however, that the impulse to create theatre is universal among humans.

Two elements of theatre are storytelling and imitation: these, along with other elements, are an important part of religious observances and rituals—formal, repeated ceremonies—in cultures around the world. An example is found in ancient Egypt, where there was an elaborate ritual concerning the god Osiris. Osiris became a ruler of Egypt, married his sister Isis, was murdered by his brother, and was eventually avenged and resurrected. The ceremony retelling the story of Osiris was performed over a period of nearly 2,000 years, from around 2500 B.C.E. to 550 B.C.E., at a sacred place called Abydos.

Another recurring theatrical element is costuming. Throughout central and western Africa, for example, striking and imaginative costumes and masks are used in a variety of ceremonies. Among the Kuba people in Zaire, there is a dance that marks the initiation into manhood. The central figure in this ceremony is the Woot, a mythical hero who wears an enormous headdress and a mask made of feathers, plumes, shells, and beads.

In certain societies, rituals, religious ceremonies, imitation, and storytelling have been combined and transformed into theatrical events. In Western culture, the first place where this occurred was ancient Greece.

GREECE

BACKGROUND: THE GOLDEN AGE OF GREECE

There are times in history when many forces come together to create a remarkable age. Such a time was the fifth century B.C.E. in Athens, Greece, when there were outstanding achievements in politics, philosophy, science, and the arts, including theatre. This era has come to be known as the *classical period* and also as the *Golden Age* of Greece.

Greece was then a collection of independent city-states, and Athens—the most important—is credited with being the birthplace of democracy (although only male citizens had a voice in politics and government). Greek philosophers, such as Socrates and Plato, tried to explain the world around them; Herodotus transformed history from a simple account of events into a social science. Also, a number of important mathematical and scientific discoveries were made: for instance, the Greek mathematician Pythagoras formulated a theorem that remains one of the cornerstones of geometry; and Hippocrates formulated an oath for physicians that is the one still taken today. Greek sculpture from this period is treasured in museums around the world, and buildings such as the Parthenon—the temple that sits atop the Acropolis in Athens—remain models for architects.

THEATRE AND CULTURE: GREEK THEATRE EMERGES

Of particular importance to Greek theatre were the ceremonies honoring Dionysus—the god of wine, fertility, and revelry. Later, Greek drama was presented in honor of Dionysus, and most (though not all) historians believe that Greek drama originated out of the dithyrambic chorus, a group of fifty men who sang and danced a hymn praising Dionysus.

A performer named Thespis is customarily credited with transforming these songs into drama in the sixth century B.C.E. by stepping out of the **chorus** and becoming an actor. He moved from simply reciting a story to impersonating a character and engaging in dialogue with members of the chorus. The contribution of Thespis is reflected in the term **thespian,** which is often used as a synonym for "stage performer."

Theatre and Religion   Greek theatre was intimately bound up with Greek religion, which was based on worship of a group of gods. Annual festivals were held in honor of the gods, and theatre became a central feature of certain Greek festivals.

Chorus In ancient Greek drama, a group of performers who sang and danced, sometimes participating in the action but usually simply commenting on it. In modern times, performers in a musical play who sing and dance as a group.

Thespian Synonym for "performer"; from Thespis, who is said to have been the first actor in ancient Greek theatre.

City Dionysia The most important Greek festival in honor of the god Dionysus, and the first to include drama.

Satyr play One of the three types of classical Greek drama, usually a ribald take-off on Greek mythology and history that included a chorus of satyrs, mythological creatures who were half-man and half-goat. On festival days in Athens, it was presented as the final play following three tragedies.

Choregus Wealthy person who financed a playwright's works at an ancient Greek dramatic festival.

In Athens, a spring festival called the ***City Dionysia*** (SIT-ee digh-eh-NIGH-see-uh), honoring the god Dionysus, incorporated tragic drama in 534 B.C.E. and comedy about 487 B.C.E. This festival lasted several days, including three days devoted to tragedies, and had time set aside for five comedies. ***Satyr plays*** were also performed; they were satiric versions of Greek history and mythology and featured a chorus of half-man and half-goats, known as satyrs. A few days after the festival, awards were given, the festival operation was reviewed by a representative body, and people who had behaved improperly or disrespectfully were judged and penalized.

Since theatre was a religious and civic event, the organization of dramatic presentations was undertaken by the government. Eleven months before a festival, an appointed official of the city-state would choose the plays to be presented and would appoint a ***choregus*** (ko-REE-guhs)—the equivalent of a modern-day producer—for each of the selected playwrights. In the early days of Greek dramatic festivals, the tragic playwrights themselves functioned as directors. A playwright would choose the actors and supervise the production, working with the chorus and conferring with the actors about their roles.

Theatre and Myth   What kind of stories were told in the plays written for the festivals? Where did the writers find these stories? The answer in most cases is Greek myths.

A *myth* is a story or legend handed down from generation to generation. In every culture, certain myths have a strong hold because they seem to sum up a view of human relationships and try to explain the problems, catastrophes, and opportunities life presents to individuals. Greece had a multitude of myths, which furnished the stories for Greek drama.

GREEK TRAGEDY

The most admired form of drama at the Greek festivals was tragedy. Approximately 900 tragedies were produced in Athens during the fifth century B.C.E., of which thirty-one have survived—all by three dramatists: Aeschylus, Sophocles, and Euripides.

Tragic Dramatists: Aeschylus, Sophocles, and Euripides

Aeschylus (525–456 B.C.E.) is considered the first important Greek dramatist and therefore the first important Western dramatist. He began writing at a time when a theatre presentation would be performed by a large chorus of fifty men and a single actor. In his own dramas, however, Aeschylus called for a second actor, who could play different parts when he put on different masks. This made possible a true dramatic exchange between characters and was the start of drama as we know it. (It should be noted that all performers were men; women's roles were played by men.) In another innovation, Aeschylus reduced the size of the chorus to twelve, making it more manageable.

The dramas of Aeschylus dealt with noble families and lofty themes and were praised for their lyric poetry as well as their dramatic structure and intellectual content. He was the acknowledged master of the ***trilogy***—three tragedies that make up a single unit. The best-known of his trilogies is the *Oresteia* (458 B.C.E.): the saga of Agamemnon, a hero of the Trojan war who, when he returns home, is murdered by his wife, Clytemnestra. She in turn is killed by their children, Electra and Orestes.

Sophocles (c. 496–406 B.C.E.), who lived through most of the fifth century B.C.E., built on the dramatic form that Aeschylus had begun. He raised the number in the chorus to fifteen, where it was to remain. More important, he realized that an additional third actor—who, again, might play several parts—would allow enormous flexibility. Because each actor, by wearing different masks in turn, could play two or three parts, the use of three actors meant that a play could have seven or eight characters.

With this newfound flexibility, Sophocles became particularly adept at dramatic construction, introducing characters and information skillfully and building swiftly to a climax. (We will see a good example when we look more closely at *King Oedipus,* which is also called *Oedipus Rex* and *Oedipus the King* in differing translations.)

The third great dramatist of the period, Euripides (c. 484–406 B.C.E.), was more of a rebel and has always been considered the most "modern" of the three. This results from several factors: sympathetic portrayal of female characters, increased realism, mixture of tragedy with melodrama and comedy, and skeptical treatment of the gods.

Trilogy In classical Greece, three tragedies written by the same playwright and presented on a single day; they were connected by a story or thematic concerns.

Tragic Structure

Let's look now at the structure of Greek tragedy, and at the plot of one tragedy—*King Oedipus*—in particular.

Pattern and Plot in Greek Tragedy

Though there are variations among the surviving thirty-one plays of the three great dramatists, the structure in most of them follows the same pattern. First comes the opening scene, after which the chorus enters. This is followed by an episode between characters; then comes the first choral song. From that point on, there is an alternation between character episodes and choral songs until the final episode, which is followed by the exit of all the characters and the chorus.

THE GREEK CHORUS
The chorus in classical Greek theatre served many functions. It provided exposition, narrated the action, interacted with the other actors, and added spectacle. Shown here is a production of *The Bacchae* by Euripides. Called *The Bacchai,* it was directed by Peter Hall at the National Theatre in London. The chorus added a visual component to the drama. The costumes and masks were designed by Alison Chitty; the lighting was by Peter Mumford. (© Donald Cooper/Photo*stage,* England)

The chorus was a key—and unique—element of Greek drama, never again being used in the same way. The characters portrayed by the chorus usually represented ordinary citizens, and they had several functions. First, they reacted the way people in the audience might react and thus became surrogates for the audience. They were a group with which the audience members could identify. Second, the chorus often gave background information necessary for an understanding of the plot. Third, the chorus represented a moderate balance between the extreme behaviors of the principal characters. Fourth, the chorus frequently offered philosophical observations and drew conclusions about what had happened in the play. It is important to note that the choral passages were sung and danced, though we do not know what the music sounded like or how the movements were choreographed.

Whether representing men or women, chorus members were always male—as were all performers in Greek theatre.

The Plot of *King Oedipus*   In Chapter 3, we discussed two basic plot arrangements developed in Western drama: climactic and episodic construction. Climactic structure, like so much else in theatre, got its start in Greek drama, and Sophocles's play *King Oedipus* (c. 430 B.C.E.) is a good example.

The story of Oedipus begins long before the opening of the play, when Oedipus—the son of King Laius and Queen Jocasta of Thebes—is born. When he is an infant, it is prophesied that he will kill his father and marry his mother, and so he is left on a

GREECE
Year, B.C.E.

THEATRE

CULTURE AND POLITICS

Age of Homer (800 B.C.E.)

Arion, harpist and poet, develops the dithyramb
(c. 600 B.C.E.)

600

Thales of Miletus begins natural philosophy (physics)
(c. 585 B.C.E.)

575

Peisistratus, tyrant of Athens (560 B.C.E.)

Thespis, supposedly first "actor" in dithyramb
(mid-sixth century)

550

Play contests begin in
Athens (534 B.C.E.)

525

Pythagoras flourishes; Doric temples of southern Italy
and Sicily (c. 525 B.C.E.)

Aeschylus (525-456 B.C.E.)
(Scala/Ministero per i Beni e le
Attività culturali/Art Resource, NY)

Athenian democracy (510 B.C.E.)

500

Pindar begins to write odes (500 B.C.E.)

Comedy introduced to City
Dionysia (c. 487 B.C.E.)

Battle of Marathon
(490 B.C.E.)

Persian Wars
(499-478 B.C.E.)

475

Aeschylus introduces
second actor (c. 471 B.C.E.)

Sophocles introduces
third actor (c. 468 B.C.E.)

Socrates born (470 B.C.E.)

Aeschylus's *Oresteia;*
introduction of skene
(458 B.C.E.)

Prizes awarded for
tragic acting (449 B.C.E.)

Hippocrates born
(460 B.C.E.)

Pericles begins rise to
power: age of Pericles
(462-429 B.C.E.)

450

Dramatic activities
incorporated into Lenaia
(c. 442 B.C.E.)

Beginning of Parthenon;
Herodotus flourishes (447 B.C.E.)

Phidias dies (500-435 B.C.E.)

Sophocles's *King
Oedipus* (c. 430 B.C.E.)

425

Peloponnesian Wars (431-404 B.C.E.)

Euripides's *Trojan Women*
(415 B.C.E.)

Aristophanes's *Lysistrata*
(411 B.C.E.)

Athenian fleet destroyed
(404 B.C.E.)

Spartan hegemony begins
(404 B.C.E.)

400

Trial and execution of
Socrates (399 B.C.E.)

Aristotle born
(384-322 B.C.E.)

Plato's *Republic*
(c. 375 B.C.E.)

375

Euripides (480-406 B.C.E.)
(© Scala/Art Resource, NY)

Spartan hegemony ends
(404-371 B.C.E.)

Theban hegemony ends
(371-362 B.C.E.)

Professional actors replace
amateurs at City Dionysia
(c. 350 B.C.E.)

Philip II, king of Macedonia
(352 B.C.E.)

350

Aristotle's *Poetics*
(c. 335-323 B.C.E.)

Theater of Dionysus
completed (c. 325 B.C.E.)

Alexander succeeds Philip II;
in 335 B.C.E., occupies Greece

From this period to
c. 100 B.C.E., Greek
theatres built throughout
Mediterranean (320 B.C.E.)

Menander's *Dyskolos*
(316 B.C.E.)

325

Hellenistic culture spreads throughout eastern
Mediterranean (c. 320 B.C.E.)

300

Alexander the Great (356-323 B.C.E.)
(© Ad Meskens/Wikimedia Commons)

Artists of Dionysus recognized (277 B.C.E.)

275

215

KING OEDIPUS

In Sophocles's *King Oedipus*—one of the most famous Greek tragedies—Oedipus becomes king of Thebes after unknowingly killing his father and marrying his mother. Upon learning what he has done, Oedipus puts out his eyes. According to Aristotle, *King Oedipus* represents the quintessential Greek tragedy. In this scene we see Alan Howard as the older Oedipus some years later in Sophocles's *Oedipus at Colonus,* in a production at the National Theatre in London, directed by Sir Peter Hall. (© Colin Willoughby/ArenaPAL)

mountaintop to die. A shepherd saves him, however, and takes him to Corinth, where he is raised by the king and queen of Corinth as their own son.

When Oedipus grows up, he learns of the oracle that prophesied that he would kill his parents. Thinking that the king and queen of Corinth are his true parents, he flees Corinth and heads for Thebes. As he approaches Thebes, he encounters, at a crossroads, a man whom he kills in a fight, not realizing that the man is his natural father, the king of Thebes. Oedipus proceeds on to Thebes and, after correctly answering the riddle of the Sphinx, he becomes king; he also marries the queen, Jocasta, not realizing that she is his mother. After a time, a plague hits Thebes.

This is when the play begins. The action takes place on one day in one place: in front of the palace at Thebes. After the play opens, there is an alternation of choral sections and episodes. The plot has many twists and turns as well as ups and downs for the characters. First, it is revealed that an oracle has said that the plague will not be lifted until the murderer of the former king is found and punished. Oedipus, not knowing that he himself is the murderer, vows to find the guilty party. After that, Jocasta says Oedipus should ignore the oracle because it stated that her husband, the king, would be killed by his son, but he was killed at a crossroads. Then Oedipus says he killed a man at a crossroads. Next, a messenger arrives from Corinth saying that the king there is dead. Jocasta points out that this proves that Oedipus did not kill his father because the father died while Oedipus was away. But then the messenger reveals that the king of Corinth was not the real father of Oedipus, and so forth, until the final revelations and conclusion—when Oedipus puts out his eyes and Jocasta kills herself.

Thematically, *King Oedipus* raises questions that have provoked philosophical discussions for centuries: questions about fate, pride, and the ironic nature of human events.

READ *Oedipus the King*

http://classics.mit.edu/Sophocles/oedipus.html

GREEK COMEDY

As we've noted, part of the seven-day City Dionysia was devoted to comedy, and comedies by five playwrights were presented during the festival. Later in the fifth century, a separate festival in the winter was devoted solely to comedy.

Greek comedy of this period has come to be known as **Old Comedy** to distinguish it from a different kind of comedy that took hold at the end of the fourth century B.C.E. and is called **New Comedy.** The only surviving Old Comedies were written by Aristophanes (c. 448–c. 380 B.C.E.).

Old Comedy always makes fun of social, political, or cultural conditions, and its characters are often recognizable personalities; the philosopher Socrates is only one of a number of prominent figures satirized in the plays of Aristophanes. The modern counterpart of Old Comedy is political satire in films and in television programs such as *Saturday Night Live, The Colbert Report,* and *The Daily Show* with Jon Stewart.

In Old Comedy, the satire is underlined by fantastic and improbable plots; this is an aspect of the comic premise, discussed in Chapter 4. In *Lysistrata,* for instance, Aristophanes condemns the Peloponnesian war, which Greece was then fighting; the women in the play go on a sex strike, refusing to sleep with the men until they stop the war.

READ *Lysistrata* in *Anthology of LIving Theatre* or at:

http://www.gutenberg.org/ebooks/7700

Unlike tragedies, most Old Comedies do not have a climactic structure. For example, they do not take place within a short span of time or in one locale, and they often have a large cast of characters. They also have two scenes not found in tragedy. One is a debate, called an ***agon*** (AG-ohn), between two forces representing opposite sides of a political or social issue. The other is a choral section, known as a ***parabasis*** (puh-RAB-uh-sihs), addressed directly to the audience; it makes fun of the spectators in general and of specific audience members.

During the Greek Hellenistic era, which began in the fourth century B.C.E., Old Comedy gave way to New Comedy. Instead of the political, social, and cultural satire of Old Comedy, New Comedy dealt with romantic and domestic problems. We will study this kind of drama when we look at Roman comedy—a direct outgrowth of Greek New Comedy.

THEATRE PRODUCTION IN GREECE

Greek drama, as we have noted, was staged in ***amphitheatres,*** which were cut out of the side of a hill and probably held between 15,000 and 17,000 spectators. At the base of the hillside was a circular playing area called the ***orchestra*** (recent excavations suggest that the earliest orchestra may have been rectangular). Behind the playing area was a scene house. The chorus made its entrances and exits on each side of the scene house through an aisle called a ***parodos*** (PAR-uh-dohs). This is the first recorded example of the thrust stage, discussed in Chapter 7. The standard scenic setting for Greek tragedy was a palace, and simple devices were used to indicate locales and to move characters on- and offstage. The audience sat in the ***theatron.*** During the classical period the hillside theatron probably had temporary wooden bleachers, but these were replaced by stone seats during the later Hellenistic era.

All the characters in Greek drama, male and female, were portrayed by men. The performers, particularly the chorus members, had to be accomplished at singing and

Old Comedy Classical Greek comedy that pokes fun at social, political, or cultural conditions and at particular figures.

New Comedy Hellenistic Greek and Roman comedies that deal with romantic and domestic situations.

Agon In classical Greek Old Comedy, a scene with a debate between the two opposing forces in a play.

Parabasis Scene in classical Greek Old Comedy in which the chorus directly addresses the audience members and makes fun of them.

Amphitheatre Large oval, circular, or semicircular outdoor theatre with rising tiers of seats around an open playing area; also, an exceptionally large indoor auditorium.

Orchestra A circular playing space in ancient Greek theatres; in modern times, the ground-floor seating in a theatre auditorium.

Parodos In classical Greek drama, the scene in which the chorus enters. Also, the entranceway for the chorus in Greek theatre.

Theatron Where the audience sat in an ancient Greek theatre.

ATHENS, 441 B.C.E. The year is 441 B.C.E. It is a morning in late March in Athens, Greece, and the citizens of Athens are up early, making their way to the Theatre of Dionysus, an open-air theatre on the south side of the Acropolis, the highest hill in Athens. On the Acropolis are several temples, including the Parthenon, a magnificent new temple dedicated to the goddess Athena, which is under construction at this very time.

The Theatre of Dionysus has semicircular seating built into the slope of the hill on the side of the Acropolis. At the foot of the seating area is a flat, circular space—the orchestra—where the actors will perform. Behind the orchestra a temporary stage house has been built, from which the performers will make entrances and exits. The facade of the stage house for the performance today represents the temple at Thebes, where the action will take place.

Priests of various religious orders are sitting in special seats at the edge of the circle opposite the stage house. Other dignitaries, such as civic and military officials, are arranged around them in the first few rows; above them sit both citizens and slaves. No one—not even those sitting in the top row—will have any trouble hearing the performers; the acoustics are so good that a whisper by an actor in the orchestra will carry to the upper reaches of the amphitheatre.

The plays performed for the citizens of Athens are part of the City Dionysia festival, an annual series of events lasting several days. During this festival, all business in Athens—both commercial and governmental—comes to a halt. On the day before the plays, there was a parade through the city, which ended near the theatre at a temple dedicated to the god Dionysus, for whom the festival is named. There, a religious observance was held at the altar.

Today is one of three days of the festival devoted mainly to tragedies. On these days, one playwright will present three tragedies and a satyr play. The three tragedies are sometimes linked to form one long play, called a *trilogy;* but sometimes they are three separate pieces—as they are today.

The play about to begin is *Antigone* by Sophocles. Its subject comes from a familiar myth: Antigone is the daughter of King Oedipus. After her father's death, her two brothers, Eteocles and Polynices, fight a war against each other to see who will become king of Thebes; during the war, they kill each other. Antigone's uncle, Creon, then becomes king of Thebes. Creon blames Polynices for the conflict and issues an edict that Polynices is not to be given an honorable burial. Antigone decides to defy Creon's order and bury Polynices. The audience members know this myth well and are curious to see how Sophocles—one of their favorite dramatists—will deal with it.

As the play begins, two actors, each wearing the mask and costume of a woman, appear in the playing area: they represent Antigone and her sister, Ismene. Antigone tells Ismene that she means to defy their uncle, the king, and give their brother Polynices an honorable burial. Ismene, unlike Antigone, is timid and frightened; she argues that women are too weak to stand up to a king. Besides, Ismene points out, Antigone will be put to death if she is caught. Antigone argues, however, that she will not be subservient to a man, even the king.

When the two female characters leave the stage, a chorus of fifteen men enters. These men represent the elders of the city, and throughout the play—in passages that are sung and danced—they will fulfill several functions: providing background information, raising philosophical questions, and urging the principal figures to show restraint. The choral sections alternate with scenes of confrontation between Antigone, Creon, and the other main characters.

As the play continues, Antigone attempts to bury Polynices, but she is caught and brought before the king. In their confrontation, Antigone defies Creon. She is sentenced to death and put into a cave to die. By the end of the play, not only is Antigone dead; so too are Creon's wife and son, who have killed themselves. In the final scene, we see Creon standing alone, wearing his tragic mask, bereft of all those whom he held dear.

READ *Antigone* in *Anthology of Living Theatre* or at:

http://classics.mit.edu/Sophocles/antigone.html

dancing as well as vocal projection. The actors may have been paid, and after 449 B.C.E. an acting contest was introduced.

The major element in Greek costuming was the mask, worn by all performers. The mask covered the entire head and included hairstyle and distinctive facial features such as a beard. Masks indicated the emotional state of the characters and also made it possible for male actors to play female characters.

Music and dance were always important elements of classical Greek theatre. By the time of Euripedes, it is believed that music was used, as in today's films, almost throughout a presentation. Dance also reflected the type of play for which it was created.

DRAMATIC CRITICISM IN GREECE: ARISTOTLE

In the fourth century B.C.E., roughly 100 years after Sophocles was at the height of his powers as a playwright, the first significant work of dramatic criticism—*The Poetics*—appeared. Its author was Aristotle (384–322 B.C.E.). Aristotle, like Socrates and Plato, was an important Greek philosopher; he was also a scientist who described and cataloged the world he saw around him, and he took the same approach in analyzing tragedy. *The Poetics* is loosely organized and incomplete, and the version we have may have been based on a series of lecture notes. It is so intelligent and so penetrating, however, that it remains the single most important piece of dramatic criticism in existence.

In *The Poetics* Aristotle describes six elements of drama: (1) plot (arrangement of dramatic incidents), (2) character (people represented in the play), (3) thought or theme (ideas explored), (4) language (dialogue and poetry), (5) music, and (6) spectacle (scenery and other visual elements). These correspond roughly to the elements of theatre we explore in Chapters 3 through 9, except that Aristotle does not include the performers. Tragedy, Aristotle suggests, deals with the reversals in fortune and eventual downfall of a royal figure.

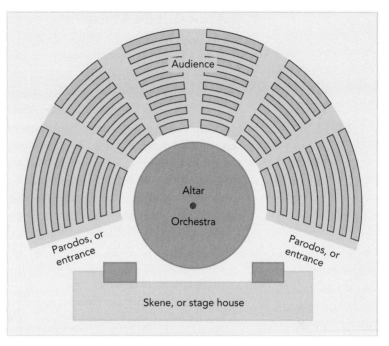

GROUND PLAN OF A TYPICAL GREEK THEATRE
The theatres of ancient Greece were set into hillsides, which made natural amphitheatres. At the base of the seating area was a circular space (orchestra) in which the chorus performed; at the center of the orchestra was an altar (thymele). Behind the orchestra was a temporary stage house (skene), at each side of which was a corridor (parodos) for entrances and exits.

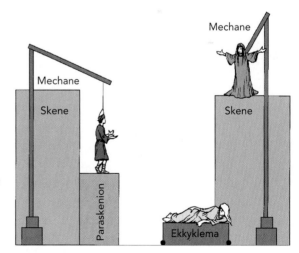

GREEK MECHANE AND EKKYKLEMA
A conjectural reconstruction of Greek stage machinery. On the left, a crane used for flying in characters located on a side wing (paraskenion) of the scene building. On the right, a mechane higher up on the roof of the skene. The ekkyklema below was a platform on wheels used to bring out characters from inside the building.

LATER GREEK THEATRE

In the two centuries after Aristotle—referred to as the *Hellenistic Age*—there were several developments in Greek theatre.

The period of great original drama was over, and revivals of plays from the past were increasingly presented. As original drama became less important, there was a shift of focus to acting and the actor. The theatre of this period saw the introduction of enlarged masks, exaggerated headdresses, and platform shoes that made the performers taller. Also, larger, more permanent stages were built, and these too directed more attention toward the actors. Emblematic of this new status for performers was the creation in 277 B.C.E. of a guild known as the Artists of Dionysus, which was the ancient equivalent of today's Actors Equity Association.

Theatre buildings proliferated throughout the Hellenistic world. We know of at least forty theatres built during this period from Asia Minor in the east to Italy in the west, many of them still standing. These were permanent structures, with both the seating area and the stage house built of stone, in contrast to the less permanent wooden structures of earlier times.

Theatre continued to flourish in Greece long after the second century B.C.E., but it was no longer purely Greek theatre—it was influenced by the omnipresent Roman civilization.

ROME

BACKGROUND: ROME AND ITS CIVILIZATION

As ancient Greece declined in power and importance, another civilization began to emerge in Europe on the Italian peninsula. Its center was the city of Rome, from which it took its name. While Greece is noted for its creativity and imagination, Rome is recognized more for its practical achievements: law, engineering, and military conquest. And just as these achievements were more down to earth than those of Greece, so too was Roman theatre. Instead of high-minded tragedy, it focused on comedy and other popular entertainments, comparable to our movies, television, and rock concerts.

Rome was founded, according to legend, around 750 B.C.E., and for more than 200 years it was ruled by kings. Around 500 B.C.E. the kings were overthrown, and a republic—which was to last nearly 500 years—was established.

During the third century B.C.E., Rome engaged in a lengthy conflict with Carthage known as the Punic Wars and finally emerged victorious. As a result, Rome controlled large parts of the central and western Mediterranean. It was at this period of conquest that Rome also came into contact with Greece and saw firsthand Greek art and culture, including theatre.

During the first century B.C.E., the Roman republic began to show signs of serious strain in attempting to govern so vast an area. In the midst of general turmoil, Julius Caesar made himself dictator. He was subsequently assassinated by a group led by Brutus, who in turn was defeated in battle by Mark Antony and Octavius. The republic could not survive these shocks, and in 27 B.C.E. Rome became an empire with one supreme ruler. This form of government continued for several centuries, during which most of the civilized Western world was unified under Roman rule.

Roman laws dealing with property, marriage, and inheritance have continued to influence Western civilization to the present day; in addition, the Romans were great

THEATRE

CULTURE AND POLITICS

Regular comedy and tragedy added to Ludi Romani (240 B.C.E.)

Plautus's *Pseudolus* (191 B.C.E.)

Terence's *Phormio* (161 B.C.E.)

Terence (c. 185–159 B.C.E.)
(New York Public Library,
Picture Collection)

Vitruvius's *De architectura* (90 B.C.E.)

First permanent theatre in Rome (55 B.C.E.)

Horace's *Art of Poetry* (24 B.C.E.)

Romans build theatres and amphitheatres throughout the empire (c. 30–200 C.E.)

Seneca (c. 4 B.C.E.–65 C.E.) writes Roman tragedies

Seneca (c. 4–65 C.E.)
(New York Public Library,
Picture Collection)

Theatrical presentations approximately 100 days per year

Council of Carthage decrees excommunication for those who attend theatre rather than church on holy days; actors forbidden sacraments (398 C.E.)

750

250

200

150

100

50

0

50

100

150

200

250

300

350

400

450

500

Traditional date for the founding of Rome (753 B.C.E.)

First Punic Wars (Greek influence on Roman culture) (264–241 B.C.E.)

Second Punic Wars (218–201 B.C.E.); Hannibal's victories (218–216 B.C.E.)

Rome defeats Philip V of Macedonia (200–197 B.C.E.)

Censorship of Cato; 1,000 talents spent on sewers (184 B.C.E.)

Roman citizens freed of direct taxation (167 B.C.E.)

Rome annexes Macedonia (147 B.C.E.)

First high-level aqueduct in Rome (144 B.C.E.)

Slave revolts in Sicily (135 B.C.E.)

Pompey suppresses piracy (67 B.C.E.)

Golden age of Roman literature (c. 58–50 B.C.E.)

Caesar's conquest of Gaul (55 B.C.E.)

Jesus crucified (30 C.E.)

Marcus Aurelius (c. 121–180 C.E.)

Marcus Aurelius rules (161–180 C.E.)

Severan dynasty; Augustan order disintegrates (193–235 C.E.)

Extensive persecution of Christians (c. 250–300 C.E.)

Constantine rules; empire reunited (324–337 C.E.)

St. Augustine born (354 C.E.)

Julian the Apostate restores paganism (361 C.E.)

Theodosius I forbids pagan worship (391 C.E.)

Sack of Rome by Visigoths (410 C.E.)

Death of Attila the Hun (453 C.E.)

Fall of western Roman empire (476 C.E.)

POPULAR ENTERTAINMENTS IN ROME
The Romans constructed large arenas for the presentation of popular entertainments, including gladiator battles, chariot races, and animal battles. Seen here is the Roman Colosseum, an amphitheatre originally built in 70 to 82 C.E., that still stands today. It was the scene of many spectacular events, including bloody combats. (Royalty-Free/Corbis)

engineers and architects, building important aqueducts and roadways. Religion was also of utmost importance to the Romans, who worshipped gods that were counterparts of the Greek deities, as well as a large number of other divinities.

THEATRE AND CULTURE IN ROME

When the Romans turned to theatre, they were strongly influenced by the Greeks, just as they were in sculpture and architecture. They borrowed freely from Greek theatre—particularly Greek New Comedy, from which they developed their own form of popular comedy. We should note that the Romans' popular entertainments were also influenced by Etruria, a civilization northwest of Rome that flourished from 650 to 450 B.C.E.

In 240 B.C.E., a festival called the *Ludi Romani,* dedicated to Jupiter (the Roman counterpart of Zeus), became the first major Roman festival to incorporate theatre. Five more official festivals eventually incorporated theatre; in addition, an increasing number of days were set aside for minor festivals and theatrical activities.

POPULAR ENTERTAINMENT IN ROME

Throughout theatre history, all civilizations have developed popular entertainments, which appeal to all levels of society, and require no educational, social, or cultural sophistication to appreciate them. Many popular entertainments are theatrical in nature, using live performers. Some historians say that twenty-first-century American culture, with its highly developed popular entertainments—television, film, rock concerts, and other less sophisticated dramatic arts—is much like Roman culture. The reason for

ROMAN COMEDY

Roman comedy, which was based on Greek New Comedy, stressed domestic travails presented humorously. Roman comedy has been the basis for comedy running through the entire Western tradition, right up to the point of today's television situation comedies. One of the most popular adaptations of ancient Roman comedy is the musical *A Funny Thing Happened on the Way to the Forum* with music and lyrics by Stephen Sondheim. The scene here is from a production at the Paper Mill Playhouse in New Jersey, with Paul C. Vogt as Pseudolus (center), the lead character. (© T. Charles Erickson)

this is that many Roman entertainments correspond to modern ones. The Romans, for example, greatly enjoyed chariot racing, equestrian performances, acrobatics, wrestling, prizefighting, and gladiatorial combats—though the gladiatorial combats were not simulated but actual battles to the death.

To house these spectacles, the Romans constructed special buildings, counterparts to our modern football and baseball stadiums. The Circus Maximus in Rome, first laid out in 600 B.C.E. for chariot races and frequently remodeled thereafter, eventually seated more than 60,000 spectators. The most renowned amphitheatre constructed by the Romans was the Colosseum, built around 80 C.E.

The Romans also developed popular entertainments that were more closely connected to theatre. Roman mime, like Greek mime, included gymnastics, juggling, songs, and dances. Short comedic skits, which were often sexually suggestive, were also presented. A unique Roman stage presentation was ***pantomime,*** which used a single dancer, a chorus, and musical accompanists and was somewhat akin to modern ballet; its performers were often sponsored by emperors and members of the nobility.

Pantomime Originally a Roman entertainment in which a narrative was sung by a chorus while the story was acted out by dancers. Now used loosely to cover any form of presentation that relies on dance, gesture, and physical movement without dialogue or speech.

ROMAN COMEDY: PLAUTUS AND TERENCE

Although theatre and drama existed in Rome for nearly seven centuries, the works of only three playwrights survive: the comedies of Plautus and Terence and the tragedies of Seneca.

Plautus (c. 254–184 B.C.E.), who based almost all his comedies on Greek New Comedy, dealt exclusively with domestic situations, particularly the trials and

ROME, 184 B.C.E. It is 184 B.C.E., and many of the inhabitants of the city of Rome are on their way to attend performances at a spring festival in honor of Jupiter. Their mood today is happy and ebullient, because they are about to see a comedy by Plautus, whose plot twists and comic invention have made his works favorites with everyone.

The Romans are heading toward a large, temporary wooden theatre building, seating several thousand, that has been erected next to a temple of Jupiter. All theatre productions in Rome now take place during religious festivals, and all the theatres are near temples. A Roman theatre—unlike the Greek theatres in the lands Rome has conquered—is a single unit, built on level ground, with the stage house attached directly to the ends of a semicircular audience area. In front of the stage house is a long platform stage; and in front of that is a half-circle surrounded by the audience.

The group converging on the theatre consists of people from all walks of life. Plautus himself has remarked that a Roman audience is a genuine mixture: in addition to well-to-do middle- and upper-class citizens, it includes government officials and their wives; children with nurses; prostitutes; slaves—in short, virtually every social group. Because this is a state festival, admission is free.

Magistrates of the state have received a grant to produce today's plays and have engaged acting troupes to present individual plays. Each troupe is under the direction of a manager, and one of these managers has bought from Plautus a play called *The Menaechmi* and has arranged for the costumes, music, and other production elements.

As the Romans enter the theatre, they see two doors onstage: one opens on the house of Menaechmus of Epidamnus (the Greek city in which Plautus has set his play); the other is the door to the house of Erotium, a woman with whom Menaechmus is having a love affair that he is trying to keep secret from his wife. The stage represents the street in front of the two houses; at one end is an exit to the port, and at the other end is an exit to the center of town.

An actor comes onstage to deliver a prologue. He asks the audience members to pay careful attention to what Plautus has to say, and then he outlines the background of the story: how the Menaechmi twins were separated when they were infants and how the twin who grew up in Syracuse is just now returning to try to find his long-lost brother. As in many of Plautus's plays, most of the dialogue is sung, somewhat like the musical numbers in contemporary musical comedies.

When the play opens, Menaechmus is shown to be the despair of his jealous wife. He confides to "Sponge," a parasite, that he has stolen his wife's dress, hiding it under his own clothes—and is going to give it to his mistress, Erotium. At Erotium's house he suggests that in return for the dress, she invite them to dinner. Menaechmus exits.

Meanwhile, the twin from Syracuse has arrived with his slave, Messenio. His master gives Messenio a purse full of money for safekeeping. At that point, Erotium steps out of her house and, mistaking the Syracuse twin for Menaechmus, makes advances to him, by which he is totally confused. Not knowing he is a twin, she is equally confused by his odd behavior. Meanwhile, the two servants of the twins are constantly confused with one another as well.

Finally, the Syracuse twin does enter the house of Erotium to have dinner, and later leaves with the dress that his twin brother Menaechmus had previously given her. Menaechmus comes back just in time to have his wife demand that he return her dress. He goes to Erotium to retrieve the dress, only to be told by her that she has already given it to him. In short, he is rebuffed by both his wife and his mistress.

The play continues like this, with the two brothers constantly being confused for one another by everyone, including the wife, the mistress, the father, and the two servants. Confusion and slapstick comedy abound until the end of the play, when everything is resolved.

READ *The Menaechmi* in *Anthology of LIving Theatre* or at:
- http://www.perseus.tufts.edu/hopper/text?doc=Perseus:text:1999.02.0101

tribulations of romance. His characters are recognizable, recurring stock types, the most popular being the parasite who lives off others and is motivated mainly by sensuality. Courtesans, lovers, and overbearing parents were also favorite characters. Most of the dialogue was meant to be sung. Plautus's comedies are farces, and they use such farcical techniques as mistaken identity. A good example of mistaken identity is found in *The Menaechmi,* which is also called *The Menaechmus Brothers* or *The Twin Menaechmi* in differing translations.

The Roman comic writer who followed Plautus was Terence (c. 185–159 B.C.E.). Although Terence's plots are as complicated as those of Plautus, his style is more literary and less exaggerated. Terence's *Phormio* (161 B.C.E.) dramatizes the attempts of two cousins to overcome their fathers' objections to their lovers. The plot complications and stock characters are similar to those found in *The Menaechmi,* but *Phormio* is less farcical and slapstick and gives more emphasis to verbal wit. Also, whereas much of Plautus's dialogue was meant to be sung, most of Terence's dialogue was spoken.

ROMAN TRAGEDY: SENECA

The most notable tragic dramatist of the Roman period was Seneca (c. 4 B.C.E.–65 C.E.). Seneca's plays appear to be similar to Greek tragedies but in fact are quite distinct. His chorus is not integral to the dramatic action; and—unlike Greek dramatists, who banished violence from the stage—Seneca emphasizes onstage stabbings, murders, and suicides. In addition, supernatural beings often appear in the dramatic action.

Although his plays were probably not performed for large public audiences, Seneca had a noteworthy influence on later authors, particularly Shakespeare. *Hamlet*—which has much onstage violence and includes a supernatural character (the ghost of Hamlet's father)—is often described as influenced by Senecan revenge tragedy.

DRAMATIC CRITICISM IN ROME: HORACE

Like Roman drama, Roman dramatic criticism was based on the work of others, especially Aristotle. Horace (65–8 B.C.E.), sometimes called the "Roman Aristotle," outlined his theory of correct dramatic technique in *Ars poetica (The Art of Poetry)*. Horace argued that tragedy and comedy must be distinct genres, or types, of drama, and that tragedy should deal with royalty, whereas comedy should depict common people. He also stressed that drama should not just entertain but also teach a lesson.

THEATRE PRODUCTION IN ROME

Roman production practices differed slightly from those of Greece. Roman festivals were under the jurisdiction of a local government official who hired an acting troupe. The ***dominus,*** or head, of a troupe—who was usually the leading actor—made financial arrangements, bought dramas from playwrights, hired musicians, and obtained costumes. Acting companies had at least six members, all male; and the Romans ignored the three-actor rule of Greek theatre. Roman acting technique emphasized detailed pantomime and broad physical gestures, necessitated by the size of Roman theatres; it also stressed beautiful vocal delivery. The Romans admired performers who specialized in one type of role and refined the characterizations of stock figures. Facial expression was unimportant since full linen head masks were worn; only mime performers appeared without masks.

Dominus Leader of a Roman acting troupe.

GREEK AND ROMAN POPULAR ARTS

Although we focus on the great dramas and comedies created during the Greek and Roman eras, we should not forget that there was a strong tradition of popular entertainment during these time periods. The types of popular arts that flourished during these eras were to have a great influence on popular culture through our own times.

During the classical and Hellenistic Greek eras, we know that there were traveling mimes who performed throughout the Greek world. Historians believe that mime may have developed in the fifth and fourth centuries B.C.E., but there is a great deal of debate over how to define the form. Greek mime is often described as dealing with domestic and sexual situations in a popular and highly bawdy manner, though it may have first been a form that parodied mythological figures and stories.

Mimes sometimes performed by themselves, but by the Hellenistic era they were usually organized into troupes. Mime was never introduced into the festivals and was seen as a lower form of theatrical art. Women eventually were performers in mime troupes, and frequently the actors in this type of popular entertainment, especially in the Hellenistic era, appeared without masks. In order to survive economically, mime troupes traveled extensively. For that reason, it is often argued that Greek mime performers influenced the development of Roman theatre and popular entertainments.

Roman theatre had great competition in the popular arts that were available to the Roman public. Mime troupes continued to perform in Roman times. The Romans also developed a form referred to as *pantomime,* in which a single male dancer interpreted classical literature, sometimes accompanied by a chorus that chanted and by musicians.

But the Romans also organized even greater spectacles. As we have noted, they created huge circuses, stadiums, and amphitheatres for popular arts. Some of the circuses, for example, had tracks for chariot races. Stadiums held animal battles, battles between gladiators, and fights between humans and animals; the Circus Maximus and the Colosseum were erected for just such events.

GLADIATOR BATTLES
Shown here is a Roman mosaic depicting a gladiator battling a leopard. Such battles between human combatants and animals were extremely popular, particularly during the Roman empire. (© Alinari Archives/Corbis)

In modern times, we can see many similarities to the popular arts of Greece and Rome. Stand-up comedians and small troupes of improvisatory comics entertain us regularly in events that are very reminiscent of the early mimes. Sports arenas, indoors and outdoors, house gladiator-like battles, such as football and boxing. And many of these events are highly theatrical, mixing pregame, halftime, and postgame performances into already highly theatricalized sports.

As we've seen, Roman theatres were based on Greek models. The Romans did not construct a permanent theatre until 55 B.C.E. Thus there were no permanent spaces for presenting the works of Plautus and Terence, the best-known Roman playwrights. Instead, elaborate temporary wooden structures, probably similar to the later permanent ones, were erected.

A Roman theatre had the same three units as a Greek theatre: (1) a semicircular, sloped seating area; (2) an orchestra; and (3) a stage house, called the *scaena* (SKAY-nah). The Roman structures, however, were different from classical Greek theatres in that they were freestanding buildings with the tiered audience section connected to the

Scaena Stage house in a Roman theatre.

THE ROMAN THEATRE AT ORANGE
The Romans built theatres throughout their empire, which circled the Mediterranean Sea. One of the best-preserved, built in the first or second century c.e., is at Orange in France, near the center of town. Note the semicircular orchestra, the large stage area, and the stage house at the back, with its ornate facade with niches for statues and other adornments. (© Vanni/Art Resource, N.Y.)

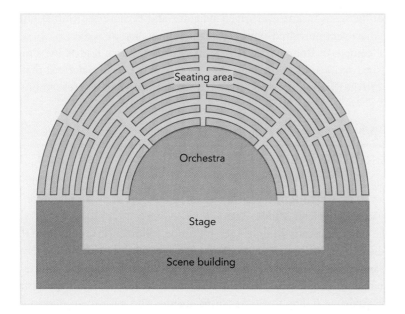

GROUND PLAN OF A TYPICAL ROMAN THEATRE
Roman theatres, in contrast to Greek theatres, were free-standing structures—all one building—with the stone stage house connected to the seating area, known as the cavea. The orchestra was a semicircle instead of a full circle as in Greek theatres. The stage was long and wide, and the stage house was several stories high with an elaborate facade.

stage house to form a single unit. The sloped, semicircular audience seating area was often larger than its Greek counterpart; the average capacity of a Roman theatre was around 25,000.

The Roman orchestra, which was semicircular (rather than circular as in Greek theatres), was rarely used for staging; rather, it was used for seating government officials or, in some theatres, was flooded for sea battles.

In front of the stage house was a large raised stage about 5 feet high whose area varied from approximately 100 feet by 20 feet to 300 feet by 40 feet. The stage house itself was a unique feature of the Roman theatre structure. Two or three stories high, it was used for storage and dressing space, and a roof extended from the scene building over the stage to protect the actors from the weather. Two side wings connected the stage house to the audience area. The facade of the stage house—the *scaena frons*—was elaborate and ornate, with statuary, columns, recesses, and three to five doorways. Because of its emphasis on the raised stage and the facade behind it, the Roman theatre moved to a point somewhere between the thrust stage of the Greek theatre and later proscenium stages.

DECLINE OF ROMAN THEATRE

In the fourth century C.E., it was clear that the Roman Empire was beginning to fall apart. In 330, Emperor Constantine established two capitals for the empire: Rome in the west and Constantinople in the east. From that point on, the center of gravity shifted to Constantinople, and the city of Rome became less and less important.

The downfall of Rome was marked in 476 C.E. by the unseating of the western Roman emperor by a barbarian ruler. It had probably been caused by the disintegration of the Roman administrative structure and the sacking of Roman cities by northern barbarians; but in any case the fall of the empire also meant the end of western Roman theatre.

Another important factor in the decline of Roman theatre was the rise of Christianity. From the outset, the Christian church was opposed to theatre because of the connection between theatre and pagan religions and because the church fathers felt that evil characters portrayed onstage taught immorality to audiences. In addition, the sexual content of Roman entertainments offended church leaders. As a result, the church issued various edicts condemning theatre and in 398 C.E. decreed that anyone who went to the theatre rather than to church on holy days would be excommunicated.

THE MIDDLE AGES

BACKGROUND: MEDIEVAL EUROPE

The period from 500 to 1500 C.E. in Western history is known as the Middle Ages or the medieval era. The first 500 years are referred to as the early Middle Ages, and the next 500 years as the later Middle Ages.

At the start of the early Middle Ages in Europe, following invasions from the north and the dissolution of Roman civilization, cities were abandoned and life throughout southern and western Europe became largely agricultural. The nobility controlled local areas, where most people worked as vassals. Gradually, several hundred years after the fall of the Roman Empire, towns began to emerge, and with them trade and crafts. Learning also slowly revived. The strongest force during this period was the Roman

Catholic Church, which dominated not only religion but education and frequently politics as well.

We should also note that theatrical activity did continue in the eastern Roman Empire, known as Byzantium, until 1453, when the region was conquered by the Islamic Turks. The theatre of Byzantium was reminiscent of theatre during the Roman Empire. The Hippodrome, a large arena in Constantinople, was the Byzantine equivalent of the Circus Maximus or the Colosseum, and popular entertainments like those of Rome flourished in the east. One contribution of the Byzantine Empire to the continuity of theatre consists of these popular presentations; another important contribution lies in the fact that Byzantium was the preserver of the manuscripts of classical Greek drama: the plays of Aeschylus, Sophocles, and Euripides and the criticism of Aristotle were saved. When the eastern Roman Empire fell in 1453, these manuscripts were transferred to the Western world and became part of the rediscovery that influenced the Renaissance.

THEATRE AND CULTURE IN THE MIDDLE AGES

During the early part of the Middle Ages, there were some scattered traces of theatrical activity, mostly based on the popular entertainments of Greece and Rome—traveling jugglers, minstrels, and mimes. In the late tenth century a nun in a convent in Germany, Hrosvitha of Gandersheim (c. 935–1001), wrote religious plays based on the dramas of the Roman writer Terence. Though her plays were probably not produced, it is still remarkable that she created drama almost in a vacuum. (Hrosvitha's work has been reexamined more fully by feminist critics.)

Essentially, though, theatre had to be reborn in the West during the latter part of the Middle Ages. Interestingly, key elements of the new theatre first appeared in the church, which had suppressed theatre several hundred years earlier. In certain portions of the church service, priests or members of the choir chanted the lines of characters from the Bible. Gradually these small segments, which were delivered in Latin, were enlarged and became short dramas—known as *liturgical dramas*—enacted in the church.

Liturgical drama Early medieval church drama, written in Latin and dealing with biblical stories.

Also, during this early period of the Middle Ages, a German nun named Hildegard von Bingen (1098–1179) wrote short musical plays that were probably performed in her convent. Hildegard wrote liturgical songs that were accompanied by texts. These dramatic musical pieces honored saints and the Virgin Mary and were written for performance on religious days. Hildegard also created a play in Latin, *Ordo Virtutum (Play of Virtues),* that seems to foreshadow the later vernacular morality plays.

Later in the Middle Ages, *vernacular drama* developed. The language of these later plays was not Latin but the everyday speech of the people. Like the brief church plays, vernacular dramas dealt with biblical stories and other religious stories. Vernacular dramas, however, were more elaborate and were usually presented as a series of one-act dramas. Also, they were presented not inside churches but in town squares or other parts of cities. Historians continue to debate whether vernacular drama evolved from liturgical drama or developed independently.

Vernacular drama Drama from the Middle Ages performed in the everyday speech of the people and presented in town squares or other parts of cities.

MEDIEVAL DRAMA: MYSTERY AND MORALITY PLAYS

Two types of religious vernacular plays were popular in the medieval period. *Mystery plays* or *cycle plays* dramatized a series of biblical religious events that could stretch from Adam and Eve in the Garden of Eden, Noah and the flood, and Abraham and

Mystery plays Also called *cycle plays.* Short dramas of the Middle Ages based on events of the Old and New Testaments and often organized into historical cycles.

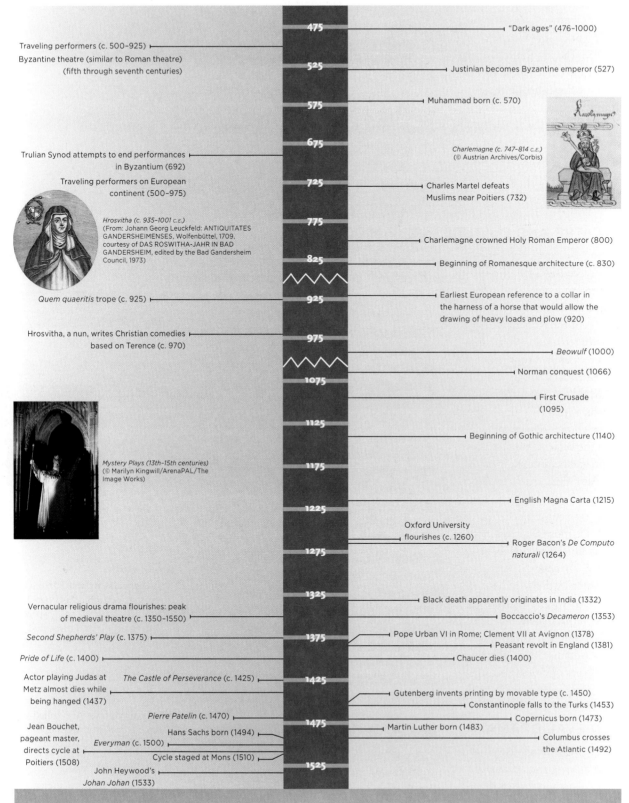

MIDDLE AGES

THEATRE

Year, c.e.

CULTURE AND POLITICS

475

"Dark ages" (476–1000)

Traveling performers (c. 500–925)

Byzantine theatre (similar to Roman theatre)
(fifth through seventh centuries)

525

Justinian becomes Byzantine emperor (527)

575

Muhammad born (c. 570)

675

Charlemagne (c. 747–814 c.e.)
(© Austrian Archives/Corbis)

Trulian Synod attempts to end performances
in Byzantium (692)

Traveling performers on European
continent (500–975)

725

Charles Martel defeats
Muslims near Poitiers (732)

Hrosvitha (c. 935–1001 c.e.)
(From: Johann Georg Leuckfeld: ANTIQUITATES
GANDERSHEIMENSES, Wolfenbüttel, 1709,
courtesy of DAS ROSWITHA-JAHR IN BAD
GANDERSHEIM, edited by the Bad Gandersheim
Council, 1973)

775

825

Charlemagne crowned Holy Roman Emperor (800)

Beginning of Romanesque architecture (c. 830)

Quem quaeritis trope (c. 925)

925

Earliest European reference to a collar in
the harness of a horse that would allow the
drawing of heavy loads and plow (920)

Hrosvitha, a nun, writes Christian comedies
based on Terence (c. 970)

975

Beowulf (1000)

Norman conquest (1066)

1075

First Crusade
(1095)

1125

Beginning of Gothic architecture (1140)

Mystery Plays (13th–15th centuries)
(© Marilyn Kingwill/ArenaPAL/The
Image Works)

1175

1225

English Magna Carta (1215)

Oxford University
flourishes (c. 1260)

1275

Roger Bacon's *De Computo
naturali* (1264)

1325

Black death apparently originates in India (1332)

Vernacular religious drama flourishes: peak
of medieval theatre (c. 1350–1550)

Boccaccio's *Decameron* (1353)

Second Shepherds' Play (c. 1375)

1375

Pope Urban VI in Rome; Clement VII at Avignon (1378)

Peasant revolt in England (1381)

Pride of Life (c. 1400)

Chaucer dies (1400)

Actor playing Judas at
Metz almost dies while
being hanged (1437)

The Castle of Perseverance (c. 1425)

1425

Gutenberg invents printing by movable type (c. 1450)

Constantinople falls to the Turks (1453)

Pierre Patelin (c. 1470)

Copernicus born (1473)

Jean Bouchet,
pageant master,
directs cycle at
Poitiers (1508)

Hans Sachs born (1494)

Everyman (c. 1500)

Cycle staged at Mons (1510)

1475

Martin Luther born (1483)

Columbus crosses
the Atlantic (1492)

John Heywood's
Johan Johan (1533)

1525

Isaac to the stories of Christ in the New Testament as well as the lives of the saints. *Morality plays* such as *Everyman* (c. 1500) used religious characters and religious themes to teach a moral lesson. Virtually all the plays were short—the equivalent of a one-act play today—and mystery plays were often strung together to form a series, known as a *cycle*.

The best-known mystery play is *The Second Shepherds' Play,* produced in England in the late fourteenth century. It concerns three shepherds who, according to the Bible, went to visit the Christ child just after his birth in a manger. The first section of the drama comically depicts the stealing of a sheep from the shepherds by a rogue, Mak. When the three shepherds search for the missing sheep in Mak's home, his wife Gil pretends that the sheep is her newborn child. When the shepherds return a second time to offer gifts to Mak's "child," they discover that the infant is the stolen sheep, and they proceed to toss Mak in a blanket. In the second section of the play, the shepherds are called by an angel to visit the newborn Christ child, to whom they also bring gifts.

The Second Shepherds' Play illustrates most of the standard dramatic techniques of medieval cycle plays. One technique is to take things out of their actual time period. Though this is a Bible story, the shepherds are not biblical characters but people of the Middle Ages who complain about their lords and feudal conditions. And even though Christ is not born until the close of the play, they pray to him and to various saints throughout the initial section. Another technique is to mix different types of drama. Though the play dramatizes the birth of the Christian savior, this serious event is preceded by an extended comic section, reflecting the influence of secular farce on medieval religious drama. In the later Middle Ages, a tradition of nonreligious folk comedies made a significant contribution to the theatrical activity of the period.

In Chapter 3, we discussed the two major dramatic structures of Western theatre—climactic and episodic. The seeds of episodic form are found in medieval religious drama. This structure has numerous episodes and is expansive rather than restrictive in terms of time, place, and numbers of characters. In *The Second Shepherds' Play,* a forerunner of this form, the action shifts abruptly from a field to Mak's hut and to Christ's manger some distance away; also, comic and serious elements are freely intermingled.

Morality play Medieval drama designed to teach a lesson. The characters were often allegorical and represented virtues or faults.

MYSTERY PLAYS
The mystery plays depicted scenes from the Bible, both the Old Testament and the New Testament. These plays were frequently presented in a cycle, a series of short dramas each of which dramatized an episode from the Bible. They were strung together over several hours or several days. The scene here shows Edward Woodward as God in a production of a mystery play at Canterbury Cathedral in England. (© Marilyn Kingwill/ArenaPAL/The Image Works)

READ *The Second Shepherds' Play*

www.calvin.edu/academic/engl/215/ssp.htm

We should mention that *secular* theatre and drama also existed during the Middle Ages. In France and Germany, for

OUTDOOR STAGES AT VALENCIENNES
A popular form of medieval staging, especially on the European continent, was a series of stage areas set alongside each other. In the one at Valenciennes, France, shown here in a color rendering of the original stage set, the action would move from one area to the next. At the far left is heaven or paradise, at the right is hell with a hell mouth out of which devils came. In between are other "mansions" representing various locales. (Bibliothèque Nationale de France)

example, many popular farces were written and performed. They are a continuation of the tradition of popular entertainment discussed earlier in this chapter. It is medieval religious drama, however, which is most remembered today.

MEDIEVAL THEATRE PRODUCTION

Large-scale productions of mystery plays took place in what is now Spain, France, the Netherlands, Belgium, and England. In some cases, most often on the continent of Europe, stages were set up in a large town square, behind which were placed the individual scenic units—the **mansions**—one for each of the plays in a cycle. In other cases, particularly in England and Spain, portable **wagon stages**—whose appearance and mode of operation are still debated by scholars—moved through towns and stopped at points along the way to present one of the plays. (We should note that a few historians even question whether the wagons actually stopped to present the plays at different points or simply paraded through the town to one central location.)

The performers, who prepared for a few weeks for their roles, were amateurs. Only men performed in England, but women were performers in some continental European countries. Craft guilds—silversmiths, leather workers, carpenters, and so forth—or laypeople who belonged to religious organizations were responsible for producing individual plays, which were presented as part of annual festivals. In some cases, individual plays were assigned to appropriate guilds: *The Last Supper* to the baker's guild; the Noah play to the shipbuilder's guild; and *The Visit of the Magi* to the goldsmiths. Frequently, they provided their own costumes, which for the most part were contemporary dress rather than historically accurate clothing. Sometimes these presentations became extremely prolonged and elaborate; a series of plays presented in Valenciennes, France, in 1547 lasted for twenty-five days.

Mansions Individual scenic units used for the staging of religious dramas in the Middle Ages.

Wagon stage Low platform mounted on wheels or casters by means of which scenery is moved on- and offstage.

1501, MONS The year is 1501. In a large town square in Mons—in the area that will much later become Belgium—a row of small stage houses called mansions have been erected. They serve as the setting for a series, or cycle, of plays based on the Old and New Testaments: dramatized Bible stories that move from the creation to the crucifixion. In the biblical plays at Mons this year, about 150 actors will perform 350 roles. They have held forty-eight rehearsals, and it will take four days to present all the plays in the cycle.

The mansions set up across the stage area are changed to suit whatever play is being performed. More than sixty different mansions—representing the Garden of Eden, the manger in Bethlehem, the temple where Christ drove out the money changers, and so forth—will be used during these four days. At each end of the stage area are two permanent mansions, symbolic of the opposing sides in this great religious drama: one is heaven and the other hell. Hell is represented by the large mouth of a monster, out of which devils and smoke pour forth at appropriate moments.

This kind of religious drama is the chief theatrical presentation in the medieval period. It takes forms that vary in theatrical setting and in staging, but in both England and continental Europe, it is widespread and popular.

The church encourages it because most people cannot read or write, and this is an excellent way for them to become familiar with stories from the Bible. The only other form of entertainment in this era is traveling troupes of jugglers, singers, dancers, and mimes. They go from place to place, performing brief dramatic sketches along with musicals and other pieces.

A good percentage of the people who live in Mons and the surrounding areas are present at the four-day cycle of religious plays. They represent a cross section of the community. The spectators either sit in temporary wooden bleachers or stand in the town square, trying to get the best possible view of the acting area and the various "mansions" from which the action of each episode begins.

The audience members have already seen dramas about Adam and Eve and about Cain slaying his brother Abel; now they will see a play about Noah, who is commanded by God to build an ark to save his family and the animals from the flood.

In the play, Noah is warned by God that it will rain for forty days and forty nights, and that he must build an ark into which he will take his family and two animals of every kind. As Noah begins building, his neighbors make fun of him, and his shrewish wife argues with him. The wife does not want

to go aboard the ark; she feels that Noah is foolish. She chides and criticizes her husband, and it is only when the rain begins to fall that she agrees to board the ark.

The spectators enjoy this comic interaction, but the moment they are waiting for is the deluge of rain, which is expected to be spectacular. At last the moment arrives, and the audience is not disappointed. On the roofs of houses behind the stage area, water has been stored in wine barrels and men are standing by, waiting for a signal to open the barrels. Now the signal is given, and the deluge begins: torrents of water fall onto the stage. The audience is completely in awe; enough water has been stored to provide a steady rain for five minutes. Water rises all around, but Noah, his family, and his animals are safe in the ark. Soon after, a dove comes, indicating that Noah can leave the ark.

During the remaining days of the cycle of plays, the spectators will see a continuing series of biblical stories, which trace episodes from both the Old Testament and the New Testament, including many events from the life of Christ. When the entire cycle has concluded, audience members will recall many highlights, but none, perhaps, more spectacular than the sensational flood in the play about Noah and his family.

Music also played a significant role, with some dramas including choruses and others featuring songs performed by an individual or group of actors. This is another reason why vocal ability was admired in the amateur players. Professional musicians provided accompaniment.

Because of the complexity of cycle plays, there developed, both on the continent and in England, a practice of having one person organize and oversee production. In England, there are records of a ***pageant master,*** who supervised the mounting of plays

Pageant master During the Middle Ages, one who supervised the mounting of mystery plays.

PAGEANT WAGONS

One form of staging for medieval religious plays was the pageant wagon, which could be rolled into a town or a nearby field. The wagon—or wagons—served as a stage, contained scenery, and had a backstage area for costume changes. We do not know exactly how a pageant wagon worked, but shown here are two suggestions or speculations. Above is a hand-colored woodcut of the performance of a mystery play on a pageant wagon in Coventry, England, at the height of medieval theatre. The wagon has a platform with a cloth covering its lower part (from which characters could emerge). The drawing at left shows a cutaway view of two wagons; one serves as a stage platform while the other, behind it, provides a place for scenery, changing costumes, and hiding special effects. (North Wind Picture Archives)

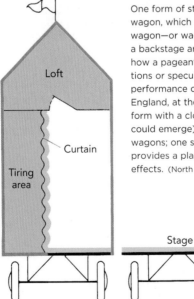

Loft

Curtain

Tiring area

Stage

Audience surrounds stage wagon

Wheels of wagons

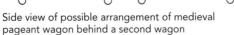

Side view of possible arrangement of medieval pageant wagon behind a second wagon

on wagons. This might include advance preparations—both for the wagons and for the rehearsals of plays to be presented on them—and the logistics of seeing that the plays unfolded on schedule.

To accommodate the abrupt changes in location that characterized the plots of mystery plays, medieval theatres used a neutral ***platform stage,*** set up either in a town square or on one of the wagon stages. This platform was not a specific locale, like a palace in Greek drama, but an unidentified space that could become whatever was designated. If the performers or the script indicated that a scene was set in a field, the platform instantaneously became a field; if it was supposed to be a ship at sea, it became a ship. This freedom of movement, based on the imagination, later became the basis of theatrical techniques perfected by Renaissance playwrights in Spain and England.

Platform stage Elevated stage with no proscenium.

Toward the end of the Middle Ages, there was a gradual decline of religious theatre. One reason was a weakening of the church, culminating in the Protestant Reformation; a second reason was that the secular qualities of drama finally overcame the religious material.

In Chapter 11, we will turn to the traditional theatres of Asia, which originated with religious ceremonies and ideas. Most are highly theatrical and stylized, and they fuse acting, mime, dance, music, and text. Among the important Asian theatres are Sanskrit drama in India; the popular Peking opera in China; and the stylized nō drama, bunraku (puppet theatre), and kabuki in Japan.

SUMMARY

The impulse to create theatre is universal. Elements of theatre exist in rituals and ceremonies in Africa, Asia, Europe, and wherever else human society develops.

On the European continent, Greek theatre set the stage for all Western theatre to follow, with the tragedies of Aeschylus, Sophocles, and Euripides and the dramatic form known as climactic structure. Aristotle's *Poetics* marked the development of serious criticism of drama and theatre. With Aristophanes's Old Comedies, the Greeks were leaders in comedy as well. Classical Greek theatre buildings were large outdoor spaces built into hillsides, which accommodated audiences attending religious festivals. All the performers were male, and the chorus was an integral element of all classical Greek drama and theatre. During the later Hellenistic period in Greece, New Comedy, which was concerned with domestic and romantic situations, prepared the way for almost all subsequent popular comedy.

The Romans borrowed many Greek conventions, including the introduction of drama and theatre into religious and civic festivals, but they emphasized domestic and romantic comedies, as in the plays of Plautus and Terence. The tragedies of Seneca are noteworthy because of their influence on later playwrights.

Roman theatres were usually huge outdoor buildings. In Roman playhouses (unlike Greek theatres), all the structural elements were connected, and the most significant element was a large raised stage with an ornate facade.

In Europe during the period from 500 to 1000 C.E.—the early Middle Ages—touring minstrels kept the theatrical tradition alive. Later in the Middle Ages, theatre was reborn, primarily in the Roman Catholic Church. Dramatic interpolations that had been added to religious services grew into plays—written in Latin and dramatizing biblical events—which were staged in churches by the clergy. In the fourteenth century, plays in the everyday language of the people developed. Mystery or cycle plays, which depicted a series of biblical tales—and which established the basis for extensive plot structure—were staged and acted outdoors by amateurs.

Thinking about Theatre

▶ Imagine yourself at the first production of *Oedipus the King*. Describe the theatre space in which the production is staged. Was there scenery onstage? What part does the chorus play in the production?

▶ The Greeks observed a *three-actor rule* in classical tragedy. What does this mean? How would three actors play all of the roles in a tragedy that you have read?

▶ Watch a skit on *Saturday Night Live*. In what way is that skit similar to Classical Greek Old Comedy?

▶ Some historians believe that in ancient Rome, popular entertainments were more prevalent than Roman theatre. Others suggest that the popular and theatrical forms were interrelated. Which of these opinions seems to be true about our own times? Name several forms of popular entertainment today. Do these performances overshadow dramatic presentations, or do they exist side by side?

▶ Describe the key similarities and differences between the classical Greek and Roman theatres both in architecture and in dramatic content.

▶ Religion played a central role in the theatre of the Middle Ages. Do you believe there is any relationship between theatre and religion today? Support your answer based on what you learned in the chapter and your own experience.

▶ Medieval theatre was frequently performed outdoors. Does this tradition survive today? Identify and describe three examples.

Key Terms

Agon In classical Greek Old Comedy, a scene with a debate between the two opposing forces in a play.

Amphitheatre Large oval, circular, or semicircular outdoor theatre with rising tiers of seats around an open playing area; also, an exceptionally large indoor auditorium.

Choregus Wealthy person who financed a playwright's works at an ancient Greek dramatic festival.

Chorus In ancient Greek drama, a group of performers who sang and danced, sometimes participating in the action but usually simply commenting on it. In modern times, performers in a musical play who sing and dance as a group.

City Dionysia The most important Greek festival in honor of the god Dionysus, and the first to include drama.

Dominus Leader of a Roman acting troupe.

Liturgical drama Early medieval church drama, written in Latin and dealing with biblical stories.

Mansions Individual scenic units used for the staging of religious dramas in the Middle Ages.

Morality play Medieval drama designed to teach a lesson. The characters were often allegorical and represented virtues or faults.

Mystery plays Also called *cycle plays*. Short dramas of the Middle Ages based on events of the Old and New Testaments and often organized into historical cycles.

New Comedy Hellenistic Greek and Roman comedies that deal with romantic and domestic situations.

Old Comedy Classical Greek comedy that pokes fun at social, political, or cultural conditions and at particular figures.

Orchestra A circular playing space in ancient Greek theatres; in modern times, the ground-floor seating in a theatre auditorium.

Pageant master During the Middle Ages, one who supervised the mounting of mystery plays.

Pantomime Originally a Roman entertainment in which a narrative was sung by a chorus while the story was acted out by dancers. Now used loosely to cover any form of presentation that relies on dance, gesture, and physical movement without dialogue or speech.

Parabasis Scene in classical Greek Old Comedy in which the chorus directly addresses the audience members and makes fun of them.

Parodos In classical Greek drama, the scene in which the chorus enters. Also, the entranceway for the chorus in Greek theatre.

Platform stage Elevated stage with no proscenium.

Satyr play One of the three types of classical Greek drama, usually a ribald takeoff on Greek mythology and history that included a chorus of satyrs, mythological creatures who were half-man and half-goat. On festival days in Athens, it was presented as the final play following three tragedies.

Scaena Stage house in a Roman theatre.

Theatron Where the audience sat in an ancient Greek theatre.

Thespian Synonym for "performer"; from Thespis, who is said to have been the first actor in ancient Greek theatre.

Trilogy In classical Greece, three tragedies written by the same playwright and presented on a single day; they were connected by a story or thematic concerns.

Vernacular drama Drama from the Middle Ages performed in the everyday speech of the people and presented in town squares or other parts of cities.

Wagon stage Low platform mounted on wheels or casters by means of which scenery is moved on- and offstage.

THEATRE ON THE WEB

For more research and to learn more about the topics in this chapter, please visit the Online Learning Center at **www.mhhe.com/livelyart8e.**

EARLY THEATRE: ASIAN

THE THEATRES OF ASIA

BACKGROUND

TIMELINE: Asia

INDIAN THEATRE

SANSKRIT DRAMA

LATER INDIAN DRAMA

CHINESE THEATRE

EARLY THEATRE IN CHINA

THEATRE IN THE YUAN DYNASTY

THEATRE IN THE MING DYNASTY

JAPANESE THEATRE

EARLY THEATRE IN JAPAN

NŌ

LIVING HISTORY: *Sotoba Komachi*

BUNRAKU

KABUKI

SOUTHEAST ASIA: SHADOW PLAYS

SUMMARY
THINKING ABOUT THEATRE
KEY TERMS
THEATRE ON THE WEB

◀ **KABUKI: CLASSIC JAPANESE THEATRE** Theatre began to develop in various parts of the world many years ago. In India, China, and other parts of the Asian continent, theatre emerged between 350 B.C.E. and 1350 C.E. It developed initially in India and China. In Japan, it appeared first during the fourteenth century. One of the three major classic forms of Japanese theatre is kabuki. Shown here is a moment in traditional kabuki theatre, which—with its stylized movements, elaborate costumes, and painted facial makeup—continues to be popular in Japan today. The actor is Nakamura Shichinosuke in the Heisei Nakamura-za troupe's presentation of *Natsumatsuri Naniwa Kagami* or *Summer Festival: A Mirror of Osaka,* a Kabuki theatre drama from the 1600s. (© Michael Kim/Corbis)

For 1,000 years, from approximately 350 to 1350 C.E., there was no organized theatre in the West. But on the continent of Asia, thousands of miles away, theatre had begun to emerge. The development of theatre began in India more than 2,000 years ago, and theatre later became well established in China while formal theatre was still moribund in the West. Theatre in Japan followed not long after. These traditions of Asian theatre, established centuries ago, continue to the present day.

THE THEATRES OF ASIA

BACKGROUND

The people who created theatre in Asia knew nothing of the theatres of Greece or Rome. In Chapter 10, we mentioned the universal tendency toward theatre; and except where theatre is expressly forbidden by religious or other laws, it is likely to emerge in any civilization. This was true in India, China, and Japan—the countries we will focus on in this chapter—and also in other Asian countries, such as Indonesia.

Each of the Asian theatres is unique, but these theatres also have aspects in common that set them apart from Western theatre. To mention two: they rely much more on dance than Western theatre does (in many instances, Asian theatrical presentations could be called *dance dramas*), and they more heavily emphasize symbolism. All the great Asian traditions—including those of India, China, and Japan—have created and sustained one form or another of what has been described as *total theatre*. In this type of theatre there is a synthesis or integration of elements—acting, mime, dancing, music, and text—more complete than in traditional Western theatre. Though each of the Asian theatrical traditions is unique and self-contained, all have qualities that may seem familiar to Westerners who have been exposed to opera in which a colorful blending of ideas, art, and technique is crucial.

One reason why this kind of synthesis developed in Asia and found continued support lies in the fact that the religious roots of theatre are still kept alive there. Each of the three Asian traditions on which we will focus—Indian, Chinese, and Japanese—reached a high point of artistic excellence at a time when religion and philosophy were central in its culture. This level of excellence has kept the focus of traditional theatre at least allied to religion and philosophy, even when society itself changed and became modernized.

We can speculate on the antecedents of theatre in India, China, and Japan, but the actual origins of theatre in each culture remain obscure. The high point, however, usually occurred when writers of poetic and intellectual ability began to create a dramatic tradition in which the text assumed a central place.

What remained in later years was usually the words rather than the production style; this is, of course, partially explained by the fact that anything written, such as a script, has some permanence, whereas a performance is ephemeral. Thus, little is known of early performance practices in China or India. Japan, on the other hand, is unique in having preserved many of the ancient techniques of acting, dancing, and singing. Still, in all three theatres the ancient traditions—interpreted and reinterpreted as these cultures developed and changed—have continued to color and shape many later experiments.

THEATRE

CULTURE AND POLITICS

100

300

500

700

900

1100

1300

1500

1700

THEATRE

Natyasastra, major critical work of Indian Sanskrit drama (200 b.c.e.–100 c.e.)

Sanskrit drama highly developed in India (320–600)

Shakuntala, famous Sanskrit drama by Indian author Kalidasa (fifth century)
The Little Clay Cart, Indian Sanskrit drama attributed to King Shudraka (fifth century)

Academy of the Pear Garden, school for dancers and singers, founded in China (714)

Development of professional theatre companies in China (960)

Indian dance drama, puppet plays, and folk plays (late twelfth century)

Decline of Sanskrit drama (1150)

Scholars and artists work in popular theatre in China (thirteenth century)

Zeami Motokiyo (1363–1444); development of nō drama

Literary and romantic drama develops during Ming period in China (1368–1664)

Kabuki's Okuni of Izumo (c. c. 1571–?)
(Bildarchiv Preussischer Kulturbesitz/Art Resource, NY)

In Japan, kabuki first performed in Kyoto (1600–1610)

Nō becomes an aristocratic entertainment and rigidly codified (1650)

Kabuki becomes popular form of theatre (1675–1750)

Chikamatsu Monzaemon begins writing for bunraku theatre (1684)

Bunraku (puppet theatre) formalized in Japan (1685)

CULTURE AND POLITICS

In India, spread of Buddhism; trade with China, Egypt, Rome, southeast Asia; Gandhara school of art flourishes (180–150 b.c.e.)

Golden age of classical Sanskrit in India (300–500)

Hindu epic, Mahabharata (c. 200 b.c.e.–100 c.e.)
(© Baldev/Corbis)

Earliest known use of zero and decimals occurs in India (600)

Tang dynasty in China (618–907)

Travels in India of Xuan Zang, Chinese pilgrim and chronicler (630–644)

Tale of Genji (c. 1000)
(© Werner Forman/Art Resource, NY)

Song dynasty in China (960–1279); flowering of arts, literature, and scholarship

Civil strife in Japan leads to military government (1100)

Beginning of Muslim rule in India (1192)

Yuan dynasty in China (1271–1368)

Marco Polo visits court of Kublai Khan, Beijing, China (1271); Polo visits Kayal, southern India (1288)

Ming dynasty in China (1368–1644)

Rule of Yoshimitsu (rules 1395–1408) in Japan; years of stability followed by civil wars

First Europeans visit Japan (1542)

Period of national unification in Japan (1568–1600)

Rule of Shah Jahan in India; construction of great buildings, including Taj Mahal (1628–1657)

Qing (Ching) dynasty in China (1644–1911)

INDIAN THEATRE

Indian history has been characterized as a succession of immigrations into the Indian subcontinent. Early traces of civilization there go back to 3000 B.C.E. The Aryans, who came into southern India 1,000 years later, left behind works in Sanskrit that constitute the basis of the great Indian literary traditions. Scholars believe that by 1000 B.C.E., certain fundamental aspects of Indian civilization were already established; one of these is the caste system under which people are classified by heredity: a person must remain in the caste to which he or she is born, and people are forbidden to change occupations.

Around 400 B.C.E., Buddhism, which had its origins in India, reached a peak of development, and soon it became a major force throughout eastern and central Asia. Based on the ideas of Gautama Buddha (c. 563–483 B.C.E.), Buddhism teaches that suffering is inherent in life but that human beings can be liberated from suffering by mental and moral self-purification. King Asoka, who ruled in India about 240 B.C.E., managed to unite the whole nation under Buddhist rule, but a period of disorder and confusion followed until the Gupta dynasty began to unite the nation again around 320 C.E.

It was at this time that another important thread in Indian history, Hindu culture, entered a golden age; and it was during the following centuries that the great Sanskrit dramas were written and performed. Hinduism stresses the belief that soul or spirit is the essence of life; that the goal of all people is to achieve oneness with the supreme world-soul, known as *Brahman;* and that the things of this life do not exist in the same way as Brahman, which is eternal, infinite, and indescribable.

SANSKRIT DRAMA

What remains from the tradition of the Indian Golden Age is a group of plays written in Sanskrit, the language of the noble classes, to be performed in various court circles. There are between fifty and sixty plays that can be reliably assigned to this period, and the greatest of them are among the finest works of classical Indian literature.

We have been provided a great insight into this early Indian theatre by a remarkable document called the *Natyasastra* (translated as *The Study of Theatre* or *The Art of Theatre*). The *Natyasastra* has been attributed to Bharata Muni but may well be by someone else, possibly by several people. Written sometime during the 300-year period between 200 B.C.E. and 100 C.E., it describes the mythological origin of theatre in India and also presents important material about the nature of Indian drama; it even includes a description of the theatre space in which performances took place.

In the course of this complex treatise, the author defines a quality called *rasa,* or flavor, which permits spectators to surrender themselves to a dramatic situation corresponding to some powerful feeling that they themselves possess. Theatre can thus serve as a means toward enlightenment; art becomes a way to move toward metaphysics and the divine.

The *Natyasastra* also serves as a kind of encyclopedia of theatrical practice. In an abstract way, every element of the complex ancient theatre is treated, from gesture and posture to music, dance, voice, and so forth. Types of characters and categories of plays are discussed, and all this specific information is related in turn to a series of metaphysical principles, which, although perhaps difficult for the modern reader to grasp, are nevertheless challenging, even humbling, to read.

SANSKRIT DRAMA
The great early drama of India was Sanskrit, and it appears to have first developed between 200 B.C.E. and 100 C.E. Sanskrit drama reached its high point between 300 C.E. and 600 C.E. Shown here is a performance, in the Shri Shri-Govindaji Temple in Imphal, of a drama illustrating episodes from the great Sanskrit epic *The Mahabharata*. (© Lindsay Hebberd/Woodfin Camp and Associates)

Although we do not know exactly how plays were performed, we learn from the *Natyasastra* that each early troupe presenting Sanskrit theatre had a leader, the *sudtradhara,* who was the chief actor and also managed all others involved in production. Men were the main performers, but women played important roles too. Acting in this type of theatre was a skill that combined voice, body, emotions, costume, and makeup in an integrated whole.

The typical theatre in which Sanskrit drama was performed was ninety-six feet long and forty-eight feet wide, divided equally into stage and auditorium, and its seating capacity was probably between 200 and 500. There were four pillars in the auditorium—colored white, yellow, red, or blue—indicating where members of different castes were to sit. A curtain divided the stage into two parts: one part for the action and the other for dressing rooms and a behind-the-scenes area. The few records available from the later period of Sanskrit drama indicate that most performances were given by troupes invited to the courts of the nobility, and performing spaces were arranged in courtyards and similar areas.

Scenery was evidently not used, although elaborate costumes probably were. Dance, symbolic gestures, and music played an important part in the productions; but again, we have no specific information about performance practices. The plays often make use of fixed characters, such as a narrator and a clown; once again, there are no details concerning how these performers appeared onstage.

From comments in a book entitled *Mahabhasya* (*Great Commentary*), some scholars believe that the main elements of Sanskrit drama, as described in the *Natyasastra,* were in place by 140 B.C.E. However, this is speculative and has not yet been proved. The earliest plays that survive, from the first and second centuries C.E., were written by Asvaghosa.

As we have noted, these plays were written in Sanskrit, the classical language of the nobility, though some of the lover characters in the later plays speak a hybrid of Sanskrit and local dialect. Thus the plays had little following among the general public, who could not understand them. The plays usually drew on themes from Indian epic literature.

From what we know, the most productive playwright of classical India was Bhasa, who may have lived around 400 C.E. Thirteen surviving plays have been attributed to him, but it is not certain they are all his. Among the best-known plays of this general era is *The Little Clay Cart,* attributed to King Sudraka, although his identity and dates have not been clearly established. He is thought by many to have lived in the fifth century C.E. *The Little Clay Cart* concerns the love between a ruined merchant and a courtesan; its style is enlivened and enriched by politics and humor. The most famous Sanskrit play, however, comes from the fourth or fifth century: this is *Shakuntala,* which is usually considered the finest classical Indian drama and whose author, Kalidasa, is the greatest of the playwrights from the classic period.

READ *The Little Clay Cart*
- http://www.gutenberg.org/ebooks/21020

Kalidasa   Though *Shakuntala* is an acknowledged masterpiece of Indian drama, almost nothing is known about its author, Kalidasa (373?–415 C.E.). Many scholars have attempted to establish his date of birth and to learn some details of his life, but they have had little success. There is no doubt, however, that *Shakuntala* is a masterwork of Sanskrit drama. In seven acts, the play recounts the romance of King Dushyanta and Shakuntala, the foster daughter of a hermit, who secretly marry and are then subjected to a long separation brought about by the curse of an irate sage. After many trials, the lovers are reunited and the king finally meets his son and heir.

Shakuntala, which is subtitled *The Recovered Ring,* has story elements such as a secret marriage, forgetfulness caused by a curse, and a magic ring. It also has ideas from Indian philosophy, religion, aesthetics, and psychology. Like all Sanskrit drama, it has both serious and comic elements and includes a large number of locations and characters. It also includes supernatural elements. In addition, *Shakuntala* has a recognition scene in which the lovers confirm their identity through signs; this recognition through signs bears some resemblance to scenes in classic Greek tragedy.

While *Shakuntala* follows traditional patterns of Sanskrit drama, it is set apart by Kalidasa's delicate lyricism. Kalidasa wrote several poems that mingle love, nature imagery, and religion. He also wrote two other plays: *Malavike and Agnimitra,* a courtly comedy about a king's love for one of the palace serving women, and *Vikrama and Urvashi,* a heroic mythological drama focusing on the love of a king and a nymph.

LATER INDIAN DRAMA

Sanskrit drama—both the plays themselves and dramatic criticism—had faded by the end of the ninth century. By the twelfth century, the Arabs had begun to invade India, and in 1206 they established the sultanate of Delhi. With this series of invasions, the Hindu Sanskrit tradition disappeared. Under Islamic rule, theatrical activities were not encouraged and the old ways of performing were no longer maintained among educated people.

However, folk dramas in the many vernacular languages of India had always been popular, and the continued performances of such works, while they may not have achieved a very high artistic level, helped to keep certain traditions alive. Many of these folk plays have continued to the present day. They used the same traditional epic materials as Sanskrit dramas, but most of them were created by dramatists whose names are now unknown, and the scripts—assuming that these dramas were written down—have not been preserved. Folk plays were extremely eclectic and emphasized spectacle rather than metaphysical profundity.

Also popular with the public were dance dramas that took up aspects of Indian myths. In the performance of such dramas, movement, rather than the spoken word, was strongly emphasized. These and other developments in later Indian theatre, including a well-known dance-drama form called *kathakali,* will be discussed in detail later.

CHINESE THEATRE

The civilization of China can be traced back to at least 2000 B.C.E., when a unified culture spread over large parts of the area that is now the People's Republic of China. The Shang Dynasty represents the first period that can be authenticated through artifacts and documents. The period following the Shang Dynasty was a turbulent era known as the Zhou Dynasty. The dates of both dynasties are somewhat disputed. Traditionally, the Shang was thought to have been from 1766 to 1122 B.C.E., but some scholars suggest either 1600 or 1523 to 1028 B.C.E. The Zhou Dynasty was dated from 1122 to 256 B.C.E., but alternative dates have been offered: 1027 to 256 B.C.E. In any event, during the later Zhou Dynasty, Confucius, Lao-tzu, and Mencius—three of the greatest Chinese philosophers—lived and wrote. They formed part of the general background of religions, philosophies, and religious practices out of which later Chinese theatre developed.

Confucianism was based on the teachings of Confucius (551–479 B.C.E.), whose ideas about the perfectibility of human beings were never wholly embraced in his lifetime but were widely adopted by later generations. Confucianism emphasized the responsibility of one individual or group to others: a ruler to his subjects, family members to one another, friends to friends. Taoism began in the sixth century B.C.E. with the teachings of Lao-tzu (born c. 604 B.C.E.), who believed in the importance of the *tao,* or path. Taoism stresses simplicity, patience, and nature's harmony; following the tao, the path of the cosmos, leads to self-realization. A key element in the philosophy of Mencius (c. 371–288 B.C.E.) is that all people are good. Their innate moral sense can be cultivated, or it can be perverted by an unfavorable environment.

Another movement that was to influence the development of theatre, in China as well as in other societies, was *shamanism,* whose rituals combined costume, song, dance, and gesture. Shamans were spiritual leaders who were thought to have magical powers to communicate with the dead and to ward off evil spirits. Buddhism, too, found its way from India to China and was added to the religious thought and practice of the time.

In terms of political developments, by 200 B.C.E. the centralized imperial system had been developed, and China was provided with a central government that continued to remain effective through many long periods of stability down to modern times.

EARLY THEATRE IN CHINA

The early development of theatre in China—as with many other forms of Chinese art—was linked to the patronage of the imperial court. Popular forms of theatre may also have flourished, though no records of early folk performances survive. Records of court entertainments, however, go back as far as the fifth century B.C.E., and such diverse activities as skits, pantomimes, juggling, singing, and dancing are frequently mentioned in ancient chronicles.

The court of the emperors during the Tang period (618–906 C.E.) was one of the high points of human culture. At this time there was a kind of actors' training institute in the capital; it was called the Pear Garden and had been founded in 714. Details of activities and performances at the Pear Garden have not been preserved, but it firmly established a tradition of training theatrical performers.

In the Song Dynasty (960–1279), which preceded the coming of the Mongols, various court entertainments contributed to the development of what are known as *variety plays.* In addition to court records, there are other documents recording the existence of traveling theatrical troupes, some permanent playhouses, and theatrical activity that involved not only actors, dancers, and singers but also shadow puppets and marionettes. Low comedy was popular as well, and its effect must have been something like our vaudeville.

A form that emerged in the province of Zhejiang, possibly in the early twelfth century, was called *nanxi,* which means "southern drama," after the region where it developed. Indications are that at this time four types of characters were predominant in Chinese theatre: the *sheng,* or male character; the *dan,* or female character; the *jing,* or painted face; and the *chou,* or clown. These were to remain staples of Chinese theatre in subsequent works.

EARLY CHINESE THEATRE
Detail from a silk scroll depicting, at the center on the right-hand side, a Chinese theatre set up for a festival in the twelfth century at Kaifeng, the northern capital during the Ching dynasty. (This scroll is an eighteenth-century copy of the original.) Note the covered stage on which performers appear, and the audience members standing on three sides of the stage observing the action. (National Palace Museum, Taipei, Taiwan, Republic of China)

A significant synthesis of art and popular tradition was to come in the dramas of the Yuan period, which followed the Song.

THEATRE IN THE YUAN DYNASTY

The Yuan Dynasty (1279–1368) was well known in the West through the writings of the Italian explorer Marco Polo. The ruler at this time was not a Chinese emperor but a Mongol, Kublai Khan, whose grandfather Genghis Khan had come down from the north to conquer China.

Although they tolerated many Chinese customs, the Mongols nevertheless dismantled much of the traditional bureaucracy. Ironically, this turned out to be an important impetus for the development of Chinese theatre. Earlier, the highly educated literati—literary intellectuals—had composed essays and poetry of the highest quality but had disdained plays as beneath their dignity. With the coming of the Mongols, many of the literati were no longer employed by the government and took up literary and theatrical work to make a living. In this way, high art and the popular theatrical tradition met. Because the complex mixture of cultural influences produced such a rich outpouring during the Yuan Dynasty, scholars have compared its theatre to that of Greece in the fifth century B.C.E. and to that of Elizabethan England.

The form of drama perfected in the Yuan Dynasty, often referred to as *zaju,* usually had four acts or—perhaps more accurately since these plays used a great deal of music—four song sequences. Rather than writing specifically for the dramas, playwrights composed their texts to suit the rhythms and meters of popular music already known to the audience. Usually the protagonist sang all the music in any act. Unfortunately, none of the music has survived.

The poetic content of these plays was considered the central factor in their success. Because of their lyrical nature, these dramas had only a few characters and avoided subplots and other complications. Accounts from the Yuan period tell us that topics chosen by the playwrights ranged from love and romance to religion and history, domestic and social themes, crimes and lawsuits, and bandit heroes.

Important Plays from the Yuan Period   Though we do not know exactly how many plays were produced during the Yuan period, there are records indicating that more than 500 dramatists were writing at this time; and we know the titles of some 700 plays, of which 168 survive.

Perhaps the most famous of the plays surviving from this period is *The Romance of the Western Chamber,* actually a cycle of plays, by Wang Shifu, who wrote in the late thirteenth century. These dramas chronicle the trials of two lovers—a handsome young student and a lovely girl of good family—who have been models for thousands of imitations down to the present century. The plays contain a certain amount of adventure and a good deal of superlative poetry.

Another popular play that has survived is *The Orphan of Chao,* which deals with vengeance, sacrifice, and loyalty. *The Orphan of Chao* was one of the first Chinese plays known in the West, as a version of it was translated into French in 1735 and was adapted for the French stage by the philosopher Voltaire.

Another popular Yuan drama, *The Circle of Chalk,* is an excellent example of the lawsuit-and-trial genre in which a clever, Solomon-like judge frees an innocent person accused of a crime. When the twentieth-century German playwright Bertolt Brecht saw a version of this play (it had been freely adapted and translated into German), he was so intrigued with the theme that he created his own version: *The Caucasian Chalk Circle.*

Theatre Production in the Yuan Period   Despite the fact that many Yuan texts survive and have been admired down to the present day, relatively little is known about how they were performed. Contemporary spectators left few records of their reactions, perhaps because theatregoing was regarded as beneath the notice of highly educated people. Nevertheless, in recent years careful scholarship has managed to piece together a certain amount of information on theatre presentations.

Professional actors and actresses performed in Yuan dramas, and on occasion both would play male and female roles. Some of the actresses performed for private entertainments at the palace, and stories of their affairs in high society were as eagerly sought out as stories about the activities of today's film and television stars. The performers were organized into troupes, some of which were run by women.

Only meager information remains about the theatres used for these performances. Evidently, there was a bare stage with two doors on each side at the rear, and a painted cloth hanging between the doors. (This arrangement is shown in a wall hanging from northwestern China painted about 1324.) Most stages seem to have been built for outdoor use and were not roofed over. Curtains and such properties as swords and fans were used, but there is no evidence of any scenery. Much of the color of performances came from elaborate costumes. Some of the stylized robes, which are illustrated in artworks of the time, resemble those in modern Peking (or Beijing) opera. Makeup was also important and was evidently applied heavily in a stylized manner.

THEATRE IN THE MING DYNASTY

By the end of the Yuan period, the level of accomplishment in theatre was very high and drama had become firmly established as a respectable art form. With the overthrow of the Mongols, however, and the establishment of the Ming Dynasty (1368–1644), a Chinese emperor was restored to the throne. At this point, the traditional patterns of social behavior were restored; highly educated scholars were still able to write plays, but they tended to confine their efforts more and more to dramas that would please the elite. The theatre tended to become ornate and artificial; it lost contact with the broad mass of the public, which had originally supported it.

What had been an active theatre in the Yuan Dynasty, responsive to general audiences, now became a kind of literary drama that emphasized poetry and was averse to sustained or powerful dramatic action. The structure of Ming plays often became far more complex than that of Yuan plays. Also, only one actor had sung in each act of a Yuan play, but several actors were now permitted to sing during an act, and the instrumental accompaniments became very elaborate.

One of the earliest and best plays written in this expanded form is *Lute Song* by Gao Ming (c. 1301–1370), dealing with questions of family loyalty in a woman whose husband has abandoned her for political reasons. *Lute Song* contains strong characterizations and beautiful poetry and has been popular ever since its composition; this story of a faithful wife even reached Broadway in a musical theatre version, also called *Lute Song,* written for Mary Martin in 1946.

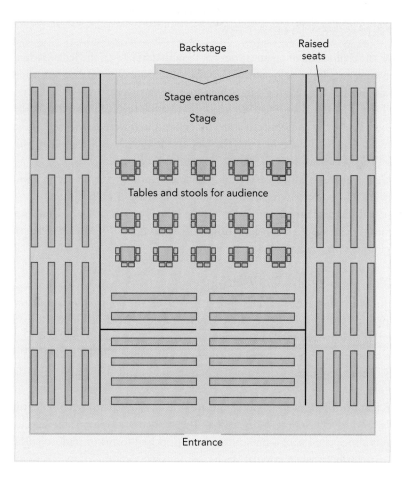

Attempts to create drama of distinction during the Ming dynasty culminated in the works of Li Yu, a scholar who failed his examinations and became instead a playwright, theatre critic, and impresario.

Li Yu Li Yu (1611–c. 1685), China's first important drama critic, believed that a playwright should write clearly, with a mass audience in mind, and should be well versed in practical stage knowledge. These conclusions were based on his own experience as a popular playwright. His writings on theatre—in which he dealt with such matters as plot construction, dialogue, music, and versification—are among the most important in the history of Chinese dramatic criticism.

As a playwright, Li Yu wrote plays for entertainment and placed little emphasis on the poetic songs that other playwrights favored. Instead, he developed well-made situation comedies with intricate plots and sophisticated dialogue. Rather than borrow his material from standard literary sources, Li created original plots based on the lives of common people. He was particularly skilled at writing strong characters for his young female performers. Most of his notable plays, including *Ordained by Heaven, Be Circumspect in Conjugal Relationships,* and *The Error of the Kite,* revolve around romantic themes.

At the end of the Ming Dynasty, theatre, which was patronized almost entirely by the rich, began to lose any real contact with the larger public, and its vitality seeped away.

JAPANESE THEATRE

Although the civilization of Japan is younger than that of China, the Japanese heritage is long and complex. The origins of the Japanese people are obscure, but anthropologists have found artifacts suggesting migrations from such diverse areas as Siberia, Korea, south China, and southeast Asia. We know that by the fifth century C.E. the southern portions of Japan were consolidated and a series of capitals were established in the vicinity of present-day Kyoto. At the time, the Japanese followed a religion called Shinto, or the Way of the Gods, closely allied to nature and spirit worship.

With the growing influence on the Japanese aristocracy of the Tang Dynasty in China (618–906 C.E.), Buddhism, a religion that was more sophisticated than Shinto in both ritual and doctrine, became a prevailing influence, first in court circles and then in the country as a whole. Influences from both Shinto and Buddhism were strong in the development of theatre in Japan.

EARLY THEATRE IN JAPAN

The earliest recorded theatrical activities in Japan are the court entertainments of the Heian period (794–1195 C.E.). These entertainments were influenced by Chinese models, but that is the only link—a very remote one—between the two traditions. Later, similar kinds of performances formed part of annual Shinto and Buddhist ceremonies. These were usually of a popular nature and included juggling, skits, dancing, and the like.

The first great period in Japanese theatre occurred in the fourteenth century, not long after similar developments in China. The sudden and remarkable development of **nō** (it is also spelled *noh*)—one of the three principal forms of traditional Japanese theatre—came about when popular stage traditions were combined with serious scholarly pursuits.

Nō Rigidly traditional form of Japanese drama combining music, dance, and lyrics.

NŌ

In the fourteenth century in Japan, there were a number of roving troupes of actors who performed in a variety of styles; some of their presentations were simply popular entertainment, but some aspired to art. One of the more artistic troupes was directed by the actor Kan'ami (1333–1384), who was also a playwright. A typical, well-known play by Kan'ami is *Sotoba Komachi* (*Komachi at the Stupa*), which was based on a familiar legend of the time. In this legend, Komachi, a beautiful but cruel woman, is pursued by a man named Shii no Shōshō. She tells him that he must call on her for 100 nights in a row, and for 99 nights he comes, in all kinds of weather. But on the hundredth night he dies.

At the beginning of the play, two priests enter, discussing the virtues of following Buddha. They then come upon an old woman—the leading actor in the mask and wig of Komachi in old age. She says that she was once beautiful but has grown old and lost her beauty. She argues with the priests about religion and then reveals who she is. She recounts the story of what she did to Shōshō.

A presentation by Kan'ami's troupe was seen by the shogun Ashikaga Yoshimitsu (1358–1408), a man of wealth, prestige, and enormous enthusiasm for the arts. Fascinated by what he saw, he arranged for Kan'ami's son, Zeami, who was then twelve years old, to have a court education in order to improve the quality of his art.

When Zeami succeeded his father as head of the troupe, it remained attached to the shogun's court in Kyoto. With a patron of this caliber, Zeami was freed from financial problems and could devote himself to all aspects of theatre: writing plays, training actors, and constantly refining his own acting style, whose outlines had been inherited from his gifted father.

Zeami Motokiyo   More than 500 years after his death, Zeami Motokiyo (1363–1443) is still considered the most important figure in the history of Japanese nō theatre. A gifted actor, Zeami brought new prestige to nō, and his plays remain an important part of its repertoire. He was most influential, however, as a theorist; in his writings, he established the aesthetic and philosophical basis of nō. Zeami became the director of his father's troupe when Kan'ami died in 1384. He continued to improve nō, borrowing elements of other, earlier, forms of dance drama. His 200 plays, 124 of which remain in the active nō repertory, incorporated his innovations.

Zeami also began writing on the theory and philosophy of nō, presenting ideas that were heavily influenced by his study of Zen. In his several volumes of theoretical works, Zeami developed the concept of *yūgen,* the mysterious inner heart or spirit behind outward form. Yūgen is the aim of nō performances; another definition of it might be philosophical and physical gracefulness.

Characteristics of Nō Theatre   Under Zeami's direction, nō became the dominant form of serious theatre in his generation, and it remained dominant well past 1600 until it was supplanted in the popular taste by bunraku and kabuki.

Nō, as perfected by Zeami, was and is a remarkably successful synthesis of various theatrical forms into a single, total experience. Nō actors (there were no actresses in Zeami's theatre) trained from childhood and became adept at singing, acting, dancing, and mime. The plays they performed were remarkably sophisticated in language and content and were all constructed around a definite series of organizational principles based on musical, psychological, and mimetic—or imitative—movements, which change gradually from a slow to a fast tempo. Many of the greatest nō plays were written by Zeami himself.

The stories considered appropriate for nō plays were often from literary or historical sources. One important source was a famous novel of Heian court life, Lady Murasaki's *Tale of Genji,* written around 1000. Another important source was *The Tale of the Heike,* a chronicle of the devastating civil wars that destroyed the power of the aristocracy in Japan at the end of the Heian period in 1185. Nō characters were generally based on literary or historical figures already familiar to the audience. A nō play reveals some working out of passions felt by a character, who often appears as a ghost or spirit.

NŌ PERFORMANCE TODAY
Traditional nō theatre is still performed in Japan and other parts of the world, and its stylized acting, minimalist settings, ornate costumes, and distinctive masks are still used. Shown here is Haruhiko Jo, as the ancient former beauty in the all-male production of *Sotoba Komachi,* under the direction of Yukio Ninagawa in a production at the Lincoln Center Festival in New York. The Japanese playwright Mishima, who killed himself in a public ritual suicide in 1970, modernized fourteenth-century Japanese nō theatre. (© Michael Kim/Corbis)

1413, KITANO TEMPLE, JAPAN

The year is 1413. In Japan, at the Kitano temple, a platform stage, with a floor of polished wood, has been set up. There is also a wooden walkway, or bridge, on which actors can move to the stage from a dressing room set up in one of the temple buildings. The spectators are on three sides of this platform stage.

The actor performing today is Zeami. He is fifty years old and has been under the patronage of the shogun of Japan since he was twelve. Zeami's father, Kan'ami, was a renowned actor before him, and Zeami has carried his father's art to even greater heights. He has studied different acting styles, perfected his own technique, trained other actors, and written plays for them to perform.

The theatre he has fashioned from all this is called *nō;* it has elements of opera, pantomime, and formal, stylized dance. In nō theatre, the main character, who wears a beautifully carved, hand-painted wooden mask, recites his or her adventures to the constant accompaniment of several onstage musicians. Toward the end of the play, the chief actor will perform a ritualistic dance that includes symbolic gestures of the head and hands and stomps of the feet on the wooden floor.

The crowd is gathered today for a special reason. Usually, Zeami performs only in a restricted theatre space for the shogun and members of his court, or at a temple for a select audience. But here at the Kitano temple, performances will go on for seven days and will be open to everyone; as one later commentator will explain: "All were admitted, rich and poor, old and young alike."

As with all nō performances, several plays will be presented each day. The play the audience awaits now, *Sotoba Komachi,* was written by Zeami's father. In it, Zeami portrays a woman. (As in ancient Greek theatre, all the performers in nō are men.) The legend of Komachi is as well known to the audience as the story of Antigone was to the Greeks. Komachi, a beautiful but cruel woman, is pursued by a man named Shii no Shōshō. She tells him that he must call on her for 100 nights in a row, and for 99 nights he comes in all kinds of weather. But on the hundredth night he dies. On that night a snowstorm is raging and he falls, exhausted, to die on her doorstep.

When the play begins, we see two priests enter. As they discuss the virtues of following Buddha, they come upon an old woman. This is Zeami in the mask and wig of Komachi in old age. She is a wretched woman approaching her hundredth birthday. Komachi tells how she was once beautiful but has lost her beauty and grown old. She argues with the priests about religion and then reveals who she is. She recounts the story of what she did to Shōshō.

As the play progresses, the audience watches Zeami's performance with rapt attention. At one point, his character becomes possessed: the spirit of Shōshō takes over Komachi, and Zeami acts this out in pantomime to a musical accompaniment. At times, he acts out Komachi's part while her lines are chanted by a chorus of ten or twelve men sitting at the side of the stage. At another point, Komachi is dressed as Shōshō and becomes him, feeling his death agony. Zeami performs this sequence as a mesmerizing, frightening dance. At the end of the play, the spirit of Shōshō leaves Komachi, and she prays to Buddha for guidance and for a peaceful life in the hereafter.

The audience members, who have heard a great deal about Zeami but have never before seen him perform, watch in awe. Throughout, he plays the various parts with astounding grace, subtlety, and understatement, developed through years of training and performance. The segments when he lets go—as in Shōshō's death agony—are all the more effective because of their contrast with the measured quality of the rest. For the audience, the play is a revelation of how moving a theatrical performance can be—an experience unlike any they have had before.

READ *Sotoba Komachi* in *Anthology of Living Theatre* or at:

http://etext.virginia.edu/toc/modeng/public/WalSoto.html

The major roles in nō are the ***shite*** (SHEE-tay), or main character, who is often masked; the ***waki,*** a supporting character; and the ***tsure,*** an accompanying role. There may be various smaller parts as well, including a ***kyōgen*** (kee-OH-gehn), or comic character.

Shite Major roles in nō.

Waki Supporting role in nō.

Tsure Accompanying role in nō.

Kyogen Comic roles in nō.

Producing Nō Theatre   The elegance, mystery, and beauty of nō have fascinated the Japanese since the time of Zeami, and the nō tradition, passed on from teacher to disciple, has been carried on to this day. In most of the larger Japanese cities, nō can be seen in excellent performances by troupes whose traditions go back to the fourteenth century—a remarkable legacy.

Even the nō stage has remained roughly the same since the time of Zeami and his immediate successors. There is a bridge, called the ***hashigakari*** (ha-shee-gah-KAH-ree), which leads from the actors' room offstage to the stage. The bridge is normally about twenty feet long. The main playing space to which it leads is about eighteen feet square; it is roofed and has a ceremonial pine tree painted on the rear wall. At the back of the playing space is a narrow section for four musicians who accompany the play on flute, small hand drum, large hand drum, and stick drum. Nō theatres were originally outdoors, and the audience sat on three sides of the stage. The modern nō theatre is built inside a larger shell as though it were a giant stage set itself, and the audience sits on two sides.

Hashigakari Bridge in nō theatre on which the performers make their entrance from the dressing area to the platform stage.

The temple roof above the stage is supported by four columns or pillars, each of which serves a definite purpose in the staging. In addition to the actors and musicians, in nō there is a chorus of ten men who serve as a very rough equivalent of the chorus in Greek theatre. Nō actors move in a highly stylized fashion that involves important elements of both dance and pantomime. During the performance of a nō text, the actors alternate sections of chanting with a kind of heightened speech that might best be compared to recitative, sung dialogue in Western opera. The costumes made for nō are usually of great elegance, and the masks worn by the shite are among the most beautiful, subtle, and effective created for any theatre.

There are occasional comic elements in nō, and these elements eventually developed as a separate form called *kyōgen.* Kyōgen plays, which use a good deal of folk humor and slapstick, are still performed and appreciated today.

The kyōgen are usually performed without special costumes, masks, or wigs, except when a nō play is being parodied, in which case the appropriate nō mask is used. Parody and satire are common in kyōgen, and no subject is sacrosanct or exempt from being

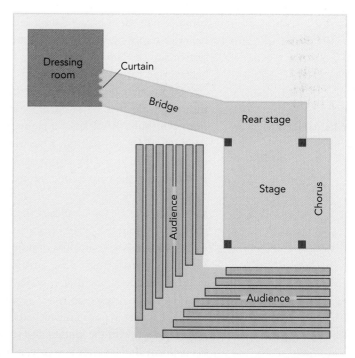

GROUND PLAN OF A TRADITIONAL NŌ THEATRE
Nō theatre of Japan—a stylized theatre originally for the upper classes—began nearly 600 years ago. It was performed outdoors; a ramp at the left led from a dressing room to the wooden platform stage. Spectators sat on two sides of the stage, to the left and in front.

treated comically. A feudal lord, monk, or friar can be the main figure; so might a drunken or stupid servant, a braggart, a shrew, or a gallant.

BUNRAKU

Nō remained the most popular theatrical form of theatre during Japan's medieval period. During the sixteenth century, civil wars and other disturbances caused political disarray of increasing gravity until a general, Tokugawa Ieyasu, unified the country in 1600. All through the long Tokugawa period (1600–1868), which bears his family name, Japan was unified and at peace, but this calm was purchased at a price. Alarmed at the political maneuvering of Japan's growing number of Christians, who had been converted by European missionaries, the Tokugawa family outlawed Christianity and cut Japan off from any extensive contact with either China or Europe until the middle of the nineteenth century.

Peace did bring a rapid development of commerce and trade that led to increasingly sophisticated urban life. As the merchant class grew, its members' wealth and their increasing leisure time allowed them to patronize various entertainments. The aristocracy and the Tokugawa family continued to support nō as a kind of private state theatre, but the merchants supported theatrical arts that more closely mirrored their own world. These entertainments flourished in large cities, such as Osaka, Kyoto, and Edo (now Tokyo).

Before we turn to puppet theatre—bunraku—and to the later kabuki, it is worth noting that both forms of theatre can be understood more fully if one takes into account certain tenets of neo-Confucianism. These tenets form the basis of rigid codes of behavior regarding such matters as sacrifice, loyalty, and revenge as found in the class system and the samurai code of the warrior aristocracy of Japan. These strict codes of behavior, in turn, are reflected in the theatrical presentations of bunraku and kabuki.

Of the new popular forms of theatre that developed in Japanese cities, puppet theatre was the first. Since the nineteenth century, this puppet theatre has been called **_bunraku_** (buhn-RAH-koo), a name that derives from a famous puppeteer. It developed in a most unusual way. One widespread form of entertainment in the medieval period was the art of the chanter—who, with his _biwa_ (a kind of large lute), would travel around the countryside intoning chronicles of wars and tales of romantic heroes and heroines. Between 1570 and 1600 the _samisen,_ a three-stringed instrument something like a banjo, replaced the biwa as the chief instrument accompanying the chanter. By around 1600, it became customary to add to these performances, as a kind of extra attraction, companies of puppeteers who would act out the stories, "illustrating" the chanter's music. The introduction of the samisen and the puppeteers made possible the development of bunraku.

The chanted texts are called **_jōruri_** (joh-ROO-ree) after the name of a popular female character in one of the recited tales. The chanters, down to the present day, have been regarded with the kind of awe reserved for opera singers in the West. The chanters perform all the voices in a play, as well as the narration, and set the general mood. Originally, they also wrote their own scripts. Eventually, however, it became customary to ask someone else to write the text.

In bunraku, the puppets representing important characters are manipulated by three people: one for the legs, one for the left arm, and the chief handler for the head

Bunraku Japanese puppet theatre.

Jōruri In Japanese puppet theatre, chanted text.

JAPANESE BUNRAKU: PUPPET THEATRE
Bunraku—puppet theatre—became a popular form in Japan in the 1600s. In bunraku, unlike traditional Western puppet theatre, the puppeteers are in full view of the audience and are always dressed in black. Often, the story is delivered by a chanter, with the puppets dramatizing the action. Because the puppets are very complex, there is usually more than one puppeteer controlling each of them, as is the case in the photo shown here. (Kyodo via AP Images)

and right arm. The chief handler is often dressed in an elaborate, gorgeous costume, but the other handlers are dressed in black and are assumed to be invisible. The puppets, which today are approximately two-thirds life-size, were originally smaller. Bunraku reached its characteristic form in the 1730s when it became a three-man form. Before that, a significant step in its development was taken in 1685, when the writer Chikamatsu began to collaborate with Takemoto Gidayu, the outstanding bunraku chanter of the day. The first and undoubtedly the best of the bunraku writers, Chikamatsu contributed enormously to the transformation of this popular form into a vehicle for great art.

Chikamatsu Monzaemon   Chikamatsu Monzaemon (1653–1725) was born to a provincial samurai family in 1653 and became the first important Japanese dramatist since the great period of nō drama 300 years earlier. His family apparently had literary interests; in 1671, they published a collection of haiku poetry that included some pieces by the future dramatist.

Chikamatsu did not begin to write plays until the age of thirty, but thereafter he was a prolific writer. His best-known dramas were written for the puppet theatre, bunraku. He is one of the world's only major dramatists to write primarily for that form. He also wrote for kabuki theatre (discussed below), and many of his puppet plays were later adapted for kabuki.

As a playwright, Chikamatsu used his knowledge of Japanese life to create vivid, detailed, and accurate pictures of his society. His history or heroic plays are loosely constructed stories about the nobility; they sometimes feature military pageantry and supernatural apparitions. In his domestic dramas he explored the problems of the middle and lower classes; many of these plays are based on actual events. Often, his domestic plays deal with unhappy lovers, who may even be driven to suicide by the problems they face. Both Chikamatsu's history plays and his domestic plays are known for the beauty of his poetry, which elevates the incidents and the characters.

Western critics have compared Chikamatsu to both Shakespeare and Marlowe because of the quality of his verse and his knowledge of society. His most famous history play is *The Battles of Coxinga* (1715). His notable domestic dramas include *The Love Suicides at Sonezaki* (1703), *The Uprooted Pine* (1718), *The Courier for Hell* (1711), *The Woman Killer and the Hell of Oil* (1721), and *The Love Suicides at Amijima* (1721).

Chikamatsu spoke of maintaining in his dramas "what lies in the slender margin between the real and the unreal," and this quality, plus his remarkable ability as a poet, has kept his plays popular. His emphasis on ordinary people, too, not only was new to the Japanese stage but also foreshadowed later developments in European theatre.

KABUKI

Kabuki Form of popular Japanese theatre combining music, dance, and dramatic scenes.

In the early seventeenth century a new form of Japanese theatre, *kabuki,* had emerged. Combining elements of nō, bunraku, and folk theatre, kabuki became the most popular form of theatre in Japan throughout the seventeenth century despite challenges and other vicissitudes. It has remained a part of the theatre scene in Japan in the centuries between and is still performed today.

Origins of Kabuki: Okuni of Izumo
According to Japanese legend, credit for developing kabuki, the most popular form of traditional Japanese theatre, belongs to a Shinto priestess, Okuni of Izumo (born in the late sixteenth century). Though little is known of her life or of the circumstances that led to the development of kabuki, tradition holds that in 1603 this priestess began kabuki by dancing on a temporary stage set up in the dry bed of the Kamo River in Kyoto.

Probably, Okuni's early dances were of Buddhist origin and had been secularized by being intermingled with folk dances. It is said that Nagoya Sanzaemon, a samurai warrior who is believed to have been Okuni's lover, taught her adaptations of dances from nō, the samurai-sponsored drama of the period. She might have used nō dances as well as elements of popular dances, but no detailed descriptions of her performances survive.

That her dances were popular, however, is shown by the fact that she and her troupe toured Japan in 1603. Okuni used a stage similar to the nō stage for the performances of her group. In 1607 she performed for the shogun. The kabuki developed by Okuni became so popular that in 1616—only a few years after she had begun her performances—there were seven licensed kabuki theatres in Kyoto.

ORIGINS OF KABUKI: OKUNI OF IZUMO
One branch of the classic Japanese theatre is Kabuki, which is supposed to have originated with the performer Okuni. In this drawing, from a 17th century Japanese scroll, Okuni (center) is seen dancing in a Shinto temple in Kyoto. (Bildarchiv Preussischer Kulturbesitz/Art Resource, NY)

Development of Kabuki   Dance was the basis of early kabuki performances, and the musical dance-dramas that developed revolved around stories that were romantic and often erotic. As a composite entertainment appealing to townspeople, kabuki was seen by some authorities as an unsettling influence on the rigid social and artistic structure.

A fascinating series of events occurred in the early days of kabuki related to social concerns and problems of gender and sex. Originally, most of the performers were women; but when social disruptions arose because of feuds over the sexual services of the women, the authorities intervened, and in 1629 women's kabuki was banned. Thereafter, young boys performed kabuki; but eventually it was felt that they, too, as sexual targets of older men in the audience, were causing problems of social and class conflicts, and so in 1652 the authorities also banned boys' troupes.

In addition to concerns about sexual relationships between performers and audience members, the authorities also worried about the mingling of different classes and improper displays by samurai at kabuki performances. After 1652, therefore, men's

KABUKI PERFORMANCE TODAY
Seen here is the kabuki actor Kankuro Nakamura performing on a special stage, set up on a beach at the break of the New Year in Naruto, Japan. Today, all roles in kabuki are performed by men; most of the actors are descended from generations of kabuki performers and train for years. Note the heavy, stylized makeup, which covers the entire face; the ornate costume; and the highly theatrical wig. The costumes, makeup, gestures, and stage configuration are part of a long-standing tradition. (© Eriko Sugita/Reuters/Corbis)

troupes, in which sexual glamour was deemphasized, became the rule—a custom that remains to the present day. Though the men's troupes were heavily regulated, kabuki flourished in the following centuries and the eroticism that had marked kabuki in the early days was reintroduced. Part of this is due to the necessary development of the art of female impersonation by the male performers.

Kabuki was greatly indebted to the plays and performance of puppet theatre, including scenes in which actors imitated puppets' movements. At least half of the current kabuki repertoire was adapted from puppet theatre. Both kabuki and the puppets were less formal and distant than nō, which remained largely the theatre of the samurai class. Still, many samurai—despite official restrictions on their doing so—secretly attended kabuki, whose action, spectacle, and rhetoric they preferred to the solemnities of nō.

As kabuki itself became popular, the playwright Chikamatsu tried writing for troupes of kabuki actors and wrote off and on for kabuki for many years. Eventually, however, he abandoned the attempt because these performers, it is assumed, unlike chanters, tended to change his lines. Kabuki actors founded dynasties, many of them still active. A kabuki dynasty that lasted through twelve generations was founded by Ichikawa Danjuro (1660–1704), who became known as Danjuro I and who began a bravura acting style known as *aragato*. Many actors came to fame in *Chushingura* or *The Forty-Seven Rōnin,* a frequently revived play originally written for puppets. It is perhaps Japan's most popular history play. The play is based on an actual historical incident in which a provincial lord was provoked into an act of violence and forced to commit ritual suicide. It traces the vendetta or revenge of the forty-seven retainers who are left behind and is a remarkable blend of adventure, pathos, and romance. Ghost stories, too, were popular dramas in the kabuki repertoire.

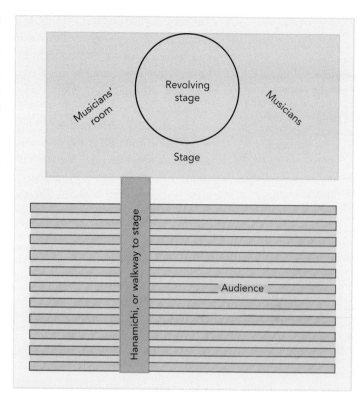

A KABUKI THEATRE
Kabuki, a 400-year-old Japanese theatre, is performed today in elaborate spaces with staging devices that include onstage turntables for shifting scenery. As shown in this ground plan, the stage covers the entire front of the theatre and is approached by a ramp—the hanamichi—on which performers make dramatic entrances and exits.

Producing Kabuki   Kabuki actors are trained from childhood in vocal technique, dancing, acting, and physical versatility. The male actors who play women's parts—these actors are called **onnagata**—are particularly skillful at imitating the essence of a feminine personality through stylized gestures and attitudes. Costumes and makeup in kabuki are elegant and gorgeous, although they may often be strikingly gritty and realistic. The effect of an actor's performance is frequently quite theatrical and a bit larger than life. Again, however, it must be emphasized that, for all its theatricality, kabuki actually expresses a wide range of styles, from the fantastical to the realistic.

The stage used for kabuki performances underwent various changes during the history of this art, but the fundamental arrangement was reached in the mid-nineteenth century and then altered somewhat after 1853, when Japan was opened to the West.

Onnagata In Japanese Kabuki, women's roles played by men.

The stage is wide and has a relatively low proscenium. Musicians—sometimes onstage, sometimes offstage—generally accompany the stage action. Kabuki features elaborate and beautiful scenic effects, including the revolving stage, which was developed in Japan before it was used in the West. Another device used in kabuki is the **hanamichi** (hah-nah-MEE-chee), or "flower way," a raised narrow platform connecting the rear of the auditorium with the stage. Actors often make entrances and exits on the hanamichi and occasionally perform short scenes there as well.

Some kabuki plays use a second or temporary hanamichi down the aisle on the audience's opposite side. The stage is also well equipped with large and small elevator traps, used to lift actors in tableaux as well as spectacular settings, which come into view as the audience watches. There is even a small trap on the hanamichi that allows supernatural characters to emerge (or disappear) in the midst of the audience.

SOUTHEAST ASIA: SHADOW PLAYS

Though we have focused on theatre in India, China, and Japan, it is important to remember that considerable theatre activity has occurred in other parts of Asia, such as Korea and the southeastern countries of Myanmar (Burma), Cambodia, Laos, Indonesia, Malaysia, Thailand, and Vietnam. Though each of these southeastern nations has its own theatrical history and tradition, all of them share certain characteristics. Most of their theatrical styles were influenced by the theatre of India and in some instances by that of China. In virtually every one of these countries we note the influence of two epics from India, the *Ramayana* and the *Mahabharata*. These stories and others are almost always performed as dance drama, classical dance, or puppet theatre. As is true in other Asian countries, theatrical presentations combine dance, song, movement, and recited text with elaborate costumes. It is worth noting that most of these countries do not even have a word in their language that denotes a dramatic form that is only written or spoken.

One type of theatrical activity that came to prominence in southeast Asia in the eleventh century is particularly significant. This was the **shadow play,** which is widely performed in Thailand, Malaysia, and Indonesia. It appears to have been developed most fully in Java, an Indonesian island. **Wayang** (WHY-young) is the term that usually refers to Indonesian puppet theatre but is also used sometimes to refer to live dance performances.

The best known form of a shadow play uses flat puppets made of leather. These figures are intricately carved to create patterns of light and shadow when their image is projected on a screen. The puppets are manipulated by sticks attached to the head, the arms, and other parts of the body. The person manipulating the puppets also narrates the drama and speaks the dialogue of the characters. Shadow plays usually take place at night—sometimes they last all night long—and are accompanied by music and sound effects.

Hanamichi In kabuki theatre, a bridge running from behind the audience (toward the left side of the audience) to the stage. Performers can enter on the hanamichi; important scenes may also be played on it.

Shadow play A play performed widely in Thailand, Malaysia, and Indonesia involving intricately carved flat leather puppets that create patterns of light and shadow when their image is projected on a screen.

Wayang Term usually referring to Indonesian shadow plays but sometimes used for live dance performances.

SHADOW PUPPETS

A longtime theatrical tradition in southeast Asia is shadow puppets. Shadow play or shadow puppetry is an ancient form of storytelling and entertainment using opaque, often articulated figures in front of an illuminated backdrop to create the illusion of moving images. It is thought to have originated in China during the Song Dynasty (960–1127), and later spread to southeast Asia, particularly Indonesia, Malaysia, and Thailand. At present, more than twenty countries are known to have shadow show troupes. The figures are manipulated by puppeteers holding sticks attached to the puppets, which themselves are intricately carved flat figures, made of leather, that create patterns of light and shadow when projected on a screen. (© Shelley Gazin/Corbis)

In various places, other theatrical forms have been developed from shadow puppets. One variation uses three-dimensional doll puppets; another uses human performers wearing masks.

In this chapter we have looked at the early development of theatre in India, China, and Japan. These theatres were formed independently of theatre in the West; in some cases, they emerged when formal theatre in Europe was dormant. We have covered a period that goes up to approximately 1700. Though this is several centuries beyond the time when theatre reemerged in the West, there was little or no contact between the two theatre traditions until considerably later.

Later we will look at further developments in Asian theatre: for example, Peking (Beijing) opera in China. We will also note the significant exchanges between Asian and Western theatre that began at the end of the nineteenth century and continued through the twentieth century and into the twenty-first.

Summary

The traditional theatres of Asia originated from religious ceremonies and concepts. Most of these theatres are highly theatrical and stylized and fuse acting, mime, dance, music, and text.

In India in the fourth and fifth centuries C.E., a theatre of a very high order—Sanskrit drama—came to full flower. Its origins and dramatic rules were outlined in a revealing document called the *Natyasastra*.

In China, an acting school called the Pear Garden flourished in the early eighth century, and professional theatre companies flourished in the tenth century. The first significant Chinese theatre from which we have surviving manuscripts emerged during the Yuan Dynasty from 1271 to 1368. During the succeeding Ming Dynasty, from 1368 to 1644, theatre became more "literary" and less in touch with ordinary people.

In Japan, the first important theatre form was nō, which emerged in the fourteenth and fifteenth centuries and is still performed today. Bunraku—puppet theatre—came on the scene in Japan in the seventeenth century, followed closely by kabuki. Both bunraku and kabuki are still performed in Japan today. Like most Asian theatres, nō, kabuki, and bunraku are complex forms; to understand them, audiences need to be aware of their intricate conventions.

Considerable theatre activity has also taken place elsewhere in Asia; one example is the shadow plays performed in Thailand, Malaysia, and Indonesia.

Thinking about Theatre

▶ Describe the origins of Asian theatres. How are they similar to the origins of the Western theatres discussed earlier?

▶ Asian theatre is often referred to as total theatre because of its mixture of drama, music, and dance. What are some examples of total theatre in today's Western theatre?

▶ Many of the Asian theatres employ puppets. Are puppets popular in today's theatre? How is the use of puppets today different from the use of puppets in the traditional Asian theatres?

▶ Many of the Asian theatres employ men to play female roles. What are your thoughts about this convention? Identify contemporary examples of men playing women in film, television, or the theatre.

▶ Some of the Asian theatres evolved into entertainment for the elite members of their societies. Name at least three examples of entertainment today that appeal primarily to a specific group of individuals.

KEY TERMS

Bunraku Japanese puppet theatre.

Hanamichi In kabuki theatre, a bridge running from behind the audience (toward the left side of the audience) to the stage. Performers can enter on the hanamichi; important scenes may also be played on it.

Hashigakari Bridge in nō theatre on which the performers make their entrance from the dressing area to the platform stage.

Jōruri In Japanese puppet theatre, chanted text.

Kabuki Form of popular Japanese theatre combining music, dance, and dramatic scenes.

Kyogen Comic roles in nō.

Nō Rigidly traditional form of Japanese drama combining music, dance, and lyrics.

Onnagata In Japanese Kabuki, women's roles played by men.

Shadow play A play performed widely in Thailand, Malaysia, and Indonesia involving intricately carved flat leather puppets that create patterns of light and shadow when their image is projected on a screen.

Shite Major roles in nō.

Tsure Accompanying role in nō.

Waki Supporting role in nō.

Wayang Term usually referring to Indonesian shadow plays but sometimes used for live dance performances.

 THEATRE ON THE WEB

For more research and to learn more about the topics in this chapter, please visit the Online Learning Center at **www.mhhe.com/livelyart8e.**

RENAISSANCE THEATRES

12

ITALY

BACKGROUND:
THE RENAISSANCE ERA

ITALIAN THEATRE: COMMEDIA
DELL'ARTE

TIMELINE: Italian Renaissance

ITALIAN DRAMATIC RULES:
THE NEOCLASSICAL IDEALS

LIVING HISTORY: Commedia dell'Arte

THEATRE PRODUCTION IN ITALY

ENGLAND

BACKGROUND:
ELIZABETHAN ENGLAND

TIMELINE: English Renaissance

ELIZABETHAN DRAMA

LIVING HISTORY: Hamlet

ELIZABETHAN THEATRE
PRODUCTION

MAKING CONNECTIONS: The Popular
Arts of Shakespeare's Time

THEATRE AFTER ELIZABETH'S REIGN

SPAIN

BACKGROUND:
THE SPANISH GOLDEN AGE

SPANISH DRAMA

TIMELINE: Spanish Golden Age

LIVING HISTORY: The King,
the Greatest Alcalde

THEATRE PRODUCTION IN SPAIN

FRANCE

BACKGROUND: FRANCE IN THE
SEVENTEENTH CENTURY

FRENCH DRAMA:
THE NEOCLASSICAL ERA

TIMELINE: Neoclassical France

THEATRE PRODUCTION IN FRANCE

LIVING HISTORY: Tartuffe

SUMMARY
THINKING ABOUT THEATRE
KEY TERMS
THEATRE ON THE WEB

◀ **THE THEATRE OF SHAKESPEARE**   In the West, the Renaissance saw a resurgence of theatre, beginning in Italy and moving through various countries of Europe and in England. An example of the vibrancy of this period is the plays of William Shakespeare, a leading English Renaissance dramatist, which continue to be immensely popular. There are frequent productions of his plays, and many have been adapted into films. Stage and film directors often set his work in a contemporary context in order to engage their audiences. Seen here is Greg Hicks as King Lear in a Royal Shakespeare Company production. (Manuel Harlan, Royal Shakespeare Company)

Renaissance is a term that means rebirth; it refers to an awakening of the arts and learning in the Western world, which occurred during the period stretching roughly from the late fourteenth through the early seventeenth century. The center of activity was Italy, which at this time was made up of a group of independent city-states. The Renaissance was also prevalent a short time later in England, Spain, and France. During the Renaissance, theatre blossomed in these countries. Before we discuss the theatrical innovations of this time period, however, let us first examine social and cultural changes.

ITALY

BACKGROUND: THE RENAISSANCE ERA

European politics changed markedly during the Renaissance. There was a rise of kings and princes, and merchants became key economic figures. As these people's wealth increased, they had leisure time to fill and also became eager to display their fortunes; consequently, they often hired artists to create lavish works for them.

Renaissance art is noticeably different from medieval art. During the Middle Ages, painting and sculpture had religious subjects. Renaissance artists, on the other hand, treated their subjects as human beings with whom we can identify. A good example is the statue of David by the Italian sculptor Michelangelo: the figure of David looks like a real person, not an otherworldly religious image. Painting also became more realistic through the use of oils and perspective, a technique that gives the illusion of three-dimensional depth on a flat canvas. In Renaissance literature, the major movement was *humanism,* which imitated the Greeks and Romans and focused on human beings rather than the gods. The printing press, which appeared in Europe in the 1450s, made this literature available to great numbers of people.

The Renaissance was also a period of exploration and invention. Discoveries in North and South America brought new wealth to Europe; at the same time, scientific advances revolutionized Western ideas about of the position of humanity in the universe. For example, the Italian astronomer Galileo argued that the sun, not the earth, is the center of the solar system.

The Renaissance also saw remarkable developments in theatre, especially in Italy, England, Spain, and France.

ITALIAN THEATRE: COMMEDIA DELL'ARTE

Italy, which led the way in Renaissance painting and sculpture, also saw radical transformations in its theatre between 1550 and 1650. These were chiefly in improvisational theatre, acting, dramatic criticism, theatre architecture, and scene design. The written drama of the Italian Renaissance is less significant: much of it was modeled after Greek and Roman plays and presented at academies or at the homes of wealthy patrons, and almost none of it left a lasting mark. Two other dramatic forms that were developed in the Renaissance and were influenced by classical subject matter and dramatic techniques were intermezzi and pastorals.

Intermezzi were short pieces depicting mythological tales; they were presented between the acts of full-length plays and were often thematically related to the full-length

ITALIAN RENAISSANCE

THEATRE

Year, c.e.

CULTURE AND POLITICS

Antonio Laschis, *Achilles* (c. 1390)

Manuel Chrysoloras opens Greek classes in Florence; beginning of revival of Greek literature in Italy (1396)

1425

Twelve of Plautus's lost plays rediscovered (1429)

Cosmo de Médici rules Florence (1432)

Founding of Platonic Academy in Florence (1440)

1450

Gutenberg invents movable type (c. 1450)

Leonardo da Vinci born (1452)

I Gelosi commedia troupe (1569–1604)
(photos12.com-ARJ)

Manuscripts of Greek plays brought to Italy after fall of Constantinople (1453)

Lorenzo de Médici rules Florence (1469)

1475

Michelangelo born (1475)

Birth of Venus by Botticelli (1484)

Columbus reaches America; Leonardo da Vinci draws a flying machine (1492)

Vitruvius's *De architectura* published (1486)

Plays by Aristophanes published by Aldine Press in Venice (1498)

Italian wars spread Italy's cultural influence but weaken Italy politically (1494)

1500

Michelangelo's *David* (c. 1504)

Leonardo da Vinci's *Mona Lisa* (1503)

Ariosto's *I Suppositi* (1509)

Machiavelli's comic play *Mandragola* (c. 1513)

Sistine Chapel (c. 1512)

Machiavelli's *The Prince* (1513)

Bibbiena's *La Calandria* (1513)

Beolco begins writing and performing (c. 1520)

Leonardo da Vinci dies (1519)

Verrazano reaches New York Bay and Hudson River (1524)

1525

Da Vinci's Mona Lisa (1503–1505)

Serlio's *Architettura* (6 vols.) (1545)

Peak of commedia dell'arte (1550–1650)

1550

Uffizi Museum at Florence founded (1560)

First performances of I Gelosi (the Andreinis) (c. 1569)

Galileo born; Michelangelo dies (1564)

Castelvetro requires unities (1570)

Palladio's *I quattro libri dell'architettura* (1570)

1575

Teatro Olimpico built (1584)

Sabbioneta theatre built (1588)

Catherine de Médicis, queen mother of France, dies (1589)

Peri's *Dafne* (1597)

1600

Mannerism begins to appear in Italy (1600)

I Gelosi troupe disbands upon the death of Isabella Andreini (1604)

Aleotti uses flat wing (c. 1606)

Teatro Farnese built (1618)

1625

Galileo Galilei (1564–1642)

Sabbatini's *Manual for Constructing Theatrical Scenes and Machines* (1638)

Torelli's pole-and-chariot system (c. 1645)

Galileo dies (1642)

267

works they accompanied. Intermezzi often required spectacular scenic effects. Although popular in the 1500s, this form disappeared in the 1600s.

The Italians also imitated Greek satyr plays—short, ribald comic pieces that had been presented as a follow-up to Greek tragedies—in a form they called a *pastoral*. The subject matter of a Renaissance pastoral is romance; the characters are usually shepherds and mythological creatures. Unlike Greek satyr plays, the Italian pastorals were not overtly bawdy or sexual. These pastorals usually deal with lovers who are threatened and often at odds with each other; while the action is serious, the endings are happy.

A third form developed during this period which, unlike the intermezzi and the pastoral, was to be of important and lasting value. This was *opera,* invented by people in Italy who believed they were recreating the Greek tragic style, which had fused music with drama. Opera is the only Italian Renaissance theatrical form that has survived. It can be defined as a drama set entirely to music. Every part is sung, including not only solos, arias, duets, trios, and quartets, but also the transitional sections between them known as recitatives. Having begun in Florence, Italy, around 1600, opera spread to other parts of Italy during the seventeenth century. After that, for three centuries, from 1600 to 1900, it spread not only throughout Italy, but throughout Europe, including France, Germany, and England. For all of its dramatic qualities, however, opera has always been considered more a part of music than theatre. This is because in opera the emphasis is always on the musical components: the composer, the singers, and the orchestra. However, opera has influenced modern musical theatre and many significant contemporary theatre directors have staged operas.

Returning to the theatre itself, we repeat that the Italian Renaissance is not distinguished for its written drama. It did, however, originate a significant and immensely popular form of improvisational theatre, closely related to many of our popular performance and comic forms today. This was *commedia dell'arte*—comedy of professional artists. Commedia dell'arte flourished in Italy from 1550 to 1750.

In commedia, performers had no set text; they invented words and actions as they went along. *Scenarios*—short plot outlines without dialogue—were written by company members.

Commedia companies, usually consisting of ten performers (seven men and three women), were traveling troupes; the most successful companies were often organized by families. Commedia companies were adaptable: they could perform in town squares, in theatre spaces, in the homes of wealthy merchants, or at court.

Commedia performers played the same stock characters throughout most of their careers. Among the popular comic personages were a lecherous, miserly old Venetian man, Pantalone; a foolish scholar, Dottore; a cowardly, braggart soldier, Capitano; and sometimes foolish servants known as **zanni** (ZAH-nee), of whom Arlecchino, or Harlequin, was the most popular. Commedia scenarios also included serious young lovers. All commedia characters used standard **lazzi** (LAHT-zee)—repeated bits of comic business, usually physical, and sometimes bawdy and obscene.

Commedia characters wore traditional costumes, such as Harlequin's patchwork jacket and Dottore's academic robes. A significant addition to Harlequin's costume was the **slapstick,** a wooden sword used in comic fight scenes; today, we still use the term *slapstick* for comedies emphasizing physical horseplay. Masks, usually covering part of the face, were a significant element of commedia costumes. The young lovers, however, did not wear masks.

Zanni Comic male servants in Italian commedia dell'arte.

Lazzi Comic pieces of business used repeatedly by characters in Italian commedia dell'arte.

Slapstick A type of comedy or comic business that relies on exaggerated or ludicrous physical activity for its humor.

COMMEDIA DELL'ARTE PERFORMERS
One of the most famous family troupes of commedia dell'arte, the improvisational Italian theatre, was known as I Gelosi. Performers from the troupe are seen here with the leading actress, Isabella Andreini, in the center. (photos12.com-ARJ)

ITALIAN DRAMATIC RULES: THE NEOCLASSICAL IDEALS

In terms of drama, critics rather than playwrights proved influential in the Italian Renaissance. Italian critics formulated dramatic rules—known as the ***neoclassical ideals***—that were to dominate dramatic theory through much of Europe for nearly 200 years.

One overriding concern of the neoclassicists was *verisimilitude,* by which they meant that drama should be "true to life." Their verisimilitude, however, was not the kind of realism we find in modern drama. Though the neoclassicists insisted that these dramas be recognizable and verifiable from real life, nevertheless they permitted stock dramatic situations and stock characters.

Another concern of the neoclassicists—in fact, their most famous mandate—was their insistence on three ***unities:*** unity of time, of place, and of action. The unities grew out of the desire for verisimilitude. Unity of time required that the dramatic action in a play should not exceed twenty-four hours. Unity of place restricted the action of a play to one locale. Unity of action required that there be only one central story involving a relatively small group of characters; this meant that there could be no subplots. The three unities are often mistakenly attributed to Aristotle, though in fact he had suggested only one unity: the unity of action.

Neoclassical ideals Rules developed by critics during the Italian Renaissance, supposedly based on the writings of Aristotle.

Unities Term referring to the preference that a play's plot occur within one day (unity of time), in one place (unity of place), and with no action irrelevant to the plot (unity of action).

1500s, ROME The time is the late 1500s; the place is a town square in Rome. Set up in the square is a wooden platform stage with a backdrop at the rear. This backdrop, or curtain, not only forms the scenic background of the action on the platform but also provides a hidden space in which the performers can adjust their costumes and from which they can make their entrances and exits.

A crowd is beginning to gather, and people are trying to get the best position to see the performance that is about to begin. In front of the stage, people are already standing several rows deep; at the sides the audience members push closer, but they won't be facing the stage directly. As the spectators look around, they can see that the audience represents a cross section of Roman citizens.

There is great anticipation in the air because the performers are members of one of the best-known theatre companies in Italy —a troupe called I Gelosi, led by Francesco and Isabella Andreini. The ten members of the company have perfected commedia dell'arte, a form of improvisational comedy that has become the most popular type of theatre in Italy.

Commedia is different from many other kinds of theatre. There is no script in the usual sense. There is an outline of the action—the characters portrayed in a scene, what happens, how the scene develops—but the dialogue is not written out. The lines the characters speak are not provided. The performers, therefore, improvise their speeches—that is, they make the dialogue up as they go along. This, plus the fact that the movements also are improvised, adds a great air of immediacy to the production. It is most challenging to the performers, and this makes the presentation all the more exciting for those now assembled to watch.

Soon the performance is under way, and the fun begins. The story is partly about an actress who is pursued by every man—unmarried or married—in town, and partly about the adulterous intrigues of her pursuers' wives. There are insults, cases of mistaken identity, and plans gone wrong, and people's misbehavior is exposed.

The characters are stock figures: an old Venetian merchant, a foolish pedant, a cowardly braggart soldier, comic servants, and young lovers. All the characters except the lovers wear masks, most of which are half masks covering the upper part of the face. Each character wears a costume that makes him or her easily recognizable: the pedant, for instance, wears academic robes; the captain wears a uniform; the young lovers are fashionably dressed. One source of great pleasure in watching the performance is seeing the pompous, self-important characters get their comeuppance during the course of the action.

The servants are a special delight. They are known as *zanni* and are usually of two types. The first, called Buffetto and various other names, is a clever, domineering intriguer who motivates the plot through various schemes. The other, even better known, is Arlecchino, or Harlequin. He wears a patchwork outfit of many colors, is given to pratfalls, and is often the victim of knockdown physical humor. Frequently, the servants outwit their masters and help the young lovers get together.

One plot twist operates around the notion that older characters attempt to thwart the desires of the young lovers, and it is only at the conclusion that the lovers achieve their objective.

The spectators crowded around the platform, knowing that the performers are improvising, are amazed at how quick on their feet the performers are and how readily they respond to the dialogue thrown at them.

The interaction of the performers is very physical. In one scene, a master beats a servant with a stick, which is hinged with a flap to make an exaggerated sound when it hits the servant's backside. In another scene, a soldier challenges a lover to a duel and becomes hopelessly entangled with his own sword; at times his sword sticks out from between his legs, taking on a sexual connotation. The more entangled he becomes, the louder the audience laughs.

At the end of the play, as they make their way home, audience members talk among themselves, sometimes laughing out loud as they recall highlights of the performance.

The neoclassicists interpreted genre very narrowly. For many of them, tragedy dealt with royalty, comedy with common people; tragedy must end sadly and comedy happily; and the two genres must never be mixed.

The function of all drama, the neoclassic critics insisted, was to teach moral lessons. Also, they held that characters must be morally acceptable to the audience.

TEATRO OLIMPICO
Completed in 1584, the Teatro Olimpico in Vicenza, Italy, is the oldest surviving theatre from the Renaissance. The stage attempted to duplicate the facade of the Roman scene house and had five alleyways leading off it. Down each alleyway, small models of buildings were created to give the illusion of disappearing perspective. This photo shows the ornate facade, a holdover from Roman theatres, with the five alleyways, two on each side of the central alleyway. (© Dennis Marsico/Corbis)

There were numerous other rules. Onstage violence was forbidden, for instance; and the neoclassicists banished the chorus and supernatural characters. They were also opposed to the *soliloquy*—a monologue through which a character reveals thoughts by speaking them aloud.

While there were significant differences among the various Italian critics, they were all highly *prescriptive,* telling authors how to write in order to create great drama. The rules of the neoclassical critics were to have particular influence on playwrights in France during the seventeenth century.

THEATRE PRODUCTION IN ITALY

A particularly significant contribution of the Italian Renaissance was made by architects who revolutionized theatre construction. Two specific buildings illustrate the gradual development of Italian theatre architecture, and fortunately both are still standing.

The oldest surviving theatre built during the Italian Renaissance—the Teatro Olimpico in Vicenza, completed in 1584—was designed as a miniature indoor Roman theatre. Its auditorium, accommodating approximately 3,000 spectators, had curved benches connected to the *scaena,* or stage house; this arrangement created a semi-circular *orchestra.* There was a raised stage, about seventy feet wide by eighteen feet deep, in front of the scaena. The ornate facade of the scene house, patterned after the Roman scaena frons, was designed to look like a street. There were five openings in the facade—three in the back wall and one on each side. Behind each opening was an alleyway or street scene that seemed to disappear in the distance. To achieve an effect of depth, in each alleyway there were three-dimensional buildings—houses and shops—that decreased in size as they were positioned farther and farther away from the opening onstage.

The most renowned theatre building of the Italian Renaissance was the Teatro Farnese in Parma, completed in 1618. The Farnese had a typical court, or academic,

TEATRO FARNESE
Completed in 1618, the Teatro Farnese was the first theatre with a proscenium arch—the opening behind which scenery and stage machinery are concealed. The auditorium is horseshoe shaped, and the orchestra is a semicircle placed between the audience and the stage. (© Ruggero Vanni/Corbis)

Pit Floor of the house in Renaissance theatres. It was originally a standing area; by the end of the eighteenth century, backless benches were added in most countries.

Box Small private compartment for a group of spectators built into the walls of traditional proscenium-arch and other theatres.

Gallery In theatre buildings, the undivided seating area cut into the walls of the building.

theatre auditorium, with raised horseshoe seating that accommodated about 3,500 spectators. What was revolutionary in the Teatro Farnese was its *proscenium-arch* stage. Despite the term *arch,* a proscenium opening is usually a rectangular frame. Realistic scenery can be placed much more effectively behind such a frame than in any other type of theatre; thus the proscenium arch, along with Renaissance innovations in scene design, became an impetus for greater theatrical realism. (See Chapter 7 for a fuller discussion of the proscenium-arch theatre.)

When we move from the stage to the auditorium, we find that the major changes occurred in the public opera houses of Venice. These were proscenium-arch houses, but—unlike court or academy theatres—they were commercial ventures that needed as many paying customers as possible; thus, they required a larger audience area. Opera houses were therefore designed with "pit, boxes, and galleries," which had already been used in France, England, and Spain. It was their combination of a "pit, box, and gallery" auditorium with a proscenium-arch stage that made the Venetian opera houses innovative. This kind of proscenium-arch theatre with pit, box, and gallery seating would later become the standard theatre space throughout the Western world and would remain so for more than 300 years.

The *pit,* in which audience members stood, was an open area on the house floor extending to the side and back walls. Built into the walls were tiers of seating. The lower tiers were usually the most expensive; they were divided into separate private *boxes* and were frequented by the upper classes. The upper tiers, which were called *galleries,* had open bench seating. The pit—a raucous area where the spectators ate, talked, and moved around—and the galleries were the least expensive accommodations.

Advances in scene design during the Italian Renaissance were no less impressive than architectural innovations. ***Perspective*** drawing, which creates an illusion of depth and which had become an important feature of Renaissance art, was introduced into theatre.

The earliest painted-perspective scenery was clumsy and not easy to shift; as a result, by the early 1600s flat wings were used to create painted-perspective settings. In this arrangement, a series of individual wings on each side of the stage, parallel to the audience, were placed in a progression from the front to the back of the stage and enclosed at the very back by two shutters that met in the middle. The final element in these perspective settings was provided by overhead borders—strips across the top of the stage that completed the picture.

The method of scene shifting used with settings of this kind is often referred to as the ***groove system*** because the wings and shutters were placed in parallel grooves on and above the stage floor. The major problem with this system was coordinating the removal of the flat wings by scene shifters at each groove position. This problem was solved with an innovative scene-changing system developed by Giacomo Torelli (1608–1678) and known as the *pole-and-chariot* system. Poles attached to the flats

Perspective Illusion of depth in painting, introduced into scene design during the Italian Renaissance.

Groove system System in which tracks on the stage floor and above the stage allowed for the smooth movement of flat wings onto and off the stage; usually there were a series of grooves at each stage position.

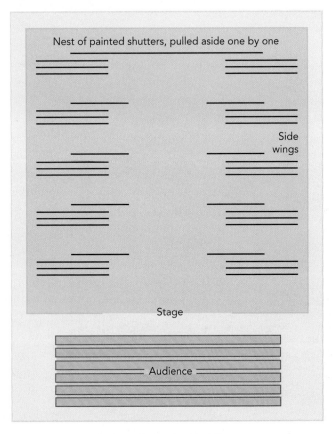

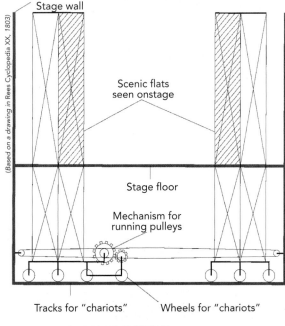

(Based on a drawing in Rees Cyclopedia XX, 1803)

GROOVE SYSTEM OF SCENE CHANGES
During the Italian Renaissance, the groove method of shifting scenery was perfected. Along the sides of the stage, in parallel lines, scenery was set in sections. At the back, two shutters met in the middle. Together, these pieces formed a complete stage picture. When one set of side wings and back shutters was pulled aside, a different stage picture was revealed.

POLE-AND-CHARIOT SYSTEM
This method of changing wings and back shutters was developed by Torelli. When a series of wheels and pulleys below the level of the stage—attached on frameworks to the scenery above—were shifted, the scene changed automatically. Because the mechanisms were interconnected, scene shifts could be smooth and simultaneous.

continued below the stage floor, where they were connected to wheels ("chariots") in tracks. In this way, the flats could be moved offstage smoothly; by connecting a series of ropes and pulleys, the entire set could be removed by turning a single winch. The pole-and-chariot system was adopted and used throughout much of the world for more than two centuries. The focus on illusion and spectacular scene shifts continues in our contemporary theatre.

ENGLAND

BACKGROUND: ELIZABETHAN ENGLAND

The English Renaissance is often called the *Elizabethan* period because its major political figure was Elizabeth I, who reigned for forty-five years from 1558 to 1603. Throughout the English Renaissance, explorations abroad were undertaken, and language and literature flourished. The English were intrigued by language—Queen Elizabeth herself was an amateur linguist—and at the heart of the English Renaissance in literature and the arts was theatre.

ENGLISH RENAISSANCE

THEATRE

Year, c.e.

CULTURE AND POLITICS

Henry VIII reigns (1509–1547)

Thomas More's *Utopia* (1516)

*King Henry VIII
(rules 1509–1547)*

Elizabeth I, queen of England, rules (1558–1603)

Sackville and Norton's *Gorboduc:*
first English tragedy (1561)

Master of revels made licenser of plays
and companies; James Burbage's Earl
of Leicester's Men founded (1574)

The Theatre built by James Burbage;
first Blackfriars opened (1576)

1550

1575

*Queen Elizabeth
(rules 1558–1603)*

Sir Walter Raleigh's
expedition to Virginia (1584)

Kyd's *Spanish Tragedy* (c. 1587)

Marlowe's *Doctor
Faustus* (c. 1588)

Alleyn's Lord Admiral's Men and
Burbage's Lord Chamberlain's Men, the
major companies in London (1594)

Second Blackfriars built by James Burbage (1596)

Shakespeare's   Globe Theatre built (1599)
Hamlet (c. 1600)

Lord Chamberlain's Men
become the King's Men (1603)

Jonson's *Volpone* (1606)

Webster's *Duchess of Malfi* (c. 1613)

Execution of Mary,
Queen of Scots (1587)

Defeat of Spanish armada (1588)

1600

James I begins reign (1603)

Jamestown, Virginia, founded (1607)   Hudson claims part
of North America for
King James Bible (1611)   United Provinces (1609)

*Inigo Jones design for a "fiery spirit" for
Thomas Campion's* Lord Masque
(© Lebrecht Music & Arts/The Image Works)

Thirty Years' War begins (1618)

Francis Bacon's *Novum
Organum* (1620)

1625

Charles I begins reign (1625)

Charles I dissolves Parliament (1629)

Inigo Jones designs masques (c. 1620)
Jacobean playwrights flourish (c. 1620)
John Ford's *'Tis Pity She's a Whore* (c. 1630)
Parliament closes British theatres (1642)

English civil war (1642)

1650

Charles I beheaded (1649)

275

ELIZABETHAN DRAMA

Christopher Marlowe and the "Mighty Line"   One of the most important of the Elizabethan playwrights was Christopher Marlowe (1564–1593), who advanced the art of dramatic structure and contributed a gallery of interesting characters to English drama; he also perfected another element that was to prove central to later Elizabethan plays: dramatic poetry. Critics speak of Marlowe's "mighty line," by which they mean the power of his dramatic verse. The meter of this verse is iambic pentameter, which has five beats to a line, with two syllables to each beat and the accent on the second beat. In Marlowe's hands, dramatic verse in iambic pentameter developed strength, subtlety, and suppleness, as well as great lyric beauty.

Marlowe wrote several important plays, including *Doctor Faustus* (c. 1588), *Tamburlaine* (Parts 1 and 2; c. 1587), and *Edward II* (c. 1592), but his promising career as a dramatist was unfortunately cut short when he was stabbed to death in a tavern brawl in 1593 at the age of twenty-nine.

William Shakespeare: A Playwright for the Ages   William Shakespeare (1564–1616) appeared on the theatre scene around 1590, just after Marlowe had made his debut. Shakespeare was a native of Stratford-upon-Avon (a town about eighty-five miles northwest of London); his father was a prosperous glove maker and town alderman, and his mother—Mary Arden—was the daughter of a prominent landowner and farmer. Shakespeare was educated in Stratford; he then married Anne Hathaway, who was several years older than he and who bore him three children.

At some point after the third child was born, Shakespeare left his family and went to London, where he worked first as an actor and shortly after that as a playwright. As a dramatist, he worked with elements that had been established in early Elizabethan drama—Senecan dramatic devices; the platform stage; powerful dramatic verse; source material from English history, Roman history and drama, and Italian literature; and the episodic plot structure that had its roots in medieval theatre. He fused these elements into one of the most impressive groups of plays ever created.

TWO PLAYWRIGHTS OF THE ELIZABETHAN ERA
Christopher Marlowe (left) and William Shakespeare (right) are the most renowned playwrights of an era that produced many great dramatists. (Marlowe: Hulton Deutsch Collection Ltd.; Shakespeare: Victoria and Albert Museum, London)

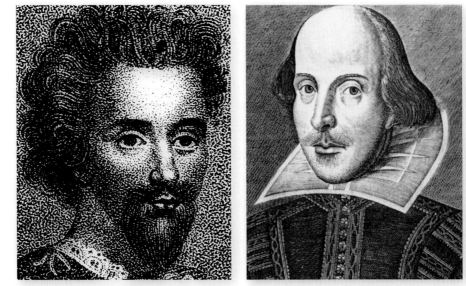

Shakespeare was an expert in many aspects of theatre. As an actor and a member of a dramatic company, the Lord Chamberlain's Men (which was London's leading troupe), he understood the technical and business elements of theatre. As a writer, he excelled in several genres, including tragedy, comedy, and history. His tragedies include *Romeo and Juliet* (1595), *Julius Caesar* (1599), *Hamlet* (1601), *Othello* (1604), *Macbeth* (1605–1606), and *King Lear* (1605–1606). His comedies include *The Comedy of Errors* (1592), *A Midsummer Night's Dream* (1595), *As You Like It* (1599), and *Twelfth Night* (1601). Among his well-known histories are *Richard III* (1592–1593); *Henry IV, Parts 1 and 2* (1597–1598); and *Henry V* (1599). Like other Elizabethan authors, he also sometimes wrote with collaborators.

His verse, especially the power of his metaphors and the music of his language, is extraordinary; and his characters are so well-rounded and carefully detailed that they often seem like living people. He was also a master of plot construction, notably episodic plot structure—which, as we have seen, stands alongside climactic structure as one of the two main forms that have been predominant throughout the history of Western theatre.

The Globe Theatre, where his plays were produced, burned in 1613; after that, Shakespeare retired to Stratford and became one of its leading citizens. He died three years later.

1600, LONDON It is early afternoon on a day around the year 1600. In London, England, people from many parts of the city are gathering along the north bank of the Thames River to be carried by boat across to its south bank. There is a special excitement in the air because most of those crossing the Thames are headed for the Globe Theatre to see the first public performance of a new play by William Shakespeare called *Hamlet*.

The Globe is one of the newest and finest playhouses serving London. The reason it is on the other side of the Thames, outside city limits, is that officials in London have forbidden theatrical performances inside the city. The first permanent theatres in England have been built to the north of London or across the Thames to the south, outside the jurisdiction of city officials.

When the spectators arrive at the theatre—more than 2,000 people all together—they can pay a penny at the main door to get in, or they can use another entrance for the more expensive accommodations. Those who use the main door move into a central courtyard, open to the sky, where they will stand during the performance around three sides of a platform stage at one end of the courtyard. Those who can afford to pay more enter one of three levels of covered gallery seats surrounding the stage and courtyard on three sides. By

paying even more, the nobility can sit on cushioned seats in boxes next to the stage. Food and drink—apples, nuts, water, ale—are being sold throughout the playhouse.

As the audience gathers, there is a great deal of conversation about the play. Some audience members already know something about *Hamlet;* they are familiar with earlier versions of the story, and they know that *Hamlet* will be a revenge play—one of their favorite types of drama. There is keen interest, too, because *Hamlet* is by William Shakespeare, a favorite playwright; and its star is Richard Burbage, who is considered by many people the finest actor in England.

At two o'clock, the play begins. Two sentinels standing watch on the parapet of a castle appear onstage, soon to be joined by Horatio, a friend of Hamlet's; the three men discuss a ghost that has been appearing every night. All of a sudden, the ghost is there: it is the ghost of Hamlet's father, and it is played by Shakespeare himself, who is also an actor with the company. Horatio and the sentinels are frightened; the ghost stays briefly and then disappears.

The scene shifts to the interior of the castle: King Claudius enters. He is the brother of Hamlet's father, the dead king, and he has married Hamlet's mother, Queen Gertrude. Onstage, too, are the other principals of the play, including Hamlet, who is

dressed in black and stands apart from the others.

The action of the play is full of twists and turns. In the next scene, Hamlet himself sees the ghost of his father, who says that Hamlet must avenge his murder at the hands of his brother, Claudius. Hamlet later has a group of strolling players present a drama that proves Claudius did murder Hamlet's father. In a later scene, Hamlet thrusts his sword through a curtain in his mother's bedroom, thinking that Claudius is hiding behind it, but the person concealed there turns out to be someone else.

As the plot continues to unfold, the audience is enthralled—all the way to the end, when almost everyone is killed: Hamlet and Laertes in a duel, Gertrude by poisoning, Claudius by stabbing. Throughout the play, the audience enjoys not only the action and suspense but also the memorable lines and speeches. Several times Hamlet stands alone onstage delivering a soliloquy.

On the way back across the Thames, after the play is over, and all evening, the audience members will continue to discuss *Hamlet*. They would like to see it again because there is more to it than they were able to take in at one viewing; they want to live through it once more to feel the thrill of the action and to sort out their thoughts about what it means.

READ *Hamlet* in *Anthology of Living Theatre* or at:

http://shakespeare.mit.edu/hamlet/full.html

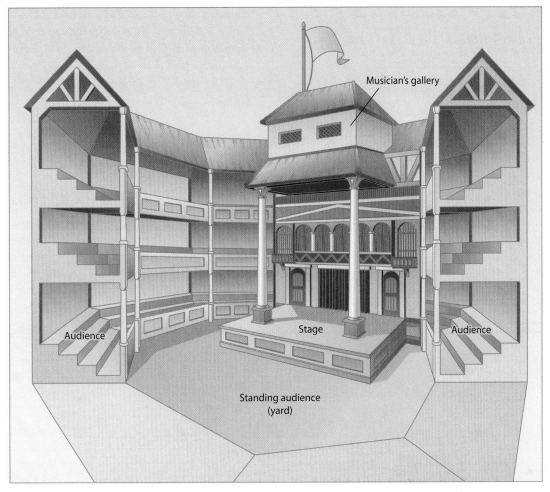

AN ELIZABETHAN PLAYHOUSE
This drawing shows the kind of stage on which the plays of Shakespeare and his contemporaries were first presented. A platform stage juts into an open courtyard, with spectators standing on three sides. Three levels of enclosed seats rise above the courtyard. There are doors at the rear of the stage for entrances and exits and an upper level for balcony scenes.

ELIZABETHAN THEATRE PRODUCTION

Public or Outdoor Theatres   The plays of Shakespeare, Marlowe, and their contemporaries were performed primarily in ***public theatres.*** Between the 1560s and 1642, at least nine open-air public theatres were built just outside the city of London. They were located just outside the city limits to avoid government restrictions. All levels of society attended productions at the public theatres. The most famous public theatre was the Globe because it was the home of Shakespeare's plays.

Elizabethan playhouses flourished 400 years ago. By a strange coincidence, within the last twenty years, the sites of three of these theatres have been rediscovered and excavated. Two theatres were close together on the south bank of the Thames River: the Rose (1587) and the Globe (1599). The third and oldest, The Theatre (1576), was northeast of the city. These discoveries have aided in understanding the size, shape, and

Public theatres Outdoor theatres in Elizabethan England.

configurations of the original theatres. Also, in 1997, a replica of the Globe Theatre opened near the site of the original Globe, and performances are held there each summer.

The stage of a public theatre—a raised platform surrounded on three sides by the audience—was closer to a contemporary thrust stage than to a proscenium stage. This platform stage was a neutral playing area that could become many different places in quick succession: a room in a palace, a bedroom, a street, a battlefield. When one group of characters left the stage and another group entered, this generally signaled a change of scene. Sometimes the characters announced where they were; at other times, the location was apparent from the action.

In the stage floor were trapdoors. Behind the raised platform was the stage house, known as the *tiring house.* This three-story building served as a place for changing costumes as well as for storing properties and set pieces. The stage house was also the basic scenic piece in an Elizabethan public theatre.

There is a great deal of debate over the configuration of the tiring house, but it is usually argued that the first level had two doorways, one on each side; and that entrances and exits through these doors indicated scene changes. For plays with scenes in which characters were concealed, there was probably an inner stage on the first level, either as part of the tiring house or within a freestanding structure. If such a special area did not exist, possibly one of the doors provided a place for concealment.

THE SWAN THEATRE
This drawing of an Elizabethan playhouse is a copy of a sketch made by a Dutch visitor to London in 1596. While the sketch shows the platform stage, tiring house, and galleries, controversial questions remain. Is the sketch complete? If so, where is the space for concealed characters? Who are the people in the gallery? Is this a rehearsal or a performance? (University Library, Utrecht)

Another feature of the Elizabethan playhouse was an upper playing area for balcony scenes. No one knows for certain what the upper playing area looked like, but it might have been an inner area on the second level of the tiring house or part of a freestanding structure at the rear of the stage. The third level of the stage house, referred to as the *musicians' gallery,* probably housed the musicians who provided accompaniment for the plays. A roof, which protected the stage, extended out from the stage house. In some theatres it was supported by pillars; in others, it was suspended from the back. A flag was flown from the top of the stage house on days when a performance was taking place.

The exact shape of public theatres varied. It is estimated that their audience capacity was between 1,500 and 3,000—the larger number is now more widely accepted.

Spectators were accommodated in the *yard, boxes,* and *galleries.* On the ground floor, in front of and on the sides of the stage, was the standing area, known as the *yard,* the front half of which sloped from the back to the stage. The lower-class audience members who stood in the yard were known as *groundlings.* The galleries were usually three tiers of seating ranged on three sides around the stage. One tier was divided into boxes known as *lords' rooms* because they were frequented by the wealthy; the undivided tiers were equipped with bench seating. Spectators—even those at the back wall of the galleries—were never very far from the actors.

Private Theatres

Elizabethan *private theatres* were indoor spaces, lit by candles and high windows. The term *private* in this context often causes confusion because today it would imply that certain classes were excluded. In Elizabethan England, however, private theatres were open to the general public, though they were usually smaller (seating about 600 to 750 spectators) and therefore more expensive than public theatres.

The pit of a private theatre, which faced the stage in only one direction, had backless benches. The platform stage extended to the side walls, with galleries and boxes facing the stage on three sides.

Scenery and Costumes in Elizabethan Theatres

The Elizabethans did not use painted scenery in their public or private theatres, and the stage space did not represent a specific locale. Instead, the extensive, episodic nature of Elizabethan drama required scenes to be changed rapidly. Sometimes actors coming onstage would bring out minimal properties, such as a throne, to suggest a locale.

Costuming followed the conventions and traditions of medieval English theatre. While their dramas exhibit a great deal of historical and geographical variety, the Elizabethans were not overly concerned with accuracy; most costumes were simply contemporary clothing, reflective of the social classes being depicted.

English Actors and Acting Companies

Throughout the English Renaissance, the monarchy exerted considerable legal control over theatre, and the number of acting companies was restricted by law.

Elizabethan acting companies—each of which had approximately twenty-five members—were organized on a *sharing plan.* There were three categories of personnel in a company: *shareholders, hirelings,* and *apprentices.* Shareholders, the elite members of the company, received a percentage of the troupe's profits as payment. Hirelings were actors contracted for a specific period of time and for a specific salary, and they usually

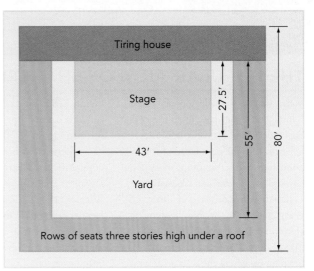

GROUND PLAN OF THE FORTUNE THEATRE
The only English Renaissance theatre for which we have a number of specific dimensions is the Fortune. From the builder's contract we know the size of the stage, the standing pit, the audience seating area, and the theatre building itself. The building was square; the backstage area ran along one side; the stage was rectangular; and the audience—both standing and sitting—was on three sides.

MAKING CONNECTIONS

THE POPULAR ARTS OF SHAKESPEARE'S TIME

When we review the history of English Renaissance theatre, we often forget that Shakespeare and his contemporaries had to battle with the popular arts for London's audiences. Two of the most popular were bearbaiting and cockfighting.

Bearbaiting consisted of a bear being chained in the middle of an arena and then attacked by trained mastiff dogs. Points were scored depending on where the dogs struck the bear. The entertainment was probably developed out of the Roman animal entertainments and the tradition of baiting bulls during the Middle Ages.

In the 1500s, bearbaiting became a commercial entertainment in London. Up until 1574, there were two baiting rings in that city. During Shakespeare's time, there was one extremely popular arena: the Bear Garden. The Bear Garden was allowed to present bearbaiting on Sundays, when the theatres were closed. Sunday attendance was so great that in 1583, parts of the building collapsed because of the large number of spectators.

Shakespeare comments on the popularity and theatricality of bearbaiting in his comedy *The Merry Wives of Windsor* (1600). The comedic character Slender comments about how much he loves the sport of bearbaiting and the audience's admiration for the great bear Sackerson:

> I love the sport well, but I shall as soon quarrel at it as any man in England. You are afraid if you see the bear loose, are you not? . . . I have seen Sackerson loose twenty times, and have taken him by the chain; but I warrant you, the women have so cried and shrieked at it, that it passed.

This form of entertainment remained popular through the English Restoration and was not made illegal until 1835.

The Cockpit, also known as the Phoenix, was opened in 1609 as an indoor space to house cockfights, another animal entertainment. Spectators would watch and bet on cocks, which were trained to fight with each other. The Cockpit became one of the best-known private, or indoor, theatres in the late English Renaissance after it was remodeled in 1616.

The popularity of cockfighting continued into the eighteenth-century English world. For that matter, the sport was popular in the early American colonies. George Washington, in his diaries, comments on attending cockfights in the new world.

Given the great competition for audiences, it is clear that the stage fights, violence, and slapstick comedy that abound in English Renaissance drama were techniques used to combat the popularity of these other forms of entertainment.

---

played minor roles. Apprentices—young performers training for the profession—were assigned to shareholders. There were no female performers; women's roles were played by boys or men. Since the plays had many characters, doubling of roles was common.

What style of acting was used by the Elizabethans continues to be debated, particularly how realistic it was—that is, how close to the speech and gestures of everyday life. Many of the conventions of the period, such as dramatic verse, seem to suggest a departure from realistic style.

An English company would rarely perform the same play on two consecutive days, and each company had to be able to revive plays in its repertory on very short notice. Thus the primary concern was not so much a carefully realized production as expert delivery of lines. Actors were provided with *sides,* which contained only their own lines and cues rather than the full script, and improvisation must have been used frequently. *Plots*—outlines of the dramatic action of the various plays—were posted backstage so that performers could refresh their memories during performances. Rehearsals were run by playwrights or leading actors; and since rehearsal time was minimal, the prompter (who stood just offstage) became an indispensable part of the productions.

POPULAR ARTS IN SHAKESPEARE'S TIME
Bearbaiting was a popular entertainment during Shakespeare's lifetime. Arenas were constructed for this form of entertainment in which bears were attacked by trained dogs. Remarkably, bearbaiting continued to attract audiences in the early nineteenth century. Shown here is an illustration of bearbaiting in Westminster, London, in the 1820s. (© Hulton-Deutsch Collection/Corbis)

THEATRE AFTER ELIZABETH'S REIGN

After Elizabeth I died in 1603, the great Elizabethan dramatists, including Shakespeare and Ben Jonson (1572–1637), continued to write plays. Ben Jonson's comic masterpiece *Volpone,* for example, was staged in 1606. In contrast to Shakespeare, Jonson championed a more literary approach to drama.

James I succeeded Elizabeth; his reign is known as the *Jacobean* period. *The Duchess of Malfi* (c. 1613–1614), by John Webster (c. 1580–c. 1630), is probably the most renowned Jacobean tragedy. These later tragedies were usually very melodramatic and emphasized violence and spectacle.

Another development in English drama in the early 1600s was a mixing of serious and comic elements. Such plays generally had many of the qualities of tragedy but ended happily. Francis Beaumont (c. 1584–1616) and John Fletcher (1579–1625), two playwrights who often collaborated with each other, excelled at this form.

An elaborate type of entertainment featured at court during the reign of James I and his successor Charles I, and not found in either public or private theatres, was the *masque.* Masques were ornate, professionally staged, mythological allegories intended

THE DUCHESS OF MALFI
The most important writer of the Jacobean period was John Webster. His drama *The Duchess of Malfi* is a passionate study of love, incest, and political intrigue in the Renaissance and contains violence, horror, grotesque comedy, and lyrical poetry. In this scene, from a production at Britain's National Theatre, directed by Phyllida Lloyd, Ray Stevenson plays the cardinal and Eleanor David is the duchess. In the play, two brothers, one of them the cardinal shown here, persecute the duchess and ultimately murder her and her two children. (© Pete Jones/ArenaPAL)

to praise the monarch; they were embellished by music and dance, and they frequently used amateur performers from the court. In the first decade of the seventeenth century, Inigo Jones (1573–1652), a designer who had studied in Italy, began to introduce the Italian style of theatre architecture and scene design into English court masques.

James I was succeeded by Charles I in 1625. Though Charles I was not deposed—and beheaded—until 1649, the English Renaissance ended in 1642. By then, a civil war had begun between supporters of Charles I and the Puritan-backed Parliament. The Puritans were vehemently opposed to theatre; they believed that playgoing was an inappropriate way to spend one's leisure time and that theatre was a den of iniquity, teaching immorality. In 1642, the Puritans outlawed all theatrical activity.

SPAIN

BACKGROUND: THE SPANISH GOLDEN AGE

The period from about 1550 to 1650 is known as the Spanish Golden Age. During this rich period, Spain, which had a formidable navy, became a leading world power, primarily because of its exploration and conquest of the new world. Spain also remained

THEATRE FLOURISHES IN SPAIN'S GOLDEN AGE

During the late sixteenth century and the early seventeenth century, Spain enjoyed an outpouring of masterworks in the arts, as well as accomplishments in many other fields. Among the well-known plays of the period is Calderón's play *Life Is a Dream,* about a king's son who is kept in prison by his father until he comes of age because it is feared he will be too dangerous and unruly. Shown here is a recent production of the play with Dominic West as the son, Segismundo; it was directed by Jonathan Munby at the Donmar Warehouse, London. (© Johan Persson/ArenaPAL)

a devoutly Catholic nation in the face of the Protestant Reformation, which had swept much of the rest of Europe. In order to keep Spain Catholic, the church instituted the Inquisition, a type of court that punished any seeming religious heresy. During this period a popular theatre, which incorporated both religious and popular secular forms, flourished.

SPANISH DRAMA

Spain was one of England's chief rivals in the late sixteenth century and the early seventeenth. At the same time that the two nations competed with each other, there were many similarities in their theatres. One important difference, however, is that the Spaniards—unlike the English—adopted the techniques of medieval religious drama and continued to produce religious dramas throughout their golden age and beyond: until 1765, in fact.

Secular drama, which flourished between 1550 and 1700, developed in Spain side by side with religious drama and was created by the same artists. Full-length secular plays, known as *comedias* (koh-MAY-dee-ahs), usually dealt with themes of love and honor; the leading characters were often minor members of the nobility. Comedias

Comedia Full-length (three-act) nonreligious play of the Spanish Golden Age.

SPANISH GOLDEN AGE

THEATRE	Year, C.E.	CULTURE AND POLITICS

Spain united under Ferdinand and Isabella (1469)

1475

Inquisition established in Spain (1481)

Jews expelled from Spain; Columbus discovers America; conquest of Granada (1492)

Columbus lands in the New World (1492)
(Library of Congress)

1500

Juan del Encina's *The Eclogue of Placida and Victoriana* (1513)

Bartolomé de Torres Naharro's *Propalladia* (1517)

Cortés conquers Aztecs (1519)

Lope de Rueda (1510?–1565)
(Biblioteca Colombina, Seville, Spain)

1525

Pizzaro takes Peru (1530)

Opening of Potosí mines in Bolivia (1545)

Jesuits begin missionary work in South America (1549)

Lope de Rueda, Spain's first popular playwright (c. 1545)

1550

Felipe II (rules 1556–1598)

City councils assume responsibilities for the staging of autos (c. 1555)

Netherlands revolt against Spain (1567)

Victory against Turks at Lepanto (1571)

1575

El Greco arrives from Greece (1575)

Corral de la Cruz, first permanent theatre in Spain (1579)

Felipe II annexes Portugal (1580)

Corral del Principe (1583)

Women licensed to appear onstage (c. 1587)

Defeat of Spanish armada (1588)

1600

Felipe III (rules 1598–1621)

Cervantes's *Don Quixote,* Part 1 (1605)

Strict censorship of plays (1608)

Expulsion of Moors (1609)

Lope de Vega's *The Sheep Well* (1614)

Felipe IV (rules 1621–1665)

1625

Felipe IV brings designer Cosme Lotti from Florence (1626)

Velázquez completes painting *Vulcan's Forge* (1630)

Cofradia de la Novena (actors' guild) established (1631)

Revolt of Catalans and Portuguese (1640)

Calderón's *Life Is a Dream* (c. 1636)

Coliseo, court theatre with proscenium arch, built (1640)

Defeat of Spanish army by French at Rocroi (1643)

Public theatres closed (1646–1651)

Number of carros for autos increased from two to four (1647)

1650

Peace of the Pyrenees; Spain's power declines (1659)

First reference to Spanish designer José Caudi (1662)

Carlos II (rules 1665–1700)

Murillo's *Immaculate Conception* (Murillo used this subject thirty times) (1678)

1675

Publication of Spanish Colonial Code (1680)

Murillo dies (1617–1682)

1750

THE IMMACULATE CONCEPTION
(Murillo) (1660–1665)

Autos sacramentales prohibited (1765)

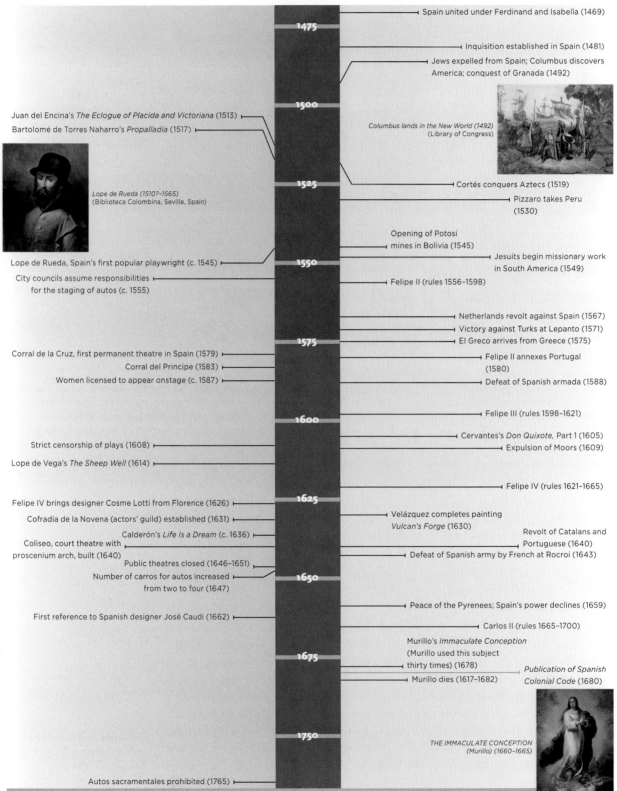

286

1620, MADRID It is four o'clock on a lovely spring afternoon in 1620. In Spain, a new full-length play by the Spanish playwright Lope de Vega is about to be performed at the Corral del Principe, one of two public theatres in Madrid. The audience has paid two entrance fees, one to the company presenting the play and the second to a charity supporting the city's hospital. The fee to the charity is one reason why government and church officials allow theatre in Madrid.

As the audience gathers inside the corral, there is great excitement about the performance that will soon begin. Those standing in the patio are a bit noisy. Many of the spectators have bought nuts, fruit, and spiced honey from the *alojero* (refreshment stand). People in the pit are jostling for the best vantage point; people in the galleries are exchanging pleasantries, speaking to friends, and looking around the theatre to see who is here this afternoon.

The audience is particularly excited to attend a new play by Lope de Vega. Some years ago, in 1609, Lope argued, in an essay titled "The New Art of Writing Plays in This Age," that the most important measure of success in theatre is the audience's enjoyment. He has certainly passed his own test for he is the most popular playwright of the day. The play about to be seen, *The King, the Greatest Alcalde,* promises to be filled with thrilling episodes.

Now the performance begins. First, before the actual play, there is a comic prologue. Then comes the play itself. It is a comedia: in Spain, this is the term for any full-length nonreligious play, serious or comic. *The King, the Greatest Alcalde* is serious, but it also has comic elements. It is about a farmer who promises his daughter Elvira to a peasant, Sancho. Sancho seeks approval for the marriage from his lord, Don Tello. Don Tello agrees, but when he sees Elvira, he wants her for himself. He postpones the wedding and kidnaps Elvira. As the play unfolds, it seems to have all the ingredients of a sparkling drama: a clash between peasants and the nobility, a wronged peasant, a kidnapping, a beautiful maiden in distress. The boisterous spectators in the pit are especially vocal in responding to each twist and turn of the plot and to the mixture of comedy and suspense, but the entire audience finds itself caught up in the story.

The actors and actresses in the theatre company play fifteen speaking roles and some nonspeaking parts, and the audience responds enthusiastically to the performances. Though the play has thirteen scenes in different locations, all the action takes place on the platform stage. It is easy to follow the action because—through a combination of dialogue and properties, such as a throne—the playwright and the performers let the spectators know exactly where they are in every scene. The scenes are divided into three acts; during intermissions between the acts, the spectators are also entertained by short comic pieces and musical interludes.

As the play continues, Sancho appeals to the king to help him regain Elvira from Don Tello; after several complications, the king arrives in disguise. When the king discovers that Don Tello has forcibly seduced Elvira, he orders Don Tello to marry her and then has him executed so that Elvira will be honorably widowed and can marry Sancho. At this conclusion, everyone in the audience—in the galleries as well as the pit—is pleased that justice has been done.

were written in three acts, and like English Renaissance plays, they were extensive or episodic in form. Comedias mix serious and comic subject matter and are very similar to modern melodrama. Thus if Spanish plays of the golden age are very close to Elizabethan drama in their dramatic form, they seem closer in their subject matter to the swashbuckling films of the 1940s, romantic novels, and television soap operas.

Besides full-length plays, the Spaniards developed many popular, short, farcical forms. A short farce of this kind would be presented on the same program with a comedia.

The major playwrights of this period were Lope de Vega (1562–1635) and Calderón de la Barca (1600–1681). Lope de Vega was born within a year of Shakespeare and was a remarkable playwright—one of the most prolific dramatists of all time. He is said to have written 1,500 plays (although 800 is a more realistic figure); 470 of them survive, one of the best-known being *The Sheep Well* (c. 1614). One of Calderón's most famous plays is *Life Is a Dream* (c. 1636).

THE CLASSIC SPANISH STAGE
The corrales were outdoor courtyard theatres used for the presentation of secular drama during the Spanish Golden Age. These playhouses were similar to the public theatres of the English Renaissance. A corral uncovered accidentally in Almagro, Spain, in 1955 is shown here. A theatre festival is staged in this space every year. (Courtesy Festival d'Almagro)

There were also a number of female playwrights in Spain during the seventeenth century, though most of their works were not produced. However, recent scholarship has shown that these women wrote texts subverting many of the traditions of the comedias and calling into question the traditional views of gender roles, love and honor, and political authority. Female playwrights of the Spanish Golden Age whose works have received significant scholarly attention are Angela de Azevedo, Ana Caro Mallén de Soto, Leonor de la Cueva y Silva, Feliciana Enríquez de Guzmán, María de Zayas y Sotomayor, and Sor Juana Inés de la Cruz.

THEATRE PRODUCTION IN SPAIN

The Corrales   Nonreligious plays by writers like Lope de Vega and Calderón were staged in public theatres known as **corrales** (the plural of *corral*). Corrales were constructed in existing courtyards; like Elizabethan public theatres, they were open-air spaces with galleries and boxes protected by a roof. These courtyard theatres were temporary at first but later became permanent spaces. The two most famous were both in Madrid: the Corral de la Cruz (1579) and the Corral del Principe (1583).

The stage in a corral was a platform erected opposite the entrance to the yard. Access to the yard was usually through a street building; there were also several entranceways for other seating areas. The yard floor or *patio* was primarily an area for standing and, like the pit of an Elizabethan public theatre, was a raucous area. At the front of

Corral Theatre of the Spanish Golden Age, usually located in the courtyard of a series of adjoining buildings.

A SPANISH CORRAL
This illustration is based on John J. Allen's research on the Corral del Principe in Madrid. Note the various elements of the corral: the yard (patio), the seating areas (boxes and galleries), and the platform stage with the tiring house behind it. Note also that in front of the yard there were benches or stools and that seats are set up at the side of stage. In addition, notice how similar the face of the building behind the stage was to the facade of the Elizabethan tiring house.

the yard, near the stage, a row of stools—later, a few benches—were set up, separated from the rest of the yard by a railing.

In the back wall opposite the stage, above the main entranceway in the yard, was a gallery for unaccompanied women known as the ***cazuela*** (cah-zoo-EHL-ah); it had its own separate entrance and was carefully guarded to prevent men from entering. Above the cazuela, there was a row of boxes for local government officials; above these boxes was a larger gallery for the clergy. Along the side walls of the yard were elevated benches and above them windows, protected by grills, from which a play could be viewed. On the next level were boxes that extended out from the buildings around the courtyard. A fourth floor had cramped boxes with low ceilings. At the back of the yard, on one side of the main entrance, was a refreshments box, the ***alojeria,*** from which food and drinks were sold.

Cazuela Gallery above the tavern in the back wall of the theatres of the Spanish Golden Age; the area where unescorted women sat.

Alojeria The refreshment box in Spanish Golden Age theatre.

A corral held about 2,000 spectators: 1,000 places for men, 350 for women, and the rest reserved boxes and other accommodations for government officials and the clergy.

Scenic conventions in Spain were similar to those in England. A two-story facade behind the platform stage was the basic scenic construction; a curtain, props, and flats might be used in conjunction with this facade. There were three openings for entrances, exits, and scenes of concealment, as well as an upper playing area. The facade, therefore, served the same function as the Elizabethan tiring house. Spoken dialogue was also used to indicate locale.

Spanish Acting Companies   In Spain during the golden age, acting troupes consisted of sixteen to twenty performers. Unlike Elizabethan companies, these Spanish companies included women. In many places on the European continent—in contrast to England—women had been allowed to act in medieval religious drama, and the inclusion of women in Spanish companies during the Renaissance was an outgrowth of this custom. The church, though, did not support the use of female performers; as a result, the Spanish government was forced to impose stringent restrictions on women working in the theatre—for instance, only a woman who was married or otherwise related to an actor in a troupe could be employed. Most Spanish acting troupes were *compañías de partes* (cahm-pa-NYEE-ahs day PAHR-teh)—sharing companies, like those of Elizabethan England. Some companies, however, were organized by a manager who contracted performers for a specific period of time.

FRANCE

BACKGROUND: FRANCE IN THE SEVENTEENTH CENTURY

Renaissance theatre did not reach its zenith in France until the seventeenth century, later than in Italy, England, or Spain. This was partly due to a religious civil war taking place in France between Catholics and Protestants, a war that was finally brought to an end in 1594 when Henry IV formulated the Edict of Nantes, which offered religious tolerance to Catholics and Protestants. With religious and political stability established in the seventeenth century, French society was able to flourish under Louis XIV, who ruled from 1643 to 1715. Among France's significant accomplishments during this period was exploration of the new world, particularly in Canada and the Louisiana Territory of the United States.

During this period, French society was greatly influenced by the innovations of the Italian Renaissance. As we shall see, French theatre in the seventeenth century adopted and adapted many of the Italian theatrical innovations.

FRENCH DRAMA: THE NEOCLASSICAL ERA

The most important seventeenth-century French dramatists were Molière, noted for his comedies; and two authors known for tragedy: Pierre Corneille and Jean Racine.

Among all the French neoclassical playwrights, the one who exerts the most influence on modern theatre is Molière (Jean-Baptiste Poquelin; 1622–1673). Molière was not only a dramatist but also an actor and the leader of a theatrical troupe. His first theatre venture in Paris was a failure, and so he toured the provinces for twelve years,

LE BOURGEOIS GENTILHOMME
One of Molière's most popular works is *Le Bourgeois Gentilhomme (The Bourgeois Gentleman)* about a self-important man who puts on airs, attempting to move into the upper class. He takes lessons of all kinds—dancing, fencing, reading—but in each case makes a fool of himself without realizing it. The scene here shows the would-be gentleman, Jourdain, on the right, fencing with his maid, Nicole, as his wife looks on. The oil painting on canvas is by Charles Robert Leslie. (Bridgeman Art Library/Victoria and Albert Museum, London)

learning firsthand the techniques of theatre and perfecting his craft as a dramatist. He then returned to establish himself as France's leading actor-manager and playwright, specializing in comedies of character.

Molière's work was strongly influenced by Italian commedia dell'arte. In plays like *Tartuffe* (1664), *The Misanthrope* (1666), *The Miser* (1668), and *The Imaginary Invalid* (1673), he creates exaggerated character types and makes fun of their eccentricities. The title character in *The Miser,* for example, is a man so greedy and so possessive of his money that he becomes paranoid when he thinks anyone knows where he has hidden it; in protecting his treasure, he even turns against his children. Molière was a master of slapstick as well as more subtle kinds of comedy, and he frequently used a *deus ex machina* to resolve his contrived plots.

Pierre Corneille (1606–1684) began his career writing comedies but soon turned to tragedy. His play *The Cid,* which opened in 1636, became a huge success. It aroused opposition from intellectuals because it did not follow the neoclassic rules established by Italian critics; despite this, it remained enormously popular and was presented frequently

NEOCLASSICAL FRANCE

THEATRE

YEAR, C.E.

CULTURE AND POLITICS

Jacques Cartier (1491-1547)
(Library and Archives Canada)

1500

Confraternity of the Passion (founded 1402)
given monopoly of Paris theatre (1518)

1525

Exploration of Gulf of St. Lawrence by
Jacques Cartier (1534-1535)

Religious plays prohibited; Hôtel de Bourgogne opens;
perspective scenery used for first time at Lyon for
performance celebrating marriage of Henri II and
Catherine de Médicis (1548)

Henri II (rules 1547-1559)

1550

Outbreak of civil war between
Protestants and royal troops (1562)

St. Bartholomew's Day massacre;
Protestants killed (1572)

*Theatre at Cardinal Richelieu's
Palace (1641)*
(Erich Lessing/Art Resource, NY)

1575

Montaigne's *Essays* (1580)

Alexandre Hardy, first professional
playwright, flourishes (1597)

Assassination of Henri III; Henri IV reigns (1589)

Henri IV abjures Protestantism (1593)

Valleran le Comte (King's Players), first
important theatrical manager (1598)

Edict of Nantes (1598)

1600

Farce players, Turlupin, Gaultier-Garguille,
Gros-Guillaume popular (1610-1625)

Permanent French outpost
in Quebec (1608)

Henri IV assassinated (1610);
Louis XIII (rules 1610-1643)

1625

Richelieu enters royal council (1624)

Théâtre du Marais (1634)

Richelieu's Palais Cardinal
opens (later renamed
Palais-Royal) (1641)

Corneille's *Le Cid* (1636)

Descartes's *Discourse on Method* (1637)

Richelieu's death (Mazarin's takeover) (1642)

New Marais with
proscenium arch (1644)

Torelli brings Italianate
innovations to France (1645)

Death of Louis XIII; Louis XIV (rules 1643-1715)

Bourgogne remodeled
(proscenium added) (1647)

Civil war (1648-1652)

1650

Molière's troupe given
Palais-Royal (1660)

Vigarini comes to France (1659)

Louis XIV ("Sun King") personal reign (1661)

Molière's *The Miser* (1668)

Jean-Baptiste Lully given monopoly of
musical performances in Paris (1672)

Founding of the French Academy
of Science (1666)

After Molière's death, Marais and his
company amalgamated by Louis XIV (1673)

Racine's
Phaedra (1677)

1675

Comédie Française
founded (1680)

Comédie Française gets new
theatre, to be used until 1770 (1689)

Revocation of Edict of Nantes (1685)

Anglo-Dutch coalition wars against
France (1689-1713)

Paris commedia troupe expelled (1697)

1700

Louis XIV dies (1715)

Racine's Phaedra *(1677)*
(© Geraint Lewis)

1725

not only in France but in other European countries. Corneille, however, stopped writing plays for four years. Because of the controversy, when he resumed playwriting, he adhered more closely to the neoclassical rules.

Jean Racine (1639–1699) was the other great writer of tragedy in seventeenth-century France. Unlike Corneille, he was comfortable with the neoclassic rules from the start; all of Racine's tragedies adhere to these rules.

One of Racine's best-known tragedies, *Phaedra* (1677), is based on a play by Euripides. In Racine's version, Phaedra, queen to King Theseus, falls in love with her stepson, Hippolytus. Upon hearing that Theseus has died, she admits her love to Hippolytus, who reacts with disgust. When Phaedra discovers that Theseus is not dead, she allows her maid to spread the rumor that it was Hippolytus who made amorous advances to Phaedra, rather than the other way around. Hearing the rumor and believing it, Theseus invokes a god to kill his son Hippolytus, after which a heartbroken Phaedra takes poison—before she dies, however, she reveals the truth.

Racine's *Phaedra* is a perfect example of climactic plot structure: it has only a few characters, and the action takes place in one place at one time. Furthermore, Racine's masterful handling of poetry and emotion established a model to be followed in France for the next three centuries.

THEATRE PRODUCTION IN FRANCE

The French were probably the first Europeans after the Romans to construct a permanent theatre building. This was the Hôtel de Bourgogne, completed in 1548. The Bourgogne was built by the Confraternity of the Passion, a religious order that had been granted a monopoly for the presentation of religious drama in Paris. When religious drama was outlawed—in the same year that the Bourgogne was completed—the Confraternity rented its space to touring companies.

The Hôtel de Bourgogne, a long, narrow building with a platform stage at one end, was the sole permanent indoor theatre building in Paris for nearly a century until the Théâtre du Marais opened in 1634. The Marais was a converted indoor tennis court. Such indoor courts were long and narrow—like the Bourgogne—and had galleries for spectators (court tennis was a popular sport); thus they could be transformed into theatres very easily.

PHAEDRA

Racine's *Phèdre* (also known as *Phaedra* in other translations) is probably the best-known neoclassical tragedy. It is the story of a queen who falls in love with her stepson, with the result that everyone involved—including these two, as well as Phaedra's husband—meets a tragic end. Shown here is Helen Mirren, in the title role, with Dominic Cooper as her stepson, Hippolytus, in a new version by Ted Hughes directed by Nicholas Hytner at London's National Theatre. (© Geraint Lewis)

1669, PARIS The date is February 9, 1669. At the Palais-Royal theatre in Paris, France, spectators are eagerly awaiting a performance of *Tartuffe,* written by France's best-known comic playwright and actor, Molière.

Tartuffe has already been the cause of an enormous controversy. Molière first read it four years ago to King Louis XIV at his palace at Versailles; the king liked it, but before it could be presented publicly, it provoked an uproar. The reason is its subject matter. The title character of the play, Tartuffe, is a religious hypocrite. He pretends to be very pious and wears clothing that looks like a religious habit, but he is actually interested in acquiring money and seducing women. He has come to live in the house of Orgon, a wealthy man who has been completely taken in by Tartuffe's false piety.

The people who oppose the presentation of *Tartuffe* include a number of religious figures (one of them is the archbishop of Paris) who say that it is an attack on religion. Molière, however, insists that his play is not an attack on religion but rather an attack on people who hide behind religion and exploit it.

The audience is aware that until now the opposition has been successful in keeping *Tartuffe* out of theatres; the king did not dare authorize its presentation as long as the forces against it were so strong. So far, the play has been presented only once, in the summer of 1667, and then for only one night. The king was out of the country at that time, and in his absence the religious authorities had it closed down. Now, however, *Tartuffe* has finally been given royal approval, and today's performance is to be its official public unveiling.

The Palais-Royal theatre, where Molière's troupe performs, is a rectangular space with a stage at one end and galleries on three sides around it. It accommodates almost 1,500 people: 300 stand in a "pit" in front of the stage, about 700 sit in a raised amphitheatre behind the pit, about 330 sit in the galleries, 70 stand at the very back, and 50 wealthy nobles sit on the sides of the stage itself. Having spectators onstage is customary in French theatres but makes things very difficult for the performers.

The stage is fitted with wings and shutters, like Italian Renaissance theatres, and scenery can be changed with a pole-and-chariot system. For *Tartuffe,* however, there will be no scene changes: the entire action takes place in the drawing room of Orgon's house.

Well aware of all the scandal and debate, the audience feels a rush of anticipation as this performance of *Tartuffe* begins. Once it is under way, though, the spectators realize that the controversial figure of Tartuffe does not even make an appearance for two full acts. Rather, it is the figure of Orgon, played by Molière himself, on whom they first concentrate. The spectators see that Orgon is thoroughly duped and pays no attention to the members of his family when they tell him how dishonest and disreputable Tartuffe is.

Finally, in the third act, Tartuffe makes his entrance. He is challenged by Orgon's family, but Orgon remains loyal to him. Only when Orgon learns for himself the awful truth about Tartuffe does he realize his error. This occurs in a scene in which Orgon, hiding under a table, hears Tartuffe try to seduce his wife. The wife has led Tartuffe on, and he exposes himself as a genuine scoundrel. As the audience members watch the scene, they think it is one of the funniest they have ever seen.

Orgon's discovery of Tartuffe's true nature seems to come too late: at this point, Orgon has already handed his house and his fortune over to Tartuffe, disinheriting his own children. At the end of the play, though, the king intervenes. This is the same Louis XIV who in real life has intervened on Molière's behalf so that the play can be presented.

A few weeks from now, both king and playwright will be vindicated: *Tartuffe* will be performed twenty-eight times in a row—an unprecedented number—and will show every sign of becoming a classic comedy.

READ *Tartuffe* in *Anthology of Living Theatre* or at:

• http://www.gutenberg.org/ebooks/2027

The Italian influence on French theatre architecture became evident in 1641, when Cardinal Richelieu, a leading political figure, erected the Palais Cardinal, renamed the Palais-Royal after his death. This is the theatre that Molière's troupe eventually used. The Palais Cardinal was the first proscenium-arch theatre in France and also had Italian-style machinery to shift scenery. Following the construction of Richelieu's theatre, the Théâtre du Marais and the Hôtel de Bourgogne were remodeled in the 1640s into proscenium-arch theatres. Painted-perspective wing-and-shutter scenery—shifted by the pole-and-chariot system—was used in the two remodeled theatres.

Early French proscenium-arch theatre buildings differed slightly from those of the Italian Renaissance: in the back wall opposite the stage was an ***amphithéâtre,*** an undivided gallery with inexpensive bleacherlike seating. In both the Marais and the Bourgogne, there was probably a small upper stage, raised thirteen feet above the main stage and was used for special effects such as flying. At the close of the seventeenth century, upper-class audience members were frequently seated onstage.

In the 1650s, Louis XIV's interest in ballet brought this form of entertainment back into prominence at court. To satisfy the royal taste for elaborate ballets and to prepare for Louis's marriage, a new court theatre was built, known as the Salle des Machines ("Hall of Machines"). It was completed in 1660 and was the largest playhouse in Europe: 52 feet wide and 232 feet long. The auditorium took up only 92 feet of the 232-foot length, leaving 140 feet for the stage and its machinery. The backstage equipment included one piece of machinery on which the entire royal family and all their attendants—more than 100 people—could be "flown" into the space above the stage. Because of its unsatisfactory acoustics, its size (especially backstage), and the expense of producing spectacles, the Salle des Machines was rarely used after 1670.

Amphithéâtre An undivided gallery with inexpensive bleacherlike seating in the back wall at the French neo-classical theatre.

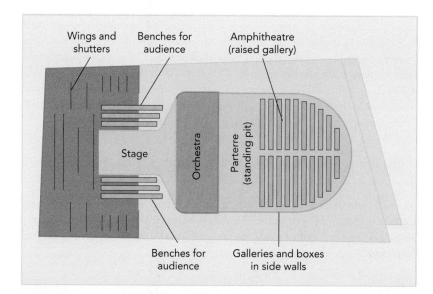

Wings and shutters

Benches for audience

Amphitheatre (raised gallery)

Stage

Orchestra

Parterre (standing pit)

Benches for audience

Galleries and boxes in side walls

GROUND PLAN OF THE COMÉDIE FRANÇAISE
The French national theatre company performed in this playhouse for eighty-one years, beginning in 1689. The theatre had a proscenium-arch stage with machinery for scene shifts, and a horseshoe-shaped auditorium for improved sight lines. The parterre was where audience members stood; the amphitheatre contained bleacherlike seating.

Another major theatre building of the French neoclassical period was the Comédie Française, which housed the national theatre. The French national theatre had been founded by Louis XIV in 1680, but the company did not move into its own building until 1689. The interior of the Comédie Française featured a horseshoe-shape construction, which meant that the sight lines were significantly better than those in other French spaces of the time.

Acting companies in French neoclassical theatres were organized under a sharing plan and had women members who could become shareholders. Rehearsals were supervised by the playwright or a leading performer or both, but troupes spent little time on rehearsals. Once a play was introduced, the troupe was expected to be able to revive it at a moment's notice, and the bill at theatres was changed daily.

The Renaissance in Italy, England, Spain, and France saw significant—even revolutionary—changes in theatrical practices. Many of these practices will be built on as we look at developments in theatre from the Restoration through Romanticism, in Chapter 13.

SUMMARY

During the Italian Renaissance, the neoclassical rules for drama were formulated. Commedia dell'arte developed as a popular theatre, based on stock characters, repeated pieces of comic business, and recognizable costumes. Painted-perspective scenery, which could be changed easily, and the proscenium-arch theatre were both introduced, leading to greater verisimilitude—the quality of being true to life—in theatre.

During the English Renaissance—the Elizabethan Age—the great plays of Shakespeare and his contemporaries were being staged. Outdoor public theatres and indoor private theatres accommodated these extensive-form dramas through the use of an unlocalized platform stage and a flexible tiring house, or stage house. Brilliant poetic language also helped set the action.

In Spain during its golden age, the secular dramas of Lope de Vega and Calderón de la Barca were performed in corrales, theatres built in courtyards. Corrales used many of the same staging conventions as Elizabethan theatres.

In French neoclassical theatre, the tragic dramas of Corneille and Racine and the comedies of character by Molière were clearly patterned after traditions established in the Italian Renaissance. French theatre architecture and design were also based on Italian models.

THINKING ABOUT THEATRE

▶ Describe the physical theatre spaces (stage configuration, scenery, audience seating) employed in each of the following eras: (a) the Italian Renaissance; (b) the English Renaissance; (c) the Spanish Golden Age; (d) the French neoclassical. What are the advantages and disadvantages of each type?

- Describe the type of drama featured (the structure and content of dramatic scripts) in each of the eras mentioned in the first item above.

- While Shakespeare's plays are considered to be classics, identify at least three similarities between his works and popular contemporary film and television.

- Molière authored comedies that focused on exaggerated comic types and their eccentricities. Identify and describe at least three examples of popular films and television shows that also focus on these types of characters and their eccentric behavior.

KEY TERMS

Alojeria The refreshment box in Spanish Golden Age theatre.

Amphithéâtre An undivided gallery with inexpensive bleacherlike seating in the back wall of the French neoclassical theatre.

Box Small private compartment for a group of spectators built into the walls of traditional proscenium-arch and other theatres.

Cazuela Gallery above the tavern in the back wall of the theatres of the Spanish Golden Age; the area where unescorted women sat.

Comedia Full-length (three-act) nonreligious play of the Spanish Golden Age.

Corral Theatre of the Spanish Golden Age, usually located in the courtyard of a series of adjoining buildings.

Gallery In theatre buildings, the undivided seating area cut into the walls of the building.

Groove system System in which tracks on the stage floor and above the stage allowed for the smooth movement of flat wings onto and off the stage; usually there were a series of grooves at each stage position.

Lazzi Comic pieces of business used repeatedly by characters in Italian commedia dell'arte.

Neoclassical ideals Rules developed by critics during the Italian Renaissance, supposedly based on the writings of Aristotle.

Perspective Illusion of depth in painting, introduced into scene design during the Italian Renaissance.

Pit Floor of the house in Renaissance theatres. It was originally a standing area; by the end of the eighteenth century, backless benches were added in most countries.

Public theatres Outdoor theatres in Elizabethan England.

Slapstick A type of comedy or comic business that relies on exaggerated or ludicrous physical activity for its humor.

Unities Term referring to the preference that a play's plot occur within one day (unity of time), in one place (unity of place), and with no action irrelevant to the plot (unity of action).

Zanni Comic male servants in Italian commedia dell'arte.

THEATRE ON THE WEB

For more research and to learn more about the topics in this chapter, please visit the Online Learning Center at **www.mhhe.com/livelyart8e**.

THEATRES FROM THE RESTORATION THROUGH ROMANTICISM

13

THE ENGLISH RESTORATION

BACKGROUND: ENGLAND IN THE SEVENTEENTH CENTURY

RESTORATION DRAMA: COMEDIES OF MANNERS

TIMELINE: English Restoration

THEATRE PRODUCTION IN THE RESTORATION

LIVING HISTORY: *The Country Wife*

THE EIGHTEENTH CENTURY

BACKGROUND: A MORE COMPLEX WORLD

EIGHTEENTH-CENTURY DRAMA: NEW DRAMATIC FORMS

TIMELINE: Eighteenth Century

THEATRE PRODUCTION IN THE EIGHTEENTH CENTURY

LIVING HISTORY: *The Marriage of Figaro*

THE NINETEENTH CENTURY

BACKGROUND: A TIME OF SOCIAL CHANGE

MAKING CONNECTIONS: Nineteenth-Century Popular Theatrical Arts

TIMELINE: Nineteenth Century, 1800 to 1875

THEATRE IN NINETEENTH-CENTURY LIFE

NINETEENTH-CENTURY DRAMATIC FORMS

THEATRE PRODUCTION IN THE NINETEENTH CENTURY

SUMMARY

THINKING ABOUT THEATRE

KEY TERMS

THEATRE ON THE WEB

◀ **EIGHTEENTH-CENTURY ENGLISH COMEDY** *The Rivals* by playwright Richard Brinsley Sheridan is a prime example of the English Sentimental or laughing comedy of the eighteenth century in which audiences were led to laugh at their foibles, excesses, and eccentricities. Shown here are Kristie Dale Sanders as Lucy and Monique Fowler as Mrs. Malaprop in a production of *The Rivals* at the Shakespeare Theatre of New Jersey. (© Gerry Goodstein)

The period from 1660 to 1875 saw radical transformations in Western society. Revolutions and nationalism led to changes in governments and the establishment of new nations. Mechanization and new technology transformed work, the workplace, and economic classes. Innovations in modes of transportation made travel easier, both within nations and internationally. Theatre mirrored the social, political, and economic issues of the times, and it too was transformed. In this chapter, we will examine the theatre of England in the late seventeenth century as well as developments in worldwide, global theatre in the eighteenth and nineteenth centuries.

THE ENGLISH RESTORATION

BACKGROUND: ENGLAND IN THE SEVENTEENTH CENTURY

After a bitter civil war lasting from 1642 to 1649, Charles I of England was removed from the throne by the Puritans and beheaded. For the next eleven years, England was a Commonwealth eventually governed by Oliver Cromwell with a Parliament that had been purged of all his opponents.

When Cromwell died in 1658, his son was unable to keep control of the government; and in 1660 Charles II, who had been living in exile in France, was invited by a newly elected Parliament to return and rule England. The monarchy was thus restored, and this period in English history—usually dated from 1660 through 1700—is therefore called the *Restoration.*

During the period of the Commonwealth, many members of the English nobility had been exiles in France; when the English monarchy returned, these people took back with them the theatrical practices they had seen in France.

RESTORATION DRAMA: COMEDIES OF MANNERS

The theatres that reopened in England represented a fusion of Elizabethan, Italian, and French stage conventions. This gave a unique flavor to every aspect of Restoration theatre: texts, theatre buildings, and set designs.

The best-known Restoration comedies, many of which were influenced by the French dramatist Molière, are referred to as ***comedies of manners.*** They poked fun at the social conventions of the upper class of the time and satirized the preoccupation of English aristocrats with reputation: most of the upper-class characters in these plays are disreputable. Emphasizing witty dialogue and filled with sexual intrigue and innuendo, the plays took an amoral attitude toward human behavior, including sex. Audiences consisted primarily of members of the nobility and the upper class, the same people whom the playwrights were satirizing.

In their dramatic structure, Restoration comedies combine features of Elizabethan theatre and the neoclassical theatre of Italy and France. For example, in *The Country Wife* by William Wycherley (1640–1715), the action is far more unified than in a Shakespearean play, with fewer scene shifts. But it does move from place to place, involves many characters, and even has a subplot. The characters in Wycherley's play are stock types with names that usually describe their distinctive personality traits. Fidget and Squeamish are nervous about their reputations; Pinchwife is a man who doesn't want his wife pinched by other men; and Sparkish is a fop who mistakenly believes himself to be a real "spark," witty and fashionable.

Comedy of manners Form of comic drama satirizing social conventions that became popular in seventeenth-century France and the English Restoration, and which emphasized a cultivated or sophisticated atmosphere and witty dialogue.

ENGLISH RESTORATION

THEATRE	YEAR	CULTURE AND POLITICS
Parliament closes theatres (1642)	1640	English civil war (1642)
	1645	
		Execution of Charles I (1649)
	1650	Hobbes's *Leviathan* (1651)
		Anglo-Dutch Wars (1652–1674)
		Protectorate under Oliver Cromwell (1653–1658)
Davenant's *The First Day's Entertainment at Rutland House;*	1655	
Siege of Rhodes (designer John Webb) (1656)		Cromwell dies (1658)
Davenant's and Killigrew's companies granted patents (women in companies) (1660)	1660	Restoration of Charles II; Navigation Acts (1660)
Lincoln Inn Fields Theatre (1661)		
Thomas Betterton foremost actor (c. 1662)		Royal Society founded (science) (1662)
	1665	
		Milton's *Paradise Lost* (1667)
Dorset Garden (1671)	1670	Treaty of Dover between Charles II and Louis XIV (1670)
		Habeas Corpus Act (1679)
New Drury Lane opens (1674)		Wren's Tom Tower, Christ Church, Oxford (1681)
Wycherley's *The Country Wife* (1675)	1675	
Dryden's *All for Love* (1677)		
Aphra Behn's *The Rover* (1677)		
	1680	
Otway's *Venice Preserved* (1682)		
	1685	
Actress Nell Gwynn (1650–1687)		James II rules (1687)
		Newton's laws of gravity (1687)
		William and Mary; Glorious Revolution (1688)
	1690	Locke's *Essay Concerning Human Understanding* (1690)
	1695	Bank of England established (1694)
Mary Pix's *The Innocent Mistress* (1697)		
Collier's *Short View of the Immorality and Profaneness of the English Stage* (1698)		
Congreve's *The Way of the World* (1700)	1700	

Thomas Killigrew (1612–1683)
(© National Portrait Gallery, London)

William and Mary
crowned (1688)

Nell Gwyn (1650–1687) with Charles II
(Bettmann/Corbis)

FEMALE PLAYWRIGHTS IN THE RESTORATION
There were a number of significant female playwrights during the Restoration. Among them was Aphra Behn, whose works are frequently revived today. Seen here is a production of her most famous comedy of intrigue, *The Rover,* as staged at Illinois State University. (© Peter Guither)

Other types of Restoration comedies included comedies of humors and comedies of intrigue. Comedies of humors followed the tradition of Ben Jonson in which characters have one trait overshadowing all others. Comedies of intrigue featured daring exploits of romance and adventure and had complicated plots. One of the most successful writers of this type of comedy was a woman, Aphra Behn (1640–1689), whose most famous play is *The Rover* (1677).

Another well-known comic playwright of the Restoration is William Congreve (1670–1729). Congreve's *The Way of the World* (1700) is often considered a bridge between Restoration comedy and the later, more traditional morality of eighteenth-century English sentimental comedy. In eighteenth-century English comedy, as we will see, the sinful are punished and the virtuous are rewarded. Like Restoration comedy, *The Way of the World* has a number of characters involved in adulterous affairs, as well as the traditional stock characters; but its two young lovers, Mirabell and Millamant, are united, while the wicked characters, Fainall and Marwood, are punished.

Following the lead of Aphra Behn, female playwrights emerged at this time. The London season of 1695–1696 saw productions by seven female dramatists. Three women, known as the "female wits," were active in the period that marked the end of the Restoration and the beginning of the eighteenth century. They included Mary Pix (1666–1706), Delarivière Manley (c. 1663–1724), and Catherine Trotter (1679–1749). Another transitional female playwright was Susana Centlivre, (c. 1667–1723), whose best-known works are *The Gamester* (1705) and *The Busy Body* (1709).

Many Restoration comedies, including *The Country Wife,* indicate that audiences of that era, unlike today's audiences, were quite spirited during theatrical presentations.

The fop Sparkish in *The Country Wife* describes how audience members bought fruit from the "orange wenches" (some of whom were prostitutes), spoke back to the performers, arranged assignations, and attended theatre to be seen rather than to see the play. These extratheatrical activities increased attacks on theatre by religious leaders, who were generally opposed to theatre anyway.

READ *The Way of the World*

http://online-literature.com/congreve/way-of-the-world/

READ *The Busy Body* in *Anthology of Living Theatre* or at:

http://www.gutenberg.org/ebooks/16740

THEATRE PRODUCTION IN THE RESTORATION

Performers and Acting Companies In theatre production, the most obvious difference between the English Renaissance and the Restoration was the appearance of women on the English stage.

Another change was that in London the sharing plan followed by companies like Shakespeare's almost disappeared during the Restoration. Instead, London performers were hired for a specific period of time at a set salary. In order to increase the set wage, an actor or actress was provided with a yearly *benefit,* a performance of a play from which he or she kept all the profits. The benefit system was used in English theatre from the Restoration through the nineteenth century.

The Restoration also saw the emergence of theatrical entrepreneurs who were often part owners of theatre buildings and companies. The rise of the entrepreneur as a powerful theatrical force was, of course, a step in the development of modern theatre business with its independent theatre owners and producers.

Government and Theatre When English theatre was restored in 1660, Charles II issued patents to two entrepreneurs, William Davenant and Thomas Killigrew (1612–1683), which in effect gave them a monopoly on presenting theatre in London.

By the early eighteenth century, this monopoly would become unenforceable, however; and in 1737 Parliament was to pass the Licensing Act, a new attempt to regulate London theatre. Under this act, only two theatres—Drury Lane and Covent Garden—were authorized to present drama for "gain, hire, or reward," and the lord chamberlain became responsible for licensing plays.

RESTORATION DRAMA: COMEDIES OF MANNERS
During the period of the English Restoration, beginning in 1660, the most popular plays were comedies that satirized the upper classes—their gossip, emphasis on dress and decorum, infidelity, sexuality, and conspiracies. In the scene here from William Congreve's *The Way of the World,* Andrew Long plays Fainall and Deanne Lorette plays Mrs. Marwood in a Restoration comedy of manners, which put a premium on language (including sexual double meanings). This production was directed by Michael Kahn at the Shakespeare Theatre Company in Washington, D.C. (© Carol Rosegg)

1675, LONDON, ENGLAND It is a raw, overcast day in January 1675, and two young men—members of the nobility—have set forth to the theatre in London. They are making their way to the new Drury Lane Theatre. Another theatre once stood at the site of the Drury Lane, but it burned in 1672; the new theatre, designed by the architect Christopher Wren and erected on the same spot, opened only a year ago, in 1674.

The play they will see is a new one by William Wycherley called *The Country Wife*. They anticipate that they will hear witty, rapier-like exchanges between the characters, and doubtless many double entendres: clever lines that operate on two levels, one ordinary and the other decidedly sexual.

It is just after two o'clock in the afternoon. The play will not begin until 3:30, but the young men want to arrive at the theatre early—to talk to their acquaintances, to flirt with the attractive young women who sell oranges and other things to eat, and even to go backstage to try to see the actresses. As they arrive at the playhouse, the young men join a carefree, pleasure-loving crowd.

The new Drury Lane—a building 58 feet wide by 140 feet long—seats 650 people, some in a pit facing the stage, others in boxes and galleries along the sides and back. Its stage is a platform about 34 feet deep; the front half of the stage is open, and the back half—framed by a proscenium—contains the scenic elements.

When the performance begins, the first person onstage is an actor named Charles Hart, who delivers a prologue; then the play itself starts. Hart plays a character called Horner, who spreads the rumor that he has been rendered impotent by a venereal disease he contracted while abroad. Horner's doctor, Quack, substantiates the rumor, and Horner uses this "cover story" to gain access to his acquaintances' wives; because of his supposed condition, the husbands will regard him as no threat. The wife he most desires is Margery Pinchwife, a naive woman whose husband usually keeps her locked away in the country and tries to disguise her as a boy when they are in town. Coming upon Pinchwife and the disguised Margery in the street, Horner realizes that the "boy" is a woman in a man's clothing and takes advantage of the situation to make amorous advances, hugging and kissing her in front of her husband, who can do nothing. During the course of the dramatic action, a subplot develops: Horner's friend Harcourt steals Pinchwife's sister Alithea away from her intended husband, Sparkish.

The young male spectators are particularly taken with Elizabeth Bowtell, who plays Margery. In France and Spain, women have appeared onstage for some time; but England forbade actresses until 1660—only a few years ago—and seeing them now is a novelty that strongly appeals to the men in the audience. Moreover, ever since women have been allowed to perform onstage in England, a favorite dramatic device is to have a woman dress as a man; parts that require this kind of cross-dressing are called *breeches roles*. Seeing a woman's legs—which are usually hidden under wide skirts—has a strong sexual fascination.

The audience is also titillated by the sexual references, especially by a scene which is to become famous—the "china closet" scene. In this scene, Horner and Lady Fidget are in a room offstage while Lady Fidget's husband is onstage listening to their conversation. Horner and Lady Fidget are supposed to be examining Horner's collection of china, but the audience soon realizes that though Horner is speaking about china, he is actually making love to Lady Fidget while her husband stands by in ignorance. Then another woman, Mrs. Squeamish, arrives, and she too asks to see Horner's china. When Horner tells Mrs. Squeamish he has no more, the audience knows that china has become a code word for sex and that Horner is unable at that moment to make love.

At the conclusion of the play, Horner's scheme has been successful: he has made love not only to Margery but to the other wives as well.

READ *The Country Wife*

http://publish.uwo.ca/~shroyer/authors/Wycherley/texts/country_wife.html

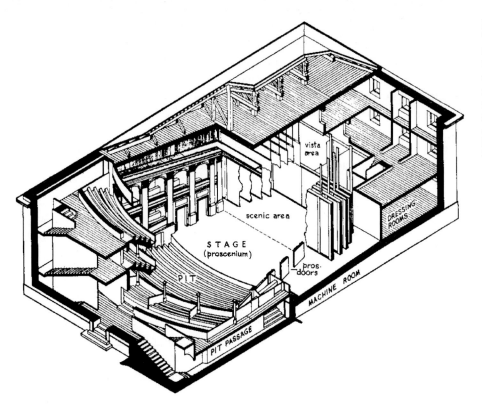

DRURY LANE THEATRE
This reconstruction of the Drury Lane Theatre in the Restoration period shows Christopher Wren's design for the Theatre Royal, Drury Lane, 1674. Note the pit for the audience and the two doors on each side of the stage. (From Richard Leacroft, in *The Theatre,* Roy Publishers, p. 34)

Theatre Architecture

During the Restoration, there were three theatres of note in London: Drury Lane (1663); Lincoln Inn Fields (1661), a converted tennis court; and Dorset Garden (1671). Though the interiors of these theatres were distinct, all three showed a unique fusion of Italian and Elizabethan features.

All Restoration theatres were indoor proscenium-arch buildings. The area for the audience was divided into pit, boxes, and galleries and had a total seating capacity of about 650. The pit, which had backless benches to accommodate spectators, was raked—or slanted—for better sight lines.

The Restoration stage was highly unusual in that it was divided into two equal halves by the proscenium arch. In the seventeenth century, only English theatres had this extended apron, and most historians believe that it was a vestige of the Elizabethan platform stage. The deep apron was a major performance area in Restoration theatres; the upstage area housed the scenery. The entire stage was raked to improve the spectators' sight lines.

Another unique element of the Restoration stage was the proscenium doors, with balconies above them. On each side of the stage there were two proscenium doors leading onto the forestage. These doors were used for exits and entrances and for concealment scenes—scenes in which one character listens from out of sight, a popular device in Restoration comedy. The balconies above these doorways could be used for balcony and window scenes.

Scenery, Lighting, and Costumes

Restoration scenery and lighting also illustrate a fusion of Italian and English stage practices. The basic scenic components were wings, shutters, which were sometimes replaced by rolled backdrops, and borders for masking. The English rarely used the pole-and-chariot system for scene changes; instead, they used the groove system. Throughout the Restoration, companies kept collections of stock sets, painted in perspective; these were reused frequently, partly because it was expensive to have new scenery painted.

Because Restoration theatres were indoors, lighting was a major concern. During the late seventeenth century, theatre performances were normally given in the afternoon so that the windows could provide some natural lighting. Candles were the source of artificial light; these were placed in chandeliers above the stage and the audience, and also in brackets attached to the fronts of the boxes. The stage and audience area were always lit, and footlights—candles on the floor along the front of the stage—were also used.

Restoration costuming followed the traditions of the English Renaissance and the French neoclassical era: contemporary clothing was used rather than historically accurate costuming.

THE EIGHTEENTH CENTURY

BACKGROUND: A MORE COMPLEX WORLD

Throughout Europe, the eighteenth century was a time of transition. As the world was slowly transformed into a global community, homogeneous, self-contained societies began to disappear. Increased manufacturing and international trade affected populations worldwide. The major eighteenth-century mercantile powers were England and France, and decisions made in these two nations directly affected people in such places as North America, India, and Africa. One effect on Africa, for example, was a marked increase in the slave trade.

Because of the growth in trade, western Europe prospered more than ever before. Profits from colonial trade filtered down to the emerging middle class, which included merchants and others in commercial enterprises and which now became a social as well as a political force.

There were so many new developments in learning and philosophy that the eighteenth century is called the *Age of Enlightenment.* Two major political and social upheavals, the American Revolution (1775–1783) and the French Revolution (1789–1799), were based on ideals of the Enlightenment. Unfortunately, the ideals of the French Revolution were compromised by the Reign of Terror; instead of liberty, equality, and fraternity, the French in 1799 wound up with Napoléon.

Much of the new knowledge that characterized this era had practical applications. Inventions of the late eighteenth century facilitated the Industrial Revolution in the nineteenth century. The flying shuttle, the spinning jenny, and the cotton gin revolutionized the textile industry; James Watt's improved steam engine revolutionized manufacturing and transportation.

Baroque Eighteenth-century art and music that emphasized ornamentation.

In the arts of the late seventeenth century and early eighteenth century, the predominant style was *baroque.* Baroque painters emphasized detail, color, and ornamentation to create a more total visual illusion. Renowned baroque composers achieved unity of mood and continuity of line, but their music—like baroque painting—was filled with movement and action.

The complexity of eighteenth-century society was mirrored in an extremely complex theatre that crossed many national boundaries and saw the rise of many new theatrical forms.

EIGHTEENTH-CENTURY DRAMA: NEW DRAMATIC FORMS

The eighteenth century did not produce outstanding drama; rather, this was a time when new dramatic forms began to appear.

In terms of genre, for instance, many eighteenth-century plays deviated from traditional definitions of tragedy and comedy. The *drame* (DRAHM), a new French form, was a serious play that did not fit the neoclassical definition of tragedy. *Bourgeois* (middle-class) *tragedy* and *domestic tragedy* are eighteenth-century examples of drame. Bourgeois and domestic tragedies ignored the neoclassical requirement that the chief characters be kings, queens, or nobles; their new tragic heroes and heroines were members of the emerging middle class. These plays were frequently sentimental and melodramatic, and they usually reflected eighteenth-century middle-class morality with the virtuous being rewarded and the wicked punished. By the close of the century, such melodrama was being written in France, Germany, and England.

The English and the French originated additional dramatic forms during this period. In England these included the satirical *ballad opera,* which employed popular music and was popularized by the success of *The Beggar's Opera* (1728) by John Gay (1685–1732), as well as *sentimental comedy.* Sentimental comedy of eighteenth-century England, like Restoration comedy, was comedy of manners, except that it reaffirmed middle-class morality. The major examples of this later form are *The Rivals* (1775) and *The School for Scandal* (1777) by Richard Brinsley Sheridan (1751–1816). In the emerging American theatre, *The Contrast* (1787) by Royall Tyler (1757–1826) was patterned after Sheridan's sentimental comedies.

There were opponents of sentimental comedy; the best-known was the English dramatist Oliver Goldsmith (c. 1730–1774), who wrote two plays: *The Good Natur'd Man* (1768) and *She Stoops to Conquer* (1773). Goldsmith advocated "laughing comedy," which would force audiences to laugh at their own eccentricities and absurdities.

SENTIMENTAL COMEDY
In the eighteenth century in England a type of comedy emerged that was much less amoral than Restoration comedy. Called sentimental comedy, it satirized social pretensions but upheld middle-class values. A good example of the form is *The Rivals* by Richard Brinsley Sheridan. Shown here in a production at the Huntington Theatre are Cheryl Lynn Bowers (as Lydia Languish) and Scott Ferrara (as Captain Jack Absolute). (© T. Charles Erickson)

READ *School for Scandal*

http://www.gutenberg.org/ebooks/1929

GOLDONI VERSUS GOZZI
In the middle of the eighteenth century, two Italian dramatists, Carlo Goldoni and Carlo Gozzi, took different approaches in adapting Italian commedia dell'arte to a more modern form. Goldoni wanted drama to be more realistic; Gozzi wanted it to be more fanciful. Seen here is a scene from Goldoni's *La Locandiera* (*The Mistress of the Inn*) presented in Lyon, France. (© Jacques Morell/Sygma/Corbis)

In the late eighteenth century, many German playwrights revolted against the neoclassical ideals. The playwright and critic Gotthold Ephraim Lessing (1729–1781), for example, was a leader in the *Sturm und Drang* (*storm and stress*) movement, in which dramatists patterned their works on Shakespeare's extensive episodic structure, his mixture of genres, and his onstage violence. "Storm and stress"—which included such plays as *Goetz von Berlichingen* (1773) by Johann Wolfgang von Goethe (1749–1832) and *The Robbers* (1782) by Friedrich Schiller (1759–1805)—was the forerunner of nineteenth-century romanticism.

In Italy during the mid-eighteenth century, there was a struggle between the playwrights Carlo Goldoni (1707–1793) and Carlo Gozzi (1720–1806) over what direction commedia dell'arte should take: Goldoni wanted to make it less artificial, while Gozzi wanted to make it even more fantastic.

THEATRE | Year, C.E. | CULTURE AND POLITICS

1700

War of Spanish Succession in France (1701–1714)

Peter the Great begins westernization of Russia (c. 1701)

Ferdinando Bibiena introduces angle perspective (c. 1703)

Susanna Centlivre's *The Busy Body* (1709)

1710

The Spectator begun by Addison and Steele (1711)

Susanna Centlivre (1670–1723)
(Billy Rose Theatre Collection, The New York Public Library for the Performing Arts, Astor, Lenox, and Tilden Foundations)

Louis XIV dies (1715)

1720

Defoe's *Robinson Crusoe* (1719)

Baroque music flourishes (Bach and Handel) (c. 1724)

Gay's *The Beggar's Opera* (1728)

Gottsched and Neuber meet (1727)

Swift's *Gulliver's Travels* (1726)

Lillo's *The London Merchant* (1731)

1730

Voltaire's *Zaïre;* London's Covent Garden Theatre built (1732)

John Key's "flying shuttle" loom patented (1733)

English Licensing Act (1737)

Rococo style flourishes (1737)

1740

Frederick the Great of Prussia, "enlightened despot" (1740)

Voltaire's *Mahomet;* Macklin's Shylock—an attempt at costume reform (1741)

Garrick becomes actor-manager at Drury Lane (1747)

1750

Goldoni's *The Comic Theatre* (1750)

Encylopédie begun (c. 1750)

Hallams in Virginia (1752)

Voltaire's *Orphan of China* (1755)

French and Indian War (1754)

Seven Years' War begins (1756)

Boulevard theatres begin to develop in France (c. 1760)

Spectators banished from French stage (c. 1759)

Voltaire's *Candide* (1759)

1760

Gozzi's *Turandot* (1762)

Piranesi continues to paint his "prison drawings" using chiaroscuro (1761)

Rousseau's *Social Contract;* Catherine the Great of Russia begins reign (1762)

Drottningholm completed; Southwark Theatre in Philadelphia (1766)

James Watt patents a steam engine (1769)

John Street Theatre in New York (1767)

Lessing's *Hamburg Dramaturgy* (1767–1769)

Declaration of Independence (American Revolution 1775–1783); Adam Smith's *Wealth of Nations* (1776)

Hamburg National Theatre (1767–1769)

"Storm and stress" movement (1767–1787)

1770

Goethe's *Goetz von Berlichingen;* Goldsmith's *She Stoops to Conquer* (1773)

Sheridan's *The School for Scandal* (1777)

THE DECLARATION OF INDEPENDENCE, John Trumbull (1776)
(Architect of the Capitol)

1780

Goya's *Don Manuel de Zuniga;* James Watt patents a locomotive (1784)

She Stoops to Conquer (1773)
(© T. Charles Erickson)

Mozart's *Don Giovanni* (1787)

French Revolution (1789)

1790

David's *Murder of Marat* (1793)

Goethe "directs" Weimar court theatre; Schiller assists (1798)

Consulate of Napoleon (1799)

Schiller's *Mary Stuart* (1800)

1800

THEATRE PRODUCTION IN THE EIGHTEENTH CENTURY

Government and Theatre   In certain countries—such as England, France, and the independent German states—the eighteenth century was marked by governmental attempts to regulate theatre. We noted earlier that in 1737 the English Parliament issued the Licensing Act, which restricted the presentation of drama in London to the Drury Lane and Covent Garden theatres and made the lord chamberlain responsible for licensing plays. Frequently, however, ingenious theatrical entrepreneurs found ways to outwit the government and get around its restrictions.

In eighteenth-century France, the government restricted what types of plays could be produced and granted monopolies to certain theatres: the Opera, the Comédie Française (the home of nonmusical drama), and the Comédie Italienne (the home of commedia dell'arte and, later, of comic opera) were the three major Parisian theatres. In 1791, the leaders of the French Revolution abolished the earlier theatrical restrictions.

In Germany, government intervention in theatre was of a somewhat more positive nature. Eighteenth-century Germany was not unified but consisted of several independent states, and German theatre became an important artistic force in the last part of the century. Subsidized theatres were organized in several German states; and this practice provided stability for theatre artists, though it also meant that the government could wield control over the content of plays.

Eighteenth-Century Theatre Architecture   The basic configuration of eighteenth-century continental theatres followed the Italian Renaissance tradition; but to accommodate the new middle-class audiences, both continental and English theatres became larger. The interiors were usually egg-shaped to improve sight lines. In England, playhouses moved more toward the continental model: the apron shrank to about twelve feet, and the area behind the proscenium became much deeper.

Throughout Europe—in such countries as Germany, Russia, and Sweden—theatre buildings proliferated during the eighteenth century. One of the most significant theatre buildings of this period is Drottningholm in Sweden, erected in 1766 outside Stockholm. Drottningholm was boarded up in the 1790s and remained closed until the twentieth century, when it was reopened. Today tourists there can explore a perfect working example of an eighteenth-century theatre.

In the United States, during the colonial era and after the American Revolution, permanent theatres were constructed following the English model.

Scenery, Lighting, and Costumes   In the eighteenth century, as in the Renaissance, Italy was the birthplace of many scenic innovations. For nearly 100 years, from 1690 to 1787, the most influential Italian designers and theatre architects of the period were the Bibienas—an extended family that included several generations of designers. One innovation by the Bibienas was *angle* or ***multipoint perspective.*** Previously, the painted sets used during the Italian Renaissance pulled the eye to a central vanishing point and appeared to be totally framed and enclosed by the proscenium arch. In the Bibienas' designs, the eye was attracted to various vanishing points, and the set seemed to extend beyond the proscenium. Typically, the Bibienas' designs were grandiose, lavish, and ornate.

Elsewhere, Italian influence was pervasive in eighteenth-century scene design. Most continental theatres used wing-and-shutter settings, painted in perspective and

Angle perspective Also known as multipoint perspective, painted settings that pull the eye to multiple vanishing points.

shifted by Torelli's pole-and-chariot mechanism. Additional elements occasionally incorporated into the painted designs included the following: (1) borders at the top; (2) *ground rows* (cutouts along the stage floor); (3) large scenic cutouts, such as painted trees; (4) rolled backdrops; and (5) *act drops*—curtains at the front of the stage.

A few historians have argued that sometime between the Renaissance and the eighteenth century, Italian designers also introduced the *box set* in which flats are used to create three sides of a room onstage. We will look at the development of the box set more closely when we discuss nineteenth-century theatre.

There were also experiments with stage lighting in the late 1700s, including attempts to mask lighting sources, to use silk screens for coloring, and to replace candles with oil lamps and other sources. These lighting sources were not easily controlled, however, and the auditorium as well as the stage had to remain lit.

Unlike scenery and lighting, theatrical costuming remained underdeveloped throughout most of the eighteenth century. Actors and actresses believed that the chief criterion for a costume was to show the performer off to the best advantage. Daring theatre artists throughout Europe experimented with historically accurate costuming, but their attempts rarely resulted in the kind of historical reconstructions we see today.

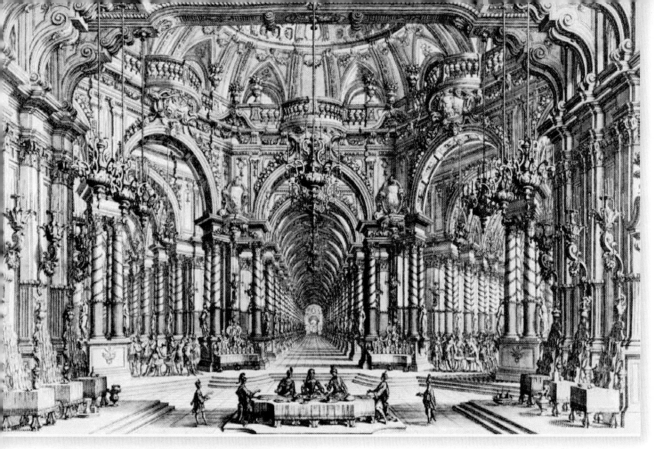

SET DESIGN BY ONE OF THE BIBIENAS
During the eighteenth century, one family dominated scene design in Europe: the Bibiena family, whose second, third, and fourth generations carried on the tradition begun by Giovanni Bibiena. This engraved stage design by Giuseppi Bibiena (1696–1757) is typical of the family's work, with its vast scale, ornateness, and elegance, and its perspective vista disappearing in several directions. (Victoria and Albert Museum, London)

Acting in the Eighteenth Century   If many of the plays of the eighteenth century were not noteworthy, the performers often were. This was an age that glorified star performers. All across Europe, successful actors and actresses developed dedicated followings.

The predominant approach to acting in the eighteenth century was *bombastic,* emphasizing the performer's oratorical skills. More often than not, performers addressed their lines to the audience rather than the character to whom they were supposed to be speaking. Standardized patterns of stage movement were necessary because rehearsal time was limited and bills were changed frequently.

In the midst of these conventional practices, however, there were some innovators. Among those who rebelled against the bombastic, conventionalized style were the English actors Charles Macklin (c. 1700–1797) and David Garrick (1717–1779). Macklin and Garrick rejected formal declamation, stereotyped patterns of stage movement, and singsong delivery of verse.

The Emergence of the Director   In terms of the future, possibly the most significant development during the eighteenth century was the first emergence of the modern director. Before then, playwrights or leading performers normally doubled

1784, PARIS, FRANCE It is a brisk spring day in May 1784. In Paris, the Comédie Française is giving a performance in its new theatre building, which opened two years ago. With great expectations, Parisians depart early so that they can arrive at the theatre before the starting time, 5:30. Tonight they are to see Beaumarchais's new play *The Marriage of Figaro*.

The Comédie Française is noted not only for traditional neoclassical drama but also for new drama by French authors. At this performance, there will be dance presentations between the acts of the play and also a short, comic afterpiece following *The Marriage of Figaro*. Not since *Tartuffe* has there been such controversy over a play.

The Marriage of Figaro—set in Spain—is about an older man's attempt to seduce a servant girl, and its key character is a comic servant; Beaumarchais introduced his characters several years ago in *The Barber of Seville*. The real point of *The Marriage of Figaro* is social and political satire, and it is this that is controversial. Because of the controversy, the king, Louis XVI, has refused to give his permission for its production. Despite this, it has been performed continuously since its opening in April and is clearly a success. People who were present on the opening night have reported that the theatre was filled hours beforehand and that some of the audience members had brought food with them so that they would not have to risk losing their seats by leaving the theatre to eat.

As the spectators enter the theatre, they are struck by its size and beauty. Remarkably, everyone in the audience now has a place to sit. In earlier French theatres, the pit in front of the stage had no seats, and people in that area stood during performances; in fact, people in the old seatless pits would move about and socialize. The new seats are controversial—Parisians enjoyed the social ambience of the old pit, and one of the leading playwrights of the day, Louis Sébastian Mercier, has publicly criticized the addition of benches. The audience area is egg-shaped; this configuration, at least, will be welcome, making it easier for everyone in the audience to see the action onstage. Like older theatres, the new Comédie Française has three rows of boxes with a row of galleries above those. Spectators who cannot afford the more expensive sections take their place in the pit, sitting on the new benches.

When the curtain rises, the spectators are impressed at once by the stage, which is large and very deep. However, it has a smaller apron than the company's previous theatres had: the actors and actresses must all perform behind the proscenium arch. The scenery is painted and will be changed by wings and shutters. As the play begins, the spectators are very excited because they are seeing performers they have heard much about.

The plot of *The Marriage of Figaro* is full of intrigue, unexpected twists, and great comic moments. Figaro, the servant, is engaged to marry Suzanne, who is also a servant; but his master, Count Almaviva, wants to sleep with her himself. The count has been unfaithful to his wife, and the audience watches with great enjoyment the various complications that develop as he tries to conquer another woman but is thwarted. At the end of the play, the count is exposed in his plotting and is humiliated; he pledges fidelity to his wife, and Figaro and Suzanne are brought together.

As the Parisians walk home, they relive many of the comic moments in the play. Yet they also understand why this seemingly simple, farcical work has caused such a political furor. It is the master who is ridiculed and frustrated: despite his social rank, his machinations are futile and his clever servants outwit him. Clearly, Beaumarchais is questioning the social structure of France. Some people are saying that this play threatens society with the same kind of revolution that has taken place in the new world. Are these people right? Was the king right to be concerned about the political implications of this comedy? These questions remain long after the evening at the Comédie Française.

READ *The Marriage of Figaro*

http://oll.libertyfund.org/index.php?option=com_staticxt
&staticfile=show.php%3Ftitle=1563&Itemid=27

as directors of stage business, and actual directing was minimal; furthermore, little time was spent on preparing a production in rehearsal. What was missing in theatre was someone to oversee and unify stage productions, assist performers, and ensure the appropriateness of visual elements. Two eighteenth-century figures are often considered the forerunners of the modern stage director: the English actor David Garrick and the German playwright, poet, and novelist Johann Wolfgang von Goethe.

Between 1747 and 1776, David Garrick was a partner in the management of the Drury Lane Theatre and was therefore responsible for all major artistic decisions. He championed a more natural style of acting and argued for careful development of characters' individual traits as well as for thorough preparation and research. In contrast to the usual eighteenth-century custom, Garrick's rehearsals were quite extended. Garrick was also a strict disciplinarian: he required his performers to be on time, know their lines, and act—not simply recite—during rehearsals. As part of his reform of stage practices, Garrick also banished spectators from the stage.

Goethe, unlike Garrick, was not restricted by commercialism and was not an actor in the company he directed. In 1775, Goethe—by then a famous author—was invited to oversee the court theatre at Weimar in Germany. Initially, Goethe did not take his theatre duties seriously, but by the 1790s he had become enthusiastic about the theatre and had become a *régisseur* (ray-zhee-SUHR), or dictatorial director. (*Régisseur* is the French term for director.)

Goethe rehearsed for long periods and expected his performers to work as an ensemble. He established rules for stage movement and vocal technique, and he also set

EIGHTEENTH-CENTURY STAR: DAVID GARRICK
The eighteenth century was an era of great stars, some of whom paid close attention to details of performance and costuming to achieve a greater sense of reality. David Garrick was both an outstanding example of this approach to acting and also a strong manager of his theatre company. In the portrait here (by Nathaniel Dance) he is shown in the title role in Shakespeare's *Richard III.* (Stratford Town Council, Stratford-upon-Avon)

Régisseur Continental European term for a theatre director; it often denotes a dictatorial director.

rules for his performers' behavior in their personal lives. He even laid down rules for the conduct of his audiences; the only appropriate audience reactions, he insisted, were applause and withholding applause.

Goethe did not advocate a completely natural style of acting; he believed, for instance, that performers should speak facing the audience rather than each other. He used routine blocking patterns, although he did emphasize careful stage composition. Goethe oversaw settings and costumes and believed in historical accuracy.

THE NINETEENTH CENTURY

BACKGROUND: A TIME OF SOCIAL CHANGE

Major social changes took place in the period from 1800 to 1875, including the Industrial Revolution, which involved technological advances such as steam power, expanded means of transportation, and new modes of communication. Another major development was the rise of nationalism.

NINETEENTH-CENTURY POPULAR THEATRICAL ARTS

As we have noted, it is hard to distinguish between the popular entertainments of the nineteenth century and the theatre of that era. Many of the popular forms were presented in theatres, and many traditional dramas were adopted for spaces that usually held mass audience entertainments.

The nineteenth century saw an explosion of museums, music halls, and circuses. The American who was world-renowned for his ability to draw mass audiences was P. (Phineas) T. (Taylor) Barnum (1810–1891), who in 1841 opened the American Museum in which he exhibited human curiosities and also staged concerts and plays, including many temperance melodramas. Later, in the early 1870s, Barnum was also instrumental in developing the three-ring circus as we know it today. But even before Barnum, there were circus rings that housed clowns, equestrian performances, trained animal acts, and pantomimes. In the early nineteenth century, dramas staged on horseback were presented in many of these spaces.

The music halls of England served food and drink and had a small platform stage for popular song and dance presentations. A master of ceremonies moved the show along, providing comic interludes. By the end of the 1800s, these early music halls evolved into theatrical spaces dedicated exclusively to the presentation of these musical performances.

The nineteenth century also saw the development of many other forms of popular entertainments, including wild west shows, vaudeville, and minstrelsy. Wild west shows (or exhibitions), popular in the last quarter of the nineteenth century, presented heroic figures of the west as well as Native Americans, most often to audiences in the eastern United States who had little real contact with that world.

Minstrel shows were variety shows that featured white performers wearing blackface, and caricaturing African Americans. Later in the nineteenth century, there were African American minstrel troupes. Vaudeville was a series of variety acts—music, sketches, juggling, animal acts—that made up an evening's entertainment.

The intertwining of the popular arts and theatre made the two almost indistinguishable. Furthermore, many of the popular forms that developed in the nineteenth century continue to have an impact on our performance arts. For example, the well-known Canadian circus troupe Cirque du Soleil stages productions that break the boundaries between popular art and theatre. Television has incorporated the tradition of vaudeville and variety.

POPULAR ARTS
During the nineteenth century, a number of highly theatrical popular entertainments developed. Among those was the circus. The American entrepreneur P. T. Barnum was a significant innovator in developing the circus as we know it today. Seen here are female trapeze artists, performing in 1890. (Library of Congress)

There was also intellectual ferment. Two especially significant theoretical works were Charles Darwin's *On the Origin of Species* (1859) and Karl Marx's *Das Kapital* (*Capital;* 1867). Darwin's work, which dealt with evolution by natural selection, led to the questioning of traditional religious concepts; Marx's work questioned the capitalist system, which was the driving economic force of the Industrial Revolution.

NINETEENTH CENTURY, 1800 TO 1875

THEATRE

YEAR, C.E.

CULTURE AND POLITICS

Talma foremost actor in France (c. 1800)

1800

Goethe's Faust *(1810)*
(© Ruth Walz)

Louisiana Purchase (1803)

Napoléon I, emperor of France (1804)

Fulton's paddle steamer *Clermont* navigates on
Hudson (1807)

Latin American independence (1808–1826)

Goethe's *Faust*, Part I (1810)
Kleist's *The Prince of Homburg* (1810)
Pixérécourt and French melodrama flourish (1810)

1810

Mme. de Stael's *Of Germany,* published in France (1810)

Beethoven's Fifth Symphony (1810)

Edmund Kean's London debut (1814)

Battle of Waterloo; Metternich system (1815)

Chestnut Street Theatre in Philadelphia
becomes first totally gaslit theatre (1816)

First Factory Act, England (1819)

1820

Daguerre exhibits
diorama (1822)

Charles Kemble's historically
accurate *King John;* Shchepkin
member of Moscow troupe (1823)

Greek war of independence (1821)

Monroe Doctrine (1823)

Decembrist uprising in Russia (1825)

Forrest's New York debut (1826)

Hugo's *Hernani* (1830)

1830

Comte's positivism (1830)

Madame Vestris's management
of Olympic Theatre begins (1831)

Upper middle class enfranchised in England (1832)

Davy Crockett killed
at the Alamo (1836)

Gogol's *Inspector General;* Büchner's *Woyzeck* (1836)
Macready manages Covent Garden (1837)

Victoria of England (rules 1837–1901)

Dickens's *Oliver Twist* (1838)

Scribe's *A Glass of Water* (1840)

1840

England's Theatre Regulation Act (1843)

Queen Victoria (rules 1819–1901)
(Ingram Publishing)

Astor Place Riot (1849)

1850

Dumas fils's *Camille;*
first production of *Uncle
Tom's Cabin;* Charles
Kean's *King John* (1852)

Adolphe Montigny innovates in
directing at Gymnase (c. 1853)

Second French Empire; Napoléon III (1852)

Crimean War (1853–1865)

Perry in Japan (1854)

Flaubert's *Madame Bovary* (c. 1857)

Darwin's *On the Origin of Species* (1859)

Sardou's *A Scrap of Paper* (1860)

1860

American Civil War (1861–1865);
proclamation of the kingdom of Italy

Bismarck becomes
Prussian prime
minister (1862)

Edwin Booth's *Hamlet* runs 100 nights
in New York (1864)

Dostoyevsky's *Crime
and Punishment* (1866)

Duke of Saxe-Meiningen begins reforms (1866)

Marx's *Das Kapital;* extension
of suffrage in Great Britain (1867)

Booth Theatre (1869)

Tolstoy's *War and Peace* (c. 1869);
American transcontinental railway (1869)

1870

Zola's *Thérèse Raquin;* preface
discussed naturalism (1873)

Henry Irving at Lyceum (1871)

German empire founded; Paris commune (1871)

Paris Opéra building completed (1874)

Zola's Thérèse Raquin *(1873)*
(© Geraint Lewis)

1880

These societal transformations had a major impact on the nature of theatre. Nineteenth-century theatre built on the innovations of the eighteenth century and paved the way for modern theatre.

THEATRE IN NINETEENTH-CENTURY LIFE

Before examining specific transformations in drama and production techniques during the nineteenth century, we should look at the unique place theatre held at that time. Between 1800 and 1875, the dramatic arts exploded. The working and middle classes who filled the fast-growing cities demanded theatre; it was a passion, a fad, and also a seeming necessity for these new audiences. Nineteenth-century theatre, therefore, was a true popular entertainment that attracted huge numbers of spectators and helped audiences to forget—momentarily, at least—the cares and drudgery of daily life.

Nonliterary forms of entertainment also attracted the masses. The American public, for example, supported such popular arts as the *minstrel show, burlesque, variety, the circus, wild west shows,* and *medicine shows.* Throughout the nineteenth century, concert halls, saloons, and playhouses presented collections of entertainments—including songs, dances, acrobatics, and animal acts—on one bill; these developed into the popular variety and vaudeville presentations at the turn of the century and in the early twentieth century. The renowned popularizer of the circus, P. T. Barnum (1810–1891), merits special mention. Barnum developed the art of spectacular advertising to attract audiences to his entertainments; when he became involved with the circus in the 1850s, he advertised it as the "greatest show on earth." The wide variety of attractions to which audiences responded in the nineteenth century is a prime example of the tradition of popular entertainments of which we have spoken in earlier chapters.

The increase in numbers of spectators and types of entertainments resulted in the construction of more and larger playhouses throughout the Western world. With improvements in rail transportation, the dramatic arts were also brought to new places and new audiences.

The passion that audiences felt for theatre helps to explain several infamous theatre riots. One of these episodes, the "Old Price Riots," took place when London's Covent Garden Theatre was remodeled in 1809 and prices for admission were raised by the actor-manager John Philip Kemble (1757–1823). Another theatre riot took place in Paris in 1830, when *Hernani* by Victor Hugo (1802–1885) premiered at the Comédie Française. Some audience members were upset by the play's break from the neoclassical form.

The most violent of the nineteenth-century riots occurred outside New York's Astor Place Theatre in lower Manhattan and grew out of rivalry between the English star William Charles Macready (1793–1873) and the American star Edwin Forrest (1806–1872). Forrest, who was noted for his portrayals of melodramatic heroes, had made an unsuccessful English tour; he blamed its failure on Macready, whose performance style was more subtle and realistic. When Macready appeared at the Astor Place Theatre on May 8, 1849, Forrest's working-class fans prevented the performance.

Macready was persuaded by his aristocratic admirers to appear again two nights later on May 10, but this performance brought out a mob of 15,000 who assembled outside the playhouse and began to attack it. The infantry was called out to disperse the mob, and by the time the riot ended, twenty-two people had been killed.

The popularity of theatre between 1800 and 1875 has not been equaled in modern times. Partial parallels could be drawn to movies and television, which present similar

kinds of entertainment, attract mass audiences, and feature popular stars. Still, the passion of nineteenth-century audiences has rarely been aroused by other forms of entertainment. In our own time, the only equivalent might be the emotional intensity of audiences at rock concerts or at professional sports events.

The Astor Place Riot and the subject matter of much popular drama also reflected growing nationalism. For example, Anna Cora Mowatt, one of America's first signifi-cant female playwrights, wrote a comedy of manners, *Fashion* (1845), that depicted the values of hardworking America as more honest than the social pretensions of Europe. The character Adam Trueman in *Fashion* was a descendant of an earlier popular stock figure in American melodramas and comedies—the "stage Yankee," a representative of diligent, unpretentious, rural America.

NINETEENTH-CENTURY DRAMATIC FORMS

Two major forms of drama that came to the fore between 1800 and 1875 were Ro-manticism and melodrama.

Romanticism   *Romanticism,* influenced by the German storm and stress move-ment, was a revolutionary literary trend of the first half of the nineteenth century. The most noted romantic dramas of the period were Goethe's *Faust* (Part 1, 1808 and Part 2, 1831) and Victor Hugo's *Hernani* (1830).

The Romantics rejected all artistic rules, believing that genius creates its own rules. Since many of the Romantics adopted Shakespeare's structural techniques, their plays were episodic and epic in scope; but unlike Shakespeare, they were often more inter-ested in creating dramatic mood and atmosphere than in developing believable plots or depth of character. The Romantic hero was frequently a social outcast—a bandit, for example—who sought justice, knowledge, and truth.

Melodrama   Another dramatic form that came to the forefront in the nineteenth century was melodrama. As was discussed in Chapter 4, *melodrama* literally means "song drama" or "music drama"—a reference to the background music that accompanied these plays.

In nineteenth-century melodrama, the emphasis was on surface effects, such as those evoking suspense, fear, nostalgia, and other strong emotions in the audience. The conflict between good and evil was clearly established: melodramatic heroes and heroines stood in sharp contrast to villains, and the audiences sympathized with the good characters and despised the bad ones. Virtue was always victorious.

To hold the audience's interest, melodramas had suspenseful plots with a climactic moment at the end of each act (the modern equivalent would be a television drama that has a car crash or a sudden confrontation just before a commercial break). Since melodrama is primarily an escapist form, visual spectacle and special effects were important.

The Well-Made Play   Many popular melodramas of the nineteenth century had a structure described by the term *well-made play.* Characteristic of such plays were tightly constructed cause-and-effect development, and action revolving around a secret known to the audience but not to the characters. The opening scenes carefully spell out the necessary background information, or *exposition.* Throughout the play, the dramatic action is clearly foreshadowed, and each act builds to a climax. In the major scene, known as the *obligatory scene,* the opposed characters confront each other in a showdown. The plot is carefully resolved so that there are no loose ends.

MELODRAMA
A type of drama that came to prominence in the nineteenth century was the well-made play. The term means a play that was carefully constructed and featured unity of action and often unity of time and place as well. It incorporated a tightly managed plot with a strong cause-and-effect sequence of events. The well-made play is particularly well suited to melodrama, a genre that also came to prominence in the nineteenth century and continues into the twenty-first century. In melodrama, the emphasis is on suspense and excitement, with good and bad characters clearly delineated. An example both of the well-made play and of melodrama is Lillian Hellman's *The Little Foxes,* in which a strong woman, Regina, attempts to control her brothers and her daughter. Shown here are Kelly McGillis (Regina) and Julia Duffy (Birdie) in the Pasadena Playhouse production. (© Craig Schwartz)

The two most famous writers of well-made plays were both French: Eugène Scribe (1791–1861) and Victorien Sardou (1831–1908).

THEATRE PRODUCTION IN THE NINETEENTH CENTURY

Performers and Acting   Even more than the eighteenth century, the nineteenth century was an era of great stars; performers throughout the world were idolized by the audiences who flocked to see them. Some of these performers amassed—and frequently lost—fortunes, and a number of them were not only national but global figures.

During the nineteenth century, the traditional *repertory company,* a troupe of actors and actresses performing together for a set period of time in a number of plays, gradually disappeared. As transportation improved, not only stars but full productions—known as *combination companies*—began to tour, replacing the local repertory troupes. At about the same time, the long run became more common: popular plays might run for more than 100 consecutive performances.

Most performers of the period acted in the classical, romantic, and melodramatic styles. Many, however, moved toward modern realism. Among such more realistic performers were the American Edwin Booth (1833–1893) and the Italian Eleonora Duse (1858–1924).

Nineteenth-Century Developments in Directing

The art of directing, pioneered by David Garrick and Johann Wolfgang von Goethe in the eighteenth century, was refined and developed in the nineteenth century. The goal of innovative nineteenth-century directors was to create a unified stage picture, particularly by allotting more time for rehearsal and paying more attention to production details. Many of them also experimented with historical accuracy in scenery and costuming.

In England and the United States, numerous performer-managers took great interest and care in creating stage productions. On the European continent, a number of people significantly developed the art of directing, including two Germans—the opera composer Richard Wagner (1813–1883) and George II (1826–1914), Duke of Saxe-Meiningen—who were not actors within their companies and thus were closer to our modern idea of the director.

Wagner's concept of a totally unified artwork—the *Gesamtkunstwerk* (guh-Zahmt-Koonst-verk)—controlled by one person influenced twentieth-century theories of "total theatre" and directing. Wagner believed that an opera, which is made up of many musical and theatrical elements, needs a controlling figure to unify it. At his Bayreuth Festspielhaus, he put this theory into practice, becoming its *régisseur*, or director. Wagner's innovations for increasing stage illusion are particularly important. Musicians were forbidden to tune their instruments in the orchestra pit, and audiences were not supposed to applaud during the course of a presentation. Wagner is also often credited with being the first director to extinguish the house lights in order to focus the audience's attention on the stage.

In 1866, the duke of Saxe-Meiningen—a small state in northwestern Germany—took control of his court theatre; and between 1874 and 1890 he made the Meiningen Players the most renowned company in the world and revolutionized stage production. He rehearsed for extensive periods of time, refusing to open a show until he believed it

EDWIN BOOTH
An outstanding actor of the nineteenth century was Edwin Booth, famous for his portrayal of Hamlet, shown here, and other Shakespearean characters, as well as for building his own theatre. As a performer, he was renowned for depth of character, grace, and freedom from mannerisms. In an age of stage posturing, he took a more natural approach to his roles. (Bettmann/Corbis)

ELEONORA DUSE: PORTRAIT BY E. GORDIGIANI
Duse was the great Italian actress of the late nineteenth century and early twentieth century. She was known for her more realistic acting style, and the English playwright George Bernard Shaw considered her a greater performer than her rival, Sarah Bernhardt. (Photo Studio Humberto N. Serra)

was ready. He was opposed to the star system and employed mostly young performers. His productions were especially famous for intricately planned crowd scenes and were also admired for their historically accurate settings and costumes. Because his company toured frequently to other countries, the duke's theatrical innovations became well known throughout Europe.

Nineteenth-Century Theatre Architecture   Between 1800 and mid-century, many playhouses, with the traditional proscenium arch and "pit, box, and gallery" arrangement, were enlarged to meet the demands of the expanding lower-class urban audiences. By the 1860s, however, there was a shift away from the construction of huge theatres.

In the United States, the Booth Theatre, completed in 1869 for the renowned American Shakespearean actor Edwin Booth, is often cited as the first modern theatre in New York City. Instead of a pit and galleries, it had a modern orchestra area and balconies, and the seats were individual armchairs. The stage in Booth's theatre was revolutionary: it was not raked, and it had no grooves. Rather, scenery could be raised from the basement by elevators or dropped in (flown in) from above, and scenic pieces were often supported by braces.

Another innovative nineteenth-century theatre building, the Bayreuth Festspielhaus, built for Richard Wagner, opened in 1876. Wagner wanted seating that would not emphasize class distinctions, and so his theatre had 1,300 individual seats in thirty raked rows, forming a fan-shaped auditorium. Audiences exited at the ends of the rows, an arrangement known as *continental seating.*

Scenery, Costumes, and Lighting   Eighteenth-century experiments with realistic devices and conventions in scenery and costuming were carried even further in the nineteenth century. Historical accuracy in sets and costumes became more common with the increasing availability of works of historical research. This new knowledge about the past—combined with the fascination with antiquity that characterized the nineteenth century—led various theatre artists, including the Duke of Saxe-Meiningen, to mount historically accurate productions.

Wing-and-shutter settings shifted by pole-and-chariot or groove systems gradually disappeared during the nineteenth century. The most significant alternative was the *box set,* an arrangement in which flats are cleated together at angles—rather than set up parallel to the audience—to form the walls of a three-dimensional room. As noted previously, the box set may have been introduced as early as the Renaissance, but it was in the nineteenth century that box sets revolutionized scene design.

During this same period, the technology of the Industrial Revolution was introduced into theatre. New means of scene shifting were developed: by the close of the century, the *elevator stage* (which allows sections of a stage floor, or even the entire floor, to be raised or lowered) and the *revolving stage* were perfected. The latter is a large turntable on which scenery is placed; as it moves, one set turns out of sight and another is brought into view.

Nineteenth-century technology also revolutionized stage lighting. In 1816, Philadelphia's Chestnut Street Theatre became the world's first playhouse to be completely gaslit. Gaslight allowed control of the intensity of lighting in all parts of the theatre; and by the middle of the century, the *gas table*—the equivalent of a modern dimmer board—enabled one stagehand to control all the stage lighting.

NINETEENTH-CENTURY THEATRE ARCHITECTURE
Significant changes took place in theatre architecture during the 1800s. This illustration of Covent Garden in London (top) shows a typical "pit, box, and gallery" theatre of the era. The photograph of Wagner's Bayreuth Festspielhaus (bottom), however, shows that by 1876 significant transformations were occurring. Wagner's theatre is much more like a modern proscenium theatre, with comfortable seating in the orchestra area, a small balcony, and a sunken orchestra pit. (top © Victoria and Albert Museum, London; bottom © ArenaPal/Topham/ The Image Works)

Thomas Edison's incandescent lamp, invented in 1879, further revolutionized stage lighting. Electricity, of course, is the most flexible, most controllable, and safest form of theatre lighting. By 1881, London's Savoy Theatre was using incandescent lighting, though some other playhouse may actually have used it earlier.

By 1875, theatre was about to enter the modern era: the seeds of theatrical realism—as well as of reactions against realism—had been gradually planted since the Renaissance. In Chapter 14, we turn to the beginnings of the modern era: the development of realism and early reactions against the new realistic theatre. In Chapter 15, we explore these and other developments in modern theatre.

SUMMARY

The theatre of the English Restoration combined aspects of English and continental Renaissance theatre. Restoration drama had elements of both Elizabethan theatre and the French theatre of Molière. The Restoration stage also had native and continental elements: its modified proscenium came from French and Italian practice, but its elongated apron came from Elizabethan theatres.

In the eighteenth century, there were many attempts throughout Europe to break away from the Italianate tradition. Theatres were still constructed as proscenium-arch spaces, but their shapes and sizes changed. Revolutionary authors—especially the storm and stress dramatists of the late 1700s—abandoned the neoclassical ideals. Many new genres that ignored the Italian Renaissance rules were developed, including bawdy Restoration comedy, sentimental comedy, middle-class tragedy, drame, and ballad opera.

There were also attempts in the 1700s to develop unity in production; these included some primitive experiments with historical accuracy, and—especially notably—the directorial controls instituted by David Garrick and Johann Wolfgang von Goethe.

The nineteenth century was the bridge to our modern era. Comfortable modern proscenium-arch theatres, such as Booth's theatre and the Bayreuth Festspielhaus, were built. Principles of modern directing were developed and were clearly manifested in the work of the Duke of Saxe-Meiningen. Historical accuracy in costuming and settings as well as expanded use of the box set added to theatrical illusionism. Theatre was also affected by technological advances, such as gas lighting.

THINKING ABOUT THEATRE

▶ Restoration and eighteenth-century sentimental comedy focus on sexual intrigue and the moral weaknesses of human beings. Identify at least three contemporary films or television shows that employ the same subject matter. Explain the similarities in your answer.

▶ How was the proscenium-arch theatre of the Restoration different from a proscenium-arch theatre on your campus?

▶ What new elements were introduced by eighteenth-century designers to aid in enhancing the illusion of reality in scene design?

▶ Why was the emergence of the director in the eighteenth century so significant?

▶ List and describe present day examples of nineteenth-century popular entertainments.

▶ Explain why a film or television show you have seen recently might be categorized as melodrama.

▶ How is a romantic film or television show today different from a nineteenth-century drama of the Romantic era? Describe any similarities.

KEY TERMS

Angle perspective Also known as multi-point perspective, painted settings that pull the eye to multiple vanishing points.

Baroque Eighteenth-century art and music that emphasized ornamentation.

Comedy of manners Form of comic drama that became popular in seventeenth-century France and the English Restoration, emphasizing a cultivated or sophisticated atmosphere and witty dialogue.

Régisseur Continental European term for a theatre director; it often denotes a dictatorial director.

THEATRE ON THE WEB

For more research and to learn more about the topics in this chapter, please visit the Online Learning Center at **www.mhhe.com/livelyart8e.**

THE MODERN THEATRE EMERGES

REALISM AND THE MODERN ERA

BACKGROUND: THE MODERN ERA

TIMELINE: 1875 to 1915

THEATRICAL REALISM

REALISTIC PLAYWRIGHTS

NATURALISM

PRODUCERS OF REALISM: INDEPENDENT THEATRES

LIVING HISTORY: *The Sea Gull*

DEPARTURES FROM REALISM

ANTIREALIST PLAYWRIGHTS: IBSEN, STRINDBERG AND WEDEKIND

SYMBOLISM

ANTIREALIST DESIGNERS: APPIA AND CRAIG

RUSSIAN THEATRICALISM: MEYERHOLD

EXPRESSIONISM

FUTURISM AND SURREALISM

THE THEATRE OF CRUELTY AND EPIC THEATRE

UNIQUE VOICES

IMPACT OF TOTALITARIANISM ON THEATRE

TIMELINE: 1915 to 1945

EXPERIMENTATION AND DEPARTURES FROM REALISM CONTINUE

LIVING HISTORY: *Waiting for Godot*

ECLECTICS

POPULAR THEATRE

AMERICAN MUSICAL THEATRE

TIMELINE: 1945 to 1975

GLOBAL THEATRE IN THE TWENTIETH CENTURY

SOME BACKGROUND ON ASIAN THEATRE

GLOBAL EXCHANGES

GLOBAL CROSSCURRENTS: Two Important International Directors

SUMMARY

THINKING ABOUT THEATRE

KEY TERMS

THEATRE ON THE WEB

◀ **THE MODERN THEATRE EMERGES** Between 1875 and the mid-twentieth century what is known as the Modern Theatre came to full flower, with both realism and departures from realism. A work that foreshadowed the modern theatre was a play by Georg Büchner, *Woyzeck*. One of the most enigmatic plays of the nineteenth century, it used romantic techniques but also elements of realism and expressionism that were to come much later. Written in 1836, it received almost no productions until the twentieth century. Shown here are Jens Jorn Spottag (Woyzeck) and Kaya Brüel (Marie) in Robert Wilson's adaptation, presented at Lincoln Center. (© Jack Vartoogian/FrontRowPhotos)

I n the modern era, usually defined as 1875 to the present, the arts have, as always, mirrored changes occurring in society. In theatre, these developments have been reflected in a great diversity of types of theatre as theatre has become increasingly global, eclectic, and experimental. Avant-garde theatre appears alongside more conventional theatre, and new plays are produced while classics from the past also enjoy great popularity. In this chapter we will focus mainly on the years 1875 to 1975.

In the theatre of the modern era, five major strands stand out. The first strand is realism; the second is departures from realism; the third strand is known as eclecticism, movements and artists who combine the various trends or are able to work across the boundaries of these trends; the fourth is a continuation of traditional and popular theatres from the past—comedies, tragedies, melodramas, and spectacular extravaganzas that nineteenth-century audiences applauded; the fifth strand is globalization. During the period of 1875 to 1975, theatre practitioners in various parts of the world—Asia (China, India, Japan, Indonesia), Europe, the United States, Central and South America—became increasingly aware of the theatrical activities and practices in other places. Often, they adopted the techniques and theatrical innovations of these other cultures. In this chapter we will examine how these five approaches developed in the modern theatre.

REALISM AND THE MODERN ERA

BACKGROUND: THE MODERN ERA

Modern theatre in the West began with the plays of three dramatists: the Norwegian Henrik Ibsen; the Swede August Strindberg; and the Russian Anton Chekhov. Their works also reflect the period in which they were written—the modern era, which began in the late nineteenth century and continues to this day. Their plays ushered in the techniques and the outlook that characterized Western theatre throughout most of the twentieth century.

In the mid-nineteenth century, profound changes began to occur in religion, philosophy, psychology, and economics. In 1859, Charles Darwin published *On the Origin of Species,* which challenged the concept that human beings are special and created by God in his own image. In 1867, Karl Marx's *Das Kapital* questioned the fundamentals of capitalism. In 1900, Sigmund Freud's *Interpretation of Dreams* suggested that we are not in complete control of our actions or even our thoughts. In 1905, Albert Einstein presented the first part of his theory of relativity, which stated that many aspects of the universe that we consider fixed and immutable are subject to variation and change. One result of this series of intellectual, religious, and moral challenges was that societies that had been unified now became fragmented.

Along with fragmentation, the first half of the twentieth century was marked by tremendous unrest, in both Europe and Asia. This era of unrest was ushered in by World War I, which lasted from 1914 to 1918 and resulted in 8.5 million deaths. Unrest also contributed to the Russian Revolution of 1917, which led to the establishment of the Soviet government. When World War I ended, it was hoped that peace would come to the Western world, but severe economic problems developed in Europe and the United States that led to the emergence of totalitarianism in Europe and the rule of fascist dictators such as Benito Mussolini in Italy, Adolf Hitler in Germany, and Francisco Franco in Spain.

1875 TO 1915

THEATRE

YEAR

CULTURE AND POLITICS

Wagner's Bayreuth Festspielhaus opened (1876)

1875

Telephone patented (1876)

Ibsen's *A Doll's House* (1879)

Edison's incandescent lamp (1879)

1880

Height of imperialism (1880–1914)

Savoy Theatre in London uses electricity (1881)

Alexander II assassinated in Russia (1881)

Wagner's Festspielhaus (1876)
(© ArenaPAL/Topham/The Image Works)

Trade unions in France legalized (1884)

1885

Stevenson's *Dr. Jekyll and Mr. Hyde* (1886)

Antoine's Théâtre Libre (1887)

Eiffel Tower completed, Paris (1887–89)

Strindberg's *Miss Julie* (1888)

Brahm's Freie Bühne (1889)

1890

Grein's Independent Theatre (1891)

The Eiffel Tower (1887-1889)
(Library of Congress)

Lugné-Poë's Théâtre de l'Oeuvre (1893)

Shaw's *Arms and the Man* (1894)

Oscar Wilde's *The Importance of Being Earnest* (1895)

1895

Chekhov's *Sea Gull;* Jarry's *Ubu Roi;* revolving stage in Munich (1896)

Dreyfus affair in France (1894)

Moscow Art Theatre (1898)

Appia's *Music and Stage Setting* (1899)

Boer War in South Africa (1899)

1900

Freud's *Interpretation of Dreams* (1900)

Marconi's first transatlantic radiotelegraph message (1901)

Williams and Walker's *In Dahomey* (1902)

Boer War ends (1902)

Chekhov's *Cherry Orchard* (1904)

Wright brothers make successful airplane flight (1903)

Synge's *Riders to the Sea* (1904)

Craig's *The Art of Theatre;* Reinhardt succeeds Otto Brahm as director of Deutsches Theatre (1905)

1905

Einstein's theory of relativity (1905)

Picasso's *Les Demoiselles d'Avignon* (1907)

First modern Japanese drama presented by Osanai Kaoru (1909)

1910

Albert Einstein (1877-1955)
(Bettmann/Corbis)

Indian playwright, Rabindranath Tagore, receives Nobel Prize (1913)

Théâtre du Vieux Colombier (1913)

Anita Bush founds Lafayette Players (1914)

Provincetown Playhouse (1915)

1915

Stravinsky's *Le Sacre du Printemps* (1913)

World War I (1914)

The extremes of fascism were frighteningly illustrated by Hitler's Nazi Germany, in which individual liberty was suppressed and millions of Jews, Roma (inappropriately referred to as gypsies), and others were exterminated in concentration camps. All together, Hitler's government murdered 6 million Jews and millions of others. Similar abuses occurred in other totalitarian states, including the Soviet Union, where Joseph Stalin (who ruled the country from 1928 until 1951) sent millions to their deaths in slave-labor camps.

After World War II, which began in 1939 and ended in 1945 with the defeat of Germany and Italy in Europe and of Japan in Asia, there was again hope for peace. The period after World War II was different from the period after World War I. For one thing, the atom bomb—which had been dropped on two cities in Japan at the close of World War II—and later the hydrogen bomb had been developed. These weapons were potentially so deadly that a stalemate developed between the United States and the Soviet Union which came to be called the cold war and which lasted for decades, not ending until the Soviet Union was dissolved at the end of 1991.

The end of World War II did not mean the end of military conflicts. From 1945 to the present, there have been numerous other wars, including the Korean War, the Israeli-Arab conflicts in the Middle East, the Vietnam War, a Soviet-led war in Afghanistan, the Persian Gulf War, the Bosnian-Serb War in the former Yugoslavia, the Rwandan civil war in Africa, and the wars in Afghanistan and Iraq—wars led by the United States. There was also a great deal of social unrest, including civil rights movements by underrepresented groups such as African Americans, women, and gays and lesbians. Also, there were wars of independence and civil wars throughout the continent of Africa during much of this period.

Another development of the postwar period was a striking increase in the industrial power of two of the defeated nations: Germany and Japan. Economically and politically, the world became more interdependent, with developments in one part of the world—such as environmental pollution or the price of oil—directly affecting other areas around the globe: Central and South America, for instance, as well as Europe, Asia, and the United States.

At the same time, tremendous problems remained: economic inequality and conflicts between rich and poor in many nations, assaults on the environment, persistent racial prejudice, and starvation and homelessness in many parts of the world. In the midst of this turmoil, theatre recovered from the ravages of World War II just as many parts of the world did.

Meanwhile, inventions continued at a rapid pace: nuclear power, for example, and computer and digital technology, which revolutionized many aspects of life, particularly communication. Earlier, this period saw the development of jet airplanes, television, and many advances in medical science. Moreover, in the post–World War II era there was a startling increase in communication across the globe, not only through radio but through television, movies, and then the Internet and other digital technologies. It was against this background that theatre became increasingly global.

THEATRICAL REALISM

As noted above, two major strands of modern theatre are realism and departures from realism. In theatre, *realism* has a specific connotation. It means that everything onstage is made to resemble observable, everyday life. How people speak, dress, and behave, as well as what kinds of rooms they live in conform as closely as possible to what

Realism One of the five strands of theatre in the modern era, realism conveys everything onstage to resemble observable, everyday life to promote a strong sense of audience recognition and identification.

we in the audience know is the way people actually speak, dress, act, and live. The power of realism lies in its credibility and in the sense of identification it creates. If we in the audience can verify from our own experience and observation the way people are acting onstage, we relate strongly to what we are observing. Realistic theatre is so effective that it has been a predominant form throughout the modern period.

The other major movement we call ***departures from realism.*** This will be discussed later in this chapter, but a few points should be noted here. At the same time that realism was becoming pervasive, there were playwrights who found it too limiting. In fact, many devices that have served well throughout theatre history are not realistic: they include poetry (a characteristic of Shakespearean drama and most other drama before recent centuries), supernatural characters such as ghosts and witches (like those in *Macbeth*), songs, fantasies, and dream sequences. Such devices do not correspond to our experience of everyday life and hence are generally excluded from realism. The division between realism and departures from realism therefore creates something of a dilemma: with realism we can have strong audience recognition and identification; but we need departures from realism if we want to use a whole range of poetic and imaginative devices that make theatre richer.

Still, these divisions are a useful way of beginning to examine our modern theatre. We will look first at realism.

Departures from realism
To overcome perceived limitations of realistic theatre, this strand of modern theatre departs from realism via non-realistic or antirealistic presentations. It often uses symbolism, non-linear narrative, dream imagery, and other ways to avoid realistic representation.

REALISTIC PLAYWRIGHTS

Henrik Ibsen   The Norwegian playwright Henrik Ibsen (1828–1906) is often considered the founder of modern realistic drama. It should be noted, however, that Ibsen wrote nonrealistic works at certain times in his career: as a young man he created romantic dramas, and near the end of his life (as discussed below) he experimented with abstract symbolist drama. He is best known, however, for his realistic works—plays like *A Doll's House* (1879), *Ghosts* (1881), and *Hedda Gabler* (1890).

As a realistic playwright, Ibsen sought to convince his audiences that the stage action in his dramas represented everyday life. But he went farther than that: he felt that drama should tackle subjects that had previously been taboo onstage—economic injustice, the sexual double standard of men and women, unhappy marriages, venereal disease, and religious hypocrisy. In his plays he refused to make simple moral judgments or resolve the dramatic action neatly. Not surprisingly, Ibsen and other realists met a great deal of opposition in producing their plays and were constantly plagued by censorship.

READ *A Doll's House* in *Anthology of Living Theatre* or at:

www.gutenberg.org/ebooks/2542

August Strindberg A second major figure ushering in the era of modern realism was the Swedish playwright August Strindberg (1849–1912). Strindberg, who was twenty years younger than Ibsen, took realism another step in plays like *The Father* (1887) and *Miss Julie* (1888): he personalized and intensified Ibsen's realism. Instead of focusing on people in a social context, Strindberg concentrated on individuals at war with themselves and with each other. In both *The Father* and *Miss Julie,* there is a war between the sexes: men and women vie with each other and attempt to dominate one another. In the end, one of them is destroyed—the man in *The Father* and the woman in *Miss Julie.* Also, Strindberg's characters are subject to the neuroses and anxieties that characterized so much of twentieth-century life. In fact, Strindberg took realistic drama closer to naturalism, a type of realism we will discuss shortly.

READ *Miss Julie*

www.gutenberg.org/ebooks/14347

Anton Chekhov The third significant playwright in the birth of modern realism is the Russian Anton Chekhov (1860–1904), whose play *The Sea Gull* (1896) was at first a failure but was later successfully revived by the Moscow Art Theatre. He wrote three other major plays: *Uncle Vanya* (1899), *The Three Sisters* (1900), and *The Cherry Orchard* (1904).

Chekhov's realism moved away from melodramatic elements such as the suicides in Ibsen's *Hedda Gabler* and Strindberg's *Miss Julie.* He also dealt with a full gallery of characters—often twelve or fourteen rather than five or six—and he orchestrated his characters in such a way that their stories overlapped and echoed one another. Chekhov also developed a blend of tragedy and comedy, employing a genre—often referred to as tragicomedy, discussed in Chapter 5—that has characterized much of modern drama.

READ *The Cherry Orchard* in *Anthology of Living Theatre* or at:

www.ibiblio.org/eldritch/ac/chorch.htm

NATURALISM

Naturalism is a form of theatre that developed alongside the realism of Ibsen, Strindberg, and Chekhov; it can be seen as a subdivision of realism or an extreme form of

AUGUST STRINDBERG
Along with Ibsen, the Swedish dramatist August Strindberg was a pioneer in developing modern realistic drama. These playwrights revolutionized the theatre of the late nineteenth century by dealing with taboo subject matter in a manner that mirrored everyday life. Much of their work was controversial and could not be produced in state or commercial theatres. (Theatre Collection, Museum of the City of New York)

THE CHERRY ORCHARD BY ANTON CHEKHOV
The Russian dramatist Anton Chekhov created a type of modern realistic drama that has had a profound influence on subsequent dramatists. Subtle, low-key, it avoided melodramatic elements but probed deeply and movingly into the hearts and souls of the characters he depicted. His final masterpiece was *The Cherry Orchard*, in which the main character, Madame Ranevskaya, unable to adjust to modern times, loses the family home and her precious cherry orchard. In this scene we see the cast, with Zoë Wanamaker as Ranevskaya, in a production at London's National Theatre, directed by Howard Davies. (© Geraint Lewis)

realism. The naturalistic movement began in France in the nineteenth century and spread to other European countries. In *naturalism,* everything onstage—characters, language, properties, settings, costumes—should seem to have been lifted directly from everyday life. Dramatic action should never seem contrived but rather should look like a "slice of life."

Many of the naturalists believed that the most appropriate subject matter for drama was the lower class, and they frequently focused on the sordid and seamy aspects of society in order to confront audiences with social problems and instigate reforms. The most famous naturalistic theorist and playwright was the French author Émile Zola (1840–1902).

The naturalists' extreme position of absolutism in form and subject matter ultimately prevented their movement from being more influential and realism was seen as a more viable theatrical form.

Naturalism Special form of realism developed in Europe in the late nineteenth century; it was not carefully plotted or constructed but was meant to present a "slice of life."

PRODUCERS OF REALISM: INDEPENDENT THEATRES

At the time when they were first written, realistic and naturalistic works were seen by the mainstream as too controversial for production; in England, for example, the Lord Chamberlain refused to allow many of these works to be performed. In order to overcome this problem, a number of independent theatres were established throughout Europe. They were exempted from government censorship because they were organized as subscription companies, with theatregoers being treated like members of a private club.

NATURALISM

An extreme form of realism is naturalism, which attempts to put onstage an unflinching, almost documentary version of people and events as they are encountered in real life. An early example is *Thérèse Raquin* (1873), a drama by Émile Zola. In the preface to this play, Zola stated the tenets of naturalism. Here we see Ben Daniels as Laurent and Charlotte Emmerson as Thérèse in a London production. (© Geraint Lewis)

The best-known of these independent theatres were the Théâtre Libre (Free Theatre), founded in Paris in 1887 by André Antoine (1858–1943); the Freie Bühne (Free Stage), founded in Germany in 1889 by Otto Brahm (1856–1912); and the Independent Theatre, founded in London in 1891 by J. T. Grein (1862–1935). In 1892, the year after its founding, the Independent Theatre introduced the Irish-born George Bernard Shaw (1856–1950) to the London public by producing his first play, *Widower's Houses*.

Possibly the most influential of the late-nineteenth-century theatres dedicated to realism was the Moscow Art Theatre, which mounted a landmark production of *The Sea Gull* as well as Chekhov's other major plays. Founded in 1898 by Konstantin Stanislavski (1863–1938) and Vladimir Nemirovich-Danchenko (1858–1943), it continues to produce drama today. In addition to giving the world an important theatre, the Moscow Art Theatre provided the first systematic approach to realistic acting: that of Stanislavski, discussed in detail in Chapter 6, which formed the basis for most realistic acting in the twentieth century.

READ *The Sea Gull*

   www.gutenberg.org/ebooks/1754

1898, Moscow It is the evening of December 17, 1898, and the Moscow Art Theatre is about to give its first performance of *The Sea Gull* by the Russian playwright Anton Chekhov. Backstage, the actors and actresses are nervous—so nervous that just before the curtain is to rise, most of them have taken valerian drops, a tranquilizer. Konstantin Stanislavski, the director of the play, who is also playing the role of Trigorin—a bored commercial writer—finds it difficult to control a twitch in his leg.

The reason for their anxiety is easy to understand. The author, Anton Chekhov, who trained to be a doctor, is one of the best-known short-story writers in Russia. So far, however, his dramatic work has not met with the same approval as his stories. In fact, when *The Sea Gull* was first produced two years ago in Saint Petersburg, the performance was a fiasco, not because of the play but because the company presenting it had not rehearsed and had produced it very badly. So devastated was Chekhov by the experience that after the performance he left the theatre in despair and swore never again to write plays or even to let *The Sea Gull* be performed.

One reason why the company in Saint Petersburg failed to give a decent performance of *The Sea Gull* is that the play was quite different from anything they were accustomed to. It takes place on a Russian country estate and is about two generations of actresses and writers. The leading female character, Madame Akardina, is a vain, self-absorbed actress. Her son Treplev, an idealistic young writer, is in love with Nina, a young woman who aspires to be an actress. Akardina's lover, Trigorin, with whom Nina falls in love, is a successful writer but dissatisfied with his life. (This is the character Stanislavski is now playing in Moscow.)

A number of other people are also involved with these four main characters, and one of the unusual aspects of the play is that the characters' lives are all closely intertwined. This orchestration of a group of characters is unlike previous nineteenth-century dramas. Another unusual aspect is an absence of melodramatic confrontations and developments, such as the murders, suicides, and sudden plot twists that had been staples of most nineteenth-century theatre. Rather, the action is subtle, modulated, and true to life.

Interestingly, the same lifelike qualities that have confused so many people have attracted a playwright and producer named Vladimir Nemirovich-Danchenko—a cofounder, with Stanislavski, of the Moscow Art Theatre. Nemirovich-Danchenko and Stanislavski want their theatre to be different from others, and Nemirovich-Danchenko feels that *The Sea Gull* is just the kind of play that will set it apart. However, when he first asked Chekhov to let the Moscow Art Theatre present this play, Chekhov adamantly refused, because of the debacle in Saint Petersburg. It has taken all of Nemirovich-Danchenko's powers of persuasion to win Chekhov's consent.

All this explains why there is so much at stake tonight in Moscow, as Act I of *The Sea Gull* begins. Chekhov himself is so worried about the outcome that he is not even here; he is far away, in Yalta—partly because of ill health, it is true, but also because of his nervousness.

Now the performers are halfway through Act I, but they cannot tell how the audience is responding. When the act ends, they are greeted by a monumental silence. Fearing failure, the actress Olga Knipper (who will later become Chekhov's wife) fights desperately to keep from breaking into hysterical sobs. Then, all of a sudden, the silence is broken; the audience breaks into thunderous, tumultuous applause. In the words of an eyewitness: "Like the bursting of a dam, like an exploding bomb, a sudden deafening eruption of applause broke out." The applause goes on and on, and Stanislavski dances a jig. The same reaction will greet the next three acts.

Both Chekhov and the Moscow Art Theatre have triumphed, and a new chapter in modern theatre has begun. So significant is this event that a century later the symbol on the curtain of the Moscow Art Theatre will still be a sea gull.

During the early decades of the twentieth century—after the initial objections and censorship had eased—realistic plays began to be presented commercially in both Europe and the United States. In the United States, however, for a long time, small, independent groups like those that developed in France, Germany, and England produced these plays. The Provincetown Playhouse, the Neighborhood Playhouse, and

THE GROUP THEATRE'S *AWAKE AND SING*
Clifford Odets's play, produced in 1935, is an example of a realistic social drama dealing with American concerns of the 1930s. It is an intense family drama set in a Bronx apartment during the Depression, and it required the realistic acting for which the Group Theatre was noted. (Vandamm Collection/The Museum of the City of New York)

the Washington Square Players, all founded in 1915 as alternatives to commercial theatre, often presented experimental, nonrealistic work; they also offered a haven for controversial or unknown realistic drama. The Provincetown Playhouse, in particular, supported the early work of the playwright Eugene O'Neill (1888–1953).

In terms of realism, the most important producing group in the United States between World War I and World War II was the Group Theatre, a noncommercial company in New York's Broadway district. Its founding members were Lee Strasberg (1901–1982), Cheryl Crawford (1902–1986), and Harold Clurman (1901–1980); and its acting company included a number of performers who became well known in movies as well as on the stage. Its resident playwright was Clifford Odets (1906–1963), whose plays include *Awake and Sing* (1935) and *Golden Boy* (1937). The Group Theatre disbanded in 1941, but its influence on realistic acting, directing, and playwriting continued for many years.

During the Depression of the 1930s, President Franklin Delano Roosevelt established the Works Progress Administration (WPA), which organized governmentally subsidized agencies to put the unemployed back to work. The Federal Theatre Project, producing both realistic and highly theatrical productions and headed by Hallie Flanagan Davis (1890–1969), a college professor, supported theatrical ventures throughout the United States and helped revitalize interest in theatre outside New York City. The Federal Theatre also assisted aspiring African American theatres and artists, supporting, for example, an all-black production of *Macbeth* directed by Orson Welles (1915–1985). For political reasons the government discontinued funding the project in 1939.

Playwrights in many countries throughout the twentieth century continued the realistic drama initiated by Ibsen, Strindberg, and Chekhov. In Europe, for example, two Irish playwrights who had a strong impact on realism were John Millington Synge

THE REALISM OF IRISH PLAYWRIGHTS

Among the important realistic playwrights in Ireland who emerged between the two world wars was Sean O'Casey. O'Casey carefully reconstructs Irish life and concerns in such plays as *The Plough and the Stars.* Shown here are Gabrielle Reidy, Tony Flynn, and Cathy Belton in a scene from *The Plough and the Stars* directed by Wayne Jordan at the Abbey Theatre in Dublin. (© Ros Kavanagh)

(1871–1909), in plays like *Riders to the Sea* (1904); and Sean O'Casey (1884–1964), in such works as *Juno and the Paycock* (1924) and *The Plough and the Stars* (1926).

In the United States, Eugene O'Neill wrote a number of realistic plays early in his career, including *Anna Christie* (1921) and *Desire under the Elms* (1924). After writing experimental plays through much of the 1920s and 1930s, O'Neill later returned to realism and wrote what many consider his finest plays: *The Iceman Cometh* (1939), *A Moon for the Misbegotten* (1947), and *Long Day's Journey into Night* (produced in 1957). Another well-known realistic playwright of the 1930s and 1940s was Lillian Hellman (1905–1984).

Between 1945 and 1975, many playwrights continued to refine the realistic form. Two important American writers in this category were Tennessee Williams (1911–1983) and Arthur Miller (1915–2005). Williams's important realistic plays include *A Streetcar Named Desire* (1947) and *Cat on a Hot Tin Roof* (1954)—both of which won the Pulitzer Prize—and *The Night of the Iguana* (1961). Miller's realistic works include *All My Sons* (1947) and *A View from the Bridge* (1955).

Some critics suggest that Miller and Williams wrote in a form known as *selective realism*—a type of realism that heightens certain details of action, scenery, and dialogue while omitting others. For example, in Miller's *Death of a Salesman* (1949), the playwright highlights selected elements of the world of the main character, Willy Loman—elements that symbolize his downfall. Moreover, scenes in Willy's mind and scenes from

REALISTIC THEATRE CONTINUES

In the second half of the twentieth century, realism continued to be a major form of drama by Western playwrights. A good example is the work of Arthur Miller. Some of his plays could be classified as "selective realism," but others were realistic in the traditional sense. A good example is *A View from the Bridge,* shown here in a recent Broadway production featuring Scarlett Johansson, Santino Fontana, and Liev Schreiber. (© Joan Marcus)

the past are interspersed with scenes in the present. Tennessee Williams combines the theatrical device of a narrator with realistic scenes in his play *The Glass Menagerie* (1945).

READ *Cat on a Hot Tin Roof*

Anthology of Living Theatre

Throughout the twentieth century, the end of realism was pronounced periodically, but the form has continued with great vigor to the present day. In 1962, another American writer, Edward Albee (1928–   ), joined the list of important realists with his play *Who's Afraid of Virginia Woolf?* (1962). Albee's style is highly enigmatic, however, and some of his plays—such as *Three Tall Women* (1991); *The Play about the Baby* (1998); and *The Goat, or Who Is Sylvia?* (2002)—combine techniques from realism and departures from realism.

In England in the 1950s, a group of antiestablishment playwrights known collectively as the angry young men dealt with the dissolving British empire, class conflict, and political disillusionment. Most of the dramas by the "angry young men" are in the traditional realistic form, slightly modified. The most famous of these plays was *Look Back in Anger* (1956) by John Osborne (1929–1994).

DEPARTURES FROM REALISM

In spite of its substantial impact on our contemporary theatre, as well as on film and television, theatrical realism is often seen as having serious limitations. For example, realistic drama excludes a number of effective, long-standing theatrical devices, such as music, dance, symbolism, poetry, fantasy, and the supernatural. Some authors argue that theatre can never truly be realistic, that the conventions of the art are always apparent. From the outset of realism, then, there have been strong countermovements.

In discussing these ***departures from realism,*** we will look at the following: early antirealist playwrights; symbolism; anti-realist designers; Russian theatricalism; Expressionism; futurism; surrealism; theatre of cruelty; epic theatre; and absurdism. In addition we will discuss other non-traditional approaches including happenings, multimedia, environmental theatre, and poor theatre.

Departures from realism
To overcome perceived limitations of realistic theatre, this strand of modern theatre departs from realism via non-realistic or antirealistic presentations. It often uses symbolism, non-linear narrative, dream imagery, and other ways to avoid realistic representation.

DEPARTURES FROM REALISM: STRINDBERG
Toward the end of his career, August Strindberg wrote plays that departed from the realistic style. These dramas were forerunners of many avant-garde texts of the later twentieth century. Strindberg's *A Dream Play* uses the structure of a dream to break many of the conventions of realistic drama. Seen here are Angus Wright, Mark Arends, and Anastasia Hille, in a new version of the play by Caryl Churchill, directed by Katie Mitchell and staged at the Royal National Theatre in London. (© Geraint Lewis)

DEPARTURES FROM REALISM—PLAYWRIGHTS: IBSEN, STRINDBERG, AND WEDEKIND

As we noted earlier in this chapter, Ibsen and Strindberg are remembered most for their realistic plays, but late in their careers they moved away from realism. In plays like *The Master Builder* (1892) and *When We Dead Awaken* (1899), Ibsen adopted many of the tenets of symbolism, discussed below; and August Strindberg's later antirealistic dramas, such as *A Dream Play* (1902) and *The Ghost Sonata* (1907), have been especially influential. As its title indicates, *A Dream Play* evokes the world of dreams.

As Strindberg says in his explanatory note to *A Dream Play,* the events of the play are dramatized in "the disconnected but apparently logical form of a dream. Everything can happen; everything is possible and likely."

READ *A Dream Play* in *Anthology of Living Theatre* or at:

www.archive.org/details/playsbyaugustst00bjgoog

The German dramatist Frank Benjamin Wedekind (1864–1918), in such plays as *Spring's Awakening* (1891), combined symbolist and grotesque elements with realistic—sometimes controversial—subject matter. This particular play was the basis for a successful 2007 musical version.

SYMBOLISM

The leading antirealistic movement between 1880 and 1910 was ***symbolism.*** Its major proponents were French, but it influenced playwrights and practitioners in many other countries. The symbolists believed that drama should present not mundane, day-to-day

Symbolism Movement of the late nineteenth century and early twentieth century that sought to express inner truth rather than represent life realistically.

activities but the mystery of being and the infinite qualities of the human spirit. They called for poetic theatre in which symbolic images rather than concrete actions would be the basic means of communicating with the audience. Symbolist plays often seem to take place in a dream world, and their most important dramatic goal is not to tell a story but rather to evoke atmosphere and mood. Probably the most renowned symbolist authors were Maurice Maeterlinck (1862–1949) in Belgium and Paul Claudel (1868–1955) in France.

The symbolists, like the realists, needed independently organized theatre companies to produce their plays. In France, two theatre companies were dedicated to antirealistic drama and production style. Théâtre d'Art was organized by Paul Fort (1872–1960) in 1890. Three years later, Théâtre de l'Oeuvre was established by Aurélien-Marie Lugné-Poë (1869–1940). (Possibly the most notorious of Lugné-Poë's presentations was not a symbolist work but a play by Alfred Jarry (1873–1907) called *Ubu the King* (1896), a takeoff in comic-book style on Shakespeare—in particular, on *Julius Caesar, Macbeth,* and the history plays. In addition to farce and satire, it employed a number of scatological references.) In Ireland, the Abbey Theatre and the poet William Butler Yeats (1865–1939), who was also a playwright, were associated with early symbolist drama.

DEPARTURES FROM REALISM— DESIGNERS: APPIA AND CRAIG

Scene designers also contributed to the departure from realistically based representations of life. Adolphe Appia (1862–1928) and Edward Gordon Craig (1872–1966), in particular, were able to present many of the symbolists' theories visually. Appia (who was born in Switzerland) and Craig (who was English) both argued against photographic reproduction as a basic goal of scene design; rather, they believed that a setting should suggest a locale but should not reproduce it. Both employed levels and platforms to design spaces that would be functional for the performer, and both took full advantage

A LANDMARK PLAY

Alfred Jarry's *Ubu Roi*, written in 1896, is often cited as a forerunner of many avant-garde movements of the twentieth century. It is an insane takeoff of *King Oedipus* and a number of Shakespeare's histories and tragedies. Shown here, with Denis Lavant as the King, is a production at the Théâtre de Gennevilliers in France. (© Jean-Paul Lozouet)

of the introduction of electricity and used light as an integral visual element. Appia and Craig influenced many of the leading twentieth-century American designers; for example, devices such as Craig's ***unit set***—a single setting that can represent various locales—have been especially important.

Unit set Single setting that can represent a variety of locales with the simple addition of properties or scenic elements.

APPIA'S DESIGN FOR *IPHIGENIA IN AULIS*

Appia's ideas of lighting and scenery were revolutionary. He moved from realistic settings to the use of shapes and levels that would serve as acting areas. He was also among the first to realize the vast possibilities of modern lighting techniques. (Billy Rose Theatre Collection, New York Public Library for the Performing Arts, Astor, Lenox, and Tilden Foundations)

RUSSIAN THEATRICALISM: MEYERHOLD

The reaction against realism also influenced a number of Russian artists. Possibly the most influential was the director Vsevolod Meyerhold (1874–1940), who was the leading Russian antirealist between 1905 and 1939 and frequently experimented with ***theatricalism.*** Theatricalists liked to expose the devices of theatre, such as the way stage machinery works, to make the audience conscious of watching a performance; they also borrowed techniques from the circus, the music hall, and similar entertainments.

The list of Meyerhold's innovations and experiments is astounding, and much of what was called avant-garde in the second half of the twentieth century can be traced back to his experiments early in the century. Meyerhold's theatre was a director's theatre: he was literally the author of his productions, and he frequently restructured or rewrote classics. He searched for suitable environments for his presentations, arguing for the use of found spaces—that is, spaces (such as streets, factories, and schools) not originally meant for theatre. He experimented with, and theorized about, multimedia in stage productions.

Meyerhold also attempted to train his performers physically by using techniques of commedia dell'arte, the circus, and vaudeville. He devised an acting system known as ***biomechanics,*** which emphasized external, physical training; the implication of biomechanics was that the performer's body could be trained to operate like a machine. Meyerhold's sets, known as ***constructivist*** settings, provided machines for his performers to work on; these settings consisted of skeletal frames, ramps, stairways, and platforms and often looked like huge Tinkertoys.

Theatricalism Exposing the elements of theatre to make the audience members aware that they are watching theatre.

Biomechanics Meyerhold's theory that a performer's body should be machinelike and that emotion could be represented externally.

Constructivism Post–World War I scene-design movement in which sets—frequently composed of ramps, platforms, and levels—were nonrealistic and were intended to provide greater opportunities for physical action.

EXPRESSIONISM

Expressionism, which flourished in Germany at the time of World War I, was a movement in art and literature in which the representation of reality was distorted in order to communicate inner feelings. In a painting of a man, for example, the lines in his face would be twisted to indicate the turmoil he feels inside.

Expressionism in drama has well-defined characteristics. Expressionist plays are often highly subjective and the dramatic action is seen through the eyes of the protagonist and therefore frequently seems distorted or dreamlike. The protagonist in a typical expressionist play is a Christlike figure who journeys through a series of incidents that may be causally unrelated. Characters are representative types, often given titles—such as Man, Woman, or Clerk—rather than names. The language of the plays is often telegraphic, with most speeches consisting of one or two lines; but these speeches alternate with long lyrical passages. Many expressionist playwrights were politically motivated, supporting socialist and pacifist causes, though some were apolitical.

The major German expressionist playwrights were Georg Kaiser (1878–1945) and Ernst Toller (1893–1939). Shortly after expressionism flourished in Europe, its influence was felt in the United State; for example, in some of Eugene O'Neill's plays, including *The Emperor Jones* (1922), as well as in *The Adding Machine* (1923), by Elmer Rice (1892–1967).

FUTURISM AND SURREALISM

Futurism originated in Italy around 1909. Unlike the expressionists, the futurists idealized war and the machine age. They attacked artistic ideals of the past, ridiculing them as "museum art" and arguing that new forms had to be created for new eras. They also believed that audiences should be confronted and antagonized.

Surrealism began in 1924. One of its major exponents was André Breton (1896–1966), and its center was France. Surrealists argued that the subconscious is the highest plane of reality and attempted to re-create its workings dramatically. Many of their plays seem to be set in a dream world, mixing recognizable and fantastic events.

THE THEATRE OF CRUELTY AND EPIC THEATRE

The two most influential theatrical theorists in Europe between the world wars were Bertolt Brecht and Antonin Artaud. Both reacted vehemently against the principles and the aesthetics of realistic theatre. Antonin Artaud (1896–1948), who was French and who had originally been associated with the surrealists, proposed a *theatre of cruelty* in the 1930s. Artaud did not literally mean that theatre artists should be cruel to their

EUGENE O'NEILL'S *THE EMPEROR JONES*
This play, like many of O'Neill's dramas of the early 1920s, uses expressionistic techniques. The audience sees the drama through the eyes of the protagonist, a Black dictatorial ruler of a Caribbean island who is fleeing from his people in the jungle. Here we see John Douglas Thompson in the title role in a production at the Irish Repertory Theatre in New York City. (Sara Krulwich/The New York Times/Redux)

Expressionism Movement in Germany at about the time of World War I, characterized by an attempt to dramatize subjective states through distortion; striking, often grotesque images; and lyric, unrealistic dialogue.

Futurism Art movement, begun in Italy about 1909, which idealized mechanization and machinery.

Surrealism Departure from realism that attempted to present dramatically the working of the subconscious.

Theatre of cruelty Antonin Artaud's visionary concept of a theatre based on magic and ritual, which would liberate deep, violent, and erotic impulses.

BERTOLT BRECHT

Brecht's epic theories and plays continue to be part of contemporary theatre; his concepts, including alienation and historification, continue to be debated and are still influential. Brecht's personal life has been no less controversial than his work: recent scholarship suggests that some of his work was plagiarized and that his political stance was perhaps hypocritical. A prime example of Brecht's work is *Mother Courage and Her Children,* shown here with Meryl Streep as Courage and Frederick Weller as Eilif in a new version translated by Tony Kushner and directed by George C. Wolfe, at the Delacorte Theatre in Central Park. (© Michal Daniel)

audiences or physically brutalize them—although some avant-garde theatre artists in the 1960s interpreted cruelty as actual physical confrontation with spectators. He felt, instead, that the viewers' senses should be bombarded. (A contemporary example of such sensory involvement would be a multimedia presentation or a sound and light show at a rock concert.)

He argued that Western theatre needed to be totally transformed because its literary tradition, which emphasized language, was antithetical to its ritualistic origins. Artaud believed that Western theatre artists should study the stylized Asian theatres. He also asserted that there were "no more masterpieces," by which he meant that the classics should be produced not for their historical significance but only if they were still relevant to contemporary audiences. For Artaud, a text was not sacred but could be reworked in order to point up its relevance. Artaud, like many of the antirealists who preceded him, wanted to reorganize the theatre space to make the audience the center of attention.

Bertolt Brecht (1898–1956), who was German, developed what he called ***epic theatre.*** Brecht's major plays—including *Mother Courage* (1937–1941), *The Good Person of Setzuan* (1938–1940), and *The Caucasian Chalk Circle* (1944–1945)—were written between 1933 and 1945, while he was in exile from Hitler's Germany. His theories, most of which were formulated in the 1930s but frequently revised, have influenced many contemporary playwrights and directors. As the term *epic theatre* implies, Brecht's plays are epic in scope. They are, accordingly, episodic in structure: they cover a great deal of time, shift locale frequently, and have intricate plots and many characters. Brecht, an ardent socialist, believed that theatre could create an intellectual climate for social change, and the goal of his epic theatre is to instruct. He believed that a production should force the audience to remain emotionally detached—or *alienated*—from the dramatic action. To prevent emotional involvement, Brecht's works are highly theatrical; the audience is always made aware of being in a

Epic theatre Form of drama associated with Bertolt Brecht and aimed at the intellect rather than the emotions in order to affect social change.

theatre. A narrator is frequently used to comment on the dramatic action, for example. To alienate the audience, Brecht also used a technique he referred to as historification. Many of his plays, such as *Mother Courage,* are set in the past, but it is apparent that he is really concerned with contemporary events paralleling the historic occurrences.

READ *The Good Woman of Setzuan*

Anthology of Living Theatre

UNIQUE VOICES

Throughout the modern period there have been playwrights who presented a unique voice, a voice that does not fit neatly into one of the categories we have been discussing. Two examples are the Italian playwright Pirandello and two French dramatists. Luigi Pirandello (1867–1936) who in *Six Characters in Search of an Author* (1921) has six characters from an unfinished play existing in a playwright's mind enter a theatre and interrupt a rehearsal, in the hope that the troupe will act out their unfinished story. In the course of the action—as in several of his other plays—Pirandello deals very theatrically with questions of appearance versus reality and art versus life.

READ *Six Characters in Search of an Author*

http://www.ibiblio.org/eldritch/lp/six.htm

Two significant French playwrights of the period between World War I and World War II were Jean Giraudoux (1882–1944) and Jean Anouilh (1910–1987). Giraudoux believed in the primacy of the word, and his language was usually eloquent as well as witty. He also stressed contradictions, ironies, and antithesis in working out the themes of his plays. Among his better-known works are *Amphitryon 38* (1929) and *The Trojan War Will Not Take Place* (1935). As can be seen from their titles, many of his plays were based on classic themes or plots. Jean Anouilh also used a classic source for his best-known play, *Antigone* (1943), a reworking of the Greek classic that spoke to the situation in Nazi-occupied France.

IMPACT OF TOTALITARIANISM ON THEATRE

Before we discuss avant-garde theatre and departures from realism in the quarter century following World War II, we should briefly discuss how the rise of totalitarianism impacted the theatre and many of the artists. In totalitarian societies—particularly the Soviet Union under Stalin and Germany under Hitler—government-supported theatres became instruments of propaganda. Courageous artists attempted to attack these regimes, but for the most part experimentation and freedom of expression were suppressed. The totalitarian rulers saw realistic art as easier to manipulate and to use for propaganda and viewed individual experimentation as dangerous because it implied freedom. Therefore, the fascists and communists vigorously attacked many of the artists who experimented with forms that departed from realism.

In Spain, for example, the playwright Federico García Lorca (1898–1936)—author of *Blood Wedding* (1933), *Yerma* (1934), and *The House of Bernarda Alba* (1936)—was killed by Franco's forces during the Spanish civil war. Productions of García Lorca's works, which poetically dramatized the oppression of Spanish women, were not allowed in Spain until after Franco's death in 1975.

Numerous German theatre artists, because of their religion or politics, had to flee Germany after Adolf Hitler's takeover in 1933. They included the directors Max Reinhardt and Erwin Piscator (1893–1966) as well as the playwrights Brecht and Toller. Many artists who opposed the Third Reich but did not leave were interned in the Nazi concentration camps.

Still, theatrical artists did resist totalitarianism; the most vivid example of such resistance was the theatre organized by inmates of the Nazi concentration camps. In

THEATRE   YEAR   CULTURE AND POLITICS

1915

Easter Rebellion in Ireland (1916)

Bolshevik revolution (1917)

Major futurist productions at
Piccolo Teatro in Rome (1918)

Prohibition in United States;
peace of Versailles (1919)

Soviet renaissance: Meyerhold,
Vakhtangov, Tairov, Erveinov

1920

Women's suffrage in United States (1920)

Toller's *Man and the Masses;*
Pirandello's *Six Characters* (1921)

O'Neill's *The Hairy Ape* (1922);
Dullin's *Atelier* (1922)

Joyce's *Ulysses;* Mussolini's march on Rome (1922)

Jouvet in *Doctor Knock*
(1923)

Hitler's beer hall putsch in Munich (1923)

Stanislavski's *My Life in Art;*
Breton's *First Manifesto;*
O'Neill's *Desire Under the Elms* (1924)

Ortega y Gassett's *The Dehumanization of Art;* Kafka's
The Trial; Thomas Mann's *The Magic Mountain* (1924)

1925

Meyerhold's *Inspector General* (1926)

Schoenberg's twelve-tone music (1926)

Meryl Streep in Brecht's Mother Courage (1938)
(© Michal Daniel/Public Theater)

Depression begins; Wolfe's *Look Homeward, Angel;*
Faulkner's *The Sound and the Fury* (1929)

Brecht's *Threepenny Opera* (1928)

1930

O'Neill's *Mourning
Becomes Electra* (1931)

Spain's monarchy collapses (1931)

Group Theatre, United States (1931)

Socialist realism declared proper style in
Soviet Union; Brecht and other German artists
emigrate (c. 1934); Gielgud's *Hamlet* (1934)

Hitler takes power in Germany;
New Deal in United States (1933)

Lorca's *House of Bernarda Alba;* Giraudoux's
The Trojan War Will Not Take Place; Federal
Theatre Project in United States (1935)

1935

Italy attacks Ethiopia; purges in Soviet Union;
Nuremberg laws against Jews in Nazi Germany (1935)

Spanish Civil War; first television broadcast (1936)

Tyrone Guthrie appointed
administrator at the Old Vic (1937)

Artaud's *Theatre and Its Double* (1938)

*Spanish Civil War (1936-1939)
Death of a Loyalist Militiaman
(Robert Capa © International Center of
Photography/Magnum Photos)*

1940

World War II (1939–1945)

Thornton Wilder's *Skin of Our Teeth* (1942)

Hemingway's *For Whom the Bell Tolls* (1940)

Othello with Paul Robeson (1943)

Camus's *Myth of Sisyphus* (1943)

Sartre's *No Exit* (1944)

1945

United States drops atomic bomb on Japan;
United Nations formed (1945)

Sartre's No Exit (1944)
(© T. Charles Erickson)

camps in conquered territories during World War II, such as Auschwitz, there were surreptitious entertainments in the barracks: these improvised presentations consisted of literature and drama recited from memory, satirical skits, and traditional songs. In the camp at Theresienstadt, in Czechoslovakia, satirical plays, operas, and cabaret entertainments were written and openly staged; this was allowed because the Nazis were using Theresienstadt as a "model" camp—they brought the Red Cross and foreign officials there in order to discredit rumors of atrocities. Most of the artists who passed through Theresienstadt were later sent to extermination centers.

EXPERIMENTATION AND DEPARTURES FROM REALISM CONTINUE

The period from 1945 to 1975 saw a great deal of experimentation with theatrical forms and techniques. Much of this experimentation was inspired by political unrest and by a desire to question political authority through the questioning of traditional theatrical practices, styles, and techniques. One of the first of the nontraditional forms to develop immediately after World War II, theatre of the absurd, was born out of the unanswerable questions this horrific conflict had left in the minds of the survivors.

Existentialism and Theatre of the Absurd   *Existentialism* is a philosophy most clearly articulated by two Frenchmen, Jean-Paul Sartre (1905–1980) and Albert Camus (1913–1960), who were reacting, among other things, against World War II. Existentialists believe that existence has little meaning; that God does not exist; that humanity is alone in an irrational universe; and that the only significant thing an individual can do is accept responsibility for his or her own actions. Both Camus and Sartre wrote plays illustrating these beliefs. The best-known are Sartre's *The Flies* (1943), an adaptation of the Greek *Oresteia;* and *No Exit* (1944), in which hell is equated with other people.

In the early 1950s, a theatrical approach emerged that combined existentialist philosophy with revolutionary, avant-garde dramatic form. Although not an organized movement, it was called ***theatre of the absurd*** by the critic Martin Esslin (1918–2002). Esslin pointed out that the playwrights in this group have certain qualities in common: the notion that much of what happens in life is ridiculous or absurd and cannot be explained logically, and the belief that this ridiculousness or absurdity should be reflected in dramatic action. Among the writers taking this approach are Samuel Beckett (1906–1989), Jean Genet (1910–1986), Eugène Ionesco (1912–1994), Edward Albee, and Harold Pinter (1930–2008).

Absurdist playwrights present our existence, including human relationships and human language, as futile or nonsensical. To reinforce this theme, they use seemingly illogical dramatic techniques. Their plots do not have either traditional climactic structure or episodic structure. Frequently, nothing seems to happen: the plot moves in a circle, concluding in the same way it began. The characters are not realistic, and the settings are sometimes strange and unrecognizable. The language is often telegraphic and sparse; the characters fail to communicate.

Existentialism   Term applied to plays illustrating a philosophy whose modern advocate was Jean-Paul Sartre and which holds that there are no longer any fixed standards or values.

Theatre of the absurd   Term applied to the works of certain playwrights of the 1950s and 1960s who expressed a similar point of view regarding the absurdity of the human condition and believed that this should be reflected in the dramatic action.

READ Samuel Beckett's *Krapp's Last Tape*

Anthology of Living Theatre   •

Waiting for Godot (1953) by Samuel Beckett is probably the most famous of these enigmatic, nontraditional dramas. As in many absurdist dramas, the plot is cyclical: the action in Act II appears to start over, with nothing having changed since Act I. The two main characters, Vladimir and Estragon, spend their time waiting; they accomplish nothing and are unable to take control of their lives. The other two men, Lucky and Pozzo, also have no control over their destiny; fate reverses their roles, transforming one from master into servant and the other from servant into master. Beckett referred to *Waiting for Godot* as a "tragicomedy in two acts," a description that reveals his tragicomic view of the human condition.

After absurdism, there were further attempts to supersede traditional theatre practices. These experiments, carried out in Europe and the United States in the 1960s and 1970s, went in many directions—a reflection, no doubt, of the fragmentation of modern life. The experiments included happenings, multimedia, and environmental theatre.

Any discussion of departures from realism after World War II must also take into account new technology in scene and lighting design. The Czechoslovakian designer

1957, CALIFORNIA The setting is San Quentin prison in California on November 19, 1957. In the prison's North Dining Hall, a stage is set up where a group from the Actors' Workshop will perform Samuel Beckett's *Waiting for Godot.* It will be the first performance at the prison in over forty years.

The Actors' Workshop is a theatre group dedicated to performing provocative, experimental, avant-garde works by both national and international playwrights. Its members have made a name for themselves not only in the San Francisco area but throughout the United States. When performing, they work closely together as an ensemble.

The performers today are nervous, not only because they are performing in a penitentiary, but also because of the play itself. *Waiting for Godot* is a drama without much action, and it is filled with literary and religious references. It has already baffled intellectuals in Europe and the United States; how, the actors wonder, will a group of restless prisoners react to it?

The setting is described simply as "A country road. A tree." In actuality, it is a barren plain. The two central characters, Vladimir and Estragon, who are also known as Didi and Gogo, are tramplike clowns who are waiting for the Godot figure. They have the vague expectation that somehow, if and when he comes, Godot will be able to help them. It is never stated who Godot is: he may be God, he may be someone else, or he may not even exist. While they wait, they try to break the painful monotony of their boring lives with bickering and occasional vaudeville routines.

The difficulty of the play is compounded by the fact that the second act seems to be almost the same as the first act. In both acts, Vladimir and Estragon try to entertain themselves; they move between hope and despair; they engage in vaudeville routines and philosophical speculation.

Meanwhile, two other characters, Pozzo and Lucky, appear. Pozzo is an overbearing creature who treats Lucky as his slave. Lucky, who has been mute, toward the end of the first act suddenly makes a long speech filled with legal terms. In the second act, the roles of Pozzo and Lucky are somewhat reversed, as Pozzo has become blind.

There is not the usual progress or story line expected in a traditional play. There is no building of suspense, no careful development of characters, no sudden plot twist, no big payoff at the end. In short, the play defies most of the conventional notions of both the content and the structure of drama.

At the end of the play, Godot's identity still has not been revealed, nor has he ever appeared. Instead, a young messenger arrives at the close of the first and second acts and announces that while Godot will not come that day, he will no doubt come the next.

The members of the Actors' Workshop have been acting together for a long time; and when they approach a play, they take their time, exploring the text, becoming familiar with the characters, and engaging in improvisation as they develop a performance. Even with this background they are apprehensive as they approach the performance at San Quentin. These, after all, are prisoners, not a sophisticated, intellectual audience, and this material is difficult for even the most scholarly spectators.

With these difficulties in mind, the performers from the Actors' Workshop begin their presentation. Shortly after the performance is under way, they have an indication that the production will go over better and be more readily understood than they had anticipated. Within the first few minutes, the audience grows quiet. A group of men sitting on some steps who had planned to leave early become engrossed and stay.

To the surprise of the performers, the audience sits in rapt attention. The prisoners follow the play closely from beginning to end and seem to understand what is happening. After the performance is over, it is clear that the prisoners have understood much of what they have seen—perhaps more than other audiences might understand. These prisoners, waiting out their sentences in boredom and frustration, have intuitively connected with the men onstage who wait for the unknown Godot, who never comes.

Josef Svoboda (1920–2002), for example, experimented with such elements as projections, multimedia, movable platforms, and new materials, including plastics. Computer technology as well has been incorporated into many modern theatre buildings and lighting systems.

Happenings were what the name suggests: unstructured events that occurred with a minimum of planning and organization. The idea—especially popular in the

Happening Nonliterary or unscripted theatrical event using a scenario that allows for chance occurrences.

Multimedia Use of electronic or digital media, such as projections, films, video, or computer animation in live theatrical presentations.

Environmental theatre A type of theatre production in which the total environment—the stage space and the audience organization—is transformed in order to blur distinctions between performers and spectators.

Poor theatre Term coined by Jerzy Grotowski to describe his theatre, which was stripped to the bare essentials of actor and audience.

Eclecticism This strand of modern theatre combines various theatrical trends or works across the boundaries of different trends.

1960s—was that art should not be restricted to museums, galleries, or concert halls but can and should happen anywhere: on a street corner, in a grocery store, at a bus stop.

Multimedia is a joining of theatre with other arts—particularly dance, film, and television. In work of this sort, which is still being produced, live performers interact with sequences on film or television. The idea here is to fuse the art forms or to incorporate new technology into a theatrical event. A current form that frequently combines theatre, dance, and media is called performance art.

The American director and teacher Richard Schechner (1934–   ) coined the term *environmental theatre* in the 1960s; many characteristics of environmental theatre, however, had developed out of the work and theories of earlier avant-garde artists, including Vsevolod Meyerhold and Antonin Artaud. Proponents of environmental theatre treat the entire theatre space as a performance area, suggesting that any division between performers and viewers is artificial. For every production, spatial arrangements are transformed. (See the discussion of created and found spaces in Chapter 8.)

The major influence on Schechner's theories is the Polish director Jerzy Grotowski (1933–1999). Works staged by Grotowski with the Polish Laboratory Theatre from its founding in 1959 until 1970 had many characteristics of environmental theatre. For each production, the theatre space and the performer-audience relationship were arranged to conform to the play being presented. In his version of *Doctor Faustus*, for instance, the theatre space was filled with two large dining tables at which audience members sat as if attending a banquet given by Faustus. As is true of Schechner, for most of Grotowski's productions existing scripts were radically modified by the performers and director. The acting style was externally based, emphasizing body and voice rather than emotions. Grotowski called his theatre *poor theatre,* meaning poor in scenery and special effects. Rather, it relied on the performers for its impact.

ECLECTICS

Some theatre artists between 1875 and 1975 tried to bridge the gap between realism and antirealism. These practitioners—known as *eclectics*—were not doctrinaire; instead, they argued that each play should define its own form. It would be impossible to list every global eclectic during this time period. Early eclectic directors included the Austrian Max Reinhardt (1873–1943) and the Russian Yevgeny Vakhtangov (1883–1922).

The English director Peter Brook (1925–   ) is a well-known contemporary eclectic. In staging *Marat/Sade* (1964), Brook applied concepts borrowed from Artaud's theatre of cruelty. His production of Shakespeare's *A Midsummer Night's Dream* (1970) was clearly influenced by Meyerhold's experiments with biomechanics and circus arts; for example, the fairy gods appeared on trapezes. Brook has tried to avoid what he calls "deadly" commercial theatre, which does not allow for experimentation, a theory he explained in his book *The Empty Space* (1968).

There have also been many directors on the European continent who have experimented with varied avant-garde theatre techniques. Some of these directors have worked only in alternative environments, but others have brought their experimental style of production into leading government-subsidized national theatres. Some have merged realistic and theatricalist techniques in their productions. They include Peter Stein (German, 1937—   ); Yuri Lyubimov (Russian, 1917–   ); Tadeusz Kantor (Polish, 1915–1990); Peter Zadek (German, 1926–   ); and Ariane Mnouchkine

PETER BROOK: INNOVATIVE THEATRE DIRECTOR
In the last half of the twentieth century, a number of creative, innovative directors emerged on the European continent and in Britain. In England, Peter Brook distinguished himself, first with Shakespeare and then with far more experimental work. One of his bold productions, influenced by the theories of Antonin Artaud, was *Marat/Sade,* shown here; the play was set in an insane asylum at the time of the French revolution. (© Dennis Stock/Magnum Photos)

(French, 1940–   ). Mnouchkine, who founded the avant-garde Théâtre du Soleil in Paris in 1964, has become one of the most widely admired directors in Europe.

POPULAR THEATRE

Popular theatre is mainstream theatre. It does not aspire to be high art or to be philosophical. It is not interested in being experimental or "cutting edge" drama. Rather, it wishes primarily to engage its audience—to keep them on the edge of their seats at a suspense drama or to entertain them with music and laughter.

Popular theatre was widespread and immensely successful throughout the 19th century. Audiences flocked to plays as well as vaudeville, circuses, and musical revues. This continued into the 20th century. In the 1927–28 season on Broadway an astounding 281 productions opened. That is more than two productions every three days. To accommodate these productions there were 65 Broadway theatres. During the 1930s, the combination of the new talking movies and the Depression cut the number of new productions sharply, but at mid-century, the number still remained higher than it is today.

Witty comedies were very much in evidence during the first four decades of the twentieth century and with writers like Neil Simon (1927–   ) well into the latter part of the 1900s. Rather than survey the entire field of popular theatre, however—melodrama, comedies, farces, and so forth—we will focus on a unique American contribution to popular theatre: the musical.

AMERICAN MUSICAL THEATRE

Antecedents   In the nineteenth century, melodrama used music to accompany the action of plays. Singing and dancing also played a key role in other forms of nineteenth-century theatrical entertainment, such as vaudeville and burlesque. Another form that developed in the late nineteenth century was operetta—a romantic musical piece featuring melodic solos, duets, and choruses interspersed with spoken dialogue. Examples of operetta include the works from Great Britain of W. S. Gilbert (1836–1911) and Arthur Sullivan (1842–1900), such as *The Pirates of Penzance* (1879) and *The Mikado* (1885). The American composer Victor Herbert (1859–1924) also composed operettas, such as *Naughty Marietta* (1910).

In the early twentieth century, the musical shows of George M. Cohan (1878–1942), such as *Little Johnny Jones* (1904) and *Forty-Five Minutes from Broadway* (1906), had songs with an American flavor and more realistic dialogue and better plot development than earlier musicals. Cohan's shows moved a step closer to today's "book" musicals—musicals that tell a story. (The dialogue and action of a musical are sometimes called the ***book,*** though the term libretto is also used.)

Book   Spoken (as opposed to sung) portion of the text of a musical play.

Around the time of World War I and in the period following, a truly native American musical began to emerge. It featured a story that was typically frivolous combined with enduring popular songs. Among the well-known composers of this period were Irving Berlin (1888–1989), Jerome Kern (1885–1945), George Gershwin (1898–1937), Cole Porter (1891–1964), and Richard Rodgers (1902–1979). Matching the inventiveness of the composers were the lyricists, including Ira Gershwin (1896–1983), who wrote lyrics for many of his brother's tunes; and Lorenz Hart (1895–1943), who teamed up with Richard Rodgers. Berlin and Porter wrote their own lyrics.

In 1927, Oscar Hammerstein II (1895–1960), who wrote the lyrics and libretto, and Jerome Kern, who composed the music, combined some of the best aspects of operetta and musical comedy to create *Show Boat.* The story was thoroughly American, rather than an exotic romantic fable, and it dealt with serious material—including the then-controversial love story of a black woman and a white man. It was also innovative in that the songs were integrated into the plot.

Another milestone of musical theatre was Gershwin's *Porgy and Bess* (1935), with a book by DuBose Heyward (1885–1940). Set in the African American community of Charleston, South Carolina, it is even more realistic than *Show Boat;* and its score is so powerful that many people consider it an opera rather than a musical.

The High Point of American Musicals   *Oklahoma!*—which was produced in 1943 and brought the team of Rodgers and Hammerstein together for the first time—heralded a significant era of the American *book musical. Oklahoma!* has been praised for seamlessly fitting together story, music, lyrics, and dances so that tone, mood, and intention became a unified whole. Its choreography, by Agnes deMille (1905–1993), included a ballet sequence that influenced many later choreographers, including Jerome Robbins (1918–1998) and Bob Fosse (1927–1987). Rodgers and Hammerstein went

SHOW BOAT: LANDMARK MUSICAL

When *Show Boat* opened in 1927, it began a new chapter in the history of the American musical. The chorus line was eliminated, miscegenation (a romance between a White man and a Black woman) was treated for the first time, and other problems facing African Americans were touched on. Also, it had a glorious score by Jerome Kern and Oscar Hammerstein. Shown here is a revival, staged by Harold Prince in 1993—a Canadian production that later moved to London and also Broadway. (© Catherine Ashmore)

on to create other significant musicals such as *Carousel* (1945), *South Pacific* (1949), *The King and I* (1951), and *The Sound of Music* (1959).

Among other notable musicals during the 1940s and 1950s were Irving Berlin's *Annie Get Your Gun* (1946), based on the life of Annie Oakley; Cole Porter's musical version of *The Taming of the Shrew*, called *Kiss Me, Kate* (1948); *Guys and Dolls* (1950) by Frank Loesser (1910–1969); *My Fair Lady* (1956), by the librettist and lyricist Alan Jay Lerner (1918–1986) and the composer Frederick Loewe (1904–1988), based on George Bernard Shaw's *Pygmalion* (1913); and *West Side Story*, a modernization of *Romeo and Juliet* which was created by the composer Leonard Bernstein (1918–1990), the lyricist Stephen Sondheim (1930–), and the librettist Arthur Laurents (1918–2011).

Some commentators believe that *Fiddler on the Roof* (1964)—with music by Jerry Bock (1928–2010), lyrics by Sheldon Harnick (1924–), and book by Joseph Stein (1912–2010)—marks the end of this era of outstanding book musicals. *Fiddler on the Roof*, about a Jewish family whose father attempts to uphold tradition in a Russian village where the Jewish community faces persecution, was directed and choreographed by Jerome Robbins. One example of changes in the musical following *Fiddler on the Roof* was the rock musical *Hair* (1967), by Galt McDermot (1928–), James Rado

HIGH POINT OF AMERICAN MUSICALS
A theatre in the long-standing tradition of American musical comedy, intended primarily for entertainment, is *Guys and Dolls,* with words and music by Frank Loesser. The story of a gambler who bets he can woo a Salvation Army worker, it features memorable melodies that run the gamut from ballads to comic numbers. An example of the latter is a song called "Sit Down, You're Rocking the Boat," shown in this scene from a production at the Paper Mill Playhouse in New Jersey. (© Gerry Goodstein)

(1932–) and Gerome Ragni (1935–1991), which had no actual story line and was a celebration of the antiestablishment lifestyle of the 1960s.

American Musicals After 1975   Although this chapter ends at the year 1975, with the musicals we are discussing it seems logical to continue tracing their development in this chapter rather than break off. We will, therefore, proceed at this point with our survey of American musicals.

   After *Hair,* the musical scene became increasingly fragmented, with fewer and fewer book musicals being written. In place of book musicals, there were other approaches, one being the concept musical, in which a production is built around an idea rather than a story. Two examples, both composed by Stephen Sondheim (1930–) and directed by Harold Prince (1928–), are *Company* (1970) and *Follies* (1971). Two of Sondheim's other works, *Sunday in the Park with George* (1985) and *Into the Woods* (1988), can also be considered concept musicals.

   Another significant trend in musicals of the 1970s and 1980s was the ascendancy of the choreographer as the director of musicals. Jerome Robbins, director of *West Side Story* and *Fiddler on the Roof,* was generally recognized as the leading director-choreographer in the United States. Following him, *A Chorus Line* was developed by

MUSICAL REVIVALS

The twenty-first century in the American theatre, as well as other parts of the world, has seen many revivals of well-known American musicals from the past. A good example is the 2008–2009 revival of *Hair*, a groundbreaking musical first produced in 1968. It was a musical celebration of the liberation and free thinking of the 1960s in the United States. Both the original production and the revival were staged by the Public Theater. Book and lyrics by Gerome Ragni and James Rado; music by Galt MacDermot; directed by Diane Paulus. (© Michal Daniel)

the director-choreographer Michael Bennett (1943–1987). Other significant director-choreographers were Gower Champion (1920–1980), responsible for *Hello Dolly!* (1964) and *42nd Street* (1980); Bob Fosse, who directed *Sweet Charity* (1966) and *Pippin* (1972); and Tommy Tune (1939–   ), who directed *Nine* (1982) and *Grand Hotel* (1989). Other contemporary director-choreographers are Susan Stroman (1960–   ), responsible for *The Producers* (2001), and Kathleen Marshall (1962–   ), director of the revival of *Anything Goes* (2010).

Still another trend of the decades since 1965 has been the emergence of British composers and lyricists. The leading figure in this movement is the composer Andrew Lloyd Webber (1948–   ), who, with the lyricist Tim Rice (1944–   ), wrote *Jesus Christ Superstar* (1971) and *Evita* (1979). Webber has also written *Cats* (1982) and *The Phantom of the Opera* (1987). Two other lavish musicals that originated in Britain are *Les Misérables* (1987) and *Miss Saigon* (1989). There has also been a movement toward revivals of earlier musicals by both American and English theatre artists.

Among several noticeable recent trends in musicals in the United States is the adaptation of films into stage musicals such as *The Producers* (2001), *Hairspray*

RECENT AMERICAN
MUSICALS
The new musical *The Book of Mormon* successfully combines traditional musical theatre elements with contemporary edgy comments and observations. It concerns a group of Mormon missionaries who visit the African country of Uganda and much of the humor arises from the clash of cultures. Written by Trey Parker and Matt Stone, the music is by Robert Lopez. The actors are (l-r:) Rema Webb, Andrew Rannelis, and Josh Gad. (Sara Krulwich/The New York Times/Redux)

(2003), *Monty Python's Spamalot* (2005), and the internationally successful *Billy Elliott* (2005). Disney's musicals, including *The Lion King* (1997) and *Aida* (1999), have also been highly successful. Still another trend has been the "jukebox," or "songbook," musical in which the well-known songs of composers or singers are the basis for the show. Examples are *Mamma Mia* (2001), featuring the music of the Swedish group ABBA, and *Jersey Boys* (2005), based on music made popular by the group The Four Seasons.

Scattered among these kinds are more traditional book musicals. The huge success of *Rent* by Jonathan Larson (1960–1996), first off-Broadway in 1995 and then on Broadway in 1996, seemed to reawaken interest in the American form. An adaptation of the opera *La Bohème, Rent* uses many musical forms (rock, jazz, Latin, opera) to tell a story about starving artists in the East Village of New York. Other more traditional musicals include: *Wicked* (2003), *Light in the Piazza* (2005), and *Memphis* (2009); in addition to other recent traditional musicals, there have been several unconventional and often irreverent book musicals, such as *Avenue Q* (2003) and *The Book of Mormon* (2011). The spectacular and controversial *Spiderman: Turn off the Dark* (2011), with music by Bono and The Edge from U2, is an attempt to create a traditional book musical based on both the popular comic book and films.

GLOBAL THEATRE IN THE TWENTIETH CENTURY

Globalism A strand of modern theatre that involves the mutual influences of theatre from around the world.

We said at the beginning of this chapter that globalization was one of the developments characteristic of twentieth century theatre. *Globalization* is the exchange of ideas, money, goods and services, art works, and languages among nations and across cultures. Advances in technology, communication, and transportation systems made possible the rapid and relatively easy exchange among people around the world of ideas and techniques in all fields, including the arts. In what follows, we will take a particular look at the exchange between Asian and Western theatre as a particularly rich example of cultural exchange; we will discuss more fully theatrical globalization in Chapter 15.

THEATRE	YEAR	CULTURE AND POLITICS

1945

Barrault's Compagnie Madeleine Renaud-Jean-Louis Barrault established (1946) — Nuremberg trials (1946)

Genet's *The Maids;* Williams's *A Streetcar Named Desire* (1947)

Ionesco's *The Bald Soprano;* Berliner Ensemble; Miller's *Death of a Salesman* (1949); Arena Stage in Washington (1949) — Orwell's *1984;* Germany divided (1949)

Vilar at Théâtre National Populaire (1951)

1950

Korean War (1950–1953)

Arthur Miller (1915–2005) (AP Images)

Beckett's *Waiting for Godot* (1953) — Stalin dies (1953)

Thornton Wilder's *The Matchmaker* (1954) — McCarthy-Army hearings; hydrogen bomb tested (1954)

1955

Osborne's *Look Back in Anger;* Dürrenmatt's *The Visit* (1956) — Russia crushes Hungarian revolt; Suez crisis (1956)

Sputnik I and II (1957)

Pinter's *Birthday Party;* Joseph Svoboda Laterna Magika (1958)

Hansberry's *A Raisin in the Sun* (1959); Grotowski founds Polish Laboratory Theater (1959)

Jerzy Grotowski (1933–1999) (AP Images)

1960

Belgian Congo granted independence (1960)

Berlin Wall (1961)

Cuban missile crisis (1962)

Café La Mama founded; Albee's *Who's Afraid of Virginia Woolf?* (1962) — Warfare escalates between North and South Vietnam; Martin Luther King arrested in Birmingham; John F. Kennedy, president of the United States, assassinated (1963)

National Theater under Laurence Olivier (1963)

Weiss's *Marat/Sade* (1964) — Khrushchev resigns (1964)

East West Players (1965)

1965

Martin Luther King, Jr. (1929–1968) (AP Images)

Ragni, Rado, MacDermot's *Hair* (1967)

The Performance Group (1968); Ontological-Hysteric Theatre (1968) — Martin Luther King, Jr. assassinated; Andy Warhol's *Campbell Soup Can I* (1968)

Lonne Elder's *Ceremonies in Dark Old Men* (1969) — American astronauts walk on moon (1969)

Dario Fo's *The Accidental Death of an Anarchist* (1970); Mabou Mines (1970)

1970

Walker's *The River Niger* (1972)

Asian-American Theatre Workshop (1973)

Nixon resigns presidency (1974)

Stopard's *Travesties* (1975)

Kathakali Traditional dance
drama of India.

Beijing opera A nineteenth-
century popular theatre form
in China which combines
music, theatre, and dance
with colorful conventions of
makeup, costumes, move-
ment, and voice production.

SOME BACKGROUND ON ASIAN THEATRE

Before we come to this artistic exchange among nations from 1875 to 1975, however, as
background we should address important events in Asian theatre that occurred prior to
that time. In Japan, for example, the three ancient forms—nō, kabuki, and bunraku—
were alive and well through the centuries and continued into the twentieth century.

In India, during the three centuries before 1900, an interesting form of dance
drama, called *kathakali,* had been prominent in the southwestern portion of the country. Kathakali is produced at night by torchlight, on a stage approximately sixteen feet
square covered with a canopy of flowers. In subject matter it heightens certain elements
of Sanskrit drama, presenting violence and death onstage in dance and pantomime. The
stories revolve around clashes between good and evil, with good always winning. A language of 500 or more gestural signs has been developed to tell these stories.

In China, a nineteenth-century development was an immensely popular form
known as *Beijing opera.* Originally, it was called Peking opera, but when the name
of the city was changed from Peking to Beijing, the newer name was assigned to the
form. This form of theatre has recently been called by other Chinese names, jingju and
xiqu being two of them. (Although mindful of the rationale for each of these, we will
use the term Beijing opera.) In Beijing opera, elements of folk drama and other genres
close to ordinary people form the basis of what is truly a popular theatre—one of the
most colorful and striking theatrical forms now practiced in Asia.

Though it is called opera, Beijing opera combines music, theatre, and dance in its
own unique way. Because of its origins in popular entertainment, it does not aspire
to be a work of high literary merit or philosophical speculation. But it preserves long
traditions of popular singing, acrobatics, and acting and thus provides insights into the
high development of performance techniques in traditional Chinese theatre. Its plays
or skits involve elaborate and colorful conventions of makeup, movement, and voice
production. In staging, Beijing opera stresses symbolism. The furniture onstage usually
consists only of a table and several chairs, but these few items are used with imagination. Depending on how they are arranged or referred to, they may represent a dining
hall, a court of justice, or a throne room. The table may stand for a cloud, a mountain,

or any other high place. A tripod on a table, holding incense, indicates a palace. When the script calls for a long journey, the performers walk in a circle about the stage. Later, this creative use of the stage impressed many Western dramatists. Well before the turn of the twentieth century, the vitality of Beijing opera had made it the most popular form of traditional theatre in China; and later its stars—including the great twentieth-century actor Mei Lanfang (1894–1961)—became performers of enormous reputation not only in China but also in the West.

GLOBAL EXCHANGES

The mention of Mei Lanfang introduces us to the exchanges in theatre between Asia and the West. Beginning in the early years of the twentieth century playwrights from China and Japan, for example, became aware of the ground-breaking work of Ibsen, Strindberg, and Chekhov in the West, and in some cases their work was influenced by their knowledge of these European playwrights. The East-West connection also worked in the other direction. In the Global Cross Currents segment in Chapter 3 (see page 56), we noted how two well-known playwrights, Thornton Wilder and Bertolt Brecht, had seen Mei Lanfang perform and had become intimately acquainted with the symbolism, scenic approach, and story-telling techniques of Chinese theatre. We described how these authors began to incorporate the elements of Asian theatre into their own work.

As the new century progressed, the vigorous exchange among directors, playwrights, actors, and designers across the full range of theatrical ideas and concepts continued, interrupted only by World War II. In the late twentieth century, excellent examples of East-West exchanges is seen in the works of Julie Taymor and Ariane

BEIJING (PEKING) OPERA
A highly formalized theatre, Beijing (or Peking) opera was developed in China in the nineteenth century. It is not like Western grand opera; rather, it is a popular entertainment filled with song, dance, and acrobatics. It makes wide use of symbols—with, for instance, a table standing for a mountain, or a blue fabric for the sea, as shown here—and is performed in highly colorful and stylized costumes like the ones we see in this performance. The production being enacted is *The Legend of the White Snake*. (© ArenaPAL/Topham/The Image Works)

TWO IMPORTANT INTERNATIONAL DIRECTORS

ARIANE MNOUCHKINE: THÉÂTRE DU SOLEIL

Since her founding of the avant-garde Théâtre du Soleil in Paris in 1964, the French director Ariane Mnouchkine (1939–) has become one of the most widely admired directors in Europe, and in fact, around the world. Although strongly influenced by Copeau, Brecht, Artaud, and Meyerhold, she is also known for her effective use of nonwestern dramatic techniques, especially those of Japan and India. She was born in a small town near Paris, France, and attended Oxford University in England, majoring in Psychology. While there, she became involved with the Oxford university Drama Society and from that point on, her interest was theatre. In the early 1960s, Mnouchkine scraped together enough money to realize a lifelong dream of traveling to the far east. In Japan, Cambodia, and other parts of Asia, she found a beauty of form and a sense of ritual that she considered indispensable to theatre. When she returned to Paris in 1963, Mnouchkine and several of her friends established a "theatrical community" which was to become the Théâtre du Soleil (the Theatre of the Sun).

The company has produced everything from loose collections of improvised materials to acclaimed versions of Shakespeare's works to a powerful 10-hour staging of the *Oresteia,* the cycle of Greek tragedies about the house of Atreus. Mnouchkine is strongly in favor of the collaborative process in creating theatrical pieces. The director, she has stated, has become all powerful. Her goal, she says, "is to move beyond that situation by creating a form of theatre where it will be possible for everyone to collaborate without there being directors, technicians, and so on." She and her company use many techniques in developing their productions. These include improvisational exercises as well as styles such as commedia dell'arte and various Asian rituals.

Among the best-known collectively created productions of the Théâtre du Soleil are *1789* (1970), which environmentally dramatized the historical background of the French Revolution; *The Age of Gold* (1975); and *Les Atrides* (1991), the adaptation of the *Oresteia.* Among her most recent productions are *And Suddenly Sleepless Nights,* (1997), which deals with the plight of illegal immigrants; the two-part, 6-hour *Le Dernier Caravansérail (Odysées), (The Last Caravan Stop)* (2003), which deals with the horrors of refugees. For this last piece, she and members of her troupe spent three years collecting poignant and tragic stories from refugees from all parts of the world which they wove into their drama. *Les Éphémères* (2009) consists of series of interwoven vignettes, chiefly about middle-class life in France.

Ariane Mnouchkine's *Le Dernier Caravanserail,* shown here, was based on interviews of refugees in camps and detention centers in many parts of the world. (© Martine Franck/Magnum Photos)

THE THEATRE OF JULIE TAYMOR

The American director and designer Julie Taymor (1952–) is known predominantly for her vibrant productions, which draw on theatrical traditions

Mnouchkine, two directors featured in the Global Cross Currents segment above. Another example of an international artist is the Japanese director, Tadashi Suzuki. After World War II, Suzuki worked frequently in the West and many American and other Western artists—actors, writers, directors—worked at his theatre in the mountains of Japan. Suzuki is discussed more fully in the next chapter.

Julie Taymor. (AP Images)

opera adaptation of *Oedipus Rex* (1992), which drew on Greek sculpture and Japanese nō costumes. However, she is best known for her productions of *The King Stag* and the Disney musical *The Lion King*.

The King Stag was written in eighteenth-century Italy by Carlo Gozzi and tells of King Derramo and his evil prime minister, Tartaglia. In order to ensure that his daughter will marry the king, Tartaglia tricks the king into transferring his soul into the body of a stag, with the prime minister then taking control of the king's body. By her own count, Taymor identifies nine different countries whose theatrical traditions she drew from in creating *The King Stag*. She used masks from eighteenth-century Italian commedia dell'arte troupes, white ruffs from Elizabethan England, Japanese prints and colors, Taiwanese paper bird kites, Indonesian puppetry, Japanese bunraku, and ancient Chinese mirror stone techniques (through her use of Plexiglas puppets). The end result was an imaginative, colorful production that could not be defined by any one theatrical tradition.

Similarly, her Broadway production of *The Lion King* used elements of numerous theatrical cultures from across Asia, especially from Indonesia and Japan; also prominent was music from South Africa. Many of the scenes combine actors, masks, and puppets, illustrating once again her distinctive fusion of numerous theatrical forms. Taymor was also the original director and co-author of the musical *Spiderman: Turn off the Dark* which proved to be Taymor's least successful venture. The show's spectacular theatricality, including characters flying over the audience, led to excessive budget overruns, delayed openings, and accidents and Taymor was eventually replaced prior to the official opening of the musical.

Owing to the wide range of sources, Julie Taymor's productions are not re-creations of any one theatrical source, but rather compositions drawn from global and historical theatrical traditions.

Prepared by Naomi Stubbs, CUNY Graduate Center.

from across the globe. Her use of puppetry (adopted predominantly from Indonesia) and her costume designs mark her as a designer who uses eastern traditions.

Taymor has traveled to Sri Lanka, Indonesia, Japan, and India, and her travels have allowed her to encounter the very different theatrical forms of those countries. Her experiences of Japanese nō, bunraku, and avant-garde theatre, and Indonesian rod puppets (wayang golek) and shadow puppets (wayang kulit), were particularly influential in her later productions. In her early experiments with blending theatrical forms, she founded the theatrical company Teatr Loh, which included performers from Java, Bali, Sudan, and the west. This blending of eastern theatrical traditions has been continued through her many productions in the east and west.

Among Taymor's productions are an adaptation of a German novella set in India called *The Transposed Heads* (1984); a production of *Juan Darien* (1988, 1990), which drew on the puppet traditions of Indonesia and Japan and the music of Australia, South America, and Africa; and an

It should be noted, too, that exchanges were not confined to East and West. South and Central America, South Africa, North Africa, Southeast Asia, Australia and New Zealand, Eastern and Western Europe, Canada: all these areas became acutely aware of what was occurring in other parts of the world, and consciously or unconsciously often incorporated it into their own work; we will highlight many of these global exchanges in Chapter 15.

Summary

Modern theatre in the West began in the late nineteenth century with the realistic plays of Henrik Ibsen, August Strindberg, and Anton Chekhov. In realism, events onstage mirror observable reality in the outside world. The characters speak, move, dress, and behave as people do in real life; they are seen in familiar places such as living rooms, bedrooms, and kitchens.

One appeal of realism is that audiences can identify with and verify people and events onstage. One disadvantage of realism is that it excludes a number of traditional theatrical devices, such as poetry, music, ghosts, and special effects. Despite this drawback, however, realism is so effective that it has been a dominant theatrical form of the past 100 years.

Because of its uncompromising presentation of life, realism was initially produced not commercially but by small independent theatres. As it became more widely accepted, it entered the mainstream of theatre.

In the twentieth century, Synge and O'Casey in Ireland, O'Neill, Hellman, Miller, Williams, and Albee in the United States, and many other playwrights worldwide wrote powerful realistic drama.

From 1875 through 1975, there were also significant movements that departed from realism: these included symbolism, expressionism, futurism, surrealism, epic theatre, absurdism, and environmental theatre. Among practitioners who attempted to transform theatre were the designers Appia and Craig as well as the director Meyerhold. Key theories arguing against realism are Artaud's theatre of cruelty and Brecht's epic theatre. Grotowski and Schechner were proponents of environmental staging.

Throughout this time period, there continued to be a strong tradition of popular theatre. The American musical flourished between 1945 and 1975.

In Asian theatre, drama influenced by the West and avant-garde, experimental theatre took their place alongside traditional forms, while writers, directors, actors, and designers in the West were strongly influenced by their Eastern counterparts.

There were many theatre companies and artists who produced new experimental works. In the United States, the off-Broadway, off-off-Broadway, and regional theatres nurtured new artists and forms.

Thinking about Theatre

▶ Discuss why you believe a TV show or film that you have seen could be considered realistic.

▶ Discuss why a TV show or film that you have seen could be considered a departure from realism.

▶ Discuss how rock concerts use multimedia and environmental theatrical techniques.

▶ Why do you think musical comedy has been more popular in theatre than in film?

▶ Do you think absurdism continues to be relevant in today's theatre? Why? Why not?

▶ Discuss how the theories of Artaud and Brecht influenced the theatre since 1945.

Key Terms

Biomechanics Meyerhold's theory that a performer's body should be machinelike and that emotion could be represented externally.

Beijing opera A nineteenth-century popular theatre form in China which combines music, theatre, and dance with colorful conventions of makeup, costumes, movement, and voice produciton.

Book Spoken (as opposed to sung) portion of the text of a musical play.

Constructivism Post–World War I scene-design movement in which sets—frequently composed of ramps, platforms, and levels—were nonrealistic and were intended to provide greater opportunities for physical action.

Departures from realism To overcome perceived limitations of realistic theatre, this strand of modern theatre departs from realism via non-realistic or antirealistic presentations. It often uses symbolism, non-linear narrative, dream imagery, and other ways to avoid realistic representation.

Eclecticism This strand of modern theatre combines various theatrical trends or works across the boundaries of different trends.

Epic theatre Form of episodic drama associated with Bertolt Brecht and aimed at the intellect rather than the emotions.

Environmental theatre A type of theatre production in which the total environment—the stage space and the audience organization—is transformed in order to blur distinctions between performers and spectators.

Existentialism Term applied to plays illustrating a philosophy whose modern advocate was Jean-Paul Sartre and which holds that there are no longer any fixed standards or values.

Expressionism Movement in Germany at about the time of World War I, characterized by an attempt to dramatize subjective states through distortion; striking, often grotesque images; and lyric, unrealistic dialogue.

Futurism Art movement, begun in Italy about 1909, which idealized mechanization and machinery.

Globalism A strand of modern theatre that involves the mutual influences of theatre from around the world.

Happening Nonliterary or unscripted theatrical event using a scenario that allows for chance occurrences.

Kathakali Traditional dance drama of India.

Multimedia Use of electronic or digital media, such as projections, films, video, or computer animation in live theatrical presentations.

Naturalism Special form of realism developed in Europe in the late nineteenth century; it was not carefully plotted or constructed but was meant to present a "slice of life."

Poor theatre Term coined by Jerzy Grotowski to describe his theatre, which was stripped to the bare essentials of actor and audience.

Realism One of the five strands of theatre in the modern era, realism conveys everything onstage to resemble observable, everyday life to promote a strong sense of audience recognition and identification.

Surrealism Departure from realism that attempted to present dramatically the working of the subconscious.

Symbolism Movement of the late nineteenth century and early twentieth century that sought to express inner truth rather than represent life realistically.

Theatre of the absurd Term applied to the works of certain playwrights of the 1950s and 1960s who expressed a similar point of view regarding the absurdity of the human condition and believed that this should be reflected in the dramatic action.

Theatre of cruelty Antonin Artaud's visionary concept of a theatre based on magic and ritual, which would liberate deep, violent, and erotic impulses.

Theatricalism Exposing the elements of theatre to make the audience members aware that they are watching theatre.

Unit set Single setting that can represent a variety of locales with the simple addition of properties or scenic elements.

THEATRE ON THE WEB

For more research and to learn more about the topics in this chapter, please visit the Online Learning Center at **www.mhhe.com/livelyart8e.**

TODAY'S DIVERSE GLOBAL THEATRE

THE DAWNING OF A NEW CENTURY

TIMELINE: 1975 To Present

TODAY'S THEATRE: GLOBAL, DIVERSE, AND ECLECTIC

PERFORMANCE ART

POSTMODERNISM

DIVERSE THEATRES IN THE UNITED STATES

AMERICAN ALTERNATIVE THEATRE

AFRICAN AMERICAN THEATRE

LATINO-LATINA THEATRE

ASIAN AMERICAN THEATRE

NATIVE AMERICAN THEATRE

FEMINIST THEATRE AND GENDER DIVERSITY

GAY AND LESBIAN THEATRE

GLOBAL THEATRE

A CONTINUING GLOBAL TREND: DOCUMENTARY DRAMA

ENGLISH AND IRISH THEATRE

CANADA AND AUSTRALIA

ASIA, AFRICA, AND LATIN AMERICA

GLOBAL CROSSCURRENTS: Tadashi Suzuki: Japanese Internationalist

GLOBAL CROSSCURRENTS: Augusto Boal: The Theatre of the Oppressed

TODAY AND TOMORROW: A LOOK AHEAD

SUMMARY
THINKING ABOUT THEATRE
KEY TERMS
THEATRE ON THE WEB

◀ **TODAY'S GLOBAL THEATRE**   The story of *11 and 12,* directed by Peter Brook, is based on the novel "Life and Teaching of Tierno Bokar." It tells the extraordinary tale of a Sufi sage in Mali. Bokar, the humble yet remarkable man at the heart of the drama, becomes caught up in an epic struggle against hatred and violence incited by the colonial powers dominating his country in the mid-twentieth century. Adapted by Marie-Helene Estienne together with Peter Brook, *11 and 12* features a multinational company of actors and a creative team that includes Japanese composer Toshi Tsuchitori. Shown here are performers Jared McNeill, and Abdou Ouologuem, Tunji Lucas. (© Geraint Lewis)

n this chapter we will examine important trends in contemporary theatre. Three words that can characterize today's theatre are *global, diverse,* and *eclectic:* global because of the extensive amount of theatre produced throughout the world as well as the interaction between national theatres; diverse because the types of theatre available to audiences are so wide-ranging, and, as we noted in Chapter 1, because the audiences themselves are so diverse; and eclectic because contemporary theatre embraces such a wide variety of styles and types. Our ultimate goal in this chapter, however, will be to consider whether theatre as we know it will survive in the twenty-first century.

In order to understand our contemporary theatre, it must be viewed against the background of the complex, unsettled, often confusing political and social turmoil of the recent past.

The Dawning of a New Century

As we noted in Chapter 14, social unrest and violence marked the second half of the twentieth century. Worldwide political, economic, and cultural turmoil continued as the century ended. Technological changes continued to make communication and personal and global interaction even more immediate.

Contemporary society was again confronted by genocide in Bosnia, Rwanda, and the Sudan, and by reports of torture of prisoners by American military or CIA personnel in the aftermath of the Iraq War, forcing us to question whether there have been any real changes in moral outlook since World War II. Although the fall of totalitarian communism was celebrated in Eastern Europe, the world has also been troubled by continued poverty, crime, and intolerance toward racial minorities.

The American presidency, under Bill Clinton, was rocked by a number of scandals and impeachment hearings. George W. Bush, while losing the popular vote, was elected president in a highly contested election in 2000, and again in 2004 in another close election. Some suggest the United States had moved toward greater racial equality with the election of the nation's first African American president, Barack Obama, in 2008. A significant economic recession affected the entire global economy, including the United States, in 2008 and its effects continue to be felt.

There has also been continuing violence in the Middle East. A culmination of this instability was the terrorist attack on the United States on September 11, 2001. The United States proclaimed a war on terror and toppled the fundamentalist Islamic regime in Afghanistan. The United States and Great Britain also deposed the regime of Saddam Hussein in Iraq in 2003. However, in 2011, the wars in Afghanistan and Iraq continued, despite the death of 9/11 mastermind Osama bin Laden. There remained unresolved conflicts between Israelis and Palestinians. And while there were demonstrations and revolts demanding democratic reform in Arab and African nations in 2011, fueled by the ability to communicate instantaneously and across the globe through the Internet on Facebook, Twitter, and YouTube, the outcomes of these protests were unclear. In the same year, the Occupy Wall Street protest, which spread to cities across the United States and the world, reflected the ongoing social unrest due to the continued economic crisis.

1975 TO PRESENT

THEATRE	YEAR	CULTURE AND POLITICS

THEATRE

Augusto Boal's *Theatre of the Oppressed* (1975)

Soyinka's *Death and the King's Horseman* (1976)

Mamet's *American Buffalo* (1977)

Sam Shepard's *Buried Child*
wins Pulitzer Prize (1979)

Fuller's *A Soldier's Play* (1981)

Fugard's *"Master Harold"... and the Boys* (1982)

Norman's *'Night, Mother* (1983)

Stoppard's *The Real Thing* (1984)

Frayn's *The Benefactors* (1985)

August Wilson's *Fences* wins
Pulitzer Prize (1987)

Lost in Yonkers, Neil Simon
wins Pulitzer Prize (1991)

Suzuki and Bogart found SIKI (1992)

Angels in America, Tony Kushner
wins Pulitzer Prize (1993)

ANGELS IN AMERICA (1993)
(Sara Krulwich/The New York Times/Redux)

Wit by Margaret Edson
wins Pulitzer Prize (1999)

Peter Stein directs *Faust*,
Berlin, Germany (2000)

Topdog/Underdog by Suzan-Lori
Parks wins Pulitzer Prize (2002)

Mnouchkine *The Last Caravan* (2003)

Kevin Spacey assumes artistic
direction of London's Old Vic (2004)

Guthrie Theatre moves
into new facility (2006)

National Theatre of Scotland's
Black Watch premieres (2006)

Harold Pinter dies (2008)

Lynn Nottage's *Ruined* wins Pulitzer Prize (2009)

Josie Rourke becomes artistic director of
Donmar Warehouse in London (2012)

YEAR

1975
1980
1985
1990
1995
2000
2005
2010

CULTURE AND POLITICS

Camp David accord reached
between Israel and Egypt (1977)

Muslim revolution in Iran (1979)

Ronald Reagan elected president (1980)

Walker's *The Color Purple* (1983)

Space shuttle Challenger disaster (1986)

Iran-Contra scandal (1987)

George H. W. Bush elected U.S. president (1988)

Chinese government crushes pro-
democracy demonstration (1989)

Berlin Wall taken down; eastern Europe
democratized (1990)

Soviet Union dissolves (1991)

Bill Clinton elected president
of the United States (1992)

World Trade Organization (1995)

Bill Clinton reelected president (1996)

Gehry's Bilbao museum opens (1997)

Gehry's Guggenheim Museum,
Bilbao (1997)
(© Inge King)

George W. Bush elected president
of the United States (2000)

Terrorist attack on World Trade
Center in NYC (9/11/2001)

War in Iraq (2003)

George W. Bush wins reelection as
president of the United States (2004)

Hamas wins Palestinian election (2006)

Barack Obama elected
President of U.S. (2008)

Recession impacts world
economy (2009)

Obama elected President
(2008)
(Official White House Photo
© Peter Souza)

Arab Spring
uprising (2011)

Today's Theatre: Global, Diverse, and Eclectic

As always, the arts have continued to reflect the world in which they are being created. Our theatre today is so complex because it mirrors the significant changes in our global society and the concerns of diverse peoples who populate our world.

In this chapter, we will first turn our attention to two key types of the contemporary global theatre, which also reflect its eclecticism: performance art and postmodernism. We will then focus on examples of theatrical diversity in the United States; in doing so, we will need to discuss early influences on these diverse contemporary theatres. We will then survey global theatres across our world, including those in England, Ireland, Australia, Canada, Asia, Latin America, and the Middle East; here, too, we will discuss earlier developments that shaped these societies' current theatres.

Finally we must always remember that it is not possible to survey all of our contemporary worldwide theatre and that these are just examples of today's vast range of global, diverse, and eclectic theatrical activity.

PERFORMANCE ART

In the past three decades, a number of artists have experimented with forms that force audiences to confront certain issues: What is performance? What is theatre? What is the subject of theatrical representation? Some of these artists are also political-minded; some are not. *Performance art* is one relatively recent form that poses these questions and then some.

Performance art has important antecedents: earlier avant-garde experiments of the twentieth century, such as dada, surrealism, and happenings, which stressed the irrational and attacked traditional artistic values and forms; the theories of Antonin Artaud and Jerzy Grotowski; and popular forms, such as clowning, vaudeville, and stand-up comedy.

During the past three decades, the term performance art has referred to differing types of theatrical presentations. In its earliest manifestations, performance art was related on one hand to painting and on the other hand to dance. In the 1970s, one branch of performance art emphasized the body as an art object: some artists suffered self-inflicted pain, and some went through daily routines (such as preparing a meal) in a museum or in a theatre setting. Another branch focused on site-specific or environmental pieces in which the setting or context was crucial: performances were created for specific locations such as a subway station, a city park, or a waterfront pier.

In some of the earliest forms of performance art, story, character, and text were minimized or even eliminated. The emphasis was not on narrating a story or exploring recognizable characters but rather on the visual and ritualistic aspects of performing. This type of theatre was often the work of an individual artist who incorporated highly personal messages, and sometimes political and social messages, in the event. The overall effect was often like a continually transforming collage. As might be expected, there was, as mentioned earlier, an affinity between this kind of theatre—with its emphasis of the visual picture formed onstage—and painting. Often, stage movement in performance art was also closely related to dance, as in the work of Martha Clarke (1944–   ).

In an article in *Artsweek* in 1990, Jacki Apple explained how the emphasis in performance art shifted in the 1970s and 1980s:

Performance art Experimental theatre that initially incorporated elements of dance and the visual arts. Since performance art often is based on the vision of an individual performer or director rather than a playwright, the autobiographical monologue has become a popular performance art form.

In the 1970s performance art was primarily a time-based visual art form in which text was at the service of image; by the early 80s performance art had shifted to movement-based work, with the performance artist as choreographer. Interdisciplinary collaboration and "spectacle," influenced by TV and other popular modes . . . set the tone for the new decade.[1]

In more recent years performance art has changed yet again. It is now often associated with individual artists who present autobiographical extended monologues or present one-person shows in which they portray various characters through interconnected monologues. There are also some performance artists who stage presentations that feature clowning and other popular slapstick techniques borrowed from the circus and other popular arts.

Several such artists—Karen Finley (1956–   ) is one of the most visible—became a center of controversy when their work was seized on by conservative groups and members of Congress as a reason to oppose funding the National Endowment for the Arts. These artists often espouse such causes as feminism and civil liberties for lesbians and gays. Often nudity and other controversial representations of sexuality or sexual orientation are used to confront audiences. Such was the case in *Alice's Rape* (1989), in which Robbie McCauley performed nude as her great-great-grandmother, a slave on the auction block. These performance artists are continuing a trend begun by early realistic and antirealistic dramatists, whose works challenged the social status quo and were often banned.

Two artists who began performing solo pieces in alternative spaces but later received commercial productions are Spalding Gray (1941–2004) and Bill Irwin (1950–   ). Gray, a monologuist who discussed issues that ranged from his own personal concerns to politics, was reminiscent of ancient storytellers who created a theatrical environment single-handedly. Irwin's performances are mime-like, and he uses popular slapstick techniques to reflect on the contemporary human condition.

Anna Deavere Smith (1952–   ), an African American performance artist, won considerable acclaim in the early 1990s for pieces dealing with racial unrest. In her works, she portrays numerous real people she has met and interviewed. For example, her *Twilight: Los Angeles 1992* presented people affected by the uprising that followed the acquittals in the first trial of police officers charged with brutalizing Rodney King.

Other well-known monologuists are Eric Bogosian (1953–   ), Danny Hoch (1970–   ), John Leguizamo (1965–   ), Mike Daisey (1973–   ), Lisa Kron (1961–   ), and Sarah Jones (1973–   ). Ping Chong (1946–   ) is an Asian American performance artist who mixes multimedia into his works.

READ Excerpts from *Freak*

Anthology of Living Theatre

A number of spaces have become recognized for their presentation of performance artists. These include two in New York City: PS 122, a converted public school in the East Village in Manhattan; and the Kitchen, also located downtown. In addition, many museums throughout the United States are known for presenting series of performance artists, including the Walker Museum in Minneapolis and the Museum of Contemporary Art in Chicago. The fact that performance art is most often presented

---

[1] Jacki Apple, "Art at the Barricades," *Artsweek,* Vol. 21, May 3, 1990, p. 21.

in converted, found spaces or museums, again reflects the eclectic nature of the form and its relationship to earlier avant-garde movements and the visual arts.

Along with those in the United States, there are also significant performance artists in most major cities around the world, such as Issei Ogata (1952–   ) in Japan and the French-Canadian Robert Lepage (1957–   ), who founded Ex Machina, a multimedia center in Quebec City.

POSTMODERNISM

Contemporary global theatre, as can be seen from the examples of performance art above, is highly eclectic. Some works focus on political concerns; others on personal issues; still others focus on formal concerns. Many works mix techniques and styles. In contemporary theatre, many such complex works are often described by critics as postmodernist.

Postmodernism, a term used to categorize much of the experimentation in theatre in the past three decades, is difficult to define. According to A. O. Scott, film critic for the *New York Times,* ***postmodernism*** is characterized by the following attributes: "a cool, ironic affect; the overt pastiche of work from the past; the insouciant mixture of high and low styles." However, we should note that some contemporary critics call into question the entire category of postmodernism and argue that each of the artists and works so categorized is unique. Still, postmodernism appears to have several characteristics.

Postmodernism questions the position of power in art and the idea of an accepted "canon" of classics: postmodernists also ask why certain artists (such as playwrights) and certain groups (such as white males) should have held positions of power and privilege throughout theatre history.

Accordingly, postmodernists rebel against traditional readings of texts, arguing that theatre productions may have a variety of "authors," including directors and even

Postmodernism A contemporary concept suggesting that artists and audiences have gone beyond the modernist movements of realism and departures of realism.

individual audience members: they argue that each audience member creates his or her own unique reading. Postmodernist directors are noted for *deconstructing* classic dramas—that is, taking the original play apart, developing a new individual conceptualization, and trying to represent onstage the issues of power embedded in the text. When a classic is deconstructed in this way, it may serve simply as the scenario for a production rather than a strictly followed script.

Postmodernist artists question categorizations of works. The term postmodernism suggests that the "modernist" interest in realism, antirealism, and form is no longer central to theatre, that artists have now moved beyond being concerned with representing either reality or abstraction. Instead, postmodernists mix abstraction and realism, so that their works cannot be easily classified. Furthermore, the distinction between "high" art and popular art can no longer be clearly defined: postmodernists mix popular concerns and techniques with those of high art.

For example, the Disney musical *The Lion King* directed by Julie Taymor, which was discussed in the previous chapter, breaks down the distinctions between popular art and high art, commercial and experimental theatre, and Asian and Western techniques.

Closely associated with the postmodernist approach to theatre is what is termed **non-text based theatre,** meaning that there is no text in a traditional sense, with dialogue written by a dramatist; rather, there is a scenario created by a director or an ensemble. The actors and the director then expand the scenario often through improvisation.

Among the most significant groups that have developed under the postmodernist banner are Mabou Mines, founded in 1970 under the artistic direction of Lee Breuer (1937–) and the Wooster Group. The Wooster Group is best known for its deconstruction of texts under the artistic direction of Elizabeth LeCompte (1944–). The film actor Willem Dafoe (1955–) began his acting career with this company and has frequently returned.

Another contemporary postmodernist company is New York's Elevator Repair Service, which was founded in 1991 and has toured throughout the United States and internationally. In 2005, it began presenting a reading of F. Scott Fitzgerald's novel *The Great Gatsby,* entitled *Gatz,* set in a dilapidated factory office; the entire novel is read and acted out by inhabitants of that office, and the performance takes more than six hours.

A postmodernist British company is Punchdrunk founded in 2000. Punchdrunk often uses abandoned spaces in which audience members follow performers to differing spaces to see sections of the productions staged. Audience members, therefore, do

A POSTMODERN PRODUCTION

As a mark of postmodernism, theatre today is eclectic and widely diversified. Periods, styles, and theatrical intentions are often mixed or coexist side by side. One such mixture of styles and material was a revival of *The Emperor Jones* by the Wooster Group, known for its experimental work. This early twentieth-century play by the American dramatist Eugene O'Neill was deconstructed and commented on at the same time that the original script was incorporated into the whole. Shown here are Scott Shepherd, Kate Valk (in the title role), and Ari Fliakos. (© Paula Court)

non-text based theatre A term meaning that there is no text in a traditional sense, with dialogue written by a dramatist; rather, there is a scenario created by a director or an ensemble, which is then usually expanded through improvisation.

not see the same "production" each evening and are actively engaged in following the performance, which is usually a deconstructed version of a classic text.

Many other alternative theatres, playwrights, and performance artists throughout the world can also be categorized as postmodernist. We will mention some of them later in this chapter.

DIVERSE THEATRES IN THE UNITED STATES

We now turn our attention to the diverse theatres found in the United States. First, we will look at the various types of alternative theatres in the United States Alternative theatres were often organized to stage works that were non-commercial, too experimental or too controversial for mainstream commercial theatre and continue to do so. The performance artists and postmodernist artists mentioned previously work in alternative theatre environments.

We will then survey the development of African American, Latino American, Asian American, Native American, feminist, and gay and lesbian theatres and artists in the United States; many were part of the alternative theatre movement in the United States since their work reflected the expanding interest in ethnicity, gender, and sexual orientation, which was often too controversial for the mainstream, commercial theatre.

AMERICAN ALTERNATIVE THEATRE

A crucial development in American theatre in the second half of the twentieth century, which continues to impact the contemporary theatre, was the creation of important alternatives to traditional Broadway commercial theatre. These alternative theatres tended to be able to offer theatre for special audiences, as well as theatre that was often more daring, bold, fresh, as well as experimental. Their offerings were often extremely eclectic in style and subject matter. Four manifestations were regional theatre, off-Broadway, off-off-Broadway, and alternative regional theatres.

Regional Theatre   An important development in the United States in the past half century has been the growth of major established regional theatres. (The phenomenon of important theatres established outside major cities is, again, a worldwide trend.) A number of significant regional theatres were founded in the 1950s and 1960s and began to flourish in large cities around the country. These are nonprofit rather than commercial theatres, but they employ professional performers, directors, and designers. They present the best dramas from the past as well as interesting new plays. In fact, in recent years nonprofit, regional theatres have been a chief source of new works in the United States. Among the best-known regional theatres are the Guthrie Theatre in Minneapolis, the Arena State in Washington, D.C., and the Goodman Theatre in Chicago.

Off-Broadway, Off-Off-Broadway, and Alternative Regional Theatres
In New York City, off-Broadway theatre began in the 1950s as an alternative to commercial Broadway, which was becoming increasingly costly. Off-Broadway theatres were smaller than Broadway theatres—most of them had fewer than 200 seats—and were located outside the Times Square neighborhood where the Broadway houses are situated. Because off-Broadway was less expensive than Broadway, it offered more opportunity for producing serious classics and experimental works.

In the past five decades, however, off-Broadway itself became more expensive and institutionalized. For example, in New York City, a group of off-Broadway theatres have become an important producing agency in the Broadway theatre district; among the best-known is Playwrights Horizons. Still, off-Broadway has and continues to present many significant playwrights and directors. Among the better-known dramatists are John Guare (1938–), Lanford Wilson (1937–2011), Marsha Norman (1947–), Wendy Wasserstein (1950–2006), as well as many of the playwrights of diverse backgrounds mentioned later.

As a result of off-Broadway's transformations, small independent producing groups had to develop another forum. The result was off-off Broadway. Off-off-Broadway shows are produced wherever inexpensive space is available—in churches, lofts, warehouses, garages—and are characterized by low prices and a wide variety of offerings. It is in these theatres, too, that much experimentation takes place, including performance art and postmodernist works. One important off-off-Broadway theatre is Café LaMama; among the significant groups that have worked off-off-Broadway are the Living Theatre, the Open Theatre, the Performance Group, Mabou Mines, and the Wooster Group.

Two experimental directors whose works were also seen off-off-Broadway are Robert Wilson (1944–) and Richard Foreman (1937–). Their work is typically unified by a theme or point of view determined by the director, and their material is often organized into units analogous to frames in television or film. Stunning theatrical images containing the essence of the ideas that interest these directors are often the key to their work.

Counterparts of the off- and off-off-Broadway movements have also sprung up in other major cities across the United States—Washington, Atlanta, Chicago, Minneapolis, Los Angeles, San Francisco, Seattle, and others—where groups perform as alternatives to the larger, established regional theatres. Presentations by these alternative theatres include classics, new plays, and experimental works. Among the best-known are Steppenwolf Theatre Company and Lookingglass Theatre Company in Chicago.

Again, this trend of creating out-of-the-way alternative theatres outside the commercial centers of major cities is taking place worldwide. In London, for example, there is a long history of "fringe" theatres: theatres outside London's commercial West End, which were originally established to circumvent the English censorship laws and which present more experimental works.

Two Contemporary American Playwrights with Roots in Alternative Theatre Two American playwrights whose work was first presented in small alternative, nonprofit theatres and who then became prominent in regional and off-Broadway theatres are Sam Shepard (1943–) and David Mamet (1947–). Like many of our contemporary playwrights, Shepard and Mamet mix concerns of high art—such as the plight of the American family and the demise of the American dream—with techniques borrowed from mass entertainments such as film, popular music, and melodrama. Also, they often blur the distinction between realism and abstraction. Many critics suggest that their work is, as discussed earlier, postmodernist.

Sam Shepard first developed his playwriting skills off-off-Broadway with works that fused surreal and absurdist styles and abandoned traditional plot structure and development. His later dramas include *Buried Child* (for which he won a Pulitzer Prize in 1979), *True West* (1980), *Fool for Love* (1982), and *A Lie of the Mind* (1985). These

plays deal with American mythology, the violence of American society, and the degeneration of the American family. His plays have naturalistic language and settings and mostly down-and-out characters whose struggles are clearly recognizable, but they do not provide the clear-cut exposition or dramatic resolutions of traditional realism.

David Mamet came out of the Chicago theatre scene. His plays have naturalistic language and settings, but they do not provide the clear-cut exposition or dramatic resolutions of traditional realism. Like Shepard's, they attack many accepted ideals of American life. Among Mamet's best-known works are *American Buffalo* (1977), *Glengarry Glen Ross* (1983), *Oleanna* (1992), and *Race* (2009). Mamet has also written and directed a number of films.

We now turn our attention to the theatres and theatre artists who reflect the great diversity of the United States and whose works reflect the sociopolitical issues of our diverse populations.

AFRICAN AMERICAN THEATRE

As we have noted previously, there are many theatres that appeal to diverse audiences with specific political viewpoints, concerns about gender, and sexual orientations. African American theatre—also referred to as Black theatre—is a prime example of a theatre that reflects the diversity of American culture and the contributions of a particular group to this culture. Since African American theatre has a long history, it will be helpful to trace its development from about 1900 on, so that we can better understand its significance and impact on our contemporary theatre.

African American Theatre from 1900 to 1950　At the turn of the twentieth century, the popular syncopated rhythms of ragtime had a strong influence on the emerging musical theatre and served as a bridge for a number of talented African Americans. Bob Cole (1864–1912) and William Johnson (1873–1954) conceived, wrote, produced, and directed the first Black musical comedy. The comedians Bert Williams (c. 1876–1922) and George Walker (1873–1911) and their wives joined composers and writers to produce musicals and operettas, in which Americans for the first time saw Blacks on the Broadway stage without burnt-cork makeup, speaking without dialect, and costumed in high fashion.

The early twentieth century also saw the formation of African American stock companies. The most significant was the Lafayette Players, founded in 1914 by Anita Bush (1883–1974), originally as the Anita Bush Players. By the time it closed in 1932, this company had presented over 250 productions and employed a number of Black stars.

Black performers and writers were also making inroads into commercial theatre in the 1920s. Twenty plays with Black themes were presented on Broadway in this decade, five of them written by African Americans. The decade also saw some Black performers achieve recognition in serious drama, among them Charles Gilpin (1878–1930), Paul Robeson, and Ethel Waters (1896–1977).

The Depression forced Black performers to find other ways of earning a living or to invent ingenious ways to create their own theatre. There were a few Broadway productions of plays by Blacks, such as the folk musical *Run Little Chillun* (1933) and *Mulatto* (1935) by Langston Hughes (1902–1967).

Possibly the most significant development for Black theatre during the 1930s was the Federal Theatre Project. This organization, discussed in the previous chapter, was meant to help theatre artists through the Depression; the Federal Theatre Project formed separate Black units in twenty-two cities, which mounted plays by Black and White authors and employed thousands of African American writers, performers, and technicians.

The 1940s saw a stage adaptation, in 1941, of the controversial novel *Native Son* by Richard Wright (1908–1960), directed by Orson Welles for his Mercury Theatre. Other important Broadway ventures included Paul Robeson's record run of 296 performances in *Othello* in 1943, and *Anna Lucasta* (1944), adapted by Abram Hill (1911–1986).

African American Theatre since 1950 The 1950s saw an explosion of Black theatre that would continue over the next five decades. *Take a Giant Step* by Louis Patterson (1922–   ), a play about growing up in an integrated neighborhood, premiered in 1953. In 1954, the playwright-director Owen Dodson (1914–1983)—a significant figure in Black theatre since the 1930s—staged *Amen Corner* by James Baldwin (1924–1987) at Howard University.

Off-Broadway, the Greenwich Mews Theatre began casting plays without regard to race and also produced *Trouble in Mind* (1956) by Alice Childress (1920–1994)—the first play by an African American woman to receive a commercial production. Possibly the most important production of the postwar era was *A Raisin in the Sun* (1959) by Lorraine Hansberry (1930–1965). It is about a Black family in Chicago, held together by a God-fearing mother, who is planning to move into a predominantly White neighborhood where the family will be unwelcome. The son loses money in a get-rich-quick scheme but later assumes responsibility for the family.

Hansberry's play was directed by Lloyd Richards (1922–2006), the first Black director on Broadway. Richards later became head of the Yale School of Drama, where in the 1980s he nurtured the talents of the Black playwright August Wilson (1945–2005), author of a 10-play cycle, chronicling African American life in the twentieth century, including *Fences* (1985), *Joe Turner's Come and Gone* (1986), and *The Piano Lesson* (1990).

READ *Joe Turner's Come and Gone*

Anthology of Living Theatre

From 1960 to the 1990s, there was an outpouring of African American theatre, much of it reflecting the struggle for civil rights. Amiri Baraka (1934–) came to theatregoers' attention in 1964 with *Dutchman,* a verbal and sexual showdown between an assimilated Black male and a White temptress, set in a New York subway. There were many other critically acclaimed African American dramas and playwrights during the 1960s and 1970s.

In 1970 the Black Theatre Alliance listed over 125 producing groups in the United States. While only a few of these survived the decade, many had a significant impact, including the Negro Ensemble Company, which was founded in 1967 and continues to produce today. One of the most notable in the contemporary theatre is Congo Square Theatre Company in Chicago, which was founded in 1999.

In addition to the emergence of these producing organizations, another major change in the 1970s was the presence of a larger Black audience at Broadway theatres, which accounted for a significant number of commercial African American productions, such as *Don't Bother Me, I Can't Cope* (1972); *The Wiz* (1975); and *Bubbling Brown Sugar* (1976).

African American artists continue to make an impact on commercial and non-commercial theatre. We mentioned August Wilson earlier. George C. Wolfe (1955–), author-director of *The Colored Museum* (1986), *Jelly's Last Jam* (1992), and *Bring in da' Noise, Bring in da' Funk* (1996), also directed both parts of the award-winning *Angels in America.* Wolfe was artistic director of the Public Theatre from 1993 to 2004. Another

African American director, Kenny Leon (1955–), in 2002 founded the True Colors Theatre in Atlanta; and in 2004 and 2010 he directed revivals of *A Raisin in the Sun* and *Fences* on Broadway. In 2011 Leon staged two Broadway productions of plays by African American authors: *The Mountaintop,* by Katori Hall (1981–), and *Stick Fly,* by Lydia R. Diamond (1969–). Thomas Bradshaw (1980–) is an African American playwright whose works have been staged in off-off-Broadway, off-Broadway, and regional theatres.

Suzan-Lori Parks (1964–), Pearl Cleage (1948–), and Cheryl West (1956–) are contemporary African American female playwrights whose works deal with issues of racism and feminism and have been produced in regional and alternative theatres. Two additional African American female dramatists whose works are politically charged are Kia Corthron (b. 1961) and Lynn Nottage (b. 1964). Nottage won the Pulitzer Prize for *Ruined* (2008).

LATINO-LATINA THEATRE

Contemporary Latino-Latina or Hispanic theatre in the United States can be divided into at least three groups: Chicano theatre, Cuban American theatre, and Puerto Rican or Nuyorican theatre. All three address the experiences of Hispanics living in the United States, and the plays are sometimes written in Spanish but are usually in English.

Chicano theatre, which originated primarily in the west and southwest, came to prominence during the time of the civil rights movements of the 1960s. The theatre troupe known as El Teatro Campesino ("farmworkers' theatre") grew out of the work of Luis Valdéz (1940–), who joined César Chavez in organizing farmworkers in California. Valdéz wrote ***actos,*** short agit-prop pieces dramatizing the lives of workers. (The term ***agit-prop*** means "agitation propaganda"; it was applied in the 1930s to plays with a strong political or social agenda.)

El Teatro Campesino became the prototype for other Mexican and Latino theatre groups such as Teatro de la Gente ("people's theatre"), founded in 1967; and Teatro de la Esperanza ("theatre of hope"), begun in 1971 in Santa Barbara, California.

Valdéz's play *Zoot Suit* (1978), about racial violence in Los Angeles in 1943, opened in Los Angeles to considerable acclaim; it later moved to Broadway. Other plays about the Chicano experience followed, one of the most notable being *Roosters* (1987) by Milcha Sanchez-Scott (1955–), in which cockfighting is a metaphor used to explore Chicano concerns and family conflicts. Luis Alfaro (1963–) is a Chicano performance artist, director, and playwright whose best known work is an adaptation of *Oedipus the King, Oedipus el Rey* (2010).

Cuban American theatre developed chiefly in Florida. The Federal Theatre Project of the 1930s resulted in fourteen Cuban American productions in 1936 and 1937. A

TODAY'S THEATRE: GLOBAL AND DIVERSE
The work of the playwright Lynn Nottage is an excellent example of theatrical diversity. *Ruined,* directed by Kate Whoriskey, was jointly produced by the Goodman Theatre in Chicago and the Manhattan Theatre Club in New York. It is set in the Democratic Republic of the Congo in the year 2000 and tells the story of Sophie (Condola Phyleia Rashad) and her horrific experiences at the hands of men. (Photo: Liz Lauren/The Goodman Theatre)

actos Short agit-prop dramas about the lives of Chicano workers.

agit-prop A term meaning agitation-propaganda, referring to plays with a strong social or politial agenda.

highly regarded Cuban American dramatist whose work began to be produced in the 1970s was Maria Irene Fornes (1930–   ). Another Cuban American playwright, Nilo Cruz (1960–   ), won the Pulitzer Prize in 2003 for *Anna in the Tropics*.

Nuyorican is a term that refers to Puerto Rican culture, mostly in New York, but elsewhere as well. Works by playwrights with a Puerto Rican background began to be produced in the 1960s and 1970s by groups such as the Teatro Repertorio Español, the Puerto Rican Traveling Theatre, and the New York Public Theatre founded by Joseph Papp (1922–1991). The Nuyorican Poets' Café presented plays by a number of Hispanic writers, including an ex-convict, Miguel Piñero (1947–1988), whose *Short Eyes,* a harshly realistic portrait of prison life, proved to be very successful and won a number of awards in the 1973–1974 season. Today many Puerto Rican playwrights have come to prominence.

The vitality of Latino theatre is also reflected in the many companies that are dedicated to the presentation of works by Latino playwrights of various backgrounds. In 1971, a network of Latino theatres across the country was established. Current examples including Teatro Vista, established by two Cuban-born theatre artists, and Teatro Luna, organized by ten Latina women, including Mexican-born playwright Tanya Saracho (1980–   ), perform works by Latino artists in Chicago. Among other writers who have dealt with wider Latino themes is Arthur Giron (1937–   ), an American writer from Guatemala.

ASIAN AMERICAN THEATRE

For most of the nineteenth century and the first half of the twentieth century, Asians appeared in dramatic offerings strictly as stereotypes. With the coming of cultural and ethnic awareness in the 1960s and 1970s, things began to change; Asian American theatre developed to represent Asian American identity on stage and to give Asian American artists opportunities not available in the mainstream theatre.

In 1965 several Asian American performers and directors founded the East West Players in Los Angeles. In 1973, two more groups were formed—the Asian Exclusion Act in Seattle and the Asian-American Theatre Workshop in San Francisco—and in 1977 the director-actor Tisa Chang (1945–   ) founded the Pan Asian Repertory

ASIAN AMERICAN THEATRE
One of the best known Asian American playwrights is David Henry Hwang, who won numerous awards for his Broadway show, *M. Butterfly.* This play is about an American diplomat in China who falls in love with a Chinese actress and has a long affair with her, only to discover later that the performer is really a man. Seen here are Tina Chilip (Suzuki), Randy Reyes (Song Liling), and Andrew Long (Rene Gallimard) in a production directed by Peter Rothstein at the Guthrie Theater. (© Michal Daniel)

Theatre in New York. These groups employed Asian American performers, produced dramas from the Asian cultural heritage, and emphasized new plays written by and for Asian Americans. More recent Asian American theatre groups include Ma-Yi Theatre Company, founded in New York in 1989; Lodestone Theatre Ensemble, founded in Los Angeles in 1999; and Mu Performing Arts, founded in Minneapolis in 1992. Silk Road Theater Project, founded in Chicago in 2003, presents works by Asian, Middle Eastern, and Mediterranean playwrights with themes related to those peoples.

A number of plays by Asian American writers were produced in the 1970s and 1980s, including a memory play by Philip Kan Gotanda (1950–) called *Song for a Nisea Fisherman* (1980). A playwright who came to prominence in the 1980s was David Henry Hwang (1957–), son of first-generation Americans who immigrated from China to California. Hwang wrote several plays that won wide recognition and in 1988, Hwang's *M. Butterfly* opened successfully on Broadway. Based on a true story, the play deals with a French diplomat who meets and falls in love with a Chinese opera singer who he thinks is a woman but turns out to be a man and a spy. Hwang has written many other successful works, including *Chinglish* (2011) which opened at the Goodman Theatre in Chicago and then transferred to Broadway.

The newer generation of Asian American playwrights includes Diana Son (1965–), Chay Yew (1965–), who in 2011 became the artistic director of Chicago's Victory Gardens Theatre, and Han Ong (1968–).

There has also been a movement to have more Asian Americans employed as performers in appropriate roles. Hwang and the actor B. D. Wong, who played the Chinese opera singer in the original production of *M. Butterfly,* led a vigorous protest against the hiring of an English actor to play the leading role in the musical *Miss Saigon.* That battle was lost; but by 1996, when a revival of *The King and I* opened on Broadway, it had a large proportion of Asian American performers.

NATIVE AMERICAN THEATRE

Strictly speaking, there was no Native American theatre tradition; rather, there were spiritual and social traditions that had theatrical elements. These were found primarily in ancient rituals and communal celebrations, which were often infused with cosmic significance. Also, in these traditions, unlike traditional Western theatre, there was no audience as such: those observing were considered participants just as much as the principal performers. Many of these ceremonies and the like were outlawed by the American government in the nineteenth century. Thus, the legacy of rituals and ceremonies, which had strong theatrical components—not to mention significant spiritual and cultural value—was forced to go "underground" if it continued at all.

The American Indian Religious Freedom Act of 1972 made it legal once again for certain ceremonies, such as the sun dance, to resume. This increased awareness of these rituals and celebrations contributed to the emergence of a Native American theatre. Two groups that led the way in the past three decades were the Native American Theatre Ensemble and Spiderwoman.

The Native American Theatre Ensemble, which was originally called the American Indian Theatre Ensemble, was founded by Hanay Geiogamah. (It is important to note that those familiar with Native American theatre invariably identify theatre companies and theatre artists not with the generic term Native American theatre, but in terms of their nations. Thus, Geiogamah is identified as Kiowa/Delaware.) Geiogamah's organization gave its premiere performance at La MaMa Theater in New York City in 1972, and later toured widely, not only in North America but also in Europe and elsewhere.

Spiderwoman Theatre comes under the headings of both Native American theatre and feminist theatre. Founded in 1975, it is the longest continually running

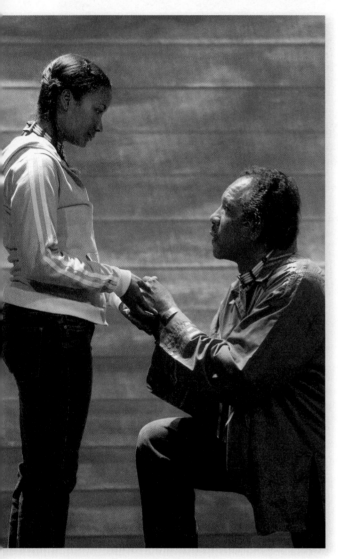

NATIVE AMERICAN THEATRE

Native American theatre, also known as indigenous theatre, is written by and for Native Americans. The participants frequently attempt to recapture not only themes and subjects appropriate to Native American culture but also the production styles and approaches of the original theatrical presentations. The scene here is from a play by William S. Yellow Robe, Jr., *Grandchildren of the Buffalo Soldiers;* it dramatizes the visit of a man, Craig Robe (James Craven), who returns to his tribe after having lived elsewhere. In this scene he is with August Jackson (Maya Washington). The drama was coproduced by Penumbra Theatre Company and Trinity Repertory Company and directed by Lou Bellamy. (Ann Marsden, 2005, Penumbra Theatre Company)

women's theatre in North America, as well as a Native American theatre. Three of its founding members—Lisa Mayo, Gloria Miguel, and Muriel Miguel—draw on storytelling and other theatrical traditions to celebrate their identities as American Indian women and to comment on stereotypes of women in general.

What is important to note about Native American theatre today is that it is not primarily historical or ceremonial. Though elements of tribal traditions may be incorporated, the emphasis among playwrights and producers is really on contemporary work, fusing the problems and aspirations of today's Native Americans with their heritage. The challenges and preoccupations of young Native American playwrights are frequently similar to those addressed by their Euro-American counterparts.

Several Native American playwrights have recently published single-author anthologies of their works. These include William F. Yellow Robe, Jr. (Assiniboine), Diane Glancy (Cherokee), and E. Donald Two-Rivers (Anishinabe). Another important contemporary playwright is Bruce King (Turgle Clan, Hodenausaunee-Oneida). King and Yellow Robe are also directors who have founded their own companies and have taught playwriting and performance at the Institute of American Indian Arts in Santa Fe, New Mexico, an organization that nurtures the next generation of Native American theatre artists.

There are also many Native American theatre organizations throughout the United States, including Thunderbird Theatre at Haskell Indian Nations University, founded in 1974; Red Earth Performing Arts, founded in Seattle in 1974; and the Tulsa Indian Actor's Workshop, founded in 1993. The American Indian Community House (ACH) in New York City uses its theatre space for Native American performing artists, hosting the Indian Summer Series, a month-long festival; ACH also keeps a database of native performers.

FEMINIST THEATRE AND GENDER DIVERSITY

In the United States, many female playwrights have questioned traditional gender roles and the place of women in American society. Of course, feminist theatre has roots in the past. One significant forerunner, for example, was the American playwright Rachel Crothers (1878–1958). Crothers wrote and directed many successful plays from 1906 to 1937; all of them dealt with women's moral and social concerns, and most of them were set in urban high society. In the summer of 1995, the Looking Glass Theatre in New York revived Crothers's *A Man's World* (1909), which attacks the sexual double standard. Rachel Crothers's plays are skillful, entertaining comedies, but she always focused on the issue of sexual equality. We also mentioned in the previous chapter other key early twentieth-century female U.S. playwrights, including Susan Glaspell and Lillian Hellman.

In the 1970s and 1980s, as the issue of women's rights and feminism came to the forefront, there were a number of successful female American playwrights. Representative works include *Fefu and Her Friends* (1977) by Maria Irene Fornes; *'Night, Mother* (1983) by Marsha Norman (1947–); *Crimes of the Heart* (1977) by Beth Henley (1952–); *The Heidi Chronicles* (1988), *The Sisters Rosensweig* (1992), and *An American Daughter* (1997) by Wendy Wasserstein (1950–2006); and *How I Learned to Drive* (1988) by Paula Vogel (1951–).

There are many contemporary U.S. female playwrights, including Sara Ruhl (1974–), as well as Rebeca Gilman (1964–). Earlier in this chapter, we mentioned four significant African American female playwrights: Suzan-Lori Parks, Pearl

For some years now, a number
of playwrights and theatre
companies have treated contemporary issues and concerns
confronting women. One of
the most notable dramatists
is Maria Irene Fornes. This is a
scene from her play *Fefu and
Her Friends,* which focuses
on eight women. During its
course, the audience is divided
into four groups and taken to
four separate locations to see
different scenes. This production was staged at the Yale
Repertory Theatre; shown in
this scene are Julianna Margulies as Emma and Joyce Lynn
O'Connor as Fefu. (© Gerry
Goodstein)

Cleage, Kia Corthron, and Lynn Nottage. There are also feminist Latina American, Asian American, and Native American playwrights.

Feminist theatre companies have encouraged audiences to reexamine their own gender biases and those of their society. Some scholars estimate that more than 100 feminist companies have been founded in the United States; these companies include At the Foot of the Mountain, Women's Experimental Theatre, and Omaha Magic Theatre. One company, Split Britches, became well known for its production of *Belle Reprieve* (1991), which made satiric references to Tennessee Williams's *A Streetcar Named Desire* and was created collaboratively with an English gay company, Bloolips.

Feminist theatre is, of course, also a worldwide phenomenon. There are many feminist playwrights and theatre companies throughout the world. In England, for ex- ample, there are a number of significant female playwrights, including Caryl Churchill (discussed later), Timberlake Wertenbaker (1946–), and Pam Gems (1925–).

GAY AND LESBIAN THEATRE

Lesbian theatre groups can be part of feminist theatre, but gay and lesbian theatre is also a distinct movement. A number of plays and performers introduced gay and lesbian themes into theatre before the 1960s. For example, in the nineteenth century and the early twentieth century there was a considerable amount of cross-dressing in performances: men often appeared in "drag" and women in men's clothing, raising questions about sexual and gender roles. Also, plays included material on this subject; one example is Lillian Hellman's *The Children's Hour* (1934), in which a presumed lesbian relationship between two schoolteachers was presented.

However, the play that first brought gay life to the forefront was *The Boys in the Band* (1968), by Mart Crowley (1935–). Crowley depicted a group of men living an openly gay life. Ironically, in 1969, the year after it opened, gay patrons of the Stone-

wall Inn in New York's Greenwich Village fought against police officers attempting to close the bar. This uprising, considered the beginning of the modern gay rights movement, changed attitudes of gay activists, who now rejected what they considered a stereotype of homosexuals depicted in *The Boys in the Band.* However, successful New York revivals in 1998 and 2010 led to a reevaluation of the play's significance in the history of gay and lesbian theatre in the United States.

In the years that followed, complex gay characters were presented unapologetically. Plays in the 1970s and 1980s included *The Ritz* (1975) by Terrence McNally (1939–) and *Torch Song Trilogy* (1983) by Harvey Fierstein (1954–). Since then, more and more plays have dealt expressly with gay issues. In these dramas, not only are the lives of gays and lesbians presented forthrightly, but frequently a gay or lesbian sociopolitical agenda is also put forward. In addition to a general concern for gay and lesbian issues, there was a sense of urgency engendered by the AIDS crisis and the ongoing gay rights issues. This has led to a number of significant dramas, including *The Normal Heart* (1985) by Larry Kramer (1935–), which was revived in a Tony award-winning production in 2011, *As Is* (1985) by William M. Hoffman (1939–), Tony Kushner's two-part play *Angels in America: A Gay Fantasia on National Themes* (1993– 1994), Terrence McNally's *Love! Valour! Compassion!* (1995), *Take Me Out* (2003) by Richard Greenberg (1958–), and *Next Fall* (2009) by Geoffrey Nauffts (1961–).

Groups that use cross-dressing to break stereotypes of gender and sexual orientation have also been extremely important in the past three decades. Among the early "gender-bender" groups were the Cockettes and the Angels of Light in San Francisco and Centola and Hot Peaches in New York. An important company in New York was the Theatre of the Ridiculous, founded by John Vaccaro, which developed an extraordinary writer and performer—Charles Ludlam (1943–1987). Ludlam rewrote the classics to include a good deal of wild parody and frequent cross-dressing; he also created the long-lived Ridiculous Theatrical Company.

READ *The Mystery of Irma Vep* by Charles Ludlam

Anthology of Living Theatre

Though a number of groups have not survived, individual performers, playwrights, and companies in gay and lesbian theatre remain very much in the spotlight in the global twenty-first century theatre.

GLOBAL THEATRE

As we noted in Chapter 1, globalization has greatly affected the contemporary theatre. We can no longer very easily categorize theatre productions and artists by strictly delineated national boundaries. The fact that communication and travel is so easy makes it difficult to define national theatres and artists. As we also noted, globalization of theatre has led to interaction, collaboration, and adaptation of theatrical styles and techniques. So as we now survey some examples of global developments in England, Ireland, Australia, Canada, Asia, Latin America, and the Middle East, we must always remember that it is not possible to chronicle all of the global theatrical activity in the twenty-first century nor discuss all of the complex ways in which these theatres interact and collaborate. One intriguing example, however, is documentary drama.

A CONTINUING GLOBAL TREND: DOCUMENTARY DRAMA

Documentary drama (or theatre of fact) Term encompassing different types of drama that presented material in the fashion of journalism or reporting. Drama that is supposedly based on factual occurrences and materials.

As we mentioned in Chapter 14 when discussing realism, certain theatrical trends and forms from past periods continue in our contemporary, global theatre. One such form is ***documentary drama*** (sometimes referred to as theatre of fact), which has roots in the classical Greek and Elizabethan theatres and in other theatres through the early twentieth century. Documentary drama reflects the diversity and eclecticism of our global theatre.

Documentary dramas are based on historical documents, which give an air of authenticity and historical reality. The goal of documentary drama was to convince audiences that they were watching history unfold, even when these dramatists had modified the documents for dramatic or political effect. One of the most famous documentary dramas was *The Investigation* (1965) by Peter Weiss (1916–1982), which dramatizes the war crimes trials of people who had been guards at a Nazi extermination camp.

Documentary drama continues to be prevalent in the twenty-first century. Today, docudramas—as they are sometimes referred to—are also popular as made-for-television movies. Still, docudramas for the stage continue to be written. A good example is *Exonerated* (2002), a documentary about former death-row inmates who turn out to be innocent. There have also been numerous docudramas dealing with the war in Iraq, including *Black Watch* (2006), staged throughout the world by the National

DOCUMENTARY DRAMA
A continuing trend in global theatre is documentary drama. This type of theatre is based on historical documents—papers, e-mails, recordings, television images—in order to give it the air of authenticity and historical reality. Some documentary presentations intersperse invented segments or dialogue, but others stick strictly to the public record. There are many documentary dramas dealing with the Iraq War. None has been more successful or more moving than *Black Watch*, the story of a 300-year-old Scottish regiment that saw combat in Iraq. A mixture of dramatic scenes, monologues, musical numbers, and horrific television footage of combat, it evoked the horror and sorrow of war. The production shown here, with Michael Nardone as Sergeant Munro, was created by the National Theatre of Scotland and first presented at the Edinburgh Festival. (© Geraint Lewis)

Theatre of Scotland. There are also examples of documentary drama from the contemporary African, Latin American, Asian, and Middle Eastern theatres. (Some of these will be noted later in this chapter.)

ENGLISH AND IRISH THEATRE

As we mentioned earlier, the diversity in today's theatre is worldwide. Alternative theatre companies and playwrights in the English and Irish theatres reflect this trend. In London, there are significant producing companies that support new playwrights and directors, some of which receive governmental support. These include the National Theatre, the Royal Shakespeare Company, the Old Vic, the Royal Court Theatre, and the Donmar Warehouse.

There is also an alternative to commercial theatre known as fringe theatre, and it is in fringe theatre that many contemporary political playwrights began their careers, though many then received productions at the subsidized and commercial theatres. These British playwrights are in the postmodernist tradition, mixing reality with theatrical techniques and fusing concerns of high art with techniques of popular art.

A good example is Caryl Churchill (1938–), the author of *Cloud Nine* (1979), *Top Girls* (1982), and *Far Away* (2002), whose work is also feminist.

THE IRISH PLAYWRIGHT MARTIN McDONAGH
British and Irish playwrights come from a long line of well-known predecessors. In the case of the Irish, there is a strong tradition going back over a century. Among the prominent younger Irish dramatists is Martin McDonagh. Often mixing comedy and cruelty and continuing the strong oral tradition of Irish writing, McDonagh includes gruesome details and creates vivid scenes and characters. The scene here shows three characters from his play *A Behanding in Spokane,* his first play set in the United States, with the actors Christopher Walken, left, Zoe Kazan, and Anthony Mackie. (Sara Krulwich/The New York Times/Redux)

READ *Far Away*

> **Anthology of Living Theatre**

Of course, there are many other significant playwrights in England. Tom Stoppard (1937–   ) continues to write dramas emphasizing wordplay and intellectual concerns. A significant number of "angry" playwrights continue to attack traditional political, social, and economic institutions; among the best known are David Hare (1947–   ) and Howard Brenton (1942–   ). More contemporary socio-politically oriented British playwrights include Patrick Marber (1964–   ), Jez Butterworth (1969—   ), and Sarah Kane (1971–1999). There is also a new generation of young Irish playwrights who dramatize social, political, and historical issues. Martin McDonagh (1970–   ) and Conor McPherson (1971–   ) have gained international attention.

An English director who has used a more experimental style of production, along with reinterpretations of texts that focus on feminist, gender, and other sociopolitical issues, is Deborah Warner (1959–   ). Warner began her career with an alternative London troupe, the Kick Theatre Company, which she founded in 1980, when she was twenty-one. She has since directed unique interpretations of the classics for the Royal Shakespeare Company and the National Theatre in London. She is best-known for the many productions she has directed that star the actress Fiona Shaw (1959–   ).

Among the other successful female directors in England is Josie Rourke (1980–), who took over as artistic director of the Donmar Warehouse in 2012.

CANADA AND AUSTRALIA

Before World War II, Canadian and Australian theatres developed commercially, presenting popular forms of entertainments that also reflected national identity. Two Australian examples are *The Squatter's Daughter,* or, *The Land of the Wattle* (1907), which focused on the Australian outlaw known as the bushranger; and the pantomime *The Bunyip,* or *The Enchantment of Fairy Princess Wattle Blossom* (1916), which included a mythological Aboriginal character.

During the same period, Australia and Canada developed "little theatres"—some professional and some amateur—that presented noncommercial, and often politically charged, works. In Australia, three such companies were Sydney's New Theatre League, established in 1936; Melbourne's New Theatre Club, founded in 1937; and Brisbane's Unity Theatre, which also opened in 1937. Hart House Theatre, founded on the campus of the University of Toronto in 1919, was one example of the Canadian "little theatre" movement. It presented many of Canada's most important theatre artists in the two decades before World War II. After World War II, the Hart House became a venue for university productions, reflecting the vitality of university theatre across Canada.

Since World War II, the theatres of Canada and Australia have seen developments that parallel the complexity of international theatre. For example, in Canada in the 1950s and 1960s, many regional theatres were established. One of the most famous is the Stratford Shakespeare Festival in Stratford, Ontario. This festival, established in 1952 under the artistic direction of Tyrone Guthrie, continues to produce classics, musicals, and contemporary works, in multiple venues. The Shaw Festival, established in 1962, stages works by Shaw, his contemporaries, and works set during his lifetime. Australia also saw the development of theatres across the nation from the 1950s through the 1970s.

Both Australia and Canada, from the late 1960s through the present, saw the development of theatre companies dedicated to new works, experimentation, and innovative revivals of classics. In 1967, Betty Burstall (1926–) established Melbourne's La Mama theatre, based on New York's famous experimental theatre. La Mama continues to function as does Company B, which was established in Sydney in 1985, and is known for presenting contemporary works and unique readings of classics. Among the stars who have recently appeared with the company are the film actors Geoffrey Rush (1951–) and Cate Blanchett (1969–). At the Sydney Theatre Company, founded in 1979, Blanchett is now the co-artistic director.

BRITISH WOMEN COLLABORATE
The director Deborah Warner and the actress Fiona Shaw (pictured here) have worked together to create several unusual and memorable theatre pieces. A good example is their production of Brecht's *Mother Courage and Her Children,* translated by Tony Kushner, for a production originating at Britain's National Theatre. (© Donald Cooper/ Photo*stage*)

Playwrights and theatre artists have dealt with the issues related to these countries' diverse populations. In Canada and Australia, there are theatres that focus on native peoples and people of African descent. For example, the Australian musical *Bran Nue Dae* (1990) dealt with Aboriginal life. Playwrights have also dramatized issues of gender and sexual orientation in these countries. Michel Tremblay (1942–   ), who was born in Montreal, focuses on working-class Canadians and gay issues. The theatre company Buddies in Bad Times, established in 1979, is committed to gay and lesbian theatre. In the 1980s, feminist theatres in Australia included Home Cooking Theatre (1981) and Vital Statistix (1984).

There are also Canadian and Australian artists who present performance art, discussed earlier in this chapter, and multimedia works. The French-Canadian Robert Lepage (1957–   ) is a well-known director, creator of theatrical and operatic productions, and actor. In 1993, he founded Ex Machina, a multimedia performance center in Quebec City. Lepage is probably best-known for *KÀ,* the Cirque du Soleil production he staged in Las Vegas in 2005. Australia also has many contemporary performance artists, such as Mike Parr (1945–   ).

ASIA, AFRICA, AND LATIN AMERICA

Theatres in India, China, and Japan   As we noted in the previous chapter, the period at the end of the nineteenth century and the beginning of the twentieth saw increasing interchange between Asian and other theatres. Particularly, Western theatre had a growing influence on the modern theatres of India, China, and Japan. However, in the past four decades, there has been a unique return of traditional forms blended into the sociopolitical sensibilities of Asian theatre artists. This return to traditional forms, in itself, is a rejection of colonial and postcolonial Western intrusions into the continent.

In India several changes occurred a few decades into the twentieth century, an important one being the advent of cinema. In India, film became extremely popular, from the standpoint of both producers and consumers. Films began to be produced in great numbers, and audiences flocked to them. At mid-century, this trend, plus World War II, led to a great dropping off of professional theatre in many parts of India.

The theatre that emerged in the latter half of the twentieth century was primarily an amateur theatre. It is estimated that Calcutta has as many as 3,000 registered amateur theatre groups, Mumbai, formerly called Bombay, perhaps has as many as 500, and Madras has at least 50. These theatres keep alive plays written by Indian playwrights, past and present, as well as plays from other nations.

In China after the civil war and Mao Zedong's rise to power following World War II in 1949, spoken drama was written, but additional emphasis was given to traditional forms of popular theatre. These traditional forms were familiar in the countryside and became a medium for carrying messages of the government to remote corners of the nation. During the cultural revolution, which began in 1966, theatrical activity—particularly spoken drama—was more restricted; increasing emphasis was placed on a few dance-dramas, elaborately staged and performed, that had very heavy ideological or propagandistic content. For the most part, theatre artists, along with intellectuals, were seen as subversive and suffered greatly during this era in Chinese history.

Since the death of Mao, and the opening up of China to the West in the late 1970s, there has been cross-fertilization between the Chinese traditions and Western drama. Theatre artists from the United States and Europe have visited and performed in China. Arthur Miller, for example, directed a production of *Death of a Salesman* in Beijing in 1983. In addition, popular traditional forms, such as Beijing (Peking) opera and other forms of classic music-drama, which were demeaned during Mao's rule, are becoming popular again. Although much of the drama still remains socialist in point of view and realistic in style, there are a number of artists who push the boundaries of subject matter and style, fusing classical traditions with contemporary forms and issues; Yu Rongjun (1971–) is one of the best known.

Since the end of World War II, contemporary theatre in Japan has been in a healthy condition. A number of truly gifted playwrights have emerged, chief among them Kinoshita Junji (1914–), whose work combines social concerns with humor and, when appropriate, elements from Japanese folk tradition.

Japan, from the second half of the twentieth century to the present, has maintained three main branches of theatre. One is traditional theatre—nō, bunraku, and kabuki—of which the most active is kabuki. It is remarkable that these three ancient theatre traditions in Japan have remained so vital and active in the present day.

A second branch consists of various manifestations of ***shingeki,*** a word that means "new theatre." Shingeki began in the late nineteenth century and in one form or another continued throughout the twentieth century. Broadly speaking, it was a modern theatre, in contrast to the traditional classic theatres. It was more realistic than the traditional theatres and banished the gods and the fantastic from theatre, partly because they had played such a large role in classic theatre. Later, after World War II, nonrealistic elements were admitted to shingeki dramas. Overall, shingeki remains a theatre in which the playwright is a central figure; in recent years it has included female playwrights, who were almost nonexistent in earlier times. Among Japan's contemporary playwrights are: Shoji Kokami (1958–), whose plays have been staged in England; Noda Hideki (1955–); and Keralino Sandorovich (born Kazumi Kobayashi in 1963).

The third strain of modern Japanese theatre has been avant-garde or experimental theatre. A good example of this movement is the work of Tadashi Suzuki (1939–), who began his work at Waseda University in Tokyo and then developed a theatre community in the mountains at Toga. Following the models of men such as Jerzy Grotowski and Peter Brook, Suzuki led a director-centered theatre that was international in its ideas and its reach. In his theatre, there was an emphasis on ensemble playing, on physical movement, and on combining the old and the new, the traditional and the experimental.

JAPANESE SHAKESPEARE

A Japanese director known for presenting Western classics in a distinctly Japanese style is Yukio Ninagawa. Ninagawa has directed not only Shakespeare but also the Greek classics and modern works. In every case he creates his own, Japanese, version of the play. Shown here are Kayoko Shiraishi (Titania) and Goro Daimon (Bottom) in a production of Shakespeare's *A Midsummer Night's Dream* by the Ninagawa Company at the Mermaid Theatre, London. (© Donald Cooper/ Photo*stage*)

Shingeki Contemporary Japanese theatre that incorporated Western ideas about playwriting and theatre production.

TADASHI SUZUKI: JAPANESE INTERNATIONALIST

Among important international theatre artists, a key figure is Tadashi Suzuki, a director, writer, and teacher who calls Japan his home but has worked with and influenced artists around the world. Suzuki first attracted attention as a part of Japan's *shōgekijō undō*, or "little theatre movement" in the 1960s and 70s. *Shōgekijō* was a response to what was seen as the restrictive realism and limited point-of-view of *shingeki*. Like proponents of "little theatre" and avant-garde movements in the West, *shōgekijō* artists largely rejected mainstream success, preferring smaller, more adventurous audiences who were willing to engage with provocative, experimental material. Other directors who were a part of this movement included Shūji Terayama (1935–1983), Shogo Ohta (1939–2007), and Yukio Ninagawa (1935–   ).

Today, Tadashi Suzuki is among the world's most famous theatre directors. His Suzuki Company of Toga, in the mountains of Japan, is well-known for combining stories and traditions from various cultures; this includes creating theatre pieces that remain distinctively Japanese while also entering into conversation with theatre across the globe. His work also frequently comments on international political situations. In addition to his own company in Japan, Suzuki co-founded the SITI company in 1992 with the prominent American director Anne Bogart.

Two examples of Suzuki's international work are his productions of Euripides's *The Bacchae*. In 1981, Suzuki worked with students at the University of Wisconsin to develop a dual-language version of the play, which he had been working on in Japan for a number of years. In this production, the American actors spoke English and the Japanese actors spoke Japanese, the characters responding as if they understood each other. The production also emphasized the cyclical nature of violence and power, suggesting that one tyrant dies only to be replaced by another.

Beginning in 1991, Suzuki introduced *Dionysus*, a new adaptation of the play that focused on the clash between religion and government. This production was widely interpreted as a comment on the escalating violence in the Middle East in general and the wars between the United States and Iraq more specifically.

Suzuki's actors are praised for their onstage presence and incredible athleticism. His actor-training system, the Suzuki method, combines elements of traditional Japanese theatre

Yukiko Saito in the title role in Tadashi Suzuki's *Electra*.
(© Jack Vartoogian/FrontRowPhotos)

techniques with the experimental work that emerged from international theatre in the 1960s and 1970s. Actors spend a great deal of time focusing on their feet and the ground beneath them, building strength, flexibility, and balance through a physical connection to the earth. Many observers feel that Suzuki's most lasting impact on world theatre will be his work on actor training.

Prepared by Frank Episale, CUNY Graduate Theatre Program.

Theatres in the Middle East Contemporary theatre in the Arab world is greatly affected by the politics of the region. Although Islam has strong prohibitions against theatre, there have always been storytelling, folkloric, and popular comic traditions throughout the Middle East, before Islamic times and since. As in Asia and Latin America, the close of the nineteenth century and the beginning of the twentieth century saw a rise in Western colonial influence on the theatres of the Arab Middle East.

After World War II and through the 1970s, there was significant development of professional theatrical activity throughout the Middle Eastern region, including Egypt, Iran, Syria, Lebanon, and Iraq. The theatres of these countries continued to be influenced by Western practices and artists, but there also developed a good deal of theatrical cross-fertilization. Iran, for example, was host to a significant international festival of avant-garde artists in the early 1970s. The festival featured works by such notable Western artists as Peter Brook, Jerzy Grotowski, and Robert Wilson, and many of these works clearly reflected the influence of Middle Eastern theatre and literature. However, the works of many Arab theatre artists were highly nationalistic during this era and returned to traditional folk materials; examples are the works by the Iraqi playwright-director Qassim Mohammed (1935–).

With the rise of Islamic fundamentalism and totalitarianism in many of these countries, theatrical activities have been halted, significantly curtailed, or rigidly controlled by the state. For example, the theatrical infrastructure in Iraq was severely damaged by Iraq's war with Iran in the 1980s, by economic hardships after the Persian Gulf War in the early 1990s, and then again with the invasion and occupation of Iraq by the United States, Britain, and their allies in 2003. In Saudi Arabia, the state-sponsored Saudi Society for Culture and Arts, established in 1972, oversees much theatrical activity; however, there is great controversy over the support of theatrical art.

Three internationally recognized contemporary Egyptian playwrights are Alfred Farag (1929–), Lenin El-Ramley (1945–), and Gamal Abdel Maqsoud (1942–). In Jordan, the ministry of culture has sponsored annual theatre festivals, and there have also been independent festivals that bring together theatre artists from many parts of the Arab world.

There has been Palestinian theatre since the 1850s, but historians have focused most on theatrical activities since the Israeli occupation in 1967. Many companies and playwrights have created theatrical works that express the Palestinian point of view in relationship to Israel's control of the West Bank and, until recently, Gaza. A Palestinian company that is gaining international recognition from its visits to the Royal Court Theatre in London is Al-Kasaba Theatre, originally founded in Jerusalem in 1970 but now located in Ramallah in the occupied West Bank. In 2001, Al-Kasaba staged *Alive from Palestine: Stories Behind the Headlines,* which consists of a series of monologues dealing with the Palestinian uprising against Israel. Two other production that reflect the Palestinians' existence under Israeli occupation, and have received global recognition, are: *The Alley* (1992), a one-woman production written and performed by Samia Qazmouz al-Bakri, which focuses on the lives of Palestinian women since 1948, and *We are the Children of the Camp* (2000) by al-Rowwad Theare for Children of the Aida refugee camp near Bethlehem. The second production, performed primarily by children, toured the United States in 2005.

THEATRE IN THE MIDDLE EAST

When the turmoil in the Middle East became increasingly intense, the Al-Kasaba Theatre in Ramallah had difficulty mounting its regular schedule. One way to keep its theatre alive was to present plays like *Alive from Palestine: Stories under Occupation,* a series of monologues developed by actors and writers responding to the situation in Ramallah. This theatre piece was later transferred to the Young Vic Theatre in London. Shown in this scene are Hussam Abu Eisheh, Mahmoud Awad, and Georgina Asfour. (© Geraint Lewis)

Israeli theatre has also developed since the founding of that state in 1948. Israeli drama has been influenced by the eastern European origins of many of its founders as well as the Middle Eastern traditions of those Jews who left Arab nations to settle in the Jewish state.

One national theatre of Israel is the Habimah, which was established in Russia in the early twentieth century and settled in what was then British-controlled Palestine in 1931. The other large national theatre in Israel is the Tel Aviv Municipal Theatre, referred to as the Cameri, founded in 1944 by the director Yossef Milo (1916–   ). There are many other active Israeli theatres throughout the country—in Tel Aviv, Jerusalem, Haifa, and elsewhere. As in Europe and the United States, there are also smaller fringe theatrical groups, which experiment with avant-garde techniques, and performance artists. Most of the theatres in Israel receive some governmental subsidy. Israeli drama also reflects the tumultuous history of the nation. The most internationally recognized Israeli dramatist is Joshua Sobol (1939–   ), whose play *Ghetto* (1984) was produced throughout the world.

African Theatre and Drama   Early African societies had many traditional performances that were connected to ceremonies and rituals and used music, song, and dance. Colorful, exotic, and symbolic costumes were also a key element of many rituals and ceremonies. African theatre artists in the twentieth century used these traditional forms and subverted forms of popular Western theatre in order to create work that reflects anticolonial struggles as well as attacks against totalitarian regimes in the new independent African nations.

Contemporary African theatre and society are divided into English-speaking Africa, French-speaking Africa, and Portuguese-speaking Africa. In all these nations, which were originally defined by nineteenth-century colonial powers, there are also attempts to experiment with the indigenous languages of the peoples of Africa. In Portuguese-speaking Africa, which includes Angola, Cape Verde, Guinea-Bissau, Mozambique, and São Tomé and Principe, missionaries introduced religious drama in order to spread Catholicism. Before independence in 1975, much of the theatre of this part of Africa was somewhat like vaudeville, although some anticolonial dramas were written. After independence, there was a greater focus on theatre that would arouse social consciousness, and plays followed the model of agit-prop dramas. In Angola, for example, the National School of Theatre was founded in 1976 and staged works that focused on African liberation.

French-speaking (francophone) Africa includes areas south of the Sahara as well as nations in northern Africa. There is a vital theatre in the sub-Saharan nations, influenced by traditional forms of storytelling and music as well as by French theatre traditions. Many of the plays written in this part of French-speaking Africa have been produced in festivals organized in Paris. The plays of this region usually focus on historical chronicles, social concerns, and political circumstances. Theatre in French-speaking Africa also received international attention when such well-known contemporary directors as Roger Blin and Peter Brook employed actors from this region in some of their productions.

English-speaking (anglophone) Africa, which included Nigeria, South Africa, Uganda, and Zambia, has had a significant international impact. Anglophone theatre became more highly developed in the 1950s because of the influence of universities in this region. Universities encouraged the work of dramatists and also organized traveling theatre troupes.

Among the influences on the theatre of English-speaking Africa are traditional forms, popular theatre, and the indigenous languages of the peoples; in fact, there has been considerable debate over whether theatre should be created in the language of the African peoples or in English. Among the leading theatre artists from anglophone Africa are the Nigerians Hubert Ogunde (1916–1990), the playwright who is often cited as the founder of modern Nigerian theatre; Moses Olaiya Adejumo (1936–   ), an actor-manager; and Olu Obafemi (1951–   ), a playwright, director, and actor. Among the leading playwrights in Zimbabwe are S. J. Chifunyise (1948–   ), Ben Shibenke (1945–   ), and Thompson Tsodzo (1947–   ). In Kenya, the playwright Ngugi wa Thiong'o (1938–   ), who has created individual and collaborative works in Kenyan languages, was arrested by the oppressive government between 1977 and 1978 and then forced to live in exile. South Africa produced many significant playwrights and theatre companies in the 1970s, including the Market Theatre, People's Space Theatre, and Junction Avenue Theatre Company; these companies frequently produced works that questioned South Africa's apartheid.

Wole Soyinka and Athol Fugard   Concern for political and social equality is at the heart of the dramatic works of the South African Athol Fugard (1932–   ) and the Nigerian Wole Soyinka (1934–   ), and these two authors have become the

WOLE SOYINKA: A NOBEL PLAYWRIGHT

Wole Soyinka, a remarkable playwright from Nigeria, is outspoken and has faced many hardships, including being jailed for his beliefs. Undeterred, he has continued to write plays, and in 1986 he was awarded the Nobel Prize for literature. The scene shown here is from his play *Death and the King's Horseman* in a recent London Production. (© Elliott Franks/ArenaPAL/The Image Works)

most internationally renowned of all contemporary African playwrights. Fugard, who is White, attacked apartheid in such plays as *The Blood Knot* (1964), *Sizwe Banzi Is Dead* (1973), *Master Harold . . . and the Boys* (1982), and *A Lesson from Aloes* (1987). Soyinka, a Black playwright, is also a poet, essayist, and novelist, who began his career with the Royal Court Theatre in London in the late 1950s. His politically charged works led to his arrest in Nigeria in 1967, and to two years imprisonment. In 1973, he adapted Euripides's *The Bacchae* for the National Theatre in England. Soyinka gained international recognition in 1986, when he received the Nobel Prize in literature. Among his best-known dramas are *The Swamp Dwellers* (1957), *The Road* (1965), *Death and the King's Horsemen* (1975), and *Play of Giants* (1985).

Latin American Theatre In the twentieth century in Latin America, and continuing today, there was a development of realistic drama, experimental theatre, radical sociopolitical drama, and popular forms, all existing side by side. Although there have been economic, political, and social problems, including periods of censorship and governmental repression (for example, in Chile during the dictatorship of Pinochet from 1973 to 1989), all the countries in Latin America have significant theatres and playwrights. Frequently these artists have responded to the political and social turmoil in their societies.

At the beginning of the twentieth century, for instance, many comedies were written throughout Latin America—and especially in Argentina—that dealt with the unique local customs of each of the Latin American nations. In the period between the world wars, the dramatists of Latin America were clearly influenced by such European styles as surrealism and expressionism but often touched on nationalistic issues.

Following World War II, many Latin American dramatists began to focus on the unique national issues and concerns that confronted their individual countries. Some of Latin America's most developed and politically active playwrights and theatre companies can be found today in Argentina, Brazil, Chile, Mexico, and Peru. The theatre artists of these countries have fused the popular styles of their peoples and the modernist styles of Western theatre, including realism, expressionism, absurdism, and performance art.

One of the most renowned is the Brazilian playwright, director, and theorist Augusto Boal (1931–2009). Boal wrote many plays and in the 1960s created works about historical figures, theatrical and revolutionary. Because of his Marxist point of view, Boal was forced into exile.

In exile, Boal traveled throughout South America and other parts of the world, experimenting with different types of theatre. He created a documentary-like drama that focused on current political issues and an environmental style of theatre that presented performances in public spaces, catching spectators by surprise. Boal became internationally known for his theoretical work *Theatre of the Oppressed* (1975), which became a manifesto for revolutionary and socially conscious theatre. Until his death, Boal continued to teach, give workshops, and lecture throughout the world.

There are significant dramatists today throughout Latin America. Four young contemporary playwrights from Argentina are David Veronese (1955–   ), Lola Arias (1976–   ), Rafael Spregelburd (1970–   ), and Federica León (1970–   ). Contemporary Mexican theatre, according to a young playwright, Richard Viqueira (1976–   ), "wants to unburden itself from the influence of European theatrical models, and is seeking to forge is own voice. The move in new writing," he says, "more and more is away from the folkloric toward the more recognizably idiomatic." Along with Viqueira, other recognized young Mexican playwrights include Javier Malpicak (1965–   ), Sabima Berman (1955–   ), Sylvia Pelaez (1965–   ), and Alberto Villarreal (1977–   ).

In Cuba, the country's communist government controls most theatres. Still, there are a number of theatre companies that have been able to present works by international playwrights and contemporary authors. These include: Teatro Studio (founded in 1959), Compañia Teatral (founded 1962), Compañia Teatral Humbert de Blanck (founded 1992), Teatro El Publico (founded 1992), and Argos Teatro (founded 1996). In recent years, several Cuban companies have toured internationally. For example, Teatro Buendia, an independent theatre that was established in 1986 and that stages adaptations of historically significant texts using Cuban contexts and music, performed at the Goodman Theatre in Chicago as part of the 2010 Latino Theatre Festival.

AUGUSTO BOAL: THE THEATRE OF THE OPPRESSED

Augusto Boal (Sucheta Das/AP Images)

If ever there was an international theatre figure in recent times it was Augusto Boal (1931–2009). Born in Brazil, Boal (pronounced Bo-AHL) attended Columbia University in the United States. Returning to Brazil, he began working in the Arena Theatre in São Paulo. At first he directed conventional dramatic works, but Boal was a man with a powerful social conscience. During his early years he began to develop his philosophy of theatre. He determined, for example, that mainstream theatre was used by the ruling class as a soporific, a means of sedating the audience and inoculating it from any impulse to act or revolt. In other words, conventional theatre was oppressive to ordinary citizens, especially the underprivileged.

Boal also became fascinated with the relationship of actors to audience members. He wished to establish a partnership between the two, and he felt strongly that spectators should participate in any theatre event, that a way must be found for them to become performers and a part of the action. In putting these theories into practice, he began to present agitprop plays, that is, plays with a strong political and social message. He experimented with several versions of such plays. One was the Invisible Theatre in which actors, seemingly spontaneously, presented a prepared scene in a public space such as a town square or a restaurant. Another was his Forum Theatre in which a play about a social problem became the basis of a discussion with audience members about solutions to the problem.

Considered an enemy of the authoritarian government in Brazil for his work in the 1960s, he was jailed in 1971 and tortured. Released after a few months, he was exiled from his native land. Following that he lived in various countries: Argentina, Portugal, and France. He decided along the way that his approach should be less didactic than it had been, that he would be more effective if he engaged the audience in the theatrical process rather than confronting them. This was the basis of his Theatre of the Oppressed, which became the cornerstone of his life's work from then on. He authored a book by that title which appeared in 1974.

In 1985 Boal returned to Brazil. From that point until his death, for the next quarter century, he traveled all over the world, directing, lecturing, and establishing centers furthering the Theatre of the Oppressed. He also authored other books that were widely read. Altogether, his approach to theatre found adherents in more than 40 countries. Wherever the Theatre of the Oppressed was established, its productions challenged injustice, especially in poor and disenfranchised communities where citizens are often without a voice or an advocate. In his later years he was looked upon by many as the most inspirational person of his time in propagating socially oriented theatre.

TODAY AND TOMORROW: A LOOK AHEAD

In the twentieth century, theatre faced a series of unprecedented challenges. First came silent films, then radio, then sound films, then television. With each new challenge, it was assumed that theatre would suffer an irreversible setback. After all, each of these new media offered drama in a form that was less expensive and much more accessible than the traditional theatre setting. When sound film appeared, for example, it was argued that anyone who went out for entertainment would go to the movies rather than theatre: film would be cheaper and would offer more glamorous stars. When television appeared, it was argued that people did not even need to leave their homes to see drama.

Inevitably, some changes in audiences' habits have resulted from new customs and from competition by films and television. For most of the eighteenth and nineteenth centuries, theatre was the main source of escapist dramatic entertainment—both comedies and suspense melodramas. Today, television, with its situation comedies, provides much of the light entertainment formerly offered by theatre, and film also provides much escapist entertainment.

Now in the twenty-first century, there is the additional concern that even newer technologies—such as interactive 3-D blu-ray and television as well as new computer, tablet, and smartphone entertainments—will further erode interest in theatre.

But despite these new media, theatre has not suffered as predicted. Much to the surprise of the prophets of doom, there is probably more theatrical activity in the United States and worldwide today—as the discussions in this chapter and Chapter 14 suggest—than at any other time.

Why is this so? First, in spite of their similarities, there is a basic difference between theatre on the one hand and these technological entertainments on the other. As we pointed out in Chapter 2, the difference is the presence in theatre of the live performer. All of these other technologies present images of people or animations, not the real thing. Human contact between audience and performers meets a profound, fundamental need that neither the large screens in movie theatres nor the small screens in our living rooms or on our computers, tablets, or smartphones can ever satisfy. The human electricity that flows back and forth between performers and audience—the laughter at comic moments and the hushed silence at serious moments—cannot be created in these other media.

Second, there is the human impulse to create theatre. Earlier, we said that this universal impulse leads every society to create its own theatrical activity, unless such activity is expressly forbidden. The need and desire for theatre will continue into the future. The diverse theatres growing out of the diverse populations in our global society reflect the intense need by audiences for theatre that focuses on their issues and concerns as well as provides them with live entertainment.

When we turn from the theatre of today to the future, a question arises: Where will theatre go from here? It is impossible, of course, to answer with any certainty. We can assume, though, that the trends described in this chapter and Chapter 14 will continue. Theatre of the future will no doubt continue to present new works alongside a rich mixture of plays from the past. In both writing and production, theatre will draw on many sources. We cannot know whether or not new plays will attain the greatness of the past, but playwrights show no sign of abandoning theatre, despite the larger financial rewards offered by other media.

We can be sure that theatre will survive in a vigorous form, no matter what challenges it faces from electronic and digital media. At the same time, modern technology will play an important role in theatre: in lighting effects, with the use of computerized lighting boards; in the shifting of scenery; and in other ways. There will also, no doubt, continue to be multimedia experiments, fusing theatre with film, video, dance, and digitally-generated media.

Theatre will also find new ways of co-opting new technologies to reach out to audiences across the globe, such as digitally streaming live performances, seeking instantaneous feedback from spectators via Twitter, as well as interacting with potential audience members by means of social media.

With all its innovations, however, theatre of the future will no doubt be an extension of theatre of the past. Theatre will continue to be enacted by women and men in person before an audience, and the plays they perform will deal primarily with the hopes, fears, agonies, and joys of the human race.

It is clear that the complexity of the global world will result in a heterogeneous theatre. Ongoing exploration of the diversity of contemporary society means that diverse theatres will continue to spring up. There is no question that in the twenty-first century, theatre will be as complex and fragmented as the world in which it exists. Yet from the start theatre has always focused on human concerns, and they will remain the source of its appeal as far ahead as we can see.

SUMMARY

Contemporary theatre is eclectic, combining styles and techniques from earlier periods as well as from other art forms. Today's playwrights and directors draw from a wide range of sources. The types of theatre available include realism and departures from realism (similar to the movements covered in Chapter 14), and additional forms of ethnic and political theatres: African American theatre, Latino-Latina theatre, Native American theatre, feminist theatre, gay and lesbian theatre, and so forth. All these exist side by side in numerous production settings, throughout the world: the rich storehouse of theatre available today is global in scope, with active theatres in Africa, Asia, Latin America, Canada, Australia, and the Middle East.

The vitality of today's theatre in the face of challenges by new technologies demonstrates the continuing appeal of live theatre and the performer-audience relationship. If the present age is not one of great drama, it is a period of tremendous activity in writing and producing, in avant-garde experimental work, and in the revival of classics.

THINKING ABOUT THEATRE

▶ Explain why some theorists might categorize a stand-up comedian as a performance artist.

▶ Discuss why a film or television show you have seen might be categorized as postmodern.

▶ Discuss key changes in communication that have had an impact on global theatre.

▶ Discuss why a film or television show that you have seen might be categorized as a documentary drama.

▶ How do you think theatre will be affected by new digital technologies? Explain your answer.

KEY TERMS

actos Short agit-prop dramas about the lives of Chicano workers.

agit-prop A term meaning agitation-propaganda, referring to plays with a strong social or politial agenda.

Documentary drama (or theatre of fact) Term encompassing different types of drama that presented material in the fashion of journalism or reporting. Drama that is supposedly based on factual occurrences and materials.

non-text based theatre A term meaning that there is no text in a traditional sense, with dialogue written by a dramatist; rather, there is a scenario created by a director or an ensemble, which is then usually expanded through improvisation.

Performance art Experimental theatre that initially incorporated elements of dance and the visual arts. Since performance art often is based on the vision of an individual performer or director rather than a playwright, the autobiographical monologue has become a popular performance art form.

Postmodernism A contemporary concept suggesting that artists and audiences have gone beyond the modernist movements of realism and departures of realism.

Shingeki Contemporary Japanese theatre that incorporated Western ideas about playwriting and theatre production.

THEATRE ON THE WEB

For more research and to learn more about the topics in this chapter, please visit the Online Learning Center at **www.mhhe.com/livelyart8e.**

Abbey Theatre, 341
Abraham Lincoln Presidential Library and Museum, 30
Absurdism. *See* Theatre of the absurd
Accessories, 181, 185
ACH, 381
Acker, Barbara F., 111
Act drops, 311
Acting
  eighteenth century, 312
  judging performances, 116
  making characters believable, 98–105
  nineteenth century, 320–321
  physical, 106–113. *See also* Physical acting
  Stanislavski system, 99–105
  synthesis and integration, 113–116
  voice and body, 106–113
Acting One (Cohen), 103
Action, 54
Actor at Work, The (Benedetti), 104
Actos, 377
Adding Machine, The (Rice), 192, 343
Adejumok, Moses Olaiya, 393
Adler, Stella, 103
Adwin, Elisabeth, 159
Aeschylus, 120, 213
Aesthetic distance, 35, 153
African American theatre, 374–377
African Theatre, 392–394
Age of Enlightenment. *See* Eighteenth century theatre
Agit-prop, 377
Agon, 217
Aguilera, Christina, 28
Aida, 29
Akalaitis, Joanne, 129
Akingbola, Jimmy, 339
Albee, Edward, 53, 70, 338, 347
Alchemist, The (Jonson), 69
Alice's Rape, 369
Alive from Palestine: Stories Behind the Headlines, 391, 392
Al-Kasaba Theatre, 391, 392
All My Sons (Miller), 26, 54, 337
All Shook Up, 28
All-purpose spaces, 152–153
All's Well That Ends Well (Shakespeare), 90

Alojera, 289
American alternative theatre, 372–374
American Buffalo, 160, 374
American Idiot, 28
American Indian Community House (ACH), 381
American Indian Religious Freedom Act of 1972, 380
American Revolution, 306
Amphitheatre, 217, 295
Amphitryon 38 (Giraudoux), 345
Amplification, 199
Ancient Greece. *See* Greek theatre
Anderson, Heather Lea, 80
Andreini, Francesco and Isabella, 270
Andrews, Patrick, 160
Angels in America: A Gay Fantasia on National Themes (Kushner), 383
Angle perspective, 310
Animal Crackers (Kaufman/Ryskind), 183
Anna Christie (O'Neill), 337
Anna Lucasta, 375
Anouilh, Jean, 61, 345
Antagonist, 71
Antigone (Anouilh), 61, 345
Antigone (Sophocles), 128, 218
Antoine, André, 334
Antony and Cleopatra (Shakespeare), 6, 63, 122
Appia, Adolphe, 341, 342
Apple, Jacki, 368
Apprentices, 282
Aragato, 259
Architecture. *See* Theatre architecture
Arena stage, 146–149
Arends, Mark, 340
Argos Teatro, 395
Arias, Lola, 395
Aristophanes
  comedy, 80
  comic premise, 83
  history of theatre, 208–209
  nonhuman characters, 70, 71
  Old Comedy, 217
Aristotle, 54, 219, 225
Arlecchino: Servant of Two Masters (Goldoni), 185
Arms and the Man (Shaw), 86
Ars poetica (Horace), 225

Arsenic and Old Lace (Kesselring), 76, 81, 82
Art
  characteristics, 10–11
  defined, 9–12
  performing arts, 11–12
Artaud, Antonin, 18, 343, 344, 350
Artistic director, 133
Artists of Dionysus, 220
As Is (Hoffman), 383
As You Like It (Shakespeare), 277
Asfour, Georgina, 392
Asian American theatre, 378–380
Asian Exclusion Act, 378
Asian theatre
  background, 240
  Chinese theatre, 245–249. *See also* Chinese theatre
  globalization, and, 17
  heavy makeup, 182
  Indian theatre, 242–245
  Japanese theatre, 250–260. *See also* Japanese theatre
  southeast Asia, 260–261
  timeline of events, 241
Asian-American Theatre Workshop, 378
Astor Place Riot, 317, 318
Ataka, 146
Audience
  aesthetic distance, 35
  as an element of theatre, 12
  diversity, 36–39
  independent judgment, 42
  participation of, 35–36
  personal interaction, 11–12, 23
  responsibility of, 39
  role of, 33–39
Auditions, 123
Australian theatre, 387–388
Auteur director, 41, 128–129
Automated light fixtures, 197
Avant-garde, 66
Awad, Mahmoud, 392
Awake and Sing (Odets), 336

Bacchae (Euripides), 212, 214, 390
Backlighting, 195
Bakkensen, Michael, 84
Ballad of Emmett Till, The, 167

Ballad opera, 307
Baraka, Amiri, 376
Barkin, Ellen, 383
Barlow, Thelma, 82
Barnum, P. T., 315
Baroque, 306
Bartolini, Niccolò, 273
Batman films, 26
Battle of Coxinga (Chikamatsu), 256
Bayreuth Festspielhaus, 323
Be Circumspect in Conjugal Relationships
    (Li Yu), 249
Bean, Jeffrey, 74–75
Bear Garden, 282
Bearbaiting, 282, 283
Beats, 102
Beaumont, Francis, 283
Beckett, Samuel. *See also* individual
    plays
    avant-garde/experimental theatre
        (*Happy Days*), 112
    patterns as structure (*Waiting for
        Godot*), 65
    theatre of the absurd, 91, 347, 348
Bedford, Brian, 85
Beggar's Opera (Gay), 307
Behn, Aphra, 302
Beijing (Peking) opera, 358–359, 389
Bellamy, Lou, 380
Belton, Cathy, 95
Benedetti, Robert, 103, 104
Benefit, 303
Bergin, Jan, 95
Berlin, Irving, 352
Berman, Sabima, 395
Bernhardt, Sarah, 321
Berry, Gabriel, 14
La Bete (Hirson), 96–97
Bibiena, Giovanni, 312
Billy Elliott, 29
Biomechanics, 109, 342
Birds, The (Aristophanes), 70, 83,
    208–209
Biwa, 254
Black box theatre, 152, 153
Black Eyed Peas, 32
Black Watch, 384, 385
Blackout, 198
Blacks, The (Genet), 182
Blanchett, Cate, 99, 331, 387
Blocking, 125
Blood Wedding (García Lorca), 159,
    176, 345
Blue Man Group, 31
Blueprint, 13
Blunt, Ed Onipeda, 80
Bly, Robert, 50
Boal, Augusto, 395, 396
Body. *See* Physical acting
Body mike, 201, 202
Bogart, Anne, 110, 128, 129

Bogosian, Eric, 369
Bolton Theatre, 140
Bombastic acting approach, 312
Bongiovanni, Giorgio, 185
Bono, 29
Book of Mormon, The, 356
Booth, Edwin, 321
Booth Theatre, 322
Border lights, 195
Bortolussi, Sophie, 151
Bourgeois drama, 89
Bourgeois (middle-class) tragedy, 307
Le Bourgeois Gentilhomme (Molière),
    291
Bowers, Cheryl Lynn, 307
Box, 272
Box set, 311
Boxes, 281
Boys in the Band, The (Crowley), 382
Brahm, Otto, 334
Brahman, 242
Bran Nue Dae, 388
Brand (Ibsen), 49
Bread and Puppet Theatre of San
    Francisco, 115
Brecht, Bertolt. *See also* individual plays
    Asian influence, 18, 56
    Caucasian Chalk Circle, The, 247
    epic theatre, 343, 344
    global exchanges, 359
    theatre and human condition, 9
    totalitarianism, impact on theatre,
        345
Breeches roles, 304
Brenton, Howard, 386
Breton, André, 343
Breuer, Lee, 123, 129, 371
Bridel, David, 110
Broadway, popular theatre, 351
Broderick, Matthew, 104
Brook, Peter
    design concept development
        (*Midsummer Night's Dream, A*),
        161
    eclectics, 350, 351
    Iran international festival (1970s),
        391
Bruder, Nicholas, 151
Brüel, Kaya, 326–327
Büchner, Georg, 326–327
Buddhism
    Chinese theatre, and, 246
    Japanese theatre, and, 250
Buddies in Bad Times, 388
Building costumes, 173
Bullock, Sandra, 26
Bunraku, 254–256
Bunyip, The, or The Land of the Wattle,
    387
Buried Child (Shepard), 373
Burlesque, 85, 317

Burstall, Betty, 387
Bush, Anita, 375
Bush, George W., 366
Bushell-Mingo, Josette, 208–209
Business, 125
Busy Body, The (Centlivre), 302
Butterworth, Jez, 386
Byzantine Empire, 229

CAD, 169, 170
Caesar and Cleopatra (Shaw), 177
Café LaMama, 373
Calcutta, 388
Calder, David, 67
Calderón de la Barca, Pedro, 285, 287
Calhoun, Jeff, 188–189
Camargo, Christian, 54
Camus, Albert, 347
Canadian theatre, 387–388
Carell, Steve, 84
Carrey, Jim, 84
Carroll, Nancy, 45
Carroll, Tim, 50
Case, Sue-Ellen, 65
Casino Royale, 105
Casting, 123
Cat on a Hot Tin Roof (Williams), 337
Caucasian Chalk Circle, The (Brecht),
    56, 248, 344
Cazuela, 289
Centering, 110–111
Centlivre, Susana, 302
Central image, 161–162
"Centrality" of the playwright, 51
Ceremony, 66
Chang, Tisa, 378
Characterization, costume design, 176
Characters. *See* Dramatic characters
Charles I, King, 283, 284, 300
Charles II, King, 300, 303
Chekhov, Anton. *See also* individual
    plays
    global theatre, 207
    realism and modern era, 328
    modern tragicomedy, 91
    Sea Gull, The, 335
    Stanislavski system, 99
Cherry Orchard, The (Chekhov),
    332–333
    ensemble playing, 102
    globalism, 207
    modern tragicomedy, 90
    Stanislavski system, 101
Chifunyise, S. J., 393
Chikamatsu Monzaemon, 255–256,
    259
Chilip, Tina, 379
Chinese theatre
    contemporary global theatre,
        388–389
    early development, 246–247

Li Yu, 249
  Ming Dynasty, 248–249
  Yuan Dynasty, 247–248
Ching Dynasty, 246
Chitty, Alison, 214
Choregus, 212
Chorus, 70, 211
Chorus, Greek drama, 214
Chorus Line, A, 354
Chou, 246
Churchill, Caryl, 340, 385
Chushingura (Danjuro I), 259
Cibula-Jenkins, Nan, 160
Cid, The (Corneille), 291
Circle of attention, 100
Circle of Chalk, The, 247
Circle theatre, 146
Circus, 315, 317
Circus Maximus, 223
Cirque du Soleil, 30, 315
City Dionysia, 212
Civil War, The, 188–189
Clarke, Martha, 368
Classical period, ancient Greece, 211
Claudel, Paul, 341
Cleage, Pearl, 381–382
Cleveland Play House, 140
Climactic structure, 59–62, 64, 65
Climax, 59
Clinton, Bill, 366
Close, Glenn, 104
Clouds, The (Aristophanes), 83
Clurman, Harold, 121, 336
Cockpit, The, 282
Cohen, Robert, 103
Cole, Bob, 374
Coleridge, Samuel Taylor, 35
Collaborative aspect of theatre, 15
Collins, Pat, 160
Color
  costume design, 179
  lighting design, 193–194
  scene design, 163
Colosseum, 222, 223
Columbus, Curt, 90
Combination companies, 320
Combs, Sean ("Puff Daddy"), 28
Comedia, 285–287
Comédie Française, 295, 296, 310
Comédie Italienne, 310
Comedies of menace, 91
Comedy, 80–86
  burlesque, 85
  characteristics of, 81–83
  comedy of ideas, 86
  comedy of manners, 85–86
  comic promise, 83
  defined, 80
  domestic comedy, 85
  force, 83–85
  satire, 85

Comedy of Errors, The (Shakespeare), 8, 277
Comedy of manners, 85–86, 300–303
Comic premise, 83
Commedia dell'arte, 69, 266–269, 270
Commercial theatre, 130–131
Commonwealth, 300
Compania Teatral, 395
Compania Teatral Humbert de Blanck, 395
Company, 354
Complication, 58
Composition
  lighting design, 193
  scene design, 162
  visual, 125
Computer-assisted design (CAD), 169, 170
Computerized synthesizers, 203
Concentration/observation, 100
Conflict, 55
Confucianism, 245
Confucius, 245
Congo Square Theatre Company, 376
Congreve, William
  comedy of manners, 85
  dominant trait (*The Way of the World*), 69
  English Restoration, 302, 303
  evolution of director, 121
Constructivism, 342
"Content-less Scene" exercise, 103
Continental seating, 322
Contrast, 63
Cool lights, 193
Cooper, Dominic, 293
Copeau, Jacques, 109
Copley, Paul, 67
Corddry, Nate, 374
Corneille, Pierre, 290, 291
Corral, 143, 288–290
Corral de la Cruz, 288
Corral del Principe, 288
Corthron, Kia, 382
Costume
  design elements, 14
  eighteenth century, 310–311
  English Restoration, 305–306
  nineteenth century, 322–324
Costume design, 172–185
  costume designer, 172–173
  designer's collaborators, 181
  designer's objectives, 173–178
  elements of, 179–181
  hairstyles/wigs, 183–184
  makeup, 181–183
  masks, 184
  millinery/accessories/crafts, 184–185
Costume shop supervisor, 181
Counterparts, 71

Country Wife, The (Wycherley), 300, 303, 304
Courier for Hell, The (Chikamatsu), 256
Covent Garden, 303, 323
Coward, Noël, 86
Cowboys Stadium, 150
Crafts, 185
Craig, Edward Gordon, 341
Craven, James, 380
Crawford, Cheryl, 336
Created space, 149–152
Crisis, 59
Crisis drama, 60
Critic/reviewer, 39–42
  criteria for criticism, 40–41
  influence decline, 41–42
  preparing for criticism, 40
Cromwell, Oliver, 300
Cross-fade, 198
Crothers, Rachel, 381
Crowley, Mart, 382
Croy, Jonathan, 107
Crucible, The (Miller), 55
CSI, 25
Cuba, 395
Cuban American theatre, 377
Cue, 198
Cumbus, Philip, 108
Cunningham, Merce, 110
Cutouts, 167
Cyc lights, 195
Cycle plays, 229
Cyclical structure, 65
Cyrano de Bergerac (Rostand), 87

Dafoe, Willem, 371
Daily Show, The, 217
Daimon, Goro, 389
Daisey, Mike, 369
Dan, 246
Dance dramas, 240
Dance Flick, 85
Daniels, Ben, 176, 334
Danjuro I, 259
Darwin, Charles, 315, 328
Das Kapital (Marx), 315, 328
Davenant, William, 303
Davi, Mara, 183
David, Eleanor, 284
Davies, Howard, 333
Davis, Hallie Flanagan, 336
Davis, Viola, 376
Day of Absence (Ward), 182
Death and the King's Horseman (Soyinka), 394
Death of a Salesman (Miller), 69, 337, 389
Deconstruction, 129, 370
Def, Mos, 28, 157
deMille, Agnes, 352

Dench, Judi, 104, 105
Departures from realism, 339–350
 antirealist designers, 341
 antirealist playwrights, 340
 environmental theatre, 350
 epic theatre, 344
 existentialism, 347
 expressionism, 343
 futurism, 343
 happenings, 349–350
 multimedia, 350
 surrealism, 343
 symbolism, 340–341
 theatre of cruelty, 343–344
 theatre of the absurd, 347–348
 theatricalism, 342
 timeline of events, 346
 totalitarianism, 345–347
 unique voices, 345
Depinet, Kevin, 160
Le Dernier Caravanserail, 360
Design. *See* Costume design; Scene
 design; Sound design; Stage
 lighting
Design concept, 161
Design elements, 14–15
Designer/front elevations, 170
Desire under the Elms (O'Neill), 337
Desperate Housewives, 85
Deus ex machina, 62
Devices, scene design, 166–168
Devil You Know, The, 370
Dialogue, 66
Diapolyekran, 165
Diary of Anne Frank, The, 171
Dick, Maggie, 162
Dickinson, Ian, 95
Digital media, 31–33
Digital technology, sound design, 203
Dimmer, 193
Dinner theatres, 39
Dionysus, 211–212, 218
Dionysus (Suzuki), 390
Direction, stage lighting, 194–195
Director, 13
 auteur director, 128–129
 dramaturg, collaboration with, 130
 duties, 127
 emergence of, 18th century, 312–314
 evolution of role, 120–121
 postmodern director, 129
 role, defined, 120
 stage manager, collaboration with,
  127–130
 at work, 121–126
Directorial concept, 121
Discher, Joe, 162
Distressing, 181
Diversity
 audiences, 36–39
 contemporary theatre, 18

Doctor Faustus (Marlowe), 107,
 109–110, 276, 350
Documentary drama (theatre of fact),
 384–385
Dodson, Owen, 375
Dollhouse, 123
Doll's House, A (Ibsen), 68, 69, 331
Domestic comedy, 85
Domestic drama, 88–89
Domestic tragedy, 307
Dominant trait, 69
Dominus, 225
Doran, Greory, 104
Dorset Garden, 305
Dos Santos, Laura, 339
Dowling, Joe, 122
Downlighting, 195
Downstage, 165
Doyle, John, 162
Draghici, Marina, 192
Drama of catastrophe, 60
Dramatic characters, 66–71
 antagonist, 71
 commedia dell'arte, 69
 costume design, and, 177
 dominant trait characters, 69–70
 extraordinary, 66–68
 internal aspects of, 115
 making characters believable,
  98–105
 minor, 70
 narrator/chorus, 70
 nonhuman, 70, 71
 outer aspects of, 114
 protagonist, 71
 representative/quintessential, 68
 stock characters, 69
Dramatic purpose, 50–52
Dramatic structure, 52–66
 action, 54
 avant-garde/experimental, 66
 climactic plot construction, 59–62
 conflict, 55
 cyclical, 65
 episodic plot construction, 62–64
 essentials of, 52–57
 patterns, 65
 plot, 53–54
 ritual, 64–65
 segments/tableaux, 66
 sequence, 57–59
 strongly opposed forces, 55–57
Dramatists Guild contract, 53
Dramaturg, 130
Drame, 307
Dream Play, A (Strindberg), 198, 340
Dreamgirls, 26
Dress rehearsal, 126
Dromgoogle, Dominic, 108
Drottningholm, 310, 311
Drumstruck, 34

Drury Lane Theatre, 303, 304, 305,
 314
Dubois, Blanche, 129
Duchess of Malfi, The (Webster), 283,
 284
Duffy, Julia, 320
Duke of Saxe-Meiningen. *See* George II,
 duke of Saxe-Meiningen
Duncan, Lindsay, 95

Eberhart, Rachel, 128
Eclecticism, 350
Edelstein, Gordon, 12
Edgardo Mine (Uhry), 125
Edge, 29
Edison, Thomas, 190, 324
Editing, sound, 202
Edmondson, James, 171
Edward II (Marlowe), 276
Ehrmann, Kurt, 160
Eighteenth century theatre, 306–314
 background, 306–307
 Marriage of Figaro, The, 313
 new democratic forms, 307–308
 theatre production, 310–314
 timeline of events, 309
Eisenhauer, Peggy, 157
Eisheh, Hussam Abu, 392
Ekkyklema, 219
El-Amin, Hassan, 177
El-Ramley, Lenin, 391
El Teatro Campesino, 377
Electra (Euripides), 49
Electra (Sophocles), 49
Electra (Suzuki), 390
Elevator Repair Service, 371
Elevator stage, 322
11 and 12, 364–365
Elizabeth I, Queen, 274, 283
Elizabethan playhouse, 279, 280
Elizabethan theatre. *See* English
 Renaissance
Elliott, Marianne, 4–5
Ellipsoidal reflector spotlight, 196
Emmerson, Charlotte, 334
Emotional recall, 103
Emperor Jones, The (O'Neill)
 dramatic characters, creation, 68
 expressionism, 343
 postmodernism, 129, 371
Empty Space, The (Brook), 350
EndGame (Beckett), 129
England, Jamie, 159
English Renaissance, 274–284
 background, 274
 Elizabethan drama, 276–278
 post-Elizabethan era, 283–284
 theatre production, 279–282
 timeline of events, 275
English Restoration, 300–306
 comedy of manners, 300–303

Country Wife, The, 304
  government, and theatre, 303
  performers/acting companies, 303
  theatre architecture, 305–306
  theatre production, 303–306
English theatre, 385–387
Enlightenment. *See* Eighteenth century theatre
Ensemble playing, 103
Environmental sounds, 201
Environmental theatre, 350
Epic theatre, 344
Episodic structure, 59, 62–64, 65
Equus (Shaffer), 27
Error of the Kite, The (Li Yu), 249
Esslin, Martin, 347
Esteinne, Marie-Helene, 364–365
Euripides. *See also* individual plays
  focus in playwrighting, 49
  Greek theatre, and religion, 212
  Suzuki's production (*The Bacchae*), 390
  tragic drama, 213, 214
Europe, globalization and theatre, 17
Every Man in His Humour (Jonson), 69
Every Man Out of His Humour (Jonson), 69
Everybody Loves Raymond, 85
Ex Machina, 388
Exaggeration, 84
Existentialism, 347
Exit the King (Ionesco), 348
Exonerated, 384
Experimental spaces, 152–153
Experimental structures, 66
Exposition, 60, 319
Expressionism, 343
Extensive structure, 59
Extraordinary characters, 66–68

Fabric, 180
Fade, 198
Farag, Alfred, 391
Farce, 83–85
Fashion (Mowatt), 318
Father, The (Strindberg), 332
Faust (Goethe), 318, 319
Federal Theatre Project, 336, 375, 377
Fefu and Her Friends (Fornes), 382
Fela!, 118–119
Feldshuh, Tovah, 182
Feminist theatre, 381
Fences, 26
Ferrara, Scott, 307
Fiddler on the Roof, 353, 354
Film, and theatre, 26–27
Finley, Karen, 369
First hand, 181
Fisher, Jules, 157
Fisher, Linda, 180
Fitchander Stage, 147

Fitzgerald, F. Scott, 371
Flat, 166
Fleetwood, Kate, 101
Fleming, Ian, 105
Fletcher, John, 283
Fliakos, Ari, 371
Flies, The (Sartre), 347
Flockhart, Calista, 104
Floodlight, 195, 197
Fly loft, 139, 166
Focus
  lighting design, 193
  playwrighting, 49–50
Follies, 354
Follow spot, 196
Fontana, Santino, 338
Fool for Love (Shepard), 373
Forbes, Tyson, 50
Foreman, Richard, 66, 128, 129, 373
Form, light, 195
Fornes, Maria Irene, 382
Forrest, Edwin, 317, 318
Fortune Theatre, 143, 281
Forty-Five Minutes from Broadway, 352
Forty-Seven Rônin, The (Danjuro I), 259
Fosse, Bob, 352
Found space, 149–152
Fourth-wall convention, 138
Foxx, Jamie, 26
France, 290–296
  background, 290
  neoclassical era, 290–293
  theatre production, 293–296
  timeline of events, 292
Frayn, Michael, 84
Free Man of Color, A (Guare), 157
Freie Bühne, 334
French Revolution, 306
Fresnel, Auguste, 196
Fresnel spotlight, 196
Freud, Sigmund, 328
Friedman, Thomas, 16
Frigerio, Ezio, 185
Frogs, The (Aristophanes), 70
Front of the house, 133
Fugard, Athol, 393–394
Funny Thing Happened on the Way to the Forum, A, 194, 223
Future outlook, 396–398
Futurism, 343

Gad, Josh, 356
Galati, Frank, 162
Gallery, 272, 281
Gallo, Paul, 192
Gamester, The (Centlivre), 302
Gao Ming, 248
García Lorca, Federico, 159, 161, 345
Garrick, David, 312, 314, 321
Gas table, 322
Gay, John, 307

Gay/lesbian theatre, 382–384
Geiogamah, Hanay, 380
Gel, 193
Gelbart, Larry, 194
Gender
  feminist theatre, and diversity, 381
  Japanese kabuki, 257
General Hospital, 25
General mike, 202
Genet, Jean, 347
Genre
  comedy, 80–86. *See also* Comedy
  defined, 76
  domestic drama, 88–89
  heroic drama, 86–87
  melodrama, 87–88
  tragedy, 77–80. *See also* Tragedy
  tragicomedy, 89–91
George II, duke of Saxe-Meiningen, 120, 321, 322
Germany
  eighteenth century, 310
  Nazism/totalitarianism, and theatre, 345–347
Gershwin, George, 352
Gershwin, Ira, 352
Gesamtkunstwerk, 321
Ghetto (Sobol), 392
Ghost Sonata, The (Strindberg), 340
Ghosts (Ibsen), 331
"Gibson girl" look, 184
Gibson, William, 182
Gidayu, Takemoto, 255
Gilbert, W. S., 352
Gilliam, Michael, 179, 188–189
Gilman, Rebeca, 381
Gilmour, Alexander, 339
Gilpin, Charles, 375
Gionfriddo, Gina, 53
Giraudoux, Jean, 345
Given circumstance, 100
Gladiator battles, 226
Glancy, Diane, 381
Glass Menagerie, The (Williams), 12, 70, 338
Glengarry Glen Ross (Mamet), 374
Global theatre, 384–398
  Asia/Africa/Latin America, 388–395
  Canada/Australia, 387–388
  documentary drama, 384–385
  English/Irish theatre, 385–387
  future outlook, 396–398
  global exchanges, 359–361
  globalism, defined, 356
  Mnouchkine, Ariane, 360
  performance art, 368–369
  post modernism, 370–371
  Taymor, Julie, 360–361
  timeline of events, 357, 367
  United States, 372–374. *See also* United States

Globalism, 356
Globalization, 15–18, 356
Globe Theatre (London)
  audience, crucial role of, 37
  Elizabethan theatre production, 277–280
  restoration of, 144
  thrust stage, 143
Goat, or Who Is Sylvia?, The (Albee), 338
Gobo, 196
Gocdc, Jay, 178
Goethe, Johann Wolfgang von, 308, 314, 318, 319, 321
Goetz von Berlichingen (Goethe), 308
Golda's Balcony (Gibson), 182
Golden Age of Greece, 211
Golden Boy (Odets), 336
Goldoni, Carlo, 185, 308
Goldsmith, Oliver, 14, 85, 307
Goldstein, Daniel, 374
Gone with the Wind, 184
Good Natur'd Man, The, 307
Good Person of Setzuan, The (Brecht), 9, 344
Good Woman of Setzuan (Brecht), 56
Goslow, Jonas, 50
Government, and theatre
  eighteenth century, 310
  English Restoration, 303
Gozzi, Carlo, 308
Grapes of Wrath, The (Steinbeck), 162
Gray, Spalding, 369
Great Gatsby, The (Fitzgerald), 371
Great God Brown, The (O'Neill), 184
Greek theatre
  amphitheatres, 107
  arena stage, 148
  Aristotle, 219
  demands of classical acting, 106
  Golden Age, 211
  Greek comedy, 216–217
  Greek theatre emergence, 211–212
  Greek tragedy, 213–216
  Hellenistic Age, 220
  historical reason to attend theatre, 8
  mimes, 226
  playwrights, 48
  theatre production, 217–219
  thrust stage, 142
Greenberg, Richard, 383
Greenshow, 36
Greenwich Mews Theatre, 375
Greenwood, Jane, 174
Grein, J. T., 334
Gromada, John, 200
Groove system
  English Restoration, 306
  Italian theatre, 273, 274
Grotowski, Jerzy
  auteur director, 128

created/found spaces, 149
environmental theatre, 350
Iran international festival (1970s), 391
physical acting, 110
Ground plan
  Chinese theatre, 249
  Comédie Française, 295
  Fortune Theatre, 281
  Greek theatre, 219
  kabuki theatre, 259
  nō theatre, 253
  playing area layout, 164
  Roman theatre, 227
  scene design, 163
Ground rows, 311
Groundlings, 281
Group Theatre, 336
Guare, John, 53, 157, 373
Guizzi, Stefano, 185
Gurney, A. R., 53
Guthrie, Tyrone, 387
Guys and Dolls, 354

Hagen, Uta, 103
Hair, 353, 355
Hairspray, 26, 175, 184
Hairstyles, 183–184
Hall, Peter, 214, 216
Hamlet (Shakespeare), 277
  contrast/juxtaposition, 63, 64
  dramatic structure sequence, 58–59
  lighting design, 195
  tragicomedy, 89
Hammerstein, Oscar, II, 352, 353
Hanamichi, 260
Hansberry, Lorraine, 9, 89
Happening, 349–350
Happy Days (Beckett), 112
Hard flat, 167
Hare, David, 386
Harper, Valerie, 182
Harry Potter films, 26, 27
Hart, Jake, 8
Hart, Lorenz, 352
Hashigakari, 253
Hathaway, Anne, 276
Head microphone, 202
Heartbreak House (Shaw), 174
Hedda Gabler (Ibsen), 71, 331
Heian period, 250
Hellenistic Age, 220, 226
Hellman, Lillian, 320, 337
Henry IV, Part I (Shakespeare), 89, 277
Henry IV, Part II (Shakespeare), 277
Henry V (Shakespeare), 277
Herbert, Victor, 352
Hernández, Riccardo, 192
Hernani (Hugo), 317, 318
Heroic drama, 86–87
Heyward, DuBose, 352

Hickey, John Benjamin, 383
Hicks, Greg, 212
Hildegard von Bingen, 229
Hilferty, Susan, 177
Hill, Abram, 375
Hille, Anastasia, 340
Hippodrome, 229
Hirelings, 281
Hirson, David, 96–97
History. *See* Theatre history
Hitchcock, Alfred, 105
Hitler, Adolf, 330, 345
Hoch, Danny, 369
Hoffman, William M., 383
Hollywood flat, 167
Holmes, Katie, 26, 54
Home Cooking Theatre, 388
Honeyman, Janice, 2, 113
Hopkins, Laura, 50
Horace, 225
Hôtel de Bourgogne, 293, 295
Hould-Ward, Ann, 157
House of Bernarda Alba, The (García Lorca), 159, 161, 345
Houston, William, 212
How to Succeed in Business Without Really Trying, 27
Howard, Alan, 216
Howe, Tina, 53
Hrosvitha of Gandersheim, 229
Huddle, Elizabeth, 159
Hughes, Langston, 375
Hughes, Ted, 124, 293
Hugo, Victor, 317, 318
Humanism, 266
Huntley, Paul, 157, 184
Hwang, David Henry, 379, 380
Hytner, Nicholas, 293

I Gelosi, 270
Ibsen, Henrik, 331–332. *See also* individual plays
  antirealism, 340
  domestic/bourgeois drama, 89
  global theatre, 17
  focus in playwrighting, 49, 50
  juxtaposition of characters, 71
  realism, and modern era, 328
  realistic acting, development of, 98
  representative/quintessential characters, 68
Iceman Cometh, The (O'Neill), 337
Imaginary Invalid, The (Molière), 291
Importance of Being Earnest, The (Wilde), 85
Impromptu of Versailles, The (Molière), 120
Improvisation, 66
Incandescent lighting, 324
Independent Theatre, 334
Independent theatres, 333–339

Indian theatre, 242–245, 388–389
Industrial Revolution, 314
Ingraham, Margaret, 159
Ingulsrud, Leon, 128
Inner truth, 100–101
Integration, 113–115
Intensity, lighting, 193
Intensive structure, 59–62
Intermezzi, 266–268
Internal aspects of character, 115
International Theatre Festival, Lincoln
    Center, 16
Interpretation of Dreams (Freud), 328
Into the Woods, 354
Investigation, The (Weiss), 384
Ionesco, Eugene, 70, 91, 347, 348
Iphigenia in Aulis (Appia), 342
Irish theatre, 385–387
Irwin, Bill, 369
Italian Renaissance, 266–274
    background, 266
    commedia dell'arte, 266–268
    neoclassical ideals, 269–271
    theatre production, 27–274
    timeline of events, 267
Ivey, Judith, 12

Jackson, LaTanya Richardson, 88
Jackson, Peter, 27
Jacobean period, 283
Jacobs, Sally, 161
James I, King, 283, 284
Japanese theatre, 250–260
    bunraku, 254–256
    Chikamatsu Monzaeman, 255–256
    contemporary global theatre,
        388–389
    early development, 250
    kabuki, 256–260. *See also* Kabuki
        theatre
    nō, 250–254. *See also* Nō theatre
    Zeami Motokiyo, 251
Jarry, Alfred, 341
Jealous Venus (Bartolini), 273
Jekyll and Hyde the Musical, 184
Jelks, John Earl, 177
Jersey Boys, 28, 29, 31
Jing, 246
Jo, Haruhiko, 251
Johansson, Scarlett, 338
John, Elton, 29
John Gabriel Borkman (Ibsen), 95
Johnson, Philip, 140
Johnson, William, 374
Jolie, Angelina, 26
Jones, Bettrys, 4–5
Jones, Bill T., 118–119
Jones, Inigo, 284
Jones, Rolin, 53
Jones, Sarah, 369
Jonson, Ben, 67, 69

Jôruri, 254
Juan Darien, 361
Judging performances, 116
Jukebox Journey, 28–29
Julius Caesar (Shakespeare), 62, 63, 277
Junji, Kinoshita, 389
Juno and the Paycock (O'Casey), 337
Juxtaposition, 63

KA, 30
Kabuki theatre, 238–239
    development of, 257–259
    origins (Okuni of Ozumo), 256
    production of, 259–260
Kahn, Michael, 303
Kaiser, Georg, 343
Kalidasa, 244
Kalman, Jean, 95
Kan'ami, 250, 251
Kane, Sarah, 386
Kani, Atandwa, 113
Kani, John, 113
Kantor, Tadeusz, 350
Kata, Takeshi, 192
Kathakali, 358
Kaufman, George S., 183
Kazan, Zoe, 386
Keeley, Keira, 12
Kemble, John Philip, 317
Kern, Jerome, 352, 353
Kerr, Walter, 34
Kesselring, Joseph, 76, 82
Khanishu, Kristine, 192
Kierkegaard, Søren, 91
Killigrew, Thomas, 303
Kinetic stage, 165
King Kong, 27
King Lear (Shakespeare), 277
    Breuer production (postmodernism),
        129
    extraordinary characters, 67
    parallel plot/subplot, 63
King Oedipus (Sophocles), 214–216
    climactic plot construction, 60, 61
    dramatic structure sequence, 58
King Stag, The, 361
King, The Greatest Alcalde, The, 287
Kitano temple, 252
Kopit, Arthur, 81
Korins, David, 14
Kramer, Larry, 383
Krass, Michael, 178
Kremer, Dan, 62
Kron, Lisa, 369
Kublai Khan, 247
Kurtz, Swoosie, 174
Kushner, Tony, 192, 344, 383, 387
Kyogen, 253

La Mama theatre, 387
Laboissoniere, Wade, 188–189

Lady Gaga, 27, 28
Lafayette Players, 375
Land of the Wattle, 387
Landau, Tina, 122, 178
Lao-tzu, 245
Las Vegas, 30
Last Supper, The, 232
Laterna magika, 165
Latin American theatre, 394–395
Latino-Latina theatre (United States),
        377–378
Lavant, Denis, 341
Law and Order, 25
Law, Jude, 109
Lazzi, 268
Lebow, Will, 61
LeCompte, Elizabeth, 129, 371
Lecoq, Jacques, 109
Left stage, 165
Leguizamo, John, 369
León, Federica, 395
LePage, Robert, 30, 369, 388
Leptis Magna theatre, 136–137
Lesbian theatre groups, 382–384
Lessing, Gotthold Ephraim, 308
Letter to Queen Victoria, A, 112
Li Yu, 249
Les Liaisons Dangereuses, 176
Libation Bearers, The (Aeschylus), 49
Licensing Act, 303, 310
Lichtscheidl, Jim, 50
Lie of the Mind, A (Shepard), 373
Life is a Dream (Calderón), 285, 287
Light plot, 198
Lighting. *See* Stage lighting
Lillo, George, 89
Lincoln Inn Fields, 305
Lindquist, Kryztov, 62
Lindsay, Katrina, 176
Line, 162, 179
Linney, Laura, 176
Lion King, The, 6, 361, 371
Literary arts, 10
Literary manager, 130
Little Clay Cart, The (Sudraka), 244
Little Foxes, The (Hellman), 320
Little Johnny Jones, 352
Liturgical drama, 229
Live television, 7
Lloyd, Phyllida, 284
La Locondiera (Goldoni), 308
Lodestone Theatre Ensemble, 379
Loesser, Frank, 354
London Merchant, The, 89
Long, Andrew, 303, 379
Long Day's Journey into Night (O'Neill),
        57, 337
Long Wharf, 145
Long, William Ivey, 175, 180
Look Back in Anger (Osborne), 339
Lookingglass Theatre Company, 373

Lope de Vega, 63
Lopez, Robert, 356
Lords' rooms, 281
Lorette, Deanne, 303
Lost Colony, The, 175, 180
Loudspeakers, 202
Louis XIV, King, 290, 295
Louis XVI, 313
Louw, Illka, 2
Love Suicides at Amijima, The (Chikamatsu), 256
Love Suicides at Sonezaki, The (Chikamatsu), 256
Love! Valour! Compassion! (McNally), 383
Lucas, Tunji, 364–365
Ludi Romani, 222
Ludlam, Charles, 384
Lugné-Poë, Aurélien-Marie, 341
Lute Song (Gao Ming), 248
Lute Song (musical), 248
Lynn, Joyce, 382
Lyons, Monica, 159
Lysistrata (Aristophanes), 83, 217
Lyubimov, Yuri, 350

M. Butterfly (Hwang), 379, 380
Mabou Mines, 371
Macbeth (Shakespeare), 277
    all-black production, 336
    contrast/juxtaposition, 63
    importance of specifics, 101
    nonrealism, 161
    site-specific theatre, 151
    tragicomedy, 89
MacDermot, Gait, 355
MacDonald, Karen, 61
MacGruber, 85
Mackie, Anthony, 386
Macklin, Charles, 312
Macready, William Charles, 317, 318
Mad TV, 217
Madison Square Garden, 150
Maeterlinck, Maurice, 341
Magic if, 101
Magnetic amplifier, 191
Mahabharata, The, 124, 243, 260
Mahabhasya (Great Commentary), 244
Mahlangu, Enock, 34
Main action of the play, 121
Makeup, 181–183
Malavike and Agnimitra (Kalidasa), 244
Malpicak, Javier, 395
Mamet, David, 26, 53, 373, 374
Mamma Mia!, 28, 29, 31
Manager. *See* Producer
Manley, Delarivière, 302
Mannis, Jenny, 183
Man's World, A (Crothers), 381
Mansions, 232

Mantello, Joe, 383
Mao Zedong, 388
Maqsoud, Gamal Abdel, 391
Marat/Sade, 350, 351
Marber, Patrick, 386
Marcell, Joseph, 157
Maréchal, Benoît, 128
Margulies, Julianna, 382
Marionettes, 115
Mark Taper Forum, 142, 145, 153
Marlowe, Christopher, 107, 109, 276
Marriage of Figaro, The (Beaumarchais), 313
Martin, Nicholas, 14, 207
Martin, Steve, 74–75
Marx brothers' films, 84
Marx, Karl, 315, 328
Mary Poppins, 26
Masks
    costume design, 184, 185
    Greek theatre, 219
Masque, 283
Mass, 162
Master Builder, The (Ibsen), 340
Materials, scene design, 166–168
Ma-Yi Theatre Company, 379
McCauley, Robbie, 369
McCullers, Carson, 88
McDermot, Galt, 353
McDonagh, Martin, 386
McGillis, Kelly, 320
McLaughlin, Ellen, 178
McLeavy, Robin, 99
McNally, Terence, 53, 383
McNee, Jodie, 67
McNeill, Jared, 364–365
McPherson, Conor, 386
McTeer, Janet, 68
Measure for Measure (Shakespeare), 90
Mechane, 219
Medicine shows, 317
Medieval Nights, 30
Medieval theatre. *See* Middle Ages
Mei Lanfang, 56, 359
Meisner, Sanford, 103
Melodrama, 87–88, 319, 320
Member of the Wedding, The (McCullers), 88
Mencius, 245, 246
Menaechmi, The (Plautus), 224, 225
Mercier, Louis Sébastian, 313
Merchant of Venice, The (Shakespeare), 190, 277
Merry Wives of Windsor, The (Shakespeare), 104, 282
Metaphor, 161–162
Metzger, Jack, 88
Meyerhold, Vsevolod, 109, 128, 342, 350
Michelangelo, 266
Microphone, 201–202

Middle Ages, 228–235
    background, 228–229
    medieval drama, 229–231
    Renaissance, compared, 266
    theatre production, 232–235
    timeline of events, 230
Middle East, 391–392
MIDI interface, 200
Midsummer Night's Dream, A (Shakespeare), 277
    Brook's production, 350
    costume design, 178
    design concept development, 161
    director at work, 122
    Japanese theatre, 389
    nonhuman characters, 71
"Mighty line," 276
Mikado, The, 352
Milam, Wilson, 77
Miller, Arthur. *See also* individual plays
    action (*All My Sons*), 54
    Chinese theatre, 389
    conflict (*Crucible*), 55
    domestic/bourgeois drama, 89
    realism, 337, 338
    theatre and human condition, 9
Millinery, 185
Milo, Yossef, 392
Mimes, 226
Ming Dynasty, 248–249
Minniti, Tommaso, 185
Minor characters, 70
Minstrel shows, 315, 317
Mirren, Helen, 293
Misanthrope, The (Molière), 129, 291
Miser, The (Molière), 291
Mishima, 251
Miss Julie (Strindberg), 60, 68, 80, 332
Mitchell, Katie, 340
Mitchell, Maude, 123
Mixing, sound, 202
Mnouchkine, Ariane, 350, 359–360
Modern era
    departures from realism, 339–350
    eclectics, 350–351
    globalism, 356–361. *See also* Global theatre
    popular theatre, 351–356
    realism, 328–339. *See also* Realism
Modern tragedy, 80
Mohammed, Qassim, 391
Molière. *See also* individual plays
    comedy, 80
    comedy of manners, 300
    contrast between individuals and social order, 82–83
    evolution of director, 120
    neoclassical era, 290–291
    satire, 85
    Tartuffe, 294
Monte, Bonnie J., 102

Mood, 191
Moon for the Misbegotten, A (O'Neill), 337
Morality play, 231
Morpurgo, Michael, 4–5
Morris, Tom, 4–5
Morrison, Malcolm, 84
Morton, Amy, 160
Morton, Liz, 88
Moscow Art Theatre, 334, 335
Mother Courage and Her Children (Brecht), 68, 192, 344, 387
Motivated sounds, 201
Mouawad, Jerry, 61
Movie flat, 167
Moving lights, 197
Mowatt, Anna Cora, 318
Mu Performing Arts, 379
Much Ado About Nothing (Shakespeare), 179
Mulatto, 375
Müller, Heiner, 128
Multiculturalism, 18–19, 38
Multifocus theatre, 152
Multimedia, 350
Multimedia theatre, 152
Multipoint perspective, 310
Mumbai, 388
Mumford, Peter, 214
Muni, Bharata, 242
Murasaki, Lady, 251
Muse, David, 62
Music
    characteristics of art, 10
    medieval theatre, 233
Musicals, 352–356
Musicians' gallery, 280
Mwangi, Franky, 208–209
Mystery plays, 229
Myth, 212

Nagoya Sanzaemon, 256
Nakamura, Kankuro, 258
Nanxi, 246
Narrator, 70
National School of Theatre (Angola), 393
Native American theatre, 380–381
Native American Theatre Ensemble, 380
Native Son (Wright), 375
Natsumatsuri Naniwa Kagami, 238–239
Naturalism, 333, 334
Natyasastra, 242
Nauffts, Geoffrey, 383
Naughty Marietta, 352
Nazi Germany, 330, 345–347
Negro Ensemble Company, 376
Neighborhood Playhouse, 336
Nelson, Richard, 207

Nemirovich-Danchenko, Vladimir, 334, 335
Neoclassical era, 290–293
Neoclassical ideals, 269
New Comedy, 217
New Theatre Club (Melbourne), 387
New Theatre League (Sydney), 387
Next Fall (Nauffts), 383
Ngaujah, Sahr, 118–119
Night of the Iguana, The (Williams), 337
Nike of Samothrace sculpture, 10
Ninagawa, Yukio, 251, 389, 390
Nine, 26
Nineteenth century theatre, 317–318
    dramatic forms, 318–320
    production, 320–324
    social change era, 314–317
    timeline of events, 316
No Exit (Sartre), 61, 347
Nō stage, 146
Nō theatre, 250–254
    characteristics of, 251–253
    production of, 253–254
    Zeami Motokiyo, 251
El Nogalar (Saracho), 19
Noises Off (Frayn), 84
Nonhuman characters, 70, 71
Nonprofit theatre, 131–133
Nonrealism, 161
Non-text based theatre, 371
Nonverbal theatre, 66
Normal Heart, The (Kramer), 383
Norman, Marcia, 53
Norman, Marsha, 373
Nottage, Lynn, 377, 382
Nuyorican, 378

Obafemi, Olu, 393
Obama, Barack, 366
Obligatory scene, 319
Observation, 100
Obstacle, 58
O'Casey, Sean, 337
O'Connell, Patricia, 180
Odets, Clifford, 336
Oedipus at Colonus (Sophocles), 216
Oedipus Rex (opera), 361
Oedipus Rex (play). *See King Oedipus* (Sophocles)
Off-Broadway, 372–373
Off-off-Broadway theatre, 373, 374
Ogata, Issei, 369
Ogunde, Hubert, 393
Oh, Dad, Poor Dad, Mama's Hung You in the Closet and I'm Feeling So Sad (Kopit), 81
O'Hara, Scarlett, 184
Ohta, Shogo, 390
Oklahoma!, 352
Okuni of Izumo, 256, 257, 258

Old Comedy, 217
Old Price Riots, 317
Oleanna (Mamet), 374
Omaha Magic Theatre, 382
On Directing (Clurman), 121
On the Origin of Species (Darwin), 315, 328
O'Neill, Eugene
    expressionism, 343
    masks (*Great God Brown, The*), 217
    Provincetown Playhouse, 336
    realism, 337
    strongly opposed forces (*Long Day's Journey into Night*), 57
    Theatre and human condition, 9
Onnagata, 259
Ooms, Richard, 50
Opening scene, 57–58
Opera, 268
Opera Theatre, 310
Orange, Roman theatre, 227
Orchestra
    Greek theatre, 217
    Italian theatre, 271
    Roman theatre, 227, 228
    theatre spaces, 138
    thrust stage, 142
Ordained by Heaven (Li Yu), 249
Ordo Virtutum (Hildegard), 229
Oresteia (Aeschylus), 213
Orghast (Hughes), 124
Ornamentation, 180, 181
Orphan of Chao, The, 247
Osborne, John, 339
Ost, Tobin, 188–189
Othello (Shakespeare), 71, 77, 277, 375
Ouologuem, Abdou, 364–365
Our Town (Wilder), 56, 70
Outdoor theatres, 279–281
Outer aspects of character, 114

Pace, 126
Pacino, Al, 104, 277
Pageant master, 233
Pageant wagon, 234
Paint charge artist, 169, 170
Palais-Royal, 294, 295
Pan Asian Repertory Theatre, 378
Pantomime, 111, 223
PAR, 195–197
Parabasis, 217
Parabolic aluminized reflector (PAR), 195–197
Parallel plot, 63
Paraskenion, 219
Parham, Keith, 192
Parker, Sarah Jessica, 104
Parker, Trey, 356
Parks, Suzan-Lori, 381
Parodos, 217
Parry, Charlotte, 85

Parry, Chris, 166
Pastoral, 268
Patio, 288, 289
Patterns, 65
Paulus, Diane, 355
Pear Garden, 246
Peer Gynt (Ibsen), 49, 50
Peking opera, 358–359
Pelaez, Sylvia, 395
Performance art, 368
Performers, 12–13, 320–321
Performing arts, 10
Perspective, 273
Phaedra (Racine), 293
Phantom of the Opera, The, 168
Phoenix, 282
Phormio (Terence), 225
Physical acting, 106–113
  centering, 110–111
  physical demands of performing, 108
  special theatre forms, training for, 111–113
  voice and body, 108–110
  warm-up exercises, 111
Physical layout, 163–166
Piñero, Miguel, 378
Ping Chong, 369, 370
Pinter, Harold, 26, 91, 347
Pirandello, Luigi, 345
Pirates of Penzance, The, 352
Piscator, Erwin, 345
Pit, 272
Pitt, Brad, 26
Pix, Mary, 302
Platform stage, 143, 235
Plautus, 223, 224, 225
Play about the Baby, The (Albee), 338
Playhouse, Papermill, 194
Playwright, 48
  centrality, 51
  film and television writers, 53
Playwrighting. *See* Script creation
Playwrights Horizons, 373
Plot, 53–54
Plots, 282
Plough and the Stars (O'Casey), 337
Plum, Paula, 61
Poetics, The (Aristotle), 219
POEtry (Wilson), 160
Pole-and-chariot system, 274
  Drottningholm, 311
  eighteenth century, 311
  Italian theatre, 273
Polyekran, 165
Poor theatre, 350
Popular theatre, 351–356
Poquelin, Jean-Baptiste. *See* Molière
Porter, Cole, 352
Postmodernism, 370–371
  auteur *vs.* postmodern director, 129
  defined, 370

Poyser, Brian, 82
Previews, 126
Prince, Harold, 353, 354
Private theatres, 281
Producer
  commercial theatre, 130–131
  noncommercial theatre, 131–133
  role, defined, 130
Production. *See* Theatre production
Prop, 168
Property, 114–115
Property designer, 169, 170
Proscenium, 138–141
Proscenium-arch stage, 272
Protagonist, 71
Provincetown Playhouse, 336
Provinelli, Mark, 123
Psychophysical actions, 101, 103
Public theatres, 279–281
Pulling costumes, 173
Punchdrunk, 371
Puppet theatre
  Japanese bunraku, 254, 255
  shadow puppetry, 260–261
  Taymor, Julie, 361
Purpose of a play, 50–52
Pye, Tom, 95

Quartett (Müller), 128
Quintessential characters, 68–69

Race (Mamet), 374
Racine, Jean, 290, 293
Radcliffe, Daniel, 27
Radio Golf (Wilson), 177
Rado, James, 353, 355
Ragni, Gerome, 354, 355
Raisin in the Sun, A (Hansberry), 28, 375
Rake, 138
Ramayana, 260
Ramsay, Remak, 180
Rannelis, Andrew, 356
Rapp, Adam, 53
Rasa, 242
Rashad, Condola Phyleia, 377
Rashâd, Phylicia, 104
Realism, 160, 328–339. *See also* Departures from realism
  background, 328–330
  Chekhov, Anton, 332
  defined, 99, 330–331
  development of (Chekhov), 98–99
  Ibsen, Henrik, 331–332
  independent theatres, 333–339
  naturalism, 333, 334
  Sea Gull, The, 335
  Strindberg, August, 332
  timeline of events, 329
Realistic acting, 98–105
Regional theatre, 372

Régisseur, 314
Reinhardt, Max, 345, 350
Relaxation, 100
Religion, 211–212
Renaissance
  England, 274–284. *See also* English Renaissance
  France, 290–296. *See also* France
  Italy, 266–274. *See also* Italian Renaissance
  Middle Ages, compared, 266
  Spain, 284–290. *See also* Spain
Rendering, 169
Rent, 356
Repertory company, 320
Representative characters, 68–69
Respect for Acting (Hagen), 103
Restoration. *See* English Restoration
Reviewer. *See* Critic/reviewer
Revolving stage, 322
Reyes, Randy, 379
Rhinoceros (Ionesco), 70
Rhyne, Aaron, 188–189
Rhythm
  director at work, 126
  lighting design, 193
Rice, Elmer, 343
Richard III (Shakespeare), 107, 277
Richards, Lloyd, 375
Richelieu, Cardinal, 295
Riders to the Sea (Synge), 337
Right stage, 164, 165
Ritual, 64–65, 66
Rivals, The (Sheridan), 70, 307
Roach, Ukwell, 108
Robbers, The (Schiller), 308
Robbins, Jerome, 352, 354
Robeson, Paul, 375
Robinson, Diane, 159
Rock and roll, 27–29
Rock of Ages, 28
Rockwell, David, 157
Rodgers, Richard, 352
Role model, 98
Roman theatre, 220–228
  background, 220–222
  comedy, 223–225
  decline of, 228
  Horace, 225
  pantomime, 226
  theatre production, 225–227
  thrust stage, 142–143
  timeline, 221
  tragedy, 225
Romance of the Western Chamber, The (Wang Shifu), 247
Romanticism, 318
Romeo and Juliet (Shakespeare), 277
  contrast/juxtaposition, 63
  costume design, 177
  dramatic structure sequence, 58–59

physical demands of performing, 108
thrust stage, 144
Roosevelt, Franklin Delano, 336
Rooth, Liv, 84
Rose Bowl, 150
Rose Theatre, 279
Rostand, Edmond, 87
Rover, The (Behn), 302
Royal Shakespeare Company, 2
Ruhl, Sara, 381
Ruined (Nottage), 377
Run Little Chillun, 375
Running, 149
Run-through, 126
Rush, Geoffrey, 348, 387
Russian Revolution, 328
Russia, 342
Ryall, David, 212
Rylance, Mark, 50, 96–97
Ryskind, Morrie, 183

Saint Joan (Shaw), 87, 177
Saito, Yukiko, 390
Salle des Machines theatre, 140, 295
Samisen, 254
Sandler, Adam, 84
Sanskrit drama, 242–244
Saracho, Tanya, 19
Sartre, Jean-Paul, 61, 347
Satire, 85
Saturday Night Live, 25, 217
Satyr play, 212
Saudi Society for Culture and Arts, 391
Savoy Theatre, 324
Scaena, 226, 271
Scaena frons, 228
Scenarios, 268
Scene design, 158–171
antirealism, 341
central image/metaphor, 161–162
design concept, 161
designer's collaborators, 169–171
designer's objectives, 158–161
elements of, 161–168
locale/period, 161
materials/devices, 166–168
physical layout, 163–166
special effects, 168
steps in process, 168–169
tone/style, 158–161
total environment design, 171
Scenery
eighteenth century, 310–311
English Restoration, 305–306
nineteenth century, 322–324
Scenic charge artist, 169, 170
Scenography, 165
Schechner, Richard, 350
Schiller, Friedrich, 308
School for Scandal, The (Sheridan), 307

Schreiber, Liev, 338
Schuman, Peter, 115
Schwartz, Scott, 74–75, 179
Schwartz, Steven, 182
Scott, A. O., 370
Screen projection, 167
Scrim, 166, 167
Script, 13
Script creation
dramatic characters, 66–71
dramatic purpose, 50–52
dramatic structure, 52–66. *See also* Dramatic structure
focus, 49–50
playwright, 48
playwrighting process, 48
subject, 49
Sea Gull, The (Chekhov), 101, 332, 334, 335
Seascape (Albee), 70
Second Shepherd's Play, The (Shakespeare), 89, 231
Secular drama, 285
Selecon 1200 Fresnel, 196
Selecon Acclaim Flood, 197
Selective realism, 337, 338
Seneca, 225
Sentimental comedy, 307
Sequence, dramatic structure, 57–59
Serial structure, 65
Sexuality, Japanese kabuki, 257
Shadow play, 260–261
Shaffer, Peter, 27
Shakespeare, William, 276–278. *See also* individual plays
bearbaiting, popularity/theatricality, 282, 283
comic/serious scenes, alternation, 64
obstacles/complications (*Hamlet*), 58
script creation, 45
strongly opposed forces, 57
tragicomedy, 89
Shakespeare Festival theatre (NYC), 153
Shakespeare Theatre (Stratford), 145
Shakuntala (Kalidasa), 244
Shamanism, 246
Shang Dynasty, 245
Shape, light, 195
Shareholders, 281
Sharing plan, 281
Shaw, Fiona, 95, 387
Shaw, George Bernard. *See also* individual plays
comedy, 80
comedy of ideas, 86
heroic drama, 87
Independent Theatre, 334
Shaw Festival, 387
She Stoops to Conquer (Goldsmith), 14, 180, 307

Sheehy, Joan, 95
Sheep Well, The (Lope de Vega), 63, 287
Sheng, 246
Shepard, Sam, 26, 373, 374
Shepherd, Scott, 371
Sheridan, Richard Brinsley, 70, 307
Shevelove, Burt, 194
Shibenke, Ben, 393
Shine, Shephanie, 8
Shingeki, 389
Shiraishi, Kayoko, 389
Shite, 253
Shōgekijō undō, 390
Short Eyes (Piñero), 378
Shotgun mike, 202
Show Boat (Gershwin), 352, 353
Sides, 282
Silicon-controlled rectifiers, 191
Silk Road Theater Project, 379
Simon, Neil, 53, 351
Sipes, John, 111
"Sit Down, You're Rocking the Boat," 354
Six Characters in Search of an Author (Pirandello), 345
Slapstick, 81, 268
Sleep No More, 151
Smith, Anna Deavere, 369
Smith, Rae, 167
Smith, Will, 26
Snider-Stein, Teresea, 166
Sobol, Joshua, 392
Soft-edged spotlights, 196
Soldier Field, 150
Soliloquy, 271
Sondheim, Stephen, 162, 194, 223, 354
Song Dynasty, 246, 261
Sophocles, 213. *See also* individual plays
Antigone, 218
Golden Age of Greece, 78
playwrighting focus, 49
Sotoba Komachi (Kan'ami), 250, 251, 252
Sound design
amplification, 199
microphones/loudspeakers, 202
sound designer, 201
sound effects, 199–200
sound recordings, 202–203
sound reproduction/reinforcement, 201–202
special effects, 203
technology, 202–203
Sound effects, 199–200
Sound recordings, 202–203
Sound reinforcement, 201
Sound reproduction, 201
Soviet Union, 330

Soyinka, Wole, 393–394
Space, theatre. *See* Theatre space
Spacey, Kevin, 104
Spain, 284–290
  Spanish drama, 285–288
  Spanish Golden Age, 284–285
  theatre production, 288–290
  timeline, 286
Spangler, Walt, 179
Sparks, Paul, 374
Speakers, 202
Special effects, 168
  lighting, 203
  scene design, 168
  sound design, 203
Specifics, importance of, 100
Spiderman: Turn Off the Dark, 23, 29, 361
Spiderwoman Theatre, 380
Spielman, Makela, 128
Spine of the play, 121
Split Britches, 382
Sporting events, 32
Sports spectacle, 150
Spottag, Jens Jorn, 326–327
Spregelburd, Rafael, 395
Spring's Awakening, 340
Squatter's Daughter, The, 387
Stafford, Nick, 4–5
Stage area, 164
Stage left, 164
Stage lighting
  eighteenth century, 310–311
  elements of, 193–194
  English Restoration, 305–306
  incandescent, 324
  lighting designer's collaborators, 198–199
  lighting designer's resources, 194–198
  nineteenth century, 322–324
  objectives of, 191–193
  special effects, 203
  theatre history, 190–191
Stage manager, 127–128, 171
Stage picture, 125
Stage right, 164
Stage type. *See* Theatre space
Stalin, Joseph, 330
Stanislavski, Konstantin, 99–105, 334, 335
Stanislavski system, 99–105
Stanton, Ben, 14
Stein, Peter, 319, 350
Steinbeck, John, 162
Steppenwolf Theatre Company, 373
Stevenson, Ray, 284
Stewart, Jon, 217
Stewart, Patrick, 101
Stock character, 69

Stockhausen, Adam, 166
Stone, Matt, 356
Stone-Fenwings, Jo, 45
Stoppard, Tom, 386
Story, 54
Story of the Chalk Circle, The, 56
Strasberg, Lee, 103, 336
Streep, Meryl, 104, 344
Street theatre, 152
Streetcar Named Desire, A (Williams), 337
  auteur director, 129
  dramatic characters, creation of, 66
  portraying a believable character, 99
  strongly opposed forces, 57
Strindberg, August, 332. *See also* individual plays
  departures from realism, 340
  domestic/bourgeois drama, 89
  realism and modern era, 328, 331
  realistic acting, development of, 98
Strip lights, 195
Strobe light, 203
Strongly opposed forces, 55–57
Structure. *See* Dramatic structure
Sturm und Drang (storm and stress) movement, 308
Style
  costume design, 173
  lighting design, 192
  scene design, 158–161
Subject matter, 49
Subplot, 63
Sudraka, King, 244
Sudtradhara, 243
Sullivan, Arthur, 352
Summer and Smoke (Williams), 200
Summer Festival: A Mirror of Osaka, 238–239
Sunday in the Park with George, 167, 354
Super Bowl, 32
Surrealism, 343
Suzuki, Tadashi, 109, 389, 390
Svoboda, Josef, 165, 349
Swan Lake (Tchaikovsky), 11
Swan Theatre, 280
Sweeney Todd (Sondheim), 162
Symbolism, 340–341
Synge, John Millington, 337
Synthesis, 113–115

Tai chi, 109, 110
Take, 33
Take Me Out (Greenberg), 383
Tale of Genji (Murasaki), 251
Tale of the Heike, The, 251
Tamburlaine (Marlowe), 276
Tang period, 246

Taoism, 245
Tapper, Zoe, 77
Tartuffe (Molière), 51, 82–83, 85, 291, 294
Taymor, Julie, 359, 360–361
Teale, Owen, 68
Teatro Buendia, 395
Teatro El Publico, 395
Teatro Farnese, 271–272
Teatro Olimpico, 271
Teatro Studio, 395
Technical director, 169, 170
Technical rehearsal, 126
Technology
  nineteenth century, 322
  sound design, 203
Tel Aviv Municipal Theatre, 392
Television
  live, 7
  theatre, and, 25–26
Tempest, The (Shakespeare), 113
Terayama, Shûji, 390
Terence, 225
Text, 13, 48
Texture, 163
Theatre
  American alternative theatre, 372–374
  as an art form, 9–15. *See also* Art
  art of, 12–15
  audience, role of, 33–39. *See also* Audience
  commercial, production, 130–131
  digital media, and, 31–33
  diversity/multiculturalism, 18–19
  everyday life drama, 24–25
  film, and, 26–27
  globalization, and, 15–18
  historical reason to attend, 8–9
  human condition, and, 9
  independent, 333–339
  noncommercial, production, 131–133
  off-Broadway, 372–373
  off-off-Broadway, 373, 374
  regional, 372
  rock and roll, and, 27–29
  television, and, 25–26
  unique quality of, 6–9
Theatre architecture
  eighteenth century, 310
  English Restoration, 305–306
  nineteenth century, 322
Théâtre de l'Oeuvre, 341
Théâtre du Marais, 293, 295
Théâtre du Soleil, 360
Theatre, elements of
  audience, 12
  design elements, 14–15
  director, 13

performers, 12–13
script/text, 13
theatre space, 13–14
Theatre history. *See also* Middle Ages;
    Roman theatre
    ancient Greece, 211–220. *See also*
      Greek theatre
    lighting, 190–191
    origins, 210–211
Théâtre Libre, 334
Theatre of cruelty, 343–344
Theatre of Dionysus, 218
Theatre of fact, 384–385
Theatre of the absurd, 91, 347
Theatre of the Oppressed, 396
Theatre of the Oppressed (Boal), 395
Theatre of the Ridiculous, 384
Theatre production
    ancient Greece, 217–219
    eighteenth century, 310–314
    Elizabethan theatre, 279–282
    English Restoration, 300–306
    France, 293–296
    Italian theatre, 271–274
    kabuki, 259–260
    Middle Ages, 232–235
    nineteenth century, 320–324
    nō theatre, 253–254
    Rome, 225–228
    Spain, 288–290
    Yuan period, 248
Theatre space
    all-purpose/experimental spaces,
      152–153
    arena stage, 146–149
    created/found space, 149–152
    defined, 13–14
    multifocus environments, 152
    proscenium, 138–141
    thrust stage, 141–146
Theatre, The, 279
Theatre-in-the-round, 146
Theatricalism, 342
Theatron, 217
Thérèse Raquin (Zola), 334
Thespian, 211
Thiong'o, Ngugi wa, 393
Thirty Nine Steps, 168
36 Views, 166
Thompson, John Douglas, 107
Three Sisters, The (Chekhov), 332
Thrust stage, 141–146
Thumbnail sketches, 168
Thunderbird Theatre, 381
Timberlake, Justin, 28
Time, lighting design, 191
Tiring house, 280
Toblini, Fabio, 179
Tokugawa Ieyasu, 254
Tokugawa period, 254

Toller, Ernst, 343, 345
Tompkinson, Stephen, 82
Tone
    costume design, 173
    scene design, 158–161
Torelli, Giacomo, 273
Torres, Adrian, 378
Total theatre, 240
Totalitarianism, 345–347
Traditional tragedy, 77–80
Tragedy, 76–80
    acceptance of responsibility, 78
    ancient Greece, 213–216
    bourgeois (middle-class), 307
    conditions for, 78–79
    defined, 76
    domestic, 307
    effects of, 79–80
    heroes/heroines, 77
    modern, 80
    traditional, 77–80
    tragic fate, 77–78
    tragic verse, 79
Tragicomedy, 89–91
Transposed Heads, The, 361
Treadmill, 166
Trestle stage, 143
Trestles, 143
Trilogy, 213, 218
Trojan War Will Not Take Place, The
    (Giraudoux), 345
Trotter, Catherine, 302
True West (Shepard), 373, 374
Tsodzo, Thompson, 393
Tsuchitori, Toshi, 364–365
Tsure, 253
Tulsa Indian Actor's Workshop, 381
Turntable, 166
TV. *See* Television
Twelfth Night (Shakespeare), 45, 277
Twilight: Los Angeles, 369
Twin Menaechmi, The. See Menaechmi,
    The (Plautus)
Two and a Half Men, 85
Two-Rivers, E. Donald, 381
Tyler, Royall, 307
Tyrone Guthrie theatre, 145, 153

U2, 28, 29
Ubu the King (Jarry), 341
Uhry, Alfred, 125
Ullmann, Liv, 99
Uncle Vanya (Chekhov), 91, 332
Underpants, The (Martin), 74–75
Unit set, 341
United States
    African American theatre, 374–377
    American alternative theatre,
      372–374
    Asian American theatre, 378–380

    Latino-Latina theatre, 377–378
    Native American theatre, 380
Unities, 269
Units, 102
Unity Theatre (Brisbane), 387
Uprooted Pine, The (Chikamatsu), 256
Upstage, 165
Uribes, Mike, 378

Vaccaro, John, 384
Vakhtangov, Yevgeny, 350
Valdès, Ariel Garcia, 128
Valdéz, Luis, 378
Valenciennes, medieval staging, 232
Valk, Kate, 129, 371
Vampires Suck, 85
van Hove, Ivo, 129
Variable Beam Profile Spot, 196
Variety plays, 246, 317
Vari*Lite VL6 Spot Luminaire, 197
Vaudeville, 315
Vaughn, Vince, 84
Verisimilitude, 269
Vernacular drama, 229
Veronese, David, 395
Verse, 79
View from the Bridge, A (Miller), 108,
    337, 338
Viewpoint theory, 109–110
Vikrama and Urvashi (Kalidasa), 244
Villareal, Alberto, 395
Viqueira, Richard, 395
Visibility, 191
Visit of the Magi, The, 232
Visual arts, 10
Visual composition, 125
Vital Statistix, 388
Vogel, Paula, 53
Vogt, Paul C., 223
Voice. *See* Physical acting
Volpone (Jonson), 67, 283

Wagner, Richard, 321, 322, 323
Wagon, 166
Wagon stage, 143, 232
Waite, Todd, 74–75
Waiting for Godot (Beckett), 65, 348,
    349
Waki, 253
Waldhart, Mary, 159
Waldrop, Mark, 194
Walken, Christopher, 386
Walker, Eamonn, 77
Walker, George, 374
Walpole, Horace, 76
Wang Shifu, 247
War Horse (Stafford), 4–5, 167
Warchus, Matthew, 96–97
Ward, Douglas Turner, 182
Wardrobe supervisor, 181

Warm lights, 193
Warm-up exercises, body/voice, 111
Warner, Deborah, 386, 387
Warren, Amy, 192
Warren, Marcia, 82
Washington, Denzel, 26, 376
Washington, George, 282
Washington, Maya, 380
Washington Square Players, 336
Wasserstein, Wendy, 373
Waters, Ethel, 375
Watts, Naomi, 27
Way of the World, The (Congreve), 69, 302, 303
Wayang, 260
Webb, Rema, 356
Webber, Andrew Lloyd, 355
Webster, John, 283, 284
Wedding ceremony, 24
Wedekind, Frank Benjamin, 340
Weiss, Peter, 384
Weller, Frederick, 344
Welles, Orson, 336, 375
Well-made play, 319–320
West, Dominic, 285
West Side Story, 177, 354
Western Hall, 150
When We Dead Awaken (Ibsen), 340
Whoriskey, Kate, 377
Who's Afraid of Virginia Woolf? (Albee), 338
Wicked, 6, 141, 182
Widower's Houses, 334
Wigs, 183–184
Wild west shows, 315, 317

Wilde, Oscar, 85, 86
Wilder, Thornton, 56, 70, 359
Will & Grace, 85
Williams, Bert, 374
Williams, Tennessee. *See also* individual plays
    domestic/bourgeois drama, 89
    Japanese theatre, 389
    realism, 337, 338
    theatre and human condition, 9
Willing suspension of disbelief, 35
Wilson, August, 9, 89, 177, 375, 376
Wilson, Lanford, 53, 373
Wilson, Michael, 200
Wilson, Patrick, 54
Wilson, Robert
    auteur director, 128
    off-off-Broadway works, 373
    Iran international festival (1970s), 391
    segments/tableaux, 66, 129
    special forms of theatre, 112
Wing-and-shutter settings, 310, 322
Winiarski, Jo, 171
Wishcamper, Henry, 183
Wolfe, George C., 157, 192, 344, 376
Woman Killer and the Hell of Oil, The (Chikamatsu), 256
Women
    English Restoration, 303
    feminist theatre, 381–382
    Spanish acting companies, 290
Women's Experimental Theatre, 382
Wong, B. D., 380
Woodward, Edward, 231

Wooster Group, 371
Works Progress Administration (WPA), 336
World Is Flat, The (Friedman), 16
World War I, 328
World War II, 330
Woyzeck (Büchner), 326–327
WPA, 336
Wren, Christopher, 304, 305
Wright, Angus, 340
Wright, Jeffrey, 157
Wright, Richard, 375
Writers, 53
Wycherley, William, 85, 121, 300, 304

Yard, 281, 289
Yard floor, 288
Yeats, William Butler, 341
Yellow Robe, William S., Jr., 380, 381
Yerma (García Lorca), 345
Yoshimitsu, Ashikaga, 250
Yuan Dynasty, 247–248
Yûgen, 251

Zadek, Peter, 350
Zaju, 247
Zanni, 268, 270
Zarkana, 31
Zeami Motokiyo, 250–252
Zhou Dynasty, 245
Zimmerman, Mary, 129
Zola, Émile, 333, 334
Zoot Suit (Valdéz), 378